DENIS HEALEY

DENIS HEALEY
A LIFE IN OUR TIMES

EDWARD PEARCE

LITTLE, BROWN

For Deanna
and all the
Zettner Women

A *Little, Brown* Book

First published in Great Britain by
Little, Brown 2002

Copyright © 2002 by Edward Pearce

The moral right of the author has been asserted.

The author and publishers would like to extend
their thanks to Denis Healey for the use of his photographs.

A CIP catalogue record for this book
is available from the British Library.

ISBN 0 316 85894 3

Typeset in Sabon by M Rules
Printed and bound in Great Britain
by Clays Ltd, St Ives plc

Little, Brown
An imprint of
Time Warner Books UK
Brettenham House
Lancaster Place
London WC2E 7EN

www.TimeWarnerBooks.co.uk

CONTENTS

INTRODUCTION

The idea of a biography of Denis Healey came from my agent, Bill Hamilton of A. M. Heath, to whom fervent thanks. The authority to make it the official life, with access to papers, came from Lord Healey himself, responding with a kind note within forty-eight hours of receiving my proposal.

I have thus worked with the diary which the young Denis Healey started to keep at the age of sixteen and has maintained ever since. It has been seen by no one else, but was of course used for Healey's vastly successful autobiography, *The Time of My Life*, a work the biographer has tried to avoid depending on, using it instead as a steadying reference.

The diary itself, cryptic, corner of the mouth, non-rambling, each day covered in a couple of sentences, with the occasional half-page for a nuclear event, has been rattled against the well-known and very different published records of Barbara Castle, Richard Crossman and Tony Benn, the fascinating, but widely overlooked, fragmentary diary of Patrick Gordon Walker and by unpublished diaries of Kenneth Younger and Edmund Dell. This record has been reinforced by relevant secondary sources, recorded below, and by a series of interviews with contemporaries also listed.

At this point, a sentence should begin with, 'It would be invidious to single out particular interviewees.' So it would, and all those who helped me with their time and recollections deserve gratitude for their guidance. But invidious or not, I shall not withhold special mention of the witty downrightness of Lord Hill-Norton, who knew and watched the Secretary for Defence; the trenchant judgements inside the Cabinet of Lord Glenamara (Edward Short) and Lord Hattersley; the revelations and insights into late events of Sir Kenneth Stowe, Principal Private Secretary to three prime ministers; and the specialist knowledge of relations between Healey and the union leadership during the successful second Social Contract of Lord Lea (David Lea) of the TUC. Crucial guidance on the Benn–Healey contest was provided by David Warburton of the GMU.

In his own category, Tony Benn requires particular thanks. Denis Healey's antipodes and Moriarty (or, he might say, Holmes), he could not have been kinder to Healey's biographer, providing stirring new details about the Suez debates. And despite regrets, one cannot resent the man declining to throw open the unpublished part of his diary from mistaken but honourable fear of occasioning hurt or gossip. Finally, both Barry Jones and Richard Heller, respectively PPS and PA to Healey in the early 1980s, added sharp flavour and substance.

This is a political life. Trufflers after scandal will be miserably disappointed. Those looking for new political facts will not. Papers I turned up at the National Museum of Labour History in Manchester, whose curator, Stephen Bird, also deserves warm thanks, reveal the Spelthorne Memorandum of 1946 and Healey's response to it, something which shows both apparatchik and polemicist in full splendour. Eyewitness views of Downing Street in August 1978 and again in December–January 1978–9 indicate a relationship between Prime Minister and Chancellor which may alter received judgements.

I say that this is a political life, but the personality has not been left out. It is an unleave-outable personality. A good deal of school and university work came into my hands, giving the full picture of a precocity not far from genius, as well as a short flowering of Marxist swagger. I have given more space than does the autobiography to the young traveller in Germany, southern France and Greece – Denis laying down the law about the contents of German art galleries, Denis in thrall to the Mediterranean, Denis cycling past the last youth hostel and sleeping in a ditch. The sources are too good, the human picture too hard to resist. Much of the *echt* Healey lies in these early pages.

Eighteen pages of autograph on Italian commercial stationery contained the experience of Captain Healey waiting at 2 p.m. off the coast of Calabria to disembark for the immediate bloody harassment of invasion. Then again, Denis and Edna Healey have enjoyed one of the great and happy political marriages. I should be sorry if my appreciation of Edna's intelligence and humorous goodness fell in any way short. What I would call a garland, privately printed and presented by family, friends and neighbours for the Golden Wedding, has been a great reservoir of incident and insight into the Healeys at home and on anarchic holiday.

But ultimately this is the life of a major politician, abler (not just in my view) than most of those taking the premiership in the last half-century. It is also a life and times, for Healey lived through a heroic era. It covers student life responding to Nazism, active and energetic military service in the war, the issues of the Cold War, the technologies and theories of nuclear strategy, direct stewardship of the second great financial crisis of the century and the Labour Party's own twilight as a force for public good.

At the end of so much, one must make judgements, especially on the question of why he was finally rejected for the top. The failure to charm, the brusqueries, the overworked preoccupation and a recurring theme of the diary, sheer physical exhaustion, all feature, though there was much countervailing affection. But perhaps more important are the quarrels of the Labour Party, the impulses which led to the SDP schism by way of what Stephen Bird calls 'the Party's period of insanity'. I have no doubt that in rejecting Healey, Labour got it wrong, but getting it wrong is the métier of political parties. At the centre of events is the man. His huge exertions, his mistakes and greater achievements, and the astonishing times he lived through, have at any rate been essayed.

Final gratitude should be expressed to the academic friends who advised on great parts of the book. Anthony Gorst of Westminster University, the last scholarly word on aircraft carriers, examined and exonerated the defence chapters. Lord Morgan (Kenneth O. Morgan), ultimate historical authority on the Labour Party, read and gave guidance on the key governmental chapters and showed inexhaustible kindness. As to production, Alan Samson, editor at Little, Brown, a considerate friend, rightly coaxed me into reducing a book, still long but now shorter. Thanks go naturally to the Healeys themselves, always welcoming in Sussex, and most of all to my dear wife, Deanna, sorter of footnotes, painstaking returner to the screen of a text corrected and reduced on hard copy during a 'holiday' away from the electronic *équipe*, also patient co-exister across the two years of its composition with more talk about Denis Healey than anyone should have to endure.

Thormanby
North Yorks
August 2001

BEGINNINGS: FAMILY AND SCHOOLING

Denis Healey is generally, almost tediously, spoken of as a Yorkshireman. But he was neither born in Yorkshire, nor into a family with Yorkshire roots. Harold Wilson, as his biographer, Ben Pimlott, pointed out, could actually give warrant to Alec Douglas-Home's gentle gibe about 'the Fourteenth Mr Wilson', tracing his family roots back centuries in the Rievaulx/Helmsley area of the North Riding.

The Healeys, like so many British families, had moved under duress or in pursuit of advantage, from other places. Denis's father, William, always known as Will, had spent his youth in Yorkshire, since it was to Todmorden, at the border with Lancashire that *his* father, John William, had come, from Clogherkilty, a village not far from Enniskillin but across a county boundary, in Co. Leitrim in what is now the Republic of Ireland.

John William was a tailor and, like hundreds of thousands of our immediate ancestors, had taken his talents and skills to where they would earn him a better living. This meant migrating to two rooms in Todmorden and long working hours. The gap between skilled and unskilled runs through working-class history as a deeper divide than any petty regional or national distinction. It is a central factor in the history of the trade unions. It was the sons of skilled men who acquired formal education and moved into the professions.

The Irish tailor and his wife, née Theresa Driscoll, had five children, all accomplished and intelligent, of whom Will, Denis's father, rose by night-school classes to an engineering degree at Leeds University, to become Principal of Keighley Technical College; his brother, Russell, would head the important textile department at Bradford Technical College.

Because of the name and the partial connection, Denis Healey is spoken of almost as commonly as an Irishman. 'His Irish dander was up,' says Barbara

Castle more than once in that indispensable diary. Will is recorded talking dilettante Irish nationalism and about the Shan Van Vocht, while John William, he told Denis, had been a Fenian sympathiser in his youth. Ironically, the tale ran, this had led him, as an admirer of Parnell, persecuted by adultery-appalled bishops, to put behind him the first badge of Irishness in England.

He had, claimed William, formally left the Roman Catholic Church. Denis Healey in his memoirs recalls the then Bishop of Leeds, John Carmel Heenan, speaking of a card index of apostasy including John William's name. But the archivist of the Leeds Diocese flatly denies there having been such an index and thinks that Heenan was trying to impress a new MP. Equally, much of what Will Healey said about his father leaving the Church as a Fenian has to be questioned. For one part of Will Healey's testimony about himself is plain wrong. He claims, and Denis reports the claim, that he, William, was brought to Ireland as a baby. Baptismal records provided by Father Anthony Grimshaw, current parish priest of Todmorden, list:

William Healey bn 4.1.1886 bp 7.2.1886
S/o James Healey and Theresa Healey (née Driscoll)
By Rev Salvator Caruccio
Godfather William Henry Driscoll Godmother Mary Margaret Driscoll

Despite 'James' for 'John William', which Father Grimshaw thinks a change of name, these are our Healeys. The baptismal register also gives James and Theresa a son, John, born 1884, and another, James Russell, born 1886. Crucially John, two years older than William, is identified with a home and presumed birthplace, 8 Mechanic Street, Todmorden. These are uncles listed by their nephew Denis; John becoming mayor of Todmorden, Russell pursuing that career at Bradford Technical College. But in his autobiography, *The Time of My Life*, Denis also lists a first son, Frank, later killed in the First World War. Frank is not on the Todmorden baptismal record and might very well have been born in Ireland.

The implication is that we should take Grandfather Healey's Fenian activities with a pinch of salt. William, capable of imagining Irish birth for himself, may perfectly well have imagined a radical past for *his* father. Certainly William was not a Catholic and his father may have formally apostasised, but if so, we do not know why.

In fact, through his mother, Denis was at least as much of a Welshman. Will Healey's career path had taken him to Gloucester where he met and married Winifred Mary Powell. Win Powell had been born (in 1889), like her father before her, in Ross-on-Wye in Herefordshire close to the Welsh border. But such have been the movements between the pits and railways on either side of the Severn that just as South Wales is full of Howes and Heseltines,

come from the south-western English counties, so Shropshire, Herefordshire
and Gloucestershire are lavishly speckled with Welsh names – like Powell and
Preece. Winifred's father was Edwin Stephen Powell and her mother, Jane,
was born Preece. Healey, Driscoll, Powell, Preece: all the roots are Celtic, not
a Metcalfe or a Bootholmroyd among them. Edwin Powell, listed on
Winifred's birth certificate as 'Railway signalman', was actually signalman,
ticket clerk and stationmaster of a tiny pre-Beeching railway halt.

To emphasise this non-Yorkshireness, Denis Winston Healey was born (on
30 August 1917) in Kent, where Will's teaching work had taken him. The
'Winston' was a paternal enthusiasm for a statesman then highly unpopular
for his role in the Gallipoli landings. Before doing other things, Churchill
would next make his mark struggling at the Treasury where Denis Healey
would follow, to better effect, fifty years later.

But whatever the antecedents, Healey was brought up in Yorkshire, being
taken there at the age of five when Will obtained the technical college
Principal's post at £600 a year. Denis spent his boyhood in Riddlesden, a village near Keighley. From 1952 to 1992 he would represent a Yorkshire
constituency, variously Leeds South East and Leeds East. And, most important, he would go to school in Yorkshire, beginning with a scholarship at eight
years old to the junior section of one of the great northern grammar schools.
And though Oxford would impose its drawl and a scattering of pained
vowels, essential, flat, emphatic Yorkshire speech would never leave him.

Bradford Grammar School was the classic northern boys' high school,
aiming at providing the best for the best. There were notable contemporaries.
At the sister school for girls was the seven-years-older Barbara Betts, first
draft of the more famous Barbara Castle. She ruefully recalls the later ageism
and heightism of Denis during a larkish moment among Cabinet ministers.
'There we were at Chequers in '64 or '65 and, in front of the staff, he picks
me up and says, "Now this little girl was in the sixth form at Bradford when
I started school there." But I still like him,' she added.* Maurice Hodgson,
later head of ICI, was there at the same time, while an elder at Bradford – by
two years – was Alan Bullock, later the biographer of Healey's unofficial boss
and mentor, Ernest Bevin.

Although Healey occasionally did the things boys are supposed to do,
being severely reprimanded by the headmaster together with his friend,
Arthur Spencer, for letting down the sixth form by slipping off to watch the
Australians at Headingley, the measure of his seriousness, as shown in
books read and essays written, is almost dismaying. But happily (and sensibly) like many boys of three generations, he first read the *Wizard* and the
Rover.

---

* Lady Castle, conversation with the author.

These papers assumed high levels of literacy and though their contributors wrote to thrill and intrigue and to recount sport, they used a substantial vocabulary. Ironically, in the 1940s and 1950s at any rate, the *Wizard* had a character running through a long series of impossible yarns. He was a Yorkshireman who dwelt on remote moors of the kind familiar to any inhabitant of Keighley. He lived on a frugal vegetarian diet, trained by running many miles every day over moorland, dressed, not in designer-tagged sportswear but a knickerbocker suit of rough worsted, spun and woven from Yorkshire wool on his own distaff and loom. He would turn up unexpectedly at the Olympic Games from time to time to win the marathon or accomplish a four-minute mile some time ahead of Dr Bannister, was about 180 years old, probably immortal – and known, with an irony only really enjoyable after 1963, as 'Wilson the Wonder Man'.

From such a solid start the young Healey graduated to detective stories, *The Saint* and *Bulldog Drummond*, before advancing, politically as well as in quality, to Raymond Chandler and Dashiel Hammett. But Healey was in the classical Sixth and would read Greats at Oxford; he recalls coming below the top in that forcing-house school in Latin and Greek, while always being top in English.

English Literature between 1930 and 1970 in any half-decent school, meant Leavis: Frank Raymond Leavis, the great refining, didactic Calvin of Cambridge who spoke of 'the great books', another elitist who laid down metallic laws of excellence which placed a handful of authors, Eliot, D. H. Lawrence, and Virginia Woolf prominent among them, on to a plateau of pre-eminence. And through 'a young man just down from Cambridge', the gospel reached Bradford.

Healey, the sixth-former, wrote an account of Leavis's *New Bearings in English Poetry*: 'The general attitude of modern poetasters towards poetry and the extravagant claims made by critics suggests that something has been wrong for fifty years; the poetry of the anthologies has no roots, does not live.' He quotes Matthew Arnold on the Augustans: 'Their poetry is conceived in their wits, genuine poetry is conceived and written in the soul.' Accordingly,

Nineteenth-century poetry was characteristically preoccupied with the creation of a dream world, e.g. Keats's 'La Belle Dame sans Merci'. The danger of such preoccupation is that even when the world which has created them has changed, they bar the true poet at the point at which the growth of the mind shows itself, from the material which is most significant to sensitive and adequate minds in his own day. Poetry can communicate experience with a subtlety and precision unobtainable by any other means. Thus it is imperative that the poetry and the intelligence of the age should keep in touch with one another. The romantic conception was out of date even in the Victorian world.

The sixth-former, Healey, is citing the doctrine direct from the preacher:

> T. S. Eliot was the first poet to show the new environment by an intensely personal technique free from preconceptions ... 'Prufrock' appeared in 1917, defying the traditional canon of seriousness; the poet assumes the right to make use of any materials which seem to him significant ... Corbière and Laforge indicated the lines on which a poet with Eliot's attitudes might work ... With him [Eliot], as with the late Elizabethans, the intellect is immediately at the tips of the senses; sensation becomes word and word sensation. Eliot's idiom and movement derive from modern speech ... 'Gerontion' has a really dramatic detachment, the impersonality of great poetry. There is no dramatic or narrative continuity; the theme is the mixture of memory and desire in present barrenness.

As for 'Ash Wednesday', 'It works by compensations, resolutions, residuums and convergences. Mr Eliot remains a directing influence.'

This essay, one of an unnervingly wide and eclectic list, is the work of a brilliant schoolboy restating the arguments of Leavis. Written in 1935 when Denis was seventeen, it is the record of a mind receiving imprints and ardently responding. The reading list recorded in the exercise book includes James, Huxley, Wells, Ibsen and Conrad, as well as studies by Herbert Grierson, Clive Bell, Woelfflin and Freud.

If this is impressive, even in a precocious sixth-former at a first-rate school, it is also greatly earnest and very slightly suggests the Max Beerbohm cartoon of Matthew Arnold anxiously addressed by his niece: 'But, Uncle Matthew, why are you not always entirely serious?'

It comes as a mild relief to find Healey going to a party and being 'smitten', as he puts it, by a girl. 'The rest of the evening was continuous flirtation. I think that the only reason I fell for Clarrie was that she fell first for me ... Pleased to find my head clear though my heart is misty.'[1] But the next day he is being serious again, listening to a friend's records. 'Heard with great pleasure Brandenburg No. 5 and Isolde's Liebestod.' And two days later, at a subscription concert, Denis at sixteen finds the programme 'patchy'. He is 'Enraptured by Delius, irritated by Rossini, bored by Vaughan Williams, amused and thrilled by César Franck', but before he can be damned for correct contemporary views, he is 'delighted by Tchaikovsky 5 – seems to be bad taste.' Tchaikovsky, like girls, provided the human element.

The passion for music would be a constant. The records bought then were the fragile, heavy, twelve-inch shellac affairs, half a dozen to a decent-length symphony. The subscription concerts took place at Bradford's St George's Hall and involved the Hallé Orchestra under either Hamilton Harty or the young Barbirolli. The instrumentalists visiting the West Riding might be

'Szigeti and Huberman on the violin, Cortot, [Edwin] Fischer and Schnabel on the piano.'[2]

But it was art that mattered. Among the expositions of the seventeen-year-old's notebook was a very reverent one about Heinrich Woelfflin's *Principles of Art History*:

> Baroque art is restless, limitless, colossal, conglomerations of parts without true independence . . . Think of water bubbling in a vessel at a given temperature. It is still the same element, but repose has given place to activity and the palpable to the impalpable. Only in this form did the baroque recognise life . . . Sixteenth-century art presents pictures which demand a united perception of the manifold, the seventeenth century a definite main motive to which everything is subordinate and even the dominant forms are detachable from their surroundings . . . Classic – an articulated whole, Baroque – a fused movement. For Holbein the cloak is as valuable as the man.

This is not a student's one-uppishness. It is the judgement of a major art historian being restated as clarification and perhaps avowal. Healey would go through the art galleries of Belgium, Holland, Germany and Austria in a year's time, ready with his own judgements and approvals. But in Bradford in 1935 he was teaching himself what to look for in art before judgements could be made.

All his life Healey would think of the other career he might have followed, as a student of the philosophy of art. At the end of his time at university it would loom quite seriously with a postgraduate scholarship which five years of military immediacy finally discouraged.

He was also at the threshold of serious political thought, his inspiration here being E. F. Carritt's *Morals and Politics*. For someone who would in due course join the Communist Party at Oxford, Healey relates Carritt's cool view of Marx quite cheerfully. Marx, having followed the Hegelian idea of opposites, history as billiard cannon, states Healey/Carritt succinctly:

> the new mental facts that come into being change the situation so that the organisation becomes ineffective, the instability necessitates an abrupt change to effect a synthesis. The next synthesis will be the classless society. Our allegiance is to the proletariat, which is the antithesis of the capitalist. But the lacunas in the philosophy, particularly the impossibility of choosing 'moments' in the elements of the trend, make it unconvincing. It differs essentially in no way from Hegelian Fascism.

Wrapping up Carritt on Marx, Healey concludes this section of his exposition: 'We make our own history; but obligation cannot be based on inevitability, but only on possibility. History is man's own active pursuit of his ends.' And again and again, in diaries and the memoirs, Healey comes back to the thinking of Kant, philosopher of duty and First Gravedigger of the rational claims of religion. The tantalising thought occurs that Healey may have become a Communist without ever having been much of a Marxist.

But Marx would weigh with Healey over the next four years while he was an undergraduate at perhaps the most political of all Oxford colleges at that time, Balliol. And before that, Healey, the holidaymaker, quite as serious minded, would set out on a cycle in the late Summer of 1936 to see Germany. He would view a great many pictures in the art galleries of Munich, but in the Germany of Hitler he would experience other things.

2

STUDYING AND CYCLING – BRADFORD

'God, the books I read at that time!' Healey would say of his sixth-form and Balliol years. But he was bursting then quite as much with furious physical energy as with intellectual curiosity. Typically for his generation, young Healey was a keen cyclist – one way to be fit and to see, if not the world, large pieces of it. At seventeen he made modest beginnings, an excursion with a friend into the Lake District. Always a collector of data, he recorded the stations of the first day, leaving Keighley at 8.40, reaching Skipton by 9.30, Settle 11.40, Ingleton 1.40, Kirkby Lonsdale 2.40, Kendal 4.30, before reaching Crossthwaite at 6.30. He overcame early regrets at the exertion, defying strong winds at Gargrave, in time to react to nature – 'Two lapwings heading a grouse off their pasture'. He was recognising and responding to things: 'Young clusters of hawthorn flowers . . . sprays of wild parsnip . . .' While, on his way to Kendal, 'pink campion and the pale forget-me-not' delighted him after Devil's Bridge, from which the climb was satisfactorily 'exhausting' before 'a delicious run down Underbarrow Scar' fully entitled him to 'a light tea' at the youth hostel in Crossthwaite – and a further walk to see the sunset. That ride continued over three days to Langdale Pikes, Coniston, Thirlmere – 'a superb view' of Skiddaw, Keswick – Egremont and Kendal.

On Sunday, after a breakfast described as 'wonderful', there was more climbing to a waterfall, then through a snow shower to a view of the sea from which 'the descent was headlong down steep grassy slopes'. Healey's Spartan and punitive narrative ends appropriately with him cycling 'in wet shoes to Endmore beyond Kendal where I spent an excellent night'.

A trip to Scotland later in the year was studded with similar exertion and enjoyments. 'Delicious supper, ham and 2 eggs, Cumberland ham, warm,

soft, thick and not very salted', a flight of lapwing above a crimson moun-
tainous sunset, 'a Turnerian sky', 'Penrith, a clean town', finally, 'Swans in St
Mary's Loch. Run through Yarrow Valley past Grey Mare's Tail to Moffat.'
He also made the discovery, real enough in 1935, that 'Sunday in Scotland is
a limbo. Everybody wanders about restless, aimless, doing nothing and wishing to do nothing. Every shop, inn, place of amusement, golf course is closed.
There is a Hobson's choice between staying at home and walking into the
country.'

Another journey, to Loch Shiel – 'a great lake running like a fjord into the
sea' – leading to a first view of Skye before they rode on to Kyle of Lochalsh,
was described with some fervour, and once on Skye, Denis resumed painting.
This day, Thursday, had been his birthday and the best day of the trip – until
Saturday. Skye itself yielded two hundred yellow-billed seagulls, a view of the
Hebrides through mist and, once they had rounded the headland, another of
'the Scotch highlands'. Rather like Johnson and Boswell, he recorded seeing
'a very Gaelic woman milking a fine red haired cow' and took photographs
of her. He also noted the thatched shielings, temporary shepherds' or fishermen's summer huts, the thatch held down against the weather by large
stones. From the boat taking him from Skye he saw the Cuillins over Loch
Scavaig, 'beautiful and magnificent'. The record of the journey ended in the
Lowlands with the abbeys of Melrose – 'picturesque Gothic ruin' – and
Dryborough – 'the style is transitional. Rude Gothic windows with Norman
doors; Gothic layout with Norman tower is competent.'

A more ambitious journey of 1936 through the Low Countries, Germany
and Austria, also had its episodes of art and salutations of landscape, but
during an unnervingly polite lull in the Hitler era, it was something quite different. Denis Healey was to spend a life devoted to foreign affairs, and on the
eve of his nineteenth birthday, he was to plunge into the country which, as
enemy then ally, would be the preoccupying neighbour. After riding seventy-
three miles from Bradford, 'left mid-afternoon, to Mansfield Woodhouse,
then 101 to Cambridge and a further 93 to Harwich', he did not actually
want for endeavour. Rising at six on shipboard next morning, Healey went
on deck to find that they were moving 'surely along the grey estuary of the
Scheldt'. It was, as he wrote at the top of the page, '1 day on Continent.' The
English students were quite taken 'by the nonchalance of the officials and by
the policemen with swords' and 'several detachments of soldiers passed in
front of the café'.

In Belgium they took against the cobbles but admired the new housing
estates 'in the modern style and extremely good – better than in England'.
They took in posters, 'Socialist, Catholic, Communist and Lib-Lab', for
English and American films 'everywhere', as well as the 'extremely fine'
tower at Mechelen. In Tongres, Denis observed a gambling room: 'eight men

and women seated silently round a green table', watched the Hunsti-Bunsti vaudeville troop from Antwerp and, at a stall, bought chips and rossignols – 'a confection like warm new doughnuts without jam'. And now, satisfactorily abroad, Healey added: 'Note for the traveller. There are few recognised lavatories in Belgium – lamp standards, walls and notice boards are used indiscriminately.'

From Maastricht, 'a beautiful Dutch town' where performances of *De Tante van Charlie* were advertised, they came through a massive thunderstorm to the German border 'to be greeted with Nazi Flags and banners of welcome'. On his first afternoon in the country, travelling to Aachen, he noticed two salient things: 'Portraits of Hitler were posted up everywhere possible' and 'in the surrounding fields conscripted civilians were practising throwing sticks like hand grenades.'

He looked with envy at German cycles, the saddles very wide and well sprung and with 'enormously wide tyres inflated soft', anti-cobble measures greatly envied. But the Cologne art gallery, apart from five pictures by Rubens and two Van Goghs, was poor, also German postage stamps were short of gum. And he noticed the uniforms: 'Everyone from wolf cubs to taxi drivers wore a national uniform of some kind.'

Although, in best Kendal and Skye form, Healey climbed the Rhineside Drachenfels, Siegfried's river did not impress him. 'The Rhine is a disappointment . . . the scenery was disappointing and the Lorelei rock utterly undistinguished.' However, on progressing and looking at the castles above the river, 'the last four miles over and into Mainz were heartbreaking'.

Although Healey talks sweepingly in *The Time of My Life* about having cycled through Germany on black bread and strawberry jam, there are encouraging contrary references in the text to 'pork cutlet, potatoes, salad, cabbage and soup for 10d'. South of Mannheim he would see his first Autostrasse (or motorway) – described in the voice of a Gulliver of modern transport as 'a straight concrete road only for motors'. By melancholy contrast, he also saw that 'most of the hay wains were drawn by beautiful, clean, buff oxen'. He found the road from Ettlingen to Herrenalb in the Black Forest wonderful, 'overhanging meadows soft with green grass with foam dew meadowsweet swimming on its trembling surface'.

But given beer and biscuits at an inn by a young man doing the Nazis' *Arbeitsdienst* (labour conscription) and a young woman, he learned something less enchanting. 'The enthusiasm which the man and she showed for Hitler was indescribable. They described seeing him *persönlich*, how the pictures gave no idea of his immense personality, their reverence approached worship.' He tried to draw them out on German hatred of the Jews and was told that 'the Volk of every country hated the idea of war and that Krieg was always due to the capitalists i.e. in Germany, to the Jews.' And Healey ends, 'We parted great friends.' He was hearing, after all, the line of a fearful regime from the mouths of entirely decent young people. Another couple, encountered in Bad Boll, 'emphasised the German hatred of the Jews and when I said the *Stürmer** was *schlecht*, were emphatic in denial'. The next sight, 'the greatest waterfall in Germany', at Triberg, got nowhere with this traveller. 'To an Englishman familiar with Scotland and Ingleton this was not extremely impressive.' However the view did win approval as he descended to Freiburg where, at the hostel, he found 'four typically querulous Yorkshiremen'.

Moving on to Donauschingen in sight of the Bodensee, then Überlingen, noting, as he went, an idyll of peasants mowing wheat and piling it on to ox wagons and gathering cherries from high ladders, peasants who could think themselves lucky not to be linked with Breughel, he was guided to a hostel 'by the kindness of a young fuehrer of Hitlerjugend' whose troop he saw being drilled outside next morning. Delighted by Lake Constance and the lakeside village of Meerburg, Healey sat in a chair by the harbour and watched as, 'over the glitter of the lake rose the Alps dim and vast, many-streaked with snow', before cycling on through clouds of dust over bad roads to the sound of cowbells. When he reached the hostel at Sondthofen, he had 'covered myself and bike with white mud . . . my legs looked like plaster casts'.

This was the point of access to Austria, in 1936 still in non-Nazi, if unengaging, clerical and constitution-suspending hands. Here he would be rewarded with his first view of Neuschwanstein castle, King Ludwig's impossible piece of real-life stage scenery, then the baroque interior of a celebrated church at Wies – inside 'white, gold, red and blue whirling with giddy carving', outside 'a gentle piece of rococo like a Louis Quinze court chair'.

By contrast, Oberammergau was 'not very interesting, rather trippy as often in Bavaria, while Garmisch too was crowded with foreign tourists'. On finally reaching Salzburg, he met a committed anti-Nazi who 'typified the Catholic opposition to Hitler – a firm conviction that the people of Germany would return to God – and the uncomfortable consciousness of the omnipresence of Nazi control.' This young man made a remark which registered strongly enough to be echoed in Healey's own memoirs: that 'the Communists were now wearing red shirts under the brown'.

Wednesday 12 August was not for cycling but for *Faust* at the Festspielhaus – the production 'throughout unforgettable and distinctive', the Mephisto superb but the music 'undistinguished', and the dancing 'though adequate was completely eclipsed by the masterly production'. Healey, exhausted after three hours standing when the play ended in the admiring

---

* The Nazi Party's official paper, edited by Julius Streicher and notorious for general obscenity as well as its anti-Semitic articles and cartoons.

silence of Salzburg custom, had spent the earlier part of the day going to an exhibition of modern art: 'very good, especially the Vlaminck and a Chagall', and seeing a film, *Savoy Hotel 217* with Hans Albers, 'undistinguished', and the accompanying Austrian newsreel: 'politically and artistically colourless'. He had also spent time talking with two sorts of Czechoslovak: an actual Czech who told him that 'Czech youth was all Socialist or Communist and very friendly with Russia' and one of the Volksdeutsch, a Czechoslovak citizen of German race, 'who was a passionate Nazi'.

In Munich, admired for its street planning, good architecture, parks and fountains and 'the beautiful Koenigsplatz' (also very cheap art books), he went to the pictures and found the newsreel to consist 'solely of a long film of the most recent events in the Olympic Games'. His reaction to this reads rather sadly now: 'The universal interest for this festival shown by the German people would be quite impossible in England.'

The following morning found Denis in the Alte Pinakothek examining Rogier van der Weyden – 'universally keen delight in all objects' – Rubens – a page of varied but positive reactions – and Van Dyck – who, after Rubens, was 'like passing from a glorious fiery sunrise to a placid skyscape of grey clouds on a pale blue heaven'. But when, in the gallery shop, Healey asked about postcards or reproductions of Matisse or Picasso, the assistant responded with 'shocked propriety', *entartete kunst* presumably.

The running political dialogue which this traveller combined with art appreciation and strenuous physical exertion, continued with an elderly German 'who wanted Germany to regain her colonies and join with England as the foremost combination in the world'. But approaching Augsburg in the late afternoon, he fell in with a young man who spoke of war 'with loathing and recognised that the scientific element would make the next war more destructive and horrible'.

The vast cathedral of Ulm, an hour and a half on from Augsburg, drew the cyclist in, but he pushed on to Geislingen for lunch (sausage and black bread), a new companion proclaiming at once his pacifism, his admiration for Hitler's brave acts in the last war and the German hatred of the Italians. This pacifist was also proud of 'Germany's excellence in modern warfare . . . and showed pride at Germany's skill in *Chemie* [chemical weapons] and gas.' This conversation Healey noted coolly as 'very illuminating'. His companion 'was devoted to the paradox that Germany wanted only living room for her nationals, that she wanted colonies for her surplus population and that she wanted a higher birth rate to maintain her *Kultur* . . . He loved Nietzsche and German philosophy and his passionate conviction [was] that the Jews were all blameworthy and wicked . . . he thought that all capitalists were Jews and vice versa.'

From Stuttgart next day Healey moved, by way of Ludwigsburg, into a particularly beautiful part of Germany, the valley of the Neckar, 'beneath trees literally bowed under the weight of fruit'. After Heilbronn he was befriended by another affable Nazi who invited him into his home, 'a picture of Hitler in every room except the living room where there were two'. On the following day the first objective was Heidelberg and the usual Matthew Arnold pattern of plain living and high thinking, bread and sausage for lunch at Neckargemünd before viewing the Altes Schloss at Heidelberg, 'possibly the best ruin I have visited', then Darmstadt where, in the city of beer and the young Brahms, he met his worst hostel, overcrowded and with outdoor taps at 32 pfennigs a night.

Frankfurt offered the Stadel's Kunst Institut, Poussin and Velázquez – 'Poussin interests me every time I see him' – and an admired post-Impressionist section. The good feeling induced by Poussin and Corot quickly departed after a mile's ride when an earlier slow puncture reappeared as a quick one. He survived that at the cost of a Reichsmark's worth of repairs until the outskirts of Mainz when his three-speed broke, costing him another two or three hours while it was repaired.

The comfort of the Mainz hostel may have been enhanced by finding someone with a new opinion, a part-paralysed French Alsatian survivor of the First World War. 'He hated the Germans much more than I have found any German hating the French and insisted that England and France must stand together; in Germany all was military uniforms and suppressed revolt – he thought that 50 per cent of the German people disliked NS [National Socialism]; in Germany was *alles verboten* – one could not even sleep with a girl – here a German youth strongly contested the point.'

Approaching the Rhine, which had failed the grade on the way out, Healey was now very much on the swing home. He reached the riverside resort of Boppard where he found 'delicious sunshine which lasted only an hour'. Sadly 'The Rhine again failed to weave any spell – it is all like one long limb of Loch Linnhe with a Fort William every mile or so.' Shades of Nazism closed on his next lap via Bonn to Aachen. At Jülich a physical culture rally was taking place, the sort of thing to put any man of sense off Nazism before the first crime was committed – 'At least 100 bronzed youths marching in ranks behind a military band'.

It might be late August and this might not be England, but it had rained a great deal and Healey was on the edge of a heavy chill. Though feeling unwell, he was pleased to see Holland and its architecture again; then, from pretty Maastricht, he pressed on into Belgium before becoming quite seriously ill: 'iron fists clutching my intestines reduced me to a pitiable state.' There was a streak of high-minded masochism in the young Healey of which the Early Church and the public schools would have approved. He registered his agony in the diary and peddled valiantly on via Saint-Trond to Assent, where he was able to eat supper and admire the landscape, 'rich dark blue, bruised here and there by a gentle pink with soft silken rolls of cloud'.

He was back among the cobbles, no longer everywhere assured of Hitler's devotion to peace, but the art galleries had never stopped – 'For the first time I began to appreciate the baroque atmospheric landscapes of Ruysdael.' And he formed a cool view of Jordaens – 'interesting – a more dissipated Rubens'. Politics flickered for a moment with a shopkeeper in Antwerp who sympathised with the Spanish rebels (the Franco people), 'a rare thing in Belgium, though the posters of the Fascist "Rex" party are a common sight in the streets'.

Apart from a last fling of modernish art at the Schoonkunst Museum, he was now winding down for departure. On shipboard, he struck up with a student from Burton-on-Trent who one-uppishly, had cycled to Budapest and back, and with an American whose racy talk was new and amusing – about Belgian cigarettes: 'Jees, these'll make your hair part in three di-rections!' Back in England, he rode from Harwich to Cambridge, the smooth roads 'a dream after the Belgian cobbles', then on to St Ives for the last political conversation of the holiday with 'a Scotch-Irish fruiterer. He had spent 18 months as a POW in Germany.' Hatreds as encountered in recent weeks did not arise but 'he greatly preferred the Saxons and Bavarians to the Belgians who were not worth two penn'orth of cold gin.' Having been in one war, this man was, succinctly, against a second.

3

STUDYING AND CYCLING – OXFORD

For all its academic standards and ambitions, Bradford Grammar had no connections, still less 'pull' with Balliol College, Oxford, which despite the Balmoral façade, can claim through its association with John Wycliffe and the High Agnostic traditions of Benjamin Jowett, to be academic Oxford much as Christ Church is social-cream Oxford, St Edmund Hall sporting Oxford, and Magdalen, Oxford *je ne sais quoi*. For the young man soaked in Woelfflin, the metaphysical poets, Freud and Kant, it was the only place. It assured him not only of outstanding teachers for the classical part of Greats – Russell Meiggs and E. R. Dodds – but a great skein of clever, interesting friends.

Healey's fellow students at Balliol would include future ministerial contemporaries: Edward Heath, organ scholar, a year older, a year ahead and in those days called 'Teddy' even by his Marxist friends, and Roy Jenkins. Apart from Jenkins, 'very much a man of the mainstream. His speeches in the Union were quiet, earnest and intellectually persuasive',[1] the only friend whom both mention in their memoirs was Julian Amery, son of the great imperialist Leopold, who would himself be an arch Suez invader and struggler against the age. But following his father, young Julian fervently opposed Munich, and he was someone many opponents found endearing.

Unlike Heath and Jenkins, Healey declined to join the Oxford Union – this nursery of politicians delightedly visited by the grown-ups on the Westminster front bench, standing out from it 'as a piece of outdated bourgeois frippery with white ties and a subscription of thirty shillings a term, the rough equivalent of £40 today'.[2] Not being part of the Union was an early manifestation of a Healey characteristic. He would rapidly become a good stump speaker when he entered electoral politics. Given a major case to argue, as in his maiden speech on the European Defence Community (see chapter 17) or over Suez, the compelling intelligence and force of personality made him formidable. But to the art of speaking, which Jenkins would invest with deft and enjoyable skills, Healey would remain indifferent; his performances would be good or mediocre according to content and circumstances. This puritan attitude he would abandon only in his last decade in politics, late-developing as the wittiest and most feared debater in the House.

His immediate passion outside art, remained philosophy. And he would rely on philosophy papers rather than what he considered a rather casual study of ancient history to get him his First in Classical Moderations – 'Mods'.[3] The intellectual efforts represented in his freshman's essays for the academic year 1936–7 are overwhelmingly literary and philosophic: 'Religion is What a Man is When He is Alone', 'Shakespeare's Sonnets', 'The Purpose of a University Education', 'Murder in the Cathedral', 'Behaviourism' and 'Macbeth' among them.

Of the fourteen serious essays preserved, only one is political and topical; it is bleakly called 'Rearmament'! Unlike anything that Healey wrote about art or philosophy, this 2000-word essay is frankly nonsense: a run-through of the glib certainties solemnly believed in by a wrong-headed generation, everything that over-education could get wrong. And in one of Orwell's great phrases, the whole thing is 'a kind of playing with fire by people who do not even know that fire is hot'.

A rearmament policy would be totally disastrous; in view of its complete moral indefensibility from every aspect and of the great additional sacrifices which would have to be made, the people of this country are justified in going to very great lengths in order to avoid taking such a policy ... The proletariat of the world is not sufficiently class-conscious to justify any war on the grounds that it may bring socialism.

Having seen real enough human beings among the polite and kindly young men in uniform with whom he had argued, he wrote that 'personal familiarity leaves no doubt that in the last event, even a Nazi domination of Europe is better than indiscriminate murder inspired by the most irreproachable of unselfish doctrines, and then the final collapse of European civilisation.'

Healey talked like this because he agreed with Stanley Baldwin, using a famous despairing remark of the Prime Minister. Indeed he went further: 'This war will be inevitable, prosecuted in the first and possibly the last place by aerial attack. There is no defence against air attack, the bomber will always get through. Therefore the only safe course is to attack first; today attack is the only means of defence.' And the fighting of a war would not bring socialism. It would cause nationalist regression. For 'the immense increase in speed and destructiveness caused largely by the development of aircraft will make the next war too short and deadly to plant seeds of anything but an immediate and fierce hatred; there will not be the humanising contact between the proletariats of combatant nations which in the last war did so much to help the Russian Revolution.'

As for vague purposes of the Woodrow Wilsonist liberal kind, Healey knew them for a nonsense. 'Collective security can provide no excuse for rearmament while this generation of politicians is in authority . . . To rearm while this government is in power is to arm not England but capitalism . . . In the present situation it is sheer madness for a socialist to arm his enemies for a struggle which the very fact of arming will make inevitable.'

Healey looked forward to one possible consequence of disarmament throughout the Empire – that Russia might seize India. Supposing moreover that India then passed under the USSR, 'that country has proved her superior competence to deal with coloured communities; what a brilliant contrast the Soviet Union presents to the fumbling injustice of British rule! . . . Whatever one may think of the suitability of Communism for an English type of society, the Soviet Union has triumphantly vindicated its supreme right to deal with more primitive communities.'[4]

All this must be taken as the work of someone nineteen years old, impossibly sophisticated about art but taking *all* his opinions indiscriminately from the most advanced, modern sources. In politics, such dominant teachers were the Webbs, H. N. Brailsford, G. D. H. Cole, Kingsley Martin of the *New Statesman*, the new wave of the silly-clever.

As for the Soviet Union, it existed, behind its own wise walls and closed doors, as an abstraction heavily promoted. There being no fool like a young fool, the officer who would be twice mentioned in dispatches and a dedicated, hard-line opponent of the Soviet Union and its friends was a natural product of his time. Happily, at the end of his first year he was ready to go on his travels again – to a real France where, outside of art galleries, better things than theories were to hand.

In the summer of 1937, Healey and a friend, Owain Rees, reached Paris on the evening of 20 June. As serious young left-wingers and this being 1937, they called almost at once on the Spanish Aid Committee, but found no work for their volunteering hands although Healey passed on a message from James Klugman, the Communist intellectual and mastermind. The Louvre was shut, the Orangerie too expensive, so Owain and Denis pushed south: the Loing, Sisley's river, 'a softer reproduction of the Neckar, grey-green poplars standing quiet over the sliding olive waters', then Vichy, 'a grand scale Harrogate', soon to be called so many worse things, Ambert and tremendous oppressive heat, Polignac and Le Puy, its Moorish looking cathedral surrounded 'by squalid tenements'.

They were now in the full south, painter's country: Nîmes with its Maison Carrée and Musée des Beaux Arts – 'Uniformly mediocre' – and

Montpellier – 'like a small block of Paris or London on a disproportionately grand scale'. And, with some enthusiasm, they saw the Mediterranean for the first time. They walked up a slope to look at a perfectly proportioned castle from the Middle Ages, picking ripe apricots as they went and, hitting the coast, 'dashed into the sea to bathe . . . the best bathe of our lives'. Going from Perpignan via Prades, they came to a hill village called Mosset.

It was at this point that a friendship was founded which went beyond even the enchantments of the south. A Quaker friend, Nick Gillett, had put Denis in touch with a couple living outside Mosset whom the Quakers had, rather cackhandedly, helped. 'Pitt Kruger and his wife Yves abominated the Nazis. They left Germany three days after the burning down of the Reichstag.'

With these people in this place, Healey fell into a kind of spiritual love affair. The Krugers lived a marginal, but sufficient, agrarian life in hard country – their cherries and vegetables and a great deal of hard physical work outside, their flutes and violins inside. Yves, Pitt's wife, whom Denis almost reverenced, could sing any Schubert song, it seemed. He wrote about them with a passionate admiration which had not waned when, in 1986, he recalled them in *The Time of My Life*.*

The Krugers, friends in Potsdam of Wilhelm Kempf, busy liberal educationalists holding seminars on new ideas, liberal socialists without party rigidities, 'had been dragged out of a cultured intelligentsia and undertaken to make a success of farming in a barren Pyrenean valley without turning disillusioned, resentful or broken spirited'. Denis was seriously affected by the Krugers, real and admirable people underfoot in the hideous new era.

Our late teens and early twenties are the time for forming our deepest prejudices or convictions. Margaret Thatcher, admiring her narrow, striving father and creditably responding to her pen-friend, Edith, a German Jewish victim, grew to be uncritically hostile to the Germans and, by extension, to most other European peoples. Denis Healey, captivated by the Krugers, recognised that other, true German civilisation and, though he would never be a *political* European, for reasons of disbelief in complex federal structures, he would be one in all the other ways.

Healey took in much more about the local life of Mosset than had been possible pushing hard through Germany. The Krugers believed in birth control, sniffed at in England, abominated by the Catholic Church. It was, Healey learned, 'so little known in France that abortion is dangerously widespread and ten thousand mothers die thus every year. Each large village has its local practitioner who works under dirty and furtive conditions.'

---

* He visited them in the late sixties to find that after bitter privations and long political imprisonment, Pitt Kruger and his wife, once reunited, had made a brilliant success of the cultural and educational institute they later established.

Never a shirker from any task if sufficiently exhausting, Healey earned his 'delicious meals' by bending his back. 'I have been working hard each day, planting and watering marrows or turning a great field of Lucerne; this is not a very pleasant task as the sun is merciless and the horseflies rather troublesome. In the evening, I climb into a cherry tree and spend an hour plucking the fruit.'

But on 9 July the young man felt he should make progress and left the Coume, the Krugers' valley, making his way back to Perpignan where he talked with a London University communist. This being a time of busy left-wing ineffectiveness, the young man's attempts to enter Spain had failed, but he 'had had an interesting time talking about non-intervention with the sailors of French and English boats'.

Never one to make life easy for himself, Denis, having swum at La Franqui, had been befriended by a Frenchman who gave him wine, red and white. But he had failed to eat, was blasted with a heavy wind picking up and driving the sand, and fell into what he calls 'a morbid melancholia, possibly caused by hunger'. After taking himself and his bike, a puncture mended yet again, to Narbonne, he cycled on to Fleury then Agde, found no youth hostel and, cycling into the night and a thunderstorm, finally, after failing to find a barn, 'lay down in a ditch by the road in my sleeping bag and went to sleep'. It beats morbid melancholy and sounds like the sort of thing the mothers of young men never thought to start worrying about.

The Stakhanovite in Healey slept through thunder and lightning in his comfortable ditch, woke at five-thirty, reached the sea near Sète at six-thirty, in time for a bathe in the rain, took in the primitive conditions of the fishermen in their shielings, then he was off to Montpellier, arriving at half past ten to find that 'the heat was already unbearable' and an examination of the Musée Fabre and its pictures, where 'a good Breughel [*Peasants Fighting*] was balanced by a bad, tricky Rubens'. After lunching in the company of a rich peasant, '. . . extraordinarily well informed on politics and economics', he cycled off 'in a burning sun' and completed the journey to Tarascon in the company of an itinerant pedlar with a look of d'Artagnan.

It will be no surprise to learn that Healey was violently ill the next day, or that 'Somehow I managed to reach Avignon.' This doggedness had its rewards, for 'I realised it was the most beautiful town I had ever seen.' Despite 'a voluble and condescending guide', the Palais des Papes reminded him of an arabesque page in the Book of Kells. As for the gardens, they were 'paradisaical – deep green, watered with fountains, pools with swans under grey grottoes, palms and fiery blue peacocks'.

Unfortunately, joy was now snapped at by low technology. He had made the distance from Avignon to Orange and had just left that town, when a pedal broke off. The next hard day's cycling, after continuous failure to hitch lifts on lorries, was eased by coming to Montélimar, 'a town which seems to exist on and by nougat alone', where he stopped and bought one, 'excellent – honey, fruit, nuts and grain embedded in a white substance which defies description'.

Heading through the Rhône valley and helped by a forceful wind to pretty Vienne, he noted, as elsewhere in France, the use of every other wall for political slogans. The road to Lyon was mostly uphill, with much bike-pushing, and finding the hostel some way beyond that city took him over ten miles of cobblestones. As the landscape on the way to a Paris where it would be raining seemed very little different to the English Midlands, he read a hundred pages of John Strachey's *Theory and Practice of Socialism* – 'exciting, convincing and thorough, but written in a schoolboy journalese'.

The point of Paris would be the Louvre, 'undoubtedly the finest museum I have ever seen' and for Denis a sort of invitation to an orgy. Degas bowled him over – 'I begin to think he is one of the two or three greatest painters of the past century . . .', while poor Edouard Manet seemed 'little better than Sargent or Lavery'. For 'my love of Manet has dissolved.' Among the painters of earlier centuries, Rubens continued in the bear market, descending after the 'glorious fiery sunrise' of Munich to 'windy and pretentious after Degas'. He is in serious, sharp earnest about all this. Rather like the general he might have become had he accepted the lieutenant-colonelcy offered him at the age of twenty-eight, when the war ended, Healey the art critic is a slightly unnerving career option.

After the Louvre, Paris was the next most interesting thing in Paris. And Paris on 14 July tried very hard. Healey watched the military parade, much taken by the overseas troops – Spahis, Senegalese, Algerians, as well as the more traditional Zouaves – and the tanks which in three years' time would be so little used, all this followed by 'Firemen, Garde Mobile, Chasseurs Alpins', and the technicians at whose chemical-container lorries a wag shouted 'Mort aux parasites'. A little later, a workers' demonstration was held – 'great banners and muslin paintings of Labour leaders' – filling the air with 'L'Internationale', followed by spectacular fireworks which he watched from a bridge, and dancing in the squares, – all rather unBritish and enjoyable.

Healey's hinterland would be expanded in the following days, not only by more art seen at the Petit Palais: Signac – not much cared for – Vlaminck and 'Picasso, of course best of all', but by the other sort of pictures. Healey would become a fairly avid filmgoer even as Minister of Defence. Now barred from the Opéra, where he had hoped to hear Berlioz, because 'not even in the 4 franc seats, could one go without dark suit and tie', he went to the cinema to see Nicholas Ekk's *The Road to Life* – 'a really fine Russian film in technique and scenario'. Paris itself was chaotic and Healey's comment cryptic: 'The traffic was overwhelming; in the Champs Elysées the Garde Mobile was out to protect the restaurants which were on strike.'

The journey home, now begun, had its own charms. He went sharply off when the turning to Giverny appeared. He had spent an hour in the Petit Palais simply letting Monet soak in. The main street here was the rue Claude Monet, the hotel the best he had yet been in. But the real interest of the visit was a conversation with a widely travelled French journalist whose 'personal political history was typical of many Frenchmen'. This man had belonged to the Croix de Feu, perhaps the least awful of the neo-fascist groups present in France during the thirties, and had come to know its leader, Colonel de la Roque. In due course 'he found fascism a swindle, de la Roque an honest dupe* and, like all the first wave of Croix de Feu, left in disgust. He carried on his forehead a scar received in the February riots.'

Later, Healey's new friend had swung leftwards, convincing himself 'that socialism is the only party for a good French patriot and he is now "pas Communiste, mais pas loin".' That would be a view common enough in France after 1945 to give Healey's future guide, Ernest Bevin (who was very *loin* indeed), serious anxieties. The journalist also thought 'that Communism was the instrument or perhaps concomitant of an intelligent nationalism; – only England, he said, with all her frontiers, could afford the luxury of a complete internationalism.'

Next day Healey made a pilgrimage to the Giverny gardens, saw 'the floating platters of water lilies in which the buds opened like white, green and pink glow worms', took photographs and saw the famous little bridge before setting out for Rouen where he stayed the night. Having looked carefully round the cathedral so minutely recorded across succeeding times of day by Monet, he went on through 'wheat, barley, apples and dairy products' towards Tôtes and eventually reached Dieppe. Getting, as he said, rather drunk – unsurprisingly after 'mussels, red wine, kirsch and anise' – he settled for the short crossing and long ride. Going north from Croydon and for the first time directly through London, he saw something new: 'my first view of Westminster Bridge and the Houses of Parliament was a real delight.' Monet of course had painted them when living in Upper Norbury. The last experience of London for this Oxford Greats student would be the expression by a street sweeper of his 'contempt for the smug, trivial middle classes who studied useless Latin and Greek'.

The education of the future Minister continued.

Another holiday two years on, in 1939, shows Denis Healey rising twenty-two, highly literate and cultivated, assured to an alarming degree, censorious, left-wing, prejudiced, strenuous, eager for experience, taking himself very

---

* A good judgement. If General Boulanger was a poor man's Napoleon, de la Roque was a poor man's Boulanger.

seriously, ardent about art and full of artistic reference, and as judgemental as ever. His travelling companion, Stephen Verney, 'looks like a small, dirty, sharp-toothed Sealyham terrier', but he likes him. The Sealyham terrier later became a suffragan bishop. His companions a day or two later, in the dining room of the Pensione Marin, in Venice, are 'four stupid-looking Germans'.

However tough he is on the passers-by, Healey is choosy about the territory. 'Lombardy appealed little to me,' he says, dismissing a major province. Travelling in the age before backpacking and regular commutes to Bhutan, Healey was in fact vastly more adventurous than the great majority of his generation. The self-doubt in someone so breezily confident is rather touching. And frank about his anxieties, he is resilient. Walking about Venice, 'within ten minutes, I was hopelessly lost, roving down dim, smelling canyons, turning suddenly into noisy nameless squares.' He asks a gendarme for directions and finds him hopeless; 'his duty seemed to be to get lost for an hour or two, then ask an inhabitant the way back to his station.'

The critical eye is turned on Venice itself, magnificent certainly but 'it attracts me less than the average Provençal town . . . nothing but stone and water . . . The buildings are either monotonously splendid or dingy tenements.' But Healey is watchful and quite ready to admit to being wrong. Leaving Venice, he is suddenly reproached. After thunderstorms, 'The colours began to glow rich gold and blues instead of the pale, flat tones they had been during my visit.' The weather 'had robbed Venice of its charm for me by killing its colour.'[5]

Having embarked on the *Abbazio* and always ready to travel rough, 'I crawled onto a pile of sacking in the hold' though a kindly steward next day guides him into a first-class cabin. Taking the electric train from Piraeus to Athens, Denis is exposed to the class enemy. Keighley Technical College, which his father, Will Healey, headed, specialised in textile art and technology. Basil Tsakos, son of a Greek millowner, had studied there and had offered help in Athens. There is a description, recurring in the memoirs – animus cheerfully sustained across fifty years – 'a flashy young man with co-respondent shoes and a rakish green hat, glittering eyes and moist bright teeth'. Don't we all have moist teeth?

There were grounds for dislike. Basil would try to involve him in helping an admiral, of all people, in changing money, and the admiral, 'a fascinating old scoundrel, a cross between Von Tirpitz and Silenus', cadged dinner and short-changed him. But the revulsion was chiefly the recurring and ad hominal Healey puritanism towards the undeserving rich. Basil's friends, with whom he drank 'Samian wine in an expensive bar', are 'a curious mixture of wilting, unhealthy, lisping rich men's sons and forceful youths on the make with a sprinkling of pretty predatory girls'.

Basil himself would explain that Greece had only two social classes. He belonged in the first, but if war came and the family business was destroyed, he would have two choices, 'retirement to the country or exile from Greece'. Liberated from Basil, Healey set out. At Mycenae his visit to what was 'superficially the dullest ruin in Greece' was made exciting by a brilliant guide, a young man had only just returned from five years' internal exile in Epidaurus. This was the Greece of the Cephalonian dictator, Metaxas; the guide was a follower of the populist democrat Venizelos. On his next stage – to Nauplia – Healey talked with a young minor political prisoner, a peasant boy off to jail in handcuffs for refusing to renounce a communism about which he seemed not to know very much.

Healey was nothing if not the strenuous sort of tourist. After a heavy day's travelling, he left the bus at Ligurio at six-thirty in the evening to walk five kilometres to the local ruins only to find the Temple of Aesculapius 'a disappointing heap of stones'. However, the adjacent theatre enjoying perfect acoustics, he stayed for an hour before making the journey back to the house of the bus driver to dine off stuffed tomatoes and retsina and to sleep, sharing a room with the children, 'the windows open to the stars'.

In Sparta – clean wide streets and bright, low, new houses – he 'dined badly in a cellar off the main street with the gramophone playing Greek music which sounded like Arabian folk-songs, until I felt quite stupid.' Healey would organise himself to do the energetic things in the mornings and late afternoon. At New Mistra he came back to his lodgings, his critical judgement of frescoes drained by intense heat, to eat 'omelette, chips, tomatoes, pears, retsina, coffee and lemonade and spent two hours in the shade' before starting on the hour-and-a-half walk to Trypi.

He was inclined to write lyrically about the Greek peasantry, admiring their features and costume.[5] But recurringly, he met the unglamorous, itinerant poor of the country. A tramp encountered in Trypi had been in America for seven years, thirty years earlier, returning in 1912 to fight in the Balkan War. 'Now friendless and dispossessed, he was wandering over the Peloponnese looking for a temporary labourer's job.' He would be met again next day working at road mending to finance his next lap.

Another exhausting day took Healey from Trypi towards Messenia through a gorge where a boulder crashed dangerously close to him; he ate sardines and drank orangeade at a roadworkers' canteen before breaking into a landscape he thought 'Bavarian – steep, blue-grey mountains thatched with fir and gorse enclosing narrow valleys'. A train connection took him to Olympia where the ruins, especially the Heraeum, made sense to him, having kept foundations and shape, and where a landscape of pines, purple flowers and 'fragrant translucent sap-green pines' seemed the best he had yet seen. He was also able to work his art critic's fastidious way through the museum which contained sculpture by Paonius – 'the drapery is brilliant', and the Hermes of Praxiteles – 'a polished listlessness'.

At Olympia, having become conscious of the orientalness and distance of

Greece earlier in the day as he listened to Turkish and Greek music, he noted how often the traveller was asked, 'How are things in Europe?' The next day he had risen at five-thirty and taken a skimped breakfast of coffee and toast, to be sure of catching a boat which then did not leave till eight-thirty, leaving him without food till eleven at night. But the journey up to Delphi 'was a wonderful experience . . . the sky was full of shining lights. Delphi away up in the mountain looked like a net of stars, since Parnassus was visible only when the lightning flashed behind it.'

We have the word 'Sybarite' deriving from the people of Sybaris, noted for extreme ease, comfort and self-indulgence. Not any longer: in pursuit of the Sybaris spring in the Pappadaio gorge, 'the descent was steep and stony . . . thorns and spikes of thistles and grass stabbed my legs', but he finds the spring and meets and talks with more Greek peasants.

A reproach to most of us, Healey, wanting to visit Osios Loukas for the monastery, is up next day at four-thirty to take the bus to Birbas, catching a sunrise 'ever more lovely . . . turning the peaks of Parnassus golden'. At six he leaves the bus and starts the two-and-a-half-hour walk up to the monastery which proved thoroughly worthwhile. The mosaics alone 'restored my interest in Byzantine art', something diminished by New Mistra – even if the apostles made him think of the Seven Dwarfs. 'A late breakfast of fresh eggs, cheese, warm brown bread, wine and celery' sounds even better than the mosaics.

But virtue is about to be punished. His espadrilles, bought the previous year when staying with the Krugers in the Pyrenees, begin to disintegrate. 'Six hours purgatory had begun . . . The further I walked, the more the stones jerked into my feet, the soles . . . already wafery, began to disappear till the heel of my left foot was bare. The fields were strewn with a particularly noxious burr, pear-shaped with hard thin spikes, which caught in my socks and pierced me at every step . . . The whole way the path was strewn with knobby pebbles and sharp flints . . . But I was feeling too healthy to collapse.' Anyway, the friendly peasants and the beauty of the landscape bring Healey back to scorn for the decadent urban rich – and *their* footwear. 'I would feel sickened on returning to Athens to see the self-conscious, egoistic, smartened middle classes, every individual affecting some pose, infesting the café bars in light suits and co-respondent shoes.'

Pain did not hamper aesthetic instinct. After reaching the extinct crater at the top of the pass above Scorpi, there was 'a superb view over the Theban plain – a perfectly flat green sea carved on all sides by mountain promontories. I reached Levadia at four in the afternoon, my feet bruised and cut, my shoulders aching with the pack.' From Levadia, 'an interesting little town, well watered and full of fruit shops', he takes a smelly train back to decadent Athens 'for an easy day', walking out to view Agora and Acropolis from the Thesaion, 'an uninspired but well-preserved Greek Temple', before meeting some English friends whose conversation proved 'as usual, trivial and mannered'.

Next day Healey, as full of drive as censure, sets out on the coast road for Sunium where 'the temple of Poseidon is wonderfully placed – about a dozen milky columns of marble visible for miles out to sea'. He delightedly joins a working-class outing – forty people come in by way of lorries, tango and waltz played by four musicians on balalaika and guitar: 'the faces were compact and handsome, not refined into the weak vapidity of the Athenian café-crawlers.'

After a busy morning in the Byzantine museum, the next destination is Mykonos where 'all the houses are faced with brilliant white plaster' and 'to wander in the maze of streets is like touring the set for an Oriental film'. But Mykonos, after a 4.30 a.m. arrival, is the merest way station for taking ship at seven-thirty for Delos, 'shattered villas with dry stalks protruding through the mosaic pavement, lizards scuttling everywhere for cover' and 'an exhausting four hours looking over the ruins with a good guide'.

After which, amazingly, 'I spent an afternoon bathing and lying in the sun' before returning to Mykonos. 'Visually, Mykonos is the most beautiful place I have ever seen.' And he meets someone there he will remember in the memoir fifty years later. Here simply 'a German painter' – he was actually called Conrad Westpfahrt. 'I have rarely met a man so immediately admirable.' Westpfahrt lived in Greece, partly for its own sake, chiefly because he abominated Hitler. They talked art. 'His favourite painters were all mine – Poussin, Chardin, Bosch, Courbet' – and books, Dostoevsky, Tolstoy and Rilke. Healey also saw and greatly admired Westpfahrt's own paintings, 'watercolour groups of people, usually from Greek Mythology'.

Santorini, the next call, left him in a clean hotel to be bitten by mosquitoes – 'I counted sixteen bites on each hand' – before making the journey on muleback to Ancient Thera and the Monastery Prophetos Elias, set on a two-thousand-feet-high cliff affording a horizon from Crete to Syra. On that day Healey again bathed and rested. On 22 July, 'unusually hot even for Greece', he wrote letters and tried, not very hard, to do some academic work, as well as inspecting the museum at Thera – the statues 'all second class, archaic, Hellenistic and Roman'.

Syra proved more like most people's idea of a holiday: a pretty boat trip, water so clear the rocks could be seen fifty feet down, a stroll on the quay and a dinner there which ended in Turkish delight. But he was still picking up opinions. A brawling itinerant pumice miner from the Italian-protected Dodecanese hated the dictator, Metaxas, as a fascist and danced with loathing for the Italians.

The weather was exceptionally hot at the end of July. Healey observed that 'two minutes after I had wiped the sweat off my face I would look as if I had just emerged from a showerbath.' It was a day for siestas and 'a shower to remove a fortnight's brine' and the enjoyment of the town. 'Both the evenings I spent at Syra bathed me with a drowsy satisfaction. The cafés poured out music, the lights swayed in the water and the population drifted ceaselessly along the quay.

The journey back to Piraeus, which he had originally compared with Grimsby, might have been anticlimactic. But quite apart from the charm of the hill above Attica and the Bay of Salamis, being arrested as a German spy tends to dispel ennui. When Denis, who had been bathing, had an altercation with abusive local urchins, a passer-by leapt to the remote conclusion that he must be illicitly photographing the terrain. He made a citizen's arrest and the two of them interrupted the siesta of a decently sceptical elderly policeman who set the prisoner free. After which Healey struck up again with his English acquaintances, and encountered one of the lights of Oxford, the aesthete and philosopher of art, Professor R. G. Collingwood who 'pranced in with beard and yachting cap – you could almost hear him saying in his sinister mild falsetto, "Once aboard the lugger and the girl is mine!"'

The journey by ship back to Britain was fourth class. The open-plan dormitory of fourth, where food was 'uniformly poor' and eaten off a rough board while diners sat on boxes, reminded him of 'an inferior doss house'. But the company fascinated him: a German Jew now resident in Palestine who cheerfully compared life there with the American Wild West, a Turkish artillery officer pretending for no apparent reason to be a Soviet citizen from Odessa, a party of Egyptians in their nightshirt-like robes, and a Greek boy on his way between relations in Greece who didn't know he had left and relations in London who didn't know he was coming.

Somehow, and very characteristically, Denis 'spent the day curled in a coil of rope and finished reading Sullivan's *Bases of Modern Science*'. At eleven at night on 31 July, they disembarked at Marseilles, 'the fourth class passengers of course leaving last'. It was an appropriate end to a voyage which had been rough and improving throughout. Apart from the Oxford finals in which he would take the expected First, Healey's next major experience of life would be the Second World War.

4

THE OXFORD BY-ELECTION

There was, in the 1930s, despite furious conviction, a certain self-conscious drabness about left-wing undergraduate activity. The Oxford Labour Club, for the first week of its programme for the Hilary term of 1939 offered what looks like a full didactic course:

ELEMENTARY SOCIALISM
Thursday in Bellamy's rooms, Queen's. Sunday at 2.30 in Sedgwick's rooms, Balliol.

and

LABOUR MOVEMENTS
Fridays at 5 p.m. in Watt's rooms C.C.C.

In the midst of this earnest life and fully active in it, Healey, the Communist, was a noted figure. It is the way of the great universities to throw up characters, presences. Kenneth Tynan in his purple suit is a fair example. They are undergraduates who are talked about. Sometimes, like Tynan, they proceed to adult stature, sometimes they slip into insubstantiality, the Oxbridge fizz going flat in the glass. Healey was not crudely famous, not what this age calls a celebrity. The witty speeches and the rough-mouthed indiscretions came later. But he was remarked. And he was interested in things beyond flat ephemeral pamphlets. In that Hilary programme, those keen to add culture to their socialism could turn to

THE HILL & KEYES GROUP
'Literature and Society 1789–1830'
Applications for invitations to D. Healey (Balliol)![1]

He was also writing arts criticism of a highly advanced sort for *Oxford Forward*. All parts of the old Marxist injunction 'Educate, organise, agitate' were served by D. Healey (Balliol).

Brought into membership of the Communist Party (CP) by the poet, Peter Hewitt, he busied himself with its enterprises. It was a time of maximum Communist influence – and a willingness to engage in 'bourgeois politics'. Alarmed by Hitler, as well he might be, Stalin had directed the infinitely subordinable parties outside the Soviet Union to seek allies among progressive people. Given the fact that alarm at Hitler was shared by these very groups, co-operation was broadly forthcoming. Though for once the Labour Party, endlessly damned for its bureaucratic rigidity, was well served against long-term infiltration following such fraternisation – by its bureaucratic rigidity. But in places like Oxford University scorning such caution, the influence of 'the Party', as it was always called, was phenomenal.

This was not surprising: 'Republican Spain is in great danger,' wrote Healey's predecessor as club chairman, John Render, in a memo to college secretaries. 'The German, Italian and Moorish allies of Franco are pressing on to Barcelona, but their advance is only possible because of the great quantity of artillery and aviation supplied by the Fascists . . .' The Oxford Labour Club would therefore send 'a mass delegation to Downing Street tomorrow (Tuesday) to demand that the right to buy arms be immediately restored to Republican Spain . . . PLEASE RALLY MAXIMUM NUMBER OF PEOPLE IN YOUR COLLEGE FOR THIS . . . BUSES LEAVE GLOUCESTER GREEN AT 12 NOON.'[2] The conflict gave Communists in Britain both credibility and opportunity to influence the rest of the left, especially the young.

The Labour Club, with its room in 'St Michael's Hall, New-Inn-Hall Street opposite St Peter's Hall',[3] as the leaflet puts it, was the target ship and it was boarded in strength. The Labour Club travelled the route urged upon the Czech and Hungarian socialist parties after the war. In the name of socialist unity it had merged (members unconsulted) with the CP-controlled October Club, retaining the company logo while being run entirely by the bidder.

At one point, the only member of the Labour Club executive *not* also a member of the Party was the Scot, Thomas Wilson, later a distinguished economist. Shrewd people like Harold Wilson belonged to the Liberal Club; Tony Crosland, in Healey's record, dithered between joining the Party and not. Only Christopher Mayhew among noted Oxford socialists was an overt anti-Communist, forming a group known as the Oxford University Democratic Socialist Group. He records the account of electoral procedures

to club office given him by an ex-Communist on the Labour Club committee at that time. The party cell decided who it wanted chosen, including
non-Communists as proof of fair play. No ballot boxes were stuffed or
weeded, the sort of thing often found out. 'The voting was fair, and so was
the counting of the votes: all the Communists did was to announce the
wrong results.'[4]

A woman contemporary of Denis Healey, herself a Communist at the
time, watched him at a distance, 'a tall man striding around, obviously
important'. 'Women at Oxford in those days,' she said, 'still did knitting.' As
a young Communist, she remembers sitting at a meeting listening to Palme
Dutt, most ferocious of orthodox Marxists, 'and there we were, all clicking
away'.[5] The Healey she saw striding around was favoured by the *apparat*
and, as he relates,[6] he was preferred to another CP member, Tom McWhinnie
of Ruskin College, whom the Party thought might turn out unreliable. Life
having its little ironies, McWhinnie would remain a loyal member for the
next forty years while Healey worked dedicatedly for the closest possible
military links with America.

The Oxford Communist cell would meet in a flat near Folly Bridge to discuss the latest events, and with the relish of teenage machiavels, consider how
they might be exploited. Iris Murdoch would later comment that of all her
fellow young Communists, the one with the best and most thoroughly devious ideas was Denis Healey.[7]

The chief political activity of Michaelmas term 1938, was the Oxford by-
election. Though not its initiators, undergraduate Communists promptly
joined up and found themselves cutting with the grain of left liberal progressive Oxford. The sitting Conservative Member, Captain R. C. Bourne,
had died in August 1938, a few weeks before Neville Chamberlain at Heston
Aerodrome would speak of reaching a settlement with Herr Hitler and hold
up 'the paper which bears on it his signature and mine'. The constituency
most adapted to impassioned argument had something to argue about. The
local Conservative Party selected as candidate one Quintin Hogg, 'a fluent
and forceful speaker'[8] who said his address with entire truthfulness.

Labour had already reselected their general election candidate of 1935,
Patrick Gordon Walker, a grim-featured academic, Tutor of Christ Church,
who was destined for electoral unhappiness (see page 256). But Oxford
being the home at least as much of baroque intrigue as of lost causes, a
number of junior dons led by Richard Crossman, who was born to such
things, and the former Conservative, Frank Pakenham, later Earl of
Longford, set out to lobby for a non-party anti-Munich candidate.

Crossman and his friends wanted the Master of Balliol, Sandy Lindsay.
Though actually carrying a Labour card, Lindsay was, if anything, a
Liberal in the Campbell-Bannerman mould, a radical Christian who got
more radical as he grew older, who held and practised anti-racist views

before the rush, to whom Hitlerism was a very evident evil walking the streets at noon. After wrestling fairly perfunctorily with doubts, Lindsay declared himself willing. As part of the Establishment *ex officio*, he was the perfect candidate against the Conservatives at a fraught moment.

The Liberals had desisted from fighting the election by a unanimous vote. Labour took longer. In a diary entry of 20 October Gordon Walker listed the causes of his discomfiture:

1   The University and middle-class element. Many of them members of the Labour Party.

2   Left Book Socialists who had recently come into the movement.

3   The Communist Party which is still making its popular front (Liberal–Communist Alliance). The CP has a considerable influence over the apparatus of the LP in Oxford. It was able to get behind it, in these circumstances, a good majority of the General Council.

4   The Labour Club, which is wholeheartedly Popular Front and which has a large delegation to the General Council.[9]

Labour politics being Labour politics, and academic Labour politics even more so, Gordon Walker added: 'Crossman, who initiated the scheme, was either consciously or subconsciously jealous of me and wanted the Oxford seat for himself as Labour candidate or independent.'[10] Without wishing to impugn any bad motive, a cheerful conceit made Richard Crossman well nigh impervious to jealousy. But Gordon Walker's reservations and the man himself are interesting. He would later, reasonably enough, earn the name of a hard right-winger. Close to Gaitskell, he lacked all populist instincts for making left-wing noises. But the Gordon Walker of 1938 was a doctrinaire socialist in the mould of Sir Stafford Cripps with whose Unity Front he had associated in 1935, essaying overtures to the Communist Party before it made them to such people itself.

He was now on deteriorating terms with the communists precisely because, after years of immured exclusiveness, they were ardent for the widest possible spread of alliance, like Popular Fronts, a government in France, a cause busily preached in Britain. 'For the last few years I have been drifting away from the CP. I have been regarding them more and more as "Liberal". They (especially recently) have been saying that, by talking Socialism, I am too sectarian.'[11] In fact, the period of such activity before the drastic step of the Ribbentrop–Molotov pact was a golden age for the British CP, its best people, such as Harry Pollitt and Johnny Campbell, able straightforwardly to fight for communism by fighting Nazism, while the clerisy – decent, liberal, educated opinion – would never before or again be so well disposed to the Party. In the reaction against Munich, it struck a resonating and emotive sequence of notes.

Gordon Walker mattered less to the CP than he thought, but his case against the Lindsay candidacy was impressive and shrewd. 'An hysterical state of mind was created largely in middle class and University circles (it was therefore stronger in Oxford than it will be in some other places) . . . The hysteria took the form of "We must *do* something." We must have something that can be successful . . . People persuaded themselves that this was important . . . Quite ludicrous ideas about the importance of Lindsay's victory were evolved. That it would check Chamberlain, lead him to alter his policy, frighten Hitler etc.'[12] He also pointed out that a Popular Front made sense in France (briefly ascendant under the attractive leadership of Léon Blum), with an electoral system in which a party is a relatively small representation of a narrow interest group like the peasants in the Radical Party. But in the tent-like communities of British parties, the cohesion of interests was already accomplished and set. He might have added that a cry in French right-wing circles, one to find full expression in 1940, had been 'Mieux Hitler que Blum'.

Less convincingly, but very much in the left-wing style of the decade, Gordon Walker wondered to his diary whether Chamberlain or Churchill was the more likely instrument of fascism. 'No one can argue that Churchill is safer than Chamberlain as a potential fascist. In the peculiar international set-up, there is always the danger to guard against, that fascists in England will march under an anti-fascist banner.'[13]

But Gordon Walker's sharply analytical though rather literalist mind could not see how much publicity mattered and what publicity the Oxford by-election was. For Labour's National Executive Committee (NEC), reassured by Lindsay that he would not stand in a general election, showed an unprecedented degree of either flair or feebleness by denying the prospective parliamentary candidate its solemn powers of veto, leaving the Oxford party to its own enterprising devices. Labour in Oxford went in with the Liberals and a progressive committee was formed to fight Chamberlain (and, very satisfyingly, 'the Hon. Quintin Hogg!' as he styled himself), choosing Lindsay as its candidate.

Among those who rallied to the Master was Harold Macmillan, then a troublesome left-wing Tory backbencher: 'If I were a voter in the Oxford constituency I should unhesitatingly vote and work for your return to Parliament at this election.'*

A noted opponent was the Member for the University, the humorist

---

* Macmillan got into serious trouble about this. As his biographer records, he 'was threatened with withdrawal of the Whip, the prospect of an official Tory candidate being put up against him at Stockton at the next election and – fate worse than death – ejection from the Carlton Club. None transpired.' (Alistair Horne, *Macmillan*, vol. 1, *1894–1956*, Macmillan, 1988, p. 119)

A. P. Herbert, who proclaimed, not very amusingly, that 'the defeat of the government candidate would be to strike a dagger labelled "Oxford" into the heart of the Prime Minister of our country at a perilous moment in our country's history.' This was balanced on the other side by the succinct, if over-enthusiastic, slogan: 'Hitler wants Hogg'.[14]

Hogg himself would contribute to the febrile gaiety of the occasion by announcing in his address that 'Mr Chamberlain has expressed the hope that the settlement of this crisis is only the first step in a programme of general European Appeasement.'[15] 'Will you not play your part in helping him to achieve the glorious goal he has set himself of permanent peace in our time.' He spoke of the Prime Minister in the way that ambitious young candidates of government parties always speak of the current Prime Minister.

In an orotund way, shortly to go out of fashion though never quite with Hogg, he observed, 'The government had been ready to fight . . . but it must never be said that we ever fought in a cause which was not wholly just or that we refused to hold out the hand of friendship while there was even the possibility of it being grasped in good faith. "Peace with Honour" is a watchword of the Party of which I am a Member.'

Although a number of heads of houses did rally round the Master, Edna Edmunds, later Edna Healey, would report another response, entirely English and even more Oxonian. After Hogg's battered return, her tutor at St Hugh's told her: 'Oh, I am so sorry. I had so wanted Dr Lindsay to win. Of course I voted for Mr Hogg. But Dr Lindsay would have made such a good MP.'[16]

Hogg would hold Oxford Borough with a majority of 3434, a swing of 3.9 per cent or a halving of his majority. 'It is Mr Chamberlain's victory,' said Hogg. 'It is a victory for democracy, for peace by negotiation, and it is a victory for a united Britain.'[17] In the vote on the Norway campaign on 7 May 1940, which destroyed Chamberlain, Quintin Hogg voted against the government's great leader.

There was something else: the whole point of an election fought against appeasement was to stop appeasing, which meant to rearm. And with the line changed soon after by Moscow, to Communist Party members all military defence became no more than preparation for an imperialist war. By January 1939, worse things had happened to the left and democratic causes than the election to parliament of Quintin Hogg. The gallant Christian gentleman and conductor of massacres, Francisco Franco, would enter Madrid on 28 March. The Hilary term, along with its workshops on Labour movements, would be marked by that lobby for arms to defend Barcelona and the films *Fight to the Last*, *Hell Unlimited* and *Madrid Today*.

The Soviet Union would draw its own conclusions from Munich, responding to the tepid next act of Chamberlain in sending a promising civil servant, William Strang, to Moscow, while Hitler sent his Foreign Minister, by concluding the Molotov–Ribbentrop Pact. The British Communist Party, after an agonising weekend at which its people of conscience, like Pollitt and Campbell, bowed to the happy clones, Palme Dutt and Rust, denounced an imperialist war which Communists should everywhere resist and sabotage. Rather less momentously, in April 1939, Healey, together with the future Earl of Longford and the city's Communist leader, Abe Lazarus, would hold a meeting to protest against conscription.

In fact there was something to learn from Lindsay. His address in the election, though it had a full share of aspirational flannel about the League of Nations, also contained something pretty succinct: 'For rearm we must to unite in defence of democracy without any holding back. First we must insist that rearmament be tackled as a truly national effort; it must not be scamped for private profit or thwarted through private control. It must make defence against air attack fundamental . . .'[18]

The Healey who would defend Ernest Bevin's stand against the Soviet Union, the Healey of the hard-nosed pamphlets, the Healey thankful that an American military base had been near enough to Korea for action in 1950, the Healey who would not flinch from British nuclear involvement, was very much the child of that conviction. Rearmament and its underpinning became his preoccupation.

SOLDIERING

'Every man thinks the worse of himself for not having been a soldier,' said Dr
Johnson. Very few people like the process of actually becoming a soldier, yet
Denis Healey actively enjoyed his early training. 931224 Gunner Healey
D. W., as he became on 13 September 1940, found that the 'most paradoxical and pleasant aspect of my life here is the complete escape from the subtly
demoralising sense of present war'. There was no politics at the Uniacke
Barracks at Harrogate and no serious talk, 'scarcely a reference to the
calamity which brought us all here, and to cope with which we are being
given a specialist's training'.[1]

War having been declared in the unplanned way of Chamberlain's last
lurch in foreign policy, volunteers like Healey were accepted in principle, but
asked to go away and do their jobs, in his case the Oxford finals, which
would secure him a Double First.

It was in fact perfectly sensible practice. The regular army was nothing like
ready to train a rush of volunteers, still less in the twilight or Phoney War in
which Hitler thankfully was attacking other people, do anything else. When
Healey actually entered the army, a full year after volunteering, France had
been conquered and the British Army had retreated via Dunkirk to Britain,
but though the RAF might be rather preoccupied, nothing much else was
happening.

But military liberalisation was real. The barracks, this volunteer noted,
were 'much more comfortable, the regime more tolerable, the NCOs more
kindly, than I had ever imagined'.[2] Only a pair of too tight boots, also too
greasy for easy cleaning, caused grief – 'Oh, they feel like leg-irons or the
Scottish Boot of King James.'[3] Healey recorded decent food, sensible battle-
dress which replaced the hellish puttees hated by soldiers of the First World

War, two film shows a week, a newly opened library offering 'everything from Jane Austen to Michael Innes' and 'infinitely less futile red tape and discipline than in the last war'.[4]

He looked round the intake more or less pleasurably, perhaps least impressed with another Oxford man, from St John's, 'a typical Rugbyan, tall, well made, glittering and immature'. This was Hugh Sebag Montefiore – who became a bishop. The conscripts, older working-class men from northern towns, were cheerful and kind, 'determined if possible, to enjoy the army';[5] one, from Leeds, said droll things such as, after lights-out, 'Strike us a match, Arthur.' 'Why, Bill?' 'To see if there are any lights showing.' There was an element present who could not read, but among them, Healey noted, 'a Good Soldier Schweik figure', Gunner Box, a pleasant little man who couldn't read or respond when orders were given, but who had serious talent as a motor engineer.

The officers, with a single exception, seemed essentially decent. 'The Colonel is a huge swollen purple bulk like a sea lion, but he gave a sensible moderate speech very free from brutal flag-flapping.'[6] The major he thought 'fatherly and sympathetic', the chaplain an obvious inoffensive fool talking about himself as 'a bloke who wears a back-to-front-collar' and was clearly waiting for Alan Bennett. But upon 'the loathsome Captain', Gunner Healey turned the full critical faculty of Healey of Balliol: 'Looks like a housemaster manqué, a foul authoritarianism, insistence on discipline and sadistic brutality of thought.'

The captain belonged to the old, bayonet-in-German-guts school. 'If you meet a German parachutist, don't offer him a cigarette. Kick him in the shins [oddly anti-climatic!]. Treat him as dirty as you know. If you treat him like a human being, our Intelligence won't get anything out of him, so give him Hell and give it him rough. Never forget he's a Hun. The Hun knows no law. Shoot as many as you can, but remember to leave a few for our Intelligence boys.'[7]

The pleasures of adjusting to army life were brought to a sharp stop by a medical examination. A hernia condition, not surprising in such a rapturous taker of violent exercise, got Healey down-graded to what the army, in its own Oxford way, called B1 and required an operation. He would for a while 'be taken away from an environment I liked, from a thrilling physical fitness to a hospital[8] . . . I had the feeling of being put off a crowded bus full of my friends to wait two months for the next one.'[9] Healey characteristically read Malraux's *La Condition Humaine* in hospital before being sent to Woolwich Artillery Barracks to await a posting.

Woolwich was not like the Harrogate barracks. It was a military slum, 'a dirty, squalid group of quasi-prison buildings with filthy mattresses called "biscuits", greasy-feeling blankets and no sheets.' The depot hadn't been destroyed but it had been hit six times, something evident in 'collapsed walls, craters in the concrete paths and shattered windows'.[10] Ten days earlier, a direct hit had killed eighteen men. Soldiers seemed to be standing up to such horrors well, but 'Everyone wants to leave this futile clearing-house where the desire for a good scrounge is gratified.'[11]

He saw that the capacity for dull, brave endurance which had been a standard British military quality, 'almost the hall-mark of the British character',[12] was there as ever, but no one had attached a purpose or wider sympathies to it. People, he thought shrewdly, 'know what they are fighting against all right, but no one believes he is fighting for better conditions'.[13] He soon received a reminder of what dull, brave British endurance was for – and his own share of it. 'The general impression of an air raid is like people noisily moving heavy furniture in the room upstairs.'[14] He saw for the first time the reaction of people used to being bombed – when in doubt, to throw themselves to the ground, behinds in the air. It reminded him of a Muslim prayer meeting.

He was relieved to find himself not scared by air raids, only startled by the first large detonation. 'Political consciousness,' he noted, 'seems non-existent,' but there was a former member of the British Union of Fascists – 'delusions of power, persecution mania . . . a good type of the psychologically unbalanced dull-wit Fascist'.[15] A happier episode which stuck with Healey until his memoirs, was the widow's-mite conduct of the bombardier with a prisoner to escort who gave him 'three Woodbines and four penny rock cakes, obviously bought specially for the purpose'.

For himself Healey was cheered by the suggestion from an officer who interviewed him that he might find a commission in the Educational Corps. Meanwhile he settled down to read and read: *Of Mice and Men*, Dashiel Hammett's *Red Harvest*, Barbusse's *Les Bourreaux*, Denis Brogan's *Development of Modern France** (chapters only), Auden's *Another Time*, Malraux's *Days of Hope* and, less intimidatingly, a detective story by Agatha Christie, *Cards on the Table*, anticipating the controversial polemic of the same title written at the height of the Cold War by Denis Healey.

Life after Woolwich would involve a succession of tasks before and after Healey – following a period at the Officer Selection Centre in Scarborough – qualified to become a second lieutenant in the General List, no splendid county regiment as yet. In and betwixt, he functioned, more or less usefully, as a traffic officer with the bureaucracy-satisfying job of spending long hours on the great railway interchange stations, counting soldiers getting on and off trains, a sort of military approach to insomnia. He would start in Swindon,

---

* Rather later he would get a pass to attend a dinner of the Balliol Leonardo Society; the guest of honour was Professor Brogan who, with the birth of his son to celebrate, got 'hopelessly drunk'. (Healey, *The Time of My Life*, Michael Joseph, 1989, p. 50)

be moved to Derby and progress as Rail Traffic Officer in places men once asked God to be delivered from – Hull and Halifax, then York, Leeds and Sheffield.

It seems to have been an amiable enough life, learning something which would actually be useful to officer and army when men were being ushered under fire on to beaches in Calabria and at Anzio by Captain Healey. Though he admits[16] to collusive fixes with the Swindon stationmaster, by which the relevant authorities would be supplied with highly adjusted information. In Sheffield he bought valuable books very cheaply and in Swindon he saw a good deal of his girlfriend from Oxford, Edna Edmunds, whose home was in Gloucestershire. And at the end of it, he was sent to Scotland for specific train-ing – as the military landing officer he would become. Coupled with the course was another in street-fighting. While there he saw, when out walking, one of the hardly remarked horrors of the war: the sinking in the Firth of Clyde of an aircraft carrier with all its men. It had hit a mine dropped by air the day before.

Eventually he was sent abroad on a Free French-manned ship to Algiers, on 12 April 1943 and arriving in Algiers on 23 April. As the ship was moving down the Clyde someone on the bank affably shouted 'Hi-di-hi'. 'The whole ship replied with a thunderous "Hi di ho" and the rest of the way, the river resounded with prayer and response like a jovial cathedral.'[17]

Healey would move about extensively in the next three months – from Spur Camp Algiers* to Beni Mansour, then for nearly a month to the Donegal Camp at Bougie before pushing on sixty miles to Djidjelli and at once another 150 to Guelma. Algiers itself was having a hard time, short of every sort of goods, including, un-Frenchly, decent alcohol. He noted later the French racial attitude towards Arabs. They seemed to look down on them in a practical way based on competence and snobbery, but not with overt racial contempt. It was 'peculiar – not imperialist in the British way, but more that of petit bourgeois toward dwellers on a council estate adjoining their garden suburb. They blackguard them as *voleurs*, *fainéants*, *vauriens*, but there doesn't seem to be much racial feeling as such or sneering at facial idiosyncrasies.'[18]

More immediately to the point was the account he heard from a friend in the Scots Guards who had been in the Tunisian landings and who com-plained bitterly about the incompetence with which the landing of troops had been managed there, 'using a platoon to test a position where a section would have done and following its massacre by pouring in larger and larger bodies in the same place'.[19] Something was being done badly which young specialist officers like Healey would have to get right.

---

* Much of Healey's reaction to Algiers was put in letters to his parents and deliber-ately left out of the diary.

When they reached Guelma, near Constantine, informed talk with Peter Larsen, the Divisional Intelligence Officer, confirmed the critical mood. But the bitterness here turned upon the inadequacies of the local commander, Anderson. 'Nearly all the time we were fighting in country which a company could hold against a battalion.' The day after General Eveleigh had taken Djedidja without trouble he had received a message from Anderson: 'Do not consider you strong enough to carry out your task.' 11 Brigade had been left at Tébourba 'under terrific dive-bombing – only one of ninety men came back out of one battalion – until an order to be withdrawn could be given.'[20] General Montgomery, he learned, had called Anderson 'A good plain cook'. Healey reported what he heard from those at the consequential end with a dash of what he saw himself: 'Anderson's name has since been mud in this division. He is a characterless, pudding-faced man with no originality or drive, unresisting to suggestions from above, sarcastic and sour to his subordinates, uninformed about the running of his own HQ and ignorant of many of his staff officers' names.'[21]

Healey was told a great deal of bad news by his friend in Intelligence. 'The parachutists had performed magnificently as infantry improperly equipped.'[22] Part two of one of their operations had been cancelled leaving them looking for ground troops which hadn't been sent; a battalion had been wiped out in a mountain ambush; during the known regular torrential rains between Christmas and March, 'one brigade pushed an attack forward for fifteen miles of mountains in the north.' There were also tales from Intelligence agents in Tunis itself, stories about that unvarying military factor, the heroic accuracy of the American Air Force. One agent had written, 'American Bombers would find mole and quays a better dumping ground than the Municipal Park.'[23] There was also much bitterness at the excess of courtly address paid to captured senior German officers, including General Von Arnim. 'The DPM officiating at a mess dinner loaded Von Arnim down with whisky, cigarettes and geniality to the disgust of other officers. The mess waiters' letters had to be returned for re-writing the following day to tone down the blistering fire of their comments.'[24]

Whatever the blunders of the whole campaign and the defects of individual British generals, Healey could see something in Guelma HQ which very much attracted him. He could see the shoots of military meritocracy, indeed of military socialism. 'Planning here is most interesting and suggests several conclusions. A group of men picked by merit, graft, service and luck can successfully plan the life of thousands down to the smallest detail in difficult country in spite of interference by the enemy and the deadweight of an apathetic civilian population. There is no unemployment or starvation in the army . . .'

Healey would note almost simultaneously soldiers too preoccupied to meet the older hierarchical instincts of the army. George VI, the War Minister Sir Edward Grigg, the General Anderson whose name was mud 'and a bevy of generals visited the division'. At Bône, the troops 'had been strung out over twenty-five miles, one every twenty yards, so no one stood to attention, saluted or cheered as he drove past. Finally he said to his aide that "If that's all they're going to do, I might just as well have stayed at home," so an armoured car was sent ahead to organise enthusiasm.'[25] But when the king reached the courtyard at Guelma 'everybody saluted which prevented them from cheering'.[26]

As troops were moved to Sousse for eventual embarkation, there was another parade for which no one sought to organise enthusiasm: 'Graves, single or in little clusters, all the way down by the roadside, with just the name in German or English on the wooden cross.'[27] Sousse had a harbour full of wrecks and all its waterfront buildings 'blasted to Hell'.

Peacetime has the two certainties: death and taxes. Soldiers at war confront a variant: death and generals. It was the privilege of all officers in Healey's division to be addressed by General Montgomery, the coming man, the future triumphant field marshal whose clipped voice speaking of hitting the enemy for six would be as celebrated by the end of the war as Churchill's low, dragging Augustan rhetoric.

Denis treated him as an interesting but not really good early-nineteenth-century French painter: 'A sharp ferret-blue face, thin-lipped mouth and very pale grey-green eyes. He has perfect self-confidence and is vain, one feels, as well as complacent.'[28] (In fairness to a general notably careful, if only in his own interests, history rates Monty as furiously vain but not all that complacent.) The gist of the lecture on generalship was that the enemy should dance to one's tune, an attacker be sufficiently balanced to absorb a counterstroke without changing a plan and the initiative taken and kept. Healey's assessment reads very well after nearly sixty years: 'a good fair weather general, but his principles of war need a definite superiority in all arms before they can be applied. They would not have met Wavell's position in Cyrenaica or Alexander's in Burma.'[29] Nor perhaps would Montgomery's principles have helped him fight as brilliant a defence as Kesselring was about to stage in the Italian theatre. He was, however, the best general we had got – 'at this time he is obviously the right type. He really is a megalomaniac who might develop very dangerously when peace robs him of his real environment.'[30] Happily, a viscountcy, a grumbling peacetime command and the Erastian tradition of British politics left Monty with nothing worse to do than mutter.

Real war would very soon start for Healey. On 28 July his group landed at Avola in Sicily. In Sicily, rather as at Woolwich, he waited for orders and, in his case, counter-orders. The next step of the Allied campaign would be the invasion of Italy at Salerno, a substantial harbour and resort well south of Naples. The force for this was to leave from Tripoli, a fact as well known to the Germans as Mountbatten's Dieppe raid. Salerno, defended from the foothills above by General Seckenius, would be a bloody and disgusting affair occasioning many more simple wooden crosses. It would also occasion a mutiny, a sit-down on the beach in the middle of unexplained moves, something handled with humour and grace by the inspired Anglo-Irish general, McCreery.[31]

Healey was ordered three times – on 31 July, 2 August and 11 August – to Tripoli in the fortnight after reaching Sicily; and three times – 1 August, 3 August and 19 August – the order was cancelled. The bureaucracy which messed Denis about probably saved his life. 'The officer who took my place in Tripoli was killed within hours of reaching Salerno's beach.'[32] Instead he was seconded as beach-master,* the job he had been trained for, to 231 Independent Brigade under a general he mightily respected, Urquhart, later commander of the Airborne Division at Arnhem.

The function of Brigade 231 was to land further south, on the coast not of Campania but of Calabria. The idea was to put down three battalions to block German attempts at counterattacking Salerno. On a map, both the first location and the second, taken up in an emergency, look horribly far south of Salerno.† The chosen objective was Pizzio, but a storm compelled a retreat to a beach close to Messina. Healey managed to get the full *équipe*, including ambulances which would be badly needed, on to the fewer ships remaining. Plans now changed again and the objective was pushed further north, closer to the main Salerno raid: a little Calabrian town called Porto Santa Venere.

In the full account which he recorded, Healey describes how at two-thirty in the morning,

> With difficulty I could construct a bleak range of mountains ahead. The commandos should at that moment be landing to secure the beaches for the assaulting battalions landing an hour later and to test the defences ... Boots sounded shuffling on the bridge. I watched and waited. Half past four. Still no sign of fighting. The darkness was almost imperceptibly reduced ... On the bridge the Brigadier was trying to contact his leading battalions.
>
> 'Hello Drake, hello Drake – are you dry yet – are you dry yet – over to you – over.'
>
> 'The Devons are ashore, sir.'[34]

---

* This term is being used for convenience but strictly it describes only the naval officer doing the job. As an army man, Healey was a transport or landing officer.

† This was part of the operation called 'Baytown'; the Salerno operation was called 'Avalanche'. The historians of the Italian campaign, Graham and Bidwell, observe drily that this, like a similar initiative, 'Buttress' near Taranto in Puglia, was acceptable to General Eisenhower 'because they made no large demands on shipping, but got troops on shore somehow on the mainland'. And in their judgement, 'The effect however was to spread the effort when it should have been concentrated.'[33]

Things were not happening as intended. The units who had gone ashore with specific objectives hadn't found them, but they were meeting little opposition. Healey prepared himself.

With my despatch cases, map-boards, haversack swinging round me, I felt absurdly dressed for action. When I came on deck again it was half-light; we all crowded up against the ramps. It seemed a small town ahead of us, the beach enclosed between the hills and the jetty, a few craft already discharging and troops running into the streets behind.

Healey was concerned to get his own landing craft discharging its bren-gun carriers, ammunition lorries and anti-aircraft guns, the first vehicles to land.

Bang!
   A loud explosion somewhere, then I saw spray settling back into the sea astern . . . For the next five minutes and until we beached there were occasional mortar shells all bursting harmlessly into the sea. At last we slid up at the village, the craft swirled onto the shingle, down rattled the ramps and we ran ashore.

In rough sync with men landing at Salerno, the first British troops were invading the continent of Europe. But

Something was seriously wrong. There should have been two LCTs in half an hour before, carrying howitzers, bulldozers, towing sledges loaded with hundreds of yards of wire track. In fact the timing had gone to hell. The commandos had landed nearly two hours late, three miles from the correct place, and no one had yet seen or heard of them.

The same thing had happened with the assault force and their beach-master, the people supposedly doing the reconnaissance to find exits to the beach. 'They had landed on the wrong beach an hour and a half late, misled by a smouldering heap of sawdust which they thought was a beach limit sign.' Things which should have happened in sequence, one part of the action clearing a way for the next, all landed in a heap on the main beach. 'Bombs now began dropping on the beach and the immobilised craft were a beautiful target. Then to pile horror upon horrors, the first bulldozer to leave the LCT with track stuck in four feet of water and stayed there.'
   The worst was avoided by improvisation. The track was hauled off by the Pioneers. 'Every LCT had safely discharged its vehicles, track was every-where laid and the enemy had not hit anything of importance.' It was seven-thirty. 'I stood at the back of the beach with Martin. We were both exhilarated by success and danger.' Martin, his naval colleague, had a minor

shrapnel wound, the beach signals commander 'had been grazed by a splinter and was limping. We all felt a bit heroic and even contemptuous of war with its clangours. Later we remembered those minutes of false security with rueful amusement.'

Martin was a regular naval lieutenant, a survivor of the Java Sea battle, something of a naval calamity. The men he commanded had an average age of eighteen. As he gave orders through his loud hailer from the roof of a bungalow, 'we all dropped to the ground as something passed just over our heads with a whining whirr and exploded beyond us. It was a heavy mortar from behind the town.'

The early shots missed but soon he was exclaiming, 'Christ, a direct hit!' While the men on the beach watched the empty ship fired on, 'one shell hit the bridge and a figure tumbled down on to the deck like a doll . . . then she turned and moved steadily out of the harbour, a shell throwing spray on her every four seconds. It was like a water beetle on which little boys drop stones continually . . . when the air clears, it is there as ever, poised on the skin of the stream.' The ship would limp back to Messina, discharge a dozen wounded and seven dead, telling the generals that the landing was opposed. A blaze higher up the beach told of another hit: 'a lorry carrying a 3.7 Ak-Ak gun had been hit, the driver killed and his mate was burning to death trapped in the cab.' As the Germans found their range, they killed the gun crew.

As Healey found out after the battle, 'the port was spread out below the German mortars like a dartboard and they could watch and interpret our every move. Our infantry was now held on the slopes of the hills and a series of little fierce section fights was taking place.' With skilfully placed machine guns protecting the mortars, the invaders' position was hopeless unless the British got their own artillery ashore. 'The Brigadier told me that he must have the LST in, no matter what the cost.' Healey and Martin signalled out to sea, the ships began to move, attracting German tracer fire before, in a mass of flame, the lead ship suffered a direct hit on one of the lorries she was carrying, creating a shower of steel splinters.

The second ship withdrew, 'the first kept straight on.' Martin realised that the ship's steering had gone and that she was bound for the far end of the beach designated 'Green'.

The beach group personnel began running to the other end of the beach to meet her. I ordered a bulldozer to lay track if she beached beyond limits. Hit after hit blew pieces from her as she drove on. Everyone was shouting and cheering . . . On her top deck, now swept by small arms fire, figures were scrambling among the trucks to play a hose on the blazing lorry. She had beached in the worst possible place, right up against the German positions accessible to small arms fire to port and to mortar fire on three sides. The next half hour was an eternity.

The ship's engine rooms were flooded, her ramps jammed, 'and as I made
a rapid assessment of the damage, a mortar shell carried an LCS away from
its clamps. Everyone was working, blind to danger, Pioneers rolling down
the heavy five-yard strips of wire matting, the bulldozer ramming the doors
wider open.' Healey recognised the lieutenant of the LST, 'a very pleasant
young Canadian I remembered from Messina'. He had climbed the steel
ladder of the ship to find out what was jamming the ramp when 'the chain
of the ramp broke and the enormous iron platform swung down to the
beach, brushing him from his hold. I scarcely dared look. He must be
smashed to pulp.' By luck or grace he wasn't. And though 'he fainted when
they went to pick him up, only his back was strained'. The artillery, twenty-
five pounders, came rumbling on to the beach, then the road. 'The day was
saved perhaps.'

The idea occurred to someone that getting on the far side of the ship might
give some protection. They had just made the move when a great explosion
brought them rushing back and they saw that 'a bomb had burst where they
had been standing.' Despite that general good fortune, the cry still went up

'Stretcher bearer, stretcher bearer.' Two men lay crumpled on the floor.
Blood was pumping from the throat of one . . . Blood flooded over
hands, tunic, face; they tried to hold the dressing firm. The other man
was gurgling horribly. The other man got up. It was Baker, the corporal's officer. Blood was drying on his face and shirt. His face was
haggard and he shook as he rose. I took him on my shoulder. 'Don't
mind me. See to my corporal. The poor fellow, the poor fellow . . . I'm
not hurt,' he kept saying in a faint voice, but insistent. He was badly
shocked. I tried to soothe him. He leaned against a wall and his corporal was carried past on a stretcher up to the BQS. His eyes were wide
open, the eyeballs turned up, only a thin slip of pupil showing under the
lid. The dressing was soaked with blood that oozed in a damp puddle.
Clots of blood dribbled from his nose. 'He'll die in ten minutes. Can't
do a thing,' said the doctor major.

Bombs were followed by a cry of 'Dive bombers'. 'My head was on the
gritty concrete. Everyone was still. I heard two, three, descending drones,
and the grass suddenly blew up in my face, the bushes moved and I felt
myself lifted off the ground . . . Then whoom! Whoom! Whoom! Whoom!
Whoom! I counted the bursts, my muscles taut, and jammed a helmet lying
on the ground on my head. Stones and earth showered round.' He took a
blow on the ankle, probably from a falling stone. 'Then I heard the drone
fading. We got up and brushed off the dirt. My ankle was numb and not
very painful.'

The record ends stoically on that anticlimax. They were stuck, but now had functioning artillery. He would next help ship two hundred casualties back to Sicily, a diversion from the Salerno assault, itself misconceived and ill-executed. It ought to be said here that Denis Healey's own account in *The Time of My Life* is an oddly flat and minimal section of an eloquent book, entirely playing down both the horror and his own part. He would in fact be mentioned in dispatches here and at the later landing, Anzio, where he was Military Landing Officer to the British Assault Brigade. The full account given here has been his private record until now. Healey, though proud of his soldiering, showed the customary reticence of good soldiers.

In ways which would become familiar to the Labour Party and in Whitehall, Healey had made himself an expert on the Italian campaign as a whole. At the end of the war he would be invited, with colleagues, to write the official history of that struggle, and a publishing proposal of some eight to nine thousand words survives. Among much else, he looks back at his own two major involvements, Calabria and Anzio, and he is, as ever, critical. Plans for landing generally came from a complexity of authorities – 'Not even "Overlord",* the assault forces for which were little if any larger, involved so many independent mounting authorities, widely separated and differing materially in organisation. The authorities included GHQ Middle East, AFHQ (and its US subordinate Natousa), the War Office in London (for the Canadian Assault Force) and the War Department in Washington (for part of the US Assault Force). Not less than a dozen ports along the full length of the Mediterranean and in the Red Sea were employed to mount an Allied Force comprising American, Canadian and British formations. He remarks that 'Baytown' (Calabria) and 'Shingle' (Anzio), both put together in three weeks, actually benefited from shortage of time. For 'the urgency thus imposed was in fact beneficial to all concerned – patience was less exacerbated by continual changes of plan and intelligence less blunted by continual wrestling with the same mass of detail.' When he writes that 'In "Baytown" it was learned that stowage plans for LSTs and LCTs need not be prepared in detail' but that it 'is essential that an officer fully familiar with the course of planning should be present at loading to give guidance and immediate decisions when for example there is a cut in craft',[35] Healey is talking about what Healey had seen and done. Witness: 'In the Bde 231 operation against Santa Venere on the other hand, it was possible to reload the whole brigade into a different craft allocation in one to suit a new tactical plan because the MLO [Military Landing Officer] was present throughout on the quayside.'[36]

The proposal which Healey drafted concerns the whole war but seen as he saw and fought it – a war of logistics reflecting his own work and area of expertise. Anzio, or 'Shingle', about which he left no diary record, is

---

* Code name for the Normandy landings.

favourably contrasted with Salerno, or 'Avalanche', where navy and army wanted different things. 'The Navy preferred to allocate [landing] craft once and for all to particular ships, the Army wanted all craft to report back to a central ship for further orders after discharging on the beach. For "Shingle" a successful compromise was reached',[37] with particular ships retained, 'but the relevant naval and army landing officers authorised to adjust allocation against new priorities'.[38] In Healey's view, Anzio was the best of the landings, picking up on previous mistakes. 'No new techniques were employed on the Movement's side, but the steady efficiency of the Naples–Anzio ferry deserves comment; – 5 Army broke down all units on its priority list into LST and LCT load serials while in the transit area.'[39]

Landing craft, variously designed and identified by initials to carry men, tanks, anti-aircraft guns and other artillery, strip-mesh track, bulldozers and other equipment were Healey's professional preoccupation as a soldier. He promised/threatened a book written lovingly about it. Possibly this was a more vital subject than it would have been an enthralling read. But when he tells us how the Anzio landings worked after the muddle and congestion of Santa Venere, it does matter. 'The Navy at sea gave maximum warning of the arrival of craft, starting berth and time available for loading after refuelling etc. The alerted serials were then called forward to the quay by Ferry Control and minimum delay was caused to all concerned.'[40]

If this sounds dry, the greater efficiency with which landings were made translated into a lower mortality rate. Anzio, planned at Caserta – Charles III of Naples's late, vast response to Versailles – was a notably less bloody affair than the Salerno operation which the Calabrian landings had supported. 'We lost fewer men than the Americans had lost on the exercise at Salerno the previous week. The surprise we achieved was so complete that we even captured some German officers in their pyjamas,'[41] wrote Healey in his memoirs, and that key undertaking weighed with him for a very good reason. In January 1944 he had been appointed Military Landing Officer to the British assault brigade at Anzio. He took a justified pride in the reduced death rate, but his recurring complaint – at Anzio as at the other landings – was that troops were needed for consolidation and that the chance of an immediate onward drive was snatched away. The real trouble at Anzio would come later, when the Germans counterattacked the beachhead which, properly manned, would no longer have been a beachhead. But concern at numbers killed was a very British priority.

The principal American general of the Italian theatre did not care for this. In the words of the historians of the campaign, 'Mark Clark in his diary and amongst his staff held the view that an attack that failed with few casualties was a poor performance.'[42] Clark, a very intelligent officer, but one sometimes flickering close to paranoia, prized a high butcher's bill as proof that an assault was serious, and was the most offensive exponent of the American view that the British commanders were soft, consequent upon their experiences between 1914 and 1917. Ironically Clark *had* fought on the Western Front in 1918. But he raged at his allies. 'The poor dumb British' he would call them a little later in the war. And the feelings of British soldiers towards General Clark were highly reciprocal. Healey's memoirs quote a marching song in which British soldiers, after listing the better men, Eisenhower and Montgomery, who had moved to larger responsibilities ahead of the invasion of France, sang of Allied Armies Italy (AAI) that:

> Even Alexander's
> Left the sinking barque
> AAI is left with
> General Fucking Clark.[43]

Incidentally, if revulsion against the mass slaughter of twenty-five years earlier seems a quite reasonable British response, Dominick Graham and his American colleague, Shelford Bidwell, point out more complex reasons for our senior officers seeking to minimise casualties. British specialist units – and Healey's transport landing groups were very much that – were teams which functioned through long working together. Any heavy slaughter meant the next job being done by an uncohesive jumble of replacements. The Americans, though, ran an industrial type of operation through which men performed a narrow function and could, without loss of efficiency, be driven and ploughed under. But what the British chiefly noticed about Salerno was that Clark had made a mess of it – and he agreed.

For Salerno had been a highly Pickwickian sort of success. The view, at the end of it, of the German commander, Field-Marshal Kesselring, is eloquent. 'He was not dissatisfied. For eight whole days he had with his scanty resources forced the Anglo-American army on to the defensive despite its air power and the support of the heavy guns of the Allied fleet; indeed he was sure he had its measure. He could repeat this manoeuvre indefinitely and had proved his point that he could fight a defensive war in central Italy.'[44]

At the start of the landings, Hitler's HQ had favoured extensive retreat to a line higher up the peninsula. But the German commander was confident that he could perform a manoeuvre repeatedly and, more important, that he could fight a defensive war in central Italy.

If Salerno was a battle won at the cost of improving the morale of those retreating, Anzio, the landing south of Rome, was an attack better carried out, but inadequately exploited and starved of troops. Healey believes that if generals, thinking too far ahead, had not withdrawn troops in readiness for D-Day, then both the beachhead and the hills immediately behind it, the Colle Laziale, could have been made secure against a counterattack.

The only virtue he sees in the general strategy was that the weakness of the undermanned beachhead provoked the Germans into a contrary mistake. They invested *too many* troops into that counterstroke and gravely weakened themselves on other fronts. Chester Wilmot takes a similar view: 'From the Balkans, Scandinavia and the Reich itself, OKW (Ober Kommand den Wehrmacht) scraped up a dozen divisions, but none was taken from the West or from Italy where all Hitler's reserves had been drawn into the battle by the timely allied landing at Anzio.'[45]

Healey's own war, after the first assault, was jerkily busy. A week after the initial landings in Calabria he was made Staff Captain (Shipping) Santa Venere. Next, after an east coast landing had been effected at Termoli early in October 1943, he was organising logistics at Bari in the heel of Italy. In November he went to Naples, then Caserta, to help plan the Anzio landings. And on 2 January came the appointment as MLO for Anzio where, a temporary acting major, he would organise his division's landing across 22–5 January.

After some time back at the staff base in Naples, a series of short logistical jobs and permanent promotion to major on 3 June, Healey found himself directing things at Porto San Giorgio at the end of June, when his next important action was indicated. Allied consolidation of southern Italy accomplished, he was sent north to Loreto on 22 July, to serve with Polish troops under General Anders (men to whom by affectionate Irish analogy, he took enthusiastically) in the investiture and capture of Ancona. He noted the ferocity of Polish hatred for the Germans, something encapsulated in a communication from Anders to Field Marshal Alexander after the fall of another city, Bologna: 'Une très jolie battaille. Nous avons tué plus que deux milles Boches . . .'[46] The Poles having taken Ancona, Healey would be attached to the British Eighth Army as DAQMG(M) (Deputy-assistant Quartermaster General), followed by some shuttling between Siena and Rome and one final, rather important but unnerving planning appointment on the Adriatic coast.

Healey later wrote from his own experience about operations in the heel and at Ancona. Armies need equipment, supplies and more men. Once they hold a port, they want it used to capacity and indicate the reinforcements and volumes of supplies they expect to receive. The forces on the east coast required Bari to discharge 5–6000 tons per day, but Bari, though an important port, had no sheltered anchorage and only four deep-draught Liberty berths, so Liberties, the major freight boats, were given five days in the Bari docks, then shifted to shallower waters to complete unloading. But signals with Augusta, the reserve harbour, were very difficult, taking as long to send – forty-eight hours – the message as to make the journey. In the absence of that sheltered accommodation at Bari, ships would find themselves being sent round the spike of the heel to Taranto. 'Thus a failure to vacate a berth by only six hours could lead to five days delay in discharging the next ship.

To crown these chronic difficulties, the air raid of 2 Dec '43 caused the loss of the equivalent of four days work over all Heel ports.'[47]

At Ancona, where he found himself later, the coasters and Liberties which brought supplies up from the heel were subject to German E-boat activity and had to complete their passage in dusk-to-dawn convoys. This left gaps in the port's function, later filled by smaller convoys designed for the purpose.

The technicalities, as so often, were essential. 'In Italy for much of the campaign two armies, one US, one British, one flanked by the Tyrrhenian and Ligurian seas and one by the Adriatic, moved forward side by side supported by lines of communications comprising coastal routes on each outer flank, a total of three main road routes and three rail routes up the leg to Italy. The mountains were again in evidence. Of the three rail routes, one finally terminated at Ortona behind the advancing Eighth Army, and its reconstruction between Ortona and Ancona was not completed until after the campaign ended.[48] They had use of road and rail going up the map, neither of them working very well, and they had the sea which was subject to German naval action, so the best possible use of all three had to be extracted. As Healey says, 'Over 100,000 troops were carried from Brindisi and Bari to Ancona between July '44 and March '45 in a five-day ferry of small ships each carrying 750 personnel.'[49]

But busy and useful as Healey was, supervising and managing major transport operations in Naples, there was also time for enjoyment. In Bari he snapped up books, as he had snapped them up in the second-hand shops of English towns when counting soldiers on and off trains. When in Siena after the fall of Ancona, he talked himself into Montegufoni, the Italian home of the Sitwells, used to store the treasures of the Uffizi, where he viewed and gloated over Botticelli's *Primavera*.

In Naples he made friends with a circle of clever and interesting people, William Chappell, the ballet dancer, Marcus Sieff, something in retail, the pleasant and unlucky Jack Profumo, their Movement's air liaison officer, and a more earnest Conservative, Viscount De L'Isle. Later, when working in the north-east of Italy, he would encounter, less agreeably, the febrile, bitter-mouthed Nigel Birch, future ally of Enoch Powell in the 1957 Treasury resignations who, by a sad turn of irony, would make a killing assault upon Macmillan in the 1963 debate following the artificial nightmare which we know as the Profumo Affair. Best of all, there was Jack Donaldson who, with his wife, Frankie, would form a close and lasting friendship with the Healeys. Such was the way of that eclectic army of all the talents, that Colonel Donaldson and Major Healey contacted the retired conductor of the San Carlo Opera Orchestra who obliged them by putting together a string quartet which played to the troops.

There was time also for a love affair which grew fiercely intense, with Lavinia, a nurse with the risibly named Female Auxiliary Nursing Yeomanry, with whom Denis took leave trips to San Gimignano and Positano, two of the most delectable places in Europe. It was a fierce wartime affair, one of tens of thousands for the soldiery, but however strong the feelings and however idyllic the settings, for historical purposes, Lavinia came between Edna and Edna.

But there were graver things to attend to, notably that planning appointment on the north-east coast. In November of 1944, Healey was sent to Pesaro, home town of Rossini, now a rather overburdened seaside resort, to help plan nothing less than the invasion of Yugoslavia. What was contemplated was more of an incursion with half a mind to territory. What the Italians called Fiume, all the warring Yugoslavs called Rijeka. Gabriele D'Annunzio, *littérateur*, proto-Fascist and killer poet, had seized the town for Italy after the First World War. The Germans held it at present. An invasion against the Germans would have been part of a wider involvement on the other side of the Adriatic and was perhaps seen in some quarters as useful pre-emption of the Communist forces.

But such thinking anticipated the Cold War altogether too quickly. Healey, for one, was highly relieved to be spared a potentially bloody undertaking. He had been designated Military Landing Officer for the island of Krk, now also a holiday place, full of hills, themselves full of death-or-glory Germans, very much like the hills above Porto Santa Venere and Anzio. When decided against by higher authority, it was a 'jolie petite battaille' happily escaped.

The formal end of Healey's own Italian campaign came early in May 1945 with a journey into Austria through Villach and Klagenfurt, then on to the Yugoslav border. 'Left Florence in the evening to cross the Apennines. Most beautiful country in the foothills, lush, glowing green woods and meadow flowers everywhere and blue sky.' But this faded into the light of common wartime day: 'Everywhere foxholes, gun pits, piles of shell cases and tangles of signal-wire. The destruction toward Bologna is complete. Every village is a shapeless heap of rubble with the strong sweet smell of dead bodies heavy in the air.'

Next day, 7 May, Healey rose early and, as he drove to Milan, he noted Partisans, essentially a Communist force 'controlling the whole area. They are everywhere, in civilian clothes with red scarves or armbands as uniform, rifles, machine-pistols and a grenade or two in the belt. Communist slogans on all the walls.' Milan, much like the River Rhine during the German cycling trip, was not esteemed, 'an enormous city very like Birmingham'.

However their city might be found wanting, the Milanese could not refrain from cheering the British soldiery, and they had a reason. On leaving at 5 p.m., 'suddenly we noticed that people were running out to clap and cheer us, bells were ringing in the villages and someone shouted "La Guerra e finita" . . .' At Verona, they passed 'Italians waving torches, lighting bonfires and Verey lights shooting up green and red in the darkness'. It *was* over and would make no end of a difference.

Heading for Udine, Healey found the Corps HQ, at which he called for information but left no wiser. He was staggered and delighted by the sub-alpine scenery: 'Like another world – great grey precipices, silky waterfalls, turf green and soft enamelled with cowslips and mountain flowers, peaks glistening with snow.' But against the grandeur, straggled the people: 'coming down the pass against us hundreds, thousands of refugees of every national- ity – Russians, Serbs, Poles, Hungarians, Italians in all costumes doggedly tramping back to Italy.'

Once in Austria, 'we sped through into an incredible dream. Hundreds of German soldiers marching up the road, German officers in staff cars, all armed, very few British about and yet no attempt to molest us.' In Klagenfurt, the next city, Denis found himself guiding and interpreting for the young lieutenant whose platoon was protecting a new local government office from the SS reprisals which its frightened officials feared. Healey was told of 2000 still armed Ustashi, the Croatian Catholic militias with a name for outrunning the Nazis in their primitive terrorism, now cornered aptly in the Adolf Hitler Platz.

Denis would have liked to go on to Trieste, but was advised against it as impossible, given Partisan control. Instead he headed for a high pass, making an incursion into Gorizia, territory held by Tito, 'superb Alpine scenery and the Yugoslav army in every village, notices in Serbian, posters of Tito, tri- umphal arches of pine branches and flags over the entrance to every hamlet'. On the way back, 'we passed a Tito division on the march – a band of tough, ragged men and women, all armed with captured weapons or British sten guns, a few officers on horses and senior officers in German cars in every type of clothing . . . but all wearing the grey forage cap with the red star.'

On 10 May he returned with his driver to Venice, then back through Ferrara and Bologna to Florence and the anticlimactic observation: 'All the shops shut for the Festa dell' Annunzione.' Even so, for Healey this whole journey had been 'just about the most exciting time of my life'.

It was now time to think of a life after the Second World War. In 1944 he had received a letter from his local Labour MP in Keighley, Ivor Thomas, suggesting membership of the candidates' list, and had let his name go for- ward. From his planning base in Pesaro he wrote a passionate letter to the GMC of one of the Tory-held seats which had shown an interest. Quite sep- arately, jobs began to loom and manifest themselves. A Harmsworth Senior Scholarship to study the philosophy of art offered earlier still stood and would have made him an Oxford don. Alternatively, David Hunt, former don and future diplomat, was collecting a team to write the history of the campaign now accomplished. Healey was invited to join it with a lift in rank which would have given us Lieutenant Colonel Healey. Aptly for an art lover who had made a special journey to see one Botticelli painting, the muses were offering three beautiful options.

6

1945 AND BEYOND

The speech of the prospective candidate for Pudsey and Otley, made to Conference at Blackpool on 21 May 1945, has been quoted before – by Tory opponents, left-wingers and Denis Healey himself in his autobiography. It came almost immediately before Bevin's. Possibly Foreign Secretaries-in-waiting do not listen to truculent speeches from the floor, Bevin never let it worry him later, but Major Healey that afternoon sounds very remote to us now.

There are two most important facts which are not very clear to people who have been living in England during the last five years. One of them is the significant fact that the Socialist revolution has already begun in Europe and is already firmly established in many countries in Eastern and Southern Europe. The crucial principle of our own foreign policy should be to protect, assist, encourage and aid in every way that Socialist revolution wherever it appears. The Labour Party must be extremely alert and vigilant in nudging its friends and enemies in Europe. It is quite easy for a person like myself who has spent the last three years in Europe to tell who are our friends and who are our enemies. The upper classes in every country are selfish, depraved, dissolute and decadent. These upper classes in every country look to the British Army and the British people to protect them against the just wrath of the people who have been fighting underground against them for the past four years. We must see that this does not happen. There is a very great danger unless we are very careful, that we shall find ourselves running with the Red Flag in front of the armoured cars of Tory imperialism and counter-revolution, very much as in the early days of the motor car a man ran with a red flag in front of the first automobiles.

The struggle for socialism in Europe has not been like the struggle for socialism in Great Britain. During the last five years it has been hard, bitter, cruel, merciless and bloody . . . We may think when occasionally facts are brought to our notice, that our comrades on the Continent are being extremist, that there is a danger of a dictatorship of the Left wing being set up. I thought I caught snatches of that sort of attitude in Mr Attlee's speech. But let us not be too pious and self righteous and say 'I am not as other men are.' Remember that one of the prices for our survival during the last five years has been the death by bombardment of countless thousands of innocent European men and women. That is a price we have all been prepared to pay. But if the Labour Movement in Europe finds it necessary to introduce a greater degree of police supervision and more immediate and drastic punishment for their opponents than we in this country would be prepared to tolerate, we must be prepared to understand their point of view.[1]

The Healey speech belonged with the exultant naïvety of that transfigured moment, though it was restrained compared with the words of Miss Wingate (sister of the Chindit leader and candidate in Holborn), 'who cried with joy "We are beginning to establish the Socialist Republic of Europe."' But, more importantly, it differed only by its vivid candour from the sort of thing which would be said across the next few years by the likes of Konni Zilliacus, John Platts-Mills and D. N. Pritt, undisputed fellow-travellers with the Soviet Union. Fellow-travellers were nowhere so animatedly brutal. They often adopted a clerical manner, and made the sleek case for a well-conducted, international, law-respecting, almost ostentatiously moderate Russia. It is worth fast-forwarding eighteen months to a debate on foreign affairs in the Commons for the views on Eastern Europe of Konni Zilliacus and the sweetened weaseling of an authentic Soviet loyalist:

The disappearance of the landowning and big business classes has meant the rise to the surface of the peasants and working class. The great problem of those countries is how to help those people to come together, and not allow them to fall apart. The way to do that is through the co-operatives and trade unions. The political dynamo is some kind of political coalition, either of Socialists or Communists, or of Communists alone in nearly all those countries. The supporters of these régimes argue for maintaining a coalition by pointing to the fact that during the war we put off the Election for five years, and that at the end of the war the Conservative Party put forward strong arguments for continuing it here in the difficult circumstances of post-war reconstruction. These people do not understand why the Conservative Party, who are such strong believers in national unity in our country, are so bent upon making

them return to party politics, when their problems are incomparably
more difficult. Part of their population is still 100 per cent hostile.[2]

The last dazzling admission made sense enough, for 'these people', the new
leaders in Eastern Europe, were Klement Gottwald in Czechoslovakia,
Matyas Rakosi in Hungary, Boleslaw Bierut in Poland and, in the Soviet
Zone of Germany, Walter Ulbricht preparing for the non-optional base of the
Socialist Unity Party inside what would be the German Democratic Republic.
They would prove less susceptible than the Conservative Party to pressure for
early free elections. The second option raised by Zilliacus, 'Communists
alone', was to be the pleasant norm for forty years.

Healey, the leftist, was as much a bruiser as Healey, the cold warrior.
There is in this early speech much of that plainness modulating into affront
as would be present in his impatient rejection of unilateral disarmament
fourteen years later: 'Can I get it into your heads, comrades, that Mr
Khruschev is not the George Lansbury type?' (Labour Conference, 1960). In
debate, Healey would say nothing with chocolates and flowers.

But his revolutionary phase was not quite over. He would continue as
apologist for revolutionary East European socialist governments by not apologising for them, glorying in short measures under necessity and speaking a
class-war language with a large streak of moralising reproach in it.

There is something of the Welsh pulpit and of Monsieur Defarge about
this Healey, alliteratively denouncing the depraved and decadent upper
classes as he ushers them towards an up-to-date equivalent of the guillotine.
But some of that class hostility had come from observation: Basil Tsakos and
his moneyed Athenian friends, the self-destructive high trash of Naples.

All healthy class-war stuff, but it was based on flesh-and-blood dislikes.
The theoretical tolerance of revolutionary short ways would vanish sharply
enough when Czech and Polish realities presented themselves; the left-wing
tone would be maintained for a while yet since the prospective candidate
now had his campaign to fight. The special meeting of the Pudsey and Otley
divisional Labour Party at the Mechanics Institute in Horsforth in February
1945 had chosen him from a shortlist of three.

Pudsey and Otley was a Conservative seat of the Elysian kind – for
Conservatives: a scatter of pleasant residential and semi-rural small towns and
villages due west and north-west of Leeds, places like Bramhope, Calverley,
Arthington, Rawdon, Horsforth and Burley as well as Ilkley and the two larger
eponymous towns. It had been represented for fifteen years by Sir Granville
Gibson,* until his recent retirement. This immediate post-war election was

---

* Gibson had lately returned from a trade mission in the US relating to the export of
goatskins!

exceptional in coming ten years after the previous one, but in 1935 Gibson had had a majority of 11,425.[3] Otley and Pudsey were ante-rooms to Leeds, but also served people not wanting to live in Bradford either. The people who lived there expected to be represented by a Conservative. The only thing they could count on in 1945 was representation by an officer in HM forces.

Such military men as survive in modern politics, drop rank and medals in an ardent wish for civilian conformity. But the contest of 1945 was an election in which anyone who sported a military title made vigorous use of it, Captain Crosland and Captain Jenkins among them. (Clement Attlee, an officer in the First World War, had as frequently been 'Major' as 'Mr' Attlee during the 1930s.) A photograph at the time brings together Major Healey (Labour), Colonel Stoddart-Scott (Conservative) and Brigadier Terence Clarke (Liberal). The Conservative candidate at P & O (what everyone called the seat) had had a creditable war. He was actually a medical man – 'A pox doctor,' said Healey, accurately if uncharitably, at one stage. But he preferred 'Lieutenant-Colonel Malcolm Stoddart-Scott' to 'Dr Malcolm Stoddart-Scott'. The Liberal out-ranked both Healey and Stoddart-Scott, but was no Liberal. Brigadier Terence Clarke, 'a Neanderthal' in Healey's view, who called himself 'Terry' for the duration of this demotic encounter, would subsequently, as Brigadier Terence Clarke, represent a Portsmouth seat as a Conservative of the most crenellated and unsympathetic sort. Healey was not impressed: 'He had been Army heavyweight boxing champion, and it showed.'[4] Stoddart-Scott was a medical man from Leeds Infirmary who had done valuable work during the war in charge of a unit screening soldiers for physical and mental health. He would be a solidly respected Conservative backbench MP.

The mood of 1945, of an election which would accomplish a social revolution, would be very well caught in the application letter which Denis Healey had, in December 1944, addressed to the local party. Stressing the difficulties for selectors and candidates in knowing the quality of the candidate, he asked that they should 'make every allowance for the difficulties of my situation. I am only one of hundreds of young men, now in the forces, who long for the opportunity to realise their political ideals by actively fighting an election for the Labour Party ... These men in their turn represent millions of soldiers, sailors and airmen who want socialism and have been fighting magnificently to save a world in which socialism is possible.' They were the people who realised 'that politics are a matter of life and death for them'.

He was speaking exactly the right language, for this was to be a khaki election in a sense quite different from that of 1900. In that letter Healey spoke credibly enough of the great reserve of Labour goodwill and votes currently obeying orders in barracks under the uneasy eye of regular officers and the encouraging one of interim junior commanders. He would also articulate the war itself to his future committee in a Yorkshire village and do so with some plagency.

We have now almost won the war, at the highest price ever paid for victory. If you could see the shattered misery that was Italy, the bleeding
countryside and the wrecked villages, if you could see Cassino with a
bomb-affected river washing green slime through a shapeless rubble
that a year ago was homes, you would realise more than ever that the
defeat of Hitler and Mussolini is not enough by itself to justify this
destruction, not only of twenty years of fascism, but too often of twenty
centuries of Europe.

There is no reason to be cynical about it. Healey had witnessed in southern
Italy a local conflict as nasty in its short, concentrated way as anything on the
larger map of the First World War. He was also placed to pick up Lloyd
George's 1918 civilian rhetoric about 'a land fit for heroes' through whose
hollow centre a cool wind of civilian prudence had swiftly blown. In 1945,
returning soldiers spoke with peculiar authority. His conclusion, notably
imprudent and committed, calling for 'a clear lead for socialism given by the
Labour Party based on generations of struggle with and for the working class'
would wear thin with the years, but it was the flame of its time.

The actual campaign of June 1945 was quite as intense. That election was
fought in the old enjoyable way of meetings, often two or three a night, at
which the candidate showed himself, spoke, answered questions and was
judged in the flesh by a few thousand voters. In the last four days of campaigning alone, Healey would speak at fifteen meetings, getting himself around
like a music-hall artiste in a cab working multiple bookings. On Sunday 7 July
he would be at the Mechanics Institute, Calverley, before going on to the
Labour Rooms at Farsley. On Monday 2 July, supported by a guest speaker,
Lord Strabolgi, he would start at seven-thirty at the Mechanics Institute, Otley,
followed by the Memorial Hall, Adel, then the National School, Pool, concluding in what is now Leeds itself, at the Council School, Alwoodley.

Tuesday brought an evening embracing the Craven Institute, Bramhope,
the Lecture Hall, Burley, the Council School, Cookridge, and the Temperance
Hall, Rawdon. The grand finale of Wednesday 4 July laid on five meetings
for the candidate. With warmers-up in the form of councillors, aldermen and
what are called stalwarts, all holding meetings scheduled to start within half
an hour of each other, Healey managed speeches at the same Mechanics
Institute in Horsforth where he had been selected, the Assembly Hall, Ilkley,
Burras Lane School, Otley, Littlemore Council School, Pudsey, and the
Methodist Schoolroom, Farsley.

Pre-television, it was surely in democratic terms a great deal better than
television. 'When the Labour candidate, Major Denis Healey spoke at the
Leeds Road Methodist Sunday School on Wednesday, the room was crowded
to the utmost capacity. He spoke for half an hour and answered questions for
another half hour,' read one report. Making so many speeches also involved

being quoted *in extenso* by the local newspaper[5] so that identical mouthings on successive nights were not on. The pressure on an uneloquent politician must have been painful. But Healey moved around the villages west of Leeds making new copy as he went.

The headline 'Major Healey at Burley' has him making an exception of Winston Churchill in his general excoriation of the Tories. 'We could not have won the war without him,' he said, before pointing out that 'his useful term of office was over'. But Churchill's policy was not Conservative policy. 'The only really strong opposition to the Yalta Conference came from the Conservatives in the House.' Healey would come in time to a view of Yalta as representing concession under pressure. But here and now in Burley, he believed, 'that the Conservative foreign policy is leading us straight into another war'.[6] 'There is a socialist revolution going on in Europe – a complete change in the class in power. The class before the war was the wealthy aristocracy and the rich who collaborated with the Germans when they took their countries. The result was that the liberation movements in each country soon found, after underground work against the Germans, that they had the same policy – a strong socialist policy – in Belgium, France, Italy and Greece.'

For the moment, we were trying to 'foist a little clique into a government which was not popular in its own country'. He said that was what we were trying to do now in Greece, Italy, Belgium among other places. The consequence of such a policy was that 'we shall find every country in Europe in five years time will regard us with the same suspicion that Russia does today.'

Healey was writing at the high point of general British good feeling towards the Soviet Union. Russia occupied Eastern Europe only as the conqueror of the Nazis. It was generally believed that Soviet withdrawal of troops would come about in the ordinary way. There had been no putsches in July 1945, no waves of arrest in Hungary or Czechoslovakia, no tanks on the street against the citizenry. The crimes within Russia before the war were cloudily reported and violently disputed. Stalin was Uncle Joe. Only two years earlier the Sword of Stalingrad had been displayed in state in Westminster Hall by the Churchill government. Across fifteen years Russia had enjoyed the steady good press of the Webbs, the *New Statesman* and Bernard Shaw.

Even Hugh Gaitskell, future paladin of anti-communism, had once dismissively said to Michael Postan, 'I hear you hold émigré views about Russia: how can you?'[7] Kingsley Amis would depict himself as a young officer shocked by an individual voicing criticism of the Soviet Union during a soldiers' mock parliament. A driving conviction far beyond the left was that the Chamberlain government had appeased Hitler out of its fear and hatred of Russia. It was a charge which Healey would repeat in his electoral address. He would also add that the 'discussions at San Francisco [the founding of the

UN] and Dumbarton Oaks were nothing but a smoke-screen behind which all the nations were busy trying to secure bases for the next world war'.[8]

This was the election of 'Whose finger on the trigger?' – a headline in the *Daily Mirror*. The element of heroism and social revolution in the Resistance was real. Jean Moulin and his Italian equivalents embodied it. Some of Churchill's local allies, notably in Greece, *were* unappetising members of a very corrupt élite – they would still be needed, without the option, to be Ernest Bevin's allies. Two years later Healey would be denounced by the *Daily Express* for being provocative to the Russians. Any young left-wing person was almost doomed in 1945 unless he had the gloomy prescience of Christopher Mayhew, to say silly things about Russia. Employing his usual vigour and openness, Denis Healey said them.

Not that it was all that he said. The problems of today, he observed at Farsley, were 'greater than in the darkest hour of 1940'. One concerned employment. 'With the demobilisation in the Services and war workers, there would probably be ten million people wanting jobs.' It was claimed that there would be 'an enormous amount of interference in the ordinary way of life'. Not so. The Labour Party proposed to plan production and he believed there would be enough jobs for everybody though they might not be just where everybody wanted them. The purpose of this was not control, it was intended so that 'the ordinary people could have houses instead of rooms, furniture at a decent price and all the things they needed in order to live decently.' In planned industry 'the only man who was adversely affected was the man who never worked in it but let his money work in it.'

At Otley he said that 'if nationalisation came into existence he would support the right of workers to strike against the state.' And in answer to another question, he favoured 'nationalisation and control of arms production – an industry which', he said, 'it had been proved had provoked wars in the past to sell their goods'.

It was a time of nonsensical insults, this election. Notoriously Churchill would accuse Labour of wanting to function like the Gestapo, a remark almost universally heard by Conservatives with wincing resignation. Labour on the whole simply sat back and enjoyed it, but individual candidates went pagerless in those unmanaged times and many of them made their own ripostes. They included Major Healey: 'Fighting men recognise Goebbels even when he smokes a cigar. Churchill has insulted the intelligence and violated the confidence of the forces.'[9]

Italy had left its mark on Healey and he would introduce Italian experience into his speeches. Answering Tory charges of coming inflation, premature as it turned out, he spoke of having himself seen 'the results of that policy [removal of controls] in Italy where only one tenth of the people's basic needs were rationed and the other nine tenths were bought by rich and poor alike on the black market at soaring prices. The cost of living has increased one hundred times since 1939, the middle classes have been wiped out and the savings of a lifetime swallowed up in a week.' That could happen here if the Tories were allowed 'to monkey with controls while there is still an acute shortage of houses, food, clothes and all that goes to make an ordinary decent life'.

But he also gave a non-political account of Italy when appearing, oddly and affably, before Otley Rotarians with a narrative of the Italian landings. Even in that left-wing year, Rotarians would not be a Labour candidate's natural audience but they would hear a remarkably candid account of what, in that bitter battle, went wrong and what went right through luck.

'The diversional operation of August 1943 was very carefully planned but owing to bad information and a difficult position, it did not go very well.' Anzio was hurriedly planned and should have been a complete failure because there were not enough landing craft . . . but it somehow 'went like an exercise' and 'was a howling success'. The real trouble came three or four days later when the Germans put in a heavy counterattack and from then onwards it became a most expensive operation.

'The President, Mr H. Howard,' reads the report, 'presided and thanked the speaker for a very interesting talk.' As well he might. Interesting? Healey was still in uniform and, despite leave to fight the election, a serving officer and what he had to say was as interesting as cogent criticism of senior officers by juniors commonly is. The Otley Rotarians were enjoying a major breach of security, King's regulations and general military discipline. But this being 1945, with millions finding the end of the war and its orders perfectly delectable, discipline could and did go hang.[10] The talk was reported in the press and Major Healey went on to his next meeting in the civilian world. That was at the overcrowded Methodist Sunday School where he stressed the need to nationalise central banking, quoting Lord Beaverbrook on 'the essential importance of the Bank of England being under the control of the Government'. It was a fond delusion but Healey enjoyed himself. 'We shall control capital in such a way as to put it where it is needed and not where there is a momentary profit.'

On railway nationalisation, Healey had quoted another capitalist less in sympathy than in the teeth. Sir Charles Hambro of the Great Western Railway had said 'to his stockholders' meeting that charges would have to be raised by 50–60 per cent'. Healey's response was that Britain simply 'couldn't afford the waste of carrying power and inflated costs caused by the way transport is run at present'.

Winston Churchill had a way of bursting back into successive speeches of Healey's. However left-wing the candidate might be, admiration for the old man was palpable, something of the fellow-feeling of one impulsive, eloquent political addict for another. 'Churchill was a very great man and his contribution during the war was unique.' But then, 'that immense store of explosives, Mr Churchill himself' was also a handy weapon against the official Tory Party. Healey took on the Cult of Churchill ploy by which the Tories were wrapping themselves not so much in the flag as in the premier's boiler suit. 'If they voted Conservative in Keighley,' he told electors tartly, 'they voted for a man called Dalrymple-White, not for Mr Churchill, and there was a big difference between the two.' The Tory candidate should be asked 'why his party never called on Mr Churchill for any help or advice during the fifteen years preceding the war'.[11]

In one respect Healey's campaign reflected a wide public fear that 1945 would echo 1918, that nothing would be done to ensure work and security for returning soldiers, that the 'land fit for heroes' would soon turn out to be Manitoba or Western Australia. Healey made this point with his usual delicacy. 'The Conservative plot was the same as it had always been – to let the men come back, spend five or six months looking for homes and living on their gratuities and then drop back on to the dole and live in a hovel or a gutter until there happened to be some work in the area . . .'

All political dialogue contains an overlap of exponentialism, the notion that what had happened must happen again. If it does not, then fear of it has usually played a major part in the escape. Healey was not much of an economist in 1945, but along with a majority of politicians he was shouting 'Wolf' in a way which made the keeping out of that particular wolf a general preoccupation.

The general left-wing tone was nothing peculiar to the candidate for Pudsey and Otley. One of his visiting speakers was Arthur Greenwood, a major orthodox party figure and Cabinet minister who, in spite of having famously been invited by Leopold Amery to speak for England, has left behind an uneloquent reputation and the name for an elderly, office-occupying mediocrity. But at Ilkley, Greenwood first of all endorsed Healey's view of Churchill and the Tories. 'He believed that as soon as Churchill had served their purpose they would discard him as they had discarded Lloyd George.' Greenwood also spoke a particular kind of deeply felt class bitterness now long drained from British politics. 'He told the story of the woman who allowed a Sunday School to meet in her kitchen and one day, when asked as part of the question "What are the laws?" gave the answer as "The laws are wise institutions to maintain the rich in their position and to restrain the vicious poor."'

Given such perceptions and feelings, the words with which Healey had opened his address, 'This is the most important election ever held in our country,' were suitable. It was a large statement and challengeable with those of 1906 or 1831, other intense, idea-charged contests. But it was highly arguable and truthfully reflected what most of those capable of thinking then thought. The outcome across Britain after the strange hiatus during which ballot boxes were locked away for three weeks until 26 July, would show the reduction of the Tories to a wretched 210 seats, untroubled rejection of Churchill, the near annihilation of the Liberal Party and a vast majority for Labour alone. It was all felt as at the edge of a great tremor in the secure, pleasant retreats of Otley, Ilkley and Pudsey.

The Conservatives had indeed retained the seat and on a hugely augmented poll (52,451, 79 per cent of the electorate), had actually increased their number of votes cast, but their majority of 1935 – 11,425 – had fallen to 1651, while the Labour vote had risen by 140 per cent. The result, counted, then announced at the Drill Hall, Rawdon, was:

Colonel Malcolm Stoddart-Scott (Conservative)	22,755
Major Denis Healey (Labour)	21,104
Brigadier Terence Clarke (Liberal)	8592
Conservative majority	1651

The local press report, fuller and more interested than we would expect today, described the count nicely. 'At 11.20 a.m. the figures (to the nearest thousand) were Conservative 15,000, Labour 12,000, Liberal 5000; at 11.40 they were Conservative 19,000, Labour 17,000, Liberal 6500. The Labour vote was creeping up and the more enthusiastic of the Socialists present were quick to see in that a good omen. "If it had not been for that far table (on which were the Liberal votes) you'd have had it," commented one to a Conservative standing alongside. "That's a matter of opinion; those votes should have been ours," came the good humoured reply.'[12]

Despite the intensity of an exceptionally important election, all sides evidently kept their civility. The local paper again: 'Compared with some occasions everybody seemed to be on their best behaviour. There were none of those little groups in which heated arguments developed as the sequel to a long and exasperating day of electioneering ... At 12.10 the candidates and their agents were drawn towards the deputy returning officer's table and while he checked the figures, Colonel Stodddart-Scott and Major Healey chatted animatedly while Brigadier Clarke, looking a little dejected, stood on the other side.'[13]

The party held later in the day was described by Healey as 'a victory social' where he spoke warmly and affectionately of the local party. 'They had a grand Labour Party in Pudsey and Otley with branches in Ilkley, Burley and Pool of an efficiency they would not have dreamed of three months before.' For himself, keeping open the option of a return, he announced that he was now returning to the army for a year and to Italy, and, he hoped, Austria.

He wasn't. He would not fight Pudsey again nor contest any other parliamentary division in the elections of 1950 or 1951. The reference to Austria concerned the option of that scholarly job with the army while he helped to write a history of the Italian campaign in an alpine schloss. He wouldn't do that either. A lifetime working for the Labour Party had only just begun.

Not winning was by far the best thing that could have happened to Healey. He had avoided the sort of squeak-in result which guarantees membership of parliament under the shadow of prospective defeat next time – what Anthony Crosland would experience in South Gloucestershire. That would have led to a stretch out of parliament in the mid-fifties with no certainty of return.

Healey got defeat out of the way at the age of twenty-seven, went away and did something else, something which gave him a vast catchment of political acquaintance and enhanced personal standing. Unstaled by the exhaustion of office – of which Kenneth Younger, another foreign affairs specialist, bitterly complained[14] – he would return fortuitously to a safe seat with a large reputation made outside the Commons but instantly recognised within it.

For though he had lost Pudsey and Otley, Healey was not short of career opportunities. He lists as options held out to him a research fellowship at Merton and that historianship of the Italian campaign as a regular officer with enhanced rank. The military career might well, twenty years later, have made Lieut. Gen. Sir Denis Healey a fearfully hard man for a reforming Defence Secretary to tangle with.* Instead, taking well-placed advice, he put in for a quite different sort of post.

The International Secretaryship of the Labour Party came as the result of nominations from Hugh Dalton, Aneurin Bevan and Harold Laski. Of the three, only Dalton could feel ideologically pleased long term with his recommendation. Perhaps like Nye Bevan, Harold Laski would have come to agree with Healey's change of view. But in 1945, Laski, the most famous don of his age, author of too many books, holder of too many opinions and finally a tragic figure, had a high, and blameless, incomprehension of what consequences flowed for people obstructing actions of which he approved in theory. 'A mousy little man', said Healey long afterwards, also noting 'his warm heart and big sorrowful brown eyes'.[15]

Laski was famous before television in the way that voluble academic popularisers have become since. He would be destroyed a year later in a libel action he should never have brought. In 1945, very like Denis Healey and large numbers of hopeful good people, Laski was an innocent optimist about 'socialist revolution'. His recommendations of Healey to the post of International Secretary in 1945 was academic praise for a high Oxford performer and for someone indulging, like him, the bombast of high tide. Laski would die soon after with the damning publicity of the court case and Attlee's famous snub at his memorial.

In some ways, Hugh Dalton was the oddest of the three nominators. Dalton could never have made Healey's Blackpool speech. If he reserved his actual hatred for the Germans, Dalton was cooler about 'the Socialist sixth of the world', as the Soviet Union proclaimed itself, than any Labour politician

---

* When this remark was casually relayed to Lord Healey, he snorted, 'Nothing less than Field Marshal.'

except perhaps Ernest Bevin. He had visited the Soviet Union and did not think that it worked.

Dalton was the persistent realist of Labour politics, but affinities with Healey were political not personal. A covert homosexual (when most homosexuals *were* covert), a dedicated hater, long out of love with his wife and mourning a child dead for twenty years, gregariously lonely, a man who steadily helped others and steadily attracted dislike, he cultivated young men – intelligent or good looking, preferably both – for wistful contemplation, occasional sexual success and for the disinterested advancement of the young and intelligent. His own sharp mind separated the categories. Anthony Crosland, to whom he was devoted and who turns up rather too often in the published diaries, may have been a lover. Healey, also handsome but reverberently heterosexual, would long after observe crisply, 'Tony was bi – tried to make a pass at me.'[16] Healey benefited from that scrupulous disinterest, while his salutations of revolutionary socialism were either discounted or not noticed.

As Healey himself acknowledges, Dalton 'was a force for good in the Labour Party'. His bleak inner character left him with less room for cant and slop than any contemporary. It also extended to a robust view of race, admiring Jews – for cleverness not victimhood – and loathing Germans. 'How many of my friends have they killed? What will happen if that dark ship puts out to sea again?' and perfect want of sympathy for Africans. He would later shock Cambridge undergraduates by applauding the 'whites only' policy of the Queensland provincial government. 'All these young men are very much against racial and colour prejudice – all for mixed marriages and miscegenation and a grey race emerging.'[17] Even Attlee looks a little bland beside that acid-traced persona.

The International Subcommittee of the National Executive of the Labour Party, subordinate offshoot of a body which would give Healey grief enough over the next forty years, met on 20 November 1945 in an unbombed room in the House of Commons to choose the party's International Officer. Laski was in the chair and present was a good tranche of the Cabinet: Aneurin Bevan, Minister of Health, Dalton, Chancellor, Herbert Morrison, Lord President, Emanuel Shinwell, the Minister of Fuel and Power, Ellen Wilkinson, Minister of Education, plus Mrs Adamson and W. A. Burke, both MPs, a Mr P. T. Hoady and the party's General Secretary, Morgan Phillips. The short-list was composed, apart from Healey, of two more temporary military men, Lieut. Col. G. A. Bamford and Major Aubrey Charles Ping, and one civilian, Graham Douglas Miller. In a vote declared unanimous, Healey was selected.

Healey's application letter listed his academic qualifications, the Domus Exhibition for his four years at Balliol, the Jenkyns Exhibition of 1939, the Firsts in Classical Moderations and finals and the Harmsworth Senior Scholarship, which would have made him a research fellow at Merton. Under languages, he lists 'Fluent French. Italian. Fair German. Some Russian. Reading knowledge of modern Greek.'

To that short-list of four should be added eighteen others (out of a grand total of 168) who did not make the final group to be interviewed. They are of a very high order indeed and include names to catch the eye: John Arthur Ford Ennals, Roy Harris Jenkins, Jack Eric Morpurgo and Dudley Seers. As a comment on the high feelings about politics at that time it is instructive and astonishing.

On the same afternoon, the committee asked Hugh Dalton to become Chairman of the International Subcommittee. It was to this body and through this politically sympathetic if sometimes difficult man, that Healey would work until early in 1952.

As the Labour Party's International Officer Healey succeeded to an empty office. His predecessor, William Gillies, an irascible Scot, had finally parted company with Transport House a year before. Gillies had views not very different from Dalton's – hating the Germans and profoundly distrusting Soviet Russia. *His* published views of the Soviet Union were the opposite of Laski's girlish enthusiasm. And as Healey would relate in his diary, Gillies was rude to all callers on principle.[18]

Having got the job, Healey proceeded to secure his wife and married Edna Edmunds. The honeymoon, after a registry office ceremony just before Christmas 1945, was a few days back in the north staying at The Buck at Buckden in Wharfedale. Edna, if this is not impertinent, was the right choice. Very able in her own right with admired books to come later in life – a biography of the philanthropist Angela Burdett-Coutts, a history of Buckingham Palace and, most recently, a study of Emma Darwin – she would also be admired all round the political circuit as the perfect political wife, perhaps just the perfect wife.

She had views of her own but didn't quarrel over them, could do the hostessing job in ministerial days without the least hint of the hard brightness often accompanying it. The word is 'intelligent' not 'smart'. Perhaps helpfully, she came like Denis's mother from the south-western borders, Coleford in the Forest of Dean. Edna endured the absences of the political day, joining for ministerial visits when and as she could. The marriage would have been strong in any circumstances, but it probably gained from Denis's lack of early parliamentary ambition. They had seven years together on something like office hours before he sought and took a seat in parliament. After Denis's election she would treat the Leeds constituency as one local official, now an MP, Harold Best, explained, utterly straightforwardly, telling officials that while the children, Jenny and Tim then Cressida, were growing up, they would take precedence. But once that was taken care of, she would put in her best efforts. And though Healey loved travel and late hard work, the successive homes they would make in Highgate, Withyham and finally Firle in Sussex, were ones that the Healey of the diary comes back to in recurring grateful relief. Healey would return to London in the new year of 1946 as Edna's husband and Labour Party man. That was how it would stay.

Denis Healey took up his post in January 1946. Labour Party Headquarters, Transport House, a matter-of-fact building in Smith Square near to Conservative Central Office and a useful pub, the Marquess of Granby, had been built by Ernest Bevin and its upper floors leased from the Transport and General Workers' Union (T&G). It housed an *apparat* under the leadership of the party's General Secretary, Morgan Phillips, a capable, hard-drinking machine minder, coercively happy with machine politics. But new and brilliant talent was coming into this dusty, underpaid *apparat*. There were Michael Young and Peter Wilmot, the future creators of *The Rise of the Meritocracy* and early practitioners of sociology in the days before its submerging in jargon and doctrine. Michael Middleton, an artist, demobbed like Healey and a future director of the Civic Trust, was hired to design publications. Middleton, though diffident about his own achievement, found Labour Party printing on his arrival 'like something done by a provincial jobbing printer in 1910'.[19] Middleton and Healey struck up an immediate friendship (artists keep turning up in Healey's circle) even though their responsibilities were far apart and Middleton noted that 'Denis seemed to be rushing out to see Ernest Bevin almost every day.'[20]

Nothing that Healey did for the institutional Labour Party, which is to say for the National Executive Committee and its grindingly heavy-handed International Subcommittee, quite compared with his role as an increasingly consulted unofficial adviser to the Foreign Secretary. He was an inferior person, in terms of hierarchy, to the Ministers of State at the Foreign Office, Hector McNeil and Christopher Mayhew. And the latter, another Oxford acquaintance, was well ahead of him in Soviet scepticism. Mayhew, as noted, had been the only member of the late 1930s Labour Club executive committee *not* to be a Communist. In the early days of his job, Healey was an adviser emphatically learning. But inferiority, hierarchical or otherwise, is not a condition to which the man ever long conformed.

Ernest Bevin was sixty-four years old, suffered from a weak heart and had already moved mountains. The eleven-year-old school-leaver from the Somerset and Devon borders who never knew who his father* was, had been a farmhand, then driven a mineral water cart through Bristol, before launching into the union work in which he would eventually create the Transport and General Workers' Union, and had held despotic (and expertly used) powers as Minister of Labour from 1940, when he was hastily bundled into parliament, until 1945.

---

* Recent research shows him to have been a local butcher called Thomas Pearce.

From domestic experience, Bevin had no love of the British Communist Party. Patronisingly, it is sometimes said that he looked upon the USSR as a branch of the T&G which was giving trouble. And during the London bus strike of 1937, the breaker of Bevin's undertakings had been Bert Papworth, a member of the CP executive and organiser of a ginger group, the 'Rank and File Movement'. But boss that he was, Bevin was bigger, more imaginative, more fundamentally serious than such superciliousness allows. And he was dealing with great if fearful affairs. His remark in 1946 to Christopher Mayhew: 'Molotov, Stalin, they are evil men'[21] spoke not intolerance but revulsion. Bevin's distrust of the Soviet Union sprang up from direct experience of dealing with the Soviet Foreign Minister, Vyacheslav Mikhailovich Molotov, in the early end-of-war conferences.

Described by Lenin as 'the best filing clerk in Moscow', Molotov was a man of ferocious, boorish obduracy with a limitless capacity for negation. As the talking presence of Stalin's probable clinical paranoia, Molotov, who taught most Westerners the one word of Russian they knew – Nyet (No) – was exquisitely cast. The other Soviet notable to whom Bevin would be exposed was Andrei Vyshinsky, chief prosecutor in Stalin's purges, a nightmarish figure on a moral par with Roland Freisler, Hitler's murderous prosecuting attorney. Their rising junior, better known to the next generation, Andrei Gromyko, had by comparison a sort of basalt charm.

At the successive conferences of Teheran, Yalta and Potsdam, the Soviets had produced bleak, untrusting demands, and in the form of curious and meaningless percentages – 90 per cent Soviet influence in Romania, for instance – had been largely deferred to. The Russians were going to do well in all circumstances as the land-war victors and consequent landholders across Eastern Europe. But all entreaties to define the limits of their ambition were met by Soviet spokesmen with what Bevin in another context would call 'a complete ignoral'.

Bevin, at that same Blackpool Conference, had used soft words which there is no reason to disbelieve.

Ever since 1920 when I formed the Council of Action to stop further war against Russia – I am not a new convert – I have always believed that the tragedy in making the last peace – or armistice which it really was – was the failure, largely out of prejudice – to bring Russia to the Conference at Versailles. Had they been brought there, the problem of the warm-water ports which is the fundamental problem of Russia's foreign policy – an absolute need for her in a great country of that kind – would have been solved.

Bevin then quoted Disraeli: 'Britain and France joined together is an insurance for Peace, but Britain, France and Russia joined together is a security for Peace ... Now,' he added, 'with the wider development of the weapons of war, we go further and our aim has been, and the insurance premium for which we have to pay in commitments, must be the United States of America, Britain and Soviet Russia.'[22]

The goodwill implied here was real – and Bevin had indeed been the union leader who, giving full official backing to London dockers in 1920, successfully barred the loading at the East India Dock of the *Jolly George*, suspected of sending munitions to Poland, then at war with revolutionary Russia. As he put it at the time: 'Whatever may be the merits or demerits of a theory of government of Russia, that is a matter for Russia, and we have no right to determine their form of government, any more than we would tolerate Russia determining our form of government.'[23]

Bevin and the government had moreover no motive in 1945 for wanting anything but amicable terms with the Soviet Union. Attlee in August 1945 would set out his thinking in a letter to the South African leader, J. C. Smuts.

> The growth of Anglo-Russian antagonism on the Continent and the creation of spheres of influence would be disastrous to Europe and would stultify all the ideals for which we have fought. But I think that we must at all costs avoid trying to seek a cure by building up Germany or forming blocs aimed at Russia . . . any suspicion – and the Russians are not slow to form suspicions – that we were trying to deal softly with Germany, or to build her up, would be such an obvious threat to Russia that we should thereby harden the Soviet government's present attitude in Eastern Europe and help to give actual shape to our fears.[24]

Those observations on arms to Poland in 1920 and Attlee's comment (advised by Bevin) made in 1945 are separated by twenty-five years. And there is no break in consistency of outlook. Bevin did not indeed like the Soviet Union. But a peace without an arms bill, and as little foreign policy commitment as possible, was to the obvious advantage of a government set upon massive reform and social redistribution. If we were to 'sell out to the Americans', as would soon be busily claimed by the left wing, it should be remembered that in 1945, there were no Americans wanting to buy. The US under Roosevelt, and with Eisenhower as an oddly unthrusting commander-in-chief, had conceded more at the early peace conferences than Churchill could stomach and missed the easy chance of getting to Prague ahead of the Red Army.

The US was, in the Europe of 1945, a force for very little. Healey, the tolerant understander of Soviet excesses of Blackpool 1945, was going to work for someone less blithe about 'the revolution in Eastern Europe', but anxious enough to make terms for a settled peace with the Soviet Union. Over two years, the bleak, uncomprehending animus of Molotov speaking for Stalin and the transformation of conquered territory into brutally subordinated near-colonies, would point both men in the same clear direction, 180 degrees from the broad hopefulness present at the war's conclusion.

But there were prophets of the Cold War even at that early date. Churchill, for one, would emerge from a switchback of euphoria about summits alternating with wild theories about immediate hot wars, to make his Fulton Declaration in 1946. More quietly compelling were the Foreign Office man, Christopher Warner, and the FO's new Permanent Under-Secretary, Sir Orme Sargent. Sargent, a steady anti-appeaser who had early assumed that where Hitler led, Stalin would wish to follow, had a full-dress sense of impending crisis. Anne Deighton, historian of the Cold War, quotes his fear that the Soviet Union might 'exploit for their own ends, the economic crises which in the coming months may well develop into a catastrophe capable of engulfing political institutions in many European countries . . . It is not overstating the case to say that if Germany is one, this may well decide the fate of liberalism throughout the world.'[25] Hitler had been that sort of man, so was Stalin. Stalin would likely do the same sort of thing. It was prejudiced, stereotypical, crude and good working practice.

Christopher Warner, assembling the accumulating evidence of Soviet conduct six months later, entitled his paper 'The Soviet Campaign against this Country and our Response to It.' The Foreign Office view and the hopes of Bevin and Attlee had one point of intersection. The Foreign Office expected the Soviets to be guileful and reassuring – in Warner's uncharacteristically banal phrase, 'attempting to pull a velvet glove over their iron hand'.[26] But the Soviet Union under Stalin was never as subtle as the elegant imaginings of Foreign Office position papers. It was crude, offensive and rebarbative. The Lancaster House Conference of September 1945 saw Molotov demanding an African colony under, amusingly, a mandate – he suggested the former Italian Tripolitania – demanding to know what 'lay behind' calls for free elections in Bulgaria and Romania which the Soviet Union entirely controlled, and asking for the admission of France and China to the UN Security Council to be rescinded.

The later dialogue at the Lancaster House Conference was not edifying, with Molotov asking, 'Why did the British want Tripolitania which did not belong to them?' and Bevin replying, 'What did the Russians want it for?'[27] Essentially Molotov, the nominated spokesman of an absolute ruler, talked a mixture of *realpolitik* and resentment. Personal relations were dreadful, with Russia observing that Anthony Eden had been a gentleman, which Bevin wasn't.[28]

What was subtly happening across the first two years of the war was a diffuse shift of attitude, political and public. The Soviet Union had in 1944–5 received officially sponsored (but real) adulation in Britain, crowds queuing in Westminster Hall to view the Sword of Stalingrad. But the warmth – this sort of British kitsch plus Dynamo Moscow playing Arsenal – receded in perplexity as Molotov and Vyshinsky, in London and New York, forever demanded, and refused, gave and took offence with an increasingly familiar sullen bombast. The *Economist* astutely compared the thrashings-about of Stalin's men not with Hitler, but with Kaiser Wilhelm and his court, uncertain of what they wanted, but distrusting the world and restless for a quarrel – great strength and a great sense of inferiority.

But the *New Statesman* thought that British and American ministers 'had done much to confirm Russian suspicions'. As for their concern about free elections in those areas of 90 per cent Soviet influence, 'they could have chosen no worse ground to stand on than the lack of "democracy" in Hungary, Romania and Bulgaria . . . the first object of Soviet policy is to preserve the peace. To believe otherwise is to display either ignorance or prejudice.'[29]

The putting of 'democracy' into quotation marks was one of the little needlepoints which would mark out the jagged line dividing the Foreign Secretary of a Labour government and the weekly journal regularly read by middle-class socialists, Labour's clerisy.

'What is to be done about Ernest Bevin?' wrote the *Statesman*'s editor, Kingsley Martin, in early 1946,[30] 'is the question I hear Labour MPs asking in the House . . . the inexcusable methods of Soviet foreign policy seem to have confirmed Mr Bevin's deep-seated loathing of everything connected with Communism and worse, since his row with Mr Vyshinsky, Mr Bevin seems to see the hidden hand of Moscow behind everything that happens . . . It is a dangerous state of mind for a Foreign Secretary . . .'

But compared with some of his correspondents, Kingsley Martin was soft-spoken. One, a Leonard Peck, responding to the 'What shall we do with Mr Bevin?' leader, wrote the next week, 'Naturally Mr Bevin has no patience with the Socialist critics in his own party. Neither had Mr Ramsay MacDonald . . . Let us have no more cant about trusting our leaders. That trust has been abused and betrayed so often in the last twenty years for it to be any longer implicit.'

There was a great deal more where that came from. The earnest rhetoric of 1945, Attlee's as much as anybody's, had been the avoidance at all costs of two camps within a divided Europe. Such division was a fact slowly acknowledged as accomplished. It would be followed by a division of the British governing party into another two camps. They would amend their complexions over the decades ahead, but the taking of a hard and a soft line towards the Soviet Union would be a touchstone between them.

Denis Healey had begun his career with what might be called a ferocious version of the soft line – not minding too much about extreme measures and all that. He would rapidly find himself equally direct, equally candid, as a champion fighter for the hard line. And hard lines began in the outer office of Ernest Bevin.

7

BUREAUCRAT AND TRAVELLER

Broadly, the Parliamentary Labour Party would endorse Bevin's foreign policy. But quite as broadly, left-wingers, themselves highly differentiable, would campaign for a different foreign policy, indeed a different stand in the world. The naïveties of 1945, of which Healey had partaken, would be diffused. The basic division lay between deferring to the simple Soviet line and an attempt to play geometry by following a course equidistant between the great powers. The intellectual theorist of this last school would be Richard Crossman. The name which this group gave to their approach had a retrospectively familiar ring – the Third Force!

A document which history has rather overlooked spells this doctrine out to perfection. Known as the Spelthorne Letter, or Memorandum, and dated 29 October 1946,[1] it was expensively published on good paper* and headed with a nice irony 'Private and Confidential – NOT for Publication', it proclaimed belief that 'British Social Democracy has an historic role to play in proving to the world by her leadership and example that democratic socialism is the only final basis of world government; and that it can therefore provide a genuine middle way between the extreme alternatives of American "free enterprise" economics and Russian totalitarian socio-political life.'

It regretted that little had been done 'to establish this middle way in a dynamic and positive sense'. The government was reactive; 'it has become more and more obvious that "security" measures taken by the USSR in expanding her "sphere of influence" in Europe and the Mediterranean are

---

* Still white after fifty years in a Labour Party archive folder in the Museum of Labour History in Manchester.

the greatest cause of preoccupation to the Government in the field of foreign affairs.' One-sidedly so, they added, since the government didn't seem to mind the creation of new US bases 'notwithstanding the United States' monopoly of the Atomic bomb, her inflated military budget, and the capitalist-expansionist nature of her economy'. Spelthorne faced the defects of Soviet policy with more restraint. 'We have no doubt that criticisms of the internal affairs in Poland and other states bordering on the Soviet, though frequently exaggerated – particularly in regard to the so-called iron curtain, have considerable foundation in fact.' But 'Gross imperfections in other states such as Greece, Spain and the United States tend to evoke but a fraction of the criticism directed Eastwards . . .' The coalitions being formed in the name of Socialist unity in East European countries should not disturb us. Our government tended to view those countries through the distorting gaze of the British Communist Party with 'its switches of "party line", its manifest desire to establish a system of government for which this county is ill-suited'.

The government should not trouble itself so much about Communists and Socialists coming together in Eastern Europe. It had been

> unaware of the fact that certain countries in the world have a social, political and economic background which will tend to favour – with or without Russian intervention – the establishment of Communist societies . . . and just as the Resistance Movement to German Fascism tended to coalesce round the Communist movements in some countries for whom Communism provided the sole workable alternative to the semi-barbarous conditions existing prior to and during the war, so too were the forces of democratic Socialism given a new coherence . . .

Yet here we were 'so fascinated by fear of Communism' that we were supporting 'the worst species of collaborators and political adventurers'. We had 'not only alienated the newly emergent Communist societies, but also brought discouragement to the democratic Socialists in countries where Western Socialism was ripe for establishment had we cared to assist them'. Asserting these views, the signatories drew themselves up to a certain height to tell Attlee: 'We feel it right and necessary to inform you of these views . . . for we must make it clear that, believing that the future of Britain and of humanity is at stake in these matters, we cannot continue to remain silent and inactive.'

The text, civil, middle class and gracefully reproachful, was above all things moralistic. Though it echoed the terrible Stalinese of Soviet liners – 'American imperialism', 'reactionaries' and so on – this is not a fellow-travelling document. It is English radicalism at its most self-preoccupied – 'the future of Britain and of humanity' – and rather mother-duckish. Not that it was all absurd. Franco in Spain and the royalist right wing in Greece *were* unlovely specimens, though across twenty to thirty years, they would dwindle or explode. But the understanding of the Soviet Union was wide-eyed and would, over the next twelve years, get its *congé* by putsch, show trial, elimination of unreliable elements and tanks in the streets.

But if the text is instructive, so are the signatories. There were twenty-one of these, including notable left-wingers of this day and later: Jennie Lee, wife of Aneurin Bevan, Bevan's PPS Donald Bruce, now an amiable peer, Harold Davies, a mild leftist who would be sent hopelessly to Vietnam by Harold Wilson, Benn Levy, only briefly in full-time politics, better known later as a playwright, J. P. W. 'Curly' Mallalieu, author of an amusing half-life autobiography *Very Ordinary Seaman*, Wyn Griffiths, par-for-the-course leftist, and Lyall Wilkes who faded later, but was at this time a markedly active left-winger. Heavier names included Sydney Silverman – to the left of the Tribune group, admirable crusader against the death penalty, but somehow unmoved by extensive Soviet recourse to it and always reliably sour – Michael Foot and Ashley Bramall, another peer who would do distinguished work as a notably moderate Chairman of the Greater London Council.

There was also Woodrow Wyatt, at this time a noisy radical, subsequently a failed provincial newspaper owner, prideless adjutant of Mrs Thatcher, 'Voice of Reason' on Mr Murdoch's *News of the World*, and faintly gruesome ultra-Tory. That particular name should give no surprise; it is in the way of flotsam to float. But at the bottom of the first right-hand column of signatories to what is a startlingly naïve and Soviet-trusting manifesto, lies, most improbably, 'James Callaghan'.

But if Callaghan would amend, Healey was amending quicker. The Danton of Blackpool and Pudsey was now on hand to put Bevin's case against Spelthorne and all its work. As a measure of Healey's future style it is very revealing. The typescript has been amended to exclude words like 'muddleheaded', 'a series of aggressions', and 'simple-minded'. The Healey of 'out of their tiny Chinese minds' was already stepping out and needed to be muted. Not that restraint reduced this riposte to any sort of niminy-piminy document. It also demonstrates a grasp with which the Ministry of Defence would become familiar so that, reasoning and stamping on feet as it goes, the paper is by turns elegant and brutal, a combination familiar to all subsequent observers of Denis Healey.

It starts with a roll of Headquarterly drums.

Dear Colleague,

It has come to the notice of Head Office that the Spelthorne Divisional Labour Party has been circulating to all Divisional Parties printed copies of a 'private and confidential' letter attacking the government's foreign policy. Its main thesis is that close collaboration with both the Soviet Union and the United States has been abandoned in favour of a line-up with American imperialism.[2]

Spelthorne was arguing, says Healey, 'that because America is capitalist and Russia socialist, therefore America constitutes a threat to world peace, while Russia could have no motive for expanding her power'.

Capitalism might contain 'tendencies which lead to war', Socialists did not however believe 'that only capitalism produces war. Capitalism is a fairly recent system in history, but war has been common for thousands of years.' The petitioners are witheringly reminded that the Soviet Union has dabbled in that sort of thing herself. Was security a Soviet concern? Yes indeed, 'Finland, the Baltic states, Poland and Romania all suffered through the Soviet desire for security.' The words 'the Soviet Union herself committed a series of aggressions' have a line through them. At such a distance, we cannot know if this is Healey raising his own tone or more probably the muffling of hard words by a prudent Morgan Phillips.

Generalisations may be unsatisfactory, Healey says, but 'it is worth suggesting that if capitalism favours war, democracy discourages it.' While *au contraire*, 'a dictatorship, even a dictatorship of the proletariat, can act first, and justify itself afterwards.' This part of the Spelthorne case had 'only to be stated clearly to be recognised as utterly wrong'.

Thus far Healey has been stating the self-evident, giving utopians a talking-to. But because at this time there existed, as far as Clement Attlee, a wish *not* to be part of a Western bloc, Healey now becomes aspirational rather than his natural, side-taking self. He quotes Attlee: 'The Government do not believe in the forming of groups – East, West or Centre. We stand for the United Nations . . . We want to have done with the suicidal game of power politics as fast as possible.' Attlee, always an earnest believer in internationalism, had meant what he had said. Healey is loyally conveying the sentiments. But the true Healey is a realist or nothing and somewhat inclined to savour power politics. 'As fast as possible' was to be quite slow. Accusing Spelthorne, not quite fairly, of wanting to side with the Soviet Union, he contemplates the straw man he has put up and machine-guns it. This argument won't 'stand examination, even in terms of strategy. Britain depends entirely on food and raw materials imported by sea.' Should we oppose 'the country which today has an overwhelming superiority in naval power but also in the mercantile marine?' Having said all this, he provokes another deletion with the words: 'The whole of this section is so simple minded that it deserves no further attention.'

At Blackpool he had talked about 'a greater degree of police supervision and more immediate and drastic punishment for their opponents'. 'In Eastern Europe,' he says now, 'the British government has only one aim . . . to ensure the carrying out of free and fair elections as agreed by all concerned so that the true minorities and majorities in the country shall be represented in the government according to their strength.'

As for Spain, Healey could say, 'Britain is the only power in the world which is continuously working both inside and outside Spain for a means of removing Franco.' But back in 1945 Ernest Bevin, in a privately circulated memorandum, had written, 'If Spain was settled, the western area would be improved and I do not believe that it is entirely love of democracy that causes Russia to want to keep the Spanish pot boiling.'[3] Bevin had also told the House of Commons[4] that while favouring the removal of Franco by Spaniards, 'HM Government is not prepared to take any steps which would promote or encourage civil war in that country.'

Defences of policy in the Middle East, Indonesia and Germany follow. The Spelthorne petitioners are then roundly told off. While 'a lively and critical interest in every aspect of government policy is vital to the success of democracy, there can be no excuse for this contradiction of the known facts which is constantly occurring in the Spelthorne Letter.' It was 'the duty of us all to see that a natural anxiety over the maladies of a war-torn world is not allowed to turn into an excited and neurotic struggle against those of our leaders who are trying hardest to cure them'.

While one might be amused at its schoolmasterly tone, the local parties had been given a reasoned case, argued out in some detail over seven pages. Spelthorne had been lectured and admonished, but also taken seriously and argued with. The whole piece belongs to a world beyond recall, one without spinning or news management. Healey's letter reposes a faith in rational discourse and indeed, for the period until the outbreak and development of the Korean War and the risks associated with General MacArthur's actions, the Labour Party would not engage in splits on foreign policy which could be called 'major'. And the conflict to which Healey had addressed himself would largely be resolved, less by argument than by events and by the common sense of Members responding to the evidence.

Benn Levy, a Spelthorne signatory, would speak the grand disillusion of many people in 1948: 'There is no longer a third choice. We must travel the Russian road or the American road ... Are we to choose the American alignment which it is widely feared may jeopardise our Socialism, or the Russian alignment which, with the object lesson of Czechoslovakia in mind, we may reasonably believe would end in the loss of our democracy? For better or worse, the choice is made ...'

Hugh Berrington, who has analysed revolt against all governments in the ten years after the war, makes this point statistically, splitting Labour backbenchers into the categories Ultra Left, Left, Centre Left and Rest, and demonstrating the refinement from the votes on a series of foreign policy divisions in the Commons.[5] The Far Left, people like John Platts-Mills, Konni Zilliacus and more tentatively, William Warbey, were the knuckle-end of the idealistic opposition to Bevin expressed by Spelthorne in 1946, what remained after Marshall Aid, the re-election of President Truman on his Liberal Democratic Fair Deal ticket and the Communist seizure of power in Czechoslovakia on 27 February 1948.

This last act would remove all credibility from the earlier statements of leftists like John Haire MP, arguing, after a visit to Hungary, that there was no question of Russia enforcing a putsch – 'the four Communist Members in the Cabinet work in close co-operation with the other members . . .' – while Lyall Wilkes had said that 'Russian policy today is a policy of self-defence.' Such language, understandable in 1945–6, was about to be invalidated in Czechoslovakia.

Healey had advanced knowledge of the situation in Czechoslovakia from his travels as International Secretary of the party. The Communists had done well in free elections – Slav fellow-feeling, liberation from the Nazis by the Red Army (after Eisenhower passed up the chance to be in Prague ahead of them), and a large working-class vote in its highly developed industrial areas. But given expropriatory trade agreements and the short ways of Soviet soldiery, that was unlikely to be sustained. The Communists did not anyway have a working majority and, under what another Communist would call 'Bourgeois Arithmetic',* the support of the Socialist Party was required.

This was proposed by way of unification, something which was to happen in a number of East European countries – in Eastern Germany, the DDR would be governed at all material times by the Socialist Unity Party! In Czechoslovakia, socialist unity was harder to accomplish. The democratic forms still stood; however menaced by Russian troops, the Socialist Party still waged arguments. Healey was present at its congress in Brno, the Moravian capital, in November 1947. He found a strike under way – called by the government to menace the under-compliance of non-Communists. The government was led by Klement Gottwald, a bigger figure in the strict hierarchy of Communist ranking than any other CP leader, a sort of Cardinal Archbishop to Stalin's Pope – and one doubling as Apostolic Delegate. He had his own nominee as leader of the Socialist Party, Zdenek Fierlinger, a former Czech ambassador to Moscow – in plain Healey terms 'universally regarded as a Soviet stooge'.

Healey had told Spelthorne that the concern of the Labour Party for Eastern Europe was that the true minorities and majorities should be represented according to their strength. Three months after that democratic vote, such luxuries were dispensed with for forty years by a straight-up-and-down military putsch. A week later Jan Masaryk, son of the founder of Czechoslovak state and Foreign Minister in the coalition government, was found dead in the courtyard of the Foreign Office, having jumped or more probably been thrown from a third-floor window. The education of Spelthorne was complete.

The experience of Czechoslovakia – where the Labour government, never mind the Labour Party, was powerless – intensified interest in areas where

---

* The later Portuguese CP leader, Amilcar Cabral.

both could hope to be listened to. The strength of the Communists in France and Italy was formidable. A major role and great prestige in the Resistance movements had added to pre-war strength in France and a quarter of votes cast in the first post-war elections had been for that party, led by the parodistically grim Maurice Thorez. The latent power of the French CP on the streets and the shop floor was frightening – power of employment, the beatings-up and maiming of opponents.*

Italy was different in many ways. The Italian Communist Party would turn, as the French one never did, into a civilised and pluralist party, though at this time it was marching to Stalin's beat. It would, in fact, be frustrated in the key elections by a murky combination of Catholic Church, US Embassy and criminal underworld which would give Italy fair prosperity and the most corrupt political class in Western Europe. But here and now, Labour concern was about the future of the Italian Socialist Party, the PSI. And Healey would be heavily involved.

The Italian problem began in late 1946 but would climax just a month after the mysterious death of Jan Masaryk in ways which directly affected the Labour Party at home. The leadership of the PSI was undoubtedly close to the PCI Communists. But a faction rejecting this link formed around Giuseppe Saragat. And the Italian party gratified the mothering instincts of Transport House with a series of appeals for involvement.

Healey had attended the Florence conference of the Socialist International in May in company with Harold Laski. The delegacy had also expanded Healey's circle of political acquaintance. He met the key party leaders including the Communist, Togliatti, and the Prime Minister and dominant figure in post-war Italy, the Christian Democrat, Alcide de Gasperi, as well as the painter Guttuso, a Communist, and the sardonic novelist, Alberto Moravia.

The Florence conference would reject what had been on offer in Prague: Socialist fusion with the Communists. But the issue here was subtler. There were at least five factions, but the bare bones were that one wing under Pietro Nenni wanted continued intensifying accommodation, if not literal unity, with the Communists, and another under Saragat violently did not. Saragat's people would soon be ready to declare their own secession, and were more tempted to make this move because, as members of the PSI, they were caught up in a sort of most-favoured-party pact which barred all criticism of the Communists and required actual defence of them.

Back in Transport House, Healey would be bombarded by requests for Labour's (and his own) involvement. He was kept up to date by analyses forwarded by Victor Schiff, Italian correspondent of the *Daily Herald* in Rome. On 26 November 1946 Schiff wrote to Healey from the Via Ajaccio. His

---

* Nowhere better described than in the novel *Uranus* by Marcel Aymé.

account conveys the fraught and apocalyptic mood of the period when world war or Communist takeover were the currency, even of such level-headed and competent people.

Schiff foresaw a party split and events leading, 'perhaps already in 1947, to a collapse of the new democratic regime, to civil war conditions and chaos and to a dangerous weakening of the British position in Italy and in the Central Mediterranean'.

Schiff pointed out how 'simply disastrous' the Socialist performance had been in recent local elections, how well organised and financed were the Communists who also had vast advantages by way of a strong press. Then again, the Socialist press was meagre and, where it existed, subservient to the Communist line and anti-British. On returning to Rome that September after three months away, the first thing which struck him had been how *Avanti*, the Socialist paper, 'never missed an occasion, either in the selection or in the presentation of news, to be disagreeable to British policy while always very careful in not offending Russia'.

'During the past four weeks, particularly since the announcement of the Pact of Action with the Communists, this tendency has been considerably accentuated . . . Sandro Pertini, the new editor, is generally described as an admirable hero, before the war as well as during the resistance in Northern Italy, but as a political simpleton.' (The same Pertini, whom Healey had met at the Florence conference, would become nearly forty years later, flourishing a briar pipe bought in England and roundly abusing members of the government, an extremely popular President of the Republic.)

Both parties, Schiff reminded Healey, were obliged under the Pact of Action to regard any attack on one party as an attack on itself, something with which the Milan edition of *Avanti* had dealt by suppressing a speech of Attlee's criticising the Italian Communists. But 'after a first moment of resignation and despair – many Socialists, both of the right-wing "Critica sociale" tendency and the pseudo left-wing "Iniziativa Socialista", have decided to unite their efforts for a supreme attempt to save the party from death and absorption by the Communists.'

They were undertaking to fight Pietro Nenni, at that time the leading Italian Socialist close to the Communists. Schiff had known him for twenty-five years, looked on him as a friend and did not give up hope that he might change his stance, but 'I must confess that his attitude in the last few days, especially his last speech at La Spezia . . . which is almost purely communist in doctrine and phraseology, have deepened the gulf which separates him not only from Saragat, but from West European Socialism.'

Meanwhile the Socialists, bound by the unity agreement, were passing up what should have been a great opportunity in not denouncing Communist acceptance of Yugoslav claims to Trieste and its territory. Terrible politics, it was 'a wonderful opportunity to beat the Communists out of the field'.

Schiff attributed Nenni's inexplicably servile collaboration with the Communists to a ploy of Togliatti. Nenni would become 'persona gratissima' in Moscow and Tito (still at this time Moscow-true) would be instructed to make 'to him, Nenni, such striking concessions that he would become the most popular man in Italy'.

However, the Christian Democrats in what was still a Catholic country were being driven, by the anti-Vatican stance of the two left parties, rightwards. There might be a strike, but the south would quickly support central government and in the much more left-wing (and advanced) north, the military and the police would back the government while the middle classes whose 'sufferings are indescribable' were, thought Schiff, overstating things, 'rallying in masses to the Qualunquists', a reactionary group using a term originally implying nostalgia and indifference to politics. Italy, he added apocalyptically, 'will thus become another Greece – engaged in civil war – on a much larger scale – or another Spain.'

Schiff was anxious that Healey, who had attended the Florence conference, should come himself to the Rome gathering, now brought forward from March to January. The same sentiment came from the British Embassy through W. H. (Bill) Braine. 'I should warn you that great importance will be attached to the presence of the British delegates and the contributions they make to the discussions; they may even be asked to discuss in open conference various aspects of the Party organisation.' Braine added gratifyingly, 'The Italians were very much impressed by Laski and yourself and say they could hope for nothing better than that you two should again be the Labour Party delegates.'

An instructive line in Braine's letter was his comment on the motives of Saragat. 'Owing to the manoeuvres of Saragat and the petty bourgeois group, the General Executive have thought it advisable to bring forward the conference . . .' (Healey had already noted during his previous visit that the British Ambassador, Sir Noel Charles, was usually drunk and that Braine did the work – 'his smoothly efficient Labour attaché, Bill Braine, made up for him.'[6]) If Braine at any rate echoed Marxist terminology, John Colville, Churchill's former Private Secretary, would be noted by Healey in his diary as hoping for the victory of the near fascist Uumo Qualunque.

But the phrase, 'petty bourgeois group' is pure Stalinist contempt. A very short, undated and unsigned memo, almost certainly from Healey to his committee having presented the options, states more neutrally: 'The British Labour attaché, Mr W. H. Braine, thinks that Nenni's policy is the best one for socialism in Italy and also for British interests.'

Such words and thinking would have enraged another correspondent, that socialist from the Abruzzi quoted by Schiff, Ignazio Silone. Author of the classic, *Fontamara* (Bitter Spring), Silone is one of the great names of modern Italian literature. A former member of the Communist Party, violently alienated from Communism by its conspirational ruthlessness, Healey writes of finding Silone 'morose . . . with flashes of brilliance' and remarks that he is more admired outside Italy for the content of his books than in that country, where his style is thought clumsy.[7]

Silone's letter was as unliterary as a missive to Morgan Phillips needed to be. Like Schiff, Braine and, it seems, the leadership of the Italian Socialists, he also urgently wanted a strong Labour delegation. The appeals by all concerned met little response from Labour's bureaucracy. Healey's attempt to get a major minister, Dalton, to go did not succeed and the split went through, leaving the Nenni group with the larger piece of the equity and its hands free for all-out co-operation with the PCI.

The Rome conference happened in January 1947. That co-operation would become a defining crisis in the British Labour Party and strategic European politics by April 1948. It would involve Healey, together with Morgan Phillips, in a central role telling key groups of Italians what to do, very much his sort of thing.

8

Cards on the Table

Healey's diary contains its share of cheerful references to excellent lunches and easy days and time spent sunning himself in Regent's Park or, as on one Saturday in late May 1947, 'Lounged all day in the sun on the roof. At night saw *A Day at the Races*.' More typically, he 'Worked hard continuously from 11.30 a.m. to 10.15 p.m. and wrote a pamphlet on Foreign Policy.'[1] That day's work is six thousand words long. But then the early career of Denis Healey is regularly marked, cairn-like, with a pamphlet, 'the flat, ephemeral pamphlet' which W. H. Auden had famously linked with 'the necessary murder' as the steady duty of a working activist. To many left-wingers, *Cards on the Table* seemed like both.

But taking on these left-wingers was now a duty. For in those days the Labour Party held conferences, furiously important conferences at which great issues – nationalisation, unilateral nuclear disarmament and, as here, alignment in the world – were fervently discussed. Sense and nonsense mingled; the voting system rested upon thirty-strong committees of trade unionists disposing half a million votes at a time; people from constituencies were allowed to make speeches criticising the leadership.

In 1947 foreign policy and Ernest Bevin personally were under assault and at Margate, with facilities far too small for a modern plastic rally, a momentous issue would be decided. The left-wing pamphlet *Keep Left* had encapsulated the opposition, in parliament and constituencies, of both utopian and fellow-travelling opinion to Bevin's great shift of alignment. Now, for the first time but not the last, Denis Healey would be called upon to make the leadership case, something he did just ahead of the conference with a pamphlet neither flat nor ephemeral.

Cards on the Table is both a defence of his boss and a spelling-out of the direction in which foreign policy must now, however regretfully, go. A pamphlet written before the events in Eastern Europe of early 1948 would have to be soft-spoken, persuasive, a temperate justification of a foreign policy for which even mainstream Labour opinion was not yet ready. It had to be significantly different from the knuckle-rapping response to the wrong-headed people in Spelthorne. Above all, it came after, and had to answer the case of, *Keep Left*, the pamphlet hurriedly produced by Foot, Mikardo and Crossman. Although there were domestic points in *Keep Left*, its chief function was a keening after the status quo in foreign affairs, the status quo of the 1945 Labour Conference, left speaking to left and avoidance of any taking of sides, the commonplaces in fact of the election speeches of so many Labour candidates.

Gladwyn Jebb at the Foreign Office, having seen *Keep Left* and given credit to Crossman, had commented to Bevin:

Much of what C says would have appeared sensible two years or even eighteen months ago. Indeed all our own papers were then based on the assumption that there should in no circumstances be any Anglo-US line-up against the USSR or indeed against Communism until such time at any rate as the Soviets should have made it abundantly clear that they did not intend to co-operate with the West. It will be recalled with what passionate conviction the FO represented this thesis to the Chiefs of Staff and what care was taken to prevent even the smallest whisper getting round that we favoured the Americans rather than the Russians . . .[2]

Keep Left, for which passionate conviction had not been cleared by events, argued for close ties with France in order to lead that Third Force 'to hold the balance of power and mediate between Russia and America'.[3]

Healey was counsel for the defence but not in a defensive way. Despite the inevitable offence given to the inevitable people, *Cards on the Table* is all the necessary things. It adopts a quiet and reasoning style and argues up to readers from contrary assumptions, recognising that 'a minority of Labour's own supporters are sincerely disturbed about the government's activities abroad . . . it is held to take sides with a Capitalist America against a Socialist Russia or to entail a diversion of men and money from home production which this country cannot afford.' Very well, they must first grasp the limitations put on policy, the destruction wrought by war and Britain's contribution to the re-creation of Europe. People had to be told, and plainly. Territorial frontiers ran together

so that no great power could increase its security without directly weakening the security of another great power. New weapons of mass

destruction like the atom bomb and biological warfare . . . threatened
to make any one part of the globe vulnerable from any other; thus no
power could feel really secure if there were an enemy anywhere on the
earth's surface. Unilateral security on the old pattern, a peace guaranteed by national power, could only be obtained by world conquest.

Level rather than flat, and hardly ephemeral in its concerns, this pamphlet
is remarkably sober, a short primer on the new brittleness of the world. The
melancholy poet of the old American South, John Crowe Ransome, had put
it well:

> Why the ribs of the Earth subsist, frail as breath,
> If but God wearieth.

Finally, 'the development of total warfare as the organised activity of the
whole state and the need for adapting industry in advance to meet the claims
of a war-machine, since an armaments programme now requires years for
fulfilment, conferred an absolute advantage on the aggressor . . . weighed the
scales heavily in favour of a nation which could plan such a crime without
interference from public opinion or democratic control.'

A good deal of what would be called games theory and planning for war –
mutually assured destruction and the like – is sketched in early in this little
party pamphlet. And for all his use of Big Three terminology, Healey has too
many devastating numbers for real illusion. 'Only thirty years since the Two
Power Naval Standard was a cardinal principle of our foreign policy, we
found our American ally with a navy six times the size of ours and a merchant fleet more than three times as large.'

We were obliged to diminish and pull back from past authority 'yet this
reduction must be carried out in an orderly way so that at no point would
we lose our power of initiative and our ability to control the process. Above
all, we must avoid creating by our withdrawal vacuums into which the
other Great Powers might surge in irresistible and world-shattering conflict.'
Twenty years later, the Secretary of State for Defence, having managed a
small, entirely justified, if not quite acknowledged, war against Indonesia,
would be called upon to make just such a decision about the British presence
in that Kipling-defined location – East of Suez.

Rallying Labour people to Labour things, Healey in 1947 lists what has
been done: 'Labour Britain has spent £750,000,000 on world reconstruction . . . Over £1,000,000,000 has been spent through UNRRA [United
Nations Relief and Rehabilitation Administration] in preventing famine and
disease – 100,000 lorries have been sent to Europe and 'in spite of destruction
infinitely worse than in 1918, there have been no epidemics and no widespread famine in Europe.' He takes leave to rebuke 'Churchill's cynical

selfishness in the debate of 12 March 1947 when he blamed the government for foregoing improvements in the British standard of living in order to save millions of Europeans from starvation and disease'.

Surveying the world which has to be met, Healey, in the way of all progressives, stresses the importance of the United Nations. 'Support of the United Nations organisation has been the key to Britain's action in all these spheres . . . British pertinacity was mainly responsible for obtaining a World Food Organisation against American reluctance and Russian indifference.' But moral points made, Healey comes to the essentials – power. If the Big Three fell out, nothing could be done. The Soviets held and used a veto which made the UN, like Poland under its Golden Constitution of unanimity, inoperative. Effectively 'the Veto power does in fact commit the Big Three to appeasement of one another so long as action is confined to the UN – a situation which puts a premium on aggressive action.'

But for here and now Healey wanted his readers to understand by what constraints the US government operated. Until very recently, 'American public opinion was deeply opposed to any policy which might conceivably lead to war.' The most damaging epithet employed against Roosevelt was 'warmonger'.

Defending America might be excused but it was when he came to Russia that Healey gave offence and ensured a row. For in respect of Russia, he was talking pure *realpolitik*. Russia had one great strength in world politics compared with America. 'The Soviet system concentrates the whole of Russian power in a few little-known men who, far from being responsible to public opinion, are capable of making it. The freedom to fit policy closely to the scientific calculation of a fluctuating national interest was demonstrated by the *volte-face* of August 1939 and gives the Soviet government an inestimable advantage.'

It was the truth; it is a banality to us. He was polite and reasonable, but he was intolerably direct. Not just to Zilliacus, but to a great many nice-minded people in the party this was no way to be. Hugh Dalton, a man of intermittent courage, would sense the unwise plainness and flinch back.

What of Russia's attitude to Britain? Healey is after all trying to explain Labour foreign policy to Labour people. Why was Russia so savagely hostile to Britain? Healey had noted from his excellent Norwegian contacts – and he would quote it again forty years later in *The Time of My Life* – a broadcast to Norway on Moscow Radio of 6 June 1946: 'This little country [England] went to war because it and its fascist reactionary leaders love war and thrive on war. The attack on Hitlerite Germany was purely incidental.' But for all that virulence, the Soviets were not engaged in a religious or ideological war on social democracy, 'for a Russia who foresaw a struggle with America, Britain was not a possible ally; for Britain could not in any circumstances adopt a policy which might lead to war against America.'

But above all else for Healey, the war theorist of 1946, fear is the spur. 'In the modern world fear for security is a sufficient motive to cause war: in 1939–1941 Russian attacks on Finland, Poland, the Baltic States and Romania were caused by fear of war.' And Russian fear, however much rendered paranoid under Stalin, was not irrational, it was geologically seated. Sounding like a man who has read his Clausewitz, Healey remarks that 'the Baltic and Black Seas are immovable salients into the heart of Western Russia.'

So much of the instinct of serious Labour Party people was internationalist. The League of Nations had been cherished, the breakdown of its international collectivism in the 1930s lamented – and blamed on Conservative Western governments. Healey makes a bob in this direction by trying to understand Russia. 'The collapse of [Maxim] Litvinov's policy when the Western democracies betrayed the League, may be responsible for the lack of faith shown so far by Russian leaders in the establishment of an international rule of law.' They had refused to join all the high-minded offshoot organisations like UNESCO or FAO (the Food and Agriculture Organisation).

And as a *realpolitiker*, Healey tells his innocent audience that Russia thought herself placed as she had been in August 1939 after the Molotov–Ribbentrop Pact. This had allowed Russia 'to cushion herself against the inevitable clash, so she sought at Yalta and Potsdam, by limiting her claims to compete with America in the Far East, to free her hands for expansion in Europe and the Middle East'. Accordingly Britain, 'this little country', over-committed and exhausted, was the target.

On the one hand, Russia opened a series of propaganda attacks through the UN and the international machine, which aimed at 'isolating Britain morally as a decadent reactionary power. British policy in Greece, Syria, Indonesia, Spain and Palestine was a special target . . . On the other hand, there was an attempt to tip the scales against Britain in important strategic areas, by diplomacy or direct action – in Trieste, Northern Persia, the Dardanelles, Greece, Turkey and Eastern Europe.'

But by 1947, it was possible to say that 'Soviet policy proved worse than a total failure'. The Labour government had stayed firm and answered charges with facts: then again 'the immoderate ineptitude with which the programme was pursued swung American public opinion into support of Britain.' The first signs had come during the 1946 Peace Conference 'when Yugoslav guns had shot down an American aeroplane'. But following the Truman declaration on Greece and Rome of March 1947, 'The world situation is now clarified and the cards are clearly on the table.'

They were, but some wisps of illusion remained as well. 'Moreover we have resisted every temptation to regard Russian policy as final. In particular, where the Tories have continually pressed us to recognise the permanent incompatibility of the communist and democratic systems to make a final decision about the frontiers of each and to build up an entirely independent Western bloc, we have fought doggedly to prevent the crystallisation of zones of influence behind rigid ideological barriers.' Healey waffling and wistful is a rare occurrence. But dogged as it might be, such resistance by Labour ministers was meaningless in the face of events. Indeed, as the Cold War would begin to simmer in 1950–51 and American reaction to hover near the control signals for invasion of China and/or the use of nuclear weapons, both the dying Ernest Bevin and the highly active Hugh Gaitskell would be concerned that 'nothing should be done to let down the Americans.'[4]

A sentence shortly afterwards would raise eyebrows today by its chutzpah. 'For so long as Britain plays a decisive part in the defence of American security, it is impossible for America to adopt a policy of world-aggression without British agreement.' The likely response is 'No, it isn't.' Britain's role in Vietnam would be one of anguished inactivity, refusing to condemn and refusing to engage. At other times Britain has looked, even to the well-disposed, very like a matching accessory. But with Attlee's government this was not necessarily the case. The Prime Minister would fly to America at the moment of greatest fear of an American-precipitated war against China and receive assurances seen by some as an actual change of intention.

In 1947 Healey is still saying that 'Ernest Bevin is seeking to obtain an alliance which will associate Britain as closely with Russia as with the United States. But the condition of such an alliance is that it should not isolate America.' This last assertion is one of those 'lapses into casuistry' which Bevin's biographer, Alan Bullock, noted in his admiring account of the pamphlet.[5] We *were* dividing into hostile blocs and we had chosen our bloc. But even Denis Healey can't quite say so. He honoured a United Nations worldview. The 'only condition on which the United Nations can operate as the guardian of world order', he wrote piously, was 'infinite tact and patience and a resolute firmness on all critical issues'. All this and 'the replacement of power politics by an international rule of law' constituted 'the only condition on which Britain can survive indefinitely'. Healey had fewer illusions and a lower threshold for self-humbug than most progressive politicians, but having talked power politics throughout the pamphlet, he felt the need for a concluding touch of uplift.

Running through this brief summary of the European situation is a very British disposition not to expect too much of the wretched continentals left to themselves. 'A few million tons of coal for export would change the face of our European policy in a night.' But things which we weren't placed to sort out could not be hopeful. 'So while we will do everything possible to restore Europe as a vital and independent factor in world politics, we cannot base our foreign policy on the assumption that this aim is already achieved.' And besides, since dependence on overseas trade made us perforce a world power, 'we will remain as much part of the Atlantic as of the European community.'

It *was* 1947 and expectations for conquered and liberated Europe would have been necessarily depressed. But the style of Healey's comments on Europe would anticipate the response to institutionally united Europe, the frigid, rather grand disinclination for enthusiasm, the steady scepticism which would mark the Foreign Office, the Conservatives (restored to office), the left wing of the Labour Party – and Denis Healey – for years to come.

In finding excuses, the Tories would stress sovereignty and what was left of imperial ties. The Labour Party would quote the United Nations and the large precluding purposes of socialism worldwide. The effect was very similar, high and far-flung reasons being cited for not doing here and now, on our doorstep, things with immediate relevance to ourselves.

There was no residual grandeur which the Healey of *Cards on the Table* did not dismissively anticipate. 'Our interests are too widespread as our principles are too international, for us to restrict ourselves to the idea of regional blocs, however constructed.'

But if Healey on power blocs was casuistic and Healey on local options De Gaulle-ishly grand, on the broad realism of Bevin's initial foreign policy, he had made a resonant case claiming that 'under disadvantages which have hampered no other British Foreign Minister since the days of Napoleon, Ernest Bevin has played a major part in saving Europe from division and collapse ... Due to British pertinacity, America has come to realise the responsibilities of her power before it was too late to assert those responsibilities except in war.'

The alternative to what Bevin had worked for was a naïve immobilism, unable to distinguish priorities or recognise threats; it was Healey's compensatory rhetoric of uplift, taking itself seriously as calamitously passive policy. The hardness of head, the commitment to defence under American leadership, whatever justified criticisms that might come to merit twenty years later, was both embarrassing and right, the foreign policy that dared not speak its name. But Healey's mix of pricks and halfpence, desperate necessities acknowledged and cherished aspirations honoured, defended this undertaking to its specific troubled audience about as well as that job could be done.

The achievement of the pamphlet in the context of its time is hard to overstate. For all the reasoned tone and pinches of incense, Healey was saying something which it was actually easier to *do*. Bevin's foreign policy, though under assault, was muffled from the sort of attack which *Cards* by its nature invited, though the advantage of *being* a pamphlet is that plain words are more easily said on paper. But he was way ahead of the game, speaking first and attracting half bricks. *Cards on the Table* was a setting-down of the good reasons for doing unwelcome things ahead of the ferocious developments which would make his point.

Healey the front-line advocate, drawing criticism and liking it, was under way. Published without delay on 22 May 1951 by Lincoln, Prager, it was to be the subject of enormous noise and heat, creating, as Healey put it, 'A ter-rific press splash over my pamphlet.' The response (not just of newspapers) was heavily mixed: '*Manchester Guardian* very favourable and full, *Times* and also *Telegraph*, angry and peevish, the *Worker* unmercifully critical.' Attending the NEC International Subcommittee the same day, he found Herbert Morrison as peevish as *The Times* – 'annoyed that he was not con-sulted about my pamphlet, I think.' The reaction rolled on from press, politicians and mandarins alike. *Express* furious, *News Chronicle* sulky but no real criticisms, Attlee was a bit anxious.' The press treatment was a bub-bling cauldron clean out of *Macbeth*. The *Daily Worker* was predictable but not less glorious in its technicolour. Across four columns, R. Palme Dutt (through whose lecture the Oxford girls had knitted), rolled his thunder. 'Its main theme is a violent and venomous attack on the Soviet Union and full-blooded support for American imperialism and world aggression . . .'[6]

Dutt, the party's leading theoretician and apologist for the Molotov–Ribbentrop Pact, who after Khruschev's secret speech of 1954 list-ing Stalin's crimes, would exclaim, 'So, there are spots on the Sun,' expanded:

Behind all the anti-Soviet bluster, the essence of the pamphlet is an apologia for surrender to American imperialism . . . the authors [sic] remain suckers still who have swallowed the old Red Bogy whole and fallen victims to the real menace of the world aggressive designs of American reaction . . . The Red scare is laid on thick. Russia is guilty of every crime in the calendar. Russia uses international institutions only to secure an immediate national advantage . . . Russia is obviously Public Enemy No. 1 in the eyes of these 'Socialists' and there is a warn-ing against 'appeasement'.

The policy of the Anglo-American bloc and submission to the Truman doctrine is not only sabotaging United Nations co-operation, but places Britain everywhere on the side of reaction against the peoples.

But the Tory press was not delighted. The *Daily Express* asked, 'Can nobody restrain the irresponsible and anonymous authors who write pam-phlets for the Socialist Party? Normally what they produce has not much importance for good or ill. But there are certain moments, there are certain subjects, where moderation and good sense are essential and should if nec-essary be imposed . . . *Cards on the Table*,' went on the *Express*, 'was either one of the most foolish or one of the most mischievous documents of its kind. It consists in part of an odious apologia, whining and self-righteous, for the Government's conduct of international business.'

The *Express*, then a major newspaper, was Conservative, but the world-view of its proprietor, Lord Beaverbrook, was idiosyncratic. Close to

Churchill, Beaverbrook shared and stoked the instinct in the old gentleman for summits and grand settlements which alternated with the early hard line at Fulton, Missouri: 'From Stettin in the Baltic to Trieste in the Adriatic, an iron curtain has descended.' Ironically, Healey the left-wing candidate in Pudsey, while ardently admiring Churchill the man, had deplored Churchill the divided-world realist.

Beaverbrook, 'the bottle-imp' as Clementine Churchill had loathingly called him, had been a pre-war appeaser. Now he hated Germany and detested the idea of a United Western Europe, hankered for summits east-wards and tended to look on the Soviet Union as his enemy's enemy. As a minister during the alliance with Russia, he had also been one of the genuine enthusiasts for the ally and for what the Russians most wanted from Britain, a second front. A wartime broadcast speech made by Beaverbrook at the Waldorf Towers was eloquent on the point.

'Communism under Stalin has produced the most valiant fighting army in Europe. Communism under Stalin has provided us with examples of patri-otism equal to the finest annals of history. Communism under Stalin has won the applause and admiration of all the western nations . . . Political purges? Of course, but it was now clear that the men who were shot down would have betrayed Russia to her German enemy . . . Strike out to help Russia! Strike out violently! Strike even recklessly!' The speech had then been fawned over by the editor of Beaverbrook's *Evening Standard*, Michael Foot, who thought it 'stupendous'.[7]

Cards on the Table, said the post-war *Daily Express* editorial,

> goes on tactfully to remind its readers that sections of the Soviet popu-lation were disloyal during the war. However according to this effusion, the Soviet Union has one great source of strength; her leaders are com-pletely without responsibility to their people. This 'handful of tyrants' had turned on the British Labour Party with, in Healey's words, 'a sus-tained and violent offensive' and doing so with 'immoderate ineptitude' had simply swung American opinion over to the support of Britain.
>
> Nothing is more calculated to embarrass Britain in her delicate nego-tiations with Russia than this unbridled account of Soviet policy and motives . . . Manners are banished, restraint forgotten. Brutally and recklessly, the cards are banged on the table.[8]

It was late May 1947 but the arch-capitalist was tiptoeing reverently around Stalin in the full spirit of Geoffrey Dawson's *Times*. The belief that Moloch could speak unto Moloch, natural in a proprietor of newspapers, had made Beaverbrook naïve on specifics. Power worship and its consequent deference found expression in rage, denying a lesson Healey had learned and Beaverbrook had not.

The Times wobbled splendidly, quoting approvingly the least credible remark in the document, that it was British policy to furnish 'a guarantee against an anti-Soviet foreign policy'. The *News Chronicle*, a left Liberal paper to be absorbed by the *Mail* in the early 1950s, was cool. Under the tepid headline 'No Aces', it observed that 'the cards are on the table, but the ace of inspiration is missing.'

The *News Chronicle* chose to read along the lines instead of between them, confusing the civilities with the substance, attributing to Healey a foreign policy which 'must strive to minimise the friction between Russian Communism and American laissez-faire capitalism'. Anyway what Britain should be doing, it said, was 'everything in its power to raise the standard of living and to strengthen the political independence and security of the 2000 million people who inhabit neither Russia nor the United States'.

Healey included the *Daily Telegraph* in his grumbles, which was hardly fair. The *Telegraph* was as clear as Zilliacus to what it was about. A leader correctly crediting Bevin with having seen off his enemies, also, though without naming him, applauded Healey.

> Mr Bevin is an immensely bigger man than his critics, even the glibbest of them. [But] in some ways the case for his policy was much better made out in the pamphlet *Cards on the Table* which gives what the Left would call the ideological background and states strategic truths with a directness the Foreign Secretary could hardly, as custom goes, indulge in. The key to our post-war policy was put in three excellent sentences:
> 'It was obvious that we must face the necessity of reducing our foreign commitments as much and as fast as possible to be consistent with our security and seek to adjust our policy to our diminished resources. Yet this reduction must be carried out in an orderly way so that at no point would we lose our power of initiative and our ability to control the process. Above all, we must avoid creating by our withdrawal vacuums into which the other Great Powers might surge in irresistible and world-shattering conflict.'

'Much of the criticism of Mr Bevin,' said the *Telegraph*, hitting a nail sharply on the head three times, 'comes from people who want us to withdraw too quickly and who want to create vacuums.'

Responsible American comment was very different. According to Joseph Phillips in the *New York Times*, the reply to *Keep Left* had now appeared: 'a remarkably lucid and informative explanation of the thinking which has guided Britain and the Labor government during these crucial past two years.' There was, he added, after citing Healey's claims for Bevin, 'no great harm in Bevin's thinking, he has persuaded us of our responsibilities. The great value of putting these "cards on the table" face up, is that in them we may read the tragedy of the two years between the end of the war and the late failure of the Council of Foreign Ministers.'

The *Christian Science Monitor* carried an assessment by Erwin Canham which applauded *Cards*: 'a realistic and frank statement has been issued. It is the kind of statement that should be prepared in Washington on American policy.' It quotes Healey saying, 'The aim of Anglo-American understanding is to prevent war by proving to Russia that an aggressive anti-British policy is doomed to frustration.' Canham turns to his readers and asks, 'With how much of that does Washington agree? In many ways it seems to be a fair statement of American policy, but let's have from Washington our own independent realistic declaration of up-to-date policy. It's about time.'

In the United States, Healey's pamphlet was being waved at the President with a call for something as clear. Back in Britain, venom from the *Daily Worker*, more venom from the *Express*, bland approbation from *The Times*, and from the earnest *Chronicle*, sounding terribly like the *Skibbereen Eagle*, which famously warned 'the Tsar of the Russians that the eye of the Skibbereen Eagle is upon him', acquiescence modulating into reproach. Finally, a grasping by the *Telegraph* of the superior case put by *Cards*: Healey was doing well enough. He was articulating a major shift in Labour policy. This involved moving away from the hopefulness of the war years and immediately afterwards of unaligned bliss, with Britain able to work equally with Russia and the US. Rival camps had been a horrid notion, not least to Attlee for whom world government was a serious aspiration. Denunciation of such a flight to the political trenches had been a commonplace. Healey's own campaign in Pudsey had been full of it. The 'malignance', as the *Telegraph* called it, of the Soviet publicity machine and even its early, pre-putsch conduct in Eastern Europe, was registering. Separate camps and American involvement were becoming inescapable.

Healey was Bevin's spokesman to the party and, at the same time, addressing a wider audience. It is possible, speaking *urbi et orbi*, to upset both city and world for quite contrary reasons. In this momentous case, it was inevitable. Healey, telling truths apparent to those who had tried to work with the Russians, was certain of giving affront. But he was to be lucky in his enemies, some of whom were equally susceptible to huge ineptitude. Arguably the pro-Soviet left, their malignancy guaranteed and underwritten, with Dutt and Zilliacus standing shoulder to shoulder, served Healey better with the uncertain middle of opinion than any other commentators.

The huddled score of Labour Party International Committee members flinched at Zilliacus's intervention and Crossman's characteristic clever question in a temporary cause. At Labour's conference opening at Margate on 26 May, Healey's diary records that the pamphlet was attacked again from the left – 'virulently by Zilliacus' and 'questioned' by Richard Crossman. In response, Dalton 'gave a cowardly pusillanimous reply which will cause trouble later'.[9] It did.

The denunciation proper was led by Wing Cdr Ernest Millington, who had earlier spoken of Ernie Bevin's 'mailed fist waved in the face of the Soviet Union'. Millington invoked the continental multitudes. There was great disquiet among the socialists of this country and Europe [sic], he said, on the failure of the Executive to express publicly its opinion on this vital matter. He wanted a clear view given of 'the Socialist policy for a United Europe'. (At this time, pre-Monnet and Schuman, 'United Europe' was nothing to do with a Common Market and was a Soviet slogan promoted by a dubious front organisation, the 'United Europe Committee'.)

K. Zilliacus (he always, Kafka-ishly, substituted the mysterious 'K' for his honest Finnish 'Konni') spoke, as generally, the straight Soviet line, avoiding the confusions of the *News Chronicle*. '*Cards* had said that the United Nations was prevented by its own constitution from dealing with disputes between the Big Three . . . and that we should line up with the United States. It said cynically that we must supply the men and the US would give the money.'

This was going it a bit, but you knew where you were with K. And in a sense, he was right. Healey, despite a few high-toned flourishes, was persuading Labour to face up to *realpolitik* precisely as Ernest Bevin, the coiner of the pamphlet's title two years earlier, was practising it. Nothing else made any sense. But the beating of left wings made far less trouble than the pertinent queries of Healey's future, and entirely untrusted, Cabinet colleague, Richard Crossman: 'Is it a discussion pamphlet or an official statement of policy? Was it written solely by Denis Healey, was it approved either by the Foreign Secretary or Foreign Office officials? Was it seen by the National Executive or the International Committee?' [*Daily Telegraph*, 24 May 1947]

Good questions which Dalton couldn't handle, prompting what the *Telegraph* reporter reasonably called a 'remarkable statement' – that *Cards on the Table* had not been considered by the Executive . . . He gave an undertaking that the Executive would do so in the next day or two and would give an opinion as to whether it supported the document or gave it a qualified support. Next day the NEC addressed its laborious collective attention to the work.[10]

The subsequent report of these deliberations, carried by *The Times*, has Dalton saying that *Cards* 'was not a statement of policy and that the Executive, while not committing itself to every detail in the pamphlet, is of the opinion that *Cards on the Table* was rightly published as a contribution to the discussion and interpretation of foreign policy'. Pusillanimous at all points, especially given Dalton's own clear convictions.

Healey, who was of course present, records the dispute about who had passed and/or read the contentious thing he had written. Herbert Morrison, reported Healey, 'forced Dalton to admit that he'd passed it for publication and the pamphlet was very conditionally accepted'.

Healey had no respect to lose for the International Committee, dismissals of which litter the diaries, and Dalton, who had both responsibilities and understanding of the issues, had let him down miserably. However, next day in the body of the kirk, with Conference back in session, the row continued, with Arthur Deakin, Boss – no other word will do – of the Transport and General – jumping in to make Dalton's life even more unhappy. Had Dalton seen it before publication? In the confusion Dalton appeared to nod, so Deakin shouted over the heads of the pressmen, 'So why the hell didn't you say so?'

By now the general panic, not just the pamphlet itself, was a news story of some dimension, being picked up by the *Evening News* who gave a credible account of the NEC's little differences. For all of which Healey acknowledged possible responsibility. He had chatted on the Tuesday evening with a heterogeneous group including Frank Pakenham, who admired it, and William Warbey, a fellow-traveller who can't possibly have done. 'Very foolishly' he had 'told Warbey something of what happened'. When Dalton was being roasted and apologising next day, Healey murmured to his diary that the *News* story 'might have come through Warbey from me'.

It didn't matter. The Subcommittee, known to the diary by adjectives like 'dull' and 'tedious', had endless unnecessary little rows, the occasional blurred revelation of which was almost their only point. This was a much bigger row and it was about something – a historic and thus anxious change of policy direction.

The only excuse Dalton had was that the same case made by a natural bureaucrat would have been duller and would have done its own flinching. Healey had been far politer than the Healey norm, but he didn't manage dullness. The terrible thing about *Cards* from a party manager's point of view was its clarity.

It was clear enough to John Gollan. Writing in the Party's journal, *World News and Views*, the future leader of the British CP would denounce 'This venomous pamphlet, a typical Transport House anti-soviet slander, produced to fight the critics . . . a diplomatic blunder, a disservice to Britain, to the cause of peace and British-Soviet relations.' Gollan cited supreme authority. 'Talk of War, Stalin has observed, is a common trick with which reactionaries get across their policies and here was a typical example.' But then, Gollan had begun his piece by conceding, 'The Margate conference has resulted in an overwhelming vote for Bevin . . .'

In this, Healey's diary agrees. His entry for 24 May reads: 'Rebels made exceptionally dull and poor speeches all morning. Bevin had one of his greatest triumphs in the afternoon – a brilliant performance.' In the evening Healey was asked back to the Foreign Minister's hotel suite 'at about 10.30

and stayed drinking whiskey till 1 am. He was in fine form – very talkative and rather like the gangster in *Born Yesterday*, especially when he kicked his shoes off for comfort.'

By however imperfect an instrument for measuring support, Bevin, with his policy spelt out in unprecedentedly lucid and unflinching terms, was confirmed by his party. His judgement articulated by Healey had been right. Events in Hungary and Czechoslovakia would, within a year, turn 'this venomous pamphlet' into a statement of consensus. As for Healey, he had done his job, could linger half a day longer at the conference, hear Nye Bevan on Friday, 'complete master of his subject and of the audience', and go home. There he would record of the following day: '31 May, Saturday. Lounged all day in the sun on the roof. At night saw *A Day at the Races*.'[11]

9

CZECHOSLOVAKIA AND FRIENDS

Denis Healey lived out of his office in Smith Square. Callers came from all angles: Finns, Austrians, Americans, Norwegians, Italians, anyone who had a Socialist party with a dispute going on inside it. On 12 June 1947, the simple entry is: 'Gilason of the Icelandic Labour Party, told me all he knew of the situation there. Otherwise a very quiet day.'[1]

He took phone calls, lunched and listened, judged quickly, sometimes correcting himself on a later meeting. Two or three times a week he and Edna went out – to concerts and theatres, but especially to films, hence the allusion to Ernest Bevin in a James Cagney role. He was in touch with ministerial colleagues like Mayhew and McNeil and with civil servants, chiefly at the Foreign Office, and he collected diplomats off the production line. Sometimes he is in receipt of gossip at a very high level, the sort of gossip which fits into history. In November 1947 he has another long talk with Ernest Bevin and finds him 'growling at Cripps and Dalton imposing a tyranny on the workers i.e. a wages stop, in Cabinet this morning'. He 'is furious with Morrison over refusal of a rise for post office workers'. But 'on foreign policy, he is more confident than when I last saw him, though he expects the November conference (Council of Foreign Ministers) to break down, including Austria.' And laconically, 'He sees a Muslim bloc from Egypt to Palestine.'[2]

But inevitably, the issues in the air at this time are Hungary and Italy (later Czechoslovakia), the better co-operation of European Socialist parties hopefully achieved through conferences, Healey's other staple, for which he travels notably to Antwerp and Zurich.

He writes – not just for the party, but for the *Economist* and the BBC, doing broadcasts which become articles in the *Listener*.[3] He is also a great receiver of complaints. Adolf Schärf, later a widely respected President of

Austria, was discounted by Healey's steady Austrian Embassy contact, Walter Wodak, as 'timid and reluctant to give himself more work'. A Major Mostyn from Japan is 'furiously indignant at Britain's neglect of East Asia'. A little later, a Hungarian calls: 'Paul Ignotus came in without any real news, then Madame Burri who is fed up with the Swiss Party' and 'Prager to tell me Lily Bier is untrustworthy, which I know'.

Joe Alsop, the terribly famous American newspaper columnist, 'looks like a shopwalker, talks like a stage Bertie Wooster, very, very conceited and arrogant, but none the less, very intelligent and a good observer'. Visiting Vienna, he has dinner with our Ambassador, 'Sir George Rendell – a rather shifty little man without much personality'. A future Cabinet minister escapes personal comment, but the diary records meeting 'Pat Gordon Walker and his dreadful wife'.

Philip Noel-Baker is Healey's private moan in residence: 'N-B was pathetic – trying to understand the Russians with a quarter mind' is par for the recurring course. More seriously, there is in the censoriousness something of the old-fashioned rectitude which would instantly bar the retired minister from the proffered chairmanship of GEC thirty-five years later. 'Lewis, the Norfolk House representative, came in – a very bad type – who wanted me to pull strings for him.'

But there is dispassionate praise too. Basil Davidson, a distinguished and controversial journalist over the next twenty-five years, is 'tall, dark and good-looking in an Irish way; he was a Col. with Tito and is now an intelligent fellow-traveller.' While Oscar Helmer, the Austrian Minister of the Interior, is 'a large proletarian, shrewd and steady from E. Austria'. (The least he could say, since another commentator on Oscar Helmer who ring-fenced the Austrian police from Communist control, spoke of an Austrian Ernest Bevin.) And with a charming nod to the future, he notes the young chairman of the Oxford Labour Club as 'a very nice young man, Tony Wedgwood Benn'!

Exposure to other countries' conferences and international Socialist ones, would give Healey more grounds for sharp observation. Attending the Zurich gathering, he observes: 'Golda Myerson made an unscrupulously demagogic speech on Palestine'. (The American Golda Myerson would in due course be the Israeli Foreign Minister then Prime Minister, Golda Meir.) With another hint to the future, he hears praise of 'Eddie Goldstücker'. In 1968, Eduard Goldstücker would be within the Czech Communist Party, the chief creative intelligence behind the Prague Spring.

But the news that mattered most, and came in snatches, was from the Eastern states where Socialist parties were, as we have seen, under pressure from Communist parties to accede to annihilatory mergers. There are telling little personal stories. One of Healey's contacts in the Polish Socialist Party, Anna Zrbowski, talks with him at length – 'She is coming to LSE in the autumn and feels a little like a deserter.' Meeting the younger Karolyi, son of the radical aristocrat Count Michael Karolyi, and his wife from Hungary, Healey thinks they are 'fishing to find out my views on Hungarian personalities. The CP collects information with which to blackmail politicians of other parties.'

He speaks with another emigrant, Tilea, a former Romanian Ambassador, about that country and passes the information to Morgan Phillips. 'It was terrible. Famine has driven the Moldavians wandering for food, the government is corrupt, incompetent and hated ... Many arbitrary arrests cause an atmosphere of terror.' Sir Knox Helme, the British Ambassador in Hungary, called on Healey during his leave. The elections in Hungary 'had been only 30 per cent fraud'. The CP had only lifted its vote from 16 to 22 per cent and Helme thought that the Socialist leader Arpad Szakasits's policy – broad subservience to the Communist Party – 'was responsible for the drop in the Socialist vote', now 15 per cent.

In Czechoslovakia, where Healey went in November, the Communists had initially played their hand quietly and skilfully. Sustained by a large following for the Communist Party in that industrialised country, and by all the post-war optimism about patriots and anti-Fascists being on the same side, the CP had done very well indeed in free elections in May 1946, taking, in its Czech and Slovak sections combined, 38 per cent of the vote, with the Social Democrats on 13 per cent, the National Socialists (nothing to do with the Nazis but a middle-class liberal reform party going back to Habsburg times) 18 per cent, the Czech populists (more Conservative and Catholic) 16 per cent and the Slovak Democrats 14 per cent. The government was a coalition involving all major parties with Gottwald, Communist leader, as Prime Minister.

Communists, by keeping a low profile, combined with economic growth helped by renewed Western trade and a good harvest, had been well placed. But in mid-1947 direct Soviet interference changed all that. The Marshall Plan had come on stream in June. The consequences of rejecting it would be exacerbated by the drought of that blazing summer, and food shortages handled extremely badly by Communist ministers. Things were made worse by a burst of draconian taxes, nationalisations and bank mergers which were effectively resisted in parliament.

It was no longer the case that the CP could more or less observe the rules of bourgeois arithmetic with confidence and hope to govern. The elections scheduled for May 1948 did not look an attractive proposition. Accordingly, the party would avoid such vulgar head-counting and require all parties to produce their lists of nominees in the proportions of the last parliament; these would then be submitted to the electorate by way of a referendum: 'Take or leave it, government or no government.' There is scary film footage of the great drab assembly in Wenceslas Square, looking fearfully like something from *Nineteen Eighty-Four*. Nominees from the non-Communist parties were put in to function on behalf of the Communists. Newspapers, universities, publishing houses, the armed forces, even sports clubs were rigorously brought in line, party-supervised and, where necessary, closed.

Totalitarianism has never been done in so straightforward and lucidly informative a way as in Czechoslovakia in the five days, 20–25 February 1948. And its educational effect upon the West, and especially on progressive and Socialist parties there, would be crucial, a crash course in Stalinism.

At the time of Healey's visit for the Socialist Conference at Brno in November 1947 there was still apparent hope in that country. Anger with the blatantly pro-Soviet leader Fierlinger as a creature of the Communists had grown, climaxing with his support for a unification pact with them. An opponent, Bohumil Lausman, was on offer arguing for resistance and party independence. Meanwhile open debate and voting were still practised.

There was an international contingent, fraternal delegates and the like. So, after watching a moderate production of Dvořak's *Rusalka* on the evening of 14 November, Healey sat up till 2 a.m. talking with Zoltan Horvath and Hochfeld. 'They are both "Marxist" socialists in fact to whom democracy in our sense is irrelevant.' At the conference he observed the reception given to the non-Marxist Vaclav Majer, 'heavily applauded for every mention of democracy or independence'. The party was effectively split, with everything turning on the post of President of the Executive, effectively leader. When it came to the vote, Lausman won by 286 to 187; Fierlinger, 'who hesitated before congratulating his rival', produced that 'wolfish snarl' which Healey would recall in his memoirs.

From another Social Democrat, Vaclav Bernard, Healey briefed himself. Fierlinger's only prominent supporters in the party were John, chairman of the constitutional committee, 'and Eugen Erban, the Gen. Sec. of the TUC who is now discredited as a crypto – most of the women also support him'. His talk and that of the Hungarian fellow-traveller, Horvath, are instructive. Bernard, a supporter of Lausman and a free Socialist Party, had been 'not very concerned by the danger of CP violence – the character of the people and above all, Beneš,* are the best defence'.

A conversation with the British Ambassador late that night revealed a tone well known to the Embassy. Pollak, Czech adviser to the British Council, 'had been arrested secretly for military espionage, and last week 60 National Socialists were arrested in Most'.

In Wroclaw for the Congress of the Polish Socialists, also affected by Soviet-conforming leaders, Healey's congressional life conformed to a Healey pattern of watching national operas, observing pro-Communists, Socialists and conferring late with briefers. In this case he saw *Halka* by Moniuszko and heard Josef Cyrankiewicz – 'spoke for 1¼ hours – dull and repetitive, but good in content'. He would observe that the spirit of that congress was 'unmistakable – very independent'. Indeed, the Communist regime in Poland,

---

* The President of the Republic and pre-war Prime Minister, Eduard Beneš.

a country so heavily Catholic and peasant, would never be quite so savage –
or so convincing – as the Gottwald and Rakosi regimes about to settle upon
Czechoslovakia and Hungary.

Healey also noted the ruin of Warsaw: 'unimaginably universal – where
the half million inhabitants live we cannot guess as you hardly ever see a
house with more than a ground floor. The ghetto is about four square miles
of formless rubble, not even a fragment of a wall remaining. But the shops
are full of good quality goods, food cheap but textiles dear.'

Healey still had visitors. Walter Kolarz, on 5 January 1948, 'thinks
Czechoslovakia will fall this year'. The Hungarian, Ries, on 12 January, was
less perceptive: 'Fusion is out of the question unless force is used – but we
will try to outflank the CP on the left.' 'Ruth Fischer came in to be exuber-
ant about her visit to Germany – 200 pre-Hitler CP people are now in leading
positions.' On the same day, he saw Peyer, the old Socialist right-winger
who did not impress: 'A vain egotistical old man with no dynamic personality and little following left in Hungary.'

Healey left his own comments on Czechoslovakia out of the diary. His
serious thinking on the subject would come by way of a radio talk transcribed in the *Listener*.[4] It is a formidable appraisal, written more than fifty
years ago when general understanding of Communist methods was casual
and naïve. But Healey had an exceptional opportunity for travelling in and
out of Hungary and Czechoslovakia and other Eastern European countries,
attending political conferences, hunching over drinks with Communists and
their opponents. Consequently, he fully understood state-of-the-art seizure of
power and set about explaining it.

The Communists had not come to power by armed rising. That had happened in Russia after 1917. 'It took the Bolshevik Party five years to establish
itself in power after the First World War . . . the operation was attended by
terrifying difficulties and dangers. Administrative collapse brought starvation
to millions.' Attracting foreign intervention, 'the revolution only survived
because Russia was geographically so remote'.

What had to be done after the Second World War was 'to capture the
bourgeois state machine rather than destroy it'. So 'they studied the anatomy
of power in a democracy. They mapped the location of strong points.'
Having applied themselves to placing supporters, police, forces, and civil
service, they 'grew expert in mobilising support for their aims through organisations in which they played no obvious part themselves'.

Under 'the Molotov plan', Russia 'encouraged the construction of a state
on the bourgeois and democratic model; these states were controlled by
coalition governments in which the Communist Party did not appear to
exercise an exclusive or even a predominating influence'. But always they
took the Interior and, directly or through trusties, the Ministry of National
Defence.

'There was intimidation and victimisation of non-Communists – sometimes the use of force, but more often the withholding of necessary privileges, the right to furniture dockets, a new flat or the right to work.' And given the flow of events, people jumped readily on to the bandwagon. 'But inside these swollen mass armies the old Communist élite remained as a general staff.' This is the exact perception of Orwell in the *Nineteen Eighty-Four* he was busy writing at this time, an inner and an outer party. They obtained a hold on the unions: 'a newspaper could be suppressed as easily by a strike of printing workers as by a decree of the Minister of the Interior.'

A little violence used judiciously also worked very well. In January 1947 the Communist Minister of the Interior announced 'a plot' in which the Smallholders' leader, Béla Kovács, was charged with complicity. 'The Smallholders fought back and used their majority in parliament to save Kovács from trial. But at the height of the argument about his parliamentary immunity, the Russian police arrested Kovács for military espionage. He has never since been seen.* This Russian intervention broke the back of Smallholder resistance.' Effectively it broke up, allowing Communist nominees to represent it, something reflected in the collapse of its vote in the next elections.

Healey is writing in the raw present continuous, at a time when people like Kolarz are sending him messages that 'It's all up in Hungary.' Accordingly, he can add, 'A prepared party congress has agreed to merge the Social Democrats finally in a single party with the Communists. Thus, although it still has only 25 per cent of the parliamentary seats, the Communist Party is now ... the only organised political force in Hungary.'

Of Czechoslovakia, Healey observes the difference was that with the Slav affinities and the role of Russia as ally against Germany, the CP were 'by far the strongest single party'. They made great efforts to obtain an alliance with the Social Democratic Party with whose support they would have had an absolute majority in parliament.' After rejection, and here Healey recounts his own eye-witness view of Fierlinger's rejection at the November conference – 'the Communists now felt certain of defeat if free elections were held, as planned for next April. In December Drtina, the Socialist Minister of Justice, produced evidence that the Communists were responsible for an attempt to assassinate President Beneš. (Drtina is said to have attempted suicide a few days ago.)' Tension was great, but the firmness and competence of the non-Communist leaders, confident that they represented the vast majority of a democratic people, made a repetition of the Hungarian débâcle seem unlikely. 'Then everything was shattered and a single party dictatorship was imposed without serious opposition.'

---

* Kovács reappeared in 1956, having been held in Soviet internment for nine years and subsequently fled to the West.

This putsch, he argues, was only possible because the police 'acted throughout as a private instrument of the Communist Party – for example, they occupied the offices of rival parties and replaced their officials by Communist stooges.' The other means to the taking of power was control of the trade unions, with sufficient loyal numbers to threaten a general strike and, if necessary, civil war. Meanwhile, 'the possibility of Soviet intervention was impressed first on the party leaders by the presence of the Soviet Deputy Foreign Minister [Zorin] who arrived when the crisis broke out, February 17, and did not leave until it was over.'

Healey was writing early in 1948. There was very real fear that what had just happened in Hungary and Czechoslovakia, and by comparable routes in Romania and Poland, might now be copied in France and Italy. The French CP had a quarter of the vote and great prestige from its role in a resistance it had joined only after the German invasion of Russia. Healey, never one for raw panic, discounts this. What distinguished the Eastern scenarios had been 'two conditions, neither of which obtain in Western Europe. First the Communists must be inside the government so that they can establish direct control of parts of the state machine. Second the Soviet Union must be able to intervene at crucial points as well as exercising an indirect influence by geographical contiguity.' What most struck Healey about the new victory in the East was 'not only that its methods resemble those of a Fascist party, but that its aim is essentially the same as that of Fascism – to protect a ruling section in the state against the possibility of its overthrow by a majority of the population. The usual word for this sort of thing is not revolution. It is counter-revolution.'

It requires a leap of the imagination to realise how bold and brutal, how deliberately offensive Healey's conclusion was. The Communist Party might be about to lose prestige in Britain. But a soft schwarm for Communism, a position to the feeble side of fellow-travelling, was well established in educated progressive circles. Healey had cheerfully shared in it during his candidacy at Pudsey. The Soviets had been 'our Russian ally', the enemy's enemy and, in consequence, our sort of friend. Here was Healey taking the word 'Fascist', still bright with the glittering evil of the previous two decades, and throwing it in the face of the Communists. But what Healey had seen and experienced and now expressed, a more general public opinion would soon echo. Nineteen forty-eight, the centenary, ironically, of the great left-wing watershed of risen and struck-down revolutions – the Year of Revolutions – was its own black marker in history. Communism had achieved wider power but would never stand in innocent eyes as it had. Denis Healey was traveller and chronicler, made expert by events, and his commitments would now be absolute.

10

HUNGARY 1947–50

Healey's role as Secretary to, and co-ordinator of, the Socialist International was the guarantee of his continuous education in foreign affairs. There is a dry little diary observation after a meeting with 'Jock' Colville, a well-placed FO man – he had been Churchill's Private Secretary – of how ignorant of events in Hungary he was.[1] Christopher Mayhew was 'still very shakey on his facts and adopts Dalton's bluff geniality to try to ignore weaknesses in his position'. Over Hungary, he noted meeting 'two English correspondents who didn't know a thing about the situation here'.[2]

On Italy, Hungary, Romania, Czechoslovakia and Finland among the fragile countries, but for that matter over Sweden, Norway and France, Healey is to be found almost every day receiving callers, lunching or settling to long conversations with politicians, many either in exile or under threat. If there is a conference of a Socialist party, he goes to it, meets, talks and listens. Nuselovici, Romanian Socialist, the Austrian journalist Walter Wodak and the future EEC Commission President Altiero Spinelli troop through the office.*

But the recurring issue and anxiety across all accounts of these contacts and their countries was the state of Social Democratic parties under varying but always noxious degrees of Soviet pressure. So conversation with Wodak yields confidence about Austria: 'things are going much better there' – the Russians are releasing their grip a good deal. In due course, Soviet involvement in Austria *would* relax, though the State Treaty confirming independent

---

* It also involved meeting Kamal Jumblatt, leader of the main Druze faction in the Lebanon. He also used the word 'socialist' and defined his objectives as, 'Drinking the blood of Lebanese Christians out of the skulls of Lebanese Christians'.

statehood on terms on international neutrality would have to wait for the warmest, wettest moment of the Thaw, 1955.

Hungary was at this time also a candidate for optimism. The Russians might be occupying the country, but their local political support was only a degree greater than in Austria. The Austrian hopes could surely be duplicated but against that clear statement of public preference stood the fact that Austria was only half-occupied. And in Austria the Russians did not have a Communist as Minister of the Interior.

The Hungarian Socialist Party understood well enough that the Armistice agreement would not be honestly conducted by the Russians and put this conclusion on record, but the party was split and frightened. The words 'fellow-travelling' and 'crypto-communist', much bandied about in the West in the most intense period of the Cold War, were in post-war Budapest at once repugnant and appropriate. Healey heard very similar views from non-Communists – Social Democrats who had lived under and faced jail from the right wing dictator Horthy. He was already persuaded that Third Force thinking must give way to *realpolitik* where the Soviet Union was concerned. Such thinking became more than a cool, strategic judgement. The people from whom he would first hear anxious but still hopeful readings, would be jailed or exiled. Men whom he had judged impressive or very intelligent, and whom his anti-Communist contacts had denied were Soviet agents, turned out to be exactly that.

At this time, Hungary becomes a preoccupation of Healey's. He is in touch with the Hungarian Socialist Party's London representative, Bede, keeping his Transport House boss, Morgan Phillips, in touch. The crisis in Hungary is in full swing – the Communist Party wants the Smallholders to expel 100 deputies and so become a minority party . . . Szakasits* is subject to CP blackmail as, of course, is Horvath.† After the destruction of the Smallholders' Party's independence, the key Communist/Soviet objective became the capture of the Socialist Party. It must not be allowed to make a firm stand against the Communists which, in a country so recently and so evidently demonstrated to be anti-Communist, would have rallied major support. To do this, it had to work through a network of obliging people, otherwise the left wing of the party – Szakasits, his deputy, Gyorgy Marosan, and Istvan Riesz who held the ever useful pre-putsch office of Minister of Justice. The talk on the left was of 'fighting fascism' which, in practical terms, meant invoking memories of Hungary's virulent old post-Habsburg military aristocratic junta under Horthy. People might be tainted and, if not, the tainting could be arranged.

---

* Arpad Szakasits, left-wing leader of the Hungarian Socialist Party.
† Zoltan Horvath, a slippery near Communist whom Healey knew well.

For the pro-Western element of the Hungarian party was led by Karoly Peyer, a capable man but vulnerable to the fact that he had done a deal with Horthy in the 1930s by which tolerance for a trade union movement had been won in return for quiescence in political opposition. But Peyer had been particularly clear-minded in his view of Communist intentions and had published a memorandum, submitted to the party's executive, which damned the left-wing leadership roundly for the extent of its concessions to the Communists. It had been rejected by the party congress and pressure was now upon the leadership to expel Peyer and his group. Accordingly, Peyer's line that co-operation with the Communists was a deadly mistake, was one which Labour at Transport House across 1945 and 1946 was slow to appreciate. It just happened to be the truth.

Close to Peyer were Lajos Lederer, Anna Kethly and Antal Ban. Lederer, after the waters closed over Hungary, would have a distinguished career as East European correspondent of the *Observer*. Ban would contribute to Healey's book, *The Curtain Falls*, in exile. Anna Kethly would stay in Hungary embodying the tragedy of her country, only escaping in the aftermath of the 1956 rising, to be met at Heathrow by Healey and Hugh Gaitskell.

In January 1947 Healey was sent as International Secretary to the conference of the Hungarian Socialist Party. He was accompanied by Jock Colville from the Foreign Office and a Mr Redward whom he scornfully identified as 'the Hungarian expert'. Redward, who had been in Hungary since 1919, had worked 'a little with SO(E) . . . a rather vulgar "old boy"-type expatriate Englishman on the make'.[3]

His impression of Peyer, despite the grumbles mentioned above, was better. If not 'an outstanding personality', the older Hungarian was still vigorous: 'he will avoid a split if compatible with his honour'. He had details of the Communist Party corruption system: 'percentages to be paid on export luxuries or even book royalties'. Meanwhile the CP ministers like Gerö* 'use their position to blackmail people into joining the party'.

Kethly briefed the Englishman. Rakosi, whom Healey called 'the Mongolian torturer', leading the CP, had demanded of Szakasits, as Socialist leader, that Peyer should be expelled. 'Szakasits had refused and agreed to a compromise of severe reprimand, but changed his mind at the last minute . . . Kethly is very worried.' As well she might be: the Socialists were facing a nightmare. Their representative in the political police had been shot in the back from a moving car. Healey records what he was told: 'he refused to go

---

* Ernö Gerö would stay loyal to (and alive) under the lethal Communist regime of Rakosi and be named as his successor in the early days of the 1956 rising, only to be instantly spat out by public loathing.

to hospital and is believed to be in hiding with the British Military Mission.' None of this had made much impression on the official British representatives. The Ambassador, Sir Alexander Knox Helme, true to the highest standards of lethargic imperception, 'liked Rakosi better than any of the Socialists'.[4]

Using his time energetically, Healey spoke to Zoltan Horvath, someone known from London 'who was dishonestly affable as usual', and 'lunched with Szakasits at his comfortable villa' and talked to his son-in-law, Paul Schiff. The message was as comfortable as Helme's; 'the general line was that they are a powerful party with mass support and have nothing to lose by close collaboration with the CP.' They also thought that 'Russia is the only guarantee against resurgent fascism while Peyer is dangerous precisely because he is respected.' Still busy, Healey dined with the dishonestly affable collaborationist, Zoltan Horvath, 'brilliant in argument ... He violently attacked Redward but said Helme is impeccable.'[5]

Healey was compiling a compressed view of twentieth-century central European history. Attending the Socialist congress at the Opera House, he met Rakosi again and shared the Royal Box with the elder Karoly, Count Michael, 'gaga but impressive, with a queer mumbling palatal speech'. Karolyi was an old-fashioned great man, a sort of Hungarian Mazzini. He was an aristocrat but also a liberal and a democrat and he had lived a disinterested life on behalf of his country, a pure and uncorrupted nationalist alien to Nazis and Soviets, Horthy and Rakosi alike.

At the Socialist conference next day, Saturday 1 February, Szakasits in tackling Peyer, killed two birds with one stone by denouncing him specifically for being friendly to the Smallholders. 'He had encouraged the Smallholders' right against his own left and damaged SP prestige abroad; he sentimentally hankered after the comfortable opportunism of pre-war and would not face the exigencies of power.'

The grim gouging of factional politics under Stalin's supervision continued with Healey as a witness observing the faces of other spectators. 'I watched Rakosi, Révai and Gerö closely – they were not satisfied that Peyer should remain in the party.' Révai he described as 'a young, very balanced but unscrupulous and unemotional intellectual', a description apt for Saint-Just, and Josef Révai as a minister under Rakosi, proclaiming to his fellow Hungarians 'Stalin is no foreign statesman', would try to live up to it.

It wasn't at this time – 1947 – generally done to see reds under the bed even when, incontestably under the bed, there were reds. When Anna Kethly, whom Healey early and subsequently trusted and liked better than any other Hungarian politician, did accuse the left wing of her party of being covert communists, Healey sounds slightly shocked: 'Anna really thinks that Bier and Horvath are crypto-Communists.' But even Antal Ban, whom Kethly admired as the ablest of the Socialist Party's younger men, 'does not think there are any cryptos in the party'.

Healey was present in Hungary at the turn of January–February 1947 and realities were crowding in on him. As soon as he arrived, he would hear from a Major Harley, just appointed military attaché in Budapest, the cryptic observation that the only armed force in Hungary was the frontier police and that 'the NKVD is all-pervasive in Hungary'.[6]

On a return visit to Hungary in the second week of May, encountering Horvath whom he liked marginally more, Healey noted: 'Much fatter and trying hard to be pleasant, not entirely without success.' He lunched with Reisz, 'as usual, the genial ruffian', and Szakasits, 'the latter seemed ill at ease', and the two Hungarians 'had a row over a new press and libel law' in front of Healey. He talked to the economist, Laszlo Farrago, then working for a Hungarian bank which, like all banks, faced nationalisation. This was something Farrago saw as 'a Communist trick to split the government on Moscow's orders'. He had another talk with Ban whose opinions at this point (May 1947), like his remarks in February, are instructive in their optimism and degree of equanimity in the face of Communist advance. Ban, after all, was a member of the right faction; as Healey records, 'His line is that while the Russians are here and there is also grave danger from the Right, the SP [Socialist Party] must work with the CP and at all costs maintain its unity and its freedom to work on as wide a basis as possible. Painful concessions must continually be made to the Left intellectuals who are running the party, but they will be swept away like paper once it is expedient to hold new elections.' The ironies coiled within that little statement are plain and bitter beyond the condescension of hindsight.

The news from the rest of Eastern Europe was less tortuous. 'I next had a conversation with a Bulgarian socialist who did not seem even himself to believe what he was saying.' While in Romania, 'the CP is making provocations to upset the coalition – denouncing "Fascists" in various ministries and generally making mischief, particularly in the factories. The SP is stressing its close co-operation with the CP in order to get at least a share of power . . .' Healey's informant, a Romanian delegate, 'had had difficulty in getting Russian permission to leave the country'.

But the full flood of events was to come a year later when, so far from the Hungarian Communists being terrified that the Russians would leave, the Soviets put pressure on the government to hold early elections under rules which allowed the Communist Party to cast 300,000 bogus votes, exclude 100,000 known Social Democrats from the register and proclaim that a Socialist/Communist union was all but settled. Technically, legally, the Russians were supposed to give up all say in internal Hungarian affairs on 15 September 1947 under the terms of the Peace Treaty. All the more reason for using the spring and summer months to place Hungarians in power who would exercise it for them.

The police, now controlled by a Communist-run Ministry of the Interior, arrested Kelemen, a prominent right-wing Socialist who was charged with treason (and later sentenced to hard labour for life), and the slogan became 'Support the Budapest resolution. Those who oppose it are anti-Soviet agents of Western imperialism and traitors to the Hungarian working class!' A packed joint congress of the two parties proclaimed fusion, thousands of members of the Socialist Party were purged, half the elected MPs barred from attending parliament, police supervision imposed on all former officials and Anna Kethly put under house arrest.

But if resisters suffered, the servers of Soviet purposes, however sophisticatedly defined, crypto-Communist or fellow-travelling, did not prosper. Szakasits would in a short flurry of moves become Chairman of a United Communist and Socialist Party, President of the Republic and be put under house arrest. Marosan would be made Secretary of the United Party followed by Minister of Light Industry and disappear during a visit to Russia. The 'affably dishonest' Horvath would *seriatim* become editor of the leading newspaper, *Nepszava*, be arrested in 1949 and eliminated.

The ultimate irony would be postponed until 1950, with a report in *The Times* of the trial of Hungarian Social Democrats which 'accused the British Labour Party of having organised Hungarian Social Democrats as spies for the British and American intelligence services' (29 October 1950). The charge came from Matyas Rakosi (Healey's 'Mongolian torturer', at this time deputy premier of Hungary). The Labour Party, reported *The Times*, straight-faced, had 'accepted the role of agents for the British intelligence service as early as 1924 . . .'

Prominent on the list of 'imperialist agents' within the Labour Party, Mr Rakosi said, were Mr Morgan Phillips and Mr Denis Healey (the International Secretary). But the acts of Phillips and Healey, the author of *Cards on the Table*, were the merest routine for obvious class traitors. The supreme betrayal of the workers and peasants of Hungary had come from a more surprising source. 'Mr Rakosi said that Mr Zilliacus became a "publicity agent" of Marshal Tito at the trial of Mr Raik* and remained in his capacity as "a whitewasher of the Marshal's past as a working class traitor". Mr Zilliacus had also acted as a link between the Labour Party and visiting Hungarian Social Democrats in Prague in 1947.'

---

* More usually Raijk – Laszlo Raijk, former Communist minister, recently hanged for treason.

11

FRANCE AND ITALY 1947–8

The Italian crisis ran parallel with these events and would come about by degrees over the next eighteen months. The Socialist Party split as predicted, though with a smaller right-wing secession than either Schiff or Silone had expected. And the new group, currently called confusingly Unita (same name as the Communist newspaper) and later called the PSDI (Social Democrats), would enter government with the Christian Democrats. The full name Unita Socialista, taken by those actually leaving the Socialist Party, had profounder ironies.

The new party mattered tactically very much in 1947–8. But long term, even under the favourable conditions of proportional representation, a breakaway party could only be a slowly dwindling force, though Saragat personally, later President of the Republic, always cut an honourable figure. Long afterwards, in 1980–81, when Labour right-wingers were gathered like swallows for the flight of the SDP, Healey would warn them against the move in his best avuncular manner, arguing from his Italian experience that it wouldn't work. For 'right-wing breakaways from left-wing parties have never come to anything. Their only important effect is to weaken the influence of common sense in the party they have deserted, and to keep Conservative governments in power.'[1]

But in 1948 the government of Italy, like the government of France, would face something close to civil insurrection by way of strikes when, a year later, the question of Marshall Aid – American financial subvention – arose. For Britain, uncomplicatedly going America's way, Marshall Aid was a simple and welcome cash bonus, a very necessary aid to reconstruction. In France and Italy it looked like, and was, a sort of influence purchase by means of which accommodating moderate governments would be obliged and kept under obligation. And in France, with its intense particularism, resentment would not just be a matter for the left. General de Gaulle, though alert to Soviet intentions at this time, held then as great a suspicion and scorn for 'Les Anglo-Saxons', the British carrying bags for the Americans, as he was to voice after coming to power in 1958. Dislike of emulsification by a transatlantic power they did not know as Cousin Jonathan or Uncle Sam was a steady factor dividing the Europeans from loyal Britain, one which would play its unspoken part in the way the EEC (European Economic Community) was created. In Italy, where emigration to America had established considerable goodwill, the distinction was different again – and simple.

But *after* Marshall Aid came NATO, an alliance of European powers with an America committed to their defence and, to that end, tucked up on near-sovereign bases from which US planes would have near-sovereign rights to fly.

It is simply not possible to overstate the fearful earnest with which this conflict was regarded. Post-war Western Europe was economically weak and politically vulnerable. The idea of states being rolled over and politically revolutionised by use of industrial action may not have been too much feared, but it was neither hysteria nor a reds-under-the-bed scare. Strikes intensified in France after a hurried visit to Moscow by Maurice Thorez to see Stalin personally.

A conflict which turned upon the disposition of trade union power was something Ernest Bevin understood and was ready for. He took the entire struggle so seriously that at his meeting with the French premier, Paul Ramadier, in September 1947 he seems to have talked the same language of possible union between France and Britain as Churchill had used in 1940. The British Ambassador in Paris, Duff Cooper, wrote: 'As we came away, Bevin said to me "We've made the union of England and France this morning." He would certainly like to and I believe if it were not for other government departments, he might bring it off.'[2]

While the French Communists demonstrated authority when they forced the resignation of Ramadier two months later, they had also painted themselves a bright, identifiable colour and scared too many people. They would now be faced with another enemy in the Hotel Matignon: Robert Schuman, backed by an anti-Communist (and very tough) Socialist, Jules Moch, at the Interior. The strike, when stood up to by Moch, collapsed and the French trade union alliance, the CGT, split into Communist and not-Communist categories at this time of preoccupying importance.

In Italy, similar but different, the disposition of the left-wing parties was vital. But in France, the Socialist Party, the SFIO, had no Nenni figure and could and did join coalitions with the centrist Catholic MRP. Togliatti, after the departure of the right-wing Unita group, had the core of the Italian Socialist Party as his ally. Interested spectators reminded themselves that the

Communist Partisans, formidable soldiers against Hitler, had effectively controlled much of northern Italy before the end of the war. The more nervous of them also looked east to Tito's Yugoslavia with its common frontier, across which assistance could conceivably come. And Tito at this date was still Stalin's ally.

Togliatti wanted to weaken the Prime Minister, De Gasperi, and force him out in the elections scheduled for April 1948. Suddenly the relations of Labour's own sister party with Italian politics became strategically important. Marshall Aid was in the offing, Bevin's own inspiration and the means of drawing in America with all that that implied. Togliatti was never to be allowed the option of grateful acceptance and making his own dispositions in the office he so nearly won, while Nenni, having made his pact with the Communists, would be obliged to count the teeth of a gift horse and talk about 'the so-called Marshall Plan'.

Healey and Morgan Phillips were sent to Italy specifically to persuade the now very left-wing PSI not to co-operate with the Communists in the elections. It was a fruitless undertaking, something which a statement from Nenni's press office makes clear in fluent intermediate Stalinese:

> The executive of the PSI has approved the report made by comrades Basso, Morandi and Vecciletti on the meeting which took place on 13th March with Morgan Phillips and Denis Healey of the English [sic] Labour Party . . . The PSI did not consider it necessary to oppose the invitation to the so-called list of 'Unita Socialista' [the Saragat group]. All the same, it was explained to the English delegation that the list consists of a secessionist group jointly responsible for the clerical and police policy of the Italian Govt. and that it had nothing to do with the Italian working classes.
>
> The executive of the Party in the spirit of the deliberations of the 26th congress which dictated a clear line against any attempt to divide the world into political and economic blocs has instructed its delegates, whether at London or at Warsaw, to make every effort to reinforce the unity of socialism on the basis of the unity of the European workers against any attempt of the capitalistic classes to divide Europe into opposing blocs.

The party, it added, 'refuses to lend itself to any attempt to use American aid as a means of pressure and blackmail of the working classes against the advance guard of Italian democracy. This finds expression in the pact of unity between socialists and communists and in the popular democratic front.'

The party believed that 'the so-called Marshall Plan ought to be discussed in the Republican parliament in the spirit of the defence of the real interests of the workers and all the people of Italy. The sole guarantee that the use made in Italy of American aid will not be in the interest of capitalistic ends, is the constitution of a democratic govt. representing the working classes.'

The appeal made by the committee of the International Socialist Conference had no more success. A memo on Healey's Transport House file records in its own bureaucratic language the complete frustration of 'a final appeal to the PSI . . . to prove by its deeds that, faced by the choice between subjection to the Comintern and free socialist co-operation in European reconstruction it had chosen the socialist way. And even after the elections had proved that co-operation with the Communists was suicidal for Socialists and after revolt among their supporters had made necessary the calling of an extraordinary congress in Genoa on 27 June 1948, the PSI sent delegates to a meeting in Warsaw on 5 June, at which all the parties represented had already fused with the Communists or were in the last stages of fusion. Moreover the Warsaw conference was called 'with the avowed purpose of attacking the policy of the International Socialist conference'. A further, more warm-blooded contribution would come by way of a letter addressed to Morgan Phillips from a former correspondent of Labour's own *Daily Herald*, Giovanni Giglio.

> Dear Mr Phillips
> I learn from the papers that at the Comisco meeting in Vienna, you were the most violent in attacking the Italian Socialist Party and that after having inter alia accused them of 'betrayal' and proposed their expulsion, out of the goodness of your heart you agreed to grant them a reprieve, on the understanding of course, that if at the Genoa conference they do not give proof of repentance, i.e. commit hari-kari, they will be summarily expelled . . . I intend to bring you, the Secretary of the Labour Party, to the bar – that is, I intend to prove that during the last three years you have constantly worked against the unity of Italian and international socialism both legally and illegally, but for the most part illegally . . . you have been the instrument of Bevin's policy . . .

If a speech by Morgan Phillips had been interesting enough to enrage comrade Giglio, then Denis Healey had almost certainly written it. An inveterate writer of other people's speeches, Healey served as Cyrano to many tongue-tied leading men. But not every Roxane appreciated them.

Despite the Punch and Judy dialogue, it was a time of further final appeals. But in due course the PSI would leave the non-Communist fold, only to return after a long exile to become almost embarrassingly flexible. Nenni would die a respected figure in mainstream Italian politics. His heirs would prove to have learned the corrupting ways of capitalistic interests rather too well. The irony of the austere Marxists behind that communiqué being succeeded by the larcenous circle of Bettino Craxi would give a twist to the earnest dispute of 1948 forty years later.

But if the expulsion of a party is a cumbersome process better delayed until yet another conference, the despatch of individual British MPs pushing their hostile associations too far could be dealt with quite crisply. With Nenni goes 'the Nenni telegram', a phrase which would echo and re-echo with approval and indignation in domestic British politics. A group of Labour MPs had signed a telegram sent to the PSI leader supporting his joint election campaign with the Communists. The original list of signatories involved thirty-seven MPs, but that dwindled as Transport House rolled out the full ceremonial of 'serious measures'. In the words of F. Anstey in *Vice Versa*, 'Serious measures is Latin for a whopping.'

The Labour Party, despite pulling authoritarian faces and periodically snapping its braces, usually has more sense and too little stomach for much in the way of expulsions and anathemas. (Hugh Gaitskell would try it a dozen years on and land a small temporary bag of obviously unsinister people, Michael Foot among them.) But in the case of the Nenni telegram, Ernest Bevin was concerned, this episode having occurred on his territory. Accordingly, Phillips was licensed to follow Elizabethan procedure and show the rack to the accused. The reaction was immediate; fifteen of the thirty-seven hurriedly announced that they had not signed at all or that there had been a misunderstanding. It wasn't all panic: some of the denials suggested that certain names really had been taken in vain. Others smelled serious trouble and hightailed it out. There remained, after the inspection of the rack, some twenty-one MPs whose names were listed in a Transport House press release.

H. L. Austin	J. D. Mack
P. G. Barstow	M. Orbach
G H. Bing	C. Royle
Tom Braddock	J. Silverman
W. G. Cove	S. Silverman
Harold Davies	S. Swingler
S. O Davies	L. J. Solley
W. Dobbie	W. Vernon
Emrys Hughes	W. Warbey
L. Hutchinson	K. Zilliacus
H. Lever	

To these members who had written in self-exculpation, the NEC in all its glory addressed a rumbling message.

The National Executive Committee has been seriously disturbed by the activities over a long period of certain members of the Party which are considered to be subversive of Party policy. The recent incident of the Nenni telegram is a flagrant example, and it was noted that among the signatories were also the names of some of those who signed the message to the Communist-controlled German Unity Congress which was later repudiated by the Parliamentary Labour Party.

In view of these and other incidents, the National Executive Committee has decided that it cannot accept as satisfactory the collective letter, the terms of which are by no means clear, signed by yourself and others.

An opportunity for repentance and recantation was given but by way of measures being serious, one member, John Platts-Mills, MP for Finsbury, was made an immediate example. Platts-Mills had been under consideration already on other counts.

In Labour Party terminology, 'The NEC had considered the political activities of Mr J. Platts-Mills MP and remitted the matter to a subcommittee for further consideration.' On 13 April, 'after a full discussion, the Committee decided that in view of his general political conduct, Mr Platts-Mills should be excluded from membership of the Labour Party.' In the course of 1948–9 the other MPs in deep, Solley, Zilliacus and Hutchinson, would be similarly expelled. All would be defeated when they stood as Independents in 1950 though Zilliacus, sometimes called the Finnish Menshevik, was allowed back into the party and parliament in the 1950s, not least because when Tito broke with the Soviets, Zilliacus had been in agreement with Tito. And a soft spot for the Marshal was permitted in the Labour Party.

Healey would be involved in this, not as part of the disciplinary process, but as a source of Italian expertise. The Labour Party was anxious to make clear exactly why association with Signor Nenni and the PSI was so heinous. Two and a half pages of quotations supplied by the International Officer were to the point.

For us Socialists the Soviet Union is not the country of the Slavs or Tartars but the country of the October revolution which smashed the repression of the capitalists and liberated hundreds of millions of men from slavery. (Nenni speech to Party Congress, 22 January 1948)

Against this Anglo-Saxon world syndicate it is Russia which today defends and guarantees our national independence and freedom. If she did not exist, it would be worth while inventing her. Do you believe that Italy would be anything but a name if it were not for the existence of Russia? (Article by Borgogni in *Avanti*, 11 February 1948)

Adherence to the Western bloc would mean starting again the power policy of Fascism and the Monarchy. (Nenni speech at Taranto, 24 February 1948)

Even the leftist optimism embodied in the Third Force, dear to many Labour MPs, had been briskly discounted by Nenni. At Ventimiglio on 5 January he had said that 'he was sceptical of the Third Force as a lie, a crime and a mystification in favour of the conservative forces'. Clearly Nenni, placing himself beyond Spelthorne, could not be a suitable associate for Labour MPs in good standing.

Healey is today doubtful of the wisdom of our having made so much of it. Italian politics, he thinks, is a complex law unto itself, so that taking a high line and getting deeply involved in the dispute was probably a mistake. But the episode illustrates the effect upon post-war politics of all the things which would mesh together and become the Cold War. Fusion of Socialist and Communist parties was frightening in Czechoslovakia, comic-disputatious in Italy.

Aid was coming coolly up by reason of the political interests it would serve, but it would do a great deal for severely impoverished peoples in battered countries. Conceived in a chance piece of rhetoric from the US Secretary of State addressing a university occasion, and hit upon by Bevin as a rope in the water, it would have the most benign and brilliant effects wherever it went. Whatever America's motives, failings or subsequent incomprehensions, the signers-up to Marshall Aid were doing the right thing. Meanwhile the rasping menace of Stalin's orders echoed through Europe with a killing fall. There was nothing for Labour to apologise for in being rid of men happy to be part of the echo.

The two blocs were now almost formed and Healey's own career path was being marked by events. The offensive letters might come to Morgan Phillips, but speeches, statements of policy objectives, assemblies of evidence and importantly pamphlets would be the work of the International Secretary. He had written *Cards on the Table* as early as 1947. It would be followed by *Feet on the Ground*, a cool response to moves for European unity, and the ironically titled *European Unity* which gave a good impression of its author not being very keen on it.

In 1951, he would commission, edit, rewrite and introduce the most famous of his pamphlets, *The Curtain Falls*. It is a dark document in a dark time. With a Polish, Hungarian and Czech essay each setting out the experience of those countries as well as Healey's own introductory piece, it has a telling foreword as mentioned above, by Aneurin Bevan:

Slowly and almost imperceptibly, the Communist Parties of the rest of the world and especially of Eastern Europe, became more and more conspiratorial, penetrating, coercing, cajoling, seducing and betraying their Social Democratic allies. In this book Denis Healey and his fellow writers describe the full fruition of this development in Eastern states in the years immediately following the end of the Second World War. It is a grim, depressing narrative, but nevertheless it is one with which the world should familiarise itself . . . the Communist Party is the sworn inveterate enemy of the Socialist and democratic parties. When it associates with them, it does so as a preliminary to destroying them.

Healey's own acknowledged contribution is cool and factual, the natural product of someone who had lived with Eastern Europe as a great part of his work for five years. It has no hysteria in the American Cold War manner, but it relentlessly spells out the realities of Soviet command extortion in what were then called, accurately enough, 'the satellite countries'.
He was writing six years after Orwell's prophetic *Animal Farm* and nature had imitated art.

'Comrades,' said Squealer, making little nervous skips, 'a most terrible thing has been discovered. Snowball has sold himself to Frederick of Pinchfield Farm, who is even now plotting to attack us and take our farm away from us. Snowball is to act as his guide when the attack begins . . .
    Four days later, in the late afternoon, Napoleon ordered all the animals to assemble in the yard . . . then he uttered a high-pitched whimper. Immediately the dogs bounded forward, seizing four of the pigs by the ear and dragged them, squealing with pain and terror, to Napoleon's feet . . . Napoleon now called upon them to confess their crimes. They were the same four pigs as had protested when Napoleon abolished the Sunday Meetings . . . When they had finished their confession, the dogs promptly tore their throats out, and in a terrible voice Napoleon demanded whether any other animal had anything to confess.

The real thing east of the Elbe is frightening enough to read now, as history, when the water under those bridges is far into the sea. This is how Healey, as a contemporary, recounted events in Czechoslovakia in 1951:

In July (1947) the Soviet Union forced the Czech Government to reverse its unanimous decision to join the Marshall Plan talks in Paris. In the autumn the Communists strained the unity of the National Front by a series of provocative and unacceptable demands – on economic issues, and in connection with the alleged discovery of a plot in Slovakia. Simultaneously they opened a campaign of terrorism against non-Communist workers in the factories. They made great efforts to obtain an alliance with the Social Democratic Party with whose support they would have had an absolute majority in the government . . . Tension grew, but the firmness and competence of the non-Communist leaders, confident that they represented the vast majority of a democratic people, made a repetition of the Hungarian débâcle seem unlikely. Then, in one week, the whole structure of post-war Czech politics was shattered, a single party dictatorship was imposed without serious opposition . . . The police acted throughout as a private instrument of the Communist Party . . . The armed mass demonstrations in Prague on February 21 performed the same function as Mussolini's march on Rome . . . the Russian Consul-General in Bratislava broadcast a statement that the Soviet people 200 million strong stood ready to support the struggle of their Czech brothers. Under the pressure of these two facts every organised opposition to the Communists crumbled.

Ironically, as a former Communist with a fair grasp of economics, Healey had additional insights. He was able to forecast accurately the consequences of Stalin's obsession with heavy industry and the Soviet Union's parasitical use of Eastern Europe. In his determination to subordinate and integrate the Eastern European economies, Stalin had vetoed the Marshall Plan for all his régimes, picking his fight with the non-Communist members of the Czechoslovak coalition on just this subject. Healey spelt out the consequences.

So Russia is forcing them to industrialise themselves largely out of their own resources. This is probably the most tragic consequence of the iron curtain. The process of self-industrialisation . . . must cause human suffering on the same scale as the Industrial Revolution in England 150 years ago. The East Europeans will have to forgo indefinitely any improvement in their own standard of living. In the age of nineteenth-century Liberalism, the social strains arising from such a process inspired Marx and Engels to make their critique of capitalist economy; in fact, they gave birth to Socialism and the trade union movement. In Eastern Europe today where the Communists wield absolute power, the same strains can only increase the rigour of the police state . . .

In 1947 I visited Eastern Europe several times. Everywhere I found the Socialists, then still in the governments, pressing the Communists in vain to reduce the merciless rise of capital investment. For democracy cannot survive the inhumanity of Communist economic theory.

He described the vicious circle of impossible demand not being met, the failure treated as sabotage and political pressure and unreason intensifying.

The freedom of the workers is progressively destroyed, efficiency falls. Managers are imprisoned as saboteurs and replaced by ignorant opportunists ... By replacing experienced technicians with safe Party men, the Communists have caused a catastrophic decline in many industries. Before the War the Romanian oil-wells produced 8,700,000 tons of oil a year. In 1946 they produced 4,800,000 tons. The yield fell a millions tons in 1947.

The fall in production is caused, above all, by resistance inside the working class ... The new Czech regime has dealt out merciless sentences for what it calls economic sabotage. Two workmen were sentenced to death in Brno in 1948 for stealing food cards.

Or as Orwell has it in *Animal Farm*: 'Then a goose came forward and confessed to having secreted six ears of corn during the last year's harvest and eaten them in the night.' A more famous quotation is: 'Comrade Napoleon is always right.' Healey quoted Moscow radio reporting the May Day celebrations of 1950: 'The name of Stalin sounded like a war cry at the demonstrations in Prague, Budapest, Peking, Warsaw and Paris.' The Stalinist régimes had one response to impossible requirements. 'In Czechoslovakia the Five Year Plan demands an increase of 18½ per cent in the industrial labour force ... The Communists set up forced labour camps for their opponents as soon as they had taken power. This year they have budgeted to spend nearly £700,000 in keeping them going. About 40,000 Czech and foreign prisoners are serving forced-labour sentences in the uranium mines alone.'

Healey's own command of detail was the product of his journeying. He had visited Eastern Europe and talked and listened at a time when very few people did so. That practice was largely confined to diplomats and a handful of privileged entrepreneurs who would make money out of the connection, men like Robert Maxwell and, more modestly, the Labour MP and East German middleman, Ian Mikardo.

A good linguist with a decent command of German, the lingua franca of Central Europe, Healey had attended conferences, especially those of the threatened Socialist Parties, but he also met many of the Communists. With a measure of immunity as an *apparatchik* himself, Healey, in our jargon, had networked. But he had networked among the victims. He was also informed by émigré opinion, émigrés who had fled for their lives. In *The Curtain Falls* Poland was described by Adam Ciolkosz, Hungary by Antal Ban and Czechoslovakia by Vaclav Majer. Ciolkosz had been a Socialist deputy in the Polish Sejm before the war, familiar with the prisons of the Germans, the Soviets and the Polish generals; Ban had been Minister of Industry and Reconstruction in Hungary for two and a half years before February 1948; Majer had been Minister of Food in Czechoslovakia from 1945 until the 1948 putsch.

Anyone reading their contributions would have found the usual British inhibitions about faraway countries and the funny names of the people who live there challenged with unanswerable and desolating detail. Majer describes the new justice after February 1948: 'More than 30,000 "lay judges" have been given a few months' training and appointed to positions on the bench where they are supposed to check the decisions by professional judges'; or the powers under 'Act No. 423 of October 1948' by which 'a three-member commission can condemn anyone to a forced labour camp on a mere accusation that he shows "a hostile attitude towards the People's Democratic Republic".'

The pamphlet is under a hundred pages long but it packs a formidable punch. It supplies facts and details to counter any smooth legend of Eastern Europe developing happily and for the best. Very few people would retain the fellow-travelling or naïve, trusting mentality after the Prague putsch, and the suppression of the Hungarian rising in 1956 had reminded the West of realities. Though as the 1960s buried the post-war years, the Soviet system would be looked upon with a sort of relaxed indifferentism. It was normality, an established state of affairs. To be against it was quite respectable but rather American, rather right-wing.

The Curtain Falls, a short concentrate of immediate history, was a source to go back to, a reminder as the unilateralist cause rolled forward and the student sixties produced their own know-nothing mentality, of a world where demonstrations took place on government orders and where 'repressive tolerance' was not a problem. Healey the hard-liner, the rough-handed debater, the unsmooth antagonist in all the debates of the years between the first Aldermaston march and the Labour crisis of 1981, had been created. On defence and foreign policy Denis Healey was going to be a hard man. He was too well travelled and well informed to be anything else.

12

FEET ON THE GROUND:
A RESPONSE TO SCHUMAN

Healey at this time functions as a pamphleteer. His writings, however much the product of their time, reread very well. He was making his reputation as part analyst, part pugilist, shoring up disputable policy with reasons, evidence and a taste for rugged, assured assertion defying all contradiction which would never leave him.

Called upon to defend Bevin's resolute line against Soviet influence, he would translate his own direct experience in Eastern Europe. Asked to set out the party's position on European integration, he was writing about an idea, an idea moreover about which the Labour government (and the Foreign Office civil servants sharing Ernest Bevin's perceptions) were as hesitant as they were apprehensive.

Feet on the Ground, published without a by-line in 1948, is a serious analysis of the current thinking in Europe which would find fruition in 1950 with the Schuman Plan. It lists five HMSO publications and four studies of the question as background and source material. It is thorough and takes each aspect of integration in turn but, despite civilities and salutes to imaginative and bold thinking, it is finally a cautionary tale whose subtitle is almost 'Better not'.

Healey begins with the observation that the idea is not new. It has been around since Dante and was last mooted by the Third Republic statesman, Aristide Briand. For that matter, Britain had never been sympathetic. 'Not only did she do her best to avoid entangling herself permanently in European responsibilities, but she frequently discouraged moves by others towards Continental unity, preferring to maintain a balance of power in Europe.'[1] But all this, he said, was going to change, not least because of the British Labour government.

Healey was writing at a time harder to appreciate today than the mid-eighteenth century. Recognisably this is our own world except for the fact that the country was desperate just to survive. Britain had been, quite simply, ruined by the Second World War. This is residually an Empire, and the vocabulary of Empire, as of a great military victor, is everywhere in evidence. But that Empire, nagged at and preached about by the United States government, is going and will soon be gone – the Raj in 1947, Africa by the early 1960s. We are hideously in debt, having position and denied the means of keeping it up. Lend Lease, the US aid tap for fighting the war, has been abruptly cut off in literal accord with the providing legislation and with no regard at all for the economic consequences. Its ersatz, Marshall Aid, is being administered at a high price in humiliation and instruction, with America laying down orders and directions.

The preoccupation of the Treasury and Board of Trade is with the dollar shortage. Healey is going to be arguing about Europe producing her own goods and substitutes to preserve dollars from expenditure in America. At the same time, the assumptions are Democratic Socialist: what is to be done must be done by way of indicative planning, regulation, quotas of materials and state ownership of key industries; and industry is, and always will be, heavy, engaged in manufacturing and a large employer of labour.

Healey speaks out of this world, this predicament.

Even if all the optimistic assumptions made by the Paris Committee on European Recovery last year are fulfilled, when Marshall Aid ends in 1952, Western Europe will be able to pay for only two thirds of her dollar needs. Yet a failure to bridge the dollar gap will compel each country to choose between a catastrophic fall in its standard of life with all the consequent political and social upheavals, and seeking further American aid at any price which is demanded.[2]

The positive side of Healey's case and the reason why Bevin himself was an activist at this stage, tied into two considerations: trade and recovery from the deep well of war exhaustion; recovery from defeat and victory. The trade advantage was external. 'But although its population numbers almost 260 million, with a further 200 million in its overseas dependencies, Western Europe could never aim at exclusiveness or self-sufficiency.' Lacking oil, foodstuffs, wool, cotton and minerals 'it would seek increasing trade with American and Russian areas. It might thus function as a bridge . . . For this reason a Western Union is of immense psychological importance.'

The peoples of Europe were 'physically and morally exhausted', they had 'lost faith in the survival of their own countries'. Without quite saying so, Healey is talking here about continental Europe. Britain with its Labour government would naturally, despite hard times, concede none of the cynicism and despair deplored here. Union, he adds Blairishly, is 'a dynamic new ideal which is fully in tune with the realities of the atomic age'. For those losing faith in their own countries, 'the idea of Western Union provides the first gleam of light at the end of a dark and gloomy tunnel.'

Such booster prose is not typical of Healey, but the preceding slightly patronising view of the neighbours expresses the fault-finding and dubiety which would increasingly mark British official attitudes as the despairing and cynical Europeans grew more serious, concrete and determined about union. Healey puts those assumptions in a couple of sentences early on. 'Britain's strength as a world power and consequently her value to a Western Union depend, above all, on the close association between herself and other members of the Commonwealth . . . The actual value of the Commonwealth to Britain is quite as great as the potential value of Western union. In particular, the Commonwealth can supply Britain's needs in food and raw materials to a degree which Western Europe could never equal.'[3]

On paper, Healey's arguments about the involvement of food-producing Commonwealth countries must have looked attractive. A Western Union, he speculated, 'might enter into long-term trade agreements with the Dominions to guarantee markets and stimulate production of goods otherwise obtainable only for dollars . . . if the Commonwealth and Europe are to derive much material benefit from Western Union, the Dominions must be closely associated with its development.'[4]

The unwisdom of downright statements about the future would duly be demonstrated by food mountains and wine lakes brought forth by the expedient of paying for them. Healey is also the first example in a long list of British politicians not understanding the motivation and set purpose of European countries to do their own thing, settle their own constituency; with us by all means and gladly, but under British leadership and guided by British preconceptions, absolutely not. Not that it inhibits him. The scheme looks promising but it 'puts the main burden on the sterling area which is the largest multilateral trading area in the world' with the Dominions being asked to supply 218 million dollars worth of goods to Europe, without immediate return, against an increase in their sterling balances in London. Perhaps Europe and the Commonwealth can be reconciled: 'But such a reconciliation is by no means automatic, and the countries of Europe must recognise the supreme importance to themselves of building a friendly association of the Commonwealth and Western Europe.'[5] Healey is speaking where he stands, where Gaitskell would also stand in his conference denial of Europe in 1961 – preoccupied by the imperial connection of 'a thousand years of history' (about 190 actually).

Contemplating Europe's and Britain's problems, he is censorious and puritan, anxious to define the correct goods for trade and enjoin them in ways to delight Sir Stafford Cripps, Labour Chancellor and Angel of Austerity. He is also a thorough-going protectionist. Any member of Balfour's Cabinet would have noted that the torch of Joseph Chamberlain was burning in Transport House. Europe needs a concentration on cheap foods rather than luxury products ... 'Many of the dollars now spent on American cheese would be saved if Europe concentrated on producing cheap cheeses for mass consumption instead of luxury cheeses like Camembert and Gorgonzola.'[6] Healey would live to laugh at himself[7] for this piece of Cromwellian economics.

But it was strongly felt. 'The decline in intra-European trade is thus caused primarily by the failure of some countries to produce the right goods for export. This failure is due to ineffective government planning which in turn is aggravated by inflation. In an uncontrolled economy, businessmen prefer to produce luxury goods because the profit margins are larger.' This in turn encourages a black market, 'So Europe's post-war trade has contained a dangerous proportion of luxuries.' Denis was not standing for such sybaritism and money-grabbing: 'If European trade is to increase, governments must co-operate to get rid of the unhealthy fat represented by all this wasteful production of luxuries – though regard must be paid to the value of less essential goods as incentives to work.'[8]

His final shot on trade generally was to contemplate with scepticism any serious improvement in the planning by which, alone, Europe might cohere. 'It may take years to complete a European production plan which will make possible multilateral trading with freely convertible currencies.'[9]

What of a customs union – the *Zollverein* upon which Germany had begun successfully assembling her many states into one in the early nineteenth century? That would mean getting rid of tariffs within Europe, imposing uniform tariffs on outside goods and common rates of excise. He was chiefly impressed by the difficulties. 'The Benelux Union, though confined in effect to two largely complementary economies, is far from complete after four years' work. A union between sixteen economies of different shapes and sizes, many of which were fiercely competitive in the past, would take much longer.'[10]

Healey may have been speaking both of his socialist convictions and of the predicament of a Britain which in the previous fifteen years had gone from the degree of Imperial preference in the Ottawa Agreements to a war economy and was now assailed by a running external payments crisis.

Everything had been done in Labour Britain against inflation and waste by 'reducing and controlling purchasing power, apart from direct taxation of incomes and profits; the chief weapon in this fight has been indirect taxation of less essential goods'. Under a customs union, he added prophetically, uniform tariffs and taxation would require 'a fixed rate of exchange so immutable that there would be no obstacle to the creation of a single European currency'.[11]

Healey sounds at times like any Tory Euro-sceptic of the 1990s. By setting up this single currency, 'individual governments would lose all control of their own financial, commercial and fiscal policies'. But where contemporary Tories object to both alien control and influence and labour-protective practices, Healey fears the economic liberal assumptions lurking in Europe.

And the institutions likely to develop will not take economic mixing. 'However desirable such a situation might be in theory, it could only work if the whole area were either a free enterprise Capitalist Utopia or a planned socialist society.'[12] In fact, as the complaints of right-wing Conservatives indicate, Europe today has managed to be a fairly free market in production, with large trade union powers and a degree of welfare more generous than our own. Anyway, says Healey, putting the aspirational cart before the working horse, if we should succeed in winning through to a planned socialist society in Western Europe, 'a complete Customs Union is the last and not the first step in the process'.

The virtue – it is the only word for it – of socialist Britain, with her punishment of unnecessary consumption and preoccupation with import substitution of plain, useful goods, would be dragged down by those in Europe combining the qualities of idle apprentice and prodigal son. Any 'removal of trade restrictions at the present time would in itself simply open the more provident planned economies to invasion by luxury goods from scent to china-dogs . . .'[13] In all this, as Edmund Dell has pointed out, Healey was almost certainly being briefed by Hugh Gaitskell and Douglas Jay, both highly resistant to liberalisation of trade, both to become long-term anti-Europeans. One memo from Jay to Cripps asks that 'ice cream spoons etc' should not be included in trade liberalisation when others were doing so much less – 'We have already gone so far unilaterally with "liberalisation".'* (Cripps, in the literal-minded way of a distinguished lawyer, replied that he did not think that ice-cream spoons would make much difference.) Jay was fervently averse to most things European, from cuisine to Roman Catholicism, but the chief influence was a conviction that trade was a thing best kept firmly under control.

Healey is a little warmer about the OEEC, the Organisation for European Economic Co-operation. The agreement concerned the share-out of the first year's Marshall Aid and a scheme for distributing 800 million dollars' worth of extra goods above their earnings to debtor countries: 'a pooling of resources on a scale unprecedented in history'.[14] The main contributors were Britain and Belgium, the chief beneficiary France, 'since she needs more than she can pay for from most of the other countries in Europe'.

That phrase explains many things. If Britain was badly knocked about,

---

* Quoted in Edmund Dell, *The Schuman Plan*, OUP, 1995, pp. 74–5.

France, conquered and humiliated, was also economically reduced to asking for extra favours. Yet so much of the impetus for European union would come from pushy French politicians. Not taking it seriously would be a cardinal error, as we shall see, but one not hard to make.

And then foreigners were so variable. 'Britain and the Scandinavian countries are ruled by Socialist governments. Belgium, Holland and Austria are ruled by coalitions between Socialist and Democratic Catholic parties. In those countries the political situation is stable and the Communists are a shrinking minority of under ten per cent. But in France the government consists of an unstable coalition between the Socialists and some centre parties.' Italy was no good, being governed by a large Catholic party unable to agree policy with progressive parties, while the Communists had a third of the vote. 'Thus the two largest countries of continental Europe are both weakened by instability and civil unrest as well as by the economic consequences of inflation.'[15]

All of this was true. Europe was run by a series of split and haphazard-looking governments, cobbled together on negative assent. Yet looking ahead, the remarkable thing would be the coherence which the countries governed by these shabby and self-contradictory coalitions would achieve – in spite of them, because of them? Such a failure of belief in continental Europe's ability to rise from humiliation, an exponential pessimism, would be widespread in British civil service and government circles at this time. And it would be deepened by the grandiose and thus clearly unrealistic nature of what was beginning to be proposed. How should a federation of Europe, something at which most of Britain strains today even when pro-European, hope to be this-worldly politics in 1948? The Americans were urging it, but America brought limited knowledge and enormous insensitivity to a continent which interested her chiefly in terms of forward defence, revived trade and cost.

The British Labour government, whom Healey reflected, believed that 'the urgent need is for immediate common action to solve critical problems'.[16] In his autobiography, Healey would cheerfully defend his opposition to federation.

'I still think that the arguments I used against federation in . . . *Feet on the Ground* in September 1948 are compelling.'[17] What had he said then? That life was unimaginably more complex in modern Europe than in the Australia which had federated in 1901 or the America of 1789, part huddle of graduate colonies, part open space. 'But today a nation's economic activities are so complicated and interwoven and the part played in them by the government so greatly increased that any attempt to disentangle separate spheres of competence for federal and state governments would involve serious dislocation of the economic and political life of the states concerned.'[18]

The British/Healey scenario is of continental abstraction and British immediacy and pragmatism. 'The European countries,' he said, 'differ much more widely in race, language, temperament, political institutions and economic organisation than states in any existing federation, and those differences are rooted in centuries of usage.'[19]

Healey was a German and Italian speaker, a student of Kant, an avid traveller in Italy, voluntary and involuntary, someone who had read about and seen more of our neighbour countries – and with a friendly eye – than almost any Englishman apart from a few exquisites and exiles. Yet he might have been more open to European integration if he had not travelled. The Italy he had come through by armed convoy from Porto Santa Venere was southern Italy, unspeakably poor and under the dirty thumbs of a narrow, uneducated priesthood. Italy itself, Healey's own particular European country, has since seen the opposite of federalism flourishing, a specifically northern, indeed Lombard party, wanting essential separation from even the south of fifty years later as a region parasitic, backward and primitive. Healey would know the amount of contempt which a north Italian, even a Roman, can pack into the word 'Napolitano'.

To believe that Denmark could be brought under the same federal roof as Italy, Zealand at one with Calabria, was against not prejudice but all reason. But Europe would be created against all reason. What Healey perhaps did not take into his calculations was the impact of defeat in Europe, even among the honorary victors. Despite the mutual friction of Britain and France, for most of Europe – bombed, starved, witness of commonplace death, caught between Hitler and Stalin – differences had never mattered so little, nor particularisms, and its pride had shrunk past keeping aloof. Europe would be jollied along quite readily by its internationalising politicians, too far for a returning General de Gaulle, a sort of grander, equestrian Denis Healey, to turn back.

And Europe's creators would plunge and go nap on immoderate solutions. The words of Britain's Foreign Secretary were too sensible for this changed reality. 'When we have settled the matter of defence, economic co-operation and the necessary political developments which must follow, it may be possible, and I think it will be, to establish among us some kind of assembly to deal with the practical things we have accomplished as governments, but I do not think it will work if we try to put the roof on before we have built the building.'[20]

Healey is sympathetic about the urge to build. He takes credit on behalf of his master for the limiting title soon to be sidelined. 'The very phrase "Western Union" is owed to Bevin's speech of 22 January 1948 in launching the Brussels Treaty on which the political side of the union is based.'[21] Britain was the country which counted, she was paying the piper, so her sort of structure, the one with the optional roof, was the one to go for. As Sir Stafford Cripps had said, 'The United Kingdom will be supplying machinery of various kinds and vehicles to Europe at a rate which will be very nearly the same as that of the USA, and large amounts of raw material will come from the rest of the sterling area as a British liability.'[22] Healey's gloss is not modest: 'Western Union has been made possible only by the achievement of the Labour Government in Britain and its future progress depends on similar achievements elsewhere.'[23]

Healey's conclusions are oddly contradictory for anyone so clear-minded. On the one hand, he speaks with unaccustomed grandiloquence: 'It is not too much to say that the future of civilisation may well depend on the success of the great enterprise to which we have pledged ourselves . . . a dramatic transformation in the whole world situation, and the nightmare which has haunted mankind since the defeat of Hitler will be forgotten in the dawning of a brighter day.'[24]

The dawning of a brighter day is not a Denis Healey locution. It is perorative and he is not the man for perorations. Much more consonant was an early remark in the same wrap-up section, again shrewd and prophetic – and again setting the hurdles high. What had been achieved so far, though creditable, surely did not deserve the title of 'Western Union'. For 'to earn that title, the European communities must agree to merge their national sovereignties in a central supra-national authority'.[25]

Any Euro-sceptic today reading Healey's pamphlet of fifty years ago would applaud the unerring lucidity, making it clear that a true union must go the whole political sovereignty-abrogating distance. It can only be a judgement, but people who actually wanted European union tended to bite less hard on the chilli. Healey is willing to write exalted platform prose about civilisation and all that if the idea should come off. But his terms for such success, though reasonably set out as a step-by-step Fabian realism, are insistently made remote and rhetorical. Like so many leading British players, not least a Winston Churchill for the moment banging on noisily about the subject, Healey was for Europe in a better than Augustinian way. With any luck, chastity might be impossible.

13

'Il Dogmatismo Laboristo'

Speaking of European projections with such iced dispassion was fine in the autumn of 1948 when Europe was a hypothesis. Healey chimed in exactly with mainstream thinking, Foreign Office and Board of Trade every bit as much as the Labour Party. America was on everybody's necks urging federalism and compliance; accordingly, generalised goodwill with all the difficulties spelt out seemed as intelligent an evasion as any.

Unfortunately the French Foreign Minister, M. Schuman, failed to go away. Healey would write again, once more be in flow with established feeling, but having affronted French and Americans in equal part would get the blame, a scapegoat much commiserated with and spoken well of, but hardly making the stage debut he can have wished.

On 9 May 1950 the Schuman Plan was launched. Robert Schuman declared:

> The gathering together of the nations of Europe requires the elimination of the age-old opposition of France and Germany. The first concern in any action undertaken must be these two countries. With this in view, the French government proposes to take action immediately on one limited but decisive point; the French Government proposes to place Franco-German production of coal and steel as a whole under a common high authority, within the framework of an organisation open to the participation of the other countries of Europe . . .[1]

The words are the foundations of modern history. Europe has been built upwards upon them. For the start of a process which would seemingly settle the wars of Louis XIV, Bismarck, Kaiser Wilhelm and Hitler into a long parenthesis, the word 'momentous' hardly says it. The immediate mechanics of Schuman involved putting the coal and iron resources of the Ruhr and Lorraine under a single supranational authority. The Ruhr and Lorraine, long-mined prosperity or triumphant marches through the other side's capital, were now one geology. They were to be worked subject to one power which was neither France nor Germany. 'The common high authority entrusted with the management of the scheme will be composed of independent personalities appointed by Government on an equal basis. A chairman will be chosen by common agreement between Governments . . .'[2]

It is a little unfair to describe the British reaction as pure rage. But it was. For Britain, meaning Ernest Bevin, had not been told. Acheson, American Secretary of State, and Adenauer, first Chancellor of the new Bundesrepublik, had both been informed, both sworn to secrecy. Britain, consequent upon a need-to-know policy of some crassness, had not. For all Britain's (and Bevin's and Attlee's) earlier foot-dragging and being difficult, it was an astonishing error of judgement and, untypically from the gentle Schuman, of manners. And Schuman and Acheson would both acknowledge the fact. As it was, Acheson who would lunch with Attlee and Bevin that day, would later write of 'Bevin's rage at his exclusion from the circle of consultation', admitting, 'I had been stupid in not foreseeing' such a reaction.[3]

Opinion back of the shop went beyond being sulphurous at being left off the guest list. Roger Makins who embodied most of the qualities which have made the Foreign Office a higher authority in its own right – one widely resented by foreigners – would write a note on 19 May which, as Edmund Dell observes, 'breathes superiority and ignorance'.

> The purpose of the scheme was Franco-German rapprochement, but the French should have tried to negotiate with us before approaching the Germans. They have not thought out how their scheme will work and we could not accept it in principle as we do not know what it would involve. The French say they are prepared to go ahead with the Germans, but they have not done so, neither have they worked out their communiqué. *We shall have to do what we can to get them out of the mess into which they have landed themselves.*

The section italicised here must come close to the high point in altitudinous imperception reached by the Foreign Office, the reconciliation of the great warring powers of the European Continent viewed through the quizzing glass of Lord Foppington.

In private, Makins suspected anti-Americanism and the left-wing cult of a neutralist Third Force. Kenneth Younger, Foreign Office Minister of State, noted in his diary: 'Makins felt we should not get committed, that the

Franco-German talks would inevitably break down sooner or later and we would then get a chance of coming in as *deus ex machina* with a solution of our own . . .' The Plan, according to Makins, 'is largely designed to get away from the "Atlantic" conception and revert to a "European" third force between USSR and USA'.[4] It wasn't, but this was a recurring Foreign Office and Bevin circle anxiety. As for the equally august Sir William Strang, 'Frankly, he thought the whole thing a nonsense and a mere French attempt to evade realities.'[5]

The personal reaction of the highly relevant minister recording all this, though less patronising, was hardly skipping. Kenneth Younger was a sensible, intelligent man with none of Douglas Jay's virulence or the hauteur of Makins, but *communautaire* he was not. 'Officially,' he wrote in his diary, 'we have welcomed the idea . . . Privately we all have doubts and misgivings.' Younger feared the plan might 'develop along old-fashioned cartel lines' or 'be just a step in the consolidation of the Catholic Black International which I have always thought was a driving force behind the Council of Europe'. Distrust of Catholicism, from a left-wing rather than a Protestant point of view, crops up from time to time; and, in fairness, the Catholic Church under the highly compromised Pius XII had recent right-wing connections and an older, obscurantist past to make socialists dubious. We were in the middle of a Marian Year! Otherwise Younger was tepidly pragmatic. 'If the scheme goes through we will have to be associated with it in some way. At present it is hard to see how we can actually join it.'[6]

'Speak for England,' Leopold Amery had said to Arthur Greenwood during the Norway debate of 1940. Denis Healey would have been hailed by official England, from Makins down, for speaking as he now fortuitously did in a pamphlet, *European Unity*, whose magisterial undersizing of the general European project had the rotten luck to come out on 12 June between the publication of Schuman's declaration and a hasty White Paper intended to make soothing noises about it. Healey's word is 'excruciating'.[7]

Conceived as an interim response to a specific proclamation, certainly not to scatter pigeon feathers, it reflected very much what most Labour politicians were saying. But its negativity, civil and reasoned though it was, said enough at a key point to send up armfuls. The reputation Healey would enjoy for the sort of candour which other people call 'engaging' through clenched teeth, would start here with maximum impact. Not many party-approved pamphlets undergoing the full tedium of distribution to, and supposed reading by, a committee including the Leader of the House and the Prime Minister, have then to be disowned by that Prime Minister.

It was a further misfortune that the Plan would be introduced, at a press conference well attended by foreign journalists, by Hugh Dalton, now Minister of Town and Country Planning. Compared to Dalton, Healey was Talleyrand in Chinese slippers. Dalton's public address system voice was wedded to settled and offensive prejudices against specific foreigners, the

Germans principal among them.* Healey and Dalton, despite their candour, did not scruple to shift blame – Healey, not unreasonably, to Dalton. 'Though I had written the first draft, using most of my earlier arguments, Dalton got the National Executive to insert a number of passages which over-emphasised the obstacles which the supranational approach would present to the economic programmes of a Labour Government' and, as if this were not enough, 'His press conference on the statement was even more aggressively sectarian.'[8]

Furore came to Dalton as a surprise, unpleasant but capable of being shrugged off. His own defence was that the pamphlet was a committee product. Drafted by Healey, it had been through many meetings. He had the old university administrator's sharp and detailed recollection. The first draft was prepared by Healey for the International Subcommittee. It was then modified a good deal and a second draft put up. The latter included several paragraphs on European basic industries, since the Schuman Plan

> had been launched on the world in the interval between the two drafts . . . Redraft was passed by International Sub[committee]. Bevan saw the redraft and initialed it . . . This redraft was sent *to all* members of NEC with other papers . . . All ministers on the executive were present. Attlee as usual, sat beside me. Morrison was there and Bevan . . . and Shinwell and Griffiths and Summerskill and Margaret Herbison. The document was unanimously approved after a short discussion.

Perhaps the key point about that meeting was that Attlee had been present and was understood to have read the paper in its second draft. His involvement was token – the wrong token. 'Only suggestion made by Attlee was that a sentence should be added, after quote from Tory programme on horticulture products, saying that he too has horticulture at heart. (This I put in.) This was practically the only amendment suggested.'[9] Despite the modifications made, it seems reasonable still to speak of Healey as author – he was, incidentally, rewriting and incorporating chunks of a piece he had published earlier in a Canadian journal. We need not speak as of unknown medieval architects, of 'the Master of Smith Square'.

One particular paragraph acted as detonator. Healey, contemplating a future assembly for Europe, a body which might supersede the consultative, or wittering, Council of Europe, fatally observed:

---

* But not just the Germans. Declining the Colonial Office, Dalton had noted in his diary 'a horrid vision of pullulating, poverty-stricken, diseased nigger communities, for whom one can do nothing in the short run, and who, the more one tries to help them, are querulous and ungrateful'.

Any such representative body in Western Europe would be anti-Socialist or non-Socialist in character. In the Consultative Assembly [of the Council of Europe] itself, the Socialists number only one in four. The proportion would be even further reduced if Communist opinion was represented in a European Parliament . . . No Socialist Party with the prospect of forming a government could accept a system by which important fields of national policy were surrendered to a supranational European representative authority, since such an authority would have a permanent anti-Socialist majority and would arouse the hostility of European workers.[10]

This is close to being a mirror image of Thatcherite denunciations of Europe as a nest of Socialists determined to clutter the well-swept hall of free-market Britain with bureaucracy and welfare for the undeserving. But the Conservatives of 1950 took the issue up with some brio, and Dalton would scornfully record Attlee 'forced into a statement that timing of publication was unfortunate'. He refused, flushed and embarrassed, to say whether he had read it or not before publication. He also reported from a conversation with Ernest Davies, P-u-S at the Foreign Office, that Bevin was happy about the pamphlet, having 'initialled and approved our first draft', also the view of two fellow northern MPs that '99 per cent of the Party thought the statement very good and the PM's line very weak'.[11]

Dalton was deluding himself. Cripps, always more open-minded on Europe, was critical. And Attlee was driven to invite in the American and French ambassadors, Douglas and Massigli, to whom he would describe 'European Unity' as deplorable, denying any knowledge of its details or the position it took. He also indicated that Britain might in principle be ready to sacrifice elements of British sovereignty outside the NATO context – by implication under the Schuman Plan.[12] Prime Ministers in dispute with colleagues enjoy a debenture holder's right of recollection. Attlee might have been shown the draft document, but if he chose to interpret dozing through everything except horticulture as *not* seeing, the privilege went with the job.

It was though, in private, a massive climb-down and repudiation and Healey was extremely lucky that Dalton had made himself as prominent as he had. Dalton's contempt for those foreigners who, not being Germans, he did not actually hate, was well known – and not unpopular in the Labour Party. Healey, whose sentiments the document, however meddled with, fully represented, was just unimportant enough for his own good.

The most embarrassing of all responses to *European Unity* came from the American administrator of Marshall Aid, Paul Hoffman, who on 15 June told Washington reporters that the paper represented 'the worst form of isolationism'. That was the sort of quotation for which Conservative politicians and newspapers hungered and thirsted. Isolationism was supposed to be a sin of the right, and of the American right at that, a case of being hoist with somebody else's petard.

Happily for Labour, Hoffman quickly acknowledged the next day that he had been commenting only on newspaper reports. Instead he declared the document to be 'a perfect diplomatic statement' (*The Times*, 16 June 1950, *passim*), adding that 'several paragraphs showed there was real interest in Britain's part in European unity' before compounding this with a nudge about Labour proving its worth by joining the European Payments Union. It was the misfortune of *European Unity* to have come out at the wrong time and be judged in advance of study. As the Cambridge aesthete, Oscar Browning, put it: 'I never read books before reviewing them. It prejudices one so.'

Healey on Schuman would provoke the same press babel as Healey on the Soviet bloc – but in splendidly contrasting ways.

The *Economist*, speaking as ever from the throne, began scornfully, chiding Labour for ineptitude. 'Once again the Labour Party has shown its almost phenomenal gift for bad timing. That Mr Attlee would make a statement on the Schuman Plan on Tuesday had been known a full week in advance. It was also known that a White Paper giving the full exchange of Notes and memoranda between the British and French governments would be published on the same day. Everything thus seemed set for a major clarification of British policy' (*Economist*, 17 June 1950, *passim*). White Paper and statement, went on the editorial, showed clearly that the Prime Minister was responsive to schemes for pooling European resources. 'Unhappily for the Prime Minister, the effects of this grand set piece of government exposition have been almost completely cancelled by the letting off the day before of a large Labour Party squib in the shape of the National Executive's document upon European Unity.' The writer then sets about Dalton, in consequence of whose 'socialism or nothing' outlook, 'every critic and commentator from Bonn to Buffalo has seized upon the National Executive's document and drawn from it the conclusion that socialist isolationism and Schachtian autarky are the real foundations of British policy. The government thus have nobody but themselves to blame if there is dismay in Paris and anger in Washington.'

But having grandly admonished Labour for 'incredibly foolish timing', the *Economist* proceeds to be understanding of the document itself. The commitment to the fullest Anglo-American understanding is fully appreciated, something which makes charges of isolationism 'nonsense'. Nor is the document criticised for its coolness towards heavy-duty integration. It is right not to want a supranational parliament with real powers. The ghostly Healey is given credit for preferring instead a confederal approach. 'Confederalism means that the existing national governments should progressively and willingly pool some of their sovereignty. Federalism means that they should have their sovereignty taken away from them and given to a supranational body.'

So why had the document created such a hostile impression? 'The reason lies partly in the tone; other nations like neither to be lectured nor to be patronised.' But the problem, following mistimed publication and hastily snatched reaction from a paper more quoted than read, also stemmed from concentration on the economics, the preoccupation with planning, which the *Economist* didn't agree with anyway. Full employment 'has been maintained partly by Marshall Aid, partly by the level of post-war demand and partly by the phenomenal prosperity of the United States. What has done the trick has not been the successful application of Socialist principles in Britain but the successful working of capitalism in America.'

This was not the view of the *Daily Worker*. The *Worker* wrote about *European Unity* in classic *Pravda* style as evidence unmasking Labour. 'Labour Party Ditches "Third Force" Bluff' read the headline to a piece by John Gollan denouncing the 'so-called Western Super-Authority' and noting that Labour would accept membership 'only if it is based on representation of governments with each government having the right of veto'. The document, he said, 'makes nonsense of the continued opposition of Bevin and the Foreign Office to the stand of the Soviet Union in the United Nations'. Whole chunks of Healey are extracted – on the right of veto, on a supranational parliament, and Britain's status as centre of the Sterling Area. Such hard-edged preoccupations laid bare Labour's real purpose. 'While in effect arguing for the special British capitalist interests, the statement goes further than any yet issued on outright defence of the war alliance with America.'

The conclusion from such brutal candour is clear: 'Labour has abandoned the United Nations and seeks to put in its place an unholy alliance of imperialist powers, near-Fascist governments, despotic, corrupt dictatorial regimes and Tory Commonwealth governments bent on war.'[13]

The *News Chronicle*, no enemy to Labour, made some nice distinctions and, satisfyingly for Healey, blamed Dalton. The pamphlet 'takes us back to where we were in 1948 when Mr Dalton said: "The success of any scheme for a United States of Europe is going to depend on Socialist groups in the individual countries achieving socialism first." No wonder M. Schuman seems surprised.' The *Chronicle* enters a gentle caveat to Dalton's (and Healey's) high line: 'Manifestly the world does not share the belief that only Socialism can save the world – and it is just possible that the world might be right.'[14] Or, as the *Corriere della Sera* put it in a concise headline of 14 June: 'Il Dogmatismo Laborista contra la solidarità europea', concluding with the tart observation that 'perhaps the salvation of Europe, England included, is much more important for everyone than the outcome of the Labour experiment.'[15]

Soviet and American expectations were nicely mirrored in a contrast between that *Daily Worker* comment and the modest, mimeographed newsletter of the Union for Democratic Action, the Liberal Democrat organisation, issued ten days after the immediate furore and, for all its rough format, a highly sophisticated analysis at proper length. The UDS *London*

Letter is unimpressed with Conservative indignation. They had sent to Strasbourg a delegation 'drawn from their small, but noisy "European" faction. The Conservative Party wasn't actually going to do anything.' (That was profoundly true. Its election programme only had that statement about protecting horticulture which had woken Attlee up.)

Into Labour's private concern with federalists, Tory and Labour, had come Schuman: 'those in charge of the European unity statement inserted some cautious though friendly language about it, but continued to act as if the public were really interested in the tricks of the Tories and the follies of the federalists at Strasbourg last year and in the sturdy common sense the Labor Party proposed to inject into the proceedings this summer.'

There followed, says the *London Letter*, 'a fantastic comedy of errors', making the pamphlet 'the most discussed and least read document of the century'. Then again, the document itself was written in parts in a specialised sort of partyspeak, exaggerating and overstating any likely step-by-step process of tariff-reduction into a ruinously accelerated crash. And anyway, 'The statement drips with the self-satisfaction appropriate to campaign propaganda.'

Healey might not have cared to be characterised as writing discountable rhetoric. But the author was actually seeing the strengths of *European Unity*. 'Once Americans have penetrated the prickly exterior, however, they will find much cause for satisfaction.' John Gollan would drink to that.

'First comes the complete rejection of the theory of Europe as a "Third Force" between the Soviet Union and the United States which has recently made some converts among French and German conservatives.' The alliance against totalitarianism which had upset the *Daily Worker* was applauded by the *London Letter*. Nor was it necessary to get into a tizz about the insistence on a Socialist consensus in Europe if it was to work. 'The trick here is in the word, "Socialist". In practice, all that British Labor requires of a government to be labelled "Socialist" is that its policies be aimed at securing full employment and that it have some measure of control over its basic industries.'

Now there were countries practising open deflation – 'Italy, Germany and Belgium' – but reports of Belgian and Italian deflation had been greatly exaggerated. The *London Letter* looked forward to an alliance among Keynesians to 'draft a full employment convention to which each European government would be invited to adhere. Meanwhile the progressive forces in Europe . . . Socialists and left Catholics and Liberals plus the small centre parties, could join supporting a minimum programme of full employment and social justice which would have the backing of the community as a whole.'

Yet in *European Unity* there was another strand, the nationalism, the 'England apart' instinct which Dalton and Jay and later Peter Shore breathed and which Hugh Gaitskell would voice in his 'thousand years of history' speech of 1962 which invoked the New Zealand dead of Vimy Ridge against EEC membership. Old Tory protectionism, surviving from the Ottawa

Agreements and wartime requirements, but deriving before that from Joseph Chamberlain, was embodied at this time in the *Daily Express* and the four million copies it sold daily. Positively radiating approval, the *Express* quoted the unnamed Healey.

> Britain is not just a small crowded island off the west coast of Continental Europe. She is the nerve centre of a worldwide Commonwealth . . . In every respect except distance we are closer to our kinsmen in Australia and New Zealand than we are to Europe.
>
> We are closer in habits and institutions, in political outlook and in economic interest. The economies of the Commonwealth countries are complementary to that of Britain to a degree which those of Western Europe could never equal.

The *Daily Express* knew what conclusion to draw. 'Shame on all the Tories who support the Schuman Plan. Those are words that should have been said by them.'

A final and soothing word on the question came in the party's own paper from the Prime Minister's press secretary, Francis Williams. Downing Street press secretaries were not then what they have become, ready to promote press understanding with a friendly head-butt. Williams was a comfortable, pipe-smoking loyalist with a non-existent boiling point who had pushed modernity and Attlee to their uttermost affinity by installing a tickertape machine at Number 10 and who existed to proclaim and sustain normality – the doing of the obviously sensible, right thing by a Labour government.

One fact above all had to be made clear: this was not a government statement, it was a party pamphlet – 'neither the content nor the phraseology of this pamphlet can be given its due weight unless it is seen in its proper context.' After that, there were four chief points to take note of, wrote Williams.

1   That it is not good, but bad socialism to imagine, as some few do here and many more on the continent still do, that Western Europe could or ought to be organised as a third and neutral force between Communist Russia and 'Imperialist' America.

2   That to talk about America as a retrogressive, imperialist power as some socialists even in Britain do – is nonsense and contrary to the known facts of American domestic and international policy.

3   That to ignore the Commonwealth as a great liberalising and peace-making force . . . is to ignore history.

4   That although the concept of European Federation has an understandable hold on the imaginations of many socialists, there are other means to European unity which may serve better the needs of democracy . . . and that to advocate these means is not to abandon

either Socialist principles or European co-operation, but may well be used to sustain them.

As for the hostile foreign reaction to which, symbolically, Williams came last: well, Hugh Dalton 'who handled the document for publicity has an ear peculiarly attuned to the controversies and triumphs of the Annual Conference of the Labour Party. The pamphlet itself – within its self-imposed limits – was an excellent analysis of the problems and difficulties in the way of European unity and the practical means to meet them in the light of conditions as they are.' As for 'the ennobling vision . . . the grand conception that this pamphlet lacks', that should be left for the Prime Minister to show his awareness of when he spoke next week.

For all the bromide of his contribution, Williams wasn't actually wrong. Half the problem with *European Unity*, apart from attracting judgements and rationalisations from people who hadn't properly read it, was that it is at least two documents.

It was particular and insistent in a conjunction of socialism and imperialism. Few newspapers read both documents. *European Unity* could be praised by the *Daily Express* which had damned the provocation of Stalin in *Cards on the Table*, and be given a cool look by the *Manchester Guardian* which had supported that pamphlet. But the *Express* thought and talked Empire free trade while the *MG* was being irritated by 'the childlike assumption that "Socialist" Britain is the most perfect of countries and that only if Europe is first remade in our own image can we begin to co-operate fully'.

The comments of the central figure in the entire brouhaha remained unruffled in ways worthy of that model of non-flapping detachment, Clement Attlee. The entries read best raw:

12 June, Monday: Lunch at US Embassy with Sam Berger, Zergotita, Gauseman. Dalton gave execrable Press conference on my pamphlet.

13 June, Tuesday: Pamphlet praised by *Times*, damned by Tories, lunch with Bernard Jacob and his Indian wife Filomena. Sam Berger came for an hour's talk on the pamphlet. Commonwealth sub cttee, dull.

14 June, Wednesday: Gilbert Harrison of a Veterans US org. wanted talk. Did recording on pamphlet for NBC. Gupta said goodbye. Eve Gibb came for talk on pamphlet. Saw poor western at night.

15 June, Thursday: Eric Wigram came about Schuman Inferno. Jim Keir for lunch. Dave Schoenbrun of CBS talked on pamphlet. Int. Sub.cttee accepted my line. Interesting meeting on German rearmament at Chatham House – sat with William Harris and Commandant of Imperial Defence College at dinner. Meeting Strasbourgeoisie afterwards – very tired.

16 June, Friday: Ernie Bevin, Ernest Davies and Phil Noel-Baker all rang
me at home. Conference began quite well – Mollet* was mollified.

On the following day, Saturday 17 June, while Mr Hoffman's corrections
were still being digested and the magisterialising of the *Economist* earnestly
reflected upon, Denis, the cause of all this activity, coolly embarked at Dover,
noting the presence of Rita Hayworth on the boat, and commenting that his
children were very happy, he set out for a holiday in Italy, pursuing the
European vision in his own way.[16]

But although European unity, even federation, were American causes at
this time, undertaken by State Department representatives in the customary
and irritating spirit of American hustle, Healey was not just an insister on a
common socialist or at any rate indicative planning approach. He profoundly
disliked French patent structures into which everything would duly and
ineluctably fall, very much a way of thinking which had made continued
membership of the Communist Party intellectually impossible for him long
before he saw the criminality of its East European methods.

Not an English patriot in the way of Gaitskell and Peter Shore, he would
live to support a 'Yes' vote in the 1975 retrospective referendum on entry. But
good friend of America that he was, he met the most ambitious schemes with
the brisk conclusion – 'Won't work.' And in practice, confederal is what
Europe has been, while federalist horror stories have been told to children,
chiefly by Conservatives, invariably devoted to the United States.

---

* Guy Mollet, General Secretary of French Socialist Party, Prime Minister 1956–7.

SCHUMAN: THE COMMONS DEBATE

Meanwhile the Conservatives, recognising a good thing when they saw it, looked about for ways of making further and better adverse publicity about *European Unity*. A debate on Schuman, scheduled for 26 June, gave them the chance. Anthony Eden, for one, had the time of his life dissecting 'this wretched khaki document'. He was also able to be upbeat and idealistic about the Schuman Plan in the most becoming way – 'I begin by submitting to the House that it is an essential British interest that the Schuman proposals should succeed.'[1]

A Conservative government with Eden as Foreign Secretary would not push this approval to the dangerous extreme of joining. But Eden was at his charming moderate best, unimaginably remote from the insensate rage to which physical pain and distress could bring him. 'Did the Prime Minister really not know the document was going to be published a fortnight ago? After all, it did not glide coyly into the world. Its arrival was heralded not only at the Press conference, but even before that, heralded and trumpeted. Did the Prime Minister really not know about it?' *He* knew about it. 'I read it in the *Observer* on the Sunday before.' Eden quoted some of the advance publicity: 'The greatest pronouncement on foreign policy that the Socialist Government have put up since the war.'[2]

But this was all delightful immediate politics. Put together the Conservative spokesman's questions and what we know from Dalton about a single amendment on horticulture, and all one really leans is that prime ministers live lives across which interminable dull paper flows.

John Maclay, another prominent Conservative, one who had been at the recent Council of Europe meeting in Strasbourg, reported that if ever there was an occasion when a whole city's mouth seemed to be hanging wide open with horrified surprise it was when news of that press conference was published in Paris.[3]

Maclay picked out a sweeping and very Healeyesque pronouncement: 'The European peoples do not want a supra-national authority to impose agreements. They need international machinery to carry out agreements which are reached without compulsion,' and had a good time: 'For sheer intolerable, self-righteous arrogance, that is unbeatable. Who are the Labour Party to speak for the peoples of Europe?' And how, he asked, could we expect Europe to take us to its arms when we said things like this: 'And many European Governments have not yet shown either the will or the ability to plan their own economies'? We have seen Denis Healey talking like this already in *Cards on the Table*. Recognisably, what one got from Healey at this time was not any old socialism, but Balliol socialism. 'The thing,' said Maclay, who had also thanked God that the document had not been translated into French, 'was simply tragic.'[4]

It was left to another Balliol man, Healey's college friend, Teddy Heath making his maiden speech, to observe quite gently that Labour were preoccupied with full employment 'and from that stems their desire not to co-operate with any government which is not a socialist one'. They had put themselves in the position of saying 'that no other country wants full employment and that no other country is capable of pursuing full employment unless it is a Socialist Government. That is obviously far from the truth.'

But the most blazing attack came from David Eccles, a very bright Tory with a Cabinet career in front of him, but whose own little superiorities – his nickname was 'Smartyboots' – probably irked enough colleagues to deny us a very able chancellor. Eccles, who had also been in Strasbourg when the story broke, was electric.

> Then came the pamphlet on European Unity. In one day . . . in a few hours, Europe understood that what they had believed to be practical and removable obstacles were, in fact, fundamental matters of disagreement. Nothing that has been said today or that can be said tomorrow can undo the disastrous effect of that document. The Prime Minister can say that he did read it or did not read it and that he likes it or does not like it. It will make not one ha'porth of difference. The doctrine of smug isolationism is there in black and white. It has fused itself into the thought of Europe and it has explained once and for all the dragging of the feet over the last few years.[5]

Not everyone on the Tory side took the liberal view of Europe. Major Harry Legge-Bourke, a legendary reactionary across decades, had a short way with such thinking. 'The nature of man as I see it, is occasioned by many factors, not least their race, the geography of their countries and the climate in which they live . . . I do not believe that common interests or even common fears are enough; there must also be common sympathies and common characteristics. Whilst those exist in the United Kingdom and in the United States, they do not exist in Europe. It is, as Disraeli once said, a matter of traditionary [sic] influences being allowed to operate.' He quoted Disraeli against 'those who in the ardour of their renovation imagine that there is a third mode and societies can be reconstituted on the great transatlantic model . . .' Such developments all ended in 'elements of destruction' and 'a due course of paroxysms'. This, thought Legge-Bourke, was 'singularly apposite to M. Schuman's proposal'.

Federation of European nations, said the Member for Ely, 'even of the six attending the conference, seems to me both impracticable and incapable of establishing what is the real aim of federation, a real solidarity against Russian communism'. Legge-Bourke had his own counterpart to the Healey–Dalton line of 'Stick with the Socialists'. The role of the Conservative Party was 'to make absolutely plain that it will not countenance, still less discuss, any steps which from the outset will restrict the right of Britain to make whatever arrangements she cares to make with other members of the Commonwealth . . . pooling of steel and coal production is inevitably an interference with that right'.

Britain would not lead Europe, as she ought, by playing 'a flat second fiddle under the baton of a third-rate Svengali in an overture that ought never to have been written'. Oddly, Legge-Bourke then accused the author of *European Unity*, whom he took to be Dalton, of setting 'the British Socialist Party ostrich to bury its head in the British Socialist sandpit . . .'[6]

The ability of Europe to scare different people in different ways was impressive. Black International Catholic fix to Younger, non-Socialist blocker of higher purpose to Healey and Dalton, Johnny Foreigner up to no good to Legge-Bourke – Europe had the quality of a political Moriarty.

Dalton, an elder indispensable, blessed anyway with imperviousness, would not get excited. He had called on Bevin at the London Clinic – he was in and out of hospital at this time – and had talked to Attlee after Cabinet. 'Both very serene,' he observed. And Dalton spoke his mind to his diary. A veteran, in odd parallel with Healey, of the Italian campaign of the First World War he voiced the preoccupations which made him a candid despiser of all European movements: 'I feel sometimes in these days as though I was living again through the thirties. Who would speak out – on Hitler, rearmament, no air force, etc? Who would hush it all up and muffle all the bells? Today there is a mush of sentimental ambiguities over "European Unity" . . . Our "European Unity" has tried to clear some of this up.'[7] As observations go, that might serve as a dictionary illustration of chutzpah.

What of *European Unity*, the pamphlet not the concept, and cause of all this grief? Taken generally, the 'socialists only' paragraph apart, it speaks the same language as *Feet on the Ground*, has the same preoccupation with dollars, takes refuge in the same standard issue uplift about international co-operation, makes remarks about the Commonwealth, acceptable, if tepid, to Major Legge-Bourke, and has running through it a vein of disbelief in the competence and civic aptitude of, at any rate, southern peoples. It also returns ever and again to something which Schuman wasn't primarily talking about: Western Europe as defensive castellation – or huddle – against Soviet expansion, 'bulwark against Communism'.

The author didn't like liberalisation of trade which would 'tend to offset the benefits of devaluation' (Britain had devalued in 1949) 'by making it easier to sell in Europe', a soft market. He feared a customs union which would create a 'protected high-cost European market and greatly hinder the solution of the dollar problem'.

Then we come to that painful political inadequacy of so much of the unhappy Continent. 'Civic and administrative traditions would prevent some countries from applying the methods of democratic socialism as practised in Britain and Scandinavia, even if their countries had a socialist majority.'[8] The tone here, even where a fair point might be made (and many Italians would hurry to make it), is unfortunate. Surveying the Continent, Healey sounds at times like a left-wing Duke of Wellington. But there is fervour as well as nonchalance – 'the flagrant injustices of a free market economy in which workers live in squalor yet see the shops bulging with goods beyond their reach, in which building materials and labour are spent on splendid villas and luxuries while millions still seek a home'.[9]

None of this was going to get the pamphlet into trouble. It was clear Labour orthodoxy put with spirit. But the burning contempt for free markets rides oddly with the recurring goodwill towards the US which, even under President Truman's Democrats (badly stymied in Congress anyway), was the place for free markets and inequality. That optimism about the United States might not have been so marked if a draft submitted to Healey by Ernest Davies, at Bevin's express request, had made it to the final text.

A further and perhaps less obvious danger is that if there is any surrender of sovereignty to Europe, an avenue of pressure through which the United States could influence Britain through Europe to accept its policies is thereby created. The Labour Party in particular is fearful of encroachment upon Britain's independence by the United States ... If Britain had to accept the majority decisions made in the Council of Europe, all the United States need do to impose its will on Britain would be to influence a majority of the European states there represented.[10]

Tailored to Bevin's understandable exasperation at much US strong-arming, this would have been the picking of one enemy too many. As it was, there would be snarls from the Republican right (Senator Knowland) at what *was* said.

What about a customs union? 'Most supporters of this policy believe that the free play of economic forces within the Continental market so created would produce a better distribution of manpower and resources. The Labour Party fundamentally rejects this theory.'[11] It would widen the dollar gap and cause 'dangerous social convulsions. Whole branches of industry and whole districts in many parts of Europe would go bankrupt and destitute. Europe today is not strong enough to undergo shock treatment of this kind ...'[12] Only Communists and fascists could benefit.

Space is then given up to anxiety about the threat of a 'Third Force between America and Russia'. But Dean Acheson, American Secretary of State, was ardently promoting Schuman; federalism with Europe was being argued unthinkingly and unreasonably by Americans. Beyond which Schuman came from the MRP – Mouvement Républicain Populaire, a Catholic, socially and economically left-of-centre, but specifically anti-Communist, grouping. Banging on about Third Force risk from such a source was entirely otiose. But bang on Healey did, hard-headed and utopian by turns. 'Britain must work at least as closely with the Commonwealth and USA as with Western Europe. There is no certainty that if Britain transferred fields of government to a European authority, she would retain her freedom to do so. It is by no means clear that a majority of Europeans recognise the need for global unity. Many people of all parties believe that Western Europe can and should stand aloof from what they see as a struggle between Russia and America for world power.'[13]

Some did, others might. Schuman didn't, Adenauer whom he had consulted, didn't. *A fortiori*, Acheson pressing, encouraging and lobbying for the whole thing, did not. This section reads slightly shrilly, a combination of invoking something nasty in the woodshed and talking largely to avoid deciding narrowly. It is reminiscent of Hugh Gaitskell's invocation of world government when, at Party Conference in 1962, he rejected membership of Schuman's inheritance, now called the European Common Market.

Much more to the point, warning is given of the perils of majority rule, pointing out Britain's difficulties with a version of the payments union proposed by the OEEC which, under majority rule, could have been imposed on her. The thinking here is sensible and has lasted. 'It is highly doubtful whether, at the present time, any European government would submit to a majority ruling against its profound conviction on an issue vital to itself. Any attempt to establish majority rule would wreck the atmosphere of confidence which already exists and revive ancient jealousies and suspicions. Co-operation between governments must be based on mutual consent.'[14]

And now, focusing on Schuman proper, the author is able to make sympathetic noises – up to a point! There was a chance here to avoid the cartels of the past, another bogey (and a legitimate fear) affecting Labour thinking. 'Europe's private industrialists fear overproduction and will try to reorganise restrictive cartels as in the past.'[15]

'Until M. Schuman's historic proposal to pool the steel and coal resources of France, German and the Saar [a French protectorate at this date] under a single authority appointed by the governments, the unwillingness of governments to control their own basic industries obviously made European planning of coal and steel impossible. The opportunity now exists to fill the greatest gap in European economic co-operation.' The Schuman proposals, it went on, should be 'shaped in the interests of the people as a whole. The decisive part in co-ordinating Europe's basic industries must be played by the governments, as trustees for their peoples.'[16]

But that said, the peoples of Europe were not to be encouraged to engage in any larger political forum. The Council of Europe was unsuitable, 'its members sit as individuals, not as official representatives of countries or even parties'. Indeed, the Assembly 'has tended to become a sort of unofficial Opposition to the European governments as a whole'. Conclusively, Healey disposes of this para-parliamentary chatter: 'For reasons already stated, the Labour Party does not favour the creation of a European Parliament with legislative powers.'[17]

The pamphlet concludes resoundingly with an underlining of Labour's natural preoccupations, full employment and social justice, words with a good deal of poignancy when read in the era of globalisation. 'Mass unemployment can no longer be considered a visitation of Providence – it is the consequence of human failure to apply measures which have long been common knowledge. Any government can choose whether or not to base its own economic policy upon the maintenance of full employment, with full hope of success unless external factors intervene.'[18]

This, like so much else, spoke Labour's sense of virtue, of doing the right thing and of the sad under-performance of other nations, give or take the Scandinavians, in showing similar keenness. Overarching talk of political and economic unity could wait until British standards, British *Labour* standards, had been matched. Meanwhile the Council of Europe, which would indeed prove a sort of glorified political coffee morning, could therapeutically reflect on the Continent's inadequacies. It speaks a great gap of sympathy. That gap would appear in many forms from many British statesmen across decades, but Healey had made a benchmark.

Two years later he would publish in *New Fabian Essays*, under the editorship ironically of Richard Crossman, stalwart of Keep Left and Spelthorne, an essay, 'Power, Politics and the Labour Party'. There is a lot of hard-headed sense here. It gently regrets the woolliness, utopianism and inwardness of socialists in respect of foreign affairs and observes that 'It is difficult to maintain that the brotherhood of men is better realised in Eastern Europe under "a peoples' democracy" than it was under the Austro-Hungarian Empire.'[19]

But about nations he is implacable. 'The fact is that the nation state is by far the most important political entity in world affairs. Nationalism is the one force strong enough to defeat all comers, whether the imperialism of the past or the totalitarianism of the present.' Nation states, he went on, 'are political entities, not moral entities; with interests and desires, not rights and duties'.[20] Only certain states could make our sort of progress: 'the policies of welfare socialism as applied with such success in Britain and Scandinavia, demand a level of civic responsibility and administrative competence which scarcely exists outside the Anglo-Saxon world and Northern Europe. Under British socialism the Welfare State is achieved by fiscal methods. This presumes that on the whole, citizens are prepared to pay taxes and that the state machinery is efficient enough and honest enough to prevent tax evasion and to administer great funds successfully.'

It is a recurring theme with Healey, a sure foundation for continuing scepticism about European developments. At one point he says that such regional in-gatherings are suitable for small states but that Britain is a world power. If there is hubris here, there is also a distinct and recurring hint of socialism in one country.

THE CASE FOR REARMAMENT – 1951

Healey's Fabian pamphlet, *Rearmament – How Far?*,[1] was actually half a pamphlet since he shared space with John Freeman. But the intellectual energy – and the scorn – is directed at *One Way Only*.[2] For this was July 1951. Bevan, with Wilson and the same John Freeman, had lately left the government after the notorious prescription charges dispute. That dispute, apart from its personality factors, had at least as much to do with defence. *One Way Only* was the first overt Bevanite publication and notably moderate. As John Campbell, in his highly critical life of Bevan, says: 'By its tone of reasoned argument, *One Way Only* and Bevan's speeches in these months, were a clear and commendable attempt to lift the debate.'[3]

Even so it won no favours from Healey. Bevan didn't dissent on the sheer menace of Soviet conduct – he would shortly provide the introduction to *The Curtain Falls* (1951) – but that gave him and his friends even less excuse in Healey's eyes for such Church Lads' Brigade sentiments. They are attached to the wheels of Healey's chariot and sent scything through the Soviet record.

'In 1948, three years ago, it was already clear that the world was divided into two camps, one of which was waging a cold war against the other. We knew at that time, as *One Way Only* admits, that Soviet policy towards the non-Stalinist world was one of unremitting and indiscriminate hostility. So far as it recognised any distinction between non-Stalinists, it put Socialists and especially left-wing Socialists first on the list for destruction.'[4] This is Healey, the unrelenting heavy.

'We also knew in 1948 that the Soviet Union had larger armed forces than all the rest of the world put together – excluding China . . .' In consequence, all neighbours of Soviet power endured 'an atmosphere of constant strain, almost of nightmare. If you went to any of these countries, to Austria, to

Berlin or to Finland, you found people living on their nerves. It was only a question of time how soon their nerves would snap.'

So the Soviet Union was fundamentally hostile to the non-Soviet world; it was very much stronger militarily than anyone else; it inspired fear and, knowing the fact, exploited it, yet was not ready to enter into general war. Why was that?

Freeman had argued that the American atom bomb had deterred the Soviets. But that argument didn't follow. It was not Soviet style, said Healey, to start wars of conquest and from 1945 to 1947 she could contemplate France, Italy, the Low Countries – demoralised, impoverished, unstable, very much fruit on the tree, so why not wait? The American atomic threat did not apply until February 1947. Finally the Soviets knew that the strength of the non-Stalinist world, however ill-assembled for conflict, was much larger, a latent force but one to be contemplated soberly.

But now the Soviet Union had the atom bomb, that provisional status quo was at an end. Healey would live to talk high countervailing force theory with its professors, where the language would be warheads and mega-strikes and, most unpleasantly, second-strike capacity. By contrast, the language in 1950 describes the options in Janet and John terms: 'Once the Soviet Union got something like one hundred atom bombs and the means to deliver them . . . from that moment the atom bomb is probably cancelled out as a deterrent factor. The Americans are unlikely to use the atom bomb if Russia is able to use it against them.'[5]

The Soviets now have the bomb, they have put Russia roughly together again, have consolidated their power in Eastern Europe so that its production is geared to Russia's. But with Marshall Aid, the Western prize is receding: we have a new status quo – and Russia is taking more risks! The Berlin blockade was the first Soviet undertaking which seriously risked war. Now there is Korea: 'I am amazed that Freeman and the authors of *One Way Only* can dismiss it so casually. Russia had been got out of Northern Persia by a diplomatic bluff, whereas in 1951 it had cost two million casualties to halt Communist aggression in Korea. Soviet adventures have grown steadily more reckless and the cost of stopping them has grown steadily higher.'[6]

Healey was never more serious. 'The attack had been stalled, but only just. It had been done at fearful cost – over a million people have died in the last year in Korea in a war deliberately planned by the Soviet rulers. We could not afford to have this sort of thing happening once a year, even if it did not involve the danger of general war.'

But there nearly had been a general war. Korea had been held by a combination of American proximity – bases in Japan, the configuration of the geography, such as the mountain ridges which could be occupied. Such a combination should not be expected next time round. 'And if Korea is repeated anywhere else in the world before the West is re-armed, we know for certain that it will not be possible to stop aggression without resorting to methods which would involve us in a third world war.'

Freeman, says Healey, is blissfully relieved and coasting. We have done the right thing and stopped the Soviets. Their experiment has been tried and failed. Slipping briefly into fairness, Healey says, 'He may be right. We don't know what lessons the Russians may derive here.' But concession goes no further, 'I am not prepared to gamble my life, the lives of my children and perhaps the civilisation, on a psychic intuition about thought processes in the Kremlin.'

We are at the high point of the Cold War – real war taking place with horrendous casualties and every hobgoblin of anticipation let out. Hindsight will show John Freeman's optimism as reasonable. A war had been fought, an enemy stalled, a long period of diminished risk and much greater Soviet circumspection would lie ahead. We were over the worst. In thinking so with the aid of retrospection, we forget the horror of 1951. Stalin lives, a prosperous gentleman, and to be at peace lies not in the prospect of belief.

Healey is geared for deterrence at the level of the worst. General MacArthur, advocate of general war, had been dismissed – blessedly since General MacArthur, latest of an apostolic line of insouciant generals, had contemplated war against China. But MacArthur and his general war were part of general deterrence, the only thing which would assuredly keep Stalin from another excursion in another, better chosen, place than Korea which the very sane General Omar Bradley had described as a war 'in the wrong place at the wrong time and with the wrong enemy'.

Healey is quite clear. 'If you base your policy on the deterrent effect of the potential strength of the Western world, you are committed to MacArthurism in a crisis.' Korea was lucky – it had geography which could be defended, it was near American resource pools. But 'if Korea is repeated anywhere else in the world before the West is re-armed, we know for certain that it will not be possible to stop aggression without resorting to methods which would involve us in a third world war.'

Such bristling realism of approach is backed by reference to the European theatre of war, just then threatened by rehearsals. Yugoslavia had deviated from the Soviet line of order and was running her own version of socialism in one country with contacts out to the West, many of them through the British Labour Party. 'It is only a few months since a leading Communist was writing in the *Daily Worker* that the Western Powers had better look out because there would be a new Korea in Yugoslavia sometime this year.'

We were at this time into the rough guessing and reassuring of strength against risk which would later be numerated with uncertain utility into the martial metrics of war theory. The Soviet Union 'has 215 divisions under arms – we have ten'.

He refers to wrong wars in wrong places. 'Russia is always present at the spot where aggression might begin, whereas her only serious military rivals are separated in Europe from the potential fighting line by something like 1000 miles and separated from other parts of the world by three, five, or ten thousand miles. This means that the countries on our side of the Soviet frontier in any part of the world are extremely frightened.' Hence the Yugoslav sense of crisis. Healey faced the Leninist query – What is to be done? – and had his own answer. 'In my opinion, the only way by which we can remove this danger of war is by producing sufficient strength at the danger spots to deter local aggression. We can do this only through a collective effort by all the countries in the Atlantic Pact, for United States co-operation in this policy is an absolute condition of its success.'

In pursuance of his strong line, Healey mounted a defence of the government's rearmament plan, very much Gaitskell's creation: that 11.4 per cent of GDP spent on defence which a Conservative government, starting with Butler, would tentatively scale down. What that undertaking meant in weaponry was that 'by 1953 we would have an army of 22 divisions, 10 regular and 12 territorial. Half of the money would be spent on manpower and the other half on the production of munitions, tanks, jet engines etc.' The money – as put in an estimate to parliament in January 1951, £4700 million – 'included our contribution toward the fifty or sixty divisions which the planners considered would be necessary to deter Soviet aggression in Europe'. This was not a force to defeat the Soviet Union. 'It would need a programme at least four times as big to do that. The aim is to deter the Soviet Union from taking steps which might lead to war and to remove the nightmare of possible Soviet attack from Western Europe. It is not to win a hot war or to win a cold war. Its single purpose is to prevent the cold war from becoming hot.'

At which point, Healey, always preferring the downright to the mealy-mouthed, made a commitment. 'A lot of people think that by doing this we are inevitably starting an arms race. The very fact that the combined resources of the Western Powers are so much superior to those of the Soviet Union, is, in my view, a guarantee that there will not be an arms race. Because if there is an arms race, the West is certain to win it.' This was literally and historically correct, would finally come true thirty-eight years later, but only after an expenditure on arms by this country (almost alone in such an attachment to the United States) of a kind to preoccupy the economy, even after the soft-line Tories got Gaitskell's spending down to 5 per cent of GDP.

Much of the rest of Healey's political life, which would involve some pulling in of military horns, was involved in facing the question: to what extent were we engaged in an arms race – and what sort of race? That question, by way of peace movements, and specifically through unilateral nuclear disarmament, would come to preoccupy British politics, the Labour Party and its specialist on defence and most unflinching defender of the line, Denis Healey.

But it is the first statement and its implication – Western strength being the guarantee that there would not be a Soviet-directed war – which was Healey's major assumption. His reasoning came from past Soviet conflict. 'Military aggression is not the traditional method used by the Soviet government since 1917. It is only used when that government is pretty confident of immediate and cheap success. We need to re-arm because the Soviet Union is always calculating wrongly what will be an immediate and cheap success.'

Memorably, he remarks that 'In 1940 they thought they could conquer Finland with a few brass bands.' He expected the Soviet Union to make these dangerous mistakes, to set challenges but be capable of being faced off. 'This time we must make sure in advance that she is not tempted to miscalculate.'

Suppose the best developments, he still has no high expectations of sunlit uplands or brotherly love – the tentative hopefulness of a world without two camps is gone for ever. 'Stalinists are never prepared, even in principle, to operate democracy with non-Stalinists. The closest Russia will move towards real co-operation is co-existence ... The Soviet World would simply exist outside the free world as an unpleasant anomaly but not a military danger, rather like Franco's Spain in Western Europe.'

Having taken account of the Soviet World, Denis turned with relish to the Labour Party – and to Aneurin Bevan and *One Way Only*. Indeed that paper was moderate enough – it did not snarl with the jutting front teeth of Konni Zilliacus. But the thinking was wispy and aspirational – a marsh light of unthought-out optimism, a wish for the world to be a better place, coupled with the belief that given goodwill and high public expenditure, it could be.

The Healey assault upon it is a dragon's doing-over of a damsel which reminds Bevan that on 15 February of that year, the defence estimates had been defended 'in a brilliant speech for the Government with the words – "We shall carry it out. We shall fulfil our obligations to our friends and allies."' He then turns round Bevan's own famous aphorism.

If Nye Bevan is right and the language of priorities is the religion of Socialism, then he himself is the first great Apostate. *One Way Only* simply refuses to discuss how much rearmament is needed to deter Soviet aggression ... Instead it says we should first decide how much to spend on welfare at home and abroad; then we should allot whatever is left to defence ... All the welfare in the world is worthless if we have another war. False teeth and spectacles are small comfort to a corpse. If there is a danger of war, then peace must come before plenty.

Healey is out of patience with the Bevanites. Unlike John Freeman who sometimes amazed him, but whose estimate of the Korean War as a line conclusively drawn, Healey respected as serious but too sanguine, *One Way*

Only seemed simply childish. 'It treats the peace budget as a fund to be raided whenever any other need arises. In fact, it is a dream book for escapists.' The Bevan people had made great play with talk of a World Plan for Mutual Aid as a way of discouraging communism and its wars. Organise mutual aid on a large scale by all means, he says, but don't delude yourself that such spending is 'the first line of defence against Communism and war'.

Yugoslavia, which was in very truth threatened with invasion, made no such mistake. She had put all such thoughts behind her because 'she can remove the danger, not by a higher standard of living, but by producing more troops.' In the litany of war-threatening crises since 1945 – Greece, Berlin, Czechoslovakia, Malaya, Burma, Indonesia, Yugoslavia – poverty had sometimes been a factor, sometimes not. 'The only constant factor in every crisis is Soviet policy.'

What *One Way Only* couldn't grasp was Russia's malicious intent. 'It seems to assume the men in the Politburo are fundamentally reasonable men whose attitude to the outside world has been distorted by harsh treatment, but who can be cured of this by a little generosity on our part.' In fact, the Soviets had enriched themselves in resources and manpower by 50 per cent in three years – 1945–8 – of East European acquisition and grown no sweeter-natured. 'It was not half the danger to world peace before the war that it is now.'

Healey also aims a swipe at chatter about steel capacity. The Soviet Union was then producing 27 million tons of steel 'which is very little compared with the Western World. But it is more than Hitler produced in 1939.' Japanese steel production in 1941 was only five million tons. 'And in spite of that she conquered the whole of South East Asia and half the Pacific.'

Healey then tried to set the Bevanites to rights about America. The Bevanites, despite some sniping, had a thoroughly dependent view of the United States, reckoning 'that the real deterrent to Soviet attack is the American guarantee through the Atlantic Pact. But it imagines that the American guarantee is effective even without adequate arms.'

Had they no recollection of Poland? Guaranteed by Britain in 1939, it had been conquered by Hitler the same year and, on his demise, had been briskly put under non-optional Soviet command.

It might have been intelligently returned to Healey that the US in 1951 was militarily quite unlike Britain in 1939. She had, or was in swift train to have, all the means to make her guarantees in Europe real. Moreover, underlying American strength lay American self-interest. She simply could not afford to see a Soviet hegemony in Italy or France.

It is an argument nowhere admitted as respectable, but the actual position of many NATO countries, especially smaller ones like Denmark and the Netherlands, is never to have been wholeheartedly committed to mutual defence, and to have tried not to think about nuclear weapons. *Per contra,*

France, always prickly towards the US, would arm like billy-o and went on doing so, never more than when at defiant arm's length from NATO. Marsupial involvement with the United States would be very British.

Healey, who was intensely close to many American political friends like Dave Linebaugh, Howard Smith and Sam Berger, was already an unflinching apostle of the connection. He argued for it in 1951 in terms of fearful options. 'America might go MacArthurite – ready like the steel-jawed general to fight the enemy at source. It might go isolationist or might stake its future on Germany and Japan rather than on its traditional allies. The approach to Franco Spain is perhaps the first fruit of Bevanism in this direction.' Fairly thin stuff, one would think, but a good burnt stick for poking in the eye of Bevanism. However the American commitment is emphatic. 'We are going to need American help everywhere if we are going to carry through the constructive policies we want in the free world.'

His Americanism was at one with his clear recognition of a threat and the marshalling of everything to contain it, the unflinching recognition that there *was* a cold war which meant an armed peace. It is a policy of high, hard nerve, self-consciously repudiating every kind of appeasement, though oddly, that epithet – since 1938 out on almost permanent loan to indignant rhetoric – is not mentioned.

The Bevanites are given one last admonitory smack. '*One Way Only* is vitiated by a schizophrenic conflict between wish and reality. Every now and then the feet of the authors touch bottom and then a billow of emotional prejudice sweeps them over and they are floating happily upside down again.' The Conservative Party was in danger of doing the opposite. 'Many of its supporters want to use blustering threats of force as the solution to every problem – even when this would involve the risk of war without the support of our allies . . . If they are now prepared to rattle an empty scabbard, what will they do when the sabre is there?'[7]

This was an extraordinarily prophetic observation. The Tory right, keen, as Healey notes, for a war-making, MacArthurish approach over crises in Persia and Egypt, would sit on the back of Anthony Eden, as Foreign Secretary, which he became again in October 1951, then as Prime Minister. And during the Suez Crisis, Eden would accede to their desires with calamitous consequences, not least alienating the United States beyond the dreams of the Bevanites. Another matter this for another chapter. And *that* episode would find Aneurin Bevan himself oddly tolerant and Healey, the hard-liner, violently against war.

FROM LEEDS TO MORECAMBE – 1952

Life could not go on being nothing but pamphlets, however vividly contentious. The job of full-time party official is not something to which a vital and active mind settles for good. Healey had not sought a seat in 1950 or 1951 (the consecutive election years marking Labour's miserable majority of six in 1950). The doubts about a political career which he expresses in *The Time of My Life* should not be treated as sham demure. Despite a talent for rough language, he was intellectually fastidious and the custard accommodations of political life would always irk him.

The servant had lost his master when Ernest Bevin died in 1951. With more votes than the Conservatives, Labour had been defeated by them in the general election of that year. A move outside party politics was of course possible, though the first post which appeared on the horizon was hardly action-packed. The chair of International Relations at Aberystwyth which had been held by the Soviet apologist, Edward Hallet Carr, was coming vacant and Healey was sought. Its location at the western edge of Wales gave it retreat potential. Professor Healey, like General Healey, did not materialise. The other tentative offer was the foreign editorship of the *Daily Herald*. In a national newspaper with a union shop, without having covered weddings and funerals for three years in Great Yarmouth, William Shakespeare would not have been eligible to report a football match. So Healey in braces was another career near-miss.

But a telegram from the Leeds South East Labour Party inviting him to apply was not. Leeds might be seen as lying between Keighley and Bradford, home and school for so long. It also lies between Dublin and Vilnius, a cosmopolitan city into which came in the time of Lord Salisbury both the Irish whom he loathed and the Jews whose entry he tried through anti-alien legislation to keep out. The 'Scum of Europe', as a leading anti-alien crusader had called them at the time,* had provided through Montague Burton's tailoring, the city's biggest employer and soon, through Fanny Waterman, would make it a European musical city. The Irish had also done well in Leeds, though they tended to be less prosperous. Behind the telegram to Healey lay the influence of Solly Pearce, editor of the *Leeds Weekly Citizen*, who persuaded Councillor Cohen to persuade Poale Zion, the Jewish socialist group affiliated to Labour, to nominate Healey.

Leeds South East was a safe seat for Labour. It had been long occupied by James Milner, who had held the Deputy Speakership since 1943 and had a fair claim to succeed Colonel Sir Douglas Clifton-Brown when he retired from the Chair in 1951. It was high time there was a Labour Speaker. But the Conservatives pushed in their own man, W. S. Morrison (known as 'Shakes' from an amiable habit of quotation), a better choice than the stiff, touchy Milner in every way. Morrison may have been the beneficiary of the skulduggery of his namesake. One young MP, in the House four years ahead of Healey, 'the charming young man who is President of the Oxford Union' thought so. Anthony Wedgwood Benn, would in *his* diaries mention having voted for Milner despite 'detesting him . . . out of disgust' at the way he had been cheated out of the Speakership by Herbert Morrison.[1] Determined on departure, Milner demanded a peerage and was made a viscount.

Healey might deserve the seat on merit, but it helped that he could pass for an Irishman and, from both parts of his name, 'Denis' and 'Healey', sounded Catholic. James Healey might not have publicly left the Church, but his grandson's principal opponent, John Rafferty, a local journalist, had. As Rafferty beat Healey on the first vote 20:10, just short of an absolute majority,[2] the regrets of communicants came in terribly handy.

Rafferty had drawn his maximum vote. Healey, the nominee of Poale Zion, had not. As outsider, Keighley being outside, and a man with a splendid CV, he was well placed for the votes of those not wanting Rafferty. Transport House did not look upon Healey as its favourite son, but had another preferred candidate. This was Aidan Crawley, cricketer (for Kent!), former Labour MP (and future Conservative MP).[3] Crawley had got nowhere, and Transport House, playing it reluctantly by the book, ordered a second poll at which all the pieces fell into Healey's hands and he was selected.

These were the days before big election swings, which came in at Orpington in 1962. Healey, opposed by a Catholic schoolmaster as

---

* Sir Howard Vivian, a former Police Commissioner and an MP (Conservative) for Sheffield.

Conservative candidate, had a quiet time, made quieter by the death of King George VI towards the end of the campaign. Healey was elected on 8 February with a majority of 7199. He was thirty-four years old.

More important than the routine campaign was the group of friends whom Healey would assemble. Most important would be Douglas Gabb, trained as an engineer and later running the engineering laboratories at Leeds University. Dougie Gabb, at that time a noted left-winger, would serve long term as agent for the constituency and would become Lord Mayor of the city. He was someone who knew all about the poverty of Leeds. As a child, he had been the beneficiary of a charity called 'Boots for the Bairns' which had provided boots and shoes for the children of the poor. He can remember a part of Leeds served by no sanitation, where in the 1920s rain was longed for as it was the only way the sewage of the court-yards would be swept away.[4] The two men struck up and stayed close. Exceptionally so, for though the engineer had at first regarded Healey as a middle-class right-winger to be argued with, when the deputy leadership was fought out thirty years later he confided that had Healey lost he would have resigned from the party.

Solly Pearce, the prime mover of Healey's case, a sophisticated journalist, would continue a long-term friend, as would Bernard Gillinson and his family. 'Stayed with the Gillinsons' is a refrain in the diaries, recording Healey's surgery visits to Leeds about which he was punctilious. Bernard and Rose, she a daughter of the St Petersburg intelligentsia, were university people and the university, one of the great ones, was important in the politics of the city. The Secretary of the party for many years was a lecturer in electrical engineering, Ashoke Bannerjee,* while a later Secretary, Doreen Hamilton, was the wife of the professor of psychiatry.[5]

But this was both a cosmopolitan and a mixed social-class party, the Gillinsons counterpointed by the Moynihans, Joe and Mary, and by Jim O'Grady, leading figures in the Irish community. What would matter to Healey in later, politically rougher years, would be the solid size and health of his local party, whether it was called Leeds South East or amended to Leeds East. When the grim Labour Party quarrel of 1979–81 arose, it would be unthinkable that Healey should leave a party nationally when locally he had so many friends in it. Equally, he would be under no threat in Leeds. Some MPs had given themselves a quiet life by letting the party dwindle and running things through a small friendly group. Such situations are a gift to infiltration. Healey's constituency party, though it often argued with him, was too large and vigorous to encourage a bedsitter infestation. Election

---

* Twenty-five years later he would give Mr Chancellor Healey astute warnings about the political implications of a low wage/benefits clash.

would make Healey a Leeds figure for forty years. It was not an uxorious relationship but it was an easy, affectionate one and, like marriage to Edna, provided him with vast security.

February 1952 was an odd time for entering parliament as a Labour MP. The party having lost office was in the process of losing its head. The quarrel which Gaitskell had picked with Bevan had gone yet more sour in opposition. The Bevanites now fought a war with the leadership and the new right led by Hugh Gaitskell. The Labour Party in its dark phases fights all the time, but it fights most bloodily, and most interestingly, at the annual conference, always held at the seaside and in those days at a rather wider selection of resorts – places like Margate, Scarborough and, in the autumn of the ferocious year 1952, at Morecambe.

That conference provided an exhilarating platform for being downright. And while Healey's parliamentary speeches were for many years to be flat and academic, full of useful information and improving matter, but not exactly bubbling, his stump speeches were commonly champagne – either fizzing in the glass or held at the neck.

The bottle-fighter in Denis always surfaced among enemies. The left had defeated a string of established figures, including Herbert Morrison, for the National Executive and were at their high point. Nye Bevan was seen as the coming leader and the recurring quarrel of the next thirty years was that week triumphantly proclaimed. Bevan from this position of strength had tried statesmanship. It was wasted on an unbelieving Healey.

> I would like to congratulate the National Executive on being completely unanimous in favour of closer economic, political and military co-operation with America because somehow the impression has got around that some members of the National Executive are anti-American . . . [and] have used very harsh words about the Americans. Indeed they could not have used harsher words if they had been talking about their colleagues in the late Labour Government . . . but now we know that the only difference between Nye Bevan and Herbert Morrison is that Nye thinks that the best way to win friends and influence people is to kick them in the teeth. That is a point of view, but I believe that even in the country of Humphrey Bogart and James Cagney, they do not understand that sort of lovemaking.[6]

Healey shared, with a whole generation of Labour right-wingers from Hugh Gaitskell to Shirley Williams, a deep affinity with democratic liberal America. They were reacting against the 1930s caricature of a green-featured Uncle Sam with the elongated physique of Abraham Lincoln, wearing dollar bills in the band of his high hat. Though Healey's account of a state of affairs in which Wall Street 'has lost every American election for twenty years and will lose this one* . . . [and] has not run America's foreign policy since the war' and his allusion to the 'blood brothers' – fifteen million men in the US unions, criticism of whom was 'a crime against international socialism', was letting exponential optimism run away with him.

Corporate capitalism would deliver the goods in the United States and would do so as unchallenged master. He would make a more measured judgement in *The Time of My Life* when he described the United States as at least five countries determined regionally, gathered into a massive single market. But Healey was on excellent ground when, during their Morecambe triumph, he accused the British left of self-preoccupied nationalism. 'A lot of it is just jingoism with an inferiority complex trying to make foreigners scapegoats for everything that goes wrong in this country.' As socialists they were supposed to believe 'in the brotherhood of man and we cannot say, "All men are brothers except the Americans"'.†

He rightly apprehended the introverted bitterness and sterility of so much in the left wing at that time. 'You cannot run a socialist foreign policy in arrogant contempt for everybody who is not an Englishman or a Welshman. Have you lost your sense of values? I ask you to throw away the stale mythology of these political Peter Pans. We are living in a harsh, dangerous and exciting world, and foreign policy is now literally a matter of life and death.' And using a phrase which Harold Wilson would make his own twelve years later, he remarked that 'we cannot solve the problems of foreign policy on a diet of rhetorical candy floss.'

---

* It didn't, Eisenhower winning for the Republicans.
† Samuel Johnson could: 'I will love any man except an American.'

MAIDEN SPEECH

The first words on Healey as a parliamentarian had better come from the man who made them, Fitzroy Maclean, war hero, author and highly unconventional Tory.

> I am sure [said Maclean] that everybody in the Committee* will agree that we have just listened to a most remarkable maiden speech . . . Hon. Members have often listened to his speeches before, but hitherto they have been delivered by other people, by his Right Hon. Friends on the Front Bench. Up to now we have known him and respected him as an expert and back-room boy. Now like other back-room boys on both sides of the committee, he has made good and emerged as an orator in his own right and an outstanding orator at that.[1]†

Party dispute hardly came into it; in what was effectively a debate on foreign affairs, Healey, speaking on the raging question of German rearmament, was at a civil distance from the Labour and Conservative leadership on specifics while sympathising with the general objectives of both.

The need to shore up Western defence against the Soviet Union had been accentuated. If Russia might even thinkably move westwards, what more

---

* Committee of Supply, a parliamentary procedure at the time.
† It was to be a good parliament for translated devillers. Reginald Maudling, Enoch Powell and Iain Macleod, the stars of Rab Butler's Conservative Brains Trust in Old Queen Street, had all entered the Commons in the general election of the previous year.

necessary step for self-protection at the huddled end of the Continent than to rearm Germany?

That was the strategic part of the argument. Parallel with it lay political questions of the purest, most unhappy and injurious nature. Labour's internal quarrel was exploited by the energetic Conservative press and hated by the leading trades unionists who stood at that time in relation to the Labour Party like the irked trustees of a wayward heir.

The Morecambe debate was inflamed when Hugh Gaitskell, fulfilling an engagement on his way back from the Lancashire coast resort, made what Labour people learned for years after to call 'the Stalybridge speech', rich in imputations of communism and fellow-travelling against part of the left.

Around Gaitskell would quickly form another faction – right wing in Labour terms, middle class, public-school educated, not without idealism, but measuring merit in terms of members' status as economists, not a little precious and closest and most content in their own company. To Bevanism there was added Gaitskellism. An important aspect of the political life of Denis Healey concerns his neither belonging to a group nor being neutral between them. For the Gaitskellites he would be rather like Mr Markby, the solicitor in *The Importance of Being Earnest*, who was sometimes invited to dinner parties – or, at any rate, came in the evenings – but a Mr Markby who *chose* when to come. However, events and evidence in his area of expertise inevitably made him an ally. Almost, where the Gaitskellites were concerned, he could have been called a fellow-traveller.

No issue divided the party more sharply, before nuclear weapons occupied centre stage, than German rearmament. This had originally taken the form of a proposal strongly supported by President Eisenhower, but undertaken largely to please the French – EDC, the European Defence Community, or as it was first called, 'The Pleven Plan'.

As an idea and, more to the point, a detailed commitment, it was very strongly federal, the thinking less of René Pleven, Prime Minister of France at the time of its inception in 1950, than of the man heavily influencing him, Jean Monnet – 'Mr Europe', arch federalist and compulsive builder of integrated structures. It was to be an army for which 'no precedent or model existed and which we had a few days to invent'.[2] The model was quite openly based upon the coal-and-steel Schuman Plan. It would be linked to a United Europe and under a single political and military command.

This was something which the British would sooner praise than join. And such a baroque community was anyway less than popular in France. It would be the French National Assembly which in 1954, to the tinkling of glass and cries of catastrophe, would with final irony reject it. Yet in fairness, even though EDC would eventually fail, it was part of a larger thinking directed by Monnet and Schuman to the high end that France and Germany should never again go to war.

France with its memory of three German conquests and occupations, France demoralised by a collaboration in which the conservative, nationalist, ostensibly patriotic part of the nation had taken the degrading lead, France with a quarter of the country voting Communist, was in a different case from Britain, never mind remote America, in her view of an armed Germany.

The Americans sought heavy defence in Europe, with the Europeans maximally involved and contributing. To get this, they pressed whatever buttons came to hand. The most important button was marked 'Germany'. But France was a 250-year dynastic enemy and 100-year victim of Germany, and her workers and students also responded to a button, one marked 'mass demonstration'. In the same month as our placid British parliamentary debate, May 1952, the new American Commander of NATO in Europe, General Matthew Ridgway, was met in Paris with a vast affray involving one death, 27 injured and 718 arrests.[3] The French government understood the necessities almost as well as it did the impossibilities. Which is why Jean Monnet and René Pleven had come forward with their plan, why a thoughtful General Eisenhower had wished EDC godspeed.

But EDC, while not placating left opposition to any German role, also conjured up the bitter resentment of French soldiers. For the means invoked in order to control Germany, Monnet's integration and supranationalism, would all too evidently also control the French. And it was proposed to do this when the French Army was fighting the long losing war in Indo-China which would end in the anabasis of 1954, Dien Bien Phu.

The irony of developments which, ten years further forward, would bring France and Germany into an alliance as strong as it would be exclusive, the bricked-out foundations of political Europe, would have to wait. For the moment, the problem was intolerable and the solution didn't work.

From the start the British Conservative government had trudged sympathetically behind the idea of EDC, but in the country at large it had few friends. Churchill spoke of 'this vast Foreign legion', calling it inimitably a 'sludgy amalgam'.[4] The Labour leadership thought it responsible to back an idea whose core support in Britain seemed at times to be Anthony Eden and Herbert Morrison. In doing so they were damaging the solid majority for their foreign policy and weakening the right wing of the party. EDC was seen on the left simply as German rearmament. Much of the impetus which would carry the old leadership to humiliation at Morecambe had derived from the fight over such rearmament, a fight in which, for once, the left had allies.

Hugh Dalton was not simply pursuing his own strand of virulent anti-Germanism when he wrote in February 1951, while Labour was still in government, 'Against this there is increasing feeling in the Cabinet. Nearly all think that though "Principle" can't at present be repudiated, application should be delayed. At least until after Russian talks – when this could, as

Bevin always intended, be used as a bargaining counter . . . Feeling in the Party is very strong on this – stronger than on China. Nye and I both encourage this.'[5]

'Nye and I' was not standard talk for Hugh Dalton. But it would continue thus, to the discomfort of Herbert Morrison. On 29 July, Dalton, never backwards in being triumphalist, wrote: 'Tremendous personal triumph, my friends say. At Party Meeting in Westminster Hall our amendment is approved 141 to 10 and the vote against the government's substantive motion by 131 to 27. When Attlee announces parliamentary committee's recommendation, and reaches 2nd vote, there is loud applause from the Bevanites and others and loud angry shouts of "no" from the German Rearmers.'[6] Approval would come narrowly and perfunctorily at, ironically, the Morecambe Conference, but amid the debris of a ruin whose chief victim would be a Morrison ejected from the Executive.

The argument over EDC was woven into the cloth of the right/left fronde, that dreadful congeries of spites, enmities, offence given and offence taken, grudges, ambition, calculation and spilt unreason now distinguishing a party which had so recently accomplished a civil and humane social revolution without spilling water, never mind blood. Both – EDC and the Labour quarrel – were destined to go on for a long time. In 1954, Aneurin Bevan's second resignation – from the Shadow Cabinet – would be in part precipitated by developments in the EDC.

But the EDC had at least the virtue of being about something. Healey's speech about it, on 4 May 1952, is an astonishing affair. Criticising EDC but accepting the motive behind it, treating Germany in a grown-up way and returning to the rejected first notion of Germany in NATO, almost every point in the 24-minute disquisition would be validated by events.

Germany was the country which mattered, both West and East wanted her. The defence of the West would simply not be possible 'if the manpower and industrial resources of Germany are lost to the Western side'. Germany might of course be taken by main force, but the risk was that we might 'lose Germany to the Western camp through the free choice of the German people themselves'.[7] Citing a deal done by the Weimar Republic and the Soviet Union at Rapallo in 1922 and the pact of 1939, he urged clear-cut recognition of Germany's great importance. 'Western Germany alone is already, in fact although not in law, the strongest single power on the continent of Europe and if and when Germany is united, as in my view is certain and is desirable, Germany will once again be a world Power [sic] of the same order as Britain herself.'[8]

The Soviet Union held the key to German unity and nothing mattered so much to the Germans themselves as that. 'The Germans themselves,' he stated dogmatically and prophetically, 'do not regard the Federal Republic as a permanent affair any more than they regard Bonn as the permanent capital of Europe.'[9] This point, made in 1952, was still incapable in 1989, year of reunification, of penetrating the three-ply prejudices of Margaret Thatcher.

But the Germans also hated and distrusted the Russians; government and opposition there were agreed that a united Germany could not be neutral. Germany should be expected to treat military alliance as we in Britain would – as a sovereign country.

Germany would not be united for another thirty-seven years and would become so only in the ruin of Gorbachev's Russia. But Healey was ready in 1952: 'We can afford to take the offensive on the question of German unity. We shall gain much and lose nothing by doing so.'

The debate had centred upon Eden's anxious argument that unless we hastened through with EDC, it was frankly so unpopular that it might never happen. Healey took issue with him. Firstly, if, as Eden argued, an EDC not achieved in the next twelve months would never be achieved, then the agreement wasn't worth having. Second, 'although public opinion in Germany is at present opposed to a defence contribution, public opinion will change very rapidly and very dramatically, possibly within the next 12 months, and once the Germans want to re-arm we shall not be able to stop them even if we want to.' (He was wrong about that. German distaste for arms and war subsists very healthily to this day, in notable contrast to the British appetite for small wars.)

Healey's next words summed up his judgement of the entire conflict: 'In other words, German rearmament in the short run is impossible; in the long run it is inevitable.'[10]

The baroque structure of the EDC, in which Germany would be an unequal member, was the wrong way to bring Germany into Western defence. 'It represents,' said Healey, 'a false start in solving the German problem, and we should be prepared to welcome the pause imposed by events in order to get back on the right road.'[11] Existing to suit France, the EDC didn't suit her. It was supposed to control Germany, but with France hideously committed in Indo-China (Vietnam mark one) and North Africa, Germany would be in practical terms the strongest member of the grouping. There was only one thing to do. It involved 'having Germany re-armed within the only framework in whose integrity Britain and America have a direct and vital interest, and that framework is the North Atlantic Treaty Organisation'.[12]

Healey caught Eden's reaction to these words. 'I see the Foreign Secretary pursing his lips. He is right. That prospect dismays the French.'[13] In which case it was really for Eden to tactfully explain to France that if she wanted Britain and America to help control Germany, then NATO, in which both countries were vitally interested, was the institution for her to join. Of course it couldn't happen at once. NATO had to be strengthened, not least with more French troops – and must tighten its structure.

Healey concluded briskly, 'I am one of those who believe that the ever closer unity of the Atlantic peoples is one of the most fruitful developments of the post-war era. And I am convinced that it offers to us the one real chance of solving the perennial problem of Germany.'[14]

The maiden speeches of future leaders vary – the collapse of Disraeli's overworked filigree dud, followed by the spark of defiance, is the best recorded. Aneurin Bevan, who would speak later and ramblingly in this debate, had made instant impact in 1929 with a burst of uncanonical passion. Healey had come with a sharp-edged option to the received policy of which government and opposition were making their uncomfortable best. He had spoken as an acknowledged expert, but, in purely political terms, his moment with the Foreign Secretary told onlookers how Denis Healey should be rated.

Anthony Eden was in his pride of day – a first-rate technician of foreign affairs, a political moderate, admired by the Opposition. Sickness and emotional pressure would soon find out the flaw in the man and widen it into tragedy. But in 1952, 1956 was further than four years away. Eden stood at the pinnacle and here was the winner of a by-election holding a short, affable, businesslike conversation with him, a little self-contained chat in the middle of a maiden speech. Healey spoke to him levelly, reasonably, with a clear indication of what Eden should now do, pleasantly confident that the Foreign Secretary would manage it very well. 'But surely it is not beyond the resources of the Foreign Secretary's diplomacy to show the French that, if they really want Britain and America involved in the long-term control of re-armed Germany, they must put Germany into the organisation in maintaining whose integrity Britain and the United States have an absolutely vital and permanent interest.' It isn't exactly chutzpah or presumption, but it is massive self-assurance.

Not rushing to get his maiden out of the way – this was three months after the Leeds poll – Healey had waited for an occasion requiring his skill and knowledge and then unblinkingly used them to address an outstanding Foreign Secretary on terms of equality. Perhaps it *was* presumption, but presumption secure upon indisputable substance.

EUROPEAN DEFENCE COMMUNITY

The context in which Healey as defence and foreign affairs specialist would find himself for the four years after Labour had left office was one all too typical of the Labour Party. Between the Bevanites, notably Richard Crossman, playing for a weak line and Dalton, as Chairman, vigorously continuing his lifelong hatred of the Germans, foreign policy was a nightmare.

Labour was supposed to be committed to German rearmament. In government she had spelt out a position which was clear enough and, under the discipline and expectations of government, had not been seriously challenged. Herbert Morrison as Foreign Secretary had approved the Washington declaration which stated that the creation of the European Defence Community with full German participation was welcome. That should have been that, but opposition was something else. Advantage would be taken of something which Attlee had said in February 1951. Labour politics at this time were literalist, not to say Talmudic, and a nice text to gnaw on gave general satisfaction. Attlee had said in the Commons by way of rough guidance, with no intention of providing such a text, that the rearmament of the NATO countries ought to precede Germany's and that the building-up of such forces should take place before the creation of German arms. German units should be 'integrated in the defence force in a way which would preclude the emergence again of German military menace'.[1]

It did not take long for the International Subcommittee, leftish and encouraged by Dalton, to take this almost casual checklist, set it up in a shrine and observe that it had not been met. The interminable taking and refining of positions which marks all oppositions with nothing better to do, produced an NEC statement of May 1952 which, though innocuous-sounding, avoided mention of the EDC which Labour in government had welcomed.

And that hellish Morecambe Conference, the one which swept out Morrison and, ironically, Dalton, bringing in Wilson and Crossman, faced the usual bouquet of motions, varying incrementally from safe to crazed. It saw off a call for abrogation of NATO and the Brussels Treaty, but settled for a soft composite, contradicting past positions, which left the NEC and its new left-wing members a happy playground. As Saul Rose, Healey's excellent replacement as International Officer, would later remark,[2] 'It is a commonplace in Transport House that one half of the year is spent clearing up after one Party Conference and the other half preparing for the next.' But a series of NEC meetings in hotels proved, as Rose puts it, 'very fluid'. However the world intervened, exactly betwixt conferences, with the death of Stalin in March.

Ahead of the Margate Conference, Bevan, with Attlee assenting, succeeded in inserting into a draft resolution the sentence: 'Conference urges that there should be no German rearmament before further efforts have been made to secure the peaceful reunification of Germany.'[3] The text had been wrestled with and emerged with a clear underlining of preconditions erected, barricade-like, against the very policy which Labour had asserted when in power.

The fact that Margate was generally reckoned a happy conference was a poor trade-off for general paralysis of will on foreign policy. And leadership and Bevanites, like preachers denouncing each other from the same text, proceeded to speak across one another. Morrison had the dropped paragraph, only after all referred back, reconsidered by the International Subcommittee. By April he had it restored in stronger form. The Labour Party at Transport House was now in a position to worry about the Scarborough Conference! Here Bevan had a resolution of his own[4] which would have had the conference say that it 'cannot agree to the rearming of Western Germany and its integration in the Atlantic bloc . . .'.

At Scarborough, the usual round dance, one beat behind the music, of unions, mandated, not mandated, or overthrowing mandates, was always going to produce a tight result. The Woodworkers', a small union given to large power plays, switched their vote from their hostile conference instructions to support the NEC resolution and thus German rearmament and Labour's coherence, giving the official resolution a majority of 248,000.

After four years of deeply futile travail, Labour was reunited with the defence policy it had followed in government. The record of what Healey would say over this period reflects the fact that he was expounding ideas about defence policy and practice in a high political wind.

Anyone who wrote seriously about defence at this time was aware that France, the centre of so much concern, was dreadfully fragile. She was visibly tottering towards crushing defeat in Indo-China. That would occur with the surrender of Dien Bien Phu, a burden which would not be finally lifted from French self-respect until the last accredited US diplomat had scuttled from roof to helicopter in Saigon twenty years later.

France was increasingly vulnerable to two sets of pressure – right-wing resentment of anything which diminished the nation, something soon to bubble up very nastily over the last colonial grief, Algeria – and Communist exploitation factitiously talking 'salle Boche' in the interests of the Soviet line.

That line was safe in the hands of Vyacheslav Mikhailovich Molotov. Stalin might be dead, but with Molotov still running foreign policy, he was around. And Molotov was holding out hope – at the Berlin peace talks – of German reunification, on terms of neutralisation but, interestingly, not military restraint. The springe was obvious and the friends of the woodcock squawked. Fear of German neutralisation as a serious option was vivid for Western politicians from Eden to Healey. They were mindful of Rapallo, and a German-Russian deal feared. As Saul Rose would write in the Labour Party pamphlet rushed out ahead of the Scarborough Conference, 'A neutralised Germany with independent forces would become the arbiter of Europe.'

The Soviets wanted to prevent, the British and Americans to accelerate, full integration of France and Germany into general (and paying) defence of Europe which, before everything else, meant accommodation with each other. For that reason, Healey's brisk dismissal of the EDC, though entirely reasonable – and, ironically, endorsed when the French Assembly finally threw the idea out – could not be followed in any official line. What Healey had said to a healthier France in 1952 could not be spoken when everyone – Americans, British government and the disorganised corporate form of the Labour Opposition – crowded round the sickbed of France.

In 1954 France died – died at any rate in the narrow context of this argument. A National Assembly, contorted with griefs and enmities, finally rejected the EDC. Accordingly, the Healey theory of unadorned NATO membership could be, and was, followed. NATO it rapidly became – with surprisingly little trouble. Eight years later and by the oddest of ironies, General de Gaulle and Konrad Adenauer would oversee France's resurrection – on the arm of Germany – an alliance still taking precedence over any other connection in Europe.

It is always satisfying to be proved right. After EDC rejection in France Anthony Eden, winding up a two-day Commons debate, said of Healey's speech the day before, 'He contrived to avoid saying, as he could so well have said, "I told you so." There is no temptation in politics more difficult to resist.'[5]

It was a nice compliment and deserved, for Healey, already winding up on the front bench for the Opposition after thirty months in parliament, had been at his most constructive and serious minded. He was also distinctly upbeat at the time when comment had varied from panic to gloating. He welcomed the substitute, the Paris Agreements, which had been committing Britain to involvement on the ground in Europe. 'They represented at least the *last* chance of solving the German problem, if not the best chance.' His own feeling, foreshadowed, as everyone knew, in his maiden speech, was that such a commitment would work better than the EDC. 'I have always shared the misgivings which finally led France to reject the treaty, that it was too supranational and that any organisation which excludes Britain is bound to be dominated by Germany.'

As a socialist, and an international one at that, Healey had to cope with the fact that the German Social Democrats had taken a stand against rearmament and were now very much against the Paris Agreements. That fact had paralysed Attlee's response to the EDC in parliament to a caution verging on immobilism. Healey was placed to jog things along. The fact was that the SDP had been heavily defeated electorally by making that initial stand. A badly defeated party 'sometimes did odd things. I remember how my party, after the great defeat of 1931, committed itself at its next annual conference to a policy of total pacifism' which, thankfully, it had dropped the following year for collective security. He was sure the SDP would calm down and take note of other socialist parties all accepting the agreements if they were not rushed into ratification. It did!

The agreements had created what was to be called Western European Union (WEU). In the light of its subsequent highly nebulous career, Healey's earlier queries seem very farsighted. 'What in fact does Western European Union mean? Is it simply to remain a kind of mechanism for arms control or nothing more than a convenient formula for avoiding a dangerous catastrophe, or does it really mean that Britain is going to have some new sort of economic and political relationship with the Continent of Europe?' It was a good question and one answered by long inconsequence. In substance, WEU was never more useful than in the first months of its existence when it provided form and gesture to cover West Germany's entry into the ranks of armed allies.

FIRE OVER SUEZ

The mid-fifties continued for the Labour Party in the customary spirit of sibilant ill-will. On Wednesday 8 June 1955, Richard Crossman held a cocktail party, a *socialist* cocktail party, at which, as Tony Benn records, 'Harold Wilson briefed us on the current position on the leadership.'[1] The questions at issue were grindingly familiar: 'Should Nye oppose Herbert for Deputy Leader? Should Jim Griffiths be put up instead? Do we really want Herbert or Hugh Gaitskell? What should Nye do about the Shadow Cabinet?' It was not Healey's scene, nor in fairness, at this time, was it Benn's: 'I found the atmosphere very depressing. The hatred for Morrison and Gaitskell is if anything stronger than their hatred for Nye . . . Pa advised me to steer clear of all intrigues.'[2]

Events would soon crowd in upon this pastoral. For a start, Gaitskell, however hated by the Bevan people, was duly elected leader, making a term to the long, sweating, anticipatory period of Attlee's late leadership, something itself expressly prolonged to accommodate an older Labour Party hatred – of Attlee in his quiet way for Morrison – concerned, as the saying went, 'to do down Herbert'.

But not all events were determined in the Parliamentary Labour Party. On 26 July 1956, President Gamal Abdul Nasser of Egypt, 'the best sort of Egyptian, and a great improvement on the Pashas of the past'[3] as Anthony Eden had called him, addressing the 1922 Committee in 1954, nationalised the Suez Canal. The effect on Britain was enormous. She was chief shareholder of the Suez Canal Company, regarding the canal as the vital trade link – 'lifeline' was the busy cliché of the time – and engaged as a Middle Eastern power in managed retreat while sustaining, in uneasy yoke with America, a group of Conservative states within the Baghdad Pact. Anxious about Soviet penetration and conscious of elements of Great Power status under threat, Britain was caught between two magnetic fields, her own old powers and obligations in the Middle East, and very great general involvement with the United States.

John Foster Dulles, US Secretary of State, had judged Egypt unworthy of the money originally agreed for a vast irrigation scheme, the Aswan High Dam. It was this into which Nasser, employed innocently enough, had invested his reputation and vast internal and neighbourhood publicity.

Irrigation by the High Dam was to feed double the current number served by Egypt's limited cultivatable area. It was to be proof to the world of what an independent Egypt, not bossed by the British, could do for itself. Intelligent investment, whether or not minutely profitable, by an American-dominated consortium, including Britain and the World Bank, made for remarkably sensible politics. In fairness to the earlier Eden, he had seen this and had been engaged in a generally conciliatory policy towards Egypt which would be muttered at as 'appeasement', a comfortable word of resort for right-wing Tories fretting in the shoals of imperial power.

Britain had, in 1954, withdrawn troops from the militarised area around the canal, an act of some courage which emphatically required all the other parts of a conciliatory policy, very much including the financing of the dam, to continue on course. It was all complicated by Nasser's sympathy, and help, for the Algerian rebels now fighting a war against colonial France. Meanwhile British pursuers of conciliation had felt themselves intolerably slighted when the heir of T. E. Lawrence, General Sir John Glubb, was dismissed as commander-in-chief of the Jordanian forces by the young King Hussein, himself mindful of Arab nationalism and the rising authority of Nasser. This was blamed on Nasser, and the fact that it was announced while Nasser was entertaining the British Foreign Secretary, Selwyn Lloyd, helped not at all.

Against this body of grievance, Nasser had an earlier encounter of his own. He had been given assurances that no attempt would be made to enlarge the defensive/hostile Baghdad Pact. Harold Macmillan, Lloyd's predecessor, with perfect disregard for promises made and his own limited authority, had engineered Jordan's entry into the Pact. The Egyptians, experiencing the specific duplicity of Macmillan, drew general conclusions about trusting the British.

The French by contrast, enraged at the Algerian connection, turned to Egypt's ultimate enemy, Israel, whose supplies of war planes she had suspended during the conciliation phase, and resumed business with the sale of twelve of the most up to date Mystères, the Mark 4, while denying the sale of mortars to Egypt 'on the ground that they might turn up in Algeria'.[4]

So when Dulles, on 13 July, informed Egypt that the USA 'were not now in a position to deal with this matter, because we could not predict what action our Congress might take and our views on the merits of the matter had now altered',[5] he had continued a train of events at a faster pace likely to end in explosion. Beset by so much unhelpfulness all round, Dulles informed the visiting King Hussein that he would cancel the loan, passing this information within the hour to the British Ambassador, Makins. Cancellation was not clever, and as Hugh Thomas, an early informed chronicler of the affair, puts it, 'Dulles had played into Nasser's hands and it is doubtful if he felt insulted.'[6]

With Russia holding back from support, Egypt's inevitable reaction was the nationalising of the Suez Canal, something which came clattering down on the frail, tribulated spirit of Anthony Eden like possession. The Prime Minister was seriously, if sporadically, ill. A duodenal ulcer had been removed in 1945, and in 1953, extraction in Boston, Massachusetts, of a stone from the bile duct, had been bungled, as would be a second operation. Eden had in consequence a plastic join in a surgically severed bile duct which subjected him to 'mysterious fevers and the normal consequences of a bad liver'.[7] He was not privately an easy man without these afflictions. However, self-control and what might unfashionably be called good breeding, had contained his temper for public purposes and kept for beneficial use his unquestionably high abilities and, ironically, his patient, moderate world-view.

He now faced the seizure of a British asset which was also a British totem (and a Conservative heirloom – the financial coup of Disraeli and the legendary grape-peeling Lord Rothschild which had purchased the canal in 1876 with as much aplomb and distress to their rivals as Nasser had now taken it back). And he had dear and avid colleagues on his neck. 'So Anthony is up. We shall see how long he stays in the saddle,'[8] Harold Macmillan had written in his best Iago manner.

Eden's misfortune was that his best efforts at making peace with an Egypt free, and therefore difficult, had been bitterly resented in the Tory press and among his own right wing. A revolt by backbenchers had marked that decision in 1954 to withdraw from the Canal Area. This body, known as 'The Suez Group', was large enough and sufficiently fellow-travelled with, to be a warning against too much moderation. Eden, thin-skinned, proud and ill-assured, was oppressed by them, and in 1956, maddened by events, would try to justify himself in their eyes and his own. It was a man thus provoked, afflicted and encircled who met parliament on 2 August to make a speech containing implied threats which was very widely approved, and uneasily handled by the Leader of the Opposition.

It is with Labour's reaction that we are concerned here. But a sense of the manic rattle of the Tory right, of what Eden was coming round to, a sense even of the times, lies in the speech, made early that afternoon, by a remorseless member of the Suez Group, Captain Charles Waterhouse. Nasser was only anticipating by twelve years the expiry of the 99-year legal agreement upon which ownership of the canal rested. No nonsense about that, it would not do for Nasser merely to withdraw his decree. 'By making that decree he has killed the very concession under which we have acted.'[9]

Waterhouse suggested that, on the model of the Panama Canal, 'a strip on either side of the Suez Canal should be declared for all time to be extra-territorial to Egypt.' The captain's way with contingencies would be brisk: 'If, as a result, there has to be some movement of population from that strip, though only the centres of Port Said, Port Suez and Ismailia are affected, it should be accomplished without too great inconvenience and in a reasonable time.'[10] Accordingly, 'as a result of this trouble, we must so play our cards as to see that the baneful influence of Colonel Nasser disappears from the Middle East . . . We have now got him on the run, and he must be kept on the run . . .'[11]

Eden's own speech at this stage was a combination of legal brief stressing rights under the Convention of 1888 and insistence on free navigation of the canal. Nasser was diverting canal revenues towards the building of the Aswan Dam. Had not Colonel Nasser, who had broken all these solemn undertakings, behaved outrageously? Having tried to do the right thing, 'Our reward has been a breach of faith, and broken promises. We have been subjected to a ceaseless barrage of propaganda. This has been accompanied by intrigue, and by attempts at subversion in British territories.'[12]

So, said Eden, to muted lower strings and a lowering of stage lights, 'Her Majesty's Government have thought it necessary to take certain precautionary measures of a military nature.' He would move certain units in all forces and recall a limited number of specialist reservists – 'Their recall will necessitate the issue of a Proclamation.'[13]

It was all being done, not war, but the intimation of war, for 'the principle of free navigation'.[14] That freedom 'and the efficiency of its operation can be effectively ensured only by an international authority. It is upon this that we must insist.'[15] That speech led on to creation of the Suez Canal Users' Authority and the discovery that most users were perfectly ready to enjoy the navigation guided by pilots quickly hired by Egypt and that the Power which mattered, the United States, had no inclination whatever for Eden's war.

If Hugh Gaitskell's reply to Eden was misunderstood by Tories – and, beginning with Waterhouse who spoke third, it would be misunderstood on a heroic scale – the fault lay partly through thick-headed backbench inattentiveness, partly by way of Gaitskell's own distribution of stress. He got in his indignation early and added the sensible caveats after the end of most backbenchers' attention span. The speech reads better analysed than taken quickly and plain. He made unexceptionable points about Nasser's delinquencies and large ambitions in the Middle East, and the claims of the international marine interest. He did not, though, at any time, encourage a militarist approach. His actual words were: 'I do not myself object to the precautionary steps announced by the Prime Minister today; I think that any Government would have had to do that, as we had to do during the Persian crisis.'[16]

And such worldliness about a routine precaution – we hadn't bombed Teheran – was double-backed with some very Labour Party international legalism, reminding the government that 'we are members of the United Nations ... signatories to the United Nations Charter ... We must not, therefore, allow ourselves to get into a position where we might be denounced in the Security Council as aggressors, or where the majority of the Assembly were against us.'[17]

For Waterhouse to stand up, two paragraphs of Hansard later, and speak of '*two* most remarkable speeches' and proclaim that 'the Leader of the Opposition, in what I think everybody will agree was an extremely courageous speech, has aligned himself with the essentials of the British attitude',[18] involved either extreme doziness or was influenced by the use in those two paragraphs of the word 'force' four times.

In fact, Gaitskell was saying that the best legal ground for force had been the stopping of Israeli ships and we hadn't used it, so we should try all the peaceful negotiating options. And he had concluded by saying that 'While force cannot be excluded, we must make sure that the circumstances justify it and that it is, if used, consistent with our belief in, and our pledges to, the Charter of the United Nations and not in conflict with them.'[19]

To a conscientious listener, Gaitskell's words could in no way be viewed as endorsement of a military course, let alone the intestinal path of deception – suppressed truth and plain lies – by which Eden finally went to war. But Conservative opinion, uncorrupted by attention, believed that he had waved them forward before turning to attack them when Waterhouse's 'British attitude' turned out to be two attitudes whose holders were throwing bottles at one another. A simmering Conservative loathing for Gaitskell, only equalling that of his own left wing, would linger for years.

The real reason for this lay in what today are called sound-bites. Those of August 1956 were quite inadvertent, items of secondary rhetoric gaudily catching the eye by way of distraction from the speech proper. 'The French Prime Minister, M. Mollet, the other day quoted a speech of Colonel Nasser's and rightly said that it could remind us only of one thing – of the speeches of Hitler before the war.'[20] And speaking a little further on of the element of shock through defiance motivating Nasser's actions, Gaitskell went on, 'It is all very familiar. It is exactly the same that we encountered from Mussolini and Hitler in those years before the war.'[21] These are the bits which were remembered against Gaitskell when the shooting started and he was in Trafalgar Square denouncing it.

As a rule of thumb, it is almost always a mistake to compare anyone with Hitler – especially Mussolini. And Nasser was, by the standards of men ruling with administrative discretion, a singularly unbloody dictator. His

rhetoric was massively discountable; the exuberance and justifiable resentment of the long-humiliated Egyptian public were never weighed by British,
French or Israelis. But Gaitskell, for all his precision, was deep in rhetoric
himself. Nothing in that speech cries out for war – it is legality, world opinion, the UN, all the obstacles in the obstacle race to conflagration.

But if you really do think someone is like Hitler, then, however pacific,
you surely *should* contemplate going early to war with him. The too-much-
ness of the words was a product of Gaitskell's own Manicheism. He had very
strong Jewish sympathies. As well as connections through his wife, he had
spent a shatteringly instructive year in 1930s Vienna and did truly care for
Israel. He was always going to dislike Nasser, wrongly, for *his* rhetoric, and
accordingly fell into his own. He used words above calibre, the only ones
which were remembered.

No such confusion would mark Denis Healey. It was his good fortune that
he was not at this early stage a member of the elected Shadow Cabinet. He
was, though, on the front bench, an adviser, a technician. As such he could,
without rebelling, diverge. And Healey diverged at this early stage on the
question of the origins of the Suez Crisis and the culpability of Nasser himself. Rising after the former Liberal leader, Clement Davies, Healey began a
sustained attack on government failure over the Middle East, moving quickly
to shift boots from feet, with Nasser's failings subordinated. Observing that
'our policy has somersaulted at least twice a year and in the last year four
times',[22] Healey unleashed a wave of facts appropriate to a foreign affairs
specialist keeping notes.

'The Government started by opposing the scuttle from Suez. Then they
made the Suez Pact and appeared to be launched on a policy of friendly relations with the new Egyptian Government. They then made the Baghdad Pact
in the full knowledge, one hopes, that nothing would be more calculated to
destroy any hope of good relations with the new Egyptian Government.'[23]
Nasser bought arms from Czechoslovakia, so Eden had rushed to the
Guildhall to warn against flirting with Britain's enemies, then he had taken a
positive, bankable view of financing the Aswan Dam.

'Within a week of that, he suddenly upset the apple cart again by trying to
force Jordan into the Baghdad Pact, an act he must have known, if he was
well advised, was calculated more than anything else to enrage Egypt against
Britain.' Healey then grew personal and deadly. 'I think that the reason for
this confusion is obvious enough. It is that we have not had a Foreign
Secretary for some time. We have a part-time diplomatist in 10 Downing
Street, but nobody across the road whatever.'[24] To put it more gracefully,
Selwyn Lloyd, under an expert if jittery boss, was not placed to exercise the
independent judgement of a proper Foreign Secretary – worse, he didn't
seem to mind.

At this point, Healey was asked by Robert Boothby if he didn't blame the

US for the muddle. Healey did, but thought that when the Cyprus problem drew them into that area, 'the Government deliberately turned the cold shoulder to the American approaches on the issue.'[25] But that was water under the bridge. What should happen now – war or peace? Waterhouse had rightly said that events brought everything to a head. Healey tried to pre-empt Eden with garlands. Outside – from the Tory press – and inside – from many backbenchers – 'the impression given to the public is that an enormous section of the Conservative Party is in favour of unilateral military action by Britain.' He congratulated Eden on standing up to his 'dinosaurs' and 'Teddy boys' and for 'making it quite clear that the solution of this issue which we are trying to achieve is an international solution by consent, by agreement with all the countries concerned, and not a national solution imposed by force of arms in direct contradiction of all the moral and legal obligations to which the Government are subject'.[26]

This was a garland full of hooks. Healey was interested in foreclosing the option of unilateral military action. He agreed with Waterhouse that everything had been brought to a head. For Waterhouse, this meant invasion and ethnic cleansing as the colonial burden was gladly taken up again. For Healey, military action would only be valid if Nasser tried to stop the movement of ships through the canal. What we should not do was to make a great issue of lesser actions – we need not be greatly agitated if Nasser increased the tolls for passage. Healey had back-of-envelope figures that a five-fold increase would only add one penny to the price of a gallon of petrol.

There were larger questions about the canal which the seizure had only underlined: traffic was increasing, the canal needed widening and modernisation. It also needed the attention of the wider community. And Nasser had ironically alerted a wider world interest in the canal. Russia could play very rough politics here if she chose. 'One thing that we ought to have learned in the last 12 months is that if the Russians want to be nasty in the Middle East they can be very nasty indeed, at little expense to themselves, and there is little that we can do about it.'[27]

All this recognised that Egypt's self-interest – revenues and an enlarged canal – massively offset any impulse to close the waterway down. But Healey's conclusion cut to the point. 'Finally, I think that the immediate reaction in this country to the seizure of the Company was very dangerous indeed. All the tremendous shouting and screaming in the Press about the insult to our national prestige and the possible use of force against the Egyptian Government have only raised the stakes without in any way making for a solution of the problem.'[28]

The final words of Healey's intervention might, in a little over three months' time, have been read over the grave of Anthony Eden's reputation. 'Let us not make a sort of Chauvinistic hullaballoo which only encourages other countries to twist the lion's tail. There is no pastime more attractive than twisting the lion's tail if one knows it will make him roar and is almost sure that it will not make him bite.'[29] The differences in Gaitskell's and Healey's speeches echo the conversation they held shortly before the debate. According to his diary, Gaitskell and his deputy, James Griffiths, had had a conversation with Eden during which Eden had flatly lied to them. The question of force was raised, supposing that 'Nasser might do some foolish thing and we had to be ready'. About plans for internationalising the canal, Gaitskell asked, '"What happens if he doesn't accept this?" Eden replied, "Well I don't want to take that hurdle yet."'[30] But as Gaitskell's biographer Brian Brivati puts it, Eden 'had already taken that hurdle. He had made clear to Eisenhower and to the Cabinet that the failure of the international-isation of the Suez Canal would lead to intervention and that military planning and preparations were under way.'[31]

Gaitskell made his speech of 2 August under many influences. He had met the Shadow Cabinet, which insisted on stressing the United Nations angle. The Israeli Ambassador had taken a hard line on Nasser and a long talk with Healey had shown him 'much more anti-government and "more pacifist, more neutralist" than he had expected'.[32] For the man who would make the 1960 Scarborough speech,* 'pacifist' and 'neutralist' were not adjectives of commendation. But his close Wykehamist friend, Douglas Jay, who had been hearing rumours of an invasion plan, had proved in discussion just as defec-tive in the gung-ho qualities.

Gaitskell also had a further encounter with Eden hours before the debate, taking away from the PM the phrase, 'I only want to keep open the possi-bility of force in case Nasser does something else.' His speech consequently created an impression of being onside with the government's warlike mode which, however objectively untrue, lingered – especially among the preju-diced. Six weeks later, after the first crisis had passed and before the balloon had gone up with invasion, Barbara Castle remarked that 'Hugh Gaitskell had let the whole Movement [sic] down by supporting Eden and getting the cheers of the Suez rebels in the debate at the beginning of August.'[33] Crossman himself rather approved of what he thought Gaitskell had said.

The amount of emotional supercharge at this period created clashes in both parties. A group of older Labour MPs, Herbert Morrison, Reginald Paget, Frank Tomney and, with particular severity, Stanley Evans essentially agreed with the ready-for-force mood of 2 August. On the Conservative side, there were rather more people out of all sympathy with the war, backbenchers like Healey's friend, Nigel Nicolson, and junior ministers like Edward Boyle, as well as the resigning Minister of State at the Foreign Office, Anthony Nutting, and just off-screen, the Minister of Defence, Walter Monckton.

---

* 'We are not the neutralists, pacifists and fellow-travellers that some people are.'

Monckton, indiscreetly confiding his disgust to Tony Benn's diary, had obtained, without open revolt, a move within the government to avoid either conducting any aspect of the war or firing openly on his own side. The period between 2 August and 30 October was one of frustration for the government and speculation for everyone else. A week before the explosion, Tony Benn recorded a story (from Francis Cassavetti of the *Daily Express*) of Walter Monckton's view that it was 'unthinkable we could use force, as a war would mean heavy casualties and the British people could not be made to believe that the differences with Egypt were great enough to justify a war'.[34]

Gaitskell, whose belief in the truthfulness of Eden was in retreat, was still being enlightened by Douglas Jay who spent time at the *Daily Herald* where the diplomatic correspondent, Bill Ewar, was telling him that a military operation was in preparation. Gaitskell accordingly gave full support* to a letter sent jointly by Douglas Jay and Healey to *The Times* in ostensible response to a spectacularly fraught and silly leader:

> Sir, If the Government resort to military force other than in self-defence or in pursuit of international obligations or the United Nations Charter, they will do so in defiance of very large sections of opinion in this country. The critical decisions now facing us can only be taken in calm understanding of the realities and not in a mood of impatience or anger.
>
> What are the realities? In nationalising the canal company, Colonel Nasser has clearly acted in an exceedingly high handed and untrustworthy fashion. But so far as your special correspondent in his article 'Company and Canal' on August 2nd points out, he has 'not violated the terms of any international treaty'. It is true that the offer of compensation so far made, appears grossly unconvincing. But this is an issue to be settled in the cool atmosphere of the law before the appropriate international forum. By no conceivable argument can one justify the use of force by one party.
>
> Secondly, Colonel Nasser's whole conduct is certainly a threat to the far more important principle of security and freedom of the canal accepted by all the main powers to the 1888 Convention. If he were to violate this, force would be justified and we might well say so. But he has not yet done this except in the sense of blockading Israeli tankers which we have connived at for years past while, as your special correspondent points out, it does not follow that because he has nationalised the company he has closed or threatened the canal.

---

* This is the view given by Brivati, 'with Hugh's strong support' (*Hugh Gaitskell*, Richard Cohen Books, 1996, p. 263) Healey does not today recall such support and sees Jay and himself as trying to move Gaitskell on from an indecisive position.

We were therefore shocked by your leading article of August 1st which says that 'quibbling over the legal issues will delight the finnicky and comfort the faint hearted' and goes on to urge with apparently no reference to our international obligations that we should 'be ready from the start to use force' if Nasser answers 'a proposal for control with a refusal'. These matters are not 'quibbles' in the eyes of most civilised nations. Such language could be used by China to excuse an invasion of North Korea, Formosa, South Vietnam or Hong Kong or by Russia to justify an attack on Finland or Persia. Action on these lines by Britain not clearly in conformity with the United Nations Charter would largely destroy in a day the moral and political force built up painfully since 1945 behind international law and order for which we all fought in Korea, which has been the basis of UK foreign policy for eleven years and which is the greatest single defence of Britain in a world which we can no longer dominate by military power. It will also array against us in the UN (where do let us remember in good time we, as well as others, can be arraigned as aggressors) not merely the Arab and Iron Curtain countries but the Eastern countries, some Commonwealth countries and many small nations.

Such an act of unilateral force would be a stupendous folly unless and until Colonel Nasser resorts to force himself. If therefore he rejects the plan for international control which emerges from the coming conference, the nations concerned should forthwith apply all effective economic and diplomatic sanctions. Should, on the other hand, Colonel Nasser accept, the way would be open for new talks on economic developments. If we thus keep the right scrupulously on our side and act resolutely we shall have by far the best chance of vindicating the essential principles at stake.

Yours faithfully
Denis Healey
Douglas Jay

Writing in the middle of August[35] Healey was even more anti-war, even less persuaded that the taking of the canal was as important as Eden (and Gaitskell) had suggested. 'What does the nationalisation of the Suez Canal Company really mean in practice? Very little. It was due to revert to Egypt in any case in 1968.'

As for Nasser, while nothing could excuse the way he had gone about his action, 'Eden's recent behaviour in the Middle East does much to explain it.' When Nasser did an arms deal with the Soviet Union, 'Eden responded to this slap in the face by moving heavily to Nasser's side on the Palestine dispute, but when, according to Selwyn Lloyd, Egypt began to improve the tone of her broadcasts about Britain, we defaulted on our promise to provide aid for the Aswan Dam.'

He was writing at a time when diplomacy appeared to have taken over, when the first bright shoots of enthusiastic war preparation had been blighted by the indifference of other users of the canal and by an American line uncharacteristically soft and sensible. With less candour than was usual in Healey, the Labour leader's performance of 2 August – belligerence redeemed by footnotes – became a splendid anti-war speech. 'Fortunately the Labour opposition spoke for sanity and international morality. Right from the very beginning in his masterly speech of August 2 Hugh Gaitskell insisted that Britain under no conditions must use force except in conformity with the United Nations' Charter'. The process of shifting Gaitskell's mood was under way: selective highlighting, with the excerpts loudly applauded, was one way of doing the trick.

It was now mid-August, a false interlude of talk and consultation. Accordingly Healey was able to write, 'It now looks as if reason and the combined pressure of his friends and enemies abroad will compel Eden to return to sanity. But the world will not easily forget the degrading spectacle presented by the Tory Press and politicians in the first few weeks of the crisis when *The Times* led once respected leaders of British opinion raging through the streets of Westminster like a Cairo mob in search of tramcars to overturn.'[36]

Suez as a conflict divides into two parts, the start in early August and the end from late October onwards when military action looms up and is taken. In between, the rabbit goes down the hole and events are largely international and unrewarding.

Tony Benn describes a meeting of the Parliamentary Party's foreign affairs group on Wednesday 24 October. Against a background of blithe talk about 'getting the Russians in', Healey changed the subject and applied himself to the Baghdad Pact, the British-centred, US-approved group of non-radical states seen by Nasser, not unreasonably, as an attempt at encircling him. 'Healey said,' writes Benn, 'that he had come to the conclusion that the Baghdad Pact was a waste of time. He thought we should be quite ready to allow it to go as part of a general settlement.'[37]

But Eden's war came, came ironically as the Russians waged theirs on Hungary. At 4.30 p.m. on 30 October Eden made his famous statement with its central and calculated lie: '. . . Five days ago news was received that the Israel Government were taking certain measures of mobilisation. Her Majesty's Government at once instructed Her Majesty's Ambassador at Tel Aviv to make inquiries of the Israeli Minister of Foreign Affairs and to urge restraint . . . news was received last night that Israel forces had crossed the frontier . . .'[38] Starting from this axial untruth – Britain having plotted the invasion of which it now heard news and against which it urged restraint – Eden behaved suitably for a great occasion.

'I must tell the House that very great grave issues are at stake and that unless hostilities can be quickly stopped, free passage through the canal will be jeopardised . . .' and announced his twelve-hour ultimatum. 'It has been made clear to them that, if at the expiration of that time one or both have not undertaken to comply with these requirements, British and French forces will intervene in whatever strength is necessary to secure compliance.'[39]

Healey made *his* intervention there and then, among the questions following the statement, a short interrogative speech positing four questions. Eden claimed to be operating under the tripartite agreement for the area: 'But the United States of America is also a signatory to that agreement . . . were the United States Government consulted when the British and French Governments took the decision which the Prime Minister has announced, and did they approve of that decision?' Since the Arab states were heavily concerned with these events, had Eden 'consulted our allies in Jordan and Iraq upon the steps which he proposes to take and do they approve?'[40] 'Had the Commonwealth Governments been told or asked anything?'

Having been cool and factual, though with questions to which there was no satisfactory answer – certainly not Eden's reply that 'We have been in close communication not only with the United States Government but also with the Security Council' – Healey dispelled the haze of statesmanly grace with a direct and biting assault.

'The British people are also vitally concerned to prevent any step being taken which may lead to general hostilities between this country and the whole of the Arab world, with a majority of the United Nations opposed to us . . .' Had Eden consulted the Opposition? 'As a backbench member of the Opposition, I should like to know what steps the Prime Minister has taken to obtain the support of at least half the country before taking so grave a step . . .' This had been 'a military ultimatum by two Governments against two others'. It was a matter of peace and war and it would be 'both a crime and a tragedy if at the moment when freedom and national independence are being suppressed by Russian tanks in Hungary, this Government did anything without international support which led to a similar impression being given to world opinion'.[41]

The savage twist of that last question anticipated the mood which Gaitskell would now show. *His* speech in the emergency debate – close questioning of Eden, tempered only by hopes of delay – was the smouldering fuse of what would come. On 31 October Gaitskell called his party together backstage and spoke a language unimaginably remote from that of 2 August.

'First we should oppose prorogation until the latest possible moment. Secondly, we should put down a motion of censure in the strongest terms for tomorrow. Thirdly, we should carry the fight to the country with an immediate national campaign and utter opposition to war . . . He warned us that we would be vilified and attacked as traitors, but that we were in a solemn duty to do this until we had brought about an end to the war.'[42]

Gaitskell had of course been steadily moving this way since the misunderstood caution of August. He was about to be exactly what he warned against – both vilified and called 'traitor' by the duller Tory patriots. Healey's response to events at this meeting was explosive in its anger. In the anthology of opinion which Tony Benn helpfully assembles, only the regulation leftists, William Warbey and Leslie Hale, are comparably vitriolic. His view, as reported, was: 'Eden has broken every pillar of British foreign policy – the Charter, the Commonwealth, the Atlantic Alliance. The Israeli attack was a put-up job. It was a tragic blunder by Israel for Eden will use her and then destroy her.'[43]

The comments of MPs were more mixed than might have been expected. Maurice Edelman, with strong Israeli sympathies, thought 'we are at fault for not being tougher with Nasser. We must not oppose the war, but only seek to end it.' Sir Leslie Plummer, sounding more cynical than he may have meant, advocated that Labour should 'take direct action, make maximum party capital and sympathy for Israel'. Reginald Paget dismissed 'the UN Charter of Disorder' and advised, 'Just attack the government on policy grounds.' But Stanley Evans expressed his contempt for the UN and did not wish to oppose the government.* Douglas Jay was as implacable as Denis, if slightly softer-spoken – 'Oppose this war all out but by political not industrial means . . . The authority of the UN is everything to us. Eden has destroyed the rule of law which is our only protection . . . We have rushed to the aid of the aggressor.'[45]

In parliamentary terms, this was a period of personalised bitterness somewhat comparable to the mood of the worst Irish debates in the late nineteenth century and shortly before the First World War. Benn records Ernest Popplewell almost coming to blows with Sir John Crowder, Gaitskell himself near to fighting with Sir Robert Cary, while Colonel Wigg did land a knock-down punch on Sir Leslie Thomas. Benn was also being told by Peter Kirk, a Tory MP, that Eden 'was now a paranoic. He was so dedicated to the cause of British greatness he was capable of anything. Kirk feared that Eden might ask for a dissolution to punish the Tory Party.'[46]

Such vivid terminology could also be found in Downing Street from William Clark who would later resign and write damningly about the whole affair. '"He is," said Clark, "a criminal lunatic." And knowing what a moderate, middle-of-the-road, wishy-washy man Clark is, I was quite surprised to hear such strong language used.'[47]

---

* Though Evans's cussed opposition to what he thought an unpatriotic line led to his voluntary resignation from parliament, his position was moderation itself compared with 'that old scandal, Hugh Dalton' whom, approaching Christmas, Benn heard 'tight as a Lord, cursing the wogs in the best Suez Group manner.'[44]

If other MPs were exchanging blows, Healey stuck to verbal violence – taken at the start and given back at the end of argument. During the morning session of Friday 2 November, after the United Nations had condemned the invasion, Gaitskell and others were angrily trying to get a statement from Eden about the ceasefire which the UN had demanded. Aneurin Bevan was behaving with vast courtly civility towards Eden – 'Suppose we assume that the Prime Minister needs more time, and suppose we accept that he cannot give an assurance now that he will be able to make a final statement on the resolution of the United Nations before the end of the Sitting. Surely he can make a statement as to what may be the result of the study he will make in the meantime, before the end of the Sitting.'[48]

Eden returned the civilities and played for time. 'The right hon. Gentleman has put his question perfectly courteously. At the same time I do not want to mislead the House. I cannot give any undertaking because I am not yet in possession even of the report of our own representative at the United Nations. These are matters upon which one must be allowed the ordinary opportunity for study. I am not prepared, and no Prime Minister would be prepared in a situation of this kind, to give any undertaking. That is my regret. I cannot do that.'[49]

Healey moved in.

> The Prime Minister has said that he does not wish to mislead the House. On Tuesday I asked the Prime Minister whether he had consulted the United States and Commonwealth Governments before taking the action he has taken and he said that he had been in close consultation with the United States Government and with the Commonwealth Governments. Reports have come in from every Commonwealth capital, and from Washington, that they were not consulted. I wish you could advise me, Mr Speaker: Could you please tell me what is the Parliamentary expression which comes closest to expressing the meaning of the word 'Liar'?[50]

The House has its own rules, including a schedule of words too offensive for use – unparliamentary expressions. Healey, on a point of order, had taken the central unparliamentary expression, 'liar' – the blackest insult on the forbidden list – and as by a billiard cannon, had bounced it off the Speaker.

Eden's reply was to insist, against the evidence, that he had stated from the beginning that Britain and France had acted on their own responsibility.[51] As the record shows, he had also said: 'We have been in close communications not only with the United States Government, but also with the Security Council . . . We have also kept in close consultation with the Commonwealth Governments.'[52]

Tory backbenchers now knew what fire to expect from this technician. On

3 November, when the bombing and invasion of Egypt were taking place, Healey had no sooner risen than his Labour colleague from Leeds, Charles Pannell, intervened to ask the Speaker if it was in order for Bernard Braine, Tory MP for Essex South East, 'to refer to my hon. Friend as a traitorous defeatist? It was said within hearing of all of us.'[53]*

Healey was good-humoured about it – 'I forgive the hon. Member. I know how strong feeling is' – before making a historical judgement which would not be disputed today. Eden had 'missed an opportunity of saving the reputation of this country and the consciences of many of our people from a mark which will last for at least a generation'.[54]

He concluded a speech of controlled anger by contrasting immediate events with those eighteen years before. 'Last night I spoke to a large meeting at the Oxford Union. Never have I seen such feeling expressed in a gathering in Oxford since I was an undergraduate there in 1938 when a similar meeting was held to celebrate the courage of one of His Majesty's Ministers in resigning from the Government in order to demonstrate his respect for international law and the rights of small nations. The name of that Minister is the name of our present Prime Minister.'

At one point Healey came as close as he would to the lower end of the 'Step outside' spectrum by turning on the Tory MP, Frederick Burden: 'I hope that the hon. Member for Gillingham will take the smirk off his face.' After Burden had claimed to be smiling and entitled to smile, Healey concluded with a deft glance at John of Gaunt's speech in *Richard II*: 'I wish to appeal to hon. Members opposite who raised grave doubts about the wisdom of the Government's policy to demonstrate their feelings in action and to show today that there are still Members of one of our two great political parties in this country who are capable of showing the same integrity as that other Eden.'[55]

In his speech of 3 November Healey drew attention to Hungary. 'On the morning of 30 October, the Soviet Government made an official statement of its readiness to withdraw its troops from Hungary . . . Twenty-four hours later Soviet policy changed. Did anything happen between the first event and the second which influenced that change in Soviet policy?'[56]

Hungary had run so level with Suez that, as Healey relates himself, while driving to a Suez protest meeting at York he heard on his radio the last pitiful Hungarian appeal to the West and 'I had to pull into the side of the road until I had stopped weeping.'[57] To say that Healey felt heavily involved is a

---

* Braine, essentially a kindly man who would become Father of the House, had a temper far outrunning any malice. He would during this crisis also call Tony Benn 'Nasser's little lackey', something which enormously amused Clement Attlee. (Benn, Unpublished Diaries)

mighty understatement. It was a country he knew, which a few years earlier
he had seen taken over by a mixture of finesse, blackmail and violent menace.
He had intervened at a pre-Queen's Speech party meeting on 30 October to
suggest that 'the whole of Gaitskell's theme should be that, in view of the
unity which the West required to meet this terrible event, the Government
should desist from its aggression in Suez.'[58]

The bombing of the Suez Canal had run almost arm in arm with the
return of tanks across the chain bridge over the Danube and the crushing of
hastily armed or not-at-all armed civilians by Russian weaponry.*

Healey would go with Hugh Gaitskell to Heathrow Airport to greet his old
friend, Anna Kethly, who had had so few illusions about the Communist
Party ten years before. She had been released from prison by Imre Nagy,
leader of the Independent Hungarian government and was now in flight from
Hungary where, two years later, Nagy and three members of his government
would be hanged. The possibility that Britain's little war had facilitated the fall
of this curtain deepened the plain rage which Healey felt. A final shot at
Eden would come with an inquiry whether he would be exchanging congratulations with the Soviet Prime Minister, Marshal Bulganin.

Certainly a subsequent course of two-handed hypocrisy brought sterility
and shabbiness East and West to a new and glittering low. The question
became one of what might be done to help Central Europe now that
Hungary was to be governed by Janos Kadar, buttressed by the Soviet loyalist, Ferenc Münnich, without a flicker of legitimacy beyond what shone out
of a tank turret?

Healey began to think anew about what adjustments and concessions
might lighten the burden. At a parliamentary foreign affairs group meeting on
Hungary on 17 December, he 'advocated withdrawal from western Germany
in return for Soviet withdrawal from the satellites'. More views had been
shaken than Healey's. Benn, who reports his new thinking, had been amused
to hear Christopher Mayhew, a harder anti-Sovietist than Healey, talking
about 'encouraging those people in the Kremlin sincerely interested in co-
existence'. As a consequence of Hungary, Healey's own thinking would
develop from unblinking cold warriordom to a more plastic view of defence
and the map of Europe, including a willingness to see parts of it, East and
West taken out of all military pacts.

The *Reynolds News* political correspondent, the left-winger Tom Driberg,
having sung the praises of Gaitskell and the softer-spoken Bevan, concluded
with an historic irony: 'On the back benches two young men have confirmed
their quality – Denis Healey and Anthony Wedgwood Benn.'[59]

---

* Something incidentally claimed by respectable sources to have been waved through
by the US State Department speaking through Tito.[59]

Events which Denis truly cared about had shifted perceptions. As he acknowledges, his speeches heretofore had been factual but not exciting. He always had ideas and information, but neither the speaking flair of a Bevan nor the emotional intensity always present under Gaitskell's brittle reserve. The blazing interventions, the contemptuous slapping down of Eden as a liar represented a newer, rougher, flesh-and-blood Healey. His qualities would always be vulnerable to cerebral excess, but they had been seen and felt. They would be back.

20

RAPACKI, GAITSKELL AND HEALEY

The trajectory of Healey is not quite like that of most politicians. Make a study of most Cabinet ministers during their time as what we used to call 'coming men', and you get a great deal of the party. Which faction did he identify with? Who was his patron? Which moves put him upward and onward for promotion? What he believed, however seriously and earnestly, may be an aspect of that faction's creed, but what he worked on is secondary, something readily compartmentalised as part of the career progression.

Asquith, Lloyd George, Baldwin, Attlee, Wilson and Major were all men who did a variety of jobs on the way up, were heavily involved in party politics, paying attention to factions even when not directly committed to one. Gaitskell, a fairly pure politician as politicians go, was never-endingly preoccupied with a grinding internal struggle. Pure politicians still belong in politics, the scrupulous – Attlee – as well as the impure, if expert – Wilson.

Healey didn't quite conform. Certainly he was unangelic, ambitious, had high abilities and a very good opinion of those abilities. Irishly, he liked a fight and Suez had seen him blazing in one. The Gaitskellites could, more or less, count him as one of theirs. But his life in the 1950s and 1960s is very much more than the record of one side's advancement and the hero's ascent with it. He was, far more than most politicians, a man for subjects. Defence and foreign affairs were cognate matters closely bound. The soldier who had gone to work for Ernie Bevin and then written pamphlets in defence of Western commitments, of NATO, the Korean War and German rearmament, and who had made his maiden speech with a closely argued case against the EDC *as a mechanism*, was preoccupied with policy – how to influence it, and ideas – how to get them accepted.

The contrast with Harold Wilson is oceanic. Wilson as a first-rate statistical economist was also an expert, but the politician dominated, continuously passing agitatedly like a needle and thread through the party robe, eternally mindful of who must be conciliated, what other group should not be fatally antagonised, once fearfully resigning on the heels of the rising faction and, as that group lost impetus, scrambling back to rejoin the group on the escalator until the moment in 1960 when, on an issue of principle – somebody else's principle – he stood for the leadership. The point of Healey is that he was Harold Wilson's antithesis; the fact that Wilson became Prime Minister and Healey did not is merely a pendant observation.

To chronicle Denis Healey is to follow an intellectual development. He knew about, and was interested in, foreign affairs and defence. He made speeches about them, more commonly gave lectures on them, wrote articles for publications like *Encounter*, the New York-based *New Leader* or *Arbeiderbladet* in Oslo; above all, he wrote pamphlets. He was the sort of batsman who spends a lot of time in the nets.

In January 1956 Hugh Gaitskell had assembled an unofficial committee to discuss foreign affairs. It consisted of Alfred Robens, Kenneth Younger, Crossman and Healey. What Healey would write now reflected the advice he was giving the leadership of the Parliamentary Party. Advice took the form of a private paper on the Diplomacy of Liberation written in the summer of that year, contributing one of the Godkin Lectures which Gaitskell would deliver in 1957, and a Fabian pamphlet, *A Neutral Belt in Europe*. What he had to say would ultimately be frustrated, but it was a major intellectual undertaking balancing a strong-nerved stand over Berlin combined with a readiness to create, through Soviet and West German concession, a non-nuclear and effectively neutral territory made up of several nations in Central Europe.

He would make contact with Adam Rapacki, Foreign Minister in the Gomulka/Cyrankiewicz government in Poland, broadly encouraging response to what would be called the Rapacki Plan. This was a call for nuclear disengagement in Central Europe, while ordinary rifle-and-pack forces on the ground were also cut back. Though Healey, as we shall see, was concerned that the central states should have decent means for short-term self-defence. His impression was that Rapacki, who spoke for a government with a fragile autonomy, had an amber light from Moscow but no stronger commitment.[1]

A recurring view in the West was that the whole thing was a Moscow-inspired ploy, no more than propaganda. But Khrushchev's Russia at this time was engaged in major defence cuts. Starting in 1955, before the Hungarian tragedy, Khrushchev had by the end of 1959 brought a total of 5,763,000 men down to 3,623,000, while a further major cut made in January 1960 would reduce the total Soviet force to about 2,420,000.

It was a shift from monstrous numbers to very large ones, but for a propaganda ploy it had a distinct look of economic needs which might make it serious. This was a period of fluidity, when the wishes of Eastern Europeans, not just Hungary and Poland but also East Germany after the workers' rising of 1953, were now known in Bonn and London. Other voices were being heard, notably that of George Kennan whose Reith Lectures would also contemplate Central European disengagement.

If there was a sea change, Healey would dive into it. By a flurry of writing and making use of his improved access to the Labour leadership since Suez, he would surprisingly quickly draw from his leader a modification of Rapacki known as the Gaitskell Plan. He was not the inventor of disengagement, but he was its most effective advocate in Britain. Not yet in the Shadow Cabinet, Healey, writing the latest Fabian pamphlet, was making policy. His thinking, though still hard-line, recognises the changes taking place in Russia beyond a dark glass and begins to wonder aloud what price Russia might ask for the reunification of Germany.

He had watched the nightmare of Stalin lift and the drive to control Eastern Europe diminish as the power blocs congealed and the prospect of sudden aggressive war looked less real. In 1956, he published a lecture given in October of the preceding year at Chatham House to the Royal Institute for International Affairs, of whose council he had been a member since 1948. The title, 'When Shrimps Learn to Whistle',* was typical Healey jauntiness, but this quotation from the new Soviet leader, Khrushchev, spoke a certain relaxing of the anxious line, almost an optimism.

It reflected, in late 1955, the things which had gone right – 'the apology to Yugoslavia, the signing of the Austrian State Treaty, recognition of the Bonn Government and the surrender of the Porkkala base to Finland'. Equally significant is the full Khrushchev quotation spoken to the East German delegation on 17 December 1954: 'We are in favour of a detente, but if anybody thinks that for this reason we shall forget about Marx, Engels and Lenin, he is mistaken. This will happen when shrimps learn to whistle . . . We are for co-existence because there is in the world a capitalist and a socialist way, but we shall always adhere to the building of socialism . . . We don't believe war is necessary to that end. Peaceful competition will be sufficient.'[2]

Healey was still cautious. It was comforting to think that 'Soviet intransigence was due to the vagaries of a mad dictator, whose death in March 1953 had transformed the international scene.' But we had been through hot and cold from the Soviets before – under Stalin! It was in Stalin's lifetime that the term 'co-existence' had been launched by way of a pamphlet with the

---

* He would use it again for a book of late opinion and reminiscence published in 1990.

leader's authority. And a civil line to the West didn't guarantee liberalisation at home. The seeking of friends in the West in the late 1930s had run level with the great purges at home.

As for the argument that the existence of nuclear weapons had necessarily foreclosed Russian adventures and risk-taking, NATO had built up a nuclear capacity to offset Soviet conventional dominance. 'Russia has acquired the power to destroy West European cities with her own atomic weapons. Within ten years she may have the power to hold American cities too against thermonuclear retaliation.' Anyway, America had been able to saturate Russia since 1949. That edge couldn't explain the change of front.

Healey didn't have far to look for a reason. The Paris Treaties, which after all the grief and fuss about the EDC, had finally brought West Germany fully into the organisation, had been ratified on 5 May 1955. 'On 11 May came the new Soviet proposals for disarmament, on 15 May, the signing of the Austrian Treaty, on 26 May, the pilgrimage of Khrushchev and Bulganin to Belgrade, a few days later, Adenauer's invitation to Moscow.' The implication of the last event, three weeks after West Germany's formal full membership of NATO, was that with a fully rearmed Germany, there might be a non-nuclear force on the Eastern front capable of making Russia think.

Ironically, after the near nervous breakdown suffered by her neighbours in accomplishing her military restoration, West Germany would in practice be an uneasy, pacific member of that alliance, guilt-ridden and prudential, her long-haired soldiery doing perfunctory duty and her government always more drawn to compromise in the East than the remote United States or bristling, good-soldierly Britain. But her reputation, a sort of monstrous historical Spenlow to the near pacifist contemporary Jorkins, came in very handy.

So, asked Healey in his brisk Leninish way, given the fact of Soviet amendment, what was to be done? 'No one will deny that we, the West, must meet the improvement in Russian manners at least half way ... A more relaxed attitude in international intercourse need not be incompatible with tenacity in the defence of fundamental principles, though we must avoid the temptation to relax tension at the expense of our security.'[3]

The conversational tone might have improved, the Russians no longer spitting on the floor, but fundamentals remained, fundamentals which to most nice Labour Party people were too unpleasant to think about. 'So far NATO has failed in its main military purpose – to produce a force in Europe which could halt a large-scale attack by the Red Army. The effective deterrent to attack in Europe is not SHAPE, but the fear of nuclear retaliation on Russian cities by the United States air force – the Strategic Air Command – which is not under NATO's orders.'

In pure military terms, said this unlikely Fabian pamphlet, the European component of NATO was a gesture or a sequence of gestures, a sort of war ballet. But there was hope for it. 'The advent of tactical nuclear weapons and the promise of twelve German divisions, has for the first time put NATO in sight of fulfilling its original purpose.' Mindful of defence, he wanted political co-operation and it hadn't been forthcoming. 'The last twelve months [he was speaking in October 1955] have shown an appalling tendency in almost all the major Western countries to sacrifice allied unity for narrow national ends. Britain in Cyprus and France in North Africa have behaved as if the North Atlantic Treaty did not exist, while the United States, dazzled by Soviet flattery of its President, has tended to treat the Four Power meetings as a Russo-American duologue.'

Outside Europe, Healey could in 1955 only be cursory and speculative. But interestingly, although he was the complete hard-liner in Europe, Healey showed himself understanding of, and sympathetic towards, the resolute non-alignment of countries like India. The Hindu gesture of praying hands might be remote from the tactical nuclear weapons and twelve German divisions he considered just the thing on the Elbe, but in the East they might represent wisdom. He had a cynical view of Western concern for poor countries. NATO had grown out of immediate and present fear of Soviet troops moving westward. The Communists would similarly promote the Chinese economy as a model for the rest of Asia, something which would help the case of people in the West who favoured extensive aid to Asia.

There was frequently an uncomprehending brutality about Western thinking. This was the time of the long, immiserating Algerian War. 'Colonialism will remain an insuperable boundary as long as, for example, France thinks it right to kill a hundred Arabs in Morocco for every murdered Frenchman.' Then again, Healey in 1955 would make an appeal for something which still hasn't happened: the granting of a seat on the UN Security Council to India.

But for all this, it was in Europe that the real game was likely to be played out. There was a world theatre of potential conflict. Issues like Formosa (Taiwan in its Portuguese disguise) had been diminished, but Russia would be most mindful of what lay close to Russia – Germany, unified or not, and Central Europe.

Meanwhile nobody should expect a quick, satisfactory deal over Germany just because the Russians were serving tea and biscuits. Basically Russia, set up inside Mitteleuropa as she now was, had cards to play, concessions to make in order to gain something. She had the Soviet Zone of Germany. The West Germans dearly wanted reunification, the West was vulnerable: 'The withdrawal of West Germany from NATO would end all prospect of any land defence for Western Europe.' 'The burglar', Healey remarked, might be offering 'to return a small part of his loot only on condition that he receives something of the same value in exchange'. But Healey was mindful that some deal might be justified. Given atomic stalemate, 'the West cannot hope to improve the *status quo* without making some concessions on its own part'.

Not to bombard the past with hindsight, neither what Healey feared nor what he contemplated doing actually eventualised. Healey knew, admired and tried hard to serve post-war West Germany and was on excellent terms with at least its Social Democratic leaders. Yet always lurking in his mind was the possibility that because she wanted reunification so passionately Bonn might make her own deal, opting out of Western defence and, in return for the lost lands, become neutral on Russia's terms. He was excessively Rapallo-minded.

There was no need. Germany had committed great crimes against Russia and had in return been defeated, raped, German sub-populations, as in the Sudetenland, ethnically cleansed – and one-third occupied. The Soviet system was understood in Karlsruhe and Hamburg precisely because, in all its despotism and dereliction, it operated in Erfurt and Leipzig.

There was something else, not much mentioned. The rulers of West Germany were Rhinelanders, Württemburgers, Bavarians, preponderantly Catholic and frequently Francophile. In 1962 two elderly Conservative Catholics, from Lorraine and the Rhineland respectively, would come together and make a deal so mutually advantageous and so binding that the British have resented it ever since. That was the new Rapallo, and possible. A German deal with Russia never was.

The passing of two years and an invasion between pamphlets would both confirm and modify Healey's Eastern anxieties. His belief that the Old Adam merely slumbered had, in the interlude, been confirmed in spades when tanks driven by reliable Central Asian troops rolled through Budapest, the Arrowcross-Fascist traitors to the Socialist homeland crushed on behalf of the workers by the Kazak soldiers of a friendly Russian government, a regime of abject collaboration installed, dead boys left in the streets, incisors appearing discreetly above the lower Soviet lip, and the spirit of Geneva dissolved into air.

Hungary wasn't the only thing which had happened. From space, Russia was now looking down on the West. Healey was clear in his conclusions. 'Two tremendous things have happened in the last twelve months – the decay of Communism in Europe and the development by the Soviet Union of long-range thermo-nuclear striking power, or to use a word to symbolise each change, Hungary and the Sputnik.'[4]

The notion that Hungary represented a 'decay of Communism' sounds like whistling in the dark after the horrors of November 1956. It was, after all, the *strength* of the Soviet Union which most people chiefly noticed, that and the brutal resolution to kill as many people as was necessary to be in control. But Healey saw the Soviet Union as a theocracy, a clerical state, dependent like the Vatican upon notions of infallibility. Khrushchev's secret speech, better known than most discourses delivered under lights and served by press handouts, had denounced the wrongdoings of Stalin in which as henchman in charge of harrowing the wretched Ukraine, he had been a major complicit performer. But now he 'had made an *ex cathedra* denunciation of papal infallibility'.

The Healeys hadn't been Catholics since grandfather James had left the Church. But he understood the logic of such an act. 'Once you have done that, nothing in the world can re-establish the doctrine.' The secret speech was, as the Marxists like to say, an internal contradiction, an attempt to treat a doctrine pragmatically. That speech 'knocked the linchpin out of international Communism as an instrument of Soviet Communism'.

However, what mattered practically was the new *status quo* in Eastern Europe. Hungary might have gone under, but Poland had managed a compromise. Having found themselves in confrontation with the previous Communist government, Poles had seen a new one under Władysław Gomułka come to power, still under obligation to the Soviets who in turn were mindful of a Polish public which had been on the streets, *not* crushed by tanks, and capable of trouble.

But the way different cards had fallen only emphasised the fragmented quality of Eastern Europe. Healey asked questions. What if 'at some stage, Polish relations with the Soviet Union might become so strained that the Soviet Union might make a threat of force against Poland in order to get her way . . .?' Then again, 'When Tito dies, and he will some day, there might be the possibility of civil war inside Yugoslavia and of outside intervention.' Indeed there might.

All this fragility and future risk existed side by side with the consequences of that first satellite in space, the Russian Sputnik. The Sputnik hadn't changed things so very much in military terms, but it had brought home to the general public what the military and governments knew anyway – 'that it is impossible to unleash thermo-nuclear retaliation against the Soviet Union without suffering crippling destruction in return'.

John Foster Dulles, the dour, lugubrious, long-stay American Secretary of State, had written an article in *Foreign Affairs* arguing for that housemaid's baby of the nuclear age, limited atomic warfare. The problem was that it wasn't anything like limited enough. There had been two military exercises, Healey recalled – the unnervingly named 'Carte Blanche' in Western Germany and the more charming 'Sage Brush' in Louisiana. Both had 'involved the total destruction of life in the areas concerned'. Even undertaken as a theoretical exercise, this was not encouraging. Healey saw it in terms of the Duke of Plaza Toro.

'A strategy which necessarily involves the atomic annihilation of the country which is attacked and which the alliance exists to defend, is not attractive to the countries in the front line, however attractive it may be to those in the rear.' Accordingly, though he could always see a case for a tactical weapons posture, Healey was drawn, like others before him, to the idea of a less terrifying limitation, limited disengagement. It was all the more appealing because, at the very time when increased reliance on conventional weapons made most sense and involved least risk, 'British and American governments have already denied that they are going to reorganise and re-equip their NATO forces so that they can only fight with nuclear weapons. And it is very hard to see how you can have, side by side on the same front, forces which can only fight with nuclear weapons and forces which can only fight without them. It seems to me that Western defence planning has, in consequence, fallen into a state of almost total paralysis.'

'Never believe anything until it has been denied' might have been a good maxim here. In the period immediately after Suez, a Britain both chastened and self-preoccupied was trying to reduce her commitments. In February 1957 she announced drastic cuts in her forces in Germany, reducing the Second Tactical Air Force Division in Europe by half while the Duncan Sandys White Paper in the spring stressed Britain's nuclear autonomy – her own nuclear programme plus V-bombers getting priority over her conventional force contribution to NATO, which would actually be reduced.

The American general in charge of Europe, Supreme Allied Commander Lauris Norstad, produced an unpublished and widely read report insisting upon those twenty-eight divisions for Europe which Healey had cheerfully saluted. This would involve France in recalling the four serving and fighting in Algeria, Britain to reverse her reductions and Germany to provide twelve. The Americans were also anxious to put down permanent bases in Europe, from which its medium-range missiles and their nuclear warheads would deter/threaten the Soviet Union. The general's message perhaps unveiled the threshold of two decades of hostility to nuclear weapons in principle and those based on national territory in particular, all of which would be coupled with the name of the Campaign for Nuclear Disarmament. The names Holy Loch and later Greenham Common would reverberate. Healey would find himself making his case for the diplomatic objective by way of a neutral non-nuclear zone while at the same time arguing inside the Labour Party for acceptance of bases.

Others had talked about neutral zones before. Winston Churchill, ardent in a broad-brush way for peace, had spoken at Aachen and contemplated the simple neutralisation of all Germany. Healey had been too devotedly concerned to get Germany armed and inside NATO to support any such gesture involving 'much greater concessions by the West than by the Soviet Union'.

But if it was not to be a narrow neutralisation, neither should we look for the sweeping continental zone which George Kennan had argued for.

Kennan, otherwise 'Mr X', was the sophisticated and independent State Department official whose mercurial mind could take him from hard line to soft in a spirit of inquisitive experiment.* As Healey remarked, Kennan and Air Chief Marshal Sir John Slessor had 'both at various times in the last few years suggested that the West could afford to accept what in effect the Russians have proposed, that is to say, the complete withdrawal of British and American forces from Western Europe in return for the complete withdrawal of the Red Army from Eastern Europe'. Healey, who had great affection for Slessor, was not convinced. Russia was much too close – 'the British would go back across the Channel, the Americans across the Atlantic, whereas the Russians would simply withdraw 500 miles across land to their own country.'

He then, as it were, put cards on the table.

> I think the most obvious line for constructing a neutral belt would have to include the Federal Republic on the Western side and Eastern Germany, Poland, Czechoslovakia and Hungary on the Soviet side and then in addition, as many other states as you could get in by bargaining. It might be that you could get in Denmark against Romania and so on. But you would have to guarantee some physical foothold on the Continent for the West as a base for military sanctions against a possible military violation of the neutral zone by the Soviet Union.

But what powers – and freedoms – would the countries of the neutral belt enjoy? They couldn't have nuclear weapons. Any state which has such capacities 'has total freedom in its foreign policy. If it wants to blackmail other countries, even large countries – it probably can.' But that said, the countries of the neutral belt positively ought to be well armed conventionally – well enough 'to defend their frontiers against local infractions'; well enough, he added, getting specific, 'to prevent a rapid *fait accompli* by the Russians'.

What Healey was driving at was the removal of a fire-provoking frontier, the separation of eyeball from eyeball by non-partisan, nuclear-free space. He was also trying to put the Soviet Union several hundred miles back from the point at which it could begin the conventional war it found so much more convenient. Hungary had been, for a week of November 1956, a neutral country with forces inadequate to fight any war against the Red Army other than by way of martyrdom.

Conventional arms sufficient to deal with 'an infraction' implied the gaining of time for at least the diplomatic intervention of powers beyond the zone. If, however, the infraction was neither a mistake nor a speculative

---

* He has recently been a sharp critic of the expansion of NATO into Eastern Europe.

nibble, but like the events faked by the Nazis on the Polish border in August 1939, then we faced a continental war with a little longer to react. The protection was not lavish, but assuming – and Healey *was* assuming this – that there was no Soviet will to opportunistic conquest of the kind he had outlined in his debate with John Freeman in 1951, something might be done.

Both sides had lived throughout the Cold War in fear of trains of consequence, of an accident or an irresponsible subordinate act and what might flow from it. For that matter, in 1914 General von Moltke had explained to the Kaiser that war, once set rolling, could not be recalled; the Kaiser's own letter calling off the invasion of Luxembourg was delayed and delivered too late. Across a couple of decades, men contemplated what is parodied in the film *Dr Strangelove*.

Disengagement hung as much upon practicalities as general strategic views. There still had to be Russian–Western alertness to each other *beyond* the zone. Healey argued that radar defences should be set up at opposite ends of that zone – Soviet ones at the western limits, those of NATO at its furthest point east. There was a flaw lurking in the argument, one which Healey acknowledged and tried to meet head-on. A neutral zone without nuclear weapons was a splendid thing given goodwill, since it removed frontier abrasion and allowed accidents to be sorted out.

But what if war were intended? What could well-wishers outside do to prevent that? Healey reflected on limited nuclear weapons, an American theoretical construction which fascinated him. It would involve 'the disincentive of punishment in limited atomic war'.

This is the theory which would be distinguished as a treacle marsh of euphemisms, among which 'disincentive' must rank as gold medallist. Healey did not put the case with much satisfaction. He would acknowledge that 'this is a frightfully difficult problem . . . and I think the Western governments, whatever their diplomatic policies for Europe, are going to spend most of the next five or ten years trying to solve it.'

The political objective was countries currently under occupation which, if the scheme worked, might become, to avoid emotive words like 'free', at any rate not occupied. This was the best you could do for Hungary and it was not utopian to think of such possibilities. The tragedy of Hungary had been preceded, eighteen months earlier, by that bland domestic play with a happy ending, Austria, first (and last) square in the projected zone. Khrushchev's Soviet Union had given up its territories in Lower Austria and the Burgenland and its famous piece of Harry Lime Vienna. For that matter, a heavily threatened Finland, led with considerable skill by Juho Paasikivi and reinforced by a military reputation won in 1939–40 for dying very hard indeed, had kept its neutrality and independence, holding the Soviet Union muttering at arm's length. If these things could be done, then surely something like them might be replicated in Central Europe.

There was, moreover, a contemporary development. What favours, apart from inspiring awe at its ruthlessness, was the Soviet Union doing itself by its dominion east of the Elbe? The satellite regimes, Healey thought, were

not a source of military strength to the Soviet Union, but a source of military danger. During the Hungarian revolution, there was consider-able fraternisation between the Hungarian rebels and the Red Army. As you know, the Russians were unable to organise effective intervention until they had replaced almost the whole of their intervention force by new troops mostly from central Asia . . . There is evidence that since last year the Russians have been systematically starving the satellite armies because they don't regard them as reliable.

The whole Healey view rested upon the notion of a dwindling Soviet interest and advantage in Eastern Europe – 'nothing like as great as it was a few years ago'. Accordingly, he thought there was a chance that the Soviet leadership, for reasons of perfect self-interest, might demote ownership of burdensome territory below economics, providing that distance and mutual guarantees stood between them and a war at their effective frontier.

The Soviet Union and the United States had lived with each other's mili-tary strength since 1945, with mutual nuclear capacity since 1949. They would never make the cool choice of going to war. The existence of subma-rine-borne nuclear missiles which could not be destroyed with assurance, settled the matter. It meant a war without a winner. 'What the big powers are worried about . . . is a war starting without their volition in a dangerous, unstable, peripheral area between them.'

The idea would flourish in one form or another for some time. After all, in early 1959 the Macmillan government engaged in the talks which eventu-ally produced the Partial Test Ban Treaty.

In a major debate on Foreign Affairs not long after (27 April 1959) Healey, summing up from the front bench after Selwyn Lloyd, the Foreign Secretary, and the now dying and gracefully conciliatory Bevan had opened, would applaud 'the British government's proposals for a zone in Central Europe in which arms will be limited and controlled'. He noted that R. A. Butler had said that he did not like using the word 'disengagement'. That was all right. The government could protect their *amour propre*. 'If this is not the first step towards disengagement, what is it?'

He found himself half-defending the government. 'First let us confess that a large part of the foreign press, particularly in Western Europe, has treated the government's proposal simply as an election stunt in Britain.' That might come into it but 'The government were too intelligent to think anything so complex would affect the outcome of such a contest.' Alternatively it was argued, notably in France, that the proposals were a ploy, 'a sort of diplomatic gamesmanship because the British are held to believe that if the Russians will not agree to anything at the forthcoming conference, it is better that they should be made to reject something which is broadly reasonable . . .' Well, that would not be too culpable – better to be reasonable than not. 'But let us treat these proposals as seriously intended to contribute towards a solution by negotiations of the present problems in Central Europe.'

In contrast to his readiness to trade alliance commitments for Western Germany, Healey would not support any deal which wrote off Eastern Germany. What did Khrushchev most want? He wanted 'to get formal sanction of the gains which Russia illegally made at the end of the war without making any concessions in return'. It was widely held that the purpose behind this was to obtain guarantees for the access of British troops and of West Germans to West Berlin.

Healey noted a wobble very much in evidence over Berlin. The three Western zones had been assailed by a Soviet blockade there in 1948 and held only by a drop of food and general supplies – the Berlin airlift. But with the passage of time and a change of Soviet government, a certain readiness to treat West Berlin as valuable exchange was at any rate feared by West Germans. John Kennedy's 'Ich bin ein Berliner' speech would create a huge relief.

To seek such an agreement, wrote Healey, would be 'to give up something of tremendous value for a price which is worth almost nothing at all'. He had perfect confidence that 'at the present time the Soviet Union is not going to risk a shooting war over West Berlin. I think it equally clear that it is not going to try again in the immediate future to impose another blockade on West Berlin.' That city 'could now survive a blockade lasting a year even if there were no airlift' and this build-up 'had taken place with Russia's knowledge and consent'. He slapped down the melancholy right-wing Tory, Viscount Hinchingbroke, who had talked in heavily defeatist terms about Berlin and Germany. He was 'exactly wrong'.

'The West,' Healey said, 'is frightening itself quite unnecessarily if it believes that the consequence of failing to surrender to a Soviet ultimatum in Berlin will be a repetition of the type of trouble we had there ten years ago . . . there is no point in paying a big price to protect West Berlin in the existing situation provided that we are prepared to maintain our present rights and position there by all necessary means.' Healey was an uncomplicated supporter of German reunification. With West Berlin isolated within a Communist state, there was 'no reason to trust any new Soviet agreement on Western access'. 'The threat to West Berlin is in the long run, and the real threat can only be met when Germany is reunited.'

The ending of occupation of Eastern Europe would be a long process and could only move forward after German reunification. 'Hon. Members on this side of the House believe that the establishment of an area of arms control in

Central Europe, however limited its scope, could be a first step . . . They had the support of the German SDP and FDP, the Opposition parties there, and individual Christian Democrats like Eugen Gerstenmaier.'*

It was Labour's policy but it was also very much Healey's policy. He had treated with the Polish Foreign Minister, had persuaded Gaitskell. He could also count, as he told the House, on support for the idea from the likes of Walter Lippmann, ultimate mandarin of the American Liberal press and the major Democratic senators, Humphrey, Fulbright and Mansfield.

But none of this ardent thinking was to be realised. Healey writes ruefully in *The Time of My Life* that a combination of Russian eccentricity and, of all things, Western investment, would turn a genuinely hopeful idea to no account. Khrushchev, in picking a fight over Berlin in 1958, authorising the Berlin Wall in 1961, and taking the sort of risk with the Cuban crisis which rational drawers of blueprints didn't envisage, 'sometimes behaved in ways which appeared to justify the anti-Soviet crusaders'.[5]

The investment point was obvious and ironic. Healey had in a modest way been part of it. The entire grief and crisis of the EDC, which had preoccupied fretting chancelleries across four years, had been about getting Germany into the Western alliance. And the effort involved had worked. As Healey himself had listed events, the Russians had over a few weeks become suddenly reasonable on a number of issues. The thought of now *dis*arming Germany, little as she liked her military role, was just too exhausting.

But such reactions apart, the neutral zone theory had been coolly received in the United States. Healey made three expositions of his thinking by way of articles in the *New Republic*, only to be damned by an old Balliol friend turned influential military analyst, James King. And in a Harvard seminar chaired by Henry Kissinger – later to push conventional weaponry to an aerial bombardment of Cambodia treble that inflicted on Japan in the Second World War – it had only one supporter, 'a pale young Pole called Zbigniew Brzezinski'.[6]

---

* Later Speaker of the Bundestag.

21

A NATO Man and the Marchers

In its early days, unilateralism did not impinge heavily upon Labour politics. That party could react to anything only if its two defining characteristics, union bloc votes and emotional impulses, managed to coincide. And, if anything, Labour politics had been pulling away quite naturally from the leftward pole of attraction. To the extent that old neutralism rested upon an optimistic reading of the Soviet Union, that magnetic field had clearly been weakened.

Hungary had shown the Soviet Union behaving under lights rather worse than people like Ernest Bevin and Denis Healey had always expected. With the correspondent of the *Daily Worker*, Peter Fryer, wiring his resignation from Party and paper with nightmarish copy of the suppression, optimism about Soviet tractability was massively discredited. Meanwhile, among the many consequences of the Suez adventure was a Labour Party united behind a leader whose own emotional outrage at the invasion was exactly that of the busiest party activists. With perfect honesty, Hugh Gaitskell had said things deeply agreeable to his natural opponents. In such an atmosphere, unilateralism was a very abstract notion – it seemed utopian even to utopians.

And to sink prospects further, Aneurin Bevan was changing his mind. Having talked unilateralism before the word was coined, he had painfully turned the tanker of personal conviction round and, at Brighton in 1957, would proclaim a categorical apostasy. As late as spring of the same year, Bevan had said, 'If Britain had any moral stature she could say "We can make the H-bomb, but we are not going to make it, we believe that what the human race needs is leadership in the opposite direction, and we are going to give it."'[1] But he wasn't. Bevan would contribute to the first major conference debate on nuclear disarmament a speech which flashed with all his deft felicity. 'But if you carry this resolution and follow out all its implications and do not run away from it, you will send a British Foreign Secretary, whoever he may be, naked into the conference chamber. Able to preach sermons, of course; he could make good sermons. But action of that sort is not necessarily the way in which you take the menace of the bomb from the world.'[2]

To the evilly disposed, of course, the key term was 'Foreign Secretary'. The blackest insult in the old Labour Party was 'careerist'. Ian Mikardo was very clear: 'I had a long talk with Nye, on the Saturday we had a drink . . . and he'd talked with Sam Watson, the miners' leader, who'd said to him that only through Nye's becoming Foreign Secretary could détente be brought about, and there was no way he could become Foreign Secretary if he stuck to the unilateralist line. And that's what I think caused the change.'

Bevan answered the charge of simple career calculation best in a passage which came shortly after 'naked into the conference chamber' and far less well known. He had suggested that unilateral disarmament should be a fall-back position for a later date if no progress was made on general disarmament. The cry went up from the floor, 'Do it now.' Bevan's response might have been the ultimate answer to the whole self-preoccupied, moral imperialist, intermittently lovable spirit of Labour Conference: '"Do it now" you say. This is the answer I give from the platform. Do it now as a Labour Party Conference? You cannot do it now. It is not in your hands to do it. All you can do is pass a resolution.'

That afternoon the unilateralist motion was put to a card vote and rejected in the Labour Party's customary style of Weimar inflation by 5,836,000 votes to 781,000, yet if notice were wanted, it was there. One might have noticed the words of the mover of the resolution, Vivienne Mendelson from Lambeth Norwood, citing: '. . . one of the most prominent members of our Party said at a Miners' Gala that the time has now come to bring the people on the streets to demonstrate against the bomb. When he said that, he said something that many of us have believed for a long time. He spoke for all of us then.'

One might also have noticed Frank Cousins. The new leader of the Transport and General Workers' Union did not have a mandated bloc of a million votes to cast at this conference, but his union had expressed a view on a similar type of resolution. As for Cousins's own opinions, this clumsily intelligent and highly moral man ended with the words, '. . . in this thing you cannot go too far or too fast for us. We are with you all the way in putting an end to this hideous, terrible nightmare that is facing the community at this time.'

For all the shift among Labour activists from earlier left-wing assumptions, perhaps almost because of that shift, a mood of emotional reaction against nuclear weapons and Britain's part in them was under way. For the people who marched against 'the Bomb', as they still called it, Russia was a sort of irrelevance, the enemy which people like Hugh Gaitskell went on about, from which we were being defended by devices which brought blinding lights and an after-flavour of strontium 90. If they had a view of Soviet Communism, it was that nothing could be so bad or so credibly a threat as to justify using such a murderous defence against it.

What was really taking place was a complete divorce of thought between people close to government, armed with or hampered by detailed and continuous study of the refinements and minutiae of nuclear deterrence as its emphases changed, and people focused upon the explosion itself.

Politics was going popular. The Aldermaston March, begun in April 1958, would balloon into a major political event, an ambling centre of attraction to the young. Something of the thirties' ardour which the young Healey had embraced had come back – clean, bright and innocent – in every sense! It was troubled with its hovering inspiritors – clerics like Mervyn Stockwood and Canon Collins, a very distinguished-looking man with iron-grey hair, an imperious style and variable judgement, Bertrand Russell, and the highly fraught double charge of Peggy Duff and Pat Arrowsmith.

There was also a body of conventional Labour politicians – Michael Foot, happy in his elemental indignation, Frank Allaun, an exasperating but rather touching idealist, and Ian Mikardo from the hardest left, sweating a bonhomie wholly faux.

But the role of left-wing MPs was parasitic, not inspirational. They joined but didn't start. For a brief period, CND had real and natural volition. In 1956, John Osborne, a marcher, had bemoaned in *Look Back in Anger* the want 'of good brave causes to fight for'. Suddenly there was one.

If you were a Labour spokesman, a specialist in defence policy, whose own moral commitments had been made by blazing events a decade earlier, you would see the world quite differently to the people now exalted by discovery of a good, brave cause. Healey probed the differences. Writing in a symposium publication for Princeton University, *NATO and American Security*, in 1959, he observed:

> Thus the fundamental argument in Britain is shifting from purely military issues to the political assumptions on which defence is based ... The division emerges most clearly in the debate about Britain's H-bomb. Some of the former group ... would like Britain to declare now that she would stop producing her own nuclear weapons in return for a sure guarantee that no countries other than the United States and the USSR would produce them in the future. Some of the latter group would like to increase the number and variety of Britain's nuclear weapons considerably before negotiation on the major problems begins in earnest.[3]

For better or worse, Healey was part of the community of military theorists whose central characteristic was an inability to meet terrible possibilities with a cry of 'Oh my God, stop it.' What he did have to say, as at the Paris parliamentary conference in July 1955, was directed to the consequences of nuclear weapons existing and the extent to which the balance of strike power increased instability by making opportunist, limited non-nuclear war thinkable. Congressman Stewart Udall, who described it as 'a penetrating speech' and 'perhaps the most discerning presentation of the entire conference',[4] placed it formally on the record of the US Congress.

Healey recognised in this address what would excite the disarmers without sharing their fraught conclusions. NATO had existed to show the Russians that if they went to war, they could be stopped by all means of war. In the sense of conventional war – soldiers and tanks – they had failed. Accordingly, NATO would have to use other means – put plain in the Healey way – 'to defeat the Soviet Union, should it engage in war, by long-range atomic bombardment of its homeland'. But this was no state to be in. Currently the only country with such means was the United States. As for the British dream of nuclear sovereignty (not yet hardened to its Duncan Sandys conclusion), it was very iffy: 'That too will not be under the control of NATO and I may say that it is a very long way at the moment from existing in Britain.'

And how credible was American involvement anyway? Always reading the latest documents, Healey had encountered a report submitted by General Matthew Ridgway, to the US Secretary of Defense, Charles E. Wilson. General Ridgway thought that with the Soviets acquiring their own capacity to devastate at long range, the US and the USSR might talk to each other as brotherly great powers, might stop calculating who would fire first – might well agree not to fire at all.

Healey quoted the general as envisaging 'a gentleman's agreement or even a formal convention' excluding mutual assault by nuclear weapons. In such circumstances, the Soviet Union's manifest superiority in men and conventional arms would put the European members of NATO into a frightened huddle, facing not so much conquest as the accommodations flowing from that acknowledged superiority. The stakes were so high, argued Healey, that commitments were harder to make believable. And now in 1955, two years ahead of the tentative formation of CND, he quoted Bertrand Russell: 'if the eight scientists who signed the declaration recently published by Lord Russell in London are right, the use of H bombs in a major war might lead to the annihilation of mankind as a whole.' Given such risk, and given the lack of NATO control over its own defence, Healey saw great danger. But he reacted to it with hopes of refining NATO till it *was* effective.

A term of abuse coined by the New Left about this time was 'Natopolitan' – citizen and/or *apparatchik* of NATO. That is what Healey was, and proud of it. Making NATO work was his central concern.

Healey quoted Senator Flanders who had called for sophistication of nuclear targets between the purely military and the civilian. Such an emphasis implied that uncertain thing, tactical nuclear war. And many people, given the atrocity of the most refined and tactful of nuclear strikes, have maintained a sullen disbelief in such a distinction. But it was the way Healey's mind was going. He was always willing to grit his teeth on nasty hypotheses, contemplating 'a rapid blitzkrieg, to make a lightning gain before the other side could make up its mind whether or not to invoke the extreme sanction'.

In other words, a new Bismarck would slip in to make limited gains while his opponents dithered between loss of face and militarised nuclear fission. Very well, said Healey, if this was going to be the pattern, the public had to be told that peace had a price. Organisationally, and in terms of cost and importance, NATO had to expand.

The objective was 'peace – not under the shadow of the H-bomb nor as an alternative to total annihilation, but a peace whose price is a reasonable one to pay – they are going to have to build up still further the unity and the strength which it has been the main purpose of NATO to provide.'

It was going to be very difficult to persuade the public of their need for an effective NATO 'so long as the Russians are smiling instead of scowling'. But his logic required both stronger conventional forces and, bluntly, a NATO credibly nuclear itself through the credible nuclear means of one or two European members.

To the unilateralists, and particularly to the left wing of unilateralism, these were corporate arguments in favour of what was good for the organisation. The world needed NATO the way the world needed Quaker Oats, consequently a strategy should be followed which kept up market share in difficult conditions. Healey would have argued that a great conflict had to be handled with nerve and consistency. The precondition of peace was credible deterrence and a clear understanding that it would not be flinched from. The First and Second World Wars had arisen in their absence.

BLUE STREAK AND LABOUR POLITICS

Healey was the product of all his experiences – the Second World War, the Soviet takeovers in Eastern Europe, his devoted service with Ernest Bevin, effectively the creator of NATO, and the outbreak, after Acheson's military disclaimer, of the Korean War. He would be ready in 1956–8 to talk with the Polish Foreign Minister, and convince his own leader that limited disengagement was worth serious undertakings, an actual set of formal proposals, the Gaitskell Plan. But he cherished NATO, saw it as the prop of peace and security, missing in 1937. He knew that the collective security which Sandy Lindsay had invoked against Quintin Hogg in the Oxford by-election, amounted to words and invocation without arms and organisation. NATO was the heir of collective security. It had worked, and if it now faced being stymied after Soviet achievement of nuclear parity, with a lesser form of war becoming a practical option, he would stand up and advocate more German divisions and whatever other undertakings would keep NATO credible in her European theatre. His belief, stated at Paris, 'that NATO should remain a united political organisation covering the frontier of the Soviet empire', reflected the lessons of his life and stood at the core of the man.

Between his learned vacations, Healey was part of Labour Party politics and the Labour Party was inundated by a rising tide of anti-bomb feeling, historically natural to it, the equivalent of the mood which had sped along the Peace Pledge Union in the 1930s and had briefly tied the party to a near-pacifist line until the theology of 'collective security' had taken it from a greater to a lesser form of unrealism.

Aneurin Bevan's apostasy had created the oddest vacuum. CND itself was made up of disparate sorts of people, some of them non-political, even anti-political. On 2 November 1957 J. B. Priestley's article called 'Britain and the

Nuclear Bombs', an oddly anachronistic title when the rocket-delivered warhead was so much the settled thing, appeared in the *New Statesman*. The left-wing weekly was close to its zenith in its circulation and influence. The response from its readership is described as 'huge',[1] and the paper's editor, Kingsley Martin, who ironically was slow to become a convert to the full disarmament cause, responded by calling a private meeting in his flat.

The company, in addition to Priestley and his wife, Jacquetta Hawkes, included George Kennan, Patrick Blackett and Denis Healey. It was proposed that a campaign should be launched, 'an all-out disarmament campaign'.[2] This was generally approved but one of those present 'told the company that they were all being foolishly utopian – this produced rather a hostile atmosphere'.[3] The relationship between CND and Denis Healey had begun as it would continue.

CND would follow its own rising course outside parliament. But the purely political group, its Moses now on good terms with the Egyptians, was at once shattered and alienated. And the movement had failed to make a breakthrough among trade union delegates; the conference of 1958 represented very little advance on that of 1957. Two motions, a pure unilateralist affair from the Fire Brigades' Union, the other condemning missile bases 'under any circumstances', were heavily defeated, the prospect of a general election helping no end.

But Labour orthodoxy depended on its Home Fleet, trade union bloc votes. And in 1959, in the words of Admiral Beattie at Jutland, there was 'something wrong with our bloody ships today'. The General and Municipal Workers', most reliable of right-wing unions under the machine-political hand of Jack Cooper, suddenly defied sun and stars by going for an anti-nuclear resolution, the motion being put by a devout Catholic, Len McNamee, expressing unaffected horror at the risks to human life.[4] The balance at Conference in 1959 left the leadership intact, but warned, its majority on the key resolution down to substantially less than 2:1.

But the Labour Party had had other things on its mind in 1959. The lead over the Conservatives which had so glittered after Suez, had diminished, was diminishing and would disappear altogether. Harold Macmillan as Prime Minister had the knack of simulating allrightness, intimating an untroubled continuity which only wild meddlers would wish to disturb. The style was in flagrant contrast with the juddering neurosis of the Macmillan diaries and their talk of eventual Communist triumph and 'things lasting for my lifetime'. But for the purposes of politics, simulation always does very well. And on 9 October 1959, the Conservatives were not only re-elected, but advanced to a parliamentary majority of 100.

On the left this created a mood of lethal introspection. Then, by way of premature reform, Gaitskell, against all conventional advice, which happened to be entirely right, launched a campaign of what the left instantly called 'revisionism'.* It involved a call for the removal of Clause Four with its sweeping commitment to public ownership of everything, something rejected even by the right-wing unions. The commitment was not believed in. But the most realistic union general secretaries were sentimentally attached to a nonsense they had long ignored and would again ignore.

At the Blackpool Conference of 1959, which would also stage preliminary exchanges of fire over unilateral disarmament, Clause Four was resoundingly upheld. For this was a conference rich in that peculiar quality of hectoring complacency familiar to regular visitors. Renée Short's outburst on women was particularly instructive about the sort of thing the undeserving public might quite reasonably have declined to vote for. 'Women in this country, I am sorry to have to say, are by and large, except in the Labour Party, politically illiterate. Our job is to get to these women and to re-educate them in the political, economic and above all, the moral base of our socialism.'[5]

The response of Denis Healey to the whole affair was very close to that of Tony Crosland, something to be echoed in the coming debates on the Common Market. Coolness allied to loyalty sums it up. 'Why draw anyone's attention to this shibboleth?' Healey, recognising the need to shift Labour, was as direct as usual and spoke of a paradox: 'we had the most enthusiastic band of workers, the most enthusiastic audiences we have had in any campaign in any election since 1945, and all over the country, candidates and party workers were convinced that on polling day we were going to do a lot better than we did. The tragic fact is that when the votes were counted, we actually did worse than in 1955 . . .'[6]

What had to be faced was that 'there is a big and growing gap between the active worker in our party and the average voter, a gap which did not exist in 1945, but which has been steadily growing ever since.' Healey had a particularly brutal truth to speak. 'We who are here at this conference do not represent the ordinary voter. Let us face it, we represent the average party worker . . .'[7]

The Dr Sacheverell of that Church in Danger, its chief protector from the heretical dragon of trying to please the voter, had been Michael Foot, darling of the activists. Foot had been cheered to the roof for his contribution, but he was yet an ejected MP of 1955 who had failed to return to his former Devonport seat in 1959. Healey could not resist a quick kick on the knee. 'Hugh Gaitskell was absolutely right yesterday when he said that what gets cheers at this conference does not necessarily get votes at elections. If it did, we would have won Devonport.'[8]

'There are,' he concluded, 'far too many people who have spoken from the

* This alluded to the revision of Marx undertaken in 1899 by the German Social Democrat, Eduard Bernstein.

rostrum in these last two days who think it is all right to do without votes.'
Gaitskell, having challenged the rubric and lost, and finding himself charged
with defacing altars, was badly placed for the coming struggle over nuclear
weapons. The next year would prove a climacteric. Part of the argument,
especially as Gaitskell and the Macmillan government saw things, stemmed
not just from membership of a nuclear-based alliance and the acceptance of
predominant American nuclear protection. It involved the 'independent
British nuclear deterrent'. The British rationale had rested upon a rocket
delivery system called Blue Streak. It was to deliver, or at any rate credibly
threaten to deliver, a nuclear warhead decently and entirely British. It was to
this end that the momentous Duncan Sandys White Paper of 1957 had
dropped conscription and committed our best efforts to nuclear defence, in
an alliance but home devised and controlled.*

Unhappily, for all sorts of reasons to do with the dubious builders' estimates put together by armed forces either squabbling or colluding, the cost
of sustaining that deterrent had got out of hand. Putting to rights the old
Spanish practices of the forces would be the first concern of Defence
Secretary Healey five years later. But what mattered in 1960 was that the
nuclear sovereignty of Britain – by our weapon controlled by us – following
a quietly delivered parliamentary message by the Minister of Defence, Harold
Watkinson, had become impossible. Blue Streak was cancelled.

Healey had hinted at doubts in Paris five years earlier. Gaitskell had
accepted Duncan Sandys's thinking. Healey's judgement of the crucial White
Paper was that it was brave, and faced many realities, but concentrated
upon nuclear capacity at the expense of conventional soldiery, the men and
tanks useful in small conflicts and holding operations. At the Paris parliamentary conference he had been thinking aloud in an entirely different way,
towards nuclear stalemate and a specifically NATO nuclear capacity which,
with wider conventional competence, should cope with that stalemate.

Sandys had been entirely modern (though he had had to cook the books to
prove that even the diminished volunteer army he now relied on was up to
numbers). The dangerous implications of his White Paper were of war
exploding sooner, with nuclear Britain a priority for taking out by an enemy
in any of those conflicts which her lack of military small change prevented
her delaying. It also gave expression, in the brute person of Randolph
Churchill, to a renewed British truculence. Healey's 1960 Fabian pamphlet
The Race Against the H-bomb, quotes Randolph addressing the American
Chamber of Commerce (London) in November 1957 when Blue Streak was
bright in prospect, in words which make their own epitaph: 'Britain can
knock down twelve cities in the region of Stalingrad and Moscow from

---

* See page 234, et seq.

bases in Britain and another dozen in the Crimea from bases in Cyprus. We did not have that power at the time of Suez. We are a major power again.'[9]

Grown-up opinion accepting an independent deterrent for a complex of better reasons light years from the toxic Randolph, nevertheless found that to defend the full Sandys package was to stand on marshland and poisonous marsh at that Healey, on the record as a sceptic, would write on the subject and on the containment of nuclear weapons in that Fabian pamphlet, parts of which had already appeared in the then liberal pages of *Commentary* (New York) in January.

The central concern was, 'Fear that the American nuclear deterrent may soon lose its validity for the alliance is the main rational ground why European countries, led by Britain and France, are beginning to produce strategic atomic weapons for themselves – though the prestige argument is no less important.' Britain hoped to replace her own 'stand-off bomb' with Blue Streak. It was to be fixed-base rather than carried by submarine because British military political opinion believed 'that by the time air warfare is carried on wholly by missiles, Russia may have an anti-missile missile – so Britain must have a missile large enough to carry not only a megaton bomb but also equipment for decoying anti-missile missiles. In other words the Blue Streak will be an anti-anti-missile missile! Even so, the 1960 defence White Paper suggests that it will be obsolete before it is operational.' And so it proved, with Harold Watkinson's announcement bringing Blue Streak to an end in the very year, 1960.

The end of the independent British deterrent meant that all the anxieties about American guarantees still stood for people trying to grapple with the strategic consequences, but also that the Labour leadership was left defending something very unpopular which wasn't there any longer. Gaitskell, who had made the strategic case for the independent deterrent early in March in the Commons, was particularly vulnerable to the scorn of the *New Statesman*. 'Mr Gaitskell,' wrote Kingsley Martin, 'is the first [leader] I have known who seems positively contemptuous of those on whose support his chance of power depends. In this of all weeks he has restated arguments rejected by the government, the military, even the experts of the Pentagon, that Britain should have its own private nuclear deterrent.'

A debate inside the Labour Party about nuclear weapons could not have taken place without politics, the politics of personality – who was up and who down, the eternal Humpty Dumpty doctrine of 'Who is to be master?'. Gaitskell, with an election lost and the false move made against Clause Four, was personally and implacably devoted to nuclear defence. His customary enemies on the left sensed more issues at stake than the narrowly humanitarian ones. With the votes put together to carry a unilateral motion, Tony Benn, then a cautious figure, observed just ahead of the 1960 Conference in Scarborough, 'The left is determined to crush Gaitskell and the right is determined to crush the left on the defence issue.'[10] James Callaghan, contemplating the compromise formula being canvassed, observed: 'I'll join the bandwagon after the Conference.'

Benn also noted Harold Wilson who was 'busy composing his speech for Sunday night, and frankly, all he's interested in is turning the situation to his own advantage. He thinks Gaitskell can be dislodged. My opinion of him drops the more I see of him.'[11] Instructively, Wilson could have been found five months earlier in avid conversation with Richard Crossman. 'A few weeks ago they were saying they would get rid of Gaitskell if there was an alternative. Now they are saying they must get rid of him, whoever takes his place. He can't last long now.'[12]

'A Student of Politics' (James Margach) in the *Sunday Times*, looking for a successor, thought adventurously ahead to James Callaghan.

Blue Streak, despite costs estimated at between £65 and £100 million in the values of the late 1950s, which after being projected in much lower terms, had been recurringly and embarrassingly reversed upwards, had been the central text. Upon its success sat the Duncan Sandys policy of minimising conventional defence and ending conscription. Gaitskell, whom Eden had described as '99.5 per cent sound' on defence, had publicly supported the principle of the independent deterrent, something which made his wider position on nuclear weapons particularly vulnerable.

The mounting mood of unilateralism bit most easily into the costly improbablism of national nuclear weapons. Actually Gaitskell privately, as Healey has insisted,[13] had 'misgivings . . . on financial and technical grounds' over an independent deterrent,[14] and favoured a NATO vehicle. He was, however, unwilling actually to attack the principle and became identified, especially on the left, with the whole independent hog.

Gaitskell underwent something of a crisis at this time. Patrick Gordon Walker, than whom nobody was more reliably hard-line on defence, wrote on 12 May, 'he is becoming distrustful and angry with his best friends and wants to take up absolute and categorical positions that will alienate all but a handful.' He goes on to describe a meeting with Gaitskell and Crosland at Roy Jenkins's flat. 'Subject of discussion was the upsurge of pacifism in the Trade Unions. G said that it was certain that a pacifist resolution would be carried at Conference. The alternatives would then be: (a) to carry the Parliamentary party into defiance of the Conference; (b) to go into opposition in the party on this issue – with perhaps 100 supporters – and fight back from the back benches . . .'[15]

Gaitskell was also vexed with George Brown – 'paying too much attention to winning Conference'.[16] Brown believed in the possibility of tempering the stand of the honest, non-conspiring Frank Cousins. Gordon Walker argued for what would actually happen – everyone in the leadership camp standing for the Shadow Cabinet after announcing disagreement with the resolution –

'a question not of a dramatic defiance of Conference, but of a long fight to get things right again . . . No one could survive who set himself against the whole fabric and structure of the party.'[17]

By contrast, Gaitskell had wanted 'to say specifically that we should retain and use nuclear weapons as loyal members of the NATO alliance'. Gordon Walker regarded such reckless candour as 'madness' and was supported by Crosland who challenged the idea of a hundred-man split in parliament. '"Perhaps 10," said G who became very angry and rounded on the other 2 sharply and implied I was a fudger of principle.'[18] Gordon Walker's melancholy reaction to the whole conversation was: 'I began to fear that G has the seeds of self-destruction in him – he almost wants to destroy himself. I said at one point that he had a death-wish.'[19]

If so, it was a death-wish which would pass when the subject applied himself to the practical business of framing a case. And the skills of Healey as a draftsman would be indispensable to reconciling the substance of British involvement in nuclear defence with avoidance of absolute and categorical statements.[20]

THE DANGEROUS ROAD
TO SCARBOROUGH

Even before the cancellation of Blue Streak Healey had written in the *Political Quarterly* about the need for interdependence, an integrated NATO, to offset what had become the French impetus towards disintegration. The trouble was that the really powerful member of the alliance lived the furthest distance from the scene of any imaginable action. Only if in some way she were part of a sovereign state would her involvement really be believed and that, equally, simply wasn't on. Yet, said Healey, 'the Western alliance had so little physical underpinning that many Europeans – and Americans – assume that if the Americans moved (back) a hundred miles within Europe, they will not stop until they reach the United States and they will never return.'

Healey's conclusion is oblique, a hint of surrendered status. 'It was Britain's bid for nuclear independence which did more than anything else to separate her from France and Germany in 1957. A substantial British move towards interdependence would find an immediate response in Germany at least.' Modified and driven by the two volcanic eruptions of 1960, it was the language and thinking which Denis Healey would soon provide for a Labour leadership obliged to adapt its thinking, yet not retreat; to be effectively part of Western nuclear defence without, as it were, giving offence.

It would be a labyrinth with monsters, but there would be a thread of sorts. From February of 1960, rumours had been circulating that Blue Streak might be terminated. When, therefore, on 13 April 1960 Watkinson finally announced cancellation, Labour, officially associated with that policy, were not placed for scoring points and indeed had to concentrate on their own crisis. The discontent had first found expression through a unilateralist motion with 24 backers in the Commons early in the year, followed in early March by the abstention of 43 Labour Members against the official Labour motion. Then in April, by way of embarrassing irony, the Liberal Party, now tentatively reviving under the sprightly Jo Grimond, had called 'for the abandonment, not only of Blue Streak but the whole independent British deterrent'.[1]

The pressure on Gaitskell was intense. He, and Healey with him, was seen as clinging obdurately to a national nuclear commitment. The very concept of 'multilateralism', a striving for mutual scaling down of nuclear defences by way of negotiation, a word which would become the password and salutation of the Gaitskell camp from 1960 onwards, was not exactly honoured at this time. Philip Noel-Baker, who annoyed Healey with his high and piping tone but who was earnestly and truly a believer in exactly such an approach, observed to the economist James Meade, 'I have never been able to make Hugh Gaitskell take a real interest in disarmament. Whenever I say to him that the only way out with the unilateralists is by running multilateral disarmament very hard, he always says "yes" and then has a perfunctory half sentence or half paragraph in the next speech. But when I have tried to urge debates in the House in which he and Healey should take part, he always says "what is there to say?"'[2]

Gaitskell was preoccupied with his enemies. The least cynical of politicians, he was determined on a hard, clear line against the unilateralists and as hard and clear a line against the Soviet Union. Policy was going to refine itself, and Healey had worked with Patrick Blackett and others to shape it. In fact, many Conservatives were unhappy with the full consequences of the Sandys doctrine. His predecessor, Antony Head, Nigel Birch and Aubrey Jones were all dubious in varying degrees about the independent line and Jones said so clearly in the Commons.

In fact, Labour's defence policy would be shifted – unilaterally one might say – by George Brown who, in Gaitskell's absence (officially in Israel, later and unofficially, in Jamaica with his mistress, Ann Fleming), made a brave, clever speech, described by an admiring *New Statesman* as 'devastating', which came fully to terms with the collapse of Blue Streak.

'Even I,' said George, acknowledging his own belligerent reputation, 'cannot be expected to go in for a policy which has no chance of ever being successful.'[3] Gaitskell was privately furious at the intrusion. But it worked, and the leadership's considered response was to redraft its thinking on the independent deterrent and, in the eternal way of politics, to 'clarify its position'. This was done in a document published on 1 July 1960.

It said in terms, 'If our strategy is to be based on military, not on prestige considerations, we must accept the truth that a country of our size cannot remain in any real sense of the word an "independent nuclear power". We believe that in future our British contribution to the Western armoury will be in conventional terms, leaving to the Americans the provision of the Western strategic deterrent.' The document, apart from the usual versicles and responses about strengthening the UN, was specific. It rejected a European deterrent – because it would widen nuclear involvement and – bobbing to good old prejudicial reasons – because West Germany would be the chief player. (In fact, such was the low level of German enthusiasm for nuclear or other military activity that this was an option never likely to have been taken up.)

Then again, in retroactive response to Sandys, it spoke of an enhanced conventional role. And there was at least one large piece of *naïveté* or rhetoric: 'We must also seek to obtain from the United States an undertaking that they will not use their strategic deterrent without the agreement of NATO.' There was also a paragraph, Philip Noel-Baker's sort of paragraph, on multilateralism, though the word wasn't used. Headed 'Disarmament, The Only Real Security', the paper asserted, 'Our aim must be general and controlled disarmament to levels which make war impossible.'

Healey was one of the drafters and the Gordon Walker diaries offer a flash of Healey, the Machiavellian. The key phrase is 'We believe that in future our contribution to the Western armoury will be in conventional terms.' It took that form because Healey argued for it. Barbara Castle, who would have liked to be rid of all American bases, had called for the wording to be 'We should' or 'We must'. Healey 'drew a distinction between a deterrent and a contribution: "will" will be proved wrong because the government will buy Skybolt. You can make a "contribution" without having a deterrent that is independent. We stuck to "will" on the ground that George B could not be expected to say that his previous policy was wrong, but only that facts led to a new conclusion.'[4]

In fact Healey was thinking ahead. 'He rang me this morning,' continues Gordon Walker, 'to explain that his real reason was to leave loopholes for when we are in office. "Should" would tie us to a policy. "Will" might well be proved wrong: then we could say that our guess about developments had been erroneous. We must keep our hands free to use Polaris.'[5]

In fact, most of Labour's problems about the deterrent, things which had kept Healey agonising in Paris, would be solved when Macmillan extracted from President Kennedy the submarine-borne Polaris system, a contribution to defence leased from America, making NATO credible at arm's length from America. Anyone moralising at Healey's deviousness is missing the point. On the eve of the Scarborough Conference Labour fully intended to maintain nuclear defence. While relinquishing unrealistic independent status, it did not think us believably defended by tanks. Healey's grasp of the auxiliary verb and its consequences kept all doors open.

Gaitskell and the people he trusted were faced with a real strategic change. The passing of Blue Streak represented a chapter ended, while a here-and-now, vividly important political crisis was blowing up inside their own party due to assemble at Scarborough in October where votes were being raked in to establish unilateralist victory at that pleasant resort. The strategic question would not budge from what Healey, with his knowledge of the running symposium of strategic thinking, had set out. In *The Race Against the H-Bomb* he had said that the decline of America's absolute guarantee after the Sputnik would set other countries looking for alternatives and increasing risks. High among those risks would be the instability caused by countries, belonging to NATO but no longer trusting the key US commitment, making their own arrangements.[6]

France, with its intense, truculent nationalism and deep aversion under General de Gaulle to the United States, was a likely leader. The essential thing for Healey, and beyond him Gaitskell, was to keep NATO together during a period of mounting anxiety and panic, of which CND, if you stopped and looked at it, was simply a component. But against that, NATO as an organisation was all over the shop. Franz Josef Strauss, the repellent Bavarian running defence in West Germany, was talking blackmail – 'when West Germany had her own atomic weapons she would be able to compel both America and Russia to take the problem of German reunification more seriously.'

But given such difficulties, the best objective being argued for by persons as disparate as Field Marshal Lord Montgomery and a busy theoretician of foreign affairs, Dr Henry Kissinger, was partial settlement, an agreement on arms limitation.

The limiting adjective was important and would emerge as reality in due course as the Partial Test Ban Treaty. Healey added that 'such an agreement with Russia would depend in part on increasing mutual confidence between the NATO allies for any limitation affecting European countries but not the Soviet Union itself, would leave the former more dependent on the United States and Britain.' To read Healey on such matters at this time is to realise the gulf between two casts of mind. The people who talked risk strategy and wondered what degree of diminished assurance from American counter-force constituted a Soviet opportunity to take a fearful risk, then balanced the plugging of such holes with national nuclear weapons against the creation of zones of disengagement, lived apart from those who hated nuclear weapons and wanted us to have nothing to do with them. The division over unilateralism was a chasm across which protagonists could only shout inaudibly.

Healey had one element of comfort for the sort of people likely to react with horror to his melancholy conclusions: the state of mind of the Soviet Union. Yes, she had Sputnik and *a fortiori* the ability to hit Washington, but just how ready were the Russians for dangerous adventures? He reverted to arguments he had used in 1951 against John Freeman.

Defending Korea must have been irrational in Russian eyes; the fact that response could be irrational had taught the Soviet Union great caution. There had been fear when Britain and America intervened in the Lebanon in 1958: 'they feared Russia might accept the challenge to fight a limited war with the West in an area where she had overwhelming superiority. But the Russians did not even dare to threaten limited war. They stuck to vague threats which no one outside the Arab world was supposed to take seriously.' As for the November 1958 crisis over Berlin, 'Experts in London and Washington . . . feared that Russia had issued her ultimatum on Berlin because she wanted an opportunity to exploit her local military superiority to inflict a demonstrative defeat on NATO. But when Western fortitude did not collapse at the first blow of Khrushchev's trumpet, Russia showed no sign of making a military challenge – instead she chose military retreat.'

Healey was pushing, for all his bleak tone, towards a sort of commonsense optimism. Its essence lay in the sentence: 'The West has always overestimated Soviet readiness to use war as an instrument of policy.' All the more reason for doing nothing by way of upsetting the boat to dissuade the Soviet Union from such an irenic outlook. For 'it was tragic that when the likelihood of attack by Russia in Europe is less than at any time since the war, European countries should be threatening the stability of the situation by demanding a degree of security which is impossible through armaments alone in the atomic age. For the problem is essentially a political, not a military one.'

But by 1960, in Britain, politics had reared its ugly head and in the name of peace there was to be political war. The atmosphere was a combination of career calculation, factionalism and genuine perplexity, with a malignant theme running vividly through it to farcical effect.

Denis and Edna Healey would spend the summer holiday of 1960 with Hugh and Dora Gaitskell, as families, an interesting closeness. Returning in September, with the Scarborough Conference looming, he was quizzed by Richard Crossman. Crossman was at first agreeably surprised. The two of them agreed, he says, 'that our aim must be not only to get a majority lined up for our document but to defeat the unilateralists on a motion explicitly demanding withdrawal from NATO'.[7]

'Denis then added,' says Crossman, 'If we can do these two things, it seems to me quite unimportant what happens to the T&G resolution.' Crossman, developing complicated purposes of his own, expressed delight. 'Oh, that's wonderful, because as long as you don't mind, you won't object to what those of us who think it important do, in order to deal with it.' 'Ah now,' Denis said, 'you're being too quick for me.'[8]

Crossman had been trying for some time to persuade the leadership to accept the T&G resolution and said as much to Healey. This resolution had been kept more vague and less conclusively unilateralist than Cousins would have wished, something which Healey acknowledged. But this did not make him a buyer in Crossman's market. 'In a different situation,' he said, 'it would be perfectly harmless, but of course we have to see it in conjunction with Cousins's known views and speeches.'[9]

Crossman, the son of a judge and given to Oxonian refinements, replied that Conference and the NEC were bound solely by the text of resolutions. Healey replied that 'if the T&G would vote for our resolution, we could vote for their resolution.' Crossman, whose skills did not include an ear for irony, said, 'So, are you willing to huckster?' and was told, 'There's no chance of it coming off.'

Crossman, excitedly full of the possibilities of a compromise – 'we dined with the Benns and Shores, all enthusiastic for the idea' – tried to sell his idea to the International Subcommittee and was brought bumpingly down to hit procedural resistance from Gaitskell and the chairman, Sam Watson, before finding wider reaction tepid. 'I got a little support from Jennie [Lee] and very much less than I had expected from Barbara [Castle]. David Ennals* sat numb and embarrassed.' The rows and leaking which followed would be part of a succession of rows and leakings, with both sides blaming each other, which would mark the whole episode.

It was hardly surprising. Crossman was engaged, for motives that seemed good to him, in the pre-emption of conflict by embracing a T&G motion which, if it was not unalloyed unilateralism, came near enough for all the purposes of the Tory press and which, further, was the offering of Frank Cousins, the most powerful trade unionist in the country, whose personal belief in unilateralism was at that moment the central fact of Labour Party politics. Crossman wanted a fudge, wanted to treat an issue involving the deepest convictions all round as only the next hurdle of the Conference, wanted a form of words less than unilateralist but acceptable to unilateralists, which the leadership could then quote to the electorate as not unilateralist. It was illustrative of everything about Crossman that Healey meant by 'no judgement' and Attlee by 'character'.

On location in Scarborough, Tony Benn, a good if earnestly engaged witness to all this, recalls the NEC meeting at the conference hotel being disturbed. 'As we met, the CND parade led by Horner,† Mikardo, Canon Collins and others, tramped by the hotel shouting "Ban the Bomb, Gaitskell must go!" It almost drowned our proceedings and induced an element of mob violence into our affairs.'[10]

It was the sort of atmosphere in which Healey the *causeur* was stood down for Healey grasping a bottle. His short floor speech to Conference was in contrast to the impassioned, exalted one which would that day register Hugh Gaitskell in minds which had had little notion of him. It was a matter of high road and low road. Gaitskell, at the end of the exhausting debate climaxing that day after the menacing acceleration of months, spoke of 'Saving

---

* International Officer.
† John Horner, leader of the Fire Brigades' Union.

the party we love' and asked 'What sort of people do you think we are?' Tony Benn, sometimes wrong-headed, always fair-minded, thought it 'magnificent' but also thought that Gaitskell threw everything away with his references to 'pacifists, neutralists and fellow-travellers'.

Healey, like many threatening speakers, began quite jovially. The abrasive cockney trade unionist, Ted Hill of the Boilermakers', had spoken in favour of unilateralism, had he? 'I rather like the picture of him walking into negotiations with the employers armed with nothing but the purity of his intentions!' This humorously lulled even the most ardent opponents for the onslaught which followed – plain, hard and direct, also *ad hominem*. Frank Cousins, who would be delivering both homily and votes on the unilateralist side, had recently lost an industrial dispute – not a common event in the fifties and sixties – by way of the London bus strike, foiled by Iain Macleod, Minister of Labour, and Sir John Eliot, who in so far as anybody did, ran London Transport. 'Is there anybody in the hall who thinks that it is so much easier to deal with Mr Khrushchev than with the Chairman of the London Transport Executive?' Then, invoking a saintly shuffling figure from Labour's legendary pacific past, he observed, 'The plain fact, you know, is that Mr Khrushchev is not the George Lansbury type. You remember at the press conference he held after the Summit collapse in Paris he boasted that when he was a boy, he used to kill cats by swinging them round by the tail and breaking their heads open against a wall ... The plain fact is that Khrushchev is probably the best Russian Prime Minister we have, but he is not a man who is going to respond to a lead for unilateral disarmament.'

The brutal metaphor, based on brutal and instructive fact, embodied the whole distinction between Healey and the disarmers. They were horrified by nuclear war, as well as they might be, and effectively wished into the space created by that wish a Soviet Union willing to respond to a moral lead. Healey's mind-set acknowledged no moral leads, only weakness and strength. Everything starkly set out in his 1951 debate with John Freeman – show weakness and they will exploit it – is present in that short, hard-knuckle paragraph. And he continued in precisely that vein. Khrushchev had talked to Gaitskell, Bevan and Healey in Moscow in 1959. They asked him how he would respond to such a lead in the way of unilateral disarmament, 'and he replied, "We do not want our grandchildren to call us fools. Do you want your grandchildren to call you fools?"'[11]

Labour conferences, to anyone who knows them, have their own culture. They are warm and sympathetic, and are regularly kept happy and warm by sympathetic – and consequently fuzzy – talk. The George Lansbury alluded to, did it from the heart. Harold Wilson had learned how to do it from the head. Healey was in violent contradiction to the whole style, like a parent confiscating sweets which will be bad for the child's teeth. His approach was substantially different from that of Hugh Gaitskell, then and generally, an odd mixture of cerebral and intellectually satisfying maker of a rational case and man as emotionally engaged as the most ardent unilateralist in the hall. Healey, though rough, was spelling out what he saw as plain sense, thick-headedly rejected by emotion and prejudice. He reserved his own emotions – and a shrewd moral blow at the left – for what he would say about Germany.

The German Social Democrats were 100 per cent in agreement with Gaitskell's new line, 'and I did not like the way, when it was mentioned yesterday by a comrade on this rostrum, there was a sneer ran round the hall. The man responsible for defence in the German Social Democratic Party is sitting on this platform now – Fritz Erler. He spent seven years in Hitler's concentration camps. When I see the man in this hall who has made the same sacrifice to defend freedom and socialism, I will be prepared to listen to his sneers, but I shall not heed them.'

Press coverage right and left had been full of speculation about what would happen when Gaitskell was defeated, as he must be. Healey anticipated his leader by indicating, Queen Victoria-like, that the possibility of defeat was something the leadership did not acknowledge: 'those of us who believe that this other policy is disastrous for the party will fight to reverse that decision and we will fight with the knowledge that we have the support, not only of the vast majority of the British people, the vast majority of the members of our party, but the whole of the Socialist Movement all over the world.'[12]

Healey was always disposed to go a touch cosmic in his rhetoric. The sharp point directed at the leader's throat would actually be beaten back in trade union gatherings of a few score people, by pamphlet and publicity, but it had begun to be reversed among the hundreds attending the Scarborough Conference. For although the unilateralist resolution would carry, it owed its success to the union bloc vote, chiefly the T&G led by Cousins and the AEU, which had temporarily bucked the right-wing norm ordained by its leader, Bill Carron. Impressively, the floor, the constituency delegates invariably to the left of the unions, the people who had brought off the Morecambe coup, voted two to one against unilateralism.

The achievement lies of course chiefly with Hugh Gaitskell, whose speech entered the written and quoted record of great political orations. But Healey's five minutes from the floor – hard, lucid and non-concessionary, demanding that people should think – had made their full contribution. The invitation to wobble or blur, to reach a conniving and incredible mixed conclusion, would never have been looked at by Gaitskell, but it fell to Healey to fire the shot which signalled resistance.

To his great advantage in argument, Gaitskell would stress as essential the aspirations of the UN and the substantiality of NATO, shifting the debate from revulsion at horrors to their logical but not-faced-up-to conclusion, departure from the defensive alliance. That approach would put the leadership on to the front foot. But Gaitskell also took pains to spell out meticulously his exact position on the independent deterrent. He thought that 'in the light of the abandonment of Blue Streak by the Tory government – with all the waste, incidentally, which was involved in trying to start it – Great Britain should give up the idea of being an independent nuclear power in the future.'

But surely he had advocated such independence in the past. 'So I have.' But he had never taken the view that the decision originally taken by Bevin and Attlee in 1945 was a matter of principle. And he reverted to his speech of 1958, that such a policy 'did not mean that we were going on and on manufacturing nuclear weapons'. He had been much denounced in *Tribune* for a speech in the Commons in March in favour of the independent deterrent. But he had also said that 'this was not, in my opinion, a matter of principle but a matter of the balance of arguments, economic, military and technical, on which a cool re-examination and reappraisal was certainly necessary from time to time.'[13]

This skeleton taken out of its cupboard and coolly looked over, Gaitskell became free to shift his argument to NATO and to the implications of leaving it, to take the logically unavoidable neutralist stand. Perhaps 'the United States may say "Well we have long-range rockets with which to defend ourselves, our own deterrent and really, with our best friends and allies out of the alliance and with the sort of difficulties – and they have them, God knows, with France and Germany – we wash our hands of Europe." Do we really want that?'

In handling the Soviet response, Gaitskell was moderate and reasoned – not the 'The Russians are coming', but 'What happens in a vacuum or where secure balances are disturbed?'

Gaitskell would end his long and compelling speech by quite deliberately switching from defence to the leadership. 'I would not wish for one day to remain a leader who had lost the confidence of his colleagues in Parliament. It is perfectly reasonable to try to get rid of somebody, to get rid of a man you do not agree with, who you think perhaps is not a good leader.' What would be wrong, said Gaitskell, 'would be to support a policy not wholly believed in to get rid of that man'.

He was touching painfully upon realities. Alongside unilateralism ran the general objectives of the left – and the private calculations which made Tony Benn so despise Harold Wilson. And what would follow, Wilson's candidacy against Gaitskell, his victory and the subsequent rerunning of the whole debate, were inherent in the whole unilateralist struggle. They were its politics.

1960 AND AFTER

The immediate consequence of events in Scarborough in the year of the Bomb was for Gaitskell to consolidate the Parliamentary Party. British parties, holding their conferences at the turn of September–October before returning to the Commons in mid-October, are well placed to respond to conference trouble. The Labour Party annually electing its leader (or Chairman of the Parliamentary Party, as he had been designated in limiting Venetian style since Keir Hardie's day) was nicely placed to settle things.

The candidacy for the leadership of Anthony Greenwood, an honest if lightweight left-winger and accredited unilateralist, would be superseded by that of Harold Wilson who was none of these things. Wilson had been urged on by Crossman, fulfilling his destiny as chief intriguer and puller at threads. Not a unilateralist, Wilson was told untruthfully by Crossman in a frantic conversation on board the Lime Street sleeper at Euston, that he must stand in their cause if he wanted to keep his precedence with the left. Sidling into the light and proclaiming himself a 'Unity candidate', Wilson confirmed every prejudice ever held about Wilson. The Shadow Chancellor made himself look shifty at a time when he was actually running fearfully to maintain a status which, outside Richard Crossman's whisperings, was unthreatened. He was also motivated by bitter feelings because Gaitskell had toyed with the idea of shifting him from the Treasury brief.

All the griefs of the Labour Party, from the split of 1951 to the manoeuvres of 1967–8, that abiding ground bass of distrust which throbbed through the party before climaxing in the great left revival which Healey would grimly inherit twenty years later, lay in that candidacy. It was a setting of faction against faction, leader against next leader. Wilson would be chosen to lead the party on Gaitskell's sudden death three years later with a substantial section of his party essentially not so much disliking as hating him. And when trouble came to his Prime Ministership, the hatred (and other men's ambitions) were waiting.

Healey, straightforwardly supporting a policy he had helped shape and a leader he worked closely with, was less emotionally affected than the immediate political family of Gaitskell. But his view of Wilson would never shift far from uncomplicated contempt. The vote itself however, rejection of the challenge by 166 votes to 81, cleared the air in parliament.

The longer struggle over unilateralism would be resolved politically by the efforts of CDS, the Campaign for Democratic Socialism, an organisation which Healey signed up to and spoke for. But this group was in many ways an affair of the younger men. Healey was forty-three; Bill Rodgers, who was its paid full-time organiser and not until 1962 a Member of Parliament, was thirty-two. Another young man, Denis Howell, who was temporarily out of a seat but exceptionally well connected in Midlands union circles, made himself enormously effective. Elder figures either financed CDS, as Jack Diamond did, putting up over thirteen months £5500 at the values of 1961,[1] or gave it the weight of their seniority, like Patrick Gordon Walker and Douglas Jay.

But arguably the people who mattered most in this struggle were trade unionists such as Fred Hayday, Jim Conway and Bill Webber. It would succeed because skilful lobbying by way of union delegate committees across the early part of 1961 turned enough key voters back to support for the leadership. Healey concentrated on drafting *Policy for Peace*, a statement adapted by the NEC and the TUC, which stressed that giving up nuclear defence must logically mean giving up membership of NATO, something which only the more ardent unilateralists entirely accepted.

This was a crucial point. Unilateralism was never again quite so strong as at that moment when Harold Watkinson killed off Blue Streak. The journey from that low point actually lightened as it approached defeat at Scarborough. Even before Gaitskell made the 'Fight, fight and fight again' speech, he had sorted out his thinking. With Healey, altogether the relevant adviser, he now had a clear and coherent view of the problem. This involved looking for, but not too officiously proclaiming, independent nuclear weapons for NATO. It stressed British membership of that alliance for the reasons Healey had been pounding out in conferences and pamphlets – Soviet ability to match US means and discourage nuclear intervention, should the Russians send tanks into Western Europe. The importance of belonging to that alliance, whatever its precise armament, was now the great theme of argument.

It was an effective position to take up, for curiously, people capable of being emotionally (and rationally) averse to national nuclear power, were reluctant to endorse neutrality. That seemed, like death, to be a very big adventure. Yet, ironically, NATO at this time was a chocolate waiting for a nuclear filling. Healey, who had played a central role in the sorting out of Labour's intellectual position on nuclear weapons, had, as we have seen, been juggling auxiliary verbs in order to keep the door open for the Skybolt/Polaris option which Harold Macmillan would negotiate.

By a nice irony, *Campaign*, the newsletter of CDS, would mark a complete break from Gaitskell's private agonies over a British weapon. It wrote: 'The failure of Blue Streak showed that a country of Britain's size cannot afford to remain an independent nuclear power in any meaningful sense, without an intolerable strain on its resources. But the Tories refused to face reality. They clung to the myth of the independent deterrent, and hoped to prolong the life of Britain's ageing force of V-bombers by buying Skybolt missiles from the United States.' Macmillan's government was not clinging but grasping. The trade in Skybolt would be withdrawn because the Americans did not want it themselves. But that temporary fiasco directly triggered in the embarrassed Kennedy a goodwill tearfully worked up by Macmillan at their Nassau meeting in 1962. In consequence, the US President agreed to sell us Polaris.

The government did not merely hope to prolong its role, it succeeded. The purchase was perhaps the best thing Macmillan ever did in government. It was cheap and it lasted a long time. And curiously, once part of Britain's defences, it ceased to be controversial. The boiling point of mid-1960 became lukewarm water and CND ceased to matter very much for nearly twenty years.

Where Labour is concerned, we are at a refinement of politics. The authors of *Campaign*, preoccupied with the party struggle, did not have Healey's grasp of pure defence policy. But between them, they and he made the leadership position ambiguous, necessarily ambiguous in the complex circumstances of new military developments and a bitter party and union struggle.

But *Policy for Peace*, whatever its disingenuous reservations or statesmanlike ambiguity, was anyway a far more rational and attractive case to put before Labour activists than stand-pat British Nuclearism. The new programme, despite the assurances of Healey's constituency ally in Leeds and editor of the *Leeds Weekly Citizen*, Solly Pearce, did not pass the National Union of Railwaymen. But such was the confusion of contradictory motions that the General Secretary, Sidney Greene, was able to throw his quarter of a million votes to the leadership. And the Engineers', a union long fought over by Communists and Catholics and their respective allies, reverted to its customary loyalist position.

With such numbers collected, the Brighton Conference of 1961 could only reject unilateralism, which now joined socialism as something which 'has not failed comrades, it hasn't been tried'. British foreign policy was placed for the future to resume its habitual function of armed normality.

The politics of 1960 and after were exceptionally hopeful. Gaitskell himself, with an outstanding speech, had caught public attention and won public respect. He didn't look any longer like a dry civil servant figure. The desiccated calculating machine had roared – and had met a friendly response. It was an interesting example of a politician reaching over his activists to the country at large. The bubbling-up of warm support across the country had given him general lift-off. The party under his leadership suddenly looked electable, and immediate personal friends like Tony Crosland saw their careers bloom with the prospect of major responsibility.

Denis Healey had little to complain about – and didn't complain. He had already, ahead of all his contemporaries, been elected to the Shadow Cabinet. Labour's annual collegiate reshuffle, a vote taken by the Parliamentary Party every autumn, was part horse race, part blood feud, wholly obsession. Healey had been closing in on the elect for some time and in 1959 he was elected. For a specialist on defence, the subject most alien to party sensibilities, it was impressive. But Healey at this stage in his career owed much to his standing as something not yet named, a technocrat. He had been blazingly effective over Suez, he was a northerner in a Parliamentary Party preponderantly northern and his abilities were self-evidently first rate.

He served as auxiliary spokesman on Foreign Affairs, directly assisting the leader, but in December 1961 he was given responsibility by Gaitskell for shadowing the Colonial and Commonwealth Offices. His own view is that Gaitskell would have been ready to give him Foreign Affairs ahead of making him Foreign Secretary in office, but that at that stage, he lacked tedious seniority.[2]

In the colonial world, the early sixties was a time of, not very principled, retreat. The Macmillan government was the product of the Suez operation. Eden's Cabinet, with Harold Macmillan as chief cheerleader, had made war as an expression of imperial authority. Its defeat, through American hostility, produced in the new Prime Minister a despondency about there being any authority left. Given to both dramatic defeatism and fly self-interest, Macmillan would accelerate the whole concept of translation from colony to state in a spirit of losses cut and responsibilities got out of.

In France, by contrast, the message was that no such things as colonies existed, there were only *territoires d'outre-mer* inhabited by Frenchmen who, black and brown, enjoyed the benefits of that high and peculiar civilisation. In Algeria, where there were a million French colonists, the conflict amounted to running war, and the message was 'Algérie française'. And echoed in five notes on car horns, that phrase would overthrow the Fourth Republic. Macmillan, watching this tragedy shuttle through several acts including the period (1954–6) when Suez had torn at British sensibilities, feared similar developments if his government had declared that we must fight open-endedly for some African or Middle Eastern interest as part of a 'mission civilisatrice'.

On the whole, Macmillan's instinct was shrewd, though it was streaked with his habitual and overdone despair, a sort of controlled panic operating long term. And the case, in Africa at least, for a real 'mission civilisatrice' – heavy funding of education and planned preparation for independence through cadres fit to govern – has been made since by developments in such places as Uganda. In fairness to him, what Macmillan would never have done, if placed in the shoes of the American President, was to fight the Vietnam War. That, by a fine irony, would become a domestic burden to the government of Harold Wilson, unwilling to asociate itself with a really serious American mistake, yet damned within its own ranks for failure to strike an attitude. Some despair is, after all, well founded.

The Labour leadership's general view of the colonies was best represented by Arthur Creech Jones, one of those quiet, genuinely expert politicians who attract little attention. Creech Jones, Colonial Secretary towards the end of Attlee's government, was an Afro-Fabian believing in the inevitability of gradualism. Healey, who greatly respected a fellow expert, quotes his private words on the prospects of a British East African colony achieving independence: 'Denis, Kenya will not be independent in my lifetime or in yours.'[3] Jones was badly out in his timing, but neither unreasonable nor wrong. Kenya had recently seen the operations of Mau Mau. Actual independent Kenya has been merely nepotistic, corrupt and tribalist, much better than might have been expected. As for Uganda, shortly to experience Mr Obote (twice) and General Amin, it would have been thought reactionary in 1961 to advocate there twenty-five years of Colonial Office direct rule plus major educational investment.

Events however had invalidated all such thinking as practice. Africa was essential to nobody's economy and, as the career of Tiny Rowland would demonstrate, all necessary exploitation could be done more effectively by bribes than by white policemen. A terminally cynical politician like Macmillan knew as much without needing to make profound calculations. Colonies with negligible European populations could go, and go quickly, Ghana first among them in 1957. Where they went did not trouble the British government.

But the larger settler groups did have a constituency in the British Conservative Party. They proclaimed themselves kith and kin, and the likes of Anthony Fell, Sir Harwood Harrison, Victor Goodhew and the Marquis of Salisbury, furiously assenting, worked up their own kind of tribal feelings. This was an issue which ran in the constituencies and at Conference. The Conservative Party could get very nasty on this topic. The jeering a few years later at a sick and dying John Davies for trying to hold to a moderate course, would be an unpleasant illustration. In fairness, the instincts of those running the Tory Party were good and went beyond Macmillan's shrugging instinct for saving us trouble.

The preoccupying question was Rhodesia, or rather Southern Rhodesia. With a white population of 220,000 and no great natural resources, it had benefited since 1953 from the 'Central African Federation' which pulled in with it Northern Rhodesia, rich in copper and with a negligible white population, and Nyasaland which had very little of either and appeared as a makeweight. The Africans of Nyasaland led by Dr Hastings Banda, wanted to leave, as did those of Northern Rhodesia led by Kenneth Kaunda. But behind these two claims lay the prospect that Southern Rhodesia, stripped of its federal assets and angry with Whitehall, might transform its *de facto* autonomy into independence by proclaiming the fact and asking Britain what she meant to do about it.

Healey would engage in a major Commons debate on the future of the Federation in December 1962.[4] He was speaking that day against one of the great men of mid-century British politics, R. A. Butler. The former Chancellor and Home Secretary was charged with dealing with the Rhodesias. Butler was famously oblique, given to the glissade where less subtle politicians aspired to advance by steps. Famous for corner-of-the-mouth ironies known as Butlerisms, he brought out in Healey on this occasion a frontal comic epigram antedating his own later, rougher-hewn Healeyisms.

Butler had deftly intimated a readiness to disengage Nyasaland from the Federation while making as yet no such suggestion about Northern Rhodesia. 'One of the things we most admire about the right hon. Gentleman,' said Denis, 'is his ability to sidle off in opposite directions at the same time without any apparent feeling of inconsistency. I know that he is a man of flesh and blood, but in his political career he gives the impression of being made of ectoplasm.'[5] It is the sort of jibe which ranks as a compliment, and Butler must have enjoyed it and Northern Rhodesia, where Kenneth Kaunda had overwhelming majority support, would become independent. The argument was taking place at a time when the patronage of Britain for Southern Rhodesia, keeping a grip on a profitable territory which didn't want to be gripped, was almost over. We were moving on to another debate at the heart of white settlers' interests.

Healey, in late 1962, was looking forward to their obvious next move, sovereign independence for their own territory, if federation should be taken from them by London. This was the objective held out by the right-wing Rhodesian Front led by a tobacco farmer, Winston Field. And the idea had friends for this purpose in Britain. Healey quoted his own neighbour, the *Yorkshire Post*, the *Daily Telegraph* of the north, which had proposed this very step. Oddly enough, Healey knew Field rather well. He had first of all been stationed with him in Keighley and later served with him in Italy. Roy Welensky, another major Rhodesian figure, and originally a trade union official, also pops up occasionally in the diaries of the International Officer.

Such acquaintance didn't show. It would be, said Healey in moralistic flight on Southern Rhodesian independence, 'a moral crime of the first magnitude to create a new South Africa in Central Africa in this way; but, not only would it be a moral crime, it would be an economic and political catastrophe for the Europeans themselves'.[6] The lines were in fact being laid down for a sixteen-year conflict.

A Healey point that afternoon that such a state would be recognised only by South Africa and Portugal, then a diehard colonial state, proved simple truth. But when, while calling on Butler to set up a new constitution to give the blacks parity with Europeans, he claimed that 'there is no other way of avoiding a new Algeria in Southern Rhodesia,' he was missing the ability of the British to fizz without exploding. Scenarios involving the descent of British paratroops to crush any move to UDI were widely canvassed at this time. The sympathies of so many right-wing Tories seemed to parallel the chants of 'Algérie française' of 1958. But of course nothing like that ever happened.

Healey would have the satisfaction of being denounced by Robin Turton, a former Health minister and pillar of the old Tory right: 'This seems to me a most untimely moment to have chosen for a debate on Central Africa. We have had, in my opinion, two most irresponsible speeches by the hon. Member for Leeds East (Mr Healey) and the right hon. and learned Member for Ipswich' (Dingle Foot). Healey 'had talked about a moral crime to create a new South Africa in Central Africa. His words, if nothing else, will do that very thing.'[7] In the debate on 3 November Healey would also be asked by Farey-Jones, Conservative MP for Watford, 'what future the coloured man has in Central Africa without the active co-operation of the white people?'[8]

But though parts of the Tory Party turned its displeasure upon Iain Macleod, the ostentatiously anti-racialist former Conservative Colonial Secretary, Rhodesia would not be a haemorrhage threatening the British state, rather a small weeping wound much consulted over. Healey himself would later pass on to a relieved Prime Minister, Wilson, the disinclination of his senior soldiers for an invasion against a government rich in old colleagues from the war, 'kith and kin' being worth rather more in certain key quarters than was ever fully recognised. While Edward Heath, though he would as Prime Minister push negotiations for a settlement with the whites rather further than Labour, would not be willing to give Mr Smith the white settlement Mr Smith wanted.

If Hugh Gaitskell, with his rigidity and fierce principles, had lived, an invasion with military men ordered to obey looks very credible. But if anyone determined the long, drab inconclusiveness of the Rhodesian issue, it was almost certainly Harold Macmillan, whose apprehension of an Algerian equivalence helped to paralyse British government, regardless of party, against anything that might have been mistaken for decisiveness.

Healey would himself in office be a prisoner of the very British response to late Empire. Nobody wanted very much wanted to die either for the settlers or the Africans. Macmillan's instincts were shared by public and political class alike, and those instincts were for not getting involved. No Algerian parallel would ever have arisen in this country. And as the dull prejudice of Mr Smith, worn down by sanctions, bush war and loss of South African patronage, finally made way under the embarrassed oversight of Mrs Thatcher for the drift into the gang violence of Mr Mugabe, the case does cross one's mind for a cynicism that dare not speak its name.

Perhaps, after forty years, the most compelling thing in Healey's Rhodesia speech is his reminder to Butler of questions he had put about the training provided in Northern Rhodesia for Africans to take up administrative posts. 'The answer was that there are three Africans on administrative courses in Britain. It is hoped to raise this to nine next year.'[9] The performance lived up to Healey's phrase, 'the immensity of past neglect'. The only figures which Healey had been able to obtain from the government were seven years out of date, those of 1955, and they showed 'only 45,000 Africans in the whole of the territory getting more than four years of schooling and that only 47 of them had two years in the sixth form'. Healey at this time, though making good points about past inactivity, was merely an early contributor to the long shouting match about Central Africa.

WILSON SUCCEEDS

On 16 January 1963 Hugh Gaitskell, who after a short illness had suddenly deteriorated, died. This meant to one group of people the loss of someone for whom attachment came close to love. When the eruptive, drink-tinged brilliance of George Brown proved too hot for a nervous party, it also meant the election of a man for whom yet others felt a contempt beyond expression. As this group would constitute the essential members of the Cabinet which Harold Wilson would form twenty-one months later, the miseries of a future Labour government were settled.

The famous view of Tony Benn that politics is about issues and not personalities would be rebutted. On issues, the differences would be minor and, ironically, on certain points, Rhodesia for example, Gaitskell would have been more likely to do the radical, left-wing thing and take up a challenge which Wilson kept shrewdly at a distance. Perhaps the ardent supporter of the Korean War might have made the contribution to America's unwisdom in Vietnam, both token and explosive, which Lyndon Johnson begged. But he would have been stubbornly slow on immigration control, provoking larger enmity from the far right. Hugh Gaitskell versus Enoch Powell is the great fight we never saw. And probably he would have been a devaluer of the pound, if not on election morning, then in a much shorter period than the three self-injuring years which Wilson took. The two men would have been at one on the liberal humanitarian front – capital punishment, divorce, homosexuality. Gaitskell's disciple, Roy Jenkins, would have the satisfaction of being the liberal Home Secretary facilitating reform on all these. Wilson, for all the derision he attracted in a smart-alec decade, was not a disastrous Prime Minister. Rather he was a victim of the expectations generated by his own rhetoric. Loyal to the United States if uncontributing over Vietnam, tied hand and foot over the sovereign currency and barred by it from any thought-out programme of social expenditure, he would be widely driven by circumstances and a desperate disappointment to the people who saluted his succession.

Between these two, personality is everything. Gaitskell was rigid and principled to a fault. One reads of the dinner for four which he and his wife, Dora, gave to Frank and Nancy Cousins after CND had been resolved[1] as something admirable, but achieved against his whole grain. Like Margaret Thatcher, in this as in nothing else, Gaitskell did divide the political world into groups – right and left, saved and damned, friends and not friends, economists and not-economists. He had intense affections and deep loathings. Harold Wilson had neither. To the personal circle of Gaitskell, Wilson was a cheap careerist, the coldest of cold fish making calculations only.

They were wrong about this in a major degree, for Wilson had a kindly side and a degree of soft-heartedness which would surprise the political world. He was also something of the outsider to both the public school coterie *and* the trade union huddle, a solitary with a weakness for bad company. But they were more wrong in thinking that Wilson, in so far as he had convictions, was a man of the left. Wilson, as his biographer Ben Pimlott has pointed out,[2] was more complicated than unprincipled. He had made judgements as a young minister – the bonfire of controls – which tended towards economic liberalism, and others on defence spending pleasing to the left, both of which were commonsense good housekeeping. A resentful antagonism towards Gaitskell personally (fully and no more creditably returned) diminished Wilson. He would be driven into the company of the left, sharing their antipathies but never their core beliefs – he really had little in common with a man like Michael Foot and would come under the influence of Richard Crossman, a genuine force for harm, one of the very few men whom Clement Attlee had bothered to hate.

Attlee would say the last, clipped word about Crossman: 'Nothing wrong with Dick's abilities; problem is character.' Crossman was curiously unmalicious in the performance of malevolent acts. In his quick-minded, almost genial way, he was entirely amoral. The business of leaking confidential business and telling outright lies he found enjoyable. Crossman was also Healey's chief aversion: 'A Machiavelli without judgement,' he called him.[3] If anyone embodied the conspiring, faction-forming, enmity-sowing spirit of mid-century Labour, it was Crossman. And Crossman, who laughed aloud at Wilson's left-wing credentials, was Wilson's bridge to the left.

Wilson would inherit power on premises at least half-false. The brighter people on the left didn't really think that the Harold who took his pipe out of his mouth and began sentences 'Quite frankly' was truly of their persuasion, but he was what they had got, and they hoped for concessions in their direction. The new leadership began with his raising a glass to make a toast. 'To the man who is not here, the man who should have done it, Nye Bevan,' words entirely without meaning, but potent. For the left this was a high point from which the rest of Wilson's time would be a long falling away.

The essence of what Gaitskell's friends felt was caught by Roy Jenkins. He had been in America during Gaitskell's sudden descent to death. Asked by the *Daily Express* for an appreciation, he felt too distressed to give one and he was told, 'But Mr Wilson who was in New York gave us a very moving one.' 'Yes,' said Jenkins savagely, 'but you must remember that he was very fond of him.'

Healey, though he did not have the visceral ties of Crosland and Jenkins, had seriously respected and admired Gaitskell, not something he did readily, and his scorn for Wilson was in its dispassion probably the most damning of all. Without disputing Wilson's intelligence, he simply couldn't begin to take him seriously.

His own immediate future would be straightforward. Nobody was more sharply defined as a military hawk, correspondent and friend of the American military, specialist attender of exotic and devilish conferences about more effective weapons of war, drafter of policy statements cleverly keeping open commitment to nuclear weapons. Who was more suitable to be given reversal of the Ministry of Defence by the candidate of the left? Wilson had drunk to the memory of Nye and it was Nye, led on by the hints and promises of Sam Watson, who had denounced unilateralism as an emotional spasm. Felicitously, it was Sam Watson who would later remark of the then Prime Minister that 'Wilson couldn't lie straight in bed.'[4]*

In fact, Healey's name was flashing up on some scoreboards for even grander promotion. On 22 February 1963, Patrick Gordon Walker would take the Foreign Affairs portfolio, something which enraged George Brown who after his defeat for the leadership had disappeared to Scotland for a few days, leaving a memorandum with Wilson asking for the Foreign Affairs brief. He and Gordon Walker had a bitter conversation two days before the official announcement. Gordon Walker tells the story:

> 'Had I been offered Foreign Affairs? . . . Was I thinking of accepting?'
> 'Yes – I think so.'
> 'I am inexpressibly shocked (repeated several times). But I am not surprised – it's not the first time . . .'
> On the 22nd, a few hours before the announcement, the conversation resumed. 'I had badly let him down. This was in character . . . I knew he wanted Foreign Affairs, but I had stopped this by telling HW I would take the job. Bevin had always said stick to your friends. I was incapable of doing this.'
> I said that when HW had made the proposal, I had said we must keep GB. HW had said if I didn't take it he would give it to Healey. To

---

* Comment at the time to the author.

stop this I said I would consider the offer – subject to talks with GB. I could not consult him as he had disappeared to Scotland.

GB: 'You should simply have refused to discuss it till GB was back. HW would never have given it to Healey.'

Wilson, according to Gordon Walker, had earlier said he would not give the job to Brown whom he and Gaitskell before him thought unsuited to the job, and that if Gordon Walker didn't take it, he would offer it to somebody else.[5]

Something of Wilson's glinting side comes from another conversation – with Crossman, whom five days earlier he had told of his proposals for Foreign Affairs and Defence. 'Wilson refused to give Healey the credit Crossman allowed him for opposing an independent deterrent: '"Not much courage on that occasion," Harold noted carefully, "since he did not say so publicly." He assented. "Nevertheless, I agree he would do well and George* would work well with him . . . As for Gordon Walker," said Wilson, "he is so stupid that by appointing him Shadow Foreign Secretary, I need not commit myself to my real Foreign Secretary when I form my Government."' Events, the defeat of Gordon Walker in a flurry of anti-immigration propaganda by a rogue Conservative candidate, would make nonsense of such intentions, if indeed they were serious. Without speculating unduly about Wilson's hypothetical intentions, Healey now occupied a notable position. Having been Gaitskell's preferred choice for the Foreign Office, though insufficiently senior, he was a combination of bogey and fall-back to Harold Wilson. Considering that in the rush of events he would never get the job, this was, at forty-six, a tribute, backhanded or otherwise, to his standing.

There was to be a third such in 1965 after Gordon Walker had been defeated at a second election and had resigned. Crossman, Healey's eternal adversary, spoke to Wilson who had told him of the appointment of Michael Stewart. 'I said that I realised that he couldn't do what I would have liked to and make Denis Healey Foreign Minister and Roy Jenkins Minister of Defence.' The compliment received a rebuttal from Wilson: 'I wouldn't trust Healey in the Foreign Office with all those professionals.'

Such tough talk was proof of one's ruthlessness, put on display for the in-house Machiavelli. Of George Brown, Crossman had written, 'Harold had said to me more than once before, and more than once after the election, that we would have to get rid of GB within six months.'[7] Brown would leave nearer five years later, very much at his own volition, for reasons of Cabinet administration which Crossman would endorse.

---

* Colonel George Wigg, whom Healey would see as 'a good but undisciplined mind', adding, 'His honesty and sincerity were never in doubt, but his arguments were often incoherent.'[6]

26

INTERVAL SCENE-SHIFTING

Richard Crossman had confided to his diaries the conviction that while Gaitskell was clinging to schemes which kept Britain involved with nuclear weapons, Macmillan and Kennedy were probably arranging things in his way – a non-nuclear Britain to be defended on the speculative sufficiency of the American arsenal. They were doing no such thing. And what they *were* doing usefully underlines the off-key nature of so much buzzing activity in the Labour Party at this time. Like Gaitskell, Macmillan believed in principle in possessing a British capability, however defined, because the huge American capacity was less guarantee against attack than helpful threat, and a threat liable to prove a bluff. Having seen enough of the Front in 1914–18 to have full, horrific understanding of conventional war, Macmillan, like any rational person, wanted weapons in the hope and prayer that having meant not using. The problems had been practicality and its near neighbour, money.

As we have seen, Blue Streak, recognised as impossible in February 1960, had been officially called off in May of that year. Humiliating and perplexing as these technical reverses and financial imposts were, the principle of direct British involvement remained. Though, with unilateralism advancing, the government was even more harassed, a man interrupted by a sermon against violence while in the business of replacing a pistol which didn't work.

The next, the only, way out was an American product, Skybolt – long range, fired from the air and, blessedly for the British, compatible with our own V-bombers. The only problem with Skybolt was that the disobliging American military had never really wanted it. Delays and unsuccessful tests fuelled the aversion until 1962, when clear indication that the weapon would not proceed finally came.

US Defense was now in the hands, under the Kennedy administration, of

Robert McNamara who would be one of Healey's key American friends
and contacts. He was, however, no friend of the irascible Defence Secretary,
Peter Thorneycroft, since McNamara strongly opposed the whole project of
a deal with Britain. A man of the highest abilities and integrity, but of
imperfect sensibility, McNamara would later sustain, for the highest
motives and made certain by expert, wrong calculation of forces, the long
continuation of the Vietnam War. In 1960, another of his certainties was
that Britain should solve her problems by joining in something called the
Multilateral Force, or MLF – mixed European sailors on missile-bearing
ships under overall American control, a baroque concept annoying to
friends and unconvincing to the enemy, conceived by politics and derided
by Macmillan (and Healey).

On top of which McNamara had no time for Skybolt, 'a pile of junk, for
which we were paying the whole bill . . .'[1] There had been a series of tests and
no completely successful performance.

Having been persuaded of the MLF alternative agenda and written off
Skybolt in principle, McNamara failed to talk clearly to Thorneycroft while
Thorneycroft failed to ask McNamara the essential questions. A prolonged
failure of communication between the two Defence ministers, and to some
extent a further gap between President Kennedy himself and McNamara,
intensified the angry uncertainty.

Macmillan needed the weapon for those declared purposes of British
autonomy. Without it, both British political parties faced prolonged crisis.
Unilateralism on the left and anti-Americanism on the right would both
flourish massively in a Britain defended only by the say-so of a United
States, either dismissing her or issuing peremptory directions. Kennedy
understood this as his advisers, broadly, did not. He also acknowledged
British arguments based on the intellectual capital contributed by Britain to
the earliest nuclear developments, upon which Macmillan made a full ren-
tier claim. But commitments made by Kennedy to Macmillan were never
made plain to, or understood by, the US Secretary of Defense. While
McNamara, by not sharing his growing scepticism about Skybolt with
Thorneycroft, created a dreadful hiatus. The news that Skybolt would not
work was communicated to Thorneycroft only on 11 December 1961 in
response to a direct question.

The abrupt answer was followed by an uninterested failure of response to
Thorneycroft's anxious inquiry about alternatives. The Anglo-American relationship at this low point, so far from being special, did not measure up to
average. Thorneycroft wanted a public row with the Americans and Britain
pulling out of all projects, beyond which would probably have lain a French
route of genuine autonomy purchased at vast expense. Intriguingly, this
might also have meant a necessary falling-in with de Gaulle's France, a building of the Force de Frappe in consort with her, circumstances which would

also have given Britain access to the EEC and on better terms than those granted eight years later. Who can know if we would have been the loser?

But Thorneycroft's rage was sidelined by the Prime Minister. Macmillan's purposes held, and at Nassau in December 1962, he got Kennedy so much on side that the President was instructing a resentful Department of Defense, military command and State Department to accommodate us.

But there were ironies even in the triumph. The central outcome of Nassau was that Britain received not Skybolt but Polaris, a submarine-based missile system, for a very modest and manageable price. Though, by a perfectly timed irony, the agreement was barely signed and Macmillan back in London before a message came from the testing grounds that for the first time Skybolt had enjoyed a 100 per cent firing. Kennedy was enraged, Macmillan wondered whether he had been 'outsmarted'[2] but with events concluded, observations were kept respectively to a poolside explosion and dark muttering into the diary.

Stationed in British water, Polaris would give us not precisely an independent deterrent, but very much that involvement in our own nuclear defence which Healey had been preaching to his party colleagues. It would last for upwards of twenty years and give credibility to Western defences – probably in Russian eyes – and certainly, which may have mattered more, in our own.

27

PREPARING FOR THE
MINISTRY OF DEFENCE

At the start of his account of life at the Ministry of Defence, Healey compares himself to a driver kept long behind a tractor on a country road, suddenly released on to the motorway. It is a good description of all those years of pamphlets, monitoring events and struggles about which attitude Labour should strike in opposition, but as Healey gets into the traffic, we need to know more about what had actually been happening on the motorway.

Harold Macmillan had briefly held the Ministry of Defence himself, one of a cavalcade of ministers each averaging about eleven months there during that Conservative era. He was sharply aware of things being ramshackle, authority diffused, factions entrenched and money strolling free. Macmillan, a good administrative minister behind the cabaret turn, combined nostalgia with bursts of peremptory action. In his first appointment to head the Ministry in 1957, he would have all the peremptory action a government could ask. Duncan Sandys was strong, assured, certain of what should be done and not terribly clever. He was also noted by Macmillan for his 'cassant manner', his way of breaking things, disregarding both civility and feelings in argument.[1] But he would be doing nothing Macmillan did not intend him to do.

Macmillan had been Chancellor during Suez and had seen the outflows of money in that crisis. In a memorandum sent when still Eden's almost melo-dramatically disloyal colleague, to the then Minister of Defence, Antony Head, he looked to the defence budget for '"substantial" savings'.[2] Thinking aloud about defence, Macmillan covers similar ground to Healey in his writings at this time. 'The true deterrent (that is to the outbreak of war with Russia) is the Americans' possession, actual or potential, of these weapons on a far greater scale than anything that we could manage.'

From the start, and mindful of cost, Macmillan wanted to cut into

American research and development. 'The relief which this would afford to our overstrained scientific resources would yield double or treble dividends.'[3] But to keep going in this field, one must concentrate resources upon it. So 'in our present position, we cannot afford to carry too many insurance policies' . . . When Macmillan, after becoming Prime Minister in January 1957, asked Head whether he could cut manpower 'down to X and costs to Y', Head, who opposed what he saw as the sacrifice of the broad function of the forces to the god of nuclear weapons, flatly resigned. Duncan Sandys and his *cassant* manner came in.

The consequence was the Sandys White Paper. Published on 4 April 1957, it proclaimed the phasing-out of aircraft carriers, 'expensive, vulnerable and largely irrelevant to national needs'.[4] It planned cuts in manpower of almost half – 690,000 troops to come down to 375,000 very quickly and the British presence in Germany to fall by 13,000 to 64,000. This was a boot resting hard on French and German insteps – very *cassant*. But Sandys also proposed more and better air transport so that in emergencies, the fewer troops could be shifted more quickly – 'firstest with the leastest', to amend General Forrest.

The longer-term cuts in manpower were to bite much deeper. Sandys had in mind a force of 165,000 which would replace the old conscript army, for he meant to end National Service. Brigadier Head and Major Healey had reservations. He did not believe that Sandys would get the numbers for the volunteer army he proposed. But Healey's greatest concern with Sandys was that his economies might undermine our usefulness in NATO. 'Britain's desire to end conscription has already led to a greater reduction in her NATO forces than her allies believe justified.'

Not that everything Sandys wanted was achieved, especially where the Navy, a prime target, was concerned. The First Sea Lord, Sir Rhoderick McGrigor, had summed up the derisive expectations of senior naval officers:

(a) In war, very little in the way of a Navy is necessary as everything will be finally decided by the H-bomb.
(b) In peace foreign stations are unnecessary. We can always warn troublemakers that if they don't stop it the RAF will deal with them.
(c) Cruisers are not needed and should be scrapped.
(d) Aircraft Carriers and Naval Aircraft are unnecessary. The RAF can do it all and it is their job.
(e) Other types of ships should be drastically reduced.
In fact the Navy is no longer needed and it is a luxury the country cannot afford.[5]

This did not desperately exaggerate the broad direction of policy, as events and money would require, across the thirteen years from the 1957 White

Paper to the end of Healey's term as Minister of Defence. It also underlined the later words of Peter Hill-Norton, a subsequent Chief of the Defence Staff, that the supposed conflict between the services was more accurately the concern of the navy not to be the victim of dismemberment. Relations between the navy and the RAF were very bad. But those between army and navy, RAF and army, were not.[6]

The First Sea Lord, Mountbatten, given, like Macmillan, to bursts of lachrymose dramatics, spoke to the Indian Prime Minister, Nehru, of a supposed remark to him: 'You were the last Viceroy of India. You will probably be the last First Sea Lord.'[7] Sandys's own proposals for the navy, when they materialised, were startling enough – the closing of the Scapa Flow naval base and four of the ten naval stations, the Naval Reserve slashed to a sixth of its size – 5000 men – and only a single battleship out of five preserved. He was also fatalistic. The Sandys/Macmillan view was go-ahead in the drastic sense of believing that war would necessarily be nuclear and all defence against it futile. Recognising this end-of-the-world principle would also save the Treasury £78 million.

Sandys as minister said and did direct and immediate things. He proposed a straight cut in the naval estimates for the next year. With a reduction in the realm of 10 per cent immediately contemplated, service chiefs, including the histrionic Mountbatten, talked of resignation. More usefully, they set about reaching the Prime Minister by going international and lobbying the United States' military, an invocation of the Seventh Fleet against the unspeakable Sandys. A British admiral (Denny) in Washington should speak to the American admiral, Radford, who should speak to the President about the effect of such cuts upon NATO.[8] The Foreign Office should pass on protest at the economic consequences if 'foreign stations' should be closed and with them the Singapore dockyard.

Behind much of this moved the hand of Lord Mountbatten. Though he hungered and thirsted for concentrations of power which, in the name of ending service rivalry, should rest safely in the hands of Lord Mountbatten, this did not make 'Dickie' any less ready to make vast trouble on behalf of the navy. It was, after all, his own service.

Sandys had hoped to rid the defence budget of aircraft carriers, things he thought useful only for anti-submarine warfare and whose number he wanted to cut by two-thirds. But a case made by the other services, with air marshals and a field marshal signing the paper, persuaded him to hold his hand. Ironically for Healey, who would be confronted by both issues, the case for aircraft carriers would rest on their utility in operations concerning all three services East of Suez.

Over integration of the services at ministerial and command level, Sandys would fail in his own time, but Mountbatten would be moving on the same side and the reform would come – in *its* time. Vain beyond belief, wondering before a function if he should wear his powder-blue and adding to a service newsletter a paragraph about the reintroduction of lace trousers, he was capable enough and a spin doctor *avant la lettre*. Mountbatten had been given the new title, Chief of the Defence Staff, and he had been seriously considered for the post of Minister of Defence. Foolish but no fool, he had declined an appointment tying him into a political administration. As CDS, he both wanted power straightforwardly for himself and genuinely believed in the concept of integration.

Macmillan did things on a rest-and-lurch basis. Harold Watkinson, the next Defence Secretary, having rested the Chiefs of Staff, would be preoccupied with the Blue Streak crisis and it was finally time under *his* successor, Peter Thorneycroft, appointed to the Ministry for the purpose, to face up to integration and lurch again, using as a starting point 'my great paper', as Mountbatten called his proposals.

Macmillan spoke scornfully of Mountbatten's actual intelligence, but was determined to use him. Charm and the semi-royal touch apart, much of the advantage in this lay in the extreme nature of Mountbatten's notions of integration. It was possible to go a long way and still claim to have compromised. A commission was appointed under two former senior officers, Lord Ismay and Sir Ian Jacob, and told to be quick. They were very quick – weeks. Ismay–Jacob proposed a unified ministry where there once stood antique titles and responsibilities, some of them reaching back to Wellington if not Pepys. The Secretary for War and the First Lord of the Admiralty should go, along with the relatively newfangled Secretary for Air.

In their place should stand subordinate Ministers of State for the separate services, under call to the Secretary of State. The new Ministry would live in a single building, one of Mountbatten's settled objectives, also to house the civilian Ministry of Aviation. But the Secretary of State himself was unequivocally exalted, promoted from referee to centre forward. On the civil service front, there would be a Permanent Under-Secretary for Defence to whom senior civil servants for the services would answer.

Macmillan, when lurching, had nothing of the grouse moor about him except perhaps as understood by the grouse. Ismay and Jacob were sent away in April and as Alistair Horne, his biographer, reports, 'By the end of July 1963, the Macmillan–Mountbatten Defence White Paper had been published, debated and accepted.'[9] The legislation for unifying the services was given its second reading on 21 November 1963 and introduced by Thorneycroft cheerfully quoting the response to an earlier proposal by the Duke of Wellington: 'this new Leviathan, A Secretary at War'. The purpose, said Thorneycroft, was 'to have one defence policy which was more than the synthesis of four different themes drawn from different sources: and secondly and also important, to improve our control over defence spending'.[10]

Into this Healey had now come officially in February 1963 as Opposition spokesman on Defence, a job on which his whole career had been converging for a decade. There is an instructive glimpse in a snappish entry of Crossman: 'Denis Healey, a very lone mover, completely on his own, running his own ideas. He, by the way, went to the Institute of Strategic Studies yesterday and delivered a fifty-minute lecture on Labour Defence policy, in which he insisted that the Minister of Defence should make it.'[11] So many of the griefs of Labour ministerial life in the sixties and seventies lie quietly in that sentence. Though, as so often, what Dick Crossman cleverly thought about policy didn't remotely matter.

There was no great love between him and Thorneycroft, something of an old-style grandee who could patronise without trying. A bad-tempered debate on the proposals followed, with George Wigg, Crossman's close ally, calling Thorneycroft 'a twister'[12] and Nigel Birch, that former comrade in Italy, did not allow this to interfere with his natural surliness, calling Healey 'a bore who could never speak for less than an hour'.[13] He had in fact spoken for forty-five minutes and taken seven substantial interventions against Thorneycroft's thirty-eight minutes with six.

Healey's response was generally cool. The Minister of Defence had extensive powers already under the Defence reorganisation of 1958 which this minister had been tardy to use. The White Paper of that date had indicated 'authority to decide . . . all major matters of defence policy affecting the size, shape, organisation and disposition of the Armed Forces'. The trouble was that Thorneycroft hadn't made effective use of the powers that he had. The real issue behind all plans for service integration was the reaching of decisions about weapons when the navy wanted one thing and the air force another.

This was something which Healey knew about in principle and of which he would soon learn more at the sharpest end of experience. Conflict between the services had proved horribly expensive and Healey cited a now largely forgotten example of military largesse, the surface-to-air missile weapon Seaslug – revealed by the Public Accounts Committee to have cost forty times the original estimate! The test which Thorneycroft had set himself was to keep military expenditure to 7.5 per cent of GNP or £2000 million. Current commitments to weapons alone would add up to more than that. The paradigm dispute between services over weapons was 'the TSR2 with an almost unlimited cost'.

That aircraft had been advanced and resisted after air force rejection of the Buccaneer: 'the RAF would never accept an aircraft originally designed for the navy – a syndrome described in the Ministry as NIH or "Not Invented Here".'[14] The TSR2 was an illustration of how it was possible to have nominal powers of central decision, but actually to spend, spend and spend again. 'I understand that when the project was first approved in 1959, the Government were assured that the total cost of research and development would be about £90 million. I understand that we have already spent about twice that amount and yet the aircraft has not yet flown.'[15]

Thorneycroft was uncommunicative, unsurprisingly, about an open-ended nightmare. But Healey could quote the stories of the *Observer*, which was talking about the aircraft having already cost £15 million each for the first eighteen ordered and the *Sunday Times* assessing the full final cost at £600 million. Healey had flown out, courtesy of the Air Minister, Hugh Fraser, and seen what the troops in Malaysia were up against. 'What those forces are crying out for,' he said, 'is helicopters, not TSR2s.'

He cited the example of the Australian government and air force which, having compared the TSR2 with another aircraft, had decisively preferred the option, the American TFX (to become the F111). Thorneycroft scornfully declined to see what the Australian example had to do with the subject. But when the Deputy Speaker intervened to remind both front-benchers that they were debating the Transfer of Functions bill, Healey said that TSR2 was dreadfully relevant. 'The Minister,' he said, 'knows better than anybody that the TSR2 project is a monument to the failure of inter-Service co-operation because if there had been proper inter-Service co-operation at the time that this aircraft was first ordered, we would not have had both a naval strike aircraft and an airforce strike aircraft performing very largely the same functions, developed totally independently with no serious attempt to render them compatible.' As Hansard remarked in its prim way, 'Mr Thorneycroft indicated dissent.'

Healey made a call for government to emulate McNamara in the US and start thinking ahead on a ten-year basis about what sort of wars, requiring what sort of equipment, it might be facing. Economies would have to be made, said Healey, contemplating a conundrum with which he would live in office. Where would they fall if the 7.5 per cent was to be met? Which system would lose out – the new transport aircraft, the P1154, supersonic strike aircraft – or the new aircraft carrier? The allusion looked back to Sandys, who had toyed with phasing that giant out, and forward to Healey who would do just that.

The speech as a whole was an evasion, entirely justified, full of heavy judgement on integration as integration. The whole undertaking was a blank cheque, but 'it will be for right hon. and hon. Gentlemen on this side of the House to cash it.'

Too much speculation would have been binding, but he did conclude with a brief critique. Firstly he saw no point in the downgrading of service ministers if the Chiefs of Staff were to remain as independent and bloody-minded as they were. Under Thorneycroft's bill, those Chiefs of Staff would retain access not just to the Secretary of State but also to the Cabinet. Many ministers of all persuasions would cringe at the prospect of those portentous waitings on the Master by which the Chiefs of Staff sought to intimidate civilian Johnnies who had got above themselves.

Even Healey, in this November 1963 debate, declared himself an opponent of so much power being concentrated in the hands of a single minister. He would be faced with 'such a colossal range of responsibilities to cover, that the prospect of his giving the time and energy required for decision on the major political issues is almost nil'. But Healey cited the words of Lord Swinton who, as Philip Cunliffe-Lister and Air Minister, had equipped the fighter pilots of 1940 to frustrate conquest by the Luftwaffe. Swinton had wanted a powerful deputy minister, whose job would be to look after the budget.

It was, overall, a skilled and expert performance reflecting the fact that Healey had been reading position papers and sitting through high-level conferences for more than a dozen years. He was in the odd and interesting position of a man watching his opponents assemble the framework of the house he would have to build. He was doing so after his party had come close to opting out of any major military role. He would not be rejecting the house Macmillan and Thorneycroft had built, but as the first tenant he reserved the right to an informed grumble.

The debate would grow more specific with the publication of a government White Paper and in late February 1964 Healey would be engaging Thorneycroft across a raft of issues, from married quarters to nuclear weapons by way of aircraft carriers. Thorneycroft was also open to the sort of question, made disagreeable by not being answerable, about shortfalls in troops, undersized battalions and the like which had haunted the Ministry of Defence since Sandys had abolished conscription.

Thorneycroft's account of weapons and vehicles to which the government was committing itself included the P1154, the Sea Vixen and, supremely, Polaris, now becoming a formal undertaking. Since Thorneycroft had been, nearly six years earlier, the Chancellor who had resigned over expenditure, his problem in containing cost was inevitably underlined by the Opposition. Healey pursued him in particular with interventions about the eternal TSR2. Could he tell the Commons whether the production programme for this plane had been negotiated? It had been authorised, the minister replied.[16]

Paradoxically, though the TSR2 would historically, in Healey's time, give great political trouble while Polaris would settle down on the hearthrug and become one of the family, it was Polaris that attracted argument in February 1964. Thorneycroft was fairly candid about the strategic situation, avoiding bombastic talk about independent deterrents. He also rejected talk of limited war, observing, 'I have rather a suspicion that if something the size of a Hiroshima bomb was dropped on a country, people would not stop to argue whether it was a tactical or a strategic one.'[17]

We were in a situation in which 'because major war would mean the destruction of the world . . . the forces of diplomacy are brought forward at a very much earlier stage in disputes, even in minor disputes.' The United States was armed with about 500 ICBMs rising to 1700 in 1966, a fleet of Polaris submarines 'and thousands, literally thousands, of tactical nuclear weapons deployed on the Continent of Europe'.[18] The Russians had their great resources, the French would follow, probably the Chinese – what should we do? Thorneycroft rightly treated the unilateralist position with more respect than Gaitskell would have done. It was an honourable point of view. But other countries simply wouldn't follow a unilateral discard of weapons.

Nuclear defence could only 'properly be considered in its real terms, the terms of a deterrent to war. There can be no other real purpose in nuclear equipment.'[19] The only defence was fear of retaliation. This had been embodied in the V-bombers. They had been formidable and must now be replaced. 'The bombers will be succeeded by the Polaris submarines. The keel of the first Polaris submarine was laid today.'[20] We should make provision for five boats, the refitting of each of which would cost £70 million.

Since he had to balance credible deterrence against cost, Thorneycroft listed the running proportion of defence expenditure which the American submarine would take up. He tentatively estimated costs at 8.4 per cent of defence spending for 1964–5, 7.6 per cent for 1965–6, about 8 per cent for the late 1960s, sinking in the 1970s to less than 5 per cent. Overall, defence costs would be kept down to 7 per cent of GNP.[21]

Healey's response in a debate rather better-tempered all round than the last, was to challenge Thorneycroft's optimism on costs. By 1968, we should have produced the bulk of our Polaris submarines, 'the average costs of which the right hon. Gentleman has admitted this afternoon, would be something of the order of £400 million'. We should also have produced 50 to 100 TSR2 aeroplanes. If the government had committed itself to keeping defence expenditure at 7 per cent of GNP, 'then we cannot conceivably find the money for the projects to which the right hon. Gentleman has committed himself and the Government during the three years ahead'.[22]

Healey, very conscious at this time that they order these things better in America, reproached Thorneycroft with not planning ahead the way McNamara did. 'We have to try now to decide where to spend money in order to get the best interests in world affairs. We cannot approach this task so long as the Defence White Paper and all the Estimates are produced in their present form.' Thorneycroft had been quite right to say that 'the problems of defence at present can be discussed only in terms of the various roles of a combined service and not in terms of the structure of individual services.'[23]

'The Estimates', said Healey, were being presented 'in terms purely of individual services and the old staff manuals which I myself had to learn in the British Army a quarter of a century ago'.[24] By contrast, McNamara was making his case to Congress for huge expenditure in '170 pages of closely reasoned argument relating every item of expenditure to the role of the particular combined force to which it relates'. There was 'a detailed account of the costs of every project . . . Above all, there is a careful assessment of the nature of the military threat for which these forces are required and a very careful judgement of the impact of this defence budget on the national expenditure as a whole.'[25]

In the same efficient planned spirit, it was for us, argued Healey, 'to decide priorities in defence expenditure according to the political judgement of what is thought to be the likely development of world affairs over the next 10, 15 or 20 years and to decide what sort of forces we are mostly likely to need and where'.[26] The problem for the combination of hubris and central planning implied by an ostensibly wise desire to cut, dry and estimate long, would come for Britain in the agonies of an economy trapped in low growth and unsuccessful defence of sterling. For the United States, it would lie in the continuance of a war in Vietnam beyond all McNamara's managerial skills to control, never mind win – everything, in short, which could be gathered under the dripping umbrella of Macmillan's melancholy dictum, 'Events, dear boy, events.'

But sharply to the immediate point, Healey faced up to our lack of resources for doing the sort of thing the Americans were doing with their pricey sea-carried brigade in the Mediterranean. 'It is no good imagining that we can do all these things and go on doing all the other things we have been trying to do and still keep the defence budget at anything like 7 per cent of the total national wealth.'[27]

In the late winter of 1963 he saw the need for things which, in 1968, he would have to dispense with. If we were to function usefully outside Europe, and he ardently assumed that we should[28] – we had to provide air cover. The government were proposing one or two very large carriers. The alternatives, many small carriers or a new form of vessel able to take VTOL (vertical take-off and landing) aircraft (a smaller carrier and/or a hybrid command carrier) were all going to be expensive. But 'These commitments are commitments which we cannot avoid and which, in my view, and, it seems in the view of both sides of the House, we should not seek to avoid in the years to come.'[29] Commitments would encounter events and be ground fine.

In fairness, if Healey would be proved over-optimistic about both our role and means, it was as a man urging scepticism and retrenchment upon the Douglas-Home government. He might have kept the door open nearly three years earlier for Polaris (and Skybolt when it was still a runner), but as a free agent he had mixed views on the submarine. Unlike Skybolt, they were undoubtedly effective and gave some evidence of being practically invulnerable but it was purely a weapon for use in strategic nuclear attack, which the Prime Minister had said was the least likely that Britain would have to face. Then there were doubts as to how independent of US control Polaris was.

Above all, Healey looked wistfully at an exchange then going on between the American and Soviet governments. It involved the prospect of freezing the number and type of strategic delivery systems. 'Does this mean that the Government would be prepared to forgo the Polaris programme if the Soviet Union and the United States would be prepared to freeze the number and type of strategic delivery systems?' Thorneycroft had better and more political fish to fry. Since Labour were sceptical about Polaris, it was worth starting a scare that they might cancel the boats and by extension leave us without a nuclear deterrent, independent or otherwise. 'Could I ask the hon. Gentleman an important and straight question? Will he cancel them or not?'[30]

Healey's answer was as candid as it was limited: 'I cannot yet say whether or not we will cancel the Polaris submarine. What I will say is that we will certainly not continue the programme in its capacity as an independent British force . . .' If Labour did cancel it, he added, they would have no hesitation in turning the actual boats into hunter-killer submarines – 'a programme of certain and immediate value to the British Navy and to national defence which has been set back five years by the Polaris programme.'[31]

He was pressed further by Thorneycroft and this brought a personal avowal. 'Speaking personally, I do not think, I do not believe that it would turn out to be a wise use of our resources to make this contribution to the alliance.' Ministers, he added, 'should make their minds up whether they believe in alliances or not'.

The argument between the parties was of a sterile and interim sort, factitious on the Tory part since Labour were never going to bow out of some form of British nuclear defence. And however much Healey might grumble about Polaris itself, what the man who negotiated it, Macmillan, had in common with the Opposition Defence spokesman was a profound sympathy and affinity with the Americans and a conviction that the only deals worth doing would be with them. The argument in the debate of 22 February was not sham, but it concerned dying embers, Thorneycroft's (and perhaps Douglas-Home's) wistful nationalism. Another ember would be Labour taking that absurd nationalism absurdly seriously. 'If the Government want to fight an election on a programme of atomic jingoism, we are quite prepared to defeat them on that programme as on any other.'[32]

On a more commonsense level, much of Healey's and Labour's want of rapture over Polaris related to cost. The British had been bitten so many times with great expectations, brilliantly sold weapons – Blue Streak, Blue Steel, Seaslug and Blue Water – whose bill of research and production had then bloomed orchidaceously. The American Skybolt had also proved an expensive failure. Polaris worked, for sure, but the idea of its ultimate bill not being a horrid multiple of the estimate was very bold thinking. In fact, estimated at £92.9 million, it would work out at substantially less. While the submarines themselves worked out only 6 per cent above estimate at £162 million.[33] Healey's caution would be unnecessary, but on the strength of past experience, was reasonable enough. Macmillan's American deal was going to be just that – American and a deal. Once seen to be that, the rhetoric on both sides would lift like fog.

28

EN FAMILLE

Whatever might go right or wrong with the Labour Party or the looming Ministry of Defence, the great success and happiness of life had been and would continue to be marriage. Edna Edmunds from Coleford in the Forest of Dean, university girlfriend – the Zuleika Dobson of Oxford – lost and found, who had married Denis on 21 December 1945, had made homes in Highgate, first at Gaisford Street, in 1952 at Langbourne Avenue, then in 1957 at Holly Lodge Gardens. There had been three children, Jennifer (Jen, Jenny or Jenjen), born first, Tim not long after, then, after a larger gap, Cressida.

From the Langbourne Avenue days a neighbour's daughter, Liz Boyd, remembers the Healey car, a blue Hillman Husky, PYN 262, and Denis swinging Tim perilously on one arm over a pond, also of being given lifts by 'the Edna taxi'. Neighbouring children were taken with Healey children by Denis to see *Henry V* at the Everyman Cinema in Hampstead and *Quo Vadis* on another occasion on which he left them, unaccompanied twelve-year-olds, watching an 'A' programme, to go to an intellectual French film down the road. There were also outings to places like Epping Forest. 'The Healeys,' says Paul Bell, another neighbourhood child of the 1950s, 'wore track suits and owned odd tents a generation before anyone else.' Not many other campers had a wobbly tooth, swung you round by an arm and a leg and sang 'Down the Sewer'. He also remembers 'the driver of the Hillman Husky on the way back with his hands off the wheel, singing "By the Light of the Silvery Moon". Another voice is saying "Denis, Denis".'

The children writing to their parents in 1995, in a family and neighbours garland to celebrate the Healeys' golden wedding,* recall 'going to the flicks'

---

* The source of all material quoted in this chapter.

with their father dressed, rather as Roy Jenkins remembered him at Oxford, in mac and black beret. They recall early hardware malfunction, appropriate in a Defence spokesman, the toy helicopter brought back from America which nearly scarred Tim for life. Jenny also remembers the volume of mail, two sacks of it waiting at the end of the summer holidays, and doing photography with her father, counting 'Mississippi one, Mississippi two', also her father's face when, by putting the wrong chemical in first, he ruined pictures he had taken of Mrs Khrushchev.

A good deal of time was spent with the grandparents on both sides in the North and the Forest of Dean. But during the Ministry of Defence period, the Healeys bought a cottage at Withyham on the Sussex–Kent borders to which they all got away for as many weekends as possible. The effort was made, in the face of the burden (and attractions) of office and politics, to be as much of a father and with the children as possible. But heavy burdens inevitably fell upon Edna. Against what is widely asserted today, this very intelligent, highly educated woman put her own creative talents aside, though not for ever, and divided her life into children, Denis, self – in that order! She had the talents of a legislator herself, but as noted above, she did not plunge into Leeds politics, making clear early on that the constituency would see more of her only when the children were grown, and then being as good as her word.

The whole relationship was summed up by Jennifer describing her mother, finding the children watching television while she worked, throwing her hands in the air with a cry of 'The ungrateful lot' and going out in the car on her own, only to turn back because she had left an apple pie in the oven and had no confidence that they would have the wit to turn it off. Denis was blessed with a lot of unfashionable devotion, the counterpart to his ferocious application to work. Cressida speaks of 'the space about Dad, the space never to be violated. "Shh, Dad's working. Don't play in the back garden, darling. Dad's working in his study'; also what the family called 'The Sacred Last Banana', the banana kept for Denis at the end of the day, together with a pint of milk.

The Healeys were something of a clan: 'Healey first and Healey last and nobody in between' was a chant Denis set up among them. (It might have been quoted at Mr Benn in 1981!) And they had something of a private language. The chair next to their father was known, after Arthurian terminology, as 'Siege Perilous'; Cressida speaks of 'a great hairy hand descending with a dad-like squeeze or a rough tickle that made you want to squirm away under the table and never sit so close again'.

A 'dicker docker' was a dictionary. Sometimes there were West Riding echoes: 'Nowt ter touch it' – an expression of deep satisfaction, and 'chiggy bread' – malt loaf; some of it was pure neologism: 'nubbly' for any pleasant taste, 'snelks' for snacks, 'weezer fizz', – any pleasant sensation as of a car going over a hump-backed bridge at speed (if that is thought pleasant). Such an undertaking might also involve 'Gritting along dreadlessly' – driving at high speed. Occasionally the language reflects Healey's affable primacy in the clan: 'Just reach out your arm' which Tim translates as: 'Get up from where you are comfortably sitting and get me a packet of crisps, my reading glasses; do a whole weekend's shopping from Sainsbury's.'

At least one piece of private Healeyese went public and delighted the nation when Denis turned to Ian Mikardo ('Not as nice as he looks' – Winston Churchill), accusing him of being 'out of his tiny Chinese mind'. It has been quoted with a mixture of reproach as dangerous directness or rejoiced in as blessed political candour. But it was apparently a standard family expression, usually put in the interrogative, and meaning 'Are you crazy?' A final echo of Yorkshire – as Lancashire would see it – was 'Healey's bounty'. This was any exiguous gift, any small grant of nothing very much. It derived from the time Denis was courting Edna. He had been eating an apple and, noting a boy watching, offered him the core. This is cognate with the Oldham account of teatime in Huddersfield: 'Have you had your tea? We've had ours.' He was, said Edna to her children, authentically puzzled. 'I would have loved a core when I was his age.' For a chancellor who would have to impose a succession of cuts, Healey's bounty was a great start.

As a family, the Healeys were keen holidaymakers. Though anything but mean, despite the above, they organised their own economy class by way of a variety of tents: the igloo, an orange one with a dome set on a pneumatic frame, a mountaineering tent for Tim. But the greatest of these was the 'Palanquin', another Healeyism, something built on Denis's specification by a Swiss company to incorporate living and cooking areas. It was celebrated for always seeing off the menace of high winds by falling down.

The pressure on Edna, also her sheer niceness, were caught by her younger daughter: 'Mum putting on a brave face,' recalls Cressida. 'Admiralty House [home when Healey went to Defence] – Mum pacing about, pulling at her hair hating how she looked, hating feeling invisible. Mum coming home from one of those fancy dinners with little packets of sugar and butter from the table and once, bless her, a little marzipan fruit from their dessert.'

The relationship between the two of them was intensely strong. At the time of the golden wedding, Cressida recalls being moved to tears 'when Dad spoke of how much he loves Mum. No artifice or fooling about in him saying how much she matters to him and how much she's given him. Hearing him worry about her when she didn't call as expected. I can't say how moved I was to see this and hear this.'

Jo, Tim's wife, who as tentative girlfriend had been first welcomed to the labyrinth of Admiralty House with great kindness and an explanation that there had been fifty ladies from Leeds in for tea so would she mind helping with the washing-up, also has a recollection of Denis. 'Not to be seen at A.H. except politely and briefly in passing, always in suit and tie. But then down at the cottage, he tapped her on the shoulder and presented her with a large black hairy-legged spider. Not being afraid of spiders and saying 'Ah, nice' she apparently passed a test. Such excesses were part of Denis's style with his children and other people's children. 'Denis, don't,' quotes Tim.

'This vain cry from Mum was a leitmotif in the Healey family life, uttered reproachfully when Dad was, for example, fiercely swinging a 6-month-old baby by its arms over a precipice or imitating a mental defective.'

It was, by the accounts of its members, a happy, noisy, experimental sort of family. Healey himself has worried that his father's inability to express affection and get across to him may have been echoed in his relations with Tim. It was also true that Cressida, the youngest and perhaps the most modern-minded of them, was unhappy at Admiralty House and spent some time at a boarding school. But the tributes hardly suggest poor relationships. Nor does the regularity with which the children turn up in the diaries, anxiously or with relief when happy or just come home.

Any serious politician, especially the head of a major department, is unbelievably busy, both with work and the sort of things ministers are supposed to do in the way of meetings and social gatherings. Family breakdown is almost a commonplace among political husbands and wives. Blessed by Edna's self-sacrifice, Denis did not have beyond his work, a second front of family unhappiness. He was boss in an abstracted busy way, but also fond, affectionate, joky and for ever able to make wife and children fall about laughing. As a pulpit phrase in the mouth of politicians, 'family values' is cant. But all the Healeys had values and lived by them. And in Denis's case, he was able to do the vast volume of work he undertook sustained by them.

At one point, Tim speaks of 'maximum extraction being a Healey motto'. It was. The crowded hour of glorious life was taken out of work and family life alike. Edna and the children were essential to Denis, however abstracted, rushing and March Hare-like the minister may have been, and they seem to have shared in the exhilaration.

29

RUN-UP TO ELECTION 1964

The Labour Party, so recently at its own throat over nuclear weapons, had seen Gaitskell's entirely unexpected defiance rally moderate opinion within the party and make friends and voters outside. The perennial problem of reconciling what the party's most ardent members wanted and what the unredeemed citizenry preferred, had eased. Labour was now tilting in directions to make for electoral success. And with Gaitskell's death, Harold Wilson, perfectly incapable of making that stand himself, would inherit the favourable territory and use it brilliantly in the one period of his career universally agreed to be wholly successful, his first Leadership of the Opposition.

Clever, adroit, twenty-three years younger than the Prime Minister, Wilson could not have succeeded without the Conservatives. Macmillan had so bamboozled opponents for years with his cunning grace and opportunist flair that the dedicated socialist cartoonist, Vicky,* had created 'Supermac', elderly party in tights swinging down from the skies, Hermes accommodated to Superman. It was meant as mockery and had been turned by Macmillan's wit, luck and political touch into an involuntary compliment. But Hermes was about to become Icarus. A few months after emerging from pure diplomatic triumph, he would get rid of a chancellor doing at last the responsible thing and replace him with a brilliant gambler picking the wrong horse. In making that shift he would turn a reshuffle into a Chicago rubbing-out. Personally blameless, he would be hit by two scandals, both sexual, both inherently absurd, one of them modest, the other calamitous. And having read his own health wrongly, he would organise his

---

* The Austrian, Victor Weiss, drawing for the *Daily Mirror* and the *New Statesman*.

succession by a sleight of hand apparent to the naked eye which provoked two resignations from the Cabinet, and do all this on behalf of the wrong candidate.

Some of the change had to do with youth coming up and refusing to be impressed. A picture of Macmillan and a group of other elderly friends spread out with their Purdys across a grouse moor belonging to Lord Swinton aroused the grand and lethal simplicities of successful photo-journalism. The very term 'grouse moor' became a rhetorical hand grenade. The fierce but gentle indignation of Vicky had never punctured the skin; the smart cruelties of the young men on *Beyond the Fringe* and its successors ran clean through man, class and generation.

The economy had never quite worked for the Tories despite the early tri-umphs of Butler as de-rationer and de-regulator and the blessings of a major shift in terms of trade. Goods had come back into the shops in the early fifties but growth was laborious and slow. The currency, devalued by Labour in 1949, turned unhealthy and potentially vulnerable again. Incomes policies were tried and, after early efflorescence, didn't stick; the balance of payments ailed.

In response, Macmillan coined the slogan 'Exporting can be fun' and established a grand guiding committee, the National Economic and Development Council. It was affectionately known as 'Neddy', but Neddy was a character in the radio show, *The Goons*, and though given their best by distinguished economists and people from both sides of industry and multi-plied into specialist areas by the 'Little Neddies' of industry groups, Neddy was essentially an aspiration. It was the elaborate alternative to deflation, very much Labour's own sort of thinking, and would be cherished by the Wilson government. But it eventually ended under Thatcher, quite out of the new drastic fashion.

The other main timber of Macmillan's economic thinking would prove alto-gether less wholesome. He had won the 1959 election for several reasons, but owed a good deal to a highly inflationary Budget from a Chancellor, Derick Heathcoat-Amory very much under the Prime Ministerial thumb. And with Macmillan one never knew where Keynesianism left off and cynicism began.

It was best judged by a future Treasury colleague of Healey's, Edmund Dell, who would write: 'caution was thrown to the winds. The overall Budget deficit projected, £730 million, was larger than any since the war . . . Yet it was already known in March that there had been a substantial fall in unem-ployment, from 2.8 per cent to 2.5 per cent . . . The stimulus was given in full knowledge of the decline in unemployment in March and clearly for politi-cal reasons.'[1]

It worked – politically, but Selwyn Lloyd, Amory's successor, would inherit the consequences. Neddy had been created in response to an inflation becom-ing endemic. But reflation was the only economic tune Macmillan really cared for and after two years of Lloyd trying to cope in a pedestrian but honest way with the fruits of voter-stimulation – higher interest rates and stagnation – Macmillan, his eyes on an election in 1963, yearned to play it again, though not perhaps with the rhapsodic frenzy of his new soloist.

The policy of his last Chancellor, Reginald Maudling, was Macmillanism without the world-weariness. Maudling believed superabundantly in expansion. He proposed – and went for – a 'dash for growth'. Edmund Dell again: 'The policy behind the 1963 Budget was a gamble fashioned by politics.'[2] It was a policy continued through 1964, despite indications that the balance of payments was going the wrong way. Seeking, as he said, 'to achieve a smooth transition from the recent exceptionally rapid rate of growth to the long-term growth rate of 4 per cent', he withheld the restraining taxation suggested even by the Keynesian National Institute, offering only a quarter of the proposed take. Maudling was confident that he was 'doing enough to steady the economy without going so far as to give a definite shock to expansion'.[3] Trade figures deteriorated across the first two quarters of 1964, and in July, the annualised estimate of the payments deficit reached £600 million.

Maudling's approach combined electoral cynicism (which Labour, flatly unwilling to challenge anything so agreeable, shared), with genuine belief that a risky break into expansion was the only hope for a stumbling economy. Electorally he was nearly right which, electorally, is never quite enough. Economically Maudling was set upon high growth, quoting 'guiding light' figures to be aimed at – higher production would mean higher productivity. It also involved tax cuts which went down delightfully with his party. But as he was expanding an economy with a shortage of skilled workers, wage pressure followed naturally. And he was using the reserves with no clear idea whether the outcome was increased investment or consumption. In this, he had been carried so far from Macmillan's own earlier objective, an overall balance of payments in surplus by £350–450 million, that the final deficit inherited by Labour would be £800 million! Labour's economic cross and its electoral jewel for the next but one election of 1966 had both been fashioned.

Under Selwyn Lloyd the wheels of the cart had turned laboriously through the mud, but it had never endangered the passengers. The event of removing Lloyd in 1962, as much as the appointment of his furiously driving successor, had done exactly that. Lloyd, a professional good servant, was told to go without any notice at all and not offered, as would have been wisdom, an alternative post. Angry and bitter, he did not observe the customary Samurai code of tight-lipped submission to the axe. The head kept talking and his great friend John Hare, Minister of Labour, responded with his own resignation. The appointment of Maudling as Chancellor bitterly disappointed Sir David Eccles, who was interested neither in a lesser post nor in staying on.

By the time Macmillan had fitted in other, quite reasonable end-of-career replacements, including the Lord Chancellor, Kilmuir, no great loss but not handled well and also aggrieved, he was seven down and awash with

resentment. At this time the left-wing press had become very keen on the
East German Berliner Ensemble which had visited recently and whose special piece was Bertolt Brecht's version of *The Beggar's Opera*. Its leading
character is the highwayman MacHeath, otherwise Mack the Knife. To
this would now be added an unkinder parallel with Hitler's massacre of difficult henchmen in 1934 – the Night of the Long Knives. As bad publicity
goes, it was terrible.

But to violence would soon be added sex. Maudling was able to run his
free-rein Budget in 1964 for the good reason that the general election had
been postponed from 1963. This had happened because sexual intercourse,
if not beginning in 1963, certainly flourished – in all the wrong places: government and the headlines.

Two cases occurred, one in a sense triggering the mishandling of the other.
Charges against a junior minister, Tam Galbraith, of homosexual involvement with a civil service clerk revealed to be a Russian informant were never
substantiated. But Macmillan, uncharacteristically angry at the entirely characteristic nastiness of the lower press, responded to the next instance with an
unwise combination of trust and vengefulness.

The involvement of John Profumo – who had of course at one stage been
Denis Healey's brigadier in Italy – with a pretty girl and quasi tart, Christine
Keeler, might have created smiles of understanding among the non-prigs of
politics. But Macmillan was so keen to get back at the men in dirty raincoats
and their proprietors that he was spoiling for a fight. Profumo, it has often
been said, lied. But the untrue answer he gave was the one the Prime Minister
wished to be told. Most important of all, it was not a question which needed
to be asked. The only employable charges related to possible involvement
with another supposed Keeler contact, the Russian diplomat Evgeny Ivanov,
and intervention in the trial of a minor West Indian heavy, 'Lucky' Gordon.
The answer to both of these was a 'no' whose truth has never been disputed. The superfluous question came from Iain Macleod and in the plainest
terms – 'Did you fuck her, Jack?'

From a clever man it was a silly question, one leading directly to the
breaking of the ninth commandment – 'Thou shalt not bear false witness' –
and the more important eleventh – 'Thou shalt not be found out.' The consequences were horrendous: formal denial in the House of Commons, Prime
Minister in attendance, libel lawyers threatened, honour invoked, all the
trumpets and drums of the governing class. R. A. Butler was appalled and
warned against the whole procedure.

The line being defended covered more than a single accused minister. A
private-enterprise sexual jaunt by Profumo would have been far less explosive than his membership of a circle of play based on Lord Astor's riverside
palazzo, Cliveden, around whose swimming pool Christine Keeler had been
pursued naked. Interest in who fell within that circle would be directed in a

speculative, word-of-mouth frenzy at other ministers, at bishops, judges, peers, royalty itself.

The press, set free by Profumo's subsequent confession, more injurious than his lie, could both construct the fantasy of an entire inheriting class occupied with late Roman excess and roll editorial thunder against it. Cliveden was a big house, people who lived in big houses clearly engaged there in promiscuous sex in all its variants at all times. And for the purposes of public debate, the people who lived in big houses were the Conservative Party.

Harold Wilson, like a shrewd man, made no points about sex. It was the lie that mattered, a lie which had only been told because sex does matter – does so by reason of being furiously interesting. When the whole episode was exhausted – Lord Denning's report, the trumpetings of *The Times* whose editor, Haley, hated Macmillan, and Viscount Hailsham waving his arms about – an election in 1963 was out of the question. Macmillan's own next stumble, acceptance of the erroneous belief of two stand-in doctors that he had cancer of the prostate, brought about his precipitate resignation.

Not only would the handling of delicate things like the economy and the election fall to a tersely gracious second-liner, the Earl of Home, but Macmillan's infallible instinct at this stage for getting things wrong meant that Home was burdened, not just by his own limitations, but as the beneficiary of a screaming fix. Macmillan had a quiet obsession that his old opponent, Butler, must never be Prime Minister. The fact that Butler had been a successful Chancellor and a major reforming Home Secretary counted for nothing. It led him to an elaborate and shabby rolling of logs and filtering of canvassed opinion, so that Home nor Hailsham, both hereditary members of the House of Lords, the one obscure, the other eccentric, should by means of cunningly prepared new legislation become eligible for a post which neither man was up to. The consequence of all that would be open schism in the party, with two major players, Macleod and Enoch Powell, resigning from the Cabinet and Macleod (who had quickly become editor of the *Spectator*) in a public indictment masquerading as a book review,* blasting the whole affair open. Bad publicity was being laid like linoleum.

Macmillan was still a formidable political figure. Butler would have been *neu-alt*, a new Prime Minister but identified across twelve years with the Tory Party's greatest achievements, and as much as Macmillan himself, with its liberal moderate reputation. Given the final defeat of the ghostly Home in October 1964 by only four seats, a workable Tory majority under a Macmillan waiting for a second opinion or under Butler rationally allowed his turn, is a fair assumption.

---

* Of Randolph Churchill's instant and Macmillan-spun account of the succession crisis, *The Fight for the Tory Leadership* (1964).

The narrow margin of the eventual Labour victory in 1964 was owing to Maudling, not Home – it was the sterling crisis which would impale Harold Wilson and his government. Would a Butler government have been wiser?

Certainly a Tory government which had been more orthodox and mindful of balance of payments deficits would have done more than benefit the economy. It would have changed history. Maudlingism was popular and played its full part in pulling the party back from a prospective heavy defeat to the photo-finish of the actual result. A prudential Tory chancellor would have made no such friends and done no such harm.

The incoming Labour government after such a course of scrupulous restraint would have had a majority of at any rate 25 to 30. It would have been able to govern comfortably for the customary four years. The £800 million deficit would have been absent as albatross and alibi. The occasion and the weapons of a second early election would have been absent. And that Labour government would not have been struggling with a devaluation crisis as Labour would do until they lost it in 1967. It would be reasonable to expect Labour to have had time and atmosphere in which to do their own thing, which in all conscience was conservative enough.

What did happen, a Conservative Party defeated by very little but just enough, with inflation given a push, a mighty overall deficit and the pound instantly under siege before the new government had found its desks, would serve as foundations for a low-rise Labour edifice and a general conduct of the economy which would be cautious and currency-patriotic to fatal excess.

'Sorry about all this,' Maudling, always as good-natured as insouciant, is supposed to have said to Callaghan on handing over. He could scarcely say less. The economic failings of the Macmillan–Home government had culminated in late arrangements for Labour to spend half its six years in office around the bed of sterling. But it would be Labour which refused surgery.

30

ELECTION 1964 AND AFTER

Healey's personal part in the election was straightforward. He had been re-elected without problems and faced a two-horse race against his opponent of 1959, John Fawcett, a Cambridge graduate working in the brewing trade. The *Yorkshire Evening Post* had kind things to say all round. Fawcett was very widely liked, Healey was 'a dark, intense but friendly member of the Shadow Cabinet' and 'Leeds knows Denis Healey of the beetling eyebrows and wide smile as the most approachable of men.' Edna was 'a vivacious brunette'. Whoever won, thought the *Post*, an attractive candidate must lose.[1]

The campaign followed this pattern. Fawcett's hardest recorded words for Healey came in a pamphlet – described as 'piquant' by the *Post*, which drew attention to Healey's absence from the constituency for a few days. Raising a couple of party points, Fawcett added rhetorically, 'Ask your Labour candidate – that is, if you can find him.'

In fact although a member of the Shadow Cabinet, Healey was not especially heavily drawn upon for the national campaign, though *The Times* lists him as speaking at two meetings in his home town of Keighley on the evening of 9 October. He also took part in a party political broadcast which involved meeting a group of people for questions in a suburban sitting room together with Gordon Walker, Ray Gunter and James Callaghan. *The Times* found the *tout ensemble* 'just a little too fluent to be true', but with the four spokesmen 'calm and untroubled throughout their inquisition'. Healey's only comment picked up by the press related to a question about teachers' pay, on which he assured viewers that a review was promised.

His only important contribution on his own subject was on 13 October, to damn the government in a testy, patriotic way for its dependence on the US for nuclear weapons. 'The Conservatives tell us that we can never be great again unless we go cap in hand to the Americans to get atomic weapons on the hire purchase system. Have we really sunk so low? We believe that greatness cannot be bought from foreigners on the instalment plan. It is something we must do by our own efforts.'

He was to be attacked by his old friend Teddy Heath. Clement Attlee had intervened with a speech endorsing the party's position on defence and, according to Heath, 'a desperate attempt to cloak with respectability Harold Wilson's surrender on defence policy to the left wing of the party'. Even the most honest politicians find themselves saying such things. Healey did genuinely dislike the Polaris deal and is still to be found grumbling *sotto voce* in his memoirs. He was also custodian of a party line which had to accommodate left-wing grumbles. Patrick Gordon Walker, a man of angular and painful honesty, would similarly imply possible rejection, saying, 'Labour wants to avoid the crippling burden of a system for whose supply and maintenance we should be wholly dependent on another power.'

But Healey had taken elaborate care to keep the option open when drafting Labour's official policy against the day of Skybolt or Polaris. Equally, he could hardly start another row inside the party by positively embracing the deal in mid-election. But continuation of the agreement was extremely likely, though Polaris would surprise him by its cheapness when he saw official figures. Perhaps disliking something to which he half expected to be shackled, he saw no harm in giving it a useful kick during the election. As for Heath, he was able to make a dubious point about the unsoundness of Labour on nuclear defence because the almost excessively sound Wilson had gone to such lengths to imply to his party that he might not be. It was a small round dance of universal disingenuousness.

The circle described by Harold Wilson during the election is harder to square. Wilson, who had been stopped in his tracks in one town – 'Why do I stress the navy?' 'Because you're in Chatham' – was even more expansive in Plymouth: 'I believe we shall need an expanded naval shipbuilding programme. How are we going to pay for it? Out of the savings made by stopping wasteful expenditure on the politically-inspired nuclear programme.'[2] Enoch Powell, who on 7 March 1966 lovingly quoted this speech in the debate following Healey's cancellation of further aircraft carriers, spelt out what this tremendously left-wing-sounding and rank-and-file-pleasing trope amounted to. 'That was the £15 million for stopping the fifth Polaris submarine.'[3] Wilson, in the same speech, talked eloquently about aircraft carriers and in this context used the phrase, 'This is taking dangerous risks with our defences.'[4] It was not in so many words a promise to keep them rolling, but in Plymouth in 1964 might have been taken for one.

While such things were said before Maudling's chickens came home to roost, Labour had already planned major defence economies and did not intend to seriously diminish its nuclear involvement. The point of aircraft carriers in 1964 was that they were built in naval yards, often in marginal constituencies, by voters Labour wanted to keep. Ironically, if Wilson had been 'frank' or 'candid', words which he kept handily by for all episodes of ambiguity, his majority of four might never have materialised, leaving the Conservative Party with the economic (and naval) consequences of the 'dash for growth', easily the best thing that could have happened to Labour.

As it was, the election would conclude, as it seemed, satisfactorily. And in Leeds East Healey's majority was pleasantly up.

Denis Healey 29,480
John Fawcett 21,474

His majority of 8006 was a solid improvement on the 4785 he had regis-tered when also running against Fawcett in the bad year of 1959. But his own total, as for many Labour victors in an anticlimactic result, had not appreci-ated very heavily. He had collected 28,707 votes in 1959.

It was enough though for the footstool of the Privy Council, for the motorway of running a great department. There had never been any serious doubt since February 1963 that he would succeed to the substantive post, as Richard Crossman had recently found out. Taking Wilson to dinner on 13 November 1963 Crossman affected to believe that 'of all Labour Party poli-cies, our defence policy is the weakest and with Denis Healey there who is a rather adventurous young man who sensationalizes everything, we are in a weak position.'[5] He shared that view with George Wigg, and both 'thought that we must get on to Harold and insist that there should be some kind of job done now, to work out a defence policy to be valid over a period of time'.

At the dinner Wilson had talked vaguely about Crossman and Wigg being able to 'knock out something on defence like the brilliant things we have done before'.[6] Crossman had said, in his usual bright, disobliging way, that 'what's really wrong is having Denis Healey as Shadow Defence Minister. Why not throw him out and put George Brown in?'[7] Wilson's reply, sounding genuinely alarmed, that that would establish victory for Callaghan over Brown on the conduct of the economy is perfect Labour politics to the last, resentful, terri-torial twitch. Healey, in his group-averse, under-political way, was not missing anything and exposed to no danger.

There was never any prospect that Healey would *not* receive the seals for Defence and its vast problems. The only alternative might have been an actual advance upon the post – to the Foreign Office. For Patrick Gordon Walker had lost his Smethwick seat to the racially unfastidious campaign of Peter Griffiths. In fact, Gordon Walker would be asked to soldier on, a min-ister without a seat until it could be found for him. This would be at Leyton where local annoyance at the inconvenience led to a second defeat and the effective end of an unlucky career.* But there was rather more to the question of the Foreign Secretaryship. Edward Short, then Deputy Chief Whip, working with his chief, Herbert Bowden, on appointments at the three levels of minister, knew what Healey really wanted. 'We spent some time together during a trip to the Middle East and he made it clear that he wanted, passionately, to become Foreign Secretary.' Ted Short's view of why this did *not* happen is instructive. 'Harold wanted to be his own Foreign Secretary. The last thing he was looking for was a strong, expert figure in that job. So he had Gordon Walker who was, well, a gentleman, and Michael Stewart who was happy to do what Harold wanted. And when he *did* get somebody strong with his own opinions, in George Brown, it was explosive.' He added that he thought that 'Denis would have been superb.'[8]

Healey, having been interviewed by a Robin Day more excited about the simultaneously announced fall of Khrushchev than the rise of Healey, went to bed at three in the morning when the majority looked good for 20 seats. By the time he and Edna got home, the majority was down to 4 and the Chinese had let off their first nuclear weapon. Shortly after his arrival, the Prime Minister called with a combined offer of the Ministry of Defence and notice that Healey's acceptance of it had been passed to the Queen.[9]

The usual splendours were laid on: Daimler Sovereign and official accommodation, a flat in Admiralty House, formerly the perquisite of the First Lord of the Admiralty who had been abolished. But there was room also for Short, now Government Chief Whip.

Accordingly *The Times* of 19 October 1964 was busy profiling the new Secretary of State. 'Denis Healey, approaching his task with characteristic zest, realises that he is faced with crucial problems.' It stressed the pressure on the new minister for a cut in the level of spending and expected a review of all programmes in the pipeline, with cancellations of some previous commitments, perhaps the P1154. *The Times* also felt that the TSR2 aircraft might be affected, though it was possible that it could form 'part of Britain's contribution to an alliance nuclear force'.

The paper noted that Healey had already exchanged telegrams with his role model, Robert McNamara, adding that 'If, as seems likely, the Government finds Polaris too far advanced to be given up without unacceptable cancellation costs, the answer might be a mixed-manned and national combined force involving Polaris and V Bombers and with Britain generally contributing a much larger share than the 10% now contemplated.'

The report was equally sure that Healey would wish to move quickly

---

* Gordon Walker would return as Education Secretary after the 1966 election but, thoroughly demoralised by his double dose of misfortune, did not make much of a fist of it and finally went altogether, a life peer before his time.

over the functional changes at the Department, and the job designations for junior ministers were an indication of this. The forecast for defence, ended the paper cheerily, was 'anything but dull – Fresh winds, cold in places, and a chance of scattered thunder storms.'[10]

Healey himself is a little droll about the buzz of ambitious backbenchers who offered their seats to Gordon Walker if only he, Healey, would make them junior something at the Army or Air. John Cronin, the MP for Loughborough, 'rang anxiously to say he would like to serve under me'. Reginald Paget, an MFH and then nearest thing Labour had to an old-style county Member, used a call to advocate proxy voting given the government's tiny majority, to drop in the thought that 'if a Minister, would be glad to go to the Lords and leave Northampton for Patrick Gordon Walker.'[11] Both would be disappointed.

First appointments brought in Frederick Mulley, who had wanted the Ministry of Aviation,[12] as both Deputy Secretary of State and Minister for the Army. And as Ministers of State, Christopher Mayhew was assigned to the Navy and Lord Shackleton to the Air Force. Mulley, though Healey early complained about anxiety and nagging, was a genuine slogging specialist who had published a relevant book, *The Politics of Western Defence*, two years earlier and would in 1974 become a perfectly competent Secretary of State himself. The normally astringent Admiral Hill-Norton has a solid respect for him, but Field Marshal Carver speaks dismissively of a 'A dear little dormouse of a man'.[13]

Mayhew, an Oxford contemporary of Healey and an anti-Communist when the Party was the height of chic, had been early spotted for brilliance and as early discounted. He possessed genuine courage, notably in a stubborn sympathy with the Palestinians, arguing their case when, to all 1960s cocktail opinion, they were no-account Arabs resisting a splendid cause. But Mayhew had neither force nor authority. At Defence he would fight his corner for the navy over aircraft carriers yet never win the respect of a key sailor like Peter Hill-Norton. He lost that argument, resigned on principle as politicians are always said not to do, became an early convert from Labour in the early days of resurgent leftism and died a Liberal peer.

Eddie Shackleton, as everyone called him, would in due course sit in the Cabinet and lead the Lords. He was much loved, never a major force in politics and no trouble. An associated minister at the Cabinet-edge was Alun Gwynne-Jones defence correspondent of *The Times* who, with a Wilsonian flourish of wish-fulfilment, was designated both 'Minister for Disarmament' and Lord Chalfont. He had been offered a Cabinet secretariat job under George Wigg and had thought it insecure.

In fact he was third choice for the Disarmament post, offered first to Kenneth Younger who had left politics in 1959, and on his declining it, to Solly Zuckerman. Both Healey and Mountbatten 'strongly advised refusal'.

Healey describes a spat with the Prime Minister over this which, in its laconic way, shows him in Attlee style. Wilson had rung up to try to force the appointment through, 'threatening to veto Mulley otherwise. Stayed firm. Home at 11.30.'[14]

There were also, in the new set-up, three parliamentary under-secretaries who were service-linked. The innocuous old leftist J. P. W. Mallalieu went to the Navy; the heavily responsible Bruce Millan, from whom across a long and rising career fitly ending in Brussels, no fire would ever be struck, served the Air Force. The Army had as its number two, Gerry Reynolds, someone of serious quality, a fast-talking, wittily combative man, arguably a George Brown without the flaws, whose death from cancer five years later, at the age of forty-two, removed a prospective Cabinet minister.

They were perhaps all wasted on Healey. Sir Frank Cooper, much later departmental Permanent Under-Secretary, but at this time Healey's Private Secretary, said of junior ministers: 'Denis was always perplexed by them. He wasn't quite sure what they were for.' Sir Frank also admiringly compared his minister to 'a selfish centre forward who wouldn't pass the ball. Anything interesting or difficult and Denis's arm went out to grab it.'[15] Lord Hill-Norton is more succinct: 'Denis didn't give a fish's tit for junior ministers.'[16]

His colleagues among the senior military would be an airman, Charles Elworthy, universally called 'Sam', originally from New Zealand and a lawyer, generally popular and admired for clarity of mind. His deputy was another trained lawyer, Air Vice-Marshal Peter Fletcher.[17] The naval head was Sir David Luce who had been involved at the start of the increasingly preoccupying operations in Borneo. Luce was also widely liked but a fundamentally moderate man who was unhappy fighting wildcat battles for a service interest, something which had won him a rap of Lord Mountbatten's lorgnette: 'though loyal, he had not the character or perception, the job is above his head.'

Few people would have been less mindful of 'Dickie's' contempt than General Sir Richard Hull, CIGS – Chief of the General Staff meaning army staff chief. Hull had been a brave active soldier who had fought in the drive on Tunis after the landings in French North Africa and, like Healey, had been engaged in Italy, doing battle painfully around Ceriano and in the assault on the Po valley in 1944. Hull despised Mountbatten, regarding him as a mountebank and liar. Hull, though capable enough, was essentially an administrative conservative very much at odds with the structural reforms now beginning to go through. Despite the animus, Hull sweetened the blow of his own elevation to Field Marshal for Mountbatten, who had tried to block it, by appointing him Colonel in the Life Guards which had a particularly fetching uniform.[18]

Mountbatten was Chief of the Defence Staff, a new title created for his predecessor but with him in mind, one presuming powers not all garnered

yet. A genuine reformer, but also a hoarder of power, he had failed calamitously in small- and medium-sized undertakings: the *Kelly*, for whose loss
any less well-connected naval officer would have been cashiered, and the
Dieppe Raid, an idea so long in the cooking that the enemy were sitting at
table when it was served. That project cost 4000 lives, mostly Canadian,
something which earned the formidable hatred of Lord Beaverbrook.
Mountbatten would begin by calling Healey 'nice', but live to take enormous
pleasure when, at General Eisenhower's funeral, an American TV commentator announced 'Lord Louis Mountbatten arriving attended by his Royal
Marine and civilian aides', 'One of whom was, joy of joys, "Denis
Healey"!'[19] Healey meanwhile was hearing other people's views. Sir Robert
Scott, the former Permanent Under-Secretary, 'dislikes and distrusts Dickie as
a dishonest Prussian'.[20]

The other key man was the Chief Scientific Officer, or in the alphabetically
crazed way of the military apparat, 'CSO', Professor Sir Solly Zuckerman, a
man of many fingers and many pies: zoologist, expert on primates, heavily
involved in running the London Zoo, whom Healey had heard as a young
don lecturing at Oxford on sexual hormone research. Zuckerman's chief
impact would lie in promoting rapidly varying ideas which, if rejected, he
would push secretly with other ministers. Two military historians put it less
delicately: 'he was also seen as an iconoclastic political manipulator with a
dangerously brilliant analytical brain and sceptical outlook.'[21]

The Secretary of State's ultimate let-out with Zuckerman would be to
dump him on Harold Wilson to advise at Number 10. Not that the ideas
were not shrewd. He was, for example, an early sceptic about the TSR2 as
too expensive too late. In this he was in agreement with Mountbatten and
there was talk of 'the Zuk-Batten axis'. Healey agreeing would, more or less
painlessly, get rid of both of them – and the plane.

On his first professional sight of his new colleagues, Healey was as criti-
cal as ever he had been about Byzantine friezes. 'Mottishead, spinsterly,
Drew no good, Army, Hull, typical cavalry officer, v. anti-Shan Hackett,
Cassels by far the best, fighting soldier but not a politician ... DCAS
Hopkins very good, Derek Stapleton Bomber Command v. good, Elworthy
good B plus, Hartley useful.'[22] He would also add cryptically that Elworthy,
though 'good and smart', was very 'Wogs have Migs'.[23] About his first
Cabinet, Healey was brisk and under-impressed. He had sat opposite Wilson
and to the left of the Lord Chancellor, Gerald Gardiner. The Home Secretary,
Frank Soskice, wasted time; Frank Cousins, brought in as one of Wilson's
anxious building blocks as Minister of Technology, was 'very friendly and a
bit talkative'.

Almost his first action in office was to tell Mountbatten, 'Most untrustworthy and faux bonhomme' and of an age to retire, that there would be no
extension; he wanted him at the end of his term to make way for Hull.

Healey noticed his reaction: 'delight and dropped eyes'. He was quickly mapping ahead the posts into which the senior military would settle, observing in an entry of 20 October a 'consensus' that Hull rather than Elworthy should serve as CDS, but for a single term only, because he was the best soldier available for many years and because Elworthy was 'irreplaceable as CAS [Chief of the Air Staff] – can be CDS soon anyway. Army feeling – Don't drop Buggins turn until Army had its best one go unless alternative was very obviously superior.'[24]

And he would have very early intimations of his concerns. He listed as 'Major issues' the NATO standing committee, a 'nuclear refitting yard location (political)' and assorted weapons and aircraft, the V235, and P1154, observing that this last was 'stymied' on the Weapons Development committee. The Chiefs were not keen on it, wanting GE Rolls-Royce engines. But the biggest preoccupation was the eternal TSR2. Healey, amid jottings about comparative costs, noted that the TSR2 was 'not v. superior to Blue Streak' and that the RAF would find it 'very difficult to man and maintain – a great strain on skilled manpower'.[25] There would also be a preliminary murmur about 'functionalism'. It was, he said, 'a dirty word, but not so dirty as "integration"'. Functionalism, the redesignation of jobs by what was done rather than which service did it, was coming to be accepted. Integration, which led logically to a single uniform single service, Canadian style, and involved 'All power to the Chief of Defence Staff à la Mountbatten', was straightforwardly detested. Healey's ultimate rejection of it would reflect his willingness to listen to his senior military advisers rather than railroad them. However radical so many of his moves might be, Healey was not an irksome new broom, changing for change's sake. Amendment and continuity was the pattern.

EARLY DAYS AS SECRETARY OF STATE

Nikita Khrushchev, ruler of the Soviet Union for ten years, had been replaced in an internal party coup. China had exploded her first nuclear bomb.

British politics had its own priorities, however, and the Labour government elected on the same day, self-preoccupied, would be affected much more by its own economic griefs than anything rattling away in another part of the Earth. And a government hit by a sterling crisis before its first breakfast in office would be thinking economy at all points. Wilson's Cabinet would be driven, across the three and a half years separating a ruling that devaluation was 'the unmentionable subject' from the day it devalued, by a need to demonstrate rectitude to the markets. As for Defence, it was torn between this priority and the other orthodoxy of being a good member of NATO, militarily significant enough to be heard by the Americans and granted that sovereign cliché – a place at the top table.

Healey's words to *The Times* about 'value for money' certainly reflected a general will to spend less on defence. This was not for nothing the least sought-after job in Labour politics. The country had also to be defended. And 'efficiency', performance for effort, has always been a good word in a political corner. But far more important, the brittle British currency, ever and again sold dear to be bought cheap by what Wilson would call 'the Gnomes of Zurich', intruded into sovereign political decisions. Labour had come in, post-Maudling, on the wrong foot. And through financial orthodoxy weakly applied, and devotion to a medium of exchange, it would fail to get on to the right one.

The wrong foot came down at a meeting on Saturday 17 October where Wilson, Callaghan and Brown and four civil servants, William Armstrong, Lawrence Helsby, Eric Roll and Donald MacDougall agreed that devaluation simply could not be contemplated. As Callaghan's biographer puts it, the very word was banned. 'Civil servants in effect removed it from their policy agendas, no papers were circulated on the topic, and there was no discussion of the topic again until July 1966.'[1]

It was a refusal to retreat which meant a requirement to defend a position which, being incapable of defence, would fall. In the intervening three years the Treasury would insist upon measures punishing and confining every department and denying its own purposes. The measures flowing from this resolute approach began with a deferral of National Insurance benefits which brought loud and effective screams from the Pensions Secretary, Margaret Herbison. When that expenditure was made after all in the Budget it started a small flood of selling, a great fall in gold and dollar reserves, and a decline in equities and gilt-edged stocks. The pattern was set.

In this sense, Healey, whatever his own choices might have been, would be confined by a prime ministerial mistake. The decision put compulsions upon defence policy as upon everything else a government might reasonably choose to do. Not at all accidentally, Wilson's own speech to the Commons on 'Defence and the Nassau Agreements' on 23 November 1964 devoted its first four and a half columns (heavily interrupted) to the question of sterling. And he would say that 'defence policy, on which the right hon. Gentleman [Sir Alec Douglas-Home] concentrated, foreign policy and economic policy are facets of a single unity.'[2]

Such considerations would indirectly affect attitudes to Polaris. Healey had always talked the submarine down in debate. But that weapon had its own flexible charm. It was representable among Conservatives as independent, and could be sold to the Labour Party as cheap. And according to his first biographers, Reed and Williams, the one piece of information provided by the Permanent Secretary at Defence, Sir Henry Hardman, which surprised him was 'the extremely low cost of this new deterrent'.[3]

Harold Wilson would use Chequers for a gathering of relevant ministers during the weekend of 21–2 November. Many aspects of defence arose and, if briefly, the whole principle of a continuing nuclear role was examined. The chief voices in favour of discontinuing the British nuclear commitment were George Wigg, whom Wilson had appointed Paymaster General where he would prove a quietly throbbing plague of intrigue and unpleasantness, and Wigg's nominee, Lord Chalfont.

According to Reed and Williams, Healey, with general support from the new Chancellor, Callaghan, and from Roy Jenkins, Minister of Aviation, saw off a never very likely lapse into nuclear opting-out. The authors speak of how Healey's 'ruthlessly logical attitude and lethal candour demolished the views of George Wigg and Lord Chalfont'.[4] Richard Crossman, a few months later, is to be found saying that Healey 'has not been dominant in Defence, but has let it be run for him by the PM and George Wigg',[5] not a credible view.

But the Chequers meeting involved much more than the ceremonial discounting of a non-nuclear Britain. It would concern itself with the future of the TSR2, with the P1154 aircraft and vexing American insistence upon mixed forces, Britain's future function East of Suez and, most immediately, with Polaris.

Healey's summing-up in the debate which Wilson had opened was even more clear about the financial pressures. 'If our defence spending imposes unacceptable strains on our economy, then it will weaken and not reinforce our influence in the world. When we decide the size and pattern of our defences, we must watch with extreme vigilance their impact both on our balance of payments and, even more important, on our productive resources, particularly in scientists and skilled manpower. . . . We must,' he added, playing the new signature tune, 'get value for money' (Hon. Members: 'Hear, hear.'). He had 'looked at the books' and he looked forward, by way of a mildly mixed metaphor, to 'discussing some of the skeletons found in the cupboard'. But party badinage apart, Healey was very serious. 'I want to share with the House and the country some of the basic facts which must govern our defence policy in the next ten years . . . unless we are to allow our defence expenditure to rise continually, not only in absolute terms, but also as a percentage of our rising national wealth, we must be prepared to reduce the calls on our military resources.'

After a nod in the direction of the pacific gods – the best possible solution being 'agreement with opponents abroad on measures of disarmament and arms control', Healey returned to what could happen. This involved looking at commitments made, observing their extent, and getting people ready for ending many of them.

One thing I have already learned from my first five weeks in office . . . is that Britain is spending more on her defence forces than any other country of her size and wealth. We are still trying to sustain three major military roles – to maintain an independent strategic nuclear striking power, to make a major contribution towards the allied defence of Western Europe and to deploy a significant military capacity overseas, from British Guiana through the Mediterranean, Africa and the Middle East to Hong Kong . . . I put it seriously to the House – and I hope that right hon. and hon. Members will listen seriously because I do not think there is disagreement between those of us who know the facts – that unless we are to impose unacceptable strains on our own economy and to carry a handicap which none of our main competitors in world trade has to bear, Britain too must decide which of these three roles should have priority.[6]

There were hints also in this speech of an issue which bothered the government: American enthusiasm for that Multilateral Force in NATO. This, generally called the MLF, had been the price to Macmillan of the Nassau Agreement. The MLF was supposed to meet the divisions within NATO, the hostility of de Gaulle to American primacy, the supposedly stirring nuclear ambitions inside West Germany – actually something of a mirage induced by the menaces the German Defence Minister, Strauss.

The practical effect would have been to provide for NATO countries without nuclear weapons to put crews of at least three different nationalities, language unspecified, into every nuclear-bearing ship – like Polaris! Healey would quote the German admiral who said 'he would rather swim than sail in it'.[7] The German Chief of Staff recalled to him that Adenauer, still incredibly running West Germany at eighty-six, had received the notion as 'a gimmick'.

The MLF was widely seen as a piece of Georgetown intellectual candy which, the German Chancellor thought, should be accepted as the sweetener to the French deal which mattered.[8] The purpose – giving West Germany some sort of involvement without scaring anyone else – looked and sounded like the political charade it was and cluttered up any military undertaking in the process. Healey and Wilson were in perfect agreement that they didn't want it, and Healey descending on Washington took advantage of uncertainty between the White House and its advisers, to urge successfully the impossibility of the MLF.

In the Commons Healey, taking on Douglas-Home who had some sympathy with the idea, noted the old Tory yearning for an independent deterrent. Home had both favoured a multilateral force and reserved the right to withdraw. 'It is no good talking, as did the right hon. gentleman today, about the need for maximum integration of forces and weapons in the Alliance if he has so little confidence in the integration that he gives the right to pull out in a crisis absolute priority over all other questions.'[9]

That sort of talk, added Healey, only made General de Gaulle's point for him. Also it helped those people in Germany who wanted an independent German nuclear deterrent 'which neither Britain nor the United States would be able to control'.[10] As far as he was concerned, the whole flurry of crisis around the MLF was an opportunity to rethink. And he paid a warm compliment to a Tory, the former Deputy Foreign Secretary Lord Carrington, who had asked, 'Did we believe that the proposal for a multilateral force should be used to prevent the spread of national nuclear forces by producing something which made national nuclear forces unwanted and unnecessary?'[11] Its replacement, in planners' minds the Atlantic Nuclear Force, pooled nuclear weapons, with British V-bombers functioning conventionally outside Europe, flourished then died its own death.

The idea was certainly going the rounds of what was not yet called the media, that Britain would submit to the plan. The *Sun*, still a decent, unsuccessful broadsheet, owned by the *Mirror* people, was convinced that a deal had been done. Wilson 'rebuked the *Sun* for sending back fictitious reports, in particular for suggesting that we had already sold out on the issue of the MLF'[12]

Crossman describing a Cabinet meeting of 13 December 1964, and with an irony not yet perceived, also quotes Wilson on Britain's still aspirant larger role. 'The most encouraging fact about the conference was America's emphasis on Britain's world-wide role; this line had been taken in particularly moving terms in a talk Denis Healey had had with McNamara on the plane to Omaha. McNamara had gone out of his way to emphasize the importance of Britain's role east of Suez.'[13]

The trip to Washington was seen as important in terms of all the British anxieties. What would the Americans do over the MLF? What would they, the British, have to do in the world? It was Wilson, after all, who would later talk about Britain having moral frontiers in the Himalayas.

TSR2

Once the government, at Callaghan's anxious urging, had settled to a threshold of £2000 million for the end of the decade, equipment – vessels and aeroplanes – would take the punishment. A large part of the military budget is pay, accommodation, pensions, training and other things not easily cut. Once a 10 per cent economy was decreed, a 40 per cent economy had to be exacted on equipment. In time that would include aircraft carriers, but for there and then – in 1964/5 – nothing was more urgent than a decision about aircraft. No aircraft was more urgently to be decided upon than the TSR2 – its initials standing for 'Tactical Strike Reconnaissance'.

As a future Chief of the Defence Staff would remark: 'Over the previous 13 years of Conservative administration, 26 major projects, costing £300m, had been cancelled, and current ones were escalating in cost and behind schedule.'[1] Labour's commitment to keep defence spending below £2000 million at 1964 prices accompanied a general readiness among the more realistic military to get out of the clutter of ordered, behind-schedule and price-escalating projects lying around. For once, the politician's cliché about clearing up the mess his opponents have left behind was a genuine sentiment. 'Healey,' said Lord Carver, 'was appalled at the mess he discovered in the aircraft field.'[2] Though, in fairness, the Conservatives themselves in their last White Paper had planned reductions to bring defence spending down by £400 million a year.

But the sources of the folly were not narrowly party-political. Lord Hill-Norton had sardonic recollections of the TSR2 as it illustrates endemic service sectarianism.

The TSR2? I can't remember where it came in the order of five aircraft the RAF never got. The RAF – I don't blame them – they thought they would *never* get one. But where the TSR2 was concerned, the Navy for once was in rather a strong position versus our light blue – allies? Opponents? *We* had the Buccaneer which was a really first-rate aeroplane. And we said to the RAF 'Why don't you have the Buccaneer for Christ's sake?' 'Oh well, we couldn't have a dark blue aeroplane. The service would go raving mad.' It was as bad as that.

Of course in the end they had to take it – and it was five years too late. If they'd taken it and modified it for land operations, they'd have been on the pig's back. Relations were so bad that they wouldn't take it for one reason and that was because it was painted dark blue. If they had taken it, the RAF would have been in a very strong position to have a new aeroplane about ten years later, the early seventies.

At the time of course they were still smarting because they hadn't got Polaris. So they were damned if they were going to have it and the fucking Navy could go to Hell. I wasn't sympathetic, I wanted to grind them down.[3]

That is just Peter Hill-Norton's rough way, but it tells a truth. The Buccaneer should have been developed jointly by air force and navy but no minister put down the necessary foot. TSR2 was a box of fascinating tricks: but production costs had increased 'to the point where the loss of a single aircraft could have been seen as a national disaster'.[4]

Healey had at the outset asked Sir William Cook, Chief Projects Officer at the Department, for economies in the programmes and budgets of the services, background to his first Defence Review. And an interim account of Cook's findings says succinctly: 'The last detailed costings available are those of summer, 1964, which assessed defence expenditure in 1969–70 on the basis of the programme then existing at £2285 m (1964 prices).'

The reporter, a more junior scientific civil servant, F. W. Armstrong, thought that figure should stand, but that a 'wedge' of about £100 million should be added to the 1969/70 figure 'to take account of extra costs'. Accordingly, the likely figure for 1969/70 would be 'expenditure of the order of £2400 m.'[5]

On previous experience, said the report with a trace of pain, insertion of an expenditure wedge was unavoidable. TSR2, P1154 and HS681 'had been at the forefront of such undertakings'. But the worst had not been reached. The heaviest spending had been 'slipping back' – presumably because production had been doing the same thing – and in the last year before full delivery, spending would be at its peak.

Using a tense which implied that a decision to cancel was inevitable, Healey concluded, 'It seems likely that if all three projects had continued, the forecast of £2400 m for 1969/70 might well have been an underestimate.'[6] If, however, all three were replaced by American purchases and a couple of other adjustments were made, then between £600 and £800 million could be saved in the next decade. Translating this into annual figures, the Department would have knocked £50 million off the starting figure, leaving it by 1969/70 at £2325 million. But if TSR2 carried on, it would put £80 million on to the current projection and, together with the wedge, would have them facing expenditure of £2500 million!

While TSR2 would have to be paid for on delivery (if delivered), they had spread payment for their option (later the F111, but then called the TFX) until 1978. During the election campaign, Healey had asked to what we had come, to be contemplating purchase from another country on hire purchase? What we had come to was a failed model with open-ended costs and a cheaper American option.

The paper had been very plain. 'At the outset therefore it would seem that the continuance of TSR2 would automatically rule out any prospect of continuing defence expenditure within £2000 m (1964 prices) by 1969/70.'[7] This was quotable authority for what Healey already knew he must do – cancel TSR2. It would be a brave decision: £400 million had already been irreversibly spent, there were jobs involved, the patriotic card would be played and Harold Wilson was not the man for brave decisions.

A central concern in the Cabinet was the position of BAC, the plane's makers, which employed skilled workers and a very fine design team. On 6 January Healey met the relevant minister, Roy Jenkins – who lived down the corridor at Aviation, and had BAC to worry about – 'over aircraft decisions which he took quite well' and faced a Cabinet committee – 'general agreement with cuts on the whole, though Cousins baffled. George meek and mild, Harold very helpful and friendly.'[8] But there would be trouble with Jenkins, whom he found anxious to keep fifty TSR2s, the financial argument for doing which Healey thought 'very spurious'.[9] There was here the start of a conflict which would only be resolved years later.

But at this time, January 1965, he paused for some brisk and physical politics. Patrick Gordon Walker, defeated in Smethwick over black immigration in the general election, had been found what should have been a safe seat in Leyton in east London. It was to be a frankly horrible election. A man, his face blackened with boot polish, turned up at the nominations with a placard saying 'Gordon Walker. The Race Mixing candidate. Make Britain Black.' And, a week later, 'Jordan dressed as a monkey was to be seen pacing to and fro outside Gordon Walker's headquarters in Leyton; he was carrying a placard which read "We immigrants are voting for Gordon Walker."'[10]

Colin Jordan, a former Coventry schoolteacher – viperous, hysterical and very soon forgotten – had espoused views to the right of the then main racist party, the National Front, forming his own British Nazi Party. Healey went down to speak for his Cabinet colleague, finding 'Hall full – about 300 of whom about 100 Nazi, Racist and Empire Loyalists.' As Healey downplays events, 'Colin Jordan got on platform. I forced him off – a lot of scuffling as police supervised expulsions.' Healey also describes 'still continuous noise when I spoke – but I roused the Labour supporters. Home without incident.'[11] It was rather stronger than this, with the Secretary for Defence[12] landing a satisfying heavy punch on the charging Jordan.*

It was magnificent but not victory. On 21 January Labour would suffer a swing of 8.7 per cent and Gordon Walker lose a safe seat by 205 votes. He would then resign as Foreign Secretary, making way for Michael Stewart.

Returning to the more civilised world of expensive military aircraft, after a Defence Council on 14 January where 'Roy had no support for TSR2 idea' and a briefing from Frank Cooper on the financial aspects, Healey on the 15th presented to the Defence and Overseas Policy Committee (DOPC) what he called his 'aircraft purge'. Over two hours, it seems to have been cheerfully received. 'Dickie said "Excellent", "first class", "splendid". Roy put TSR2 case, Jim Callaghan strongly supported. Cousins talked of past crimes of the Tories. Douglas Jay argued [that it was] too expensive in dollars and doubted TFX–TSR2 figures.'

As for the Prime Minister, 'Harold Wilson did a Macmillanesque ramble towards compromise', after which he informed Healey that he couldn't put him into the Foreign Office just yet as Gordon Walker might come back after the general election. In fact, Healey had made up his own mind to postpone any sort of crunch on TSR2 and to sort out the sort-outable first. He was already clear in his mind that one major project, the P1127, should definitely be kept and cherished.

On 25 January he is conferring with Henry Hardman and Sam Elworthy. Usefully, for the key voice of the air force and ablest of the Chiefs, makes a crucial admission: 'Sam at last agreed Air Staff now prefer TFX to TSR2 on *military* grounds.' And on the same day a still 'gloomy' Jim Callaghan was prepared to accept delay on the TSR2/TFX decision. Healey was making quiet and measurable progress even if all he had to show for it was agreement about delay.

At this time he was living a life delightfully packed, as a burst of diary jottings indicate. He rushes off to a lunch for the Japanese Foreign Minister where he talks with a FO expert on Russia. Back at the office, he has half an hour with a Malaysian minister – 'pressed him on deal with the Philippines' – then had another half-hour 'with Dick Hull and General William Sterling, C in C Northern Europe and BAOR – nice man'. After which he goes home (the Admiralty) and picks up his son, Tim, to show him the Ministry before

---

* There would be another fist fight at the Walthamstow by-election in 1968, when the National Front men attacked Healey who vigorously and physically defended himself, something watched admiringly by a future Conservative Chief Whip, Richard Ryder.

spending the evening at the theatre watching the Marat/Sade: 'brilliant production but confused play – Brecht plus *Oh What a Lovely War*.'[13]

Events of 28 and 29 January give a good idea of the way political things are actually done. At the Cabinet on the 28th,[14] after a *tour d'horizon* from the Chancellor, gloomy but in the light of history not gloomy enough, Healey announces to colleagues that 'he had managed to prune the increase in defence expenditure for 1965–6 from 5 per cent as envisaged by the previous administration, to 3.7 per cent'; this figure would be further reduced to an increase of less than 1 per cent if the economies he had proposed in military aircraft were accepted. He concluded by saying that 'a more rigorous and realistic appraisal of our defence commitments should now be made in the light of the situation described by the Chancellor of the Exchequer.'[15]

On 29 January, a 'marathon' DOPC agreed to Healey's own firm commitment to four Polaris boats, something achieved 'over George Brown who didn't want an independent deterrent and Jim Callaghan who wanted to save money'.[16] This was followed by a long wrangle on aircraft – 'finally accepted all I wanted, except TSR2 decision delay with 20% differential'. Even in Wilson's febrile and argumentative Cabinet, decisions approved in the appropriate committee would generally go through, and on Monday 1 February, Healey reports: 'the Cabinet finally agreed the aircraft package.'[17]

That is to say they approved the limited package, cancelling the less fiercely defended aircraft. The postponement of TSR2 in February, the price paid for moving against the other planes, meant that the meter of expenditure was kept running. As Healey himself observes, 'I had to keep development going for purely political reasons at a cost of £4 million a week until April 6th; I was deeply conscious of what could have been done with the £40 million for more useful purposes.'[18]

Healey, so often lazily tagged as a bully, was dealing with a dithery Cabinet whose Prime Minister had a fatal weakness for counting heads. He also had to engage in a conciliatory and inescapable process of reports, and spellings-out of evidence to his airmen and the civilian manufacturers, everyone who had major commitments to aircraft projects. Again, although it was not a popular innovation, Healey's habit of going to military/civil service meetings which Watkinson and Thorneycroft had largely kept away from, meant that he was not dependent on a Sir Humphrey-like filtering from his Permanent Under-Secretary. 'Hardman worried' is a minor motif of the diary.

Healey's approach went down well with the people off-Olympus with whom he would work for six years. His patience and involvement would produce a consensual view of their minister's excellence, including the opinion of Admiral Hill-Norton that he was 'by far the best Secretary of State since at least 1945'.[19] It made perfect sense to deal first with the less defensible aircraft projects. As Healey would tell parliament on 9 February: 'the estimated cost of the HS681 has doubled since the operational requirement was first issued nearly four years ago. In the case of P1154 the estimated cost has trebled in under three years.'[20]

Throughout this period with TSR2 as the elusive major target, Healey was of course juggling other things and picking up news at right-angles. The question of the future of the Valiant bombers comes up in the Commons – 'Rushed to House for Questions on Valiants – knocked Thorneycroft for six – Harold cleaned up afterwards.'[21]

After attending Winston Churchill's funeral on 30 January and getting his package through the Cabinet, he goes back to the DOPC to discuss his White Paper. 'Wigg difficult, but got Part 1 through.' By Thursday he has to start worrying about the Chancellor because Callaghan is worried. But on the Friday, with help from Michael Stewart, Callaghan's concern about the sales agreement with the US was allayed, only for a fresh crisis to blow up over the prospects of putting Spey engines into US Phantom planes which has Healey ringing the works at Workington for the latest information and keeping Stewart abreast of what he learns. At the end of that day he goes to Leeds on a late train, does his Saturday surgery, sleeps in the afternoon and goes to a couple of local Labour clubs in the evening – essential north of England Labour Member's business – and on the Sunday, 'Worked all morning. Good AGM in the afternoon, 5.35 train home. Read *The Collector* and *The Drowned World*.'[22]

Otherwise life at the Ministry of Defence went on in its bustling discordant way. A decision on TSR2 had been delayed, but Healey continued to work on the preoccupying case for cancelling it and replacing it with TFX/F111. On the Wednesday (24 March) he reports a 'bad meeting with PM on economy test – conditional agreement – on TSR2 – all against TFX, but prepared to axe TSR2. Callaghan weak, Brown away because father ill. Chalfont very awkward over need for either.'[23]

'The meeting,' he recalls, 'broke up inconclusively' and Cabinet enemies of the American deal would have been mortified had they known of Healey's next call – immediately after this meeting: a US Embassy reception, where he has 'a word with Averell Harriman and met Bob Corner for first time since Princeton'. Life at this time is made up of good meetings and bad meetings. There was a good one (of the DOPC) on the 29th – good in the way any harassed minister might wish: 'agreed my line to try for decision on Thursday but all but Stewart against choice of TFX', and Healey sensibly goes off to hear 'Cav. and Pag.'[24]

On the 25th, Healey enjoyed, or otherwise, a call from Mountbatten, the retiring Chief of Defence Staff, followed separately by those of his unforgiving colleagues, the Chiefs of the General Staff and the Air Staff: '3/4 hour with Dickie Mountbatten, bronzed and tricky as ever', he says. And without drawing breath, continues, 'CAS & CGS in to oppose him becoming Field Marshal and Marshal of RAF. Hull in earlier to oppose use of Queen's flight after retirement.'[25]

Healey finally won through. But not without enormous last-hurdle effort. The Cabinet meeting of Thursday 1 April broke into two distinct parts. At the first, Wilson was still against a decision to take the TFX, as was Jenkins.[26] As argument spilt over and went on, the meeting was put off until late that night. Healey went to meet his soldiers and civil servants: 'Debriefed to the boys' – and not just the boys, the US Secretary for Defense! 'Started to negotiate an extra year's option, McNamara reluctantly agreed. A lot of work on a new paper–draft statement.'[27]

And the gathering which convened at ten in the evening was 'a very delicate meeting'. As Healey tells it,[28] those present were at first equally divided between 'cancelling TSR2 without an option, cancelling with an option [on the TFX] and not cancelling'. Shifts of commitment continued, he says, 'to the last minute'.

The final resolution was reached effectively on second preferences. 'At first equal division between cancelling TSR2 without option, cancelling with option and not cancelling – shifts up to last minute – finally 12–10 division between A and C' – presumably 'cancelling without an option' and 'not cancelling'. He lists the final majority list as himself, Bottomley, Stewart, Callaghan, Brown, Gardiner, Soskice, Pakenham, Jenkins, Castle, Crosland, Gunter and Griffiths. The thing had been done after interminable unstable debate, a tribute to Wilson's conduct of his government. But it had been done, and after a modest military and civil service celebration with Hardman, Cooper, Nairne and Elworthy, the minister got to bed at 1.30 a.m.[29]

Or, as Crossman spitefully put it, 'it was more and more clear that he [Healey] has become a McNamara boy and that the Chiefs of Staff hate the TSR2 and are determined to get the F111A as a replacement.'[30] Not true, of course. The RAF (or Elworthy) had had to be persuaded that the F111A was better business and 'hate' is an absurd word. But Crossman's account of how his group was finally defeated is instructive. It was, he claimed, 'based on an assurance by Denis Healey that in taking out an option for the F111A we need not assume any obligations or commitments of any kind. Was this assurance true or not? I don't know. I doubt whether it was . . . I happened to know from George Wigg that Harold was for postponement, but he didn't put his view very clearly and allowed us to be defeated.'[31]

The F111 option would not of course be taken up, the unrelated outcome thirty-three months later of the next-but-one financial crisis. The only merit of Crossman's observations is that he demonstrates, without acknowledging it, the flabby calamitousness of Wilson at his worst. Wilson was capable of talking his won sort of dream imperialism – moral frontiers on the Himalayas and the like – and quite incapable of making a clear-minded end of East of Suez. Meanwhile Healey would be arguing over TSR2, carriers and the F111, for the best realistic involvement in a limited role East of Suez as an equally limited ally of the Americans. Given Wilson's point of departure, what Healey was doing was the best deal he was going to get. But Wilson needed the goodwill of left-wingers. They were also the vital core of Cabinet resistance, so the left had to be encouraged with time-consuming gestures. It was the sort of futile deviousness which would rack them again and again, angering left and right equally, a major contribution over time to the deep unhappiness of government and party.

The Conservative response was explosive. The actual announcement, apart from leaks which started the next day, came on 6 April in Callaghan's Budget. His Rt. Hon. friend, the Secretary for Defence, hoped to catch the Speaker's eye later. He did, and made a statement in the Chancellor's immediate wake, a piece of timing which made the Conservatives very excited.

The diary's comment, 'I had very difficult House of continuous interruptions over TSR2 – ten minute speech'[32] almost understates the case. There are eleven hostile interventions, many of them doubled and trebled with re-interjections *before* the egregious Robin Maxwell-Hislop, knowledgeable about procedure and one of the silliest men of his generation, stopped the House dead by spying strangers. After resumption there were, not counting friendly Labour appeals to the Chairman, twenty-four further interruptions, many of them multiple, something which dragged proceedings for a speech of less than five columns' length to twenty-six columns and so extended its own intended duration of ten minutes that Healey, rising at 6.20 p.m. rather than the 7.00 p.m. which Callaghan had indicated, finally concluded at 7.29.[33] 'Mr Healey rose' is a phrase wearily iterated by the Hansard reporter.

But the message was plain enough as it came through in kebab lengths. The programme of building TSR2s would have cost £750 million for research, development and production, so that an order for 150 planes would have meant that each of them cost £5 million; for 100, the price for each would have been £6 million. (We are living, of course, before the great take-off of inflation.) The government had waited a further two months after the earlier cancellations to obtain better information. (In fact, they hadn't been able to make up their minds.) And as Wilson had told the Commons back on 2 February, it was the rising cost of TSR2 which had caused the present review to be undertaken.

The Conservatives responded by rising like a Mexican wave: Sir Alec Douglas Home, Leader of the Opposition for a few more months, Sir Robert Cary, Douglas Home again, then Michael Foot trying to be helpful and Tories once more – Hugh Fraser, W. R. Davies, Christopher Soames, Healey's pleasant opposite number, before a hundred or so words from the Secretary of State, soon trodden underfoot by Neil Marten, Sir Arthur Vere Harvey, Quintin Hogg, Peter Emery and John Farr. Healey then got in almost a full column of Hansard to point out that though the manufacturers had been offered a fixed price against the present escalator, they couldn't manage one.

So there was 'no assurance that Her Majesty's Government's ultimate financial liability would have been limited'.[34]

Finally, after another flurry of interventions, Healey reached a key point. The government had 'secured from the United States Government an option on the F111A at a price per aircraft which even on a full scale programme, would represent less than half the estimated total of TSR2 research, development and production cost'. Having done all the sums, the government had learned that a full programme based on the F111 would cost £300 million less than the corresponding TSR2 programme. 'The option entered into allowed the British the rest of the year to decide on taking it up'[35] and it would not be necessary to place a follow-up order until April 1967. After another rally of outraged Conservatives (three-and-a-half columns of them), Healey reached his promise that a part of the money saved would be rerouted to other parts of the aircraft industry, spelt out the favourable credit terms obtained from the US, and made the point which for some members dare not speak its name.

'At the end of 1964 the aircraft industry was absorbing too large a proportion of the country's resources and the military aircraft programme was placing an impossible burden on the economy and the defence budget.' Henceforth the government meant to retain an 'aircraft and equipment industry of a size consistent with our resources and needs, both in military and civil aviation'. ('Hon. Members: "Resign."')

After meeting a yet further ripple of harrumphing discontent, Healey concluded that the decision was 'of crucial importance, not only to the military, but also the economic future of the country, but I must say that anyone who has sat here for the last hour would not have thought that hon. and rt. hon. Gentlemen opposite thought so.

'Hon. Members: "Resign."'[36]

That was the last thing he was going to do.

He would encounter the Conservatives again in formal debate on the aircraft industry a few days later, on 13 April. Captain Litchfield of Chelsea playfully cited 'dark rumours that the rt. hon. Gentleman the Paymaster General was behind the operation'[37] ('George Wigg difficult' is a Healey comment on that minister while negotiating cancellation), but Litchfield acknowledged his own doubts about the TSR2.

However, Christopher Soames, Opposition spokesman, would illustrate why Harold Wilson, that purely political animal, had dragged his feet over the decision. By one of those chances of politics, the previous Aviation Minister, the old Suez Grouper and traditional nationalist, Julian Amery, had represented a seat, Preston North, directly concerned with the manufacture of the TSR2. During the election, Amery had said in plain terms that TSR2 would be cancelled by an incoming Labour government. A pamphlet had appeared in Preston saying that it would not. The phrase 'Harold Wilson tells

TSR2 workers "Your jobs are guaranteed under Labour"' gave the Conservatives a good deal of pleasure. But it was the mild Soames who pushed this legitimate party point into a fair illustration of what preconception can do to judgement.

Also stressing a sinister role for George Wigg, 'Highly regarded in the Labour Party as a sort of witch doctor of defence . . . it was plain to us that he would get his way over the TSR2', Soames said that it had been a certainty that Labour would cancel the TSR2 for two reasons. 'The first was that it had a nuclear capability and that was enough to horrify the Prime Minister. He was going to have difficulty enough disposing of Polaris submarines in a way which would satisfy his CND supporters without having another nuclear weapons system on his hands. The second reason was that the Paymaster General has always been against it.'

He was missing the entire point. George Wigg was a bit player. More importantly, against the aircraft had been Lord Mountbatten, the Air Staff, who had said as much to Conservative ministers in office, Solly Zuckerman, the Cook/Armstrong report, the unidentified Air Vice-Marshal who had said that 'the TSR2 cancellation was an inevitable decision which made perfect sense from whatever angle you approached it'[38] . . . and Denis Healey.

But Amery as Member for a Preston seat could recall with horrible relish Harold Wilson coming to that Lancashire town in June of 1964 – before the election. 'Mr Amery is always spreading rumours that Labour will cancel the TSR2. I repudiate these rumours. Our position with the TSR2 is exactly the same as the Government's. If it works and does what is asked of it at a reasonable cost we shall want it though not in the nuclear role. We look forward to its success although we shall not know for many months whether it is successful. We look forward to its production.'

For Amery, 'Only two things could possibly have justified the Government's cancelling the TSR2 after that statement. One would have been if the aircraft had failed to perform adequately and the other would have been if, when the right hon. gentlemen opposite came into power, the costs had proved to be very different from what they thought they were at the time.' The reality was that the costs of TSR2 had been too high and rising for a long time; also that Harold Wilson's impulse to please, by no means only at election time, had hung anticipatory fetters upon his ministers and that Healey had been resolute enough to break them.

The Secretary of State personally was sidelined by opponents roasting the Prime Minister or demon-hunting the Paymaster General, and suffered little more than a casual knock from the eternally sour Angus Maude, for whom Healey had been 'downgraded to playing in McNamara's band'.[39] Maude also talked at a high level of improbability about the possibility of selling the TSR2 to the Americans!

Much of the Opposition argument was badly informed, as when Neil

Marten, otherwise best known as an anti-European of the jammed needle sort, argued that the TSR2 had the 'ability to penetrate very deeply, carrying the nuclear deterrent . . . Was not one of the Government's reasons for cancelling the TSR2 their dislike of the nuclear deterrent?' When Healey derided this piece of bogey-talk, Marten appealed tragically for the protection of the Chair. 'The rt. hon. Gentleman has accused me of not taking this matter seriously.' 'I tell him,' said Healey, 'as he should have known, that the TSR2 is designed purely for a conventional role.' The Tories had 'discovered a nuclear bonus when Skybolt collapsed and they found it necessary to dress up the pretence of a nuclear deterrent for purely political purposes'.[40]

On the substance, however, he was talking less about strike capacity than money. Saving £300 million was 'the pessimistic view'. He hoped to increase it because he was cutting out the research, development and production costs of the TSR2, something which made a smaller order for the F111 increasingly advantageous.

Essentially he was arguing that decisions had to be taken and that the decision on TSR2, difficult and controversial as it was, should have been faced up to by the Conservatives – 'one which they themselves would have taken years before if they had had any sense of financial responsibility and an ounce of political courage . . . They funked the decision when they should have taken it. We did not. It is as simple as that.' The tone is partisan but the conclusion hard to dispute.

CARRIERS AND RHODESIA

The great issue of aircraft carriers waited upon the reports and upon all the minor delays about which Healey had warned the Defence Council of 7 October. Meanwhile he records a litter of more casual encounters, not all of them military. For example, 'Queer hour with Tam Dalyell, claret etc – completely impervious to argument.' Little did he know how many queer hours lay ahead, for Dalyell, who in his dour dry way would have returned the compliment, had hardly begun to be impervious to Healey's arguments.*

Then there was 'Long Cabinet on S. Rhodesia, Harold very smug . . . 11% lead in NOP and dishing Tories by flight to Balmoral.' Healey attends another 'appalling *News of the World* dinner – row with John Burgess over TA . . . and Bill [Comyns-] Carr on Rhodesia'. He was engaged in drastic reform of the Territorial Volunteers. Wilson's tactically unwise open dismissal of military intervention (29 October) had pre-empted his own bluff and would make UDI an accomplished fact. Healey, in his memoirs, reckoned that he had believed since March of 1965 that a declaration of independence was inevitable.

The recurring entry at this time is 'Worked hard on Defence Review.' Almost as frequently, he records somebody – Michael Stewart, Andrew Wilson, or Alastair Hetherington with Clare Hollingworth and many more – all, in Healey's recurring phrase, 'in on Defence Review'. But for ministers in

---

* Tam Dalyell, consulted, believes that this conversation may have related to his insistence that the boundaries being defended in the confrontation with Indonesia were 'completely artificial'. His own definition of relations with the minister is 'Complete imperviousness on both sides'.

the Wilson Cabinet, everything kept coming back to Rhodesia, a process which accelerated until 11 November, Armistice Day having been chosen for his great gamble by a market-shrewd Ian Smith, the Battle of Britain pilot, as a date dripping with goodwill. Healey doesn't let the news get above itself. 'Long Cabinet. UDI announced in middle. PM up all night ringing Smith. DOPC on Rhodesia. Lunch with Leeds MPs and Harry Smith and daughters, down for his OBE.'

He was not the only one with a sense of perspective. The next meeting of Wilson's main ministers on 18 November was 'Very difficult Cabinet again on services pay'. In fact, services pay became, in the short run, an even bigger preoccupation, involving a series of 'difficult meetings'; one with Wilson, privately, was 'unfruitful'. Meanwhile Sir Ronald Melville, Second Secretary at Defence, was liaising for him on the problem with Aubrey Jones, the former Conservative Minister appointed by Wilson to head his Prices and Incomes Board. The sort of language – commitments against capabilities – used to the Defence Council obviously came into the pay dispute, for fear of money needed for carriers or F111s being eaten into by a careless definition of expenditure. Another meeting on the same day, 22 November, involved Wilson, Callaghan and Brown, and when, over pay, 'I insisted on including commitments in terms of reference' he provoked quite different trouble. 'George blew up when I said I'd spoken to Jones.'

Healey was also conferring at about this time with a more exalted Tory than Jones: 'Long talk with Rab Butler.' The former Chancellor and Home Secretary who, under Macmillan, had settled the status of the old Rhodesian federation, was characteristically liberal and as characteristically frugal with loyal party feeling – 'Usual mixed feelings about Heath's performance, sound on Rhodesia.'

November 23 followed November 22 with a 'Very difficult meeting' on services pay. 'Had to accept a reference, but got "commitment" in – nearly saddled PM with statement in the House on it. Meeting on Rhodesia first.'[1]

The possibility was now being seriously mooted, not of military intervention but of a military presence in next-door Zambia, the former Northern Rhodesia. 'I let fly over the Suez atmosphere of Zambia. Callaghan against aid, Brown in favour only if we go the whole way, [Lord Chancellor] Gardiner doubtful – long Cabinet chats on wage-related benefits.' But there were startling things said by surprising people – 'Michael Stewart wants force,' for example. While Crossman was convinced that Wilson's excited talk about how 'the Rhodesian government will be treated as traitors and the Queen will take over the government'[2] was essentially blather. By 'Socratic cross-questioning' Crossman elicited the fact that despite 'elaborate contingency plans for action, nobody wanted to reveal what they were'. Only one thing was clear. 'I managed to extract from Harold Wilson the admission that he was still determined not to send in troops even as part of a United Nations force.'[3]

As for a presence in Zambia, Healey records: 'Crossman strongly in favour – and for a quick kill. Houghton very worried. Agreed to go ahead.' Crossman writes, 'I heard Douglas Houghton pleading against reinforcement and wanting to placate the white settlers, and I heard James Callaghan wanting much stronger measures. He is concerned because the crisis is costing us a lot and might undermine confidence in the pound. The PM very much in the middle. Afterwards, talking to Denis Healey, I learnt that the inner group in cabinet which "runs" Rhodesia has been pressing Harold for stronger action, with Healey on Callaghan's side.'[4]

However, rescuing the damsel from the dragon involved getting the damsel's permission. Healey lists events immediately afterwards: 'Further meeting to give message to Kaunda' and concludes the day's entry with, 'Told at 2 a.m. Kaunda would not agree to our ground troops.' Kenneth Kaunda, the Zambian leader, had in fact more to fear from Smith, who could turn off the electricity, than he had to hope for even from Crossman and Healey. The next day's Cabinet, 30 November, reflects a half-action, gesture politics very much in Harold Wilson's style. The Cabinet 'agreed to put in the Royal Scots along Kariba [dam] and warn Smith we would not stand idly by if he cut off power to Zambia – look at striking power lines South. Very turbulent day.'

'Not standing idly by' is a phrase dear to politicians seriously worried about the consequences of moving at all. But on the next day the Cabinet was agreeing to send a task force to Zambia, and Healey records international gossip, ministerial quirks and political theatre: 'Kaunda is losing ground to OAU [Organisation of African Unity]. George very cantankerous. PM told House of "our offer-threat over Kariba".' That message had been 'very strong with us – divided Tories.'

Healey briefed his service ministers – they were already in the middle of another row, the Tory-inspired drill hall tantrum over plans to reform the Territorials where Fred Mulley, Minister for the Army, caught most of the flak. 'Awkward meeting with Fred about taskforce – frightened by TA row.' And over Rhodesia, he had to keep the soldiers sweetened – 'Talked with Dick Hull – reassured him, stroked head of CGS as well.' That was Wednesday. On Thursday (2 December), Hull would behave as a solid prop during another 'long difficult meeting with Mulley, Cassels and Drew on taskforce. Hull Helpful.'[5] So, briefly, was Kaunda who, on the same day, finally agreed to the flying in of RAF Javelins, gratifyingly in time for Wilson to tell the Commons at three-thirty.

Gradually Rhodesia would settle into place. The risk of her taking punitive measures against Zambia would not materialise, though whether as a result of all the warlike scurrying and 'sending in' by the London government or the lack of any Rhodesian need for them is unclear. There would be no end of Rhodesia meetings. And ineffective sanctions, including an oil ban bypassed with ease, would be solemnly instituted, but no intervention with troops against what Whitehall now called 'the Smith Regime' would ever take place. It would take much later American pressures on South Africa, and South Africa's withdrawal of support, to destroy UDI a decade and a half later. The Wilson government had been confined to open-ended rhetoric and an elaborate pageant of arms. had no illusions. He knew his military men and, though loyal, they were in broad emotional sympathy with Smith, the fighter pilot, and the ex-servicemen settled in Rhodesia. He speaks in his memoirs of rebuking the CGS (Cassels) on the subject. The French example, an alienated military turning against the central government over Algeria, wouldn't be given the chance of happening. What had scared Macmillan, scared Wilson.

All the entries about 'working hard on Defence Review' came to interim fruition when, on 24 November, in the middle of all the Rhodesian stage smoke, the Defence Committee responded to memoranda circulated by Healey relating to that Review but confined to commitments – most of them, East of Suez. The meeting, in the Prime Minister's Room at the House of Commons, was attended by Wilson, Brown, Callaghan, Home Secretary Soskice, Commonwealth Secretary Bottomley, Colonial Secretary Greenwood (for whom Healey had non-stop, hedge-slashing contempt), Privy Seal Lord Longford, Mulley, Fred Lee at Power and George Wigg plus the service Chiefs, Hull, Cassels, Luce and Elworthy.

Over planes and carriers, Healey simply notified colleagues that the revised structures which would be necessary were being prepared, but that this revision would not need to be in place before the Prime Minister went to see President Johnson – something with which Wilson readily agreed as long as a decision was reached on his prime concern, the purchase of the American F111, either before 31 December or the date of any extension to that option.

Placed in an annexe to the minute, Healey's memorandum proposed, along with the obvious – continued commitment in Berlin and to NATO, together with the not yet controversial retention of the base at Simonstown in South Africa and the Hong Kong garrison – a number of brisk steps down from the old military posture. 'We should withdraw all our forces from the Caribbean except for a company in British Honduras and a frigate.' There should be no further naval commitment in the Mediterranean. The Indo-Pacific commitments set out in a previous paper were affirmed, but subject to 'the specific assumptions limiting our tasks in that area listed in the annexe'.[6] On Malta, Cyprus and the Persian Gulf, Healey offered options. One of those was 'That we withdraw from the Persian Gulf entirely and have no commitment to return in any circumstances.' Another was to keep up support for most of the Gulf States but to uncouple from Kuwait.

The Defence Committee responded by agreeing with Healey about the Mediterranean, subject to some renegotiation of the matter with NATO. It agreed to 'seek to persuade the United States government to take over our commitment in respect of Libya' while offering very minor forces 'to secure a point of entry and staging facilities at El Adem. This would require very small forces, the cost of which would not be significant.'[7]

On Aden*, Healey won approval for the withdrawal he wanted, something which was by now almost preordained. 'It was agreed that when South Arabia becomes independent in 1967 or 1968 we should not maintain any obligations to, or defence facilities of forces in Aden or the South Arabian federation.' It is a momentous decision, presented in three lines.

On both Cyprus and the Persian Gulf, the options Healey had set out presumably reflected those 'Michael Stewart in for chat on Defence Review' diary entries. Stewart was anxious in one of the classic modes of British foreign policy: 'We had two objectives: to prevent the area in and around the Persian Gulf from falling into disorder; and to prevent a change of allegiance by Iran. Either event would have serious consequences for our position, not only in the Middle East, but also in the Indian Ocean.'[8] One cannot read those earnest words decades later without reflecting that Iran *did* change allegiance, turning, not to the Soviet Union but to herself and her religious traditions and against a United States so ardently concerned to guide her.

It was subsequently the object of United States policy, with Britain's mute approval, to undo that shocking fact. And from her anxious concern have flowed the Iran–Iraq war, and the rise and influence within the region of Saddam Hussein. Perhaps not giving two buttons whether Iran changed her allegiance or not might have been simple wisdom.

Britain was a sort of customer/uncle to those statelets on the Gulf usually described in newspapers as 'oil-rich'. CENTO (Central Treaty Organisation) was the American-sponsored but British-useful military guarantor of these states, with Iran as its most important local member. Stewart judged that 'Our military presence in the Gulf has been a major factor in keeping the peace in that area and, although we should not envisage remaining indefinitely, time would be needed if we were to create the necessary conditions in order to leave a stable situation when we withdrew[9] . . . We should therefore plan to retain the CENTO commitment and to build up our forces in the Persian Gulf to the extent necessary when we withdrew from Aden.'[10]

There was some argument over this, with fears expressed that we might get stickily enmired maintaining internal security in Bahrain. But the arguments which seemed to weigh most concerned 'the effect on the Kuwait sterling balances and the disruption which disorder might cause to the supply of Middle East oil, and to our oil investments'.[11] There was also a problem over planned military facilities for that region at Masirah. On this there would be a

---

* See below, page 312 et seq.

bill for the big or little option of either £16 million or £22 million, and it would take five years to get them established. There was, it was stressed, a risk of creating a hiatus of capacity at the very moment of asserting involvement.

Summing up the section, Wilson left the Masirah development open for further consideration, but on the larger question, said that 'there was general agreement that we should maintain a military presence in the Persian Gulf after withdrawing from Aden.'[12] To that end, we should adopt Healey's fourth option on the Persian Gulf and his second option on Cyprus. The second option had been to acknowledge no obligations to Cyprus itself, but to keep Akrotiri as a base from which we would 'provide nuclear support for CENTO'. Meanwhile, following Healey's option four, we would be accepting that 'Our commitments to the Persian Gulf States including Kuwait continue as at present.'[13]

Arguing policy over commitments East of Suez as against choice of military craft, Healey was servicing a committee. He would never be without opinions, but true to his repeated doctrine that commitment defines capabilities, he was telling Wilson and other colleagues the details of a tariff. They could be committed to more or to less. But more would require additional matériel and cost extra money. They should choose. It was in this spirit that on 14 January he circulated a paper to the Defence Committee.[14] He had been asked on 24 November to set out 'a revised structure of forces and weapons systems to be prepared and costed to meet the agreed pattern of commitments for the 1970s'.[15] This paper represented his own thinking on a single aspect of it: aircraft carriers.

Its opening sentence is a plain working truth according to the rules which the Cabinet had proclaimed within weeks of coming to office: 'In the course of devising a new force structure it became clear that there was no way of accommodating expenditure on the maintenance of a viable carrier force throughout the 1970s within a defence budget of £200 million in 1969/70 without a most drastic reduction in our land and air forces.'[16]

The cheapest option involving aircraft carriers, he said, required a refit of *Ark Royal* so that she could run until 1974, plus the building of one new ship – to enter service in 1973. That would keep a viable carrier fleet at sea until 1980, but after 1974 they would be exactly where the last government had left them. With three ships, one of which, after 1974, would be *Hermes*, the maximum strike complement would be seven aircraft plus twelve fighters – and without their building a second carrier, that force would cease to be viable after 1980. 'Studies have shown,' Healey reported:

(a) that a single carrier's endurance in intensive operations is four days, after which she requires two days for recuperation (though at the level of intensity envisaged in maritime operations, her endurance could be sustained for 30 days).

(b) that a single carrier would be vulnerable when operating against significant organised opposition.[17]

To make proper use of a carrier, they would need reinforcement. If, to avoid strain, it was proposed to keep two carriers West of Suez in peacetime, getting the second ship to the scene would take up to a fortnight. And to do things on this plan would cost £1100 million.

What about the notion of a second carrier – CVA 02 to join CVA 01 so as to replace *Hermes* in 1974? The amount of effective air power this would bring about would be modest: 28 strike and fighter aircraft before 1974 and 32 thereafter. (The reinforced deployment would be 63 aircraft up to 1974 and 77 thereafter.) It would cost £12 million in 1969/70 and £120 million over the costing period. Yet going for a second carrier only made sense if they were planning to run a carrier force right through the 1980s.

It was up to the Defence Committee to decide if the needs of foreign policy required them to buy the goods and 'whether against the background of the new Indo-Pacific strategy which is now envisaged, expenditure of this order would be justified on a carrier plan with the limitations I have described.'[18] Other things being equal, 'carrier-borne aircraft can be regarded as between two and three times as expensive as land-based aircraft.' It was agreed that Britain should not attempt alone to engage in 'operations involving intervention against sophisticated opposition'. Healey added his own codicil to this. 'I believe that we must also accept that the United Kingdom must renounce tasks that carry any risk of our forces having to extricate themselves from operations in similar circumstances.'

Basically, Healey was saying that Britain could not go into any war which needed invasions or landings without the US Navy and *its* carriers. 'Having weighed most carefully the likely consequences, both military and political so far as they can be foreseen, of abandoning carriers in the middle 1970s, I have reached the conclusion that from the point of view of the force structure as a whole, this is one of the less damaging ways of taking a further major step towards our defence budget target.'[19]

Healey had a strong sense of the gravity of this decision, a gravity beyond strategic calculations. The navy mattered as an institution – and as a set of people. One reason why he favoured hanging on to carriers into the mid-seventies was 'the need to allow time for the least damaging transition to a Navy without them. The whole of the Navy's weapon policy since the war has been centred around carriers, which have been the heart of the Fleet's offensive and defensive capability.'

The Fleet would have to be reshaped and Healey wanted to see the navy make its adjustments while the carriers were still helpfully there. Command-and-control facilities at sea, about which Mayhew and Elworthy had clashed, and something then only possible for carriers, would have to be reprovided. But the navy would have to be 'given some measure of independent striking power' against an enemy equipped with missiles as Indonesia was. And with a whole new practice of maritime roles being filled by aircraft flying from land, once carriers had gone, a great deal of experiment and practice would be needed 'to establish finally and convincingly the overall soundness and eventual cost of a completely new and complex system'.[20] If sea command-and-control were to change hands, he would need, in the interim, to convert Tigers (cruisers) then to find successor ships. And to accomplish the whole task, he would need limited purchase of Phantoms and Buccaneer 2s. That programme would not cost less than £150 million over the costings period.

There were to be no new carriers, they needed time and keeping the old ones to their natural term provided time. 'For all these reasons, I believe we must continue with carriers until 1974/5 or so.' And he detailed the schedule of the phase-out. It mattered now even more that *Ark Royal* should be refitted, otherwise, when *Victorious* went in 1972, they would be down from three to two carriers before their own expiry date. But *Ark Royal* would go in 1974, *Hermes* in 1975 and *Eagle* in 1976.

He also tackled manpower. The gradual and late phase-out meant keeping strength at 100,000. The navy reckoned that a decision to keep the Fleet Air Arm, plus a satisfactory pay agreement, would have kept general naval strength up to that level, but if the FAA were to be phased out as well, there would be a serious manpower problem.

It was the crisis of an interim. 'We shan't need you after a certain date and we can't get you for the period until then when you *are* wanted.' The air force was now looking forward to swing-wing aircraft while the FAA only employed fixed-wing. It wasn't realistic to recruit aircrew for a trade which should be played out by 1976, yet, given that complex phase-out, they would still need to be training such people until 1971. According to navy sources, quite soon – from 1968 – the FAA would be borrowing pilots from an RAF already stretched. That might be over-pessimistic, but some special benefits would have to be found if the navy were to continue recruiting fixed-wing aircrew for the carriers. Otherwise they would find themselves responsible for carriers they had made inoperable.

Healey returned to the issue later, giving his colleagues no excuse for not facing up to contingent risks. Shortage of aircrews or naval manpower before the mid-1970s would leave the navy unable to handle the missiles or the long-distance aircraft which were to take over the old cruiser work.

Healey set off savings from cancellation with the new costs which cancellation made necessary. Over the seven years 1969/70–1975/6 (when Chancellor Healey would start worrying), they would be at their highest, £40 million in the first year, dwindling to nothing over the next four to five years as new cruisers, helicopters and missiles were of necessity procured. 'From

1972/3 onwards, however, these savings are largely offset by RN and RAF re-provisioning and they are more than offset thereafter.'[21]

The ironic implication of all this would be the creation of an optimum period in those early years when the carriers would be operating but no replacement had to be paid for and when extensive aircraft costs, capital and running, were being taken out. In this period, the Chancellor would have his savings and there would still be operational carriers East of Suez. The government would be making their move for the financial advantages of a five-year period which would start in another three years' time. That did not invalidate what was being done, but was the perspective in which the whole exercise had to be seen.

Appropriately enough, Healey looked next at 'operational implications' – how much we could do when we had less to do it with. The gap would first show after 1975, with the decommissioning of *Ark Royal*. And, in parallel, the Buccaneer 2 would be able progressively to do less as it became more vulnerable over land from 1970 onwards. Increasingly, the function of the carrier would be to give maritime protection 'though they would continue to have a useful residual capability against land targets which are not strongly defended'.[22]

Healey reminded his colleagues of their own clear undertaking to pull back from the sort of world role which had led to overstretch in the first place. The world would see a signal and would take it. 'In general, the phasing out of carriers would be interpreted abroad as meaning that the UK intended in future not to undertake any substantial military operations in areas East of Suez or any operations from which we could not easily extricate ourselves.'[23] This might activate political troublemakers, though there were not many areas at risk in this way where we couldn't operate without carriers. Operations would be down, but 'the whole concept of the redeployment proposed in the Defence Review is one of reduction of our capabilities for independent operation and limitation of our military responsibilities.'[24]

There was no flinching in Healey's report. He had set out the risks of giving up carriers and was personally reluctant to abandon them 'any sooner than we have to. There are, in any case, special risks in attempting to do so.' But the government had

> decided to attempt to reduce our commitments over the next four years and the force structures have been devised on the basis of the reduced level of tasks in the Indo-Pacific area. We should be able to minimise our dependence on sea-borne air power; and so to make heavy capital expenditure on the Fleet Air Arm and on CVA 01 in particular unnecessary. I propose therefore to cancel CVA 01; and to reduce expenditure on the Fleet Air Arm to what is necessary, in effect, to work out the lives of our existing carriers.

That was it, the ministerial decision. And what Healey had set out by memorandum, he would argue on 14 February directly to Cabinet (a slightly reshuffled Cabinet, with Jenkins taking over from the anxious and reactionary Soskice at the Home Office while Mulley replaced him at Aviation but outside the Cabinet).

Ministers had been presented with a last-ditch move by the Board of Admiralty to keep carriers and allegedly meet something like government numbers. But by the time their own proposals were discussed in Cabinet, the figures had lost all credibility. 'It was now accepted,' said Healey, 'that the extra cost of the Admiralty Board's proposal would be much higher than they had originally estimated.'[25] Capital spending on the CVA 01 over the next three years would be £30 million and in 1969/70 the extra cost looked like being not the projected £9 million, but £20 million. And between 1973 and 1975, the retention of carriers would involve another £100 million. The whole proposal would in fact let them in for another £150 million overall. Yet such a compromise, construction of a single carrier, would give no additional military capacity until 1973 when it would come into service, the very point at which foreign policy was geared to reduction of commitments in the Far East. Even its advocates wanted this carrier only until 1980. They would have created a ship which had only six or seven years of life, for which the cost simply could not be warranted.

There were no Cabinet takers for the Admirals' scheme and Wilson summed up, gently but without reservation. It was clear that the plan proposed by the Admiralty Board would break the limits laid down. The Cabinet approved the proposal by the Secretary of State for Defence for maintaining the existing carrier force, if possible until 1975.

On New Year's Day 1966 Healey had gone back to Leeds, a more real world than the one where, with or without control-and-command, he might make 'interventions'. He faced 'long surgery, mainly housing' on the Saturday, and on the next day 'worked in hotel, quiet meeting of GMC. Home at 10 p.m.' Next day, his genial army junior minister turned up. 'Gerry Reynolds in on TA – keen to spend extra £3m' (he got it a few days later). Henry Hardman and Hull were 'in on Defence Review – Rumours of Chris [Mayhew] wanting to resign over carriers.' A 'Difficult last meeting with Navy'[26] involved 'Pollock,* combative' and 'Chris Mayhew, odd. Asked for 5 carrier programme.'

On Wednesday it was Elworthy's turn to come in 'to oppose Lightnings for Zambia – keen to keep 1127 [the Harrier] after all!' On Friday 'Fred Mulley in – must fight for P1127' and after 'Tough meeting' on US credits, the message is formal: 'Chris in to tell me he must resign on CVA 01 on grounds [that we]

---

* Admiral Sir Michael Pollock.

should not stay East of Suez. Good tempered.' Sunday's home entry: 'Walk in cold sun. Chess. Worked quite hard'[27] sums things up rather well.

But politics, not pure, not simple, also intervened – instructively. On 10 January, early for St Valentine's, comes a massacre, or at any rate a heroic burst of knight- and bishop-swapping to accompany ministerial shifts. 'Helsby in,' he records. 'Harold still nagging against Henry [Hardman]. Wants Otto Clarke out of Treasury. Barbara wants Padmore out of Transport – suggests Clarke to MOA, Henry to job abroad, Dunnett from Labour to MoD, Padmore to Labour – agrees Solly unsuitable.'

This translates as Sir Lawrence Helsby, head of the civil service (otherwise 'That awful creature, Helsby'[28]) saying that Sir Richard Clarke (the 'Otto' derived from his barking manner), might go to Aviation and Sir Thomas Padmore move to the Ministry of Labour (where he did not go, though Mrs Castle, with reverberating consequences, ultimately did). Healey, despite his peaceful relations with staff, did manage something as he put Solly Zuckerman into the back yard of Number 10 as adviser to the Prime Minister.

Helsby's speculations accurately forecast the replacement of Healey's Permanent Secretary, the untroublesome Sir Henry Hardman, by Sir James 'Ned' Dunnett, described by Peter Hill-Norton as 'Everything it ever said in *Yes Minister* about civil servants'.[29] Defence was gaining an outstanding intriguer, whose fixing lunches may have inspired the programme, while Mrs Castle did not in fact succeed in getting rid of the public servant whose entry in the index to her *Diaries* reads: 'Padmore, Sir Thomas (Permanent Secretary Transport) fails to greet Barbara, 82 ... Barbara's abortive attempts to remove, 89, 92–3, 94, 114, 115, 116, 117, 122, 156.' Healey's 15 January entry seems very natural – 'At home all day, watched Moore and Cook.'

The military, by contrast with such angry politicians, are simply worried: 'Parker in worrying about 1127,' 'Dick Hull worried about PM's Rhodesia minute.' And Healey himself, though thinking Mayhew 'odd' and on the brink of losing both him and the First Sea Lord, Luce, is still spending time pleasantly with his naval minister. On 12 January he 'worked late on Defence Review papers then to Chris Mayhew's for supper'. That supper party, quite apart from the 'very nice Mayhew children', sounds like the social equivalent of particle-bombardment: 'Clare Hollingsworth, the *Guardian*'s tigerish Defence correspondent, Ruth Dalton, Hugh's widow, much older now but still very sharp, and Cecil King of the FO, not the dreadful other Cecil, also a frequent caller, Jackie and Becky Roosevelt' and 'Pat Gordon Walker, very sad'.

In fact, the Mayhew departure would be something of a saga. On Monday 17 February, Healey records spending 'three quarters of an hour with PM and Chris on carriers – PM cagey.' On Tuesday 25 January he was also informed by the Navy Minister that he had been to see the Prime Minister about resigning, his entrenched arguments being, as Healey puts it, that 'Britain must not be East of Suez, must keep carrier there if it is.'[30]

When Healey returned from an extended and exhausting visit to the United States, Australia and the Far East, ready to apply himself grindingly to the issue paralleling carriers, purchase of the F111A swing-wing plane, Mayhew and the other protester, Admiral Luce, were still there, and still leaving. February 10 had him seeing Luce 'to edge him off resignation – very overwrought, but did leave it open'. Saturday and Sunday are disturbed by press stories – *Daily Express* followed by *Sunday Telegraph* – on the prospective resignations. On the 14th, day of a momentous Cabinet meeting on carriers and F111, he saw both men: 'Tried to hold Chris at least till DWP [Defence White Paper].' On Wednesday the 16th it is a case of 'Saw Harold about Chris – great efforts to hold him back – agrees to wait till Saturday – very angry about all the trouble.' On that Saturday, back from a flying visit to the US to see McNamara and McNaughton 'very worried about position on F111's specification', 'saw PM with David Luce, tried to get all under control.'[31]

It was to no avail. Both men went, Luce having been bullied by his own service to make the gesture, Mayhew earnest with his own idiosyncratic convictions. Mayhew was replaced with J. P. W. Mallalieu – 'Curly Mallalieu quite OK' as Healey put it, Luce with Admiral Sir Varyl Begg, who instantly resumed the naval moan about the carrier.

Mayhew's gesture of resignation was a muddled one since he wished firmly *not* to be East of Suez. On 22 February he made the customary resignation statement, a ten-and-three-quarter-column cosmic ramble. At the end, he invoked the Munich argument: 'The basic mistake of the Defence Review has been the classic crime of peacetime British Governments of giving the Armed Forces too large tasks and too few resources . . . This has all happened before.' Recalling his own war service, Mayhew said, 'Most of the men whom I knew then came back safely through Dunkirk. But more would have come back if they had had the tanks and air support which they needed and deserved,* if they had not been let down by the nation, by Parliament and by their Service ministers. I am convinced the House will never allow that kind of thing to happen again.'[32]

'Overwrought', the word Healey used about Luce, will do very nicely here. Healey's diary comment is 'appalling'. Although Mayhew had begun with a sound, or at any rate beguiling, point, that an arbitrary limit of £2000 million is a bad way to resolve one's defences, he seemed as cut off as any wardroom blowhard from the actual pressures on James Callaghan as custodian of a glass currency. His own minimalism – talk about cutting all commitments East of Suez and coming up with a services budget £200 million below the required figure ignored every small thread attaching us

---

* Not true actually. A British Expeditionary Force three times as well equipped would have been in much the same hole, given the French collapse.

Gulliverwise to a United States who, whatever her mistakes, was the chief ally and who at her own low point of international fortune, passionately desired us to stay in the theatre and make what contribution we could.

Mayhew had persuaded himself that there were only two answers, total roll up or total commitment. He also believed that carriers were indispensable if we were to function in the East. His tone is alternately *Boy's Own Paper*ish – 'We can ask our troops to go on fighting . . . without the resources necessary to enable them to get a victory' or resentful, 'or, this is the heart of the matter – we could run to the Americans for help.'[33]

What he could not understand was that Healey was accepting economic limits because they were there, because it was one driving way to get a decision, and because facing that barrier, he had created an intelligent compromise – partial retreat from East of Suez while keeping a function there which helped the Americans. Healey intended a continuing role for the British forces, made flexible between the East, Europe and whatever events threw in their way, with the best military equipment which happened to be airborne, and made feasible by the US stretching a dozen points in the sale of F111s. On top of which everything was to be done rallentando, a long withdrawal, then a slipping into the lesser role with the next generation of aircraft. It was the skilled playing of a limited hand. The whole point of Healey, as it was to be of his friend, Helmut Schmidt, was that he was a *Macher*, someone who does things – in this case finding an optimal position with the means then available.

'Suez' is an apt place-name to be linked with the major policy change now taking place. In the grand, resonant sense at any rate, we would forsake 'East of Suez', a phrase conceived when we commanded and cruised there as a blue-water power. But giving up the vast space on the map it denoted was actually the curtain on the last act after the invasion of Suez itself in 1956.

It was a reluctantly but earnestly considered and argued-through retreat from the open-ended costs of open-ended commitments and a provisioning for what *could* be done, a facing up to facts. Peter Hill-Norton, with all the built-in assumptions of not just a sailor, but the former commander of the *Ark Royal*, put it downrightly. 'Healey's strength was his mind, his determination and his courage. We lost that battle. I forget what Healey said, but he was right and thank God we did take that decision.'[34]

BETRAYING THE TERRIERS

The drastic changes Healey was bringing in were always bound to be contentious, however rational the replacement. The sensible act of military rationalisation also involved major sacrilege to a large lobby of part-time soldiers, the military equivalent of Sunday painters.

On 29 July 1965 it was formally announced that the government saw no role in home defence for the Territorial Army. Apart from the odd cryptic 'meeting about reserves' with individual Chiefs and recording one account to Cabinet, Healey says little about this development in the diary. He does, though, describe a lunch at *The Times* on the day before: 'Oliver Woods and Charlie Douglas-Home – softened them up on the TA.' As for his own statement to the House, he comments only: 'Went well – Soames doltish.'[1]

Healey was proposing that the Territorial Army should merge with the far more professional Army Volunteer Reserve and that the number of TA drill halls and assembly points be slashed. Instead he offered 8600 full members of the reserve, with 42,000 on call 'when warlike operations are in preparation or in progress',[2] while a further 23,000 would be available for exclusive home defence. This last group would be described by Field Marshal Carver as 'a sop to the Council [of the TA] which allowed it to keep in existence a number of units for which full military equipment could not be provided'. Two years later it was got rid of.

Response to the proposed changes took the form of a great chuntering, its high point a letter to *The Times* signed by eight retired field marshals. Like the much later salvoes on monetarism between alternative equal-numbered groups of economists, this conveyed more brass harmony than melodic line. But the whole performance was to be expected. The Territorial Army was, politically speaking, something of a Tory base. Membership was seen among

Conservatives as a patriotic gesture by the citizen. Descended from the old yeomanry and, behind that, the county militias, its weekends and fortnights provided an agreeable sense of contribution.

The fact that people had once stood ready to serve as fall-back resistance if Hitler's troops had landed, gave a warm, suffusing sense of cockeyed gallantry to the undertaking, cheered by the happy fact of that encounter never having taken place. Under-equipped, over-manned, scattered and not very useful, the TA in 1965 was producer-led, a form of recreational patriotism more satisfying to its own members than troubling to any sensible enemy. Younger professional soldiers, *not* retired field marshals *not* writing to *The Times*, shared Healey's judgement. But among Conservatives, defence of the drill halls as shrines to the nation was a deeply gratifying cause, and the image of Healey, the pinko subversive, undermining the fabric of the nation firmly established itself among dimmer understandings.

'Threat to the Terriers' was one of the few issues on which the Conservative Defence spokesman, the former Brigadier Powell, could be united with his leader, the former Lieutenant-Colonel Heath. The question was, in fact, a pretext for ceremonial contest, tournament style, of the tribal prejudices of the two parties. Labour people, including non-grudgers of military expenditure and preparedness, viewed the TA as a snobbish attempt by businessmen in khaki to play at soldiers, learn to talk in clipped accents, drink a good deal of gin and stroke their moustaches before coming back to the golf course to talk about doing their bit. In fairness, Labour had in Richard Crawshaw, MP for Liverpool Toxteth, a former regular soldier and a sincere believer in the Territorial system who made a vigorous defence of it against his own Whips. Leslie Lever, brother of the less famous and cleverer Harold, and a busy local populist, also came close to rebellion.

Interestingly, Crossman, who reported the debate which finally took place on 16 December[3] as 'really a very exciting affair', had supported Healey in Cabinet Committee and acknowledged having watched the defeat there by Healey of his chief opponent, the Home Secretary, Sir Frank Soskice, 'no match for this rough, rather ruthless young man'.

The Conservatives saw the TA as part of that British national thing which, through a grasp of the naming of parts, plenty of fresh air and respect for the Crown, indisputably did something for what they still tended to call 'England'. Their mood in the Commons debate was always liable to slip into mysticism. Edward Heath, declaring an interest in his own TA involvement, added: 'It is, I think, known to the House that for four years I commanded a regiment of the Honourable Artillery Company, the oldest regiment in the British Army'.

Heath spoke of 'an outbreak of spontaneous hostility'.[4] There was also 'disbelief that anyone can be so certain about the nature of future warfare as to entitle him to be as dogmatic as the Secretary of State is about the need to abolish the Territorial Army'.[5] And he moved from a familiar grumpiness to the frankly rhapsodic. The saving of £20 million by 1970 did not weigh with Heath. There is a 'deep-seated instinct in the British people . . . a disciplined, effective volunteer force, opportunities for voluntary service . . . reinforcing the life of the community'. More substantially, Heath argued from the requirements of civil defence. Healey would speak of civil defence politely but without much fervour, and a belief in the possibility, never mind the utility, of any such thing would divide right and left in the years ahead. But for Heath, 'the Territorial Army is an essential insurance policy against the uncertainties of future warfare, and it is required to meet the home defence requirements for which the right hon. Gentleman admits there is a place.'[6] It was the word 'essential' which jarred.

But compared with the insouciance in the face of nuclear fission shown by some of his backbenchers, Heath was a model of sober realism. Sir John Smythe, Jacky Smythe, a lovable ex-brigadier holding the VC, faced the eightyfold Hiroshimas in prospect with sang froid: 'Whether we should have a dose of nuclear bombs or not is a matter of opinion. But my point is that it is just when there is widespread damage that the Territorial Army will be called in.'[7] One circumstance called in aid was the prospect of the Red Air force taking over the M4. 'We have become much more vulnerable to that sort of attack now because of the enormous number of new motorways.'[8]

In a burst of enthusiasm, Sir John concluded his speech by comparing Healey with a notable admiral, Jellicoe. 'It was said of the First World War that Admiral Jellicoe was the only man who could have lost the war in one afternoon. The Secretary of State for Defence is the only man who could lose the next war in the Division lobby tonight.'[9] But the high note of hysteria was reached by Peter Bessell, later charged with Jeremy Thorpe in the Norman Scott affair: 'My opinion and the opinion of the vast majority of people in Britain, of the White Paper is best summed up like this – I tear the document to shreds.'[10]

Healey, on this occasion, would tread a soft and non-partisan course, so it was left to Fred Mulley to say cutting things on the Labour side. He drew a comparison with the Conservative amendment made when Haldane as Liberal Minister of War had set up the Territorial Army in 1907, regretting that 'destroying the Militia, discouraging the Yeomanry and imposing new and uncertain liabilities on the Volunteers, would not in a period of national peril provide an adequate force for home defence, or prompt support for the Regular Army in the Field'. He observed that 'Tanks, aeroplanes, nuclear weapons and guided missiles have all evidently failed to produce a change in basic Conservative defence thinking in the last 60 years. This is not Conservatism, it is catalepsy.'

To Enoch Powell, now Opposition spokesman on defence, the future of the TA was 'a question of transcendent importance' and he begged Healey to rethink his plans 'in the name of the nation'.[11] The serious part of Powell's case was a claim that the decision was not part of rational reorganisation, but something done at the injunction of an anxious James Callaghan desperate for another £20 million.

An altogether less exalted view would be expressed in perspective long after by a real working soldier, Field Marshal Lord Carver. The bringing together of the Territorial Army with the Army Emergency Reserve, originally the proposal of Colonel Hugh Beach, was 'a rational, sensible proposal'. The objective was 'not to produce a separate volunteer army as traditionally the TA had sought to be, but to bring the regular army from a peace to a war footing'.[12] The proposals, said Carver, had been approved by the Army Board, but 'ran into strong opposition from the TA supported by the Conservative Party in opposition. They were represented as a politically inspired blow at the traditional basis of Britain's defence and I became one of the principal targets of the lobby fuelled by the County TA associations . . . almost all retired regular army officers, usually of the rank of colonel whose jobs were threatened.'[13]

Carver's view of the utility of the old TA was brisk. Its theoretical organisation 'was far larger than was needed, could be recruited or could be equipped, trained or even clothed . . . The overheads of its administration by a plethora of county associations with drill halls scattered all over the countryside, wasted the little money that could be spared.'[14]

The field marshal had become convinced through contacts with TA units that *their* officers were in favour of the change.[15] His only regret was that the name 'Territorial' would be retained in the new Territorial and Volunteer Reserve, from which the Tories would party-politically later drop the 'Volunteer'. 'The Blimps at least won that battle,' said Carver.

A fair and scrupulous man, Carver would in his memoirs speak of the pusillanimity of his superiors in the Army Department 'in failing to fight harder for the reorganisation and letting the odium for it be deflected on to Healey and Mulley'.[16]

Healey's parliamentary response in winding up the debate was soft spoken and with only a token flutter of partisanship at conclusion. He had been willing to argue in the early 1950s for very large numbers – twelve German divisions and all that. The Conservatives, as he pointed out, despite Sandys's abolition of conscription, were using arguments in favour of the old Territorial Army which belonged with the assumptions of those days.

'We did not need our Defence Review to help us on the most important fact governing our decisions. It is one of the most important facts of the modern age: the radius of destruction of a megaton bomb.'[17] Government had to make provision for what might be done in the debris. But 'the major function for our reserve forces must be to provide a usable reserve for the conventional Regular Army.'[18] This included commitments in any limited war outside Europe about which, anyway, the Opposition didn't disagree. A reserve which provided teeth for such purposes was positively useful. They would 'As a result of these proposals . . . substantially increase the conventional capabilities of our forces for action in those contingencies where the conventional capability is most likely to be required.'[19]

But he had not felt it worth continuing to spend money on what were called the 'teeth units' of the TA because, if there were a nuclear attack, it would be 'an unimaginable disaster, and it is difficult to conceive of the survivors of such a force providing a contribution commensurate with its cost'. Some provision for civil defence was needed, but it should be both civilian and 'trained to organise such help as may be available in that unimaginable situation in which it is impossible to predict who will survive and what channels of command will remain'.[20]

We had to try to predict what risks were most likely and concentrate resources on them. The idea of a catch-all spread simply meant costs going crazily out of control. What were the options to be – 'another 50 wings of strategic bombers, or another 40 regiments of Centurion tanks'?[21] Jacky Smythe had talked about a conventional invasion. For Healey, 'such a conventional invasion of the country could not happen except in one situation, and that would be after the Alliance as a whole had been defeated in a conventional war on the continent of Europe.'[22]

Every Soviet spokesman had said that in the event of a war the Russians would use nuclear weapons. The USSR had 735 medium-range ballistic missiles targeted on Britain. That being the case, 'if both sides use tactical atomic weapons, we should need about 50 per cent more men in NATO in order to fight for more than a few days against the Soviet forces; but if neither side uses nuclear weapons, NATO would have to go back to the Lisbon goals of 1951. That would mean at least twice as many men as NATO has at present and, quite frankly, the British capability to contribute 70,000 half-trained volunteers would be totally irrelevant.'[23]

Nothing illustrates the driving clarity of Healey's mind more than the exchange which shortly followed with Enoch Powell. Powell might best be described as a man *capable* of logic, something which the romantic impulse always limited to an option. Was Healey not in danger, he asked, 'of arguing that an eventuality cannot arise, or is not probable, because it would be inconvenient, expensive or burdensome to have to meet it?'[24] That, said Healey, was 'a temptation to which any Minister of Defence in a government with scarce resources is always open'. But what would the Tories do? 'Are they prepared to double the defence budget? Are they prepared to bring back conscription? Are they prepared to provide the forces without which the Territorial Army, in the role that he conceives, has no sense whatever?'[25]

'My point,' he continued, 'is that paying another £20 million for 70,000 Territorial volunteers is not an insurance premium against that unforeseen. If we want that insurance premium, it will be £2000 million on top of the £2000 million we are already spending. That is why I must reject the arguments put so sincerely and with such great feeling by back benchers on both sides of the House.'[26] It was perfect logic and there was no arguing with it.

Not that logic counts for much in a parliamentary debate, and in its absence, Crossman was right about the excitement. Labour were working on their 1964 majority and the measure passed by a margin of one, 292 to 291.

FIII

An attempt has been made in the section of this book devoted to Ministry of Defence questions, to keep the running arguments on different aircraft and ships apart so that the highly technical detail of one should not clog that of another. But historically TSR2, CVA 01 and the FIII are part of a single garment, even though far from seamless and later badly slashed when mismanagement of the economy and factionalism culminated in a burst of dramatic cuts.

At the Cabinet which authorised the cancellation of a new carrier, Healey also obtained the statement: 'The Cabinet approved the proposal to make an agreement with the United States Government for the purchase of 50 FIIIAs on the terms proposed by the Secretary of State for Defence.'[1] This was the logical conclusion of what had been decided a year earlier, together with the cancellation of the TSR2, the advance from option to purchase. The statement did not stop there but rolled on through an undulating downland of successive clauses – 'provided that it was made clear to the United States Government that if the offset operations were not successful in meeting virtually the whole cost in foreign exchange, the government would be forced, through their paramount need to conserve foreign exchange, to make corresponding reductions in overseas defence expenditure, with all that this involved in terms of overseas commitments'.[2]

The caveats with which this authorisation bristles, to the limits of grammatical coherence, indicated the financial fears and political divisions of the Wilson government. It was also a recital of promises negotiated by Healey and a measure of his skill, breadth of transatlantic contacts, above all, of his close association with Secretary of Defense Robert McNamara, that a deal as favourable as this had finally been brought off. Healey's diary had recorded across the preceding months a number of journeys to Washington and other American centres. One of them, at a time when the carrier cancellation had just been resolved, involved the stalling in San Francisco of the British Comet carrying his team. Lord Hill-Norton relates that a member of the group cheekily asked if he should call up an aircraft carrier. There is no record of his being struck dead. In fact, Healey's journey, unlike so many of the scurryings of ministers and prime ministers, was about practical affairs. He was able to spell out the results to Cabinet colleagues on 14 February 1966.

But the compelling case for F111, as Healey saw it, was its suitability and excellence. 'Strategic reconnaissance, long range, a high ceiling and supersonic speed were essential and there was no alternative to the F111A in this role.'[3] The RAF were mindful of the likely military opposition of the 1970s and that meant low-level operation. As a strike plane, the F111A could operate at long range, something which had made it an alternative to the carrier-plus-short-range-plane combination. Not only did the RAF regard it as the best instrument for what they might be asked to do, it was a long bridge over the hiatus which would occur before Britain and France might bring forward the proposed 'variable geometry aircraft' which the two countries hoped to see in the second half of the next decade. 'The question was how to bridge the gap between 1970 and 1975.'[4]

Healey had trimmed and sophisticated his earlier plans and thinking. It had originally been proposed by Thorneycroft to build 150 TSR2s and his own first thoughts had been of 110 F111As. Steering tight in the pinched British economy, he now said that 'The solution he proposed was to purchase 50 F111As' and to supplement them 'by the transfer of V-bombers to the tactical role until they were replaced by [Anglo-French Variable Geometry] VG aircraft'.[5]

There had been two alternatives to this package – the Spey/Mirage combination or a developed version of the Buccaneer. Spey/Mirage would be at least two years late and would cost more than F111, most of it in foreign exchange. It was anyway, by original design, a high-level bomber not intended for the tropics where it might be needed. It was, into the bargain, a long take-off plane, needing a lot of concrete runway, something about which Healey and his airmen friends were increasingly fastidious. The Buccaneer was altogether a better bet, not much more expensive than the F111A and our own, but it couldn't be delivered on time and no guarantee attached to the projected delivery date. On top of which, developing the Buccaneer would be uneconomic unless we bought it in full for the strike role, 'which would conflict both industrially and financially with the Anglo-French VG project'. What Healey did not add was that the slowness of the RAF to respond earlier to that navy-blue plane and embrace it, had set a brilliant piece of engineering sadly back.

The Americans, as sellers off the peg, were by contrast able to offer a bargain. Not least there would be credit for all British purchases of aircraft at that shop at 4½ per cent interest, something which Callaghan had approved, and negotiations near to completion indicated a ceiling price for the whole batch of fifty aircraft working out at about £2.5 million each. On top of which, the Americans were trading with guaranteed delivery dates, a sad deficiency in most British operations – twelve aircraft would be delivered by the end of 1968, all fifty by January 1970. As for foreign exchange, Healey had negotiated with the Americans a guarantee, over twelve years, of British sales – stores and spares worth $725 million – and the US government had agreed to an annual monitoring of such sales. By a partial waiver of the US protectionist tariff, British firms 'would for the first time be able to compete on equal terms with United States industry for United States defence contracts; this offered a real opportunity for longer-term sales'.[6] The first bite would be a US invitation to tender for $50 million of naval auxiliaries.

If they were still worried about foreign exchange, they should note that both Spey/Mirage or Buccaneer would be dearer, including heavy expense in 1969/70, making the year-by-year spread lumpier (a point clearly aimed at Callaghan who had annual figures to worry about). Were they worrying about upsetting the French and, therefore, prospects for the variable geometry project? He had received a letter from the French Minister of Defence suggesting further Anglo-French talks about shared projects the following month.

The decision taken laboriously by the government had been to reduce its commitments, including the grand role East of Suez, but not to forsake a presence for limited purposes in the Indo-Pacific region. It had been argued, said Healey, that once we had withdrawn from Singapore, that role would dwindle to next to nothing by 1970, the very year the FIII would come into service. So why did we need it at all? Healey quoted a consensual view that even in those circumstances 'it would still be desirable for the United Kingdom to maintain a military presence in the Far East because of our Commonwealth interests and our concern for world-wide stability and because the maintenance of such a presence might be a necessary counterpart to the continuance of a United States military role in Europe.'[7]

This last, which by Healey's sharp standards reads pretty vaguely, has to be seen in terms of British anxiety about American sulking – cosmic sulking. After all, we were not going to send troops into Vietnam. 'Not a chance in a million,' Healey confided in conversation a year later.[8] Lyndon Johnson, who had boasted that he 'had Wilson's pecker in his pocket', had been very sour at its retraction. And Dean Rusk, his doggedly belligerent Secretary of State, evidently said to *The Times* journalist, Louis Heren: 'All we needed was one regiment. The Black Watch would have done. But you would not, well, don't expect us to save you again. They can invade Sussex and we won't do a damn thing about it.'[9]

Not having had much American help when Sussex very nearly was invaded in the spring of 1940, Britain might have taken such muttering into Texan beer very coolly. But the relationship with the US had continuing urgency for Wilson's ministers, and a modest availability in the region was seen as a handy ersatz for the forsworn folly of sending the Black Watch or indeed a solitary pipe major to the mud and napalm of Vietnam. For that matter, Healey had been urged by McNamara very strongly to do as much East of Suez as possible. The old American resentment of British imperialism had been replaced by the need for somebody else to be reassuringly out there. The terms for the F111 which, beyond any need to hype, were very good indeed, owed something to the suitability of that weapon for welcome service in the region. Healey's talk about a British presence 'being the counterpart to a continued US military presence in Europe' was a guiding British doctrine. As the scholar Herbert Nicholas put it, 'Britain's overwhelming concern, second only to that of not getting involved herself, was to prevent the USA from becoming bogged down in a hopeless and costly struggle that would divert her attention, her will and her resources from her primary tasks, as Britain saw them, elsewhere in Europe.'[10]

Continuous if residual involvement in and about the Far Eastern theatre meant that if we did not have carriers, we had to have something else. The new strategy was bases, islands, somewhere handy in Western Australia, for which these long-range aircraft were suitable. Not that Healey was tying his military doctrine to the dubious buoy of an East of Suez presence. Whatever might happen – in Europe, the Indo-Pacific area, Africa, in the event of a conflict between China and India or for UN peacekeeping purposes – 'we should not be wholly dependent on our allies for reconnaissance in such events'. Satellites were coming but not yet; meanwhile, this was the best reconnaissance plane about.

Healey's retreat was to be a Fabian one. The reduction of commitments contained in the Defence Review 'was a further step in the process of United Kingdom withdrawal from extensive world-wide commitments after the Second World War. This process would continue further but, if our withdrawal were carried out too rapidly, grave danger might result to world stability and to our interests there, and there would be a serious risk that we should be in no position to play a role appropriate to our standing and interests.'[11]

That sentence to those reading it at the turn of the century might have looked hubristic, a clinging-on to British self-importance. But this was 1966, the Vietnam War was getting serious and the domino theory with it, the Malayan emergency was a major event of very recent years, Mao Tse Tung was offering the wide-screen dementia of the Cultural Revolution with who knew what adventures in the neighbourhood. There also existed, in Pentagon circles, a right-wing military view of the Far East, something to do with 'bombing them back into the Stone Age', the sort of thing which had terrified Kenneth Younger at the Foreign Office in 1950–51. The

Johnson government, despite irk and irritation, was a good enough friend and rational, if dead wrong, in its Vietnam commitment. *Not* washing our hands overnight was, as a judgement in the context of its times, surely, if one dare use the word, responsible.

But even in the rigid language of printed minutes one can sense a terrible tension. The Cabinet discussion compressed here is downright jittery:[12] preoccupied, as we have seen, with cost, the guarantees and the offsets and threatening those overseas cuts which looked so tempting. The message to Healey was clear: 'You got us into this, Denis. You make jolly sure the guarantees stick.'

There was a subtext, usefully recorded by Richard Crossman:

> The things we really argued about were the decision to buy the American F111 and the British role East of Suez. As for the F111, it soon became clear that all the details were now cut and dried, and that the papers for the agreement with the Americans on the purchase of the plane were awaiting signature when Healey flew off to Washington tonight . . .* Of course there were some Ministers like Barbara Castle who took up postures of protest. But the rest of us felt that there was nothing we could do and that the procedure under which we had been excluded was not unreasonable. Fourteen of our twenty-three members of Cabinet are members of the Defence Committee . . .[13]

Crossman asked his keenest questions about

> our role East of Suez . . . extracting from the PM a very characteristic chain of utterances. First he repeated time after time that the Americans had never made any connection between the financial support they gave us and our support for them in Vietnam. Then about ten minutes later, he was saying, 'Nevertheless, don't let's fail to realize that their financial support is not unrelated to the way we behave in the Far East: any direct announcement of our withdrawal, for example, could not fail to have a profound effect on my personal relations with LBJ and the way the Americans treat us.'[14]

Crossman had also picked up the fact that the Chiefs of Staff were working on an assumption of withdrawal from Singapore long before 1970. 'Indeed it is only on this assumption that we can possibly keep our defence budget within the limit the Cabinet has set.'[15] Expenditure, he thought, was kept under that threshold by being deferred to the years after 1970 and, on

---

* Healey flew to Washington two days later, on Wednesday.

withdrawal, would never take place. Healey's own private record is far less chatty. There were in fact two sessions of the Cabinet, with FIII put off to the evening. Healey observes, 'Morning Cabinet on DWP – agreed political role without much trouble. Evening Cabinet difficult on FIIIA – esp. Crossman, Cousins, Ross* but Wilson helpful.'[16]

Healey himself had been working at a rate very hard for most men to shoulder. His recurring references to being 'very tired' or to having 'worked hard on Defence Review' reflected the fact that his all-day, two-part, hinged Cabinet devoted to the Defence Review was followed by 'Very hard work completing revision of DWP' [Defence White Paper], a lunch with a group of American journalists – 'quite relaxed', 'Boring meeting with [Sir Evelyn] Shuckburgh and others on NATO nuclear committee. Worked till late then voted at 10 p.m.'[17]

On the Wednesday he held a wind-up meeting on the Review with the Chiefs of Staff, saw Wilson again about trying to keep Mayhew and set off for the airport, his visit to the US – and the curse of the time zones.

'Washington at 5.30 (10.30). Very tired. Briefing meeting and working dinner Did not sleep too well!'[18] After a day's work and a transatlantic flight, he sat down to a working dinner at what must have been midnight GMT. Two days of American business involved the nuclear planning working group, a quiet lunch with the Ambassador, briefings most of the afternoon, an encounter with his friends the Linebaughs, 'Dinner with McNamara and Andreotti' (certain to have been a working one), 'very late to bed and slept badly'. Next day, briefings at the Pentagon, lunch with Hassel, 'cleared NPW [a press conference] by 3.30', a short meeting with McNamara and another official, McNaughton, who had serious problems about the FIII specification which was changing for the USAF, then he 'met the UK press' before finding himself 'back on PanAm . . . slept 3 hours'. Next day, a Saturday, after he had given a press conference at the airport, only fog prevented him flying to Leeds. Instead he had another meeting with Wilson and Luce to try to stop the admiral's resignation.[19]

---

* William Ross, Secretary of State for Scotland.

DEFENCE DEBATE – MARCH 1966

'Massacred Enoch Powell,' Healey gaily concludes his diary entry for 22 February 1966. Doing that in the short parliamentary discussion after the Defence Review statement was easier than it sounded. The member for Wolverhampton South-West was more than two years away from 'The black man will have the whip hand' speech which would carry him out of front-bench politics for ever. Over Defence, his official Opposition brief, he laboured under the more creditable but complex belief and corollary that the British Empire, especially the Indian part of it, ought never to have been abandoned, but that we should not now maintain any presence East of Suez. It was a point of view remarkably close to Christopher Mayhew's and moti-vated by a similar resentment of the United States.

Essentially a disciple of Joseph Chamberlain, Powell in his speech at the Brighton Conservative Conference in 1965 had taken an unorthodox line, casting doubt on the utility of Britain's overseas entanglements. The grandeur and duty of Empire departed, he was utterly unpersuadable that bit-part engagements containing undesirable developments in the Gulf were worth the candle. Especially was he unwilling to have us function as handmaiden and ladder-holder to a United States for whom he had conceived a perfect loathing.

However, on the day which accommodated Healey's Defence Review statement with Mayhew's valedictory speech, Powell as Opposition spokesman was obliged to make capital out of the resignation. And before 1968, what Enoch Powell was best known for was resigning. He had done so over £50 million worth of expenditure in the Budget of 1957 and, more understandably, over the mystical assent to the Prime Ministership of an Earl of Home, as astonishingly translated into Sir Alec Douglas-Home. What particularly snagged Powell's current show of outrage was that the modest item of too much spending which had offended him in 1957 had been in the defence budget!

When he spoke scornfully – as Mayhew publicly and Crossman privately did about the fixed limit – he showed himself vulnerable. Had not decisions, he asked of Healey, 'been forced on the Government by their own absurd preoccupation with fudging a figure of £2000 million in 1969–70 regardless of the consequences for the morale of the Services or the defence of the country?' Healey could respond with quiet deadliness. 'I am surprised that the right hon. Gentleman should have made the last point since he himself resigned from the previous government because they did not fix a limit for defence expenditure.'

Sweetly tossing Mayhew the customary garland of regrets and respect for a stand of principle in that 'appalling' speech, Healey was able to invite Powell to do likewise, prophetically wondering 'how the right hon. Member for Wolverhampton South-West can remain a member of a party shortly to stand in an election when he disagrees with its defence policy, its foreign policy, its social policy and its economic policy.'[1] This being the gospel truth, there was nothing more to say.

Heath, speaking after Powell, was a milder affair, and as leader, he was at any rate in agreement with his own defence policy. But he was ponderous and long – above a column in what was supposed to be a question session – and the words were stately processional beasts – 'a statement which has the most momentous imputations for the future for the defence of this country and for Britain's place in the world as a whole', 'constitutional crisis of the resignation of the First Sea Lord' – probably elephants.

His arbitrary remark about carriers was particularly tempting. What Healey was doing, said Heath, was to reduce 'the amount of the gross national product which is spent on defence which gives great pleasure to his right hon., and hon. friends but does not consider the defence of this country or its position in the world.'[2] This, spoken in Heath's strangulated, Kent-suppressing voice, was the sort of TA colonel's parody which did the Conservative Party no favours. Healey's response to this airing of the subject was cool. He welcomed the wide public debate which Heath had also proclaimed. But 'as regards the future of the carrier force, I am well aware that the party opposite never wished to take a decision on this issue ever. This is the reason why no new carrier has been laid down in the last 20 years and why it is impossible for the Royal Navy to have a carrier as would have made sense – in 1968 or 1969.'[3]

It was a formidable point. The Conservative Party was both exploiter and captive of military rhetoric. Where the *Royal* Navy was concerned, it did 'Hearts of Oak' on request, but it could do its sums and had been baffled by the same problem as Healey had been lately wrestling with. The undertow to all argument on the Defence Review, one difficult for intelligent Conservatives to deny, was that faced with the common, long-continuing dilemma of spending and commitments, Healey had at least made decisions.

The argument of 22 February, a structured little scuffle round the ministerial announcement, was only the preliminary event. The next week the Tories put down an amendment denouncing the Review and set about a two-day debate across 7–8 March. Powell spoke again, more effectively this time, directing much of his fire at Wilson and Callaghan. They had decreed the £2,000,000 limit and had done so in 'the financial panic into which the government were plunged in the early days of their administration'. It was all being done because of the need at that moment 'to stem the loss of confidence in sterling'.[4] This sounded more credible than it was. Labour's motives for the constraints were not wholly pure, but they were established well before the economic consequences of Reginald Maudling had broken over the heads of incoming Prime Minister and Chancellor.

Jim Callaghan used a less than felicitous metaphor when speaking just before the White Paper appeared: 'Defence spending was speeding ahead like a runaway train out of control. We had to fix a target.'[5] But, said Powell, this hadn't been so. In the last few years of Tory government (since 1957–8), annual expenditure as a percentage of GDP had been 7.3, 7.1, 6.8, 6.9, 6.9, 6.9, 6.6 and 6.5 and for the year of the election, there was a slight increase back to 6.6, the same percentage as was estimated for the current year. Powell also made great play of the breach of a commitment to stay in Aden and when Healey pressed him to say if the Conservatives 'would keep a military base in Aden even if Britain has no requirement for one and the local population does not want one there?'[6] Powell said flatly that they would. 'We regard that as being a binding commitment which the Government have broken and which, if we replace them as a result of the General Election, we shall regard as binding on us.'[7] How authorised and well received by the leadership was this piece of instant fettering is not clear.

On the issue of carriers, Powell found himself ambushed and rather knocked about by Ted Leadbitter, Member for Hartlepool, who quoted Duncan Sandys eight years earlier. 'We have no aircraft carriers large enough to operate the long-range bombers which would be needed for an effective strike operation. We could not contemplate building more and bigger carriers which, with their aircraft, would cost over £100 million each.'[8] Indeed Sandys, though turned aside from his first instincts, had been cool about carriers, a crypto-Healey. Flustered by the question, Powell, in an unfinished sentence, blundered into a statement which, given his superfine scholastic ear for English, was startlingly inexact. 'It was a great mistake to have scrapped the aircraft carrier under construction. The government should have gone on with the aircraft carrier in accordance [*Interruption*]. Already £3½ million had been spent on it. The plans had been made and announced.' To which Leadbitter responded simply, 'Which carrier?'[9]

After more aggressive floundering, Healey was able to intervene: 'I hope that the right hon. gentleman will agree that it will help hon. Members if I tell them that not only is there no carrier under construction, but that no tenders have ever been invited for contracts for a new carrier.'[10] Powell protested, 'It was in March or April of this year that tenders, if this project was to be proceeded with, were due to be called for . . . The right hon. gentleman took the wrong decision and we should have taken the right decision . . .' Without making too much out of a stumble over the facts, it was an odd failure to grasp in someone so pedantic, not to say exquisite, as Powell could be, and hard not to feel that over his Shadow brief, that strong mind was not fully focused.

What did stir in his speech, after a long wrangle about unit costs, was resentment of the usurping F111 so clearly intended for use in the East. He then made as if to pounce in his best stage-villain manner. 'There is something left over. There is a part of the independent nuclear deterrent which is not to be internationalised. There is a part which is to remain operational under our control outside Europe. Presumably this is the key . . . to the use which is to be made of these deep-striking, deep-penetrating aircraft in the Far East far into the 1970s.'[11] And the underlying feeling which drove him came to the surface in his conclusion. The Labour Party, he said, had 'taken decisions which will reduce the strength of our conventional forces and which will render us for a whole range of our requirements the prisoners of the United States.'[12]

Healey's main purpose in this debate was to show the whole problem of commitment and spending to be what it was, a seamless, not to say elastic, garment, a problem afflicting Conservative Defence ministers quite as much as him. Powell had claimed that expenditure was not running away. And if he, Healey, was setting a target figure, so had the Conservatives – they had set targets, but had not been able to keep to them. According to the White Paper on Public Expenditure of 1963: 'The average annual growth in defence expenditure envisaged was only 3½ per cent, the following year's defence estimates showed an increase at constant prices of 5½ per cent and . . . for the financial year 1965–66 showed an increase in expenditure of 5.1 per cent.'[13] The Conservatives had made forward plans for defence spending which put the defence budget for 1967 at £2200 million and for 1969/70 at £2400 million. Those targets were too high, and as the leap of 2 per cent in growth from the Public Expenditure White Paper demonstrated, they had shown no sign of being able to stay within them.

It wouldn't do for Reginald Maudling to intervene, as he did at this point and say that the proportion of GNP devoted to defence had actually fallen during the last years of the Tory government. 'What happened,' he said, 'was that they failed to carry out the programme as fast as they wished, and they simply pushed the expenditure to the right, thereby incurring a tremendous bulge in defence expenditure during the last years of this decade.'[14] Maudling was after all, by profession, an accountant.

Next, Powell had argued that the spending target set by Labour was too low. In doing so he was ignoring the general direction of Conservative thinking on defence by policy-making ministers since Suez. Healey responded with an old debating device:

> The point I want to put is the quite simple one that for twelve years we have been attempting to do more than our resources could manage and, in the process, we have been gravely weakening ourselves. We have in a sense been trying to do two things at the same time. First we have sought to be a nuclear power, matching missile with missile and anti-missile with anti-missile, and with large ... conventional forces in the Far East, the Middle East and the Atlantic ... At the same time we have sought to maintain a Welfare State at as high a level as – sometimes at an even higher level – than that of the United States ... The simple truth is that we have been spending more money that we should.[15]

The words echoed those of Peter Thorneycroft speaking in 1958 after his resignation as Chancellor in protest against over-spending. That historically momentous quarrel, like the shilling on teeth and spectacles before it in 1951, had nominally been based upon a straw, a £50 million increase in expenditure – and £50 million was a straw in Treasury terms even then. But Healey was right. The two parties shared a common horrified preoccupation with costs. Both looked to defence for fundamental reductions and Powell had talked himself into commitments to spend *more* than the £2400 million of previous Conservative estimates.

Healey again spoke of Britain honestly facing 'the natural limitations which the facts impose on our foreign policy and military capacity in the 1970s.'[16] The first conclusion to draw from this was 'that it would be a mistake to try to keep a base in Aden after independence in 1968, particularly when we do not need that base to carry out our commitments outside South Arabia'.[17] But he was hanging on to his partial involvement policy in the East. Challenged by the old-line leftist, William Warbey, about engaging in military operations in Asia at all in the 1970s, Healey had been robust. 'If the capacity to engage in small-scale military operations can prevent large-scale disaster, as undoubtedly it did when we intervened under the previous Government in East Africa in 1964, it is well worth a people with any sense of international responsibility paying something to be able to do it.'[18]

Healey had his own highly concentrated projection of Britain's function, that with 'a small increase in our forces already stationed in the Persian Gulf ... we can carry out our commitments to support Kuwait and the other states of the Gulf to which we have obligations.'[19] 'Obligations' was an uncharacteristically weaseling word for Healey. We had obligations in all but narrow advocate's terms in Aden/South Arabia, but that part of the world was in the process of becoming a violent mess and, from rational self-interest, we were well out of it. By contrast, Kuwait and other Gulf states had large quantities of oil, thus providing us with a compelling obligation to ourselves.

But Healey, for all that, was arguing his pragmatism pretty candidly. The carrier-keepers, if they had their way, would have a three-ship force which meant only one stationed East of Suez with another available as reinforcement at fifteen days' notice. A carrier functioned for four days of intensive operation and thirty of sustained operation. And the cost of this three-carrier force would be £1400 million over ten years. Given the limitations of one ship, *Hermes*, only able to take seven strike aircraft, then even with her carrying the best available of these, the Buccaneer Two Double Star, 'they would only have the capability of about three land-based F111As, costing a tiny fraction of the cost of the carrier force.'[20]

Carriers, so expensive and short-winded, could only be justified in particular extremities. He quoted the studies which had 'shown that the attributable cost of the Navy's front-line carrier aircraft tends to be between two and two and a half times higher than that of comparable aircraft based on land.'[21]

Validation of carriers lay only in the circumstances of invasion – or withdrawal: the landing or pulling-out of troops 'in enemy territory in the face of air attack outside the range of our own land-based aircraft'.[22] Just like Suez, he added. And he did not believe that 'any government in their senses would undertake such operations outside the range of land-based aircraft, if the amount of protection we could provide for our troops would be only that available from the sort of carrier force I have just described'.[23]

Assorted Conservative backbench comment in this debate was not terribly constructive. Sir John Smythe observed that 'if this country is no longer prepared to contribute for something approaching 7 per cent of its gross national product for our security and world peace there must either be something very wrong with the gross national product or else the British people are getting their priorities wrong.'[24] Brigadier Terence Clarke, Healey's old opponent in Pudsey, talked in a tabloid way about the minister having 'bought a lot of American aircraft on hire-purchase and . . . put a lot of our own men out of employment'.

Jacky Smythe had accused Healey of antagonising the House, but on the first day, though harassing, debate was civil enough. What followed the next day, 8 March, began civilly on the Conservative front bench, with the quiet-spoken Robert Carr, 'nice, but lacking bite', as Healey put it,[25] and the relaxed cerebration of Reggie Maudling, 'very good in wind-up'.[26] But his own speech at the end of the debate hit unpleasantness. Healey had not been impressed with himself on day one, 'not my best',[27] and much preferred his second speech: 'good, but drowned by Heath's claque in last ten minutes.'[28]

A certain drunken truculence late at night is a reliable link between the modern Commons and the eighteenth-century model. Anyone rising at 9.29 p.m. risks finding himself asking, as Healey did on this occasion, 'Please let me get on.' During the first day he had been interrupted forty times.[29] He declined to take an intervention from Dr Wyndham Davies, the race-card-playing Conservative MP for Perry Bar and, as his peroration hit its last couple of minutes, also declined to take one from Heath himself.

The shouting match had begun before Heath rose to intervene at the very end, something ruinous to a coherent wrapping-up of thoughts and thus a favourite time. When Healey refused to make way, a hail of shouting brought him to a halt, with the Speaker, Horace King, making forlorn appeals. When Healey resumed, Heath rose again to shouting, cries of 'Order' – and, from the busy Ted Leadbitter, the entirely parliamentary observation, 'Chuck him out.' Healey managed to finish with the straightforwardly political point that building the additional aircraft carrier which the Tories wanted would cost the whole of the further £250 million which they had publicly allocated for defence spending and that their defence proposals alone would multiply by four the costs they acknowledged for the expenditure listed in their election manifesto. It was 8 March and the election was scheduled for the 31st!

But beyond the inevitable party knockabout, Healey, in the two days of public argument, was making a coherent case. Carriers were a hugely expensive brittle instrument of war most useful in conflicts which, effectively, we couldn't fight alone. He had spread the money available among the forces, the Chieftain tank and a further 120 helicopters, bumping it up to a force of 300, going to the army, with the RAF receiving 'the largest injection of new aircraft that it has had for fifteen years'.[30]

As for Aden, though Healey had used Jesuitical language about the commitment there, unconvincingly stressing the changing identity of the local partner, he was making a rational case for evacuation from something hot, sticky and interminable. As far as the country, never mind the Labour Party, was concerned, in a year when the Vietnam War was turning into political wallpaper of a vibrant and jarring sort, there were no problems and Conservative objections were perfunctory. But the carrier, coupled with Aden, was an emblem, a motif; discarding it was part of a more general coming discard of old military involvements with the wider world.

Conservative speeches of the first decade of the twentieth century speak recurringly of 'the greatest Empire the world has ever seen'. Britain had gone through one horrendous war and a second necessary but ruinous. We were now, twenty-one years later, confronting inevitable, irreversible retreat, something the Conservatives had known about since Suez. It was being managed quite well in exceptionally difficult circumstances with a tired and limping economy. Some opposition was technical – Yes, the carriers do have utility! – some of it nostalgic and resentful, especially of the usurping Americans. 'Chauvinistic anti-American propaganda,'[31] Healey had called Powell's speech. But retreat it was and few people deluded themselves. As one of the Scots commissioners of 1707 had exquisitely put it, 'There's the end of an auld sang.'

AFTER SUEZ, EAST OF SUEZ

The phrase of course is Kipling, in *Mandalay* –

> Ship me somewhere east of Suez, where the best is like the worst,
> Where there aren't no Ten Commandments, an' a man can raise a
>   thirst

The generations of Macmillan, and for that matter of Wilson and Healey
born almost a quarter of a century later, knew Kipling by reading him. And
Healey, as an Oxford Marxist, would almost certainly have once curled a lip
at the irresistible old imperialist. But he appears twice, quoted at length for
his perceptions, in *The Time of My Life*.

Being a friend of Britain would become bad politics in many places for
a long time. As the long shudder of authority lost at Suez ran through the
East generally when the troops sent there by Anthony Eden withdrew from
the isthmus, effectively on orders from the United States, the government
of Harold Macmillan had to assemble the broken bits, a reasonable enough
assignment when Macmillan had been pricking instigator of the invasion,
key defector and chief beneficiary. He had in particular to deal with a set
of places and crises where British influence, allies and interests would be
threatened for a decade and more after 1957.

Egypt would henceforth be governed by native junior officers, mindful of
how it had been for them when the British Ambassador could smash down
the palace gates. But more shatteringly, less than two years after Suez,
Britain's greatest friend in the Middle East, the senior statesman, Nuri es
Said, and the young King of Iraq, Faisal II, were dragged through the streets
of Baghdad and dismembered. A revolutionary government was established

under the half-crazed Colonel Abdul Karim Kassim. Iraq was no longer one of ours. The wise young King of Jordan had already got rid of his British military adviser, Sir John Glubb, in order to quieten the people liable to drag him through the streets, and would live for another forty-five years, to be succeeded unchallenged by his son.

Denis Healey who had acquired acquaintance with the Easts, Middle and Far, when he became Shadow Colonial Secretary, wrote later about the effectiveness of small bodies of British troops in handling small wars and the hopelessness of large numbers of British troops resisting even peaceful independence movements which had genuine local support.[1] He had had India in the 1930s and again at the end of the Second World War very much in mind. But the distinction would be as true of the options then coming up for Britain. Healey's view of East of Suez was characteristically complex and many-sided. But, as we shall see elsewhere, complete disengagement from East of Suez was something which he fought almost too furiously, believing as he did in a selective and partial involvement, precisely the commitment or availability of those small bodies of British troops which he knew to be effective. The struggle over South Arabia and the war of confrontation with Indonesian forces in Sarawak and Sabah in the Malaysian Federation, and the further involvement to sustain a noisily fearful Singapore and reassure a United States, jittery and imperious by turns as it descended into the open pit of Vietnam, were as different from each other as different got.

But not everything the British did defensively after Suez was either doomed or a failure. There was a brief, effective intervention in the Middle East in 1958. When in 1961, as later, Iraq made a pitch at the Kuwait she had always viewed as a sort of Gibraltar with oil, a sensible show of British military strength saw her off. A brigade quickly established itself in the desert and Iraqi plans were quietly dropped. (Macmillan had declined the wishes of an extremist group in the Cabinet to invade Iraq and reverse the coup.[2]) This modest, but effective *démarche* would occasion, not long after, the dragging through the streets and dismembering of Colonel Kassim.

The answer to many problems, thought the Conservatives, lay in bases. One of these had been Kenya, still in the years after Suez a colony. 'Kenya can't go independent because it's a fortress colony,' proclaimed its Governor, Sir Evelyn Baring, in 1959.[3] But after the Conservatives won the election that year, Kenya did go independent on the decision of Macmillan and Iain Macleod and before long, Macleod was telling Conservative backbenchers privately that Britain should reconcile herself to losing the Kenya base. But she still held and cherished Aden and Singapore.

President Nasser, frustrated in Syria with which Egypt had briefly joined in the unconvincing United Arab Republic, next applied himself with rather more success to the Yemen. A land set back in the unserene antiquity of the old Scottish Highlands, under an Imam, despotic on an uncertain writ, while competing chiefs engaged in the steady brigandage and war of ancient custom, the Yemen was physically next door to the hinterland of Aden. Aden had been a coaling station to the British Empire, but though it lacked glamour, was sophisticated and cosmopolitan. And Aden, strengthened as a military centre during another averted crisis, the one affecting the Sultan of Oman in 1957, was turning at speed into a base for operations in the Gulf, on a par in status-conscious military eyes with the Cyprus base. The airborne part of the action for Kuwait was made from its much improved airfield, conveying troops to combine with others delivered by HMS *Bulwark* and a brigade flown in from still operative Kenya.[4]

The commitment which the Conservatives would make was large scale and expensive. The airstrip at Khormaksar would be vastly expanded after 1959. The building of yet more barracks was undertaken. In 1956, the junior Colonial Minister, Lord Lloyd, had responded to a call by a moderate nationalist political party for an elected legislature and ministry, in old, adamantine imperial terms. 'Her Majesty's government wish to make it clear that the importance of Aden both strategically and economically within the Commonwealth is such that they cannot foresee the possibility of any fundamental relaxation of their responsibilities for the colony.'[5]

Old-fashioned imperial high hand this might be, but on its own terms it had a certain grim coherence, not a condition which would last. Behind Aden lay rough mountain territory very similar to the Yemen, if not rougher, and out of all imaginable sympathy with the city below them. Healey's cherished expression 'hinterland', meaning the reading and cultural interests behind the man in the office, took on in Southern Arabia a whole new meaning.

The old British writ had been enforced with some brusqueness. As late as 1955, Lord Lloyd had said: 'The destruction from the air of the property of lawless tribes is, in our opinion, the most effective and probably the most humane way of punishing them when they refuse to pay a collective fine.'[6]

It was the decisive and wrong act of Macmillan and Sandys to establish, and then sustain with British troops, the Federation of South Arabia, incorporating with the Hill sheikhdoms the city of Aden. It was all to be authentic liberal democratic politics. There was to be independence in 1968, there should be a Federal Council, a Code of Fundamental Rights, and British government subsidies. More hard-headedly, there was a British right to exclude any part of Aden from the Federation. This was done with a view to a worst-case option of setting up sovereign bases, Cyprus-style.

There was something to be said for direct colonial mastery in Lord Lloyd's style, a good deal more to be said for establishing a sovereign base straight off. For using Aden was one thing; tying it in constitutionally with the neighbours, something else. Violence took off in Aden as the moderate political party which had asked Lord Lloyd for autonomy became less moderate, and groups yet more extreme were formed beyond it. Essentially the Adenis were scared of the hill tribes and the hill tribes scared of the Adenis and, in turn, the Arabs of Aden hated the Indian and Pakistani minority favoured when Aden had been ruled by the British from Bombay. They turned for patronage (and weapons) to the Egyptians.

A senior military opinion would point out that operations in South Arabia, though fought on behalf of the federal government and in conjunction with the federal regular army, were without the support of the local people 'who were Nasser supporters almost to a man'.[7]

It had been wrong to think that the South Arabian Federation could be kept together by force or guile – or even by well-intentioned advice. Britain had allies, friends even, among the Adeni merchant class and, in an erratic fashion, among the sheikhs. But they had nothing in common and trying to put them together with instructions to govern an artificial state of irreconcilable people was a certain disaster. The virtue of our not doing something, the benign neglect of Lord Durham's dictum in Canada, would be nicely demonstrated. Macmillan, on-target in Kuwait, had been off-course in Aden/South Arabia, and the Labour government was stuck with the consequences.

The official line after 1964, proclaimed – by Anthony Greenwood, Colonial Secretary, but supported by Healey – was that Labour intended to maintain the base but did not feel obliged to prop up what it called 'federal sultans' and hoped to bring the Adeni resistance into 'happy democratic association with the federal rulers'.[8] The imperious injunctions of Sandys were thus replayed through a Fabian filter. The change of policy would be hailed by the *Economist*, in its magisterial way, as 'realistic'. When Greenwood went to Aden in November, several bombs were exploded and two British soldiers were killed. A statement was made by a group of ministers in the federal and Adeni governments, praising 'a unitary sovereign state on a sound democratic basis'. Trevaskis, the High Commissioner who in December 1963 had narrowly escaped assassination at the airport, had more doubts. He retired in December 1964 and was replaced by Sir Richard Turnbull.

In mid-June 1965, Healey went with a team to Aden, having first discussed things at Chequers with Wilson, Michael Stewart and other ministers concerned.* It was his second journey there as he had visited Aden (and Borneo) in the latter days of Opposition. He would encounter a vicious muddle of enmities and fiefdoms which could be called Byzantine or Balkan,

---

* Almost his last act before the trip was an unrelated conversation with Roy Jenkins recorded in cryptic and tantalising fashion: 'mainly on political situation – frightened of catastrophe, but what to do?'

but could not be solved by either force or sweet talking. The problem of setting up the Federation at all had been complicated by the undertaking in 1964, by Sir Alec Douglas-Home, that the unhappy amalgamation should become independent in 1968. This was more realistic than the original Macmillan designation of troops being committed to Aden 'permanently', though a military treaty was promised. But the local contenders and their forces, respectively of clan and mob, were now preoccupied as to who on that date should be master.

On seeing a group of hill country sheikhs (three sultans and a rajah) before rushing off to Government House to meet Aden ministers, Healey commented in the diary that it was like coming 'from the seventeenth century Scottish Highland Chiefs to Glasgow Town Council in 1918'.[9] The Federation itself, which he crisply calls 'misbegotten',[10] was under infiltrated political pressure from Nasser-controlled Yemen and had contrary friends in Saudi Arabia, or Muscat and Oman. British or British-directed troops could maintain transient order in an area at the risk of being murdered and mutilated from time to time. But when they moved on, the old disorder returned. The military force serving the Federation functioned as a free-range Sisyphus.

After a day flying the country, a succession of meetings – with Sharif Hussein, a federal army commander, Colonel Ahmed, and the American consul, Healey dined with his service chiefs and, like Drake but in near equatorial light, 'played bowls till midnight'.[11] He would also at this time encounter in Philip Moore a young man who greatly impressed him and whom he soon made his private secretary.

As with Jenkins and British politics, the situation was frightening, but what to do? The first concern of these conversations ran outside the Federation and concerned Saqr, a local princeling, who was being financed by the Arab League. The Foreign Office thought this connection 'catastrophic'[12] but didn't care for most of the proffered solutions. Options run through with Healey included diversion of the plane carrying the money, deposing Saqr (vetoed by the Foreign Office) and the bleak injunction, 'Withdraw protection from Saqr and let his brothers kill him'[13] which very properly induced 'cold feet'. Another plan was to withdraw protection and encourage, not murder, but a takeover by Dubai. This was jointly vetoed by Healey in person and the FO in a telegram. Hardly more civilly, they contemplated getting Saqr's family to depose him and put in Khalil, a brother, while Saqr was merely deported to Dubai. Alternatively he might either be surrounded at a meeting of the Majlis (tribal court and assembly) or tricked out of his fortified palace, with the same destination of Dubai. It all sounds like G. A. Henty with additional material by John Webster.

Healey took in the remote, austere charm of the area as he was driven across an 'appalling dust road' to Shibam, capital of the Hadhramaut, and looking around, saw 'bad dust storms, milky sky'[14] before dining with the

Terry and Dennis between grandfathers.

Denis with Gran: looked after by his father's mother, Theresa *née* Driscoll.

At the piano: Denis watched by younger brother Terry.

The Classical Sixth Bradford Grammar (Healey third right, front row).

La sorridente signora Hernshaw, é il marito, personalità laburista, accompagnano Lasky nel suo viaggio.

Ms Hernshaw mistaken. Not Hernshaw, Healey: visiting Italy for Socialist International Meeting, 1947.

With Jenny, 1948.

Shorts, tent and mountains. Denis, Cressida, Edna, Jenny and Tim.

The Small Platoon: Edna, Tim, Cressida and Jenny Healey.

Hinterland: with Edna in the Dolomites.

The best political marriage in Westminster.

"Went home and mowed grass."

Rural retreat: Healey in Sussex.

'In the forest something stirred.' Denis in a jeep in woods near Siena.

Major Healey speaks for the Left: conference speech welcoming revolution, Blackpool, 9 June 1945.

Parla il compagno Heeley rappresentante del Labour Party

Parla il compagno Healey: addressing Italian Socialist Party Conference, 1947.

The coming man: Healey in the fifties.

The battle dress conference. Major Healey and Captain Jenkins at Blackpool in 1945 with former conscientious objector Emanuel Shinwell, shortly to become Minister of War.

Side view of an apparatchik. Healey assists Morgan Phillips (standing) and Emanuel Shinwell (centre) at the Socialist International Conference, Bournemouth, November 1946.

NOW I REALISE

I have taken far too much for granted. Our community is what we make it—what I make it.

I shall use my vote and am giving it to the candidate who is pledged to do his utmost for the people.

I shall give it to the candidate who believes in equality of opportunity in education, in fair shares in a better and fuller life.

I have studied the policies of all the parties and the records of the candidates.

There is only one thing I can do. That is to

VOTE
LABOUR

BALLOT
BOX

With a lady not his wife:
Labour propaganda old style,
Transport House leaflet, 1950.

The candidate and the workers. Canvassing building
workers during his Leeds S.E. by-election, February 1952.

The candidate: Healey in 1952 (age 34),
the year of his election in Leeds South East.

The Second Wilson Cabinet, 1967.

The Defence ministerial team: Healey unveils his 1966 white paper (left to right: Gerry Reynolds [Army], who died soon after, Lord Shackleton [RAF], J.P.W. Mallalieu [Navy], replacing the resigning Christopher Mayhew).

M. le Ministre: Healey inspects French troops with (left) Pierre Messmer, the French Defence Minister.

MR. HEALEY WITH SHIPS AND MEN OF THE WESTERN FLEET

Meeting the chaps.

The Young Minister.

A hopeful little tune on the recorder.
Denis in Ankara for NATO
planning group.

'Diplomatic Discomfort':
probably Aden/S. Arabia.

Somewhere East of Suez.
Healey with Tunku Abdul
Rahman, Prime Minister
of Malaysian Federation
and a close ally.

Healey demonstrates the
F111 to Wilson and Foreign
Secretary Michael Stewart.
It had actually been cancelled
a few days earlier.

DENIS
HEALEY

Vicky's view, 1966. Victor Weiss, cartoonist of the *Daily Mirror* and *New Statesman*, who drew Denis here, later committed suicide from despair at the political situation, especially Vietnam.

'Naked into the conference chamber': Roy Jenkins persuading Harold Wilson to kill the F111 and commitment East of Suez.

Taking early morning press conference: Harold Wilson and Labour, 1970.

Healey as German Joker, Rhine Festival, 1970.

The Chancellor at No.11.

The Treasury Team (mid seventies): Derek Mitchell, Alan Lord, Healey, Douglas Wass, Brian Hopkin, Leo Pliatzky, Joel Barnett.

Treasury between spending ministers: Eric Varley (Industry) and Roy Mason (Defence) flank a weary Chancellor, 1970s.

BEWARE PAY POLICY QUICKSAND

"DON'T STRUGGLE ANYONE — YOU'LL ONLY SINK FASTER!"

Travails of the Seventies (clockwise: Healey, Shore, Callaghan, Foot, Hattersley, Shirley Williams, Merlyn Rees)

'Cheerfulness kept breaking in.'
Healey on his way to the (too
cheerful) April 1975 budget.

Minister of Defence takes over Treasury.
Healey did not attempt to reflate but faulty
statistics had that effect.

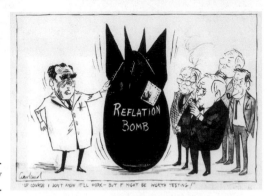

A moment of optimism.
Franklin's account, 23 March 1976.

'We're not sinking. We're just finding our
level.' Jensen at the height of the crisis.

No, not that, it's "Firstly, secondly…"
Healey attacks Tony Benn at Brighton
during the 1981 deputy leadership contest.

'The hurley-burley of the chaise-longue.'

Healey's Eye: photographer shoots Callaghan, Foot and Castle (centre left and centre right:
Audrey Callaghan, Jill Craigie [Foot] at Michael's 80th).

Sultan of Saiyun 'on Terrace of Summer Palace, eating with right hand', before making the idyllic reference 'Slept on roof under stars, dogs barking.'[15] His admiration for that fertile valley, especially as caught in pink light at dawn, was unlimited: 'two of the most enjoyable days of my life.'[16]

Central to the political problem was the unwillingness of the parts to settle into the designated whole. But there was still talk of expansion. Would the Hadhramaut join the Federation once it became independent? The Sultan, 'a tiring little man', told Healey next morning after he had woken at five-thirty and walked round the town which he found 'beautiful', that he wanted '50 more men to add to 130 KAC (Kathari Armed Constabulary), but still sitting on fence over federation'.[17] There were stories told to Healey of the Sultan being close to the Saudis who also wanted to play a hand, and of 'Indonesian-earned wealth and wives'.[18]

He spent the following day in the company of Turnbull, the sardonic British Governor of Aden and a prominent local figure, Abdollah al Asnai, who wanted a British Resident Minister and progress towards democracy in the sheikhdoms. But though these were intelligent men, Healey was increasingly aware that the influences throughout the artificial Federation came from elsewhere – Saudi Arabia eyeing the western territories, Egypt rattling a stick among the poor of Aden's slums and even Indonesia, Muslim and meddling.

Meanwhile, in Aden itself, the Crater district would soon catch the attention of the British press as Lieut.-Col. Colin Mitchell, a brave if politically unsophisticated officer and his Argyll and Sutherland Highlanders, struggled to maintain control of that blazing slum. The Egyptians, established in Yemen at Sa'ana and Taiz, sent weapons to the opposition in Aden. The British superintendent of police, Barrie, and the Speaker of State Legislature, Charles, also British, but liberal and popular with Adenis, were both murdered. But the central reason why the terrorism of the opposition groups could not be fully suppressed was that the Federation was a state split between autonomy and colonial guidance. As its chronicler, Tom Little, put it succinctly: 'The High Commissioner was committed to the suppression of terrorism and the Chief Minister to condoning it, so Britain was compelled to dismiss the government or abdicate.' In choosing to impose direct rule, the British had in effect admitted their open confrontation with their extreme opponents, and there could be no turning back short of complete defeat.[19] Extremism works if it is extreme enough. And after the natural death of Hassan Ali Bayoomi, the one resolute and uncompromising Aden statesman, every other man of any note in politics moved across the spectrum to support violence and did so in fear of unnatural death.

British ministers got the message. On the afternoon of 24 November 1965 the Defence and Overseas Committee had before it a draft of Healey's Defence Review. 'It was agreed that when South Arabia became independent in 1967 or 1968 we should not maintain any obligations to, or defence facilities in, Aden or the South Arabian Federation.'

In mid-January 1966 two of the Adeni physical force groups, OLOS and the NLF, formally came together to form the Front for the Liberation of South Yemen which was given the imprimatur of both the Arab League and Egyptian-ruled Yemen. On 14 January Healey remarked in Cabinet, 'The question is: how soon do we announce our intention to leave Aden and on what terms?' Because discontinuation of public building works would signal intentions, the government 'should announce in the White Paper that we do not believe that we shall require to maintain a military base there after 1968.' Independence had been planned by the Conservatives, but all understanding, not specifically rejected by the Labour government, had been for a military commitment afterwards. On 2 February, the White Paper was published and stated that all British troops would be withdrawn from Aden by December 1968.

The decision was a bleak piece of *sauve qui peut*. Federation had accelerated the terrorist violence of Aden. The situation could be judged precisely as one observer listed acts of terrorism: 'One incident in 1963, 36 incidents in 1964, 286 in 1965 and almost double this figure in 1966.'[20] Politicians with whom Healey had talked in June on the assumption that they would function constitutionally were already making their dispositions. And that trip seems, for all its charms, to have dissuaded him from maintaining commitment either to the Federation or even to the base. For within five months of it, Britain gave up the idea of holding the Federation together, making clear that British troops would not remain to catch any more flak.

Macmillan's biographer, Alistair Horne, describing his subject's anger at the withdrawal which would eventually follow, observes that 'Both Macmillan and Home always considered the Denis Healey policy of disengagement from East of Suez to be "the most disastrous thing that has happened in twenty years".'[21] This is startlingly unhistorical. No one familiar with the Cabinet struggles of 1967–8 would, in general terms, recognise 'the Denis Healey policy of disengagement' as anything of the sort. Overall, it was more like the Healey policy of affordable targeted commitment amended into the Treasury policy of disengagement, nagged on by left-wing backbench protest and finally accomplished after a financial crisis by Wilson moved by a short-term personal grudge.

They would catch a good deal of flak before the departure date. The Sheikh of Beihan with whom Healey had exchanged elaborate courtesies on the June 1965 visit found himself fighting a local civil war with a member of his family, armed and bankrolled by the British for quite other purposes.[22] The local constabulary, the South Arabian Armed Police, rioted and before they had done, killed nine British soldiers. The rationale at the end was that Aden had been a useful military base, apt for purposes in the Persian Gulf.

But with her own population dominated by Pan Arab nationalists violently opposed to such operations, Aden alone would have had to be coerced in ways not worth the distasteful trouble and mounting expense.

The sheikhdoms had been conservative enough and often, in a fickle, charming way, friendly enough to the British. But the notion of diluting Aden with those sheikhdoms was an attempt to blend things mutually repellent. It seems to have been one conflict which Healey had few pangs about withdrawing from, convinced as he was that a republic of chalk and cheese could not be sustained by tear gas, casualties and retaliation.

There would be a fraught search over the next couple of years for islands or corners of Australia from which any part might be played by us in the Persian Gulf. In human terms, British withdrawal abandoned the chiefs to their enemies and the shopkeeper class of Aden to the Leninist moves of the ultras, executed with great speed and ferocious will. What remained at the end, the People's Republic of South Yemen, was a state of furious revolutionary violence producing instant anachronism. In the famous words of a witness at the 1957 bank rate tribunal, withdrawal was immoral and wrong but, on balance, it made sense.

Singapore and Malaya were something quite different, actually, two things quite different, and snappishly distinguishable from each other. The city, which in 1942 General Percival first incompetently defended, then wretchedly surrendered to a savage Japanese army, had generally been seen by twitchy American *geopolitikers* as a high-ranking candidate for 'going Communist'. In the fifties and early sixties, it was very far from rich; and, being a city, was worryingly urban, full of talk and subversive whispers, full also of Chinese, all said to be looking to Mao for leadership. And it was the Chinese who had provided the men in the jungles who had made the Malayan Emergency of the early fifties, put down in his exemplary way by the glass-crunching General Templer. It had an active Peking-sympathetic grouping, the Barisan Sosialis, whom the Americans and the British left wing, in their different ways, expected to inherit.

Malaya, independent since 1957, was a different world – slow, Muslim, given to the lethargic ill-humour towards foreigners generally, and Chinese in particular, memorably captured by Anthony Burgess in his *Malayan Trilogy*. The Malays disliked the Chinese who despised the Malays. It was therefore inevitable that Macmillan and Duncan Sandys, knowing what was best for people, should after much fussing have delighted to bring Malaya and Singapore together in 1962 as the 'Malaysian Federation'. In fairness, although the British ministers ran hard with the ball, it was first picked up by the Malay leader, Tunku Abdul Rahman, and was the original idea of Lee Kwan Yew of Singapore. It was a mistaken move, but less foolish than creating the South Arabian model. The Communists had been defeated in Malaya – would probably have been defeated even without General

Templer's severities – because no Malay of standing would be long involved in a movement run by Chinese and looking for patronage to China itself. The Malaysian Federation would fail because the Malays conceived of it as being too energetic, too abrasive, too talented, too Chinese. It would also fail because the Tunku, a shrewd, humorous aristocrat, vividly disliked the dazzling but fraught Lee.

But for a long time external threats made for coherence more pressingly than internal hostilities made for dissolution. Ironically, the assembly of bits and pieces by which Macmillan/Sandys federations worked, had provided the external menace which would for a while keep the Federation together. For, added to the mixture, had been Sarawak and Sabeh, another name for North Borneo, home of, among others, primitive head-hunters – the Healeys would on their first visit be presented with the shrunken head of a Japanese soldier which, found in a plastic bag behind a sofa, would cause their cleaning lady, very reasonably, to pass out.

These people had nothing in common with either Malays or Chinese. But neither had they had anything in common with the Indonesians whose ambitions to take these territories over would occasion a small war, much trouble and, as long as the threat lasted, more unity than the founders of the Federation quite deserved. As Field Marshal Carver would write, 'The formation of Malaysia was seen by Macmillan and Sandys ... as yet another means of divesting Britain of its direct responsibilities in the hope that not only would subversive movements be defused, but that the new amalgam of territories would be capable of looking after its own security, otherwise than from a direct threat by a major power such as China or the Soviet Union.' 'SEATO,' the field marshal adds with the faintest of ironies, 'existed for that.' Meanwhile the US attitude to British military activity, with Vietnam beginning its first toddler's steps to calamity, had changed significantly since Suez. They were only too eager to find partners to share the White Man's Burden in 'containing the spread of Communism in the developing world'.[23]

Healey himself had been more sceptical about British military commitment than he would become in government, having wondered aloud in parliament on 15 May 1961 if 'certain substantial British overseas commitments were not politically or strategically irrelevant in the contemporary context'.[24] But this was a time of anxiety about communist expansion. Senior Labour figures at this time, Patrick Gordon Walker and Arthur Bottomley, were respectively talking of 'maintaining the balance of stability in this part of the world' and saying that 'Malaysia is being created to contain Communism'.[25]

'Malaysia' it was, not Malaya, the new name being employed to signify the federal union. Initially the US and an anxious Australia had had hopes of drawing Malaya into that same SEATO (South-East Asian Treaty Organisation), an American construction which the Tunku shrewdly resisted. What he wanted, entirely sensibly, was the best of both worlds – outside support, primarily Commonwealth, and no interference. He was also extremely concerned about the stability of Singapore, poor, left wing, milling with extremist factional politics and Chinese. Healey was very taken with the Tunku's dictum on war: 'If you have an enemy you can defeat on your own, fight. If you have an enemy you can defeat with allies, fight. If your enemy is China, surrender.'[26]

The foundation of military defence had been AMDA, the Anglo-Malaysian Defence Agreement. Agreed in 1957 and a major commitment, it was sometimes called by Britain a blank cheque, or unequal burden, involving two countries to be supported, one country to give the major guarantee and two neighbours, Australia and New Zealand, chipping into the undertaking. It was not, like SEATO, a Dullesian 'bulwark against Communism' reliant upon constituent parts no more savoury than the neighbouring Philippines where incredible comic criminal would succeed incredible comic criminal in an apostolate of '*our* bastards'. This was instead a sensible, if onerous, undertaking, a natural extension of old British connections, a practical carry-over from the old imperial power giving support against a shared threat. It was a modest survival of colonial obligation, indeed of the White Man's Burden – in the white man's enlightened self-interest.

The move to federation derived from the Indonesian threat and from movements in Singapore. The rising political party there was Lee's People's Action Party motivated by Chinese fear of Chinese communism. What interested the Australasians and Britain most immediately was the excellence (for friend or enemy) of Singapore as a military harbour. In 1959 Lee had won the elections on a campaign for merger with the mainland while giving expression, by ironic paradox, to a general left-wing mood in the island. Tunku Abdul Rahman, despite a career-long dislike of Lee, shrill, parvenu, too clever by half, tricky, Chinese, had no wish for something worse, more radical, more Chinese.

Though, with equal irony, it was only when two years later Lee's power seemed to be waning, that the Tunku proposed the creation of an assembly serving a federation of Malaya and Singapore. For her allies, what mattered most at this time, the Singapore base, would seem to have been ensured. And the Tunku quoted the British saying that 'With the situation as it is in South East Asia . . . there is an absolute necessity for Britain in connection with this base to maintain confidence in this part of the world.'

More succinctly, Britain could only keep Australia and New Zealand happy with their commitments if she was the active user of that base. As for the Indonesian threat, it was typical of the regime which has misgoverned that country for forty years. A nation in which Suharto succeeds Sukarno is drawing serial short straws. The recent record of the Indonesians in East Timor casts a backward light of great credit upon all those discouraging Indonesian expansion anywhere. At this time, the leader was Sukarno, Bung (or Brother) Karno, redeemer, beloved leader, syphilitic, fiscally unsound, proclaimer of 'Guided Democracy' (with Sukarno guiding). He sustained a raggedy state on the rhetoric and, more marginally, the substance of war. Bankrupt regimes need external enemies for rally purposes.

At that time, the Indonesian Communist Party (PKI) was very large and threatening. Accordingly, the United States in the early sixties, Kennedy time, had put their money on Sukarno. The feeling was that he needed an external triumph to score off the Communists and what better object than a Malaya whose British-educated patrician leader showed such distaste for SEATO? Philip Moore, who turns up again as Deputy High Commissioner in Singapore, would spend a fruitful three hours with Robert Kennedy on this topic. After hearing the 'Damn British' duly damned Irish-American style, Moore patiently explained the real balance of forces, the personalities concerned and the risks involved. Much to his pleased surprise, Kennedy, properly briefed, became wholly rational, saw the argument and undertook to go home and instruct his brother, something he successfully did.*

As for the Communist problem in Indonesia, that would be put right in 1965 by a handy act now handily forgotten, the massacre of a majority of the membership of the Communist Party, a figure put at the time at half a million. The full extent of US complicity remained unclear, but something about such cleansing calls to mind an old phrase about 'good Indians'.

Sukarno's ambitions concerned Sarawak and Sabah which were geographically contiguous, sharing with Indonesian territory the island known as Kalimantan. The term 'Confrontation' would not be coined until Sukarno's Foreign Minister, the no more engaging Dr Subandrio, employed it in a speech of 20 January 1963. In doing so he was ringing bells throughout the region. It was the word Bung Karno had used in his successful campaign against the Dutch in West New Guinea or, as the Indonesian regime called it, West Irian. But his first ploy was to make a pitch at another corner of Kalimantan, Brunei, an independent sultanate with large oil resources. He supported a local rebellion there in December 1962 which took control of the Seria oilfields, attacked government buildings and took European hostages. This coup, run by a politician A. M. Azahari, had been promptly put down by the gentle Admiral Luce, later Healey's unhappy Chief of Naval Staff, from the Singapore base. Brunei would be wanted by the matchmakers for a constituent part of Malaysia. But the Sultan, able to get British military backing anyway, stayed polite and independent.

Healey, as we have seen, had been unsure as Shadow Colonial Secretary that further heavy involvement was a good idea and his doubts were shared, not only by the predictable Crossman, but by Christopher Mayhew and,

---

* Private information.

surprisingly, George Brown. By December 1964, with Labour in power, Confrontation was heavily under way and Healey, having talked the nature of our commitment through in a long ministerial meeting with McNamara, would give a formula to Cabinet which encapsulated his whole thinking East of Suez. Crossman records: 'Healey replied that what they wanted us to do was not to maintain huge bases but keep a foothold in Hong Kong, Malaya, the Persian Gulf, to enable us to do things for the alliance which they can't do.'[27] Reflection also made it clear that Indonesia had an army of 300,000 men, a navy equipped by the Soviet Union, an air force which had 400 planes; she was pushing armed patrols along the approaches to Malaya and claimed to have '"Indonesian volunteers" massing on the Borneo border'.[28]

The British response to mounting threats was to dispatch that future Defence Chief, General Sir Richard Hull, a blunt, honourable despiser of diplomatic refinement who would talk openly about Britain being committed '500 per cent if need be', before going off to Canberra to jolly the Australians into line.[29] Healey, more than most men, was able to make his own mind up, but in 1964 he would have close to his elbow two Chiefs with direct (and invigorating) experience of resisting Indonesia.

Malaysia, the Federation, would have a short and melancholy life, a political chrissom created in 1962 and ended in 1965 (ended *de facto* in 1963). But in practice, such severance made no difference to the *realpolitik* of the commitment. As long as Britain was good for playing any world role, perhaps especially the jobbing one which Healey and McNamara were agreed on, it needed Singapore as a base. Malaya, however difficult, was worth saving; Singapore harbour, both for access and denial, was a military jewel, Sukarno the sort of inferior windbag with whose adventures it would be humiliating to comply. Besides, in pure military terms the war was going sweetly.

For the conflict had, in a buzz-word of the era, escalated. Attempts had been made to keep firepower down and to entice the Malay people with the idea, originating with Macapagal of the Philippines, of a pan-Malay fatherland embracing the more racially mixed Philippines in something called Maphilindo, a hypothesis happily fizzling out, but one which played its part in alienating Lee and Singapore. This having come to nothing, Sukarno next put terrorists into Sarawak.

The war, into which sporadic action mixed with diplomatic feints now drifted, would by its nature coin a new military expression, 'low-level operations', of which the chief exponent would be the brilliant, if eccentric, Sir Walter Walker, commander of indispensable Gurkhas. It was very much irregular soldiering – counter-insurgency, guerrilla fighting, and involved crossing into enemy territory which, in the absence of a declared war, was *not* enemy territory. These operations – incursions of between 5000 and 20,000 yards – known collectively as 'Claret' – received Healey's carefully judged authorisation, as a proposal for bombing did not. It was the sort of war which had to be fought hard but discreetly, without either public relations or high-altitude killing of civilians. Far more useful was the extensive employment of undercover intelligence, especially within the groupings of Chinese communist families – allegedly 5000–7500 supporters of the 1950s insurgency now settled in Sarawak.

Although Malay troops were of course engaged, this was primarily the business of the British military supported by battalions of Australians and New Zealanders. It was very much a war of cunning and courage in the field, officers using their initiative, enemy soldiers outmatched by soldiering, a small war won in a quite decent cause. There had been a lobby for counter-invasion which, a year or two earlier, 'had very nearly succeeded in persuading the Conservative Government to escalate the conflict'.[30]

As Healey wrote with a certain pride, 'At a time when America was plastering Vietnam with bombs, napalm, and defoliant, no British aircraft ever dropped a bomb in Borneo.'[31] Though, as he adds, 'the presence of ships and aircraft probably stopped the Indonesians from escalating the war.'[32] The price paid in life, though no such tally may ever be called light, was 114 killed and 181 wounded from 17,000 servicemen against Indonesian figures of 590 killed, 222 wounded and 771 captured – a fair measure of the old fighting against the new American sort which furnished a vast war memorial in Washington.

However this was an unstable war, capable of sudden demands on manpower, like the 10,000 men rushed into Sarawak after an air attack on a settlement in September 1965 which ominously paralleled the endless calls of General William Westmorland for more troops in Vietnam. There were 50,000 troops in Borneo, the land border was 1000 miles long and British and Commonwealth patrols also had to cover 3000 miles of coastline with the support of fifty naval craft.

A different temptation – to get out – came from the dissensions of the local principals. As Healey told his first biographers, 'I was very tempted when, in the middle of Confrontation – in the summer of 1965 – the Tunku and Harry Lee* gave us an opportunity for getting out, by breaking their own Federation behind our backs. But you just couldn't do it. There wasn't a political solution as long as Sukarno was there.'[33]

Federation had always been irrelevant. It was worthwhile defending Singapore and worthwhile defending Malaya; so it went on being done after the arranged marriage promoted by Macmillan and Sandys had ended in total and irreconcilable breakdown. And unlike the South Arabian conflict, this war seemed to have an end, the peace, a shape.

There flowed from the conflict, as Field Marshal Carver drily notes, all

---

* Lee liked to be known by this pet name, at least among Westerners.

sorts of arguments for Britain East of Suez. It pleased Mountbatten because the services in Sarawak and Sabah were functionally integrated in the best Mountbatten manner; a case could be made for the commando carrier which got men to places effectively (and against it in that, once there, they stayed put and didn't use it again). And the Labour government in this glad, confident morning was glad to demonstrate 'soundness' while easing the Labour conscience with the reflection that a Norwegian resolution at the UN Security Council deploring Indonesian actions had been supported 9–2. Perhaps best of all, this reputable but preoccupying engagement provided an additional and canny excuse for not obliging America in Vietnam.

Healey's longest visit to the operations came in the summer of 1966, precisely as economic crisis was about to drive Wilson and Callaghan back on their heels. Their July Measures, the first stone on the government's jarring road downhill, were put together while Healey was whisked around in helicopters, briefing and being briefed, rebuking a journalist, Ian Ward, sniffing after a split with the Tunku, was 'a bit rough'[34] with a British official, 'totally wrong on his facts about Hong Kong', and inspected equipment – Sea Vixens and Buccaneers – over whose affordability he had wrangled in the office.

On one occasion he received a nineteen-gun salute, more than Jim Callaghan was getting. On another he was delayed because his driver was playing poker with the King of Malaya![35] The first officers he met impressed him almost all round for quality and quick-mindedness. A visit to Brunei and the Sultan's brother had the opposite effect – 'Very dull and futile social conversation'.[36] But he spent more time with Gurkhas and their officers who briefed him on their 'Claret' operations.

The war was actually almost won. Sukarno, who had gambled on intimidation and incursion winning him an inexpensive victory, had lost prestige in the inner cliques of Indonesian politics as war painfully continued despite the change of party in Britain. He went and, for all purposes, Confrontation with him, in August 1966.

A month before Healey's visit, the Parliamentary Labour Party, the democratic representative of the governing party not always quite ready to endorse that government's policy, had met in Committee Room 14 of the Commons. It was to debate the Vietnam War (Britain's failure to denounce) and, very sweepingly, East of Suez. The left led the argument, but non-leftists with agendas of their own, Woodrow Wyatt and Christopher Mayhew, joined in. Wilson made the case, very much his own version, that 'though he would reduce the number of troops East of Suez, he would never deny Britain the role of a world power'.[37] The motion was heavily rejected (225:54) but with many abstentions, a full complement of the ministerial payroll and sundry peers present and in a mood of despondency with commitments. The economic crisis had not yet struck, but it would fall on politically soggy ground with a great splash.

What was true of Healey throughout this time was that he saw the Far East from a different angle to Wilson. The Prime Minister, plagued by a US president (and by the Australians who had troops in Vietnam) demanding at least token support in that conflict and by a party which would tolerate no such thing, saw himself as a peacemaker, an airport profile, a comer-and-goer between world capitals, helping to resolve the conflict. His defence of foreign policy took on great platonic sweeps of language, but wandered perilously close to implying unthinkable nuclear guarantees to the Indian subcontinent against China. With Wilson, where furtiveness towards the US left off and unmerited self-belief took over, was never clear.

Healey was a pragmatist in the creditable sense of the world. What should be done? What *could* be done? If sentiment came into things at all, then in Malaya/Singapore a liking for the local peoples and for both Lee and the Tunku, played a part.*

Healey had been briefed to cut the defence budget and called upon to fight a medium-sized local war. He wanted the job accomplished, the British to linger near the stage as reinsurance and reassurance to our local partners. But unlike his Conservative predecessors, he had to do the accountancy. 'World peace' was a large expression. Healey was content with achieving stability in one place where the means were available. Left to himself, he wanted troops there until well into the 1970s.

For all his practicality, the Secretary for Defence would speak in too sanguine a way to the Commons on 8 March: 'We shall be able to carry out a large range of peace-keeping tasks like that in East Africa two years ago, entirely on our own, while maintaining a powerful deterrent against intervention by others, and we shall also be able to make a powerful contribution to allied operations if we so decide.'[38] That was what Healey *wanted* to do. In pursuit of it, he was telling journalists in Hong Kong as late as July 1966 that 'Britain would stay in Singapore and Malaysia as long as she was wanted on acceptable conditions.'[39] Such talk was temperate beside Wilson's imaginings, but still aspired too far. Four months after the debate, days after the press conference, economic failure would assume control of events and shades of the prison house surround the most reasonable of undertakings East of Suez.

---

* Philip Moore, a close observer of both men, says simply that the two most brilliant minds he has ever encountered were Lee Kuan Yew and Denis Healey! (Conversation with the author.)

1966–7 – CRISES

Her Majesty the Queen spoke of 1992 as an *annus horribilis*. Harold Wilson, if the phrase had occurred to him, would probably have designated 1966 by the same term – until 1967. But it hardly started that way. On 31 March, Labour won its second general election, its majority moving from three to 97. The government was placed to win because it stood in the happiest of relationships with the electorate, that of a new ministry, hampered and protected by a small majority which served as an alibi for doing very little. Indeed, Wilson's Cabinet could follow the Gilbertian maxim of doing nothing in particular and doing it very well. On top of which, anxious inactivity could be squared with much tutting and head-shaking at those reckless excesses of Reginald Maudling which had never been seriously criticised by Labour when they were happening.

Wilson was able to say, 'Look, we are perfectly competent, quite moderate, a government governing much like other governments. It's safe to vote for us.' The unstated thesis that there was nothing to frighten the horses might be unheroic, but given those thirteen wasted years (wasted for Labour at any rate), given also the tendency of Conservatives to play the fear and atrocity card and mutter about revolutionary danger, stroking the horses' heads had much to be said for it.

The election was sufficient of a readjustment of 1964's short lease to provide very few thrills. Walter Terry of the *Daily Mail* coined the phrase 'non-event' in its honour. Ted Heath, the new Tory leader, made a little joke about Wilson's fondness for stunts, saying that doubtless in a month's time he would be entertaining a pregnant panda to tea in Number 10, a very human flash of the subconscious conveying the sort of submission which Opposition leaders fighting elections try to avoid. Enoch Powell, for reasons making sense only to himself, announced at Falkirk five days before the poll that the government was about to commit troops to Vietnam.

Healey, just through with his February Defence Review, had a busy election, being more widely used than in 1964. He was a Cabinet minister of nearly two years' standing, the Leeds seat safe as safe seats come; he was free to travel a little. He was able to break away from DOPCs, from discussing the sale of Lightnings to Saudi Arabia and the future of the P1127. Such half-holidays – he still saw a good deal of the office – allowed him to write articles for the *Yorkshire Post* and the *Daily Telegraph,* attend a St Patrick's Night at Harehills, Leeds, and start a round of wider election appearances.

At Newcastle and then Sunderland on 21 March, he spoke for Geoffrey Rhodes and Gordon Bagier – 'a lot of heckling but went very well'. In Stanmore and Mill Hill he spoke on 23 March for Roy Roebuck and Ernest Wistrich – 'good, lively meetings'. Friday the 25th found him in the north-west, at Hyde, then at Stockport and Ellesmere Port before touching base with a Leeds meeting and being inducted as president of Helton Moor Social Club, before, on the Sunday – 'tremendous gales and very cold' – he canvassed the Monkswood flats in his constituency and spoke at 'a good town hall meeting' for the other Leeds Labour candidates. Returning by way of Manchester, he did an ITV interview with Julian Haviland on Vietnam followed by evening meetings at Halton and Halton Moor.

After a few other assemblies near to home, he would be told by his agent, Pat Crotty, to expect a favourable swing of 6 per cent. The swing was 3.5 per cent. Perhaps symbolically where the young candidate, even the aspirant minister, eagerly recorded his own majority down to the spare numbers, the now slightly blasé Cabinet minister would write on the Friday morning simply: 'Majority 97.'

But apart from Bobby Moore's team winning the World Cup, something which brought Wilson on to the players' balcony like an additional self-associated manager, 31 March was all the glad, confident morning the government was going to get. Just as the election campaign was starting, on 9 March, there had been a bitter exchange between Wilson and the Governor of the Bank of England, Lord Cromer, a man rich in City of London unpleasantness and offensive to the detriment of the cause he argued, but not actually wrong, about his proposal of a 2 per cent increase in the bank rate. Wilson was furious and inclined to talk constitutional outrage; Callaghan, deeply worried about prospective trade figures which in 1966 did worry chancellors, argued – in Cabinet, with Cromer gone – for 1 per cent.

He didn't get it but the pressure for such a move, having gone, came back. The pleasant football result of June was followed by the unpleasant statistics of July – falling reserves, scary cat stock market, a run for gold and, on 12 July, a vertical pound hitting its lowest point since November 1964 when of course it had all been Reggie Maudling's fault. On 14 July, Callaghan got his interest rate increase – to 7 per cent. But the crisis demanded more, especially as on the same day, the trade deficit increased from 28 million to 57 million, something which, even allowing for the building-in of thirty-four years of inflation, would not cause distress today.

Also the government lost a by-election in Wales at a time when lost by-elections still counted. This seat, Carmarthen, was marginal, having only been won in 1957 by the personal appeal of Lady Megan Lloyd George whose death had now lost it. Yet Wilson seemed too preoccupied for making decisions. With his usual grasp of inessentials, the Prime Minister was due to make a formal visit to Moscow to cut a figure in meaningless world states-manship over Vietnam, about which he could do nothing. Arguably there was something to be said for insouciance, given the way the economic end of the world occurs at comfortable intervals in any government's life. But insou-ciance was the last thing for which George Brown, Roy Jenkins, Tony Crosland, Barbara Castle, George Wigg and Harold Wilson were equipped. Conspiracy and suspicion of conspiracy played in the heavens.

Were Jenkins and the Gaitskellites plotting to make an end of Wilson? Was Callaghan a party to any such activity and looking towards his own succes-sion? His biographer, Kenneth Morgan, believes that almost certainly he was not. Did Wilson *believe* that there was a conspiracy, with Callaghan the intended and intending beneficiary? Quite as certainly he did. In the late six-ties, conspiracy and paranoia were ships passing and re-passing in the night with all lights blazing. Certainty about dirty works at the crossroads comes from Ted Short, who holds Wilson in respect as 'always as straight as a dye with me' and thinks of Callaghan as 'the most devious politician of the lot'. He recollects an arm round his shoulder and the observation, 'We'll have to think about what to do if the roof falls in.'[1] Asked if Callaghan had been conspiring in 1966, he replied, 'Of course he was, he never did anything else!' And Roy Hattersley insists there *was* a meeting to discuss moves against Wilson, that Callaghan and Jenkins were present, and that it ended with Jenkins saying he saw 'little point in an undertaking whose outcome would be to make Callaghan Prime Minister'.

Healey at this time was the prisoner of events, a departmental minister watching the running, not to say institutional, griefs of the economy while having no influence over them. He had agreed at Chequers in November 1964 over the £400 million to be taken off defence spending by the end of the decade. That had been his brief, and with difficulties, he had effectively accomplished it.

In October 1965 he had talked to the Chiefs at that Defence Council about having to disabuse the political masters of the illusion that 'the neces-sary economies in Defence could be secured solely by cutting capabilities not commitments'.[2] But Healey's central argument about relating capabilities to commitments would increasingly seem mere departmental fastidiousness to a chancellor and prime minister who, having got the economy wrong, looked around for cuts, any cuts, to make up an inadequate deflationary package.

Wilson's obdurate refusal even to contemplate devaluation and the general consensus, in which Healey would have shared, against imposing the stark deflation which had to come whether it attended a devaluation or ruled alone, ensured a pattern of delayed pain. Failure to act produced in the first three Wilson years a succession of such packages, painful, imposing irrational strictures upon spending departments, but not deflationary enough.

And bad news always came as a surprise. Labour's election victory in March 1966 was followed not only by Callaghan's Budget of 4 May, 'brilliantly successful' according to Richard Crossman,[3] which contained the pointlessly punitive Selective Employment Tax, by that victory in the World Cup, by the seamen's strike, a major fall of the stock market and another fall (to the lowest point since November 1964) of sterling. What would follow last and least was the deflationary package to end all deflationary packages – before the one in November 1967, accompanying devaluation of sterling, and the one after that. In July 1966 Callaghan looked to defence expenditure as natural victim, proposing at a meeting of 'the paramount ministers' (Edmund Dell's phrase) an abandonment of commitments East of Suez.[4]

Healey was a participant in none of the events of July. Before the crisis broke, he had set out on a visit to the Far East by way of Aden. He was not missing anything very useful. The government was giving itself up – at the top anyway – to a prolonged fit of paranoia, alleged to be conspiring, accused of conspiring, conspiring. The Wilson government was literally at its unhappiest. It was Healey's good fortune to have been occupied at all relevant times on 16–17 July safely and respectably in Bahrain.

As for the previous weekend, 9–10 July, also pretty fraught in London, Healey had been visiting the Sultan of Brunei, that 'very dull and futile social conversation'. He even had witnesses: 'Talked to [General] Nigel Bagnall and Brigadier House about MoD reorganisation.' Also 'nice Shell man, Wheeler with awful wife, Mrs Wheeler' (what else would she have been called?).

Returning on Sunday the 17th, he would soon be briefed by the official briefer. George Wigg, 'at the PM's request', related the response to the deflationary package which Callaghan had announced to the Commons on Wednesday 14 July. 'Brown would not agree to decision without devaluation, Callaghan wanted devaluation later but not now.'[5] Which, historically, was what, in November 1967, Callaghan would get.

On the Tuesday, Healey recorded a four-and-a-half hour Cabinet on devaluation. 'Brown, Benn, Castle, Jenkins, Crosland for – most rather against now, but no real evidence on which to base a judgement.'[6] Healey himself, with sixteen others headed by Wilson, voted against. It was noticed that most people involved in foreign affairs, the Colonial Secretary and the Commonwealth Secretary, supported Wilson, something which may or may not tie in with George Brown's bitter complaint to Crossman that 'there was no chance whatsoever of Wilson agreeing because he was now bound personally and irrevocably to President Johnson and had ceased to be a free agent.'[7] Benn records Wilson at the end of the meeting saying 'he was glad the meeting had gone against devaluation as he would have had to consider his position if it had gone in favour.'[8] This devaluation was not a left/right division. Roy Jenkins was as ardently in favour of a floating pound as Barbara Castle, and had said to Dick Crossman, 'If we go on as we are, we remain prisoners of the situation and prisoners of our own weakness.'[9] Crosland had the longest record of devaluationist thinking, and George Brown came very close to resignation on its behalf.

Of the next day's four-hour Cabinet, Healey comments ambiguously, 'Got away too lightly with minimal cuts.' On that day he reported, 'George Brown tottering on edge of resignation' and on 21 July that 'George Brown decided to stay.'[10]

Healey might be faulted for a passive, incurious view of the economy, for being so heavily a departmental minister, forming no clear view on the central issue of all policy. But the devaluers were never going to get devaluation through argument. It would come through collapse of the castle. The substantial point was that Brown, a devaluer for some time, would not face the pain of heavy deflation while Callaghan, who had been applying deflation often, but not enough, would soon snap out of his brief flirtation with a lower pound.

He would obtain financial backing from the Bank of England, the US Federal Reserve and the Bundesbank. There would next be a reshuffle, with George Brown leaving the near defunct DEA in order to become, for a couple of years and many more threats of resignation, Foreign Secretary. The government had failed and been seen to fail. The people who, believing that a currency will go down, sell it, would not fail in that belief, and when the support packages were heavily drawn upon and the deflationary packages had made no impact, would sell again, betters on a certainty.

Parallel with anxieties in the Treasury, the party reared its high-minded head at Conference. In Brighton in early October, Frank Cousins, who had discharged himself from the Cabinet in the way of a recalcitrant patient, would in his sincere, heavy way, urge 'conference to realise that we are already spending more than we spend on education, roads and overseas aid put together, in our defence commitment . . . If you cannot afford a 10s increase in pay, you cannot afford to take £3 a week from the wage packet of each family and spend it on defence.' He was joined by the now thoroughly alienated Mayhew, who described Britain's military commitments as 'a sure road to bankruptcy' and accused the government of making Britain 'a junior dependent partner of the Americans in Asia'.

For all Mayhew's obsessive anti-Americanism, he and Cousins spoke for the respectable, economy-led mainstream of argument. But a whiff of the old Far Left instinct, the Spelthorne Manifesto, came in a resolution from Brighton Kemp Town moved by a Mr W. Adams. It 'called on Labour to re-examine our attitude to Europe with a view to withdrawing from NATO and to grant full recognition to the German Democratic Republic at the earliest possible moment'. If we wanted to achieve 'true greatness for our country', what was needed was 'a drastic and real cut in our arms expenditure'. The speaker was a rank-and-file banger-on, and Kemp Town constituency party had a name for excess, but the sentiments, a muttered obbligato here, would be played much louder in a few years' time.

Healey not being a member of the NEC at this time, the case against all this was put with impressive moderation and cogency (also to much applause) by George Brown. And despite so many grand naïveties, the hostility to defence expenditure shown by Conference (which passed the resolution by 500,000 dead soul votes) was not very far from the Treasury view.

Healey had spoken cryptically about the Ministry of Defence 'getting away too lightly with minimal cuts'. He would not speak so when coping with the demands which had appeared by the end of the year. Already, as one military study put it fairly enough, events had 'turned Healey's original Defence Review into a rolling programme of retrenchment'.[11] A memorandum of Healey's, dated 23 November 1966, states that 'the Chancellor of the Exchequer has indicated the need to consider further large reductions in the defence budget by 1970/71 . . . Savings of this magnitude', he wrote, 'following so closely on the Defence Review, would be difficult to achieve; and it is not clear if they could be reconciled to an effective defence and foreign policy.'[12]

Policy being policy, he would offer the options for which studies would be made. Although the paper breathes unhappiness, Healey offered five pillars, pillars now to be shortened:

(a) a cut of one third in Defence Review force levels in Europe;
(b) a cut of one half in Defence Review force levels in the Far East, including Hong Kong;
(c) a reduction in Defence Review force levels in the Persian Gulf;
(d) a reappraisal of the value of CENTO in the longer term and of our position in Cyprus;
(e) cuts in supporting forces and facilities in the United Kingdom.[13]

His accompanying introduction was horribly eloquent of the instability of Britain's function as ally or guarantor. 'A leak about these studies could be very damaging. In view of the sensitivity of our allies and the risk to Service morale, it is especially important that there be no external or internal refer-ences to any new target figures. In answers to questions we should take the line that the Defence review is a continuing process.'[14]

The makers of the study, which usually meant the devilling Vice-Chiefs, acknowledged that they would have to find cuts of between £200 million and £300 million by 1970/71, a figure best seen as 50–75 per cent over and above the cuts undertaken in the first Defence Review. They also knew that cuts in spending outside the UK were at a premium. We had to ask how many 'teeth units' of army and RAF might actually be needed in the UK after general British reductions worldwide. Healey's indication of CENTO, the creaking Off-Middle Eastern military commitment, as a possible target, would involve thinking about Libya and Cyprus. 'By 1973' the studiers expected 'our Libyan commitment to be at end'. This was sanguine. Sooner than anyone imagined Libya would cease to be part of anybody's financial obligation when, in 1969, the young Colonel Quadaffi, freelance enemy of Western interests, would seize power which, at the time of writing, the older Colonel Quadaffi still holds.

As for Cyprus, with its British military contribution, 1.3 army units and four RAF squadrons, we were advised to think seriously about 'the longer-term value of and prospects for CENTO and the case for the retention of the Sovereign Base Areas in the mid-1970s'.

In the Middle East, across Bahrain and Sharjah and the Gulf waters, Britain's 3 frigates, 6 minesweepers, 2.6 major army units, an RAF maritime reconnaissance squadron transport aircraft and 6300 personnel had serious political significance. When deciding to leave Aden, 'we laid great stress to our friends and allies, both in the area and further afield, on our intention to increase our forces in the Gulf and to stand by our remaining commitments there.'

In the Far East our ten major army units had been expended for the protection of Singapore and Malaysia, to keep Australia and New Zealand if not assured, then comforted, and to make the US Department of Defense imperfectly happy, all in the larger context of what China might do. We are speaking pre-Nixon when Korea was a green memory, the islets of Quemoy and Matsu had created an international crisis, the time of the Vietnam War. With the sort of biting irony which a very plain statement often innocently contains, the report says, 'We cannot assess the political and military consequences of cutting our forces in South East Asia by about half.' Nor could they 'make recommendations on the best means of presenting such a cut to our allies until we have seen what kind of forces emerge from the military studies to be undertaken on the basis of previous paragraphs'. Policy directed by financial stringency would seek the best ways of doing less and give new importance to the unNelsonian art of public relations.

The way out of those paragraphs involved conflating Britain's contribution to the Commonwealth Strategic Force with its contribution to SEATO. The CSF was the military group of Australians and New Zealanders who had been valuable during Confrontation. The shuffle involved was almost a polite way of getting the numbers counted twice, as we would be making 'no plans or specific provision for "teeth" arm reinforcement of SEATO'.[15] Then again, the locals should be asked to do more. That strange deformity, the teeth arm, might be strengthened as we considered 'to what extent Australia and New Zealand could be invited to increase their support for the Commonwealth Strategic Force'.[16]

There was of course the more drastic option of simply going home from Malaysia and Singapore. 'But the Australians would object violently and would command American sympathy and support, at least until there has been a Vietnam settlement.'[17] And if the Australians thought that helping us out with base facilities would move us more quickly out of Singapore, they would be unhelpful; 'they would be reluctant to provide, let alone contribute to the cost of, alternative facilities in Australia.'[18] Healey had been put in the melancholy position of a bodyguard asking for a fee curiously proximate to the cost of his ticket home.

The economic failures of the paramount British ministers would expose the Ministry of Defence to humiliating requests while beating a retreat. The best that could be done in the hole where Healey and the Chiefs of Staff found themselves was to study reductions, 'to work out new force levels for the Far East aimed at reducing Defence Review forces by about a half'.[19] They could take comfort from the fact that Confrontation with Indonesia had ended in 1966 and was unlikely to be resumed. For the next thirty-two years the fantasising General Sukarno would be replaced by the corrupt General Suharto. For any future adventure, the UK 'could expect considerable notice'.[20]

Accordingly, for the defence of Malaysia and Singapore, 'we should only keep in the area forces adequate to maintain a secure entry to both countries and ensure the local security of our forces and facilities, together with naval forces for maritime patrol activities.'[21] They should also look, said the studiers, for withdrawal of forces from the Sultanate of Brunei by 1970, keeping out of 'major operations without our allies', 'external defence of Eastern Malaysia or Brunei', and 'internal security other than defence of British installations'. 'No forces would be supplied specifically and solely for SEATO.'[22]

Six months later, on 4 April 1967, Healey was reporting conclusions: 'There was no hope that by making recommendations for cuts in our forces, but without major changes in our overseas policies, we could reduce planned defence expenditure in 1970/71 by £200–300 million in addition to the reduction achieved during the previous defence review of £400 million for that year.'[23] He confirmed that most economies would have to come in the Far East where it would be possible to reduce forces in Singapore/Malaysia 'by about half by 1970/71. If the Cabinet wanted more savings there would have to be more cuts.'[24]

Larger savings would be possible if the rundown could be made part of a firm plan to withdraw all our forces from Singapore/Malaysia no later than 1975–6 with, if necessary, a military presence in the Far East consisting of small naval and air forces based in Australia.[25] So drastic and decisive a withdrawal could give the Chancellor an edging-up of the planned Defence Review savings of £100–125 million to something between £150 and 200 million. And by 1975/6 some other Chancellor would see the total savings raised to £300 million. The Chancellor of that date, Denis Healey, would need every penny of it.

But the here-and-now politics of getting out would have to be accelerated. Healey told colleagues that he wanted a decision by July so that Services would be working from a firm plan. It would be necessary to speak to the US, Australia, New Zealand and Singapore. He was due to have a meeting with Robert McNamara later in the week, but 'he had agreed with the Foreign and Commonwealth Secretaries that this should not be the occasion on which to discuss with him even the general shape of our plans.'[26] It was agreed that the Cabinet, not wanting to commit itself straight away, would leave such early intimations until the SEATO council meeting on 18–20 April, and give itself time to make its mind up on the major withdrawal proposed. The usual recommendation of secrecy from Wilson was reinforced with the all too credible warning that otherwise 'we should face united opposition from them'.[27]

Discussion was continued a week later, on 4 April 1967, with George Brown as Foreign Secretary arguing that the proposals he and Healey had made should be 'presented to our allies as a major change of policy, not as a reduction of forces dictated by economic considerations alone'.[28] But almost everything the Wilson government did or stopped doing was dictated by economic considerations. Brown's argument, he claimed, derived from his fears that we should be under pressure to maintain commitments 'and we should then be unable to make the reductions in defence expenditure that were needed'.[29] One might have thought that being broke was a robust answer to any pressure. But for Brown the fact that the economies depended upon 'a decision to leave the mainland of Asia and on giving up the capability to intervene there with reinforcements'[30] was a reason for not admitting that such economies *were* so dictated. Stripped of the fuzzy code, he was saying that the economic defeat triggering withdrawal from a continent was a failure that dared not speak its name.

Callaghan took his turn to support Healey's and Brown's intentions by the brisk expedient of saying that they did not go deep enough. He wanted consideration of further defence cuts, 'including the possibility of disbanding forces withdrawn from Germany rather than earmarking them for assignment to the North Atlantic Treaty Organisation'.[31]

Not that Callaghan stopped there. It was important, he said, 'also to know whether the proposal to maintain a maritime and air presence in the Far East would prevent us from making substantial economies in the equipment

programme of the service, for example, in the purchase of the F111 aircraft . . .!'
From a military point of view, Callaghan wanted blood, arterial blood.

The Cabinet minute speaks without names of the discussion which followed, expressing fear of falling between stools. Speaking to old allies of a
general shift of focus to Europe, 'We might find that we did not enter the
EEC and that at the same time we had succeeded in estranging ourselves
from the United States and from the Commonwealth countries.'[32] But, on the
other hand, it records the argument – presumably from Callaghan or
Healey – that unless we started planning at once on the evacuation of
Singapore/Malaysia at least by 1975/6, the sort of savings which had been
mooted had no chance of being achieved.

Richard Crossman reported that six ministers wanted to keep a presence
in the Far East, saying that we 'shouldn't make any drastic cuts or try to get
off the mainland by 1975. Everybody else felt equally strongly that the cuts
were not radical enough.' Brown, in this report, complained – reasonably
enough – that he was being asked 'to negotiate with our allies . . . in terms of
a slow, orderly process of withdrawal when most of the Cabinet wanted a
drastic revision of policy next July'.

The business of actually telling Lee Kuan Yew would fall to Healey, who
describes doing so on the Singapore government yacht in April 1967 and of
Lee's concerned resignation, 'asking only that I should try to delay our departure until at least 1975'.[33] In May he was to be found in Cabinet arguing
both for a clear decision soon and putting Singapore's case. He quoted Lee's
letter to Wilson, fearing that 'by announcing an intention to leave Singapore
in the middle 1970s we should cause a complete loss of confidence in the
area'.[34]

Anxiety that a quick turning-off of jobs at the garrison would create what
the age euphemistically called 'industrial unrest' came naturally to a Labour
government. And Healey spoke in dark terms of the consequences. If we *were*
to announce on the planned date of July that we would be gone by the mid-
seventies, then 'the present administration in Singapore might collapse in the
next twelve months.'[35] He was not asking for hard numbers now of what
might be spent, but surely out of a budget (at 1964 prices) of £1800 million,
'a useful capability could be provided for this purpose'.[36]

Healey was mindful of the dimensions of the retreat he was being invited
to superintend. The reductions involved 'were the largest we had ever made
in so short a period except immediately after a World War'.[37] Getting the
reductions meant bigger shifts of commitment than had ever been contemplated, telling our allies that we would have withdrawn by 1975–6. And after
the resistance and hostility shown all round, we knew that 'we could not
hope to obtain the acquiescence of our allies in a withdrawal from mainland
Asia by that date unless we were now to give them a commitment that we
would maintain a military capability for use in the Far East thereafter.'

Without the consent of our allies, we would face two options: having to stay longer than planned and thus losing the economies or by pulling out precipitately, 'jeopardising local politics and business confidence, risk the overthrow of the existing regime in Singapore . . . We could thus be letting ourselves in for *increased* defence expenditure and taking risks with the lives of the forces and British residents.'

But if Healey was under pressure at the end of May, a month later he was trying to keep a niggle from the Chancellor translating into Treasury tanks on his lawn. 'The studies which had been carried out on the reduction of defence expenditure indicated that it might not be possible to achieve a greater saving than £200 million by 1970–71.' If therefore he, Callaghan, were to achieve his overall purpose of £500 million worth of cuts, 'it would be necessary to effect a reduction of £300 million in civil expenditure.'[38]

Callaghan was not the man to rant and, despite his dreams of leaving East of Suez, was appreciative of the MoD's problems. But this was a proper Labour government. Civil expenditure was houses and hospitals – good things. They directly affected 'our people'. The implication of Defence – air vice-marshals, military bureaucrats, foreign countries and the Americans – causing civil cuts to go deeper was simple abomination. Anthony Crosland expressed much of this by arguing that the demand for £500 million in cuts overall was excessive and unnecessary. A total of £350 million all told would do nicely and since cuts in defence were fine, £200 million could come through them.

Healey fought his corner. His comment: 'I spoke up and got off not too badly.' The defence budget was carrying expenditure not previously included in it. If these extraordinary items were stripped out, then he could demonstrate that 'the changes would provide for a saving in defence expenditure of £250 million.' Furthermore, simply by sticking to the plans established up to the year 1970/71 over six years, the government would have 'cut defence expenditure by 5 per cent whereas in the same period, government civil expenditure would increase by 25 per cent'.[39] There were studies which 'showed that our overseas commitments could not be reduced at a faster rate than was now planned and that we could not reduce our military capability except in step with the reduction of commitments'.[40]

He had spent time already with Wilson, explaining things to the visiting Lee. On the day before, a Monday, he speaks cryptically of 'Lee and PM – Lee very eloquent and able – PM left it all to me.'[41]

The business trundled on. Healey's diary across July 1967 as he prepared for publication of his own White Paper, is eloquent:

6 *July* Cabinet on DWP (Defence White Paper), went fairly easily – congratulations.
7 *July* Friday Talks with Tengku [(Tunku) Abdul Rahman, Malaysian Prime Minister] all morning.

10 July, Monday Another meeting with Tengku and Tan Siew Sin
   [Office?].
11 July Long Cabinet on oil etc . . . up all night in the House.
12 July, Wednesday Cabinet on civil cuts.
13 July, Thursday Cabinet on Transport axe.
14 July, Friday Very tired.
15 July Off to Leeds, worked on train. Surgery with AVF? shop stewards, Fabian Society Tea. (Unclear name) brought me back to
   Doncaster then train . . . arrived midnight, very tired.

On the 18th he would emerge to a chorus of press and TV attention with
his White Paper. This document[42] announced planned cuts in the defence
budget by 1970/71, reducing it to £2200 million, and by the mid-seventies to
£2100 million, with the armed forces reduced overall by some 75,000 men.
British forces would be withdrawn from Malaysia and Singapore by the
middle of the decade, with Britain concentrating her military commitment on
NATO. Healey, in the battering circumstances of financial crisis and panic,
had done as much as could wisely be done by way of cuts, more than he quite
wanted by way of retreat; and he had demonstrated in the struggle that mixture of cheerful grasp and masterful personality for which he would be both
admired and disliked. He was inclined to see himself as having done the job
and made the concession necessary for orderly and unhurried withdrawal. It
was a reasonable conclusion but not an accurate one.

If the government seemed anxious and wobbling in their divisions and
indecisions about defence and foreign policy, they are owed the recollection
that this debate took place not just during a period of acute economic
fragility, but at a time when Singapore, now one of the most formidable small
economies on earth, was an intensely vulnerable place, fearful of Peking's
attentions. It had been making major economic strides lately, but had been
subjected to riots fomented by local Communists. Malaysia had been the
scene in the early 1950s of a Chinese-inspired jungle war made by
Communists from among the Chinese minority.

But against the instincts of Labour's chattering classes, Healey and Wilson
had rightly continued discreet and effective military support for regimes
which had a good claim to be supported. They had been applying a decent
political responsibility and the essential lines having been drawn, the precipitate flight from commitment soon to follow would not produce disaster. But
if financial crisis had come in 1964 and the economisers had had their way
at once, Sukarno's opportunistic aggression could well have been validated,
the Singapore riots and strikes successful.

A great deal of what would follow from the retreat now, with
Confrontation won and the British economy shell-shocked, would be
desirable. The seeing-off of Sukarno's forces in a low-level operation of great

skill was over and done. America had attempted to create a South East Asian Treaty organisation modelled on NATO, but in its preachy cynicism, had embraced immeasurably corrupt despots whose only virtue was a fly and clamorous anti-Communism. It was reminiscent of the US in South America and something best kept clear of. Beyond all that, as Healey gloomily understood, there was to be a general retreat, a hauling down of the flag in the Far East. But it was all being done too soon and for the wrong reasons. An orderly diminuendo in the British military role had to be expected. But this was a crisis measure rolled into an emergency package by a prime minister and finance minister unwilling to devalue against the next run on the pound.

The retreat would be a march to a band accelerating from *largo* to *allegro* as the money ran out. And Healey would be passing on, insistently, the advice of his military advisers that this change of tempo should not be disclosed until ways of explaining it to allies could be very carefully considered. What had been set in motion would not happen all at once. In November 1966, the march was no quicker than *andante*. But harder things were being thought in response to the medium-sized crisis embodied in the July Measures of that year.

However, back in that autumn of 1966 with Brown, an enthusiast for Europe, at the Foreign Office, and Wilson looking for something to fill up space, Britain would announce her intention of seeking to join the EEC. Healey would be against it, if not as much as the President of the Board of Trade, Douglas Jay. 'Jay in,' reads a laconic diary entry, 'still obsessed.'[43] So, more to the point, would be General de Gaulle. But the Wilson government were as serious about the undertaking as they were about anything, and the existence of this unsuccessful project did much of Healey's and the FO's work in telling the Australians and Lee Kuan Yew that, for quite respectable reasons, we would soon be occupied elsewhere.

The fifteen months after the July Measures constituted a period of lull, the Wilson government's success-substitute. The wage freeze which Callaghan had imposed appeared to be working well. Unemployment stood at 2 per cent, the 450–500,000 mark. Across this period, Callaghan would relax things, cutting bank rate by 1 per cent, increasing various government grants and proclaiming a special premium for employment in the declining towns called development areas. He also got rid of a crisis measure from November 1964, the temporary import surcharge. The temporary quality had simply kept importers holding back until it should be withdrawn and had thus given Callaghan a surplus on the balance of trade as wholly misleading as it was gratefully believed.

Callaghan 'became, at least in his own mind, the skipper who had weathered the storm'. This illusion provoked a famous observation. 'We are back on course. The ship is picking up speed. The economy is moving. Every seaman knows the command at such a moment. "Steady as she goes".'[44]

By late autumn, the command would be 'Women and children first'. They would be helped into the boat by the decision of the DEA, under Michael

Stewart, to end the statutory restrictions on prices and incomes – not in the first place a good idea, but better than precipitate cancellation, accompanied as it was by a further half per cent cut in interest rates. Soon afterwards Wilson, in a reshuffle, 'took over economic affairs', assuming the chairmanship of E Committee and what was left of the DEA's economic brief. So empowered, he proceeded, against the wishes of Bank and Treasury, to ease hire purchase conditions.

Not that, even during this light-hearted interlude, Conference ever stopped going on about defence spending. Brighton 1966 was followed by Scarborough 1967 where the platform managed to beat off a call from the Draughtsmen's Union to 'drastically reduce its military commitments and in the interest of restoring our economy to severely slash our military expenditure overseas'. 'If we initially reduce defence spending,' said the mover, Ron Huzzard, 'to the Western European average of 4 per cent, Jim Callaghan would have £700 million a year more in the kitty to pay for, yes, capital investment in the electricity industry, expanding housing, education and so on.' When the time did come, very soon, to 'slash our military expenditure', it wouldn't be quite like that.

But as long as the lull held up, prevailing opinion in the Cabinet, with Healey absolutely no exception, was that the deflationary pudding was flat and unappetising and that considered measures of reflation were needed. An economy, at best convalescent and still vulnerable to speculative sales, was told in the evangelical style never far from Harold Wilson, to take up its bed and walk. Considered steps would be taken in the wrong direction.

What followed, by way of a European Commission Report in October suggesting the need for devaluation before entry into the EEC, the seven-week-long seamen's strike of September/October 1966, a too small increase in bank rate (19 October) and at Party Conference an upbeat speech by Callaghan applauded by both *Guardian* and *Daily Telegraph*, and described in the *Sunday Times* as showing 'near-greatness' in the Chancellor,[45] would be an annual deficit on the balance of payments of £417 million. But long before that computation could be made, another figure – a trade deficit of £107 million – would resolve things. The Treasury, little disposed to command ministers, made the impossibility of the present course clear. Alec Cairncross of its economic section, hardly the sort of civil servant keen to boss ministers, would tell Callaghan on the afternoon of 25 October, 1967 that devaluation was now the only option available. Devaluation had been resisted so long and often that the actual decision seemed the more stunning. Roy Jenkins for one was angrily convinced that the column would be dodged and told Healey as much over a lunch for both families after, aptly, the Armistice Day wreath-laying. 'Roy wants to force issue on devaluation. Fears new sell-out to the Americans instead. Rather emotional.'

And, indeed, on that Sunday there would be a brief scramble after more foreign loans. But when Wilson and Callaghan had attended the Lord Mayor's Banquet, 'We met at 11.15 [p.m.] on 13 November after Guildhall and *decided finally*.'[46] In the early morning of 16 October 1964 they had also met and decided that in no circumstances would they ever devalue. It was rather a tragic story than otherwise, for all the temptation to mock.

On a historic analysis of economic argument, Healey could not complain too bitterly. The central economic policy had had his general endorsement. Such reflections did not stop him from also being rather emotional when, on the evening of Tuesday 14 November, Callaghan announced devaluation to an advance meeting of key ministers in advance of telling the Cabinet. This group involved Brown, Healey, Crosland and Shore, together with Prime Minister and Chancellor. As William Armstrong, who had been present, told Alec Cairncross, Healey was the one who exploded, asking Callaghan 'why anyone should trust him or believe his forecasts after all he has dragged the party through'.[47]

Healey, in his clipped way, acknowledges the event: 'Was insubordinately rude to Jim who provoked me on F111A.' But mindful of American pressure, which feared for the dollar being hurt in the rush, he adds at once, 'Still risk of being bought off by very big loan.'[48] George Brown, he notes as 'oddly subdued'. And since Healey's own rage did not subside – he was described as 'fearfully angry' – it was this pleasingly irenic George who next morning undertook, successfully, to calm him down over breakfast, ahead of the yet further secret and restricted meeting which agreed the actual level of devaluation – 14.3 per cent – 'the maximum not to provoke reciprocation'.[49]

It was not until Thursday 16 November that, with a little twirl of personal feeling, the Chancellor told Cabinet: 'I have decided that the pound must be devalued. If Cabinet agrees, the necessary machinery will be set in motion and devaluation will be announced on Saturday. This is the unhappiest day in my life.'[50]

When Callaghan came to the package of expenditure cuts to be made, in addition to hiking interest rates to a crisis level of 8 per cent, he did so at great and flustering speed, leaving colleagues desperately trying to keep their own scribbled record of how he hoped to save £500 million. He gave no hint of anger, singling Healey out for thanks and explaining that he had been speaking to the Defence Secretary since August about 'the possibility of further cuts in defence expenditure. The Defence Secretary had now indicated that he could secure reductions of £110 million in the planned expenditure for 1968–69. A reduction of this order would bring the total expenditure on defence in that year below this year's expenditure in money terms; and this would be the first time we should have achieved a year-to-year reduction of this kind.'

It was an achievement, but cutting so much had been the last grief. It was now going to start all over again, for from the £500 million of cuts Callaghan was asking for, Defence would have to find the cream. In fact, there were to be additional cuts, also hitting Defence, which the Chancellor had yet to announce. Healey, talking to his Chiefs next day, would, perhaps fortunately, be dealing only with the earlier part. 'Grim meeting with Chiefs and had to tell them about £500 million. Not too bad. Home, felt very ill.' Intense tiredness and physical illness recur heavily at this time in his personal record – 'dog-tired', 'very tired', 'felt very ill'. They will appear again in this narrative. Healey under pressure worked as intensely as he worked long, felt the pangs of exhaustion, but seems to have had the art of re-creation through sound sleep.

Tiredness didn't diminish his partisan feelings during the media show which followed. 'Heath like aggressive skinny crow on TV.' He was also hearing odd rumours. George Brown told him that Callaghan 'would leave Treasury for back benches within a week and campaign from backstage as Treasurer of the Party!'[51] This was an elective post and one with ironical implications for someone having trouble with the national finances.

The comments of Healey, preoccupied with an unwelcome task, are calm and dispassionate. The contrast with more fraught ministers is blazing. Barbara Castle's account of the left-wing reaction to Callaghan's speech to the Commons on 22 November catches everything. It was, she acknowledged, 'astonishing to see Jim completely command the House . . . He clearly had the Tories almost eating out of his hand and our people gave him a great ovation too. But the more sophisticated of us could see his ploy standing out as obvious as the Albert Memorial. Tommy [Balogh] caught up with me after the Vote and hissed at me, "Did you ever see the knife put more deliberately into a leader's back?" and he almost spat out the word "Casca".'* Jennie Lee said indignantly to me, 'That was a coalition speech.'[52]

Crossman, calm enough himself about the speech, records another reaction. 'Knowing how Harold would be feeling, I slipped along to his room and found him there with Gerald [Kaufman] and Marcia [Williams] and then, along with Tommy who came along a little later, for a very long time we discussed the meaning of Jim's speech. They all thought Jim was intriguing with the Tories and the City . . . I've never been in one of these discussions with Harold and his kitchen Cabinet and I felt that his suspicions of conspiracy were unduly strengthened by it.'[53] Denis Healey's diary entry says: 'Harold flopped on devaluation – brilliant debating but worthless. Callaghan more impressive by contrast.' And of the previous night's presentations to the Parliamentary Party, he says simply, 'Meeting went easily . . . Jim better than Harold.'

The distinction is central to any understanding of the man in the murderous, if toothless, context of the Labour Party at that time. Healey didn't plot;

---

* The first assassin to strike at Julius Caesar: 'Speak, hands, for me!', Shakespeare's *Julius Caesar*.

he didn't see plots. He admits to a pang of regret when the Treasury chalice, poisoned or otherwise, passed to Jenkins. But his contemporary comment is Roman. Between a note about a military Air evaluation being complete and a junior colleague, Alan Lee Williams, coming in for 'a chat about Vietnam', he neutrally observes, 'Roy and Jim swop jobs – some relief.'[54]

But the stoic qualities would be needed. The exchange with Callaghan was less important for the anger and the reproaches than the occasion. Healey and Callaghan, both notably sane and rational, would work together with the utmost trust down a darker defile than this one. 'He provoked me over F111A'. That aircraft, upon which Healey's judgement and that of such people as Sam Elworthy, now Chief of the Defence Staff, had been carefully focused, was a natural target to an economiser in a hurry. It had been painfully authorised through a questioning Cabinet. It was soon to be contested again. At the same time, while £100 million did not, at a blow, end the limited role East of Suez which Healey and the Chiefs wanted to retain, it would soon combine with events to do pretty much that.

In his latest (July) White Paper, Healey had written with characteristic blitheness: 'We have been working continuously for almost three years on a major review of defence, revising Britain's overseas policy, formulating the role of military power to supplement it, and planning the forces to carry out this role. This statement marks the end of the process.' It didn't.

39

FI11 AGAIN:
'APPALLING DAY AT NUMBER 10'

The new Chancellor would stand in an odd relationship to Healey. The sympathies of Balliol for Balliol and Oxford First for Oxford First had kept them on civil and social terms. But they were very different types. Jenkins had a social radar on which the friendship of hostesses and patrician figures like Lady Violet Bonham Carter, Asquith's Edith Evans-like and rather stupendous daughter, regularly figured. His speech had lost any tincture of Wales, where Healey's was a random mixture of Oxford and the West Riding. One might be tempted to oppose Jacob with Esau, but this would be profoundly unfair to Jenkins who would show, more than once, a disposition to make a stand and trouble at the same time. Like Healey, Jenkins had great talents beyond politics and where Denis did photography and soaked himself in the poetry and art later celebrated in *My Secret Planet*, Roy Jenkins had, since 1954, been writing history of a deft and lapidary sort: *Mr Balfour's Poodle* (1954) and *Asquith* (1964). With *Gladstone* (1997) and *Churchill* (2001), he still is.

None of this mattered intrinsically. What did count was that Jenkins, as he has candidly said, was a much more refined politician, cheerfully ready to cabal. And most important of all, in the years since 1963, he had become securely the heir at law of Hugh Gaitskell. Healey, as we have seen, was never more than a country or associate member of Gaitskellism. He contracted, he was called in, he was rightly trusted. But he belonged to no congregation. As for the posthumous club, Healey is not a joiner and, with the second most onerous job after the Treasury, he had had no time to spend on moves for which anyway he had no taste. Jenkins had been devotedly close, shattered by Gaitskell's death, and had first given thought to leaving politics altogether to take up the editorship of the *Economist*. And commanding the

Gaitskellites was a commitment not unlike a spiritual leadership. David Marquand, Bill Rodgers, Robert Maclennan, David Owen and John Mackintosh, for example, were ardent people, through whom a charge of sympathy and identity ran at a fair voltage. Though generally much nicer, they had their affinities with 'Tommy', 'Marcia' and 'Gerald' talking over with Barbara Castle what Jim had meant by his speech.

The Gaitskellites would become, in a precious journalistic phrase, F.O.R.J, the Friends of Roy Jenkins. More remotely, they would become the Social Democratic Party. Such solidarity would work to Jenkins's advantage and it would work against it. Equally uncertain in its consequences would be a liberal press opinion whose effusive support for Jenkins worked against him in the party to which he belonged.

Denis Healey was as ambitious as the next man, had a high opinion of his abilities and could convey an overpowering masterfulness. But he was unconspiratorial, uncliquey, a bustling minister, almost too happy in the work of his office and its outside duties, not good at looking for political moves and openings ahead. Not for nothing was he generally most admired – very like Rab Butler – by civil servants and by the senior military men who worked with him. For all his GBH partisanship, he was not the party politician in the Department.

Then again, though capable of making a superb speech, as over Suez, and always a forceful, effective speaker, he did not linger over the art's refinement. He would keep his genius out of debate until the epilogue to his political career. Then, the derider of tiny Chinese minds would suddenly blaze forth from hopeless Opposition as a nationally admired personality. The step from the arid to the luscious aspect of politics came very late.

Healey and Jenkins also differed in their relationships to what Gaitskell, at the emotional climax of his anti-CND speech, had called 'the party we love'. It is no discredit to Jenkins that by degrees – degrees of its folly, squabbling and self-destruction – he came *not* to love the Labour Party. It was a rational and honest conclusion. But through every kind of thick and all forms of thin, Healey continued to be fond of and loyal to the Labour Party. I once said to him in his garden near Alfriston, 'You know what you are. You're a good party man.' He paused for a moment, then acknowledged the fact. 'Yes,' he said with some pride. 'I *am* a good party man.'[1]

The differences were going to matter on and off over the next fifteen or so years. Wilson had passed over Anthony Crosland – as the Gaitskellites, though they would not admit it, had also passed him over. Very clever, intellectually daring, proud, sulky, volatile, too conscious of his own election, Crosland had the best economist's qualifications for the Treasury, as Jenkins readily acknowledges, but Wilson, for a variety of Wilsonian reasons, would not have him. Any follower of the political turf would have known after November 1967 that, leaving Callaghan out of the calculations, the race between younger men was between Healey and Jenkins.* It was not to be a stupid relationship of knifings and counter-knifings. Despite the civilities, rivalry now overhung disputes of however rational a sort.

As Chancellor inheriting a devaluation, Jenkins, though, according to one critic, he dawdled in getting down to digging,[2] once he grasped what he should do, also knew that it should have maximum impact. Devaluation, like patriotism, was not enough. Jenkins would understand the need for accompanying it with deflation and with a determined show of hard-knuckle economy for the benefit of the markets – cutting things. He had in mind four targets: a delay in the raising of the school-leaving age, that cherished, emblematic Labour thing, reimposition of prescription charges, cancellation of the F111 and withdrawal from East of Suez. The last two both assuaged the anger of the left at the first two and were also mutually dependent. The case for the F111 would be mightily diminished by surrender of commitments in the Far East.

Jenkins himself was an opponent in Cabinet of both undertakings. And they fitted in with another distinction between the two men. Healey was close to America, American politicians and academics. It was of course, a particular kind of America that he admired – East Coast, liberal and very much associated with the Democrats. The sort of feelings which produced a terrifying photograph of Mrs Thatcher, eyes raised to the United States flag beside Ronald Reagan – an ensemble resembling one of those Soviet pictures faked in the 1930s of Lenin in perfect harmony with his great disciple – were not his.

But essentially, Healey did look to America and, for all the Byzantine friezes and Renaissance *pietàs* he had ever hurried to inspect, he had and has no natural sympathy with the European political itinerary. Jenkins was affable towards things American, but not close, while his commitment to Europe as institution and sympathetic place, went down the line and still does. The idea of missing an opportunity to underpeg the pound by continuing to buy American aircraft with which to sustain the likes of Lee Kuan Yew and please the US Department of Defense quietly appalled him.

Jenkins knew that Healey was a mighty obstacle and speaks of the need for good relations. He also set up for 14 December a lunch to break the ground with his intentions and try to sell them. A 'softening-up lunch', he calls it, at Brown's Hotel in Dover Street. 'I disclosed my broad thoughts, which he took in without fainting or blustering and we arranged to have a return luncheon the following Tuesday.'[3]

Healey had superficially many strengths and allies for resistance to the designs of Jenkins, notably Brown and the FO, and George Thomson at the

---

* Though Callaghan was born only five years before Healey and eight before Jenkins, he was actually older than Wilson – and fell irresistibly into the senior group.

Commonwealth Office. But he also had the disadvantage of recently having engaged in a major conflict with Wilson. The Prime Minister had earlier supported the Foreign Office and Ministry of Defence over their readiness to sell arms to South Africa. In their view, the sophisticated Simonstown base and refitting centre was useful and the very large sales welcome to any economy on a saline drip. In response to the furious protests of the left wing Wilson did a policy flit, but found himself taken on and beaten in Cabinet, principally, by the efforts of Denis Healey.

Wilson would respond by setting his Chief Whip, John Silkin, to organise a backbench revolt against the Cabinet decision. Brian Walden recalled being approached for his support. The Chief Whip, though he seeks to assure the government of its parliamentary majority, is not supposed to be the creature of the Prime Minister against his ministerial colleagues and Walden thought that Silkin's reputation had been destroyed.[4] Wilson violently reacted to this resistance. Healey's indignant, open anger had done him more harm than any amount of conspiratorial whispering.

Richard Crossman found the PM on 15 December 'full of the wickedness of Denis Healey and how he must get rid of him. I said that it was time for him to consider Healey's successor and that I was the only person who could really do the job of cutting our military commitments.'[5]* Wilson had behaved unconstitutionally and in ways to destroy confidence in his fitness to be Prime Minister, but he was Prime Minister yet and was minded straightforwardly for revenge.

At the Cabinet of 15 December, he intended, writes Crossman, 'to split his opponents and if possible to isolate Healey and Brown, whom he was quite determined to be rid of'.[6] Instead the three chief opponents, Brown, Crosland as Trade Minister and Healey, stuck furiously and effectively together. 'George Brown thundered against character assassination . . .'[7] 'George threatened to read PM's letter in July. I *did* read PM's approval letter at DOPC.'[8] The terrible thing for Wilson was that, although by way of a favourable (deferring) compromise engineered by Callaghan, he would eventually get most of his way; he had not merely been devious, he had been seen being devious. 'He had reckoned,' wrote Crossman, 'that they would be devastated by the exposure to which they had been submitted in the press and by the clear evidence that the party was fully organised against them. But not at all. They came back at him one after the other . . . They hit back extremely effectively and in concert.'

---

* Crossman, combining charity with his customary brass neck, recommended that Healey should not be got rid of, only treated 'like Callaghan and moved to another job where he'll be safe'. The safeness of Callaghan in another job would be fully demonstrated when, in 1969, he annihilated Wilson and Castle's trade union legislative proposals.

Having been damned in the daily press by Wilson's people, the triumvirate had had their people, notably Brown's press man, Bill Grieg, damn him back in the Sundays. On the Sunday, Crossman talked to Wilson again and was 'struck by his bitterness against Denis for his ruthlessness, for his behaviour as a stooge of McNamara'. Even Crossman was moved by Wilson's behaviour to remark to his diary, 'Why did he sit there with his coterie? He certainly didn't make things easy for himself.'[9]

One of the things which Healey records from his first lunch with Roy Jenkins, which took place in the middle of this running fight, was the Chancellor's remark that 'You are now Harold's P[ublic] E[nemy] No. 1'[10] and he adds, 'We agreed not to let him split us.' His overall and laconic comment was, 'Quite useful, but Roy still more a politician than a chancellor.'[11] However, Wilson's rage at the furious resistance to his own cheating, perfectly fashioned him to be Jenkins's ally, discreetly this time, against Healey. He could not of course 'get rid of him'. Even before the row, he had been regularly offering alternative jobs to his Defence Secretary – perhaps in response to Crossman; most recently, it had been the Commonwealth Office held by Denis's close friend and ally, George Thomson – and they had all been casually declined.

Wilson did not begin to have the nerve for sacking a heavyweight. But he could spite one. And on that Sunday night he had also said to Crossman 'that he was now certain that he would get the big defence cuts he'd always wanted'.[12] He had wanted nothing of the sort but, like most of Wilson's remarks, he believed it at the time. Meanwhile Roy Jenkins wanted to ease pressure on sterling with convincing cuts, those at Defence high among them. He was politician enough to make himself the sort of Chancellor he wanted to be. Circumstances made Jenkins, for the interim, Healey's opponent. Wilson was already his enemy. Objectively, as Marxists used to say, they were united.

Sterling remained weak. The tantrum over South Africa was briefly interrupted by the more important news that the deficit on the balance of trade had risen to £158 million. This made Jenkins's point and the Chancellor circulated a paper – 'sloppy paper from Jenkins'[13] noted Healey cheerfully – stressing the 'menacing' nature of the situation. As Jenkins equally cheerfully says, both phrase and paper were 'motivated by the desire to create a suitable mood of malleable apprehension'.[14] Healey noted, 'Roy's minatory demand for cuts.'[15] Malleability being the natural condition of Cabinet in a panic, it worked in general terms, sloppy or minatory.

The trouble came with the particular, and none were more stubbornly particular than F111 and East of Suez. The passionate resistance of Defence, Foreign Office and Commonwealth Relations was guaranteed. George Brown set up a meeting on his own turf, his room at the House of Commons. Healey and Thomson were present with their officials: Healey had brought his Chiefs of Staff. Jenkins, who felt himself arraigned before a Grand Assize of Empire, recalls that his most reasonable opponent – as he sees it – was

George Brown. Healey, he describes as 'mainly engaged in speaking, or shouting, for the benefit of his Chiefs of Staff'.[16]

Jenkins might feel that this inquisition had knocked him 'around like a squash ball',[17] but the South African rumpus had given Wilson good reason for supporting any enemy of Healey or indeed of Brown and Thomson. Jenkins himself had not been an opponent of the arms sellers during the Cabinet argument. It didn't matter. The core offenders in that dispute had caught a swiveller out in mid-swivel and were damned for it.

On the afternoon of the Cabinet fight, Wilson called in Jenkins for an hour-and-a-half's private conference, offering him an acceleration of withdrawal from East of Suez to 1970–71 which would make the argument in favour of cancelling the fifty FIIIs correspondingly stronger. Wilson also gave Jenkins general backing on the issues which did not concern his enemies – delay in raising the school-leaving age and higher prescription charges – only holding back for the moment over the housing cuts, expenditure which he had earlier described in full Wilsonic flight as 'not a promise but a pledge'.[18] Which pledge would, in a few weeks' time, become another and perfectly manageable swivel.

Jenkins recalls a course over eight Cabinet meetings of the Prime Minister's steady support. 'I did not admire the way in which he got the package through ... His own patience being apparently limitless, he allowed the Cabinet to bore itself into exhaustion. But his quiet, almost resigned loyalty was impeccable when it came to votes and in other ways.'[19] Jenkins was also aware that he was being caught up on the side opposite to a group of men he generally liked and normally agreed with. His economic purposes and his own European-preoccupied coolness towards the ex-imperial military theatre and its US connection had made this inevitable. He was being signed up with the votes of the Cabinet left and the Wilson payroll 'in order to defeat a substantial part of the old Labour right'.[20] He found himself telling Crossman, surely tongue-in-cheek, that he ought to be Foreign Secretary. The shift involved an unquantifiable weakening of solidarity on the right wing of the party which would show horridly when things began to crumble in the early seventies.

An earlier conversation passed on to Healey by Ned Dunnett about William Armstrong, just out of the Treasury, reveals something striking. He writes on 5 January, quoting Dunnett, 'Willie Armstrong delighted to be leaving Treasury because no one ever took his good advice. PM had refused a package of measures to go with devaluation.'[21]* What cuts the supposed package contained, and how far they exceeded the limited steps taken at that time by Callaghan, is not clear. But money had continued to pour out for days

---

* Edmund Dell, quotes Jenkins, complained about not being at once urged by civil servants to make cuts or told of Callaghan's thoughts in that direction.[22]

after devaluation. So if Armstrong was rightly understood, major economies which Wilson would not give the Treasury as policy in the immediate aftermath of devaluation, he would give to Jenkins in an hour-and-a-half's confabulation a month later – *after* the quarrel on South African arms.[22]

Did Wilson's fear of doing the politically unpopular thing at the worst moment of crisis and a yearning for personal revenge combine and cause him, by mid-December to wave through measures he had rejected at the high point of the crisis? Jenkins could take the responsibility; Healey, Brown and Thomson would get the knocks. If so, the conclusions about Harold Wilson are dismaying. The stewing hatreds of those long hours with his kitchen Cabinet spill into the making of economic and foreign policy.

The battles themselves were recorded by Healey in detail larger than his cryptic norm. Before the end of the year there were relays of meetings with Brown, Thomson, the Chiefs, Dunnett and everyone else concerned. This included Wilson, of course, whom he reminded on 20 December of the need to warn the Australians about the cuts which they would hate. As for the Chiefs, they on the same day gave Healey 'a very rough meeting . . . all ready to resign'.[23] Healey had one idea clear in his mind: that win or lose, he would not pretend to powers if they were taken away from him. Britain could now function in the Gulf and the Far East only if she had the F111s. If she should not have them, all pretence of 'maintaining a presence', fulfilling a role, had to be set aside. Wilson had regularly fantasised about a moral imperial role, the latest episode being the serious thought of a naval drive on Cairo during the Israeli–Egyptian War. If the Prime Minister was now, for whatever reason, bent upon economy with the means, Healey would state the limit of the ends. Even so, he would first of all fight.

His description of the grand inquisition of Roy Jenkins on the same day is of a 'very rough meeting', lots of those at this time, though Healey's recollection of Brown as the Chancellor's chief antagonist – 'George, a bit drunk at first, gave Roy a very rough ride'[24] – contradicts Jenkins's. He then continued a day which would end by way of dinner at Lord Rothermere's and votes at 11 p.m., with a meeting to rally sympathetic backbench MPs.

Christmas that year took place over a weekend, but on the Sunday, Christmas Eve, the main social event was 'Drinks with George and Grace Thomson', reciprocated on Christmas Day when Frank Cooper, a key Ministry aide,* also phoned. There would, on the 27th, be a special pre-Cabinet meeting at Downing Street of what Jenkins calls 'a curious *ad hoc* inner Cabinet of eleven which the Prime Minister thought would form a phalanx to ease the passage of the economy measures through the whole Cabinet.'[25] In fact, the Treasury case had a much better time in Cabinet

---

* Later, as Sir Frank, Permanent Under-Secretary at Defence.

proper when the left-wing residualists on Wilson's payroll were whistled up. At this meeting Healey simply noted, 'Jenkins very equivocal on FIIIs.'[26]

He heard next day, the 28th, that Paul Nitze, US Under-Secretary for Defense, had made an offer of a further $100 million for 'teeth' specifically to underpin the FIIIs. Profit was the last thing the Americans were trying to make out of the deal. He also talked to Stephen Hastings, managing director of Handley Page, who would write a strong letter supporting the offer to the unsympathetic *Times*. For, as Healey remarked, 'Handley Page's survival depends on it!'[27] Not surprisingly during a period of intensive work and struggle, by the end of Friday the 28th Healey was physically ill, susceptible to a bug, which had also waylaid Edna. But on New Year's Day, he was back with his Chiefs persuading them to present arguments on cutting forces. They were awarded marks in the customary way: 'Varyl good, Cassels dumb, Grandy couldn't see how to oppose.'[28]

In addition to all his troubles, Healey had been having a hard time with this man, Air Marshal Sir John Grandy, over the French-deserted Anglo-French variable geometry or swing-wing aircraft which the CAS favoured soldiering on with alone. The comment is 'Got them to admit no future for VG (Variable Geometry)!'[29] He was caught at this time in a Wildean paradox, between soldiers who could see only the value of Defence and Cabinet colleagues obsessed with its price.

On 3 January 1967 he would be told – at the Ritz – by the journalist Peter Jenkins 'that Harold hated me and would not give me FO'. Assessing the story's provenance, he comments scientifically, 'a leak, not a plant, probably Chalfont'.[30] He tried to bargain for support from Tony Benn at Technology who might need it himself over Concorde, but found him undecided. Benn observed a Denis 'surrounded by some of his senior people who were in a very angry mood and his language was full of f— this and f— that. He said that the defence cuts were mad, that they were just being done to make it possible to introduce prescription charges.' But Benn thought that Healey's direct offer of swapping support for Concorde for his backing of the FIII 'very crude politicking'.[31]

These and meetings with Thomson, Brown and Dunnett preceded the first Cabinet encounter of 4 January – 'Appalling day at No. 10.'[32] The first dispute, much of it carried by Brown and Thomson, concerned the date of withdrawal from Singapore, which would now be a matter of 1971 or 1972. 'Fierce argument . . . went badly for the Georges – 6–13 on 72 v 71, but 4 of 13 seemed prepared to switch if necessary.'[33] They didn't and George Thomson would tell him that night that he was ready to resign if he 'could not get 72. I said end of 71.'[34] He then talked late with George Brown, 'amazingly sober but really set on resignation at the right time',[35] before going off to what must have been a melancholy party at the Ministry to bring his military colleagues up to date. The Chiefs at this time have a startling resemblance to Tom

Stoppard's Rosencrantz and Guildernstern – men of intermittent relevance hanging around in well appointed places waiting to be told the worst.

The argument on key detail continued next day, 5 January. The security of Polaris lurked as Jenkins played with the possibility of getting rid of it. This, Healey knew, was a ploy. 'But in end, obvious even PM doesn't want to cancel Polaris – nor Roy if he could get F111As. A good steam and blood-letting.'[36] Jenkins knew that as well and, when it had been successfully bartered a week later, commented, 'I always had that up my sleeve.'[37] The Defence Secretary was able to argue through the blood and steam that $80 million would have to be paid to the Americans for nothing more than the after-scent of a cancelled plane, that in the first year no savings would be made and that no compromise such as part-purchase of the agreed number existed – it was all or nothing.

Tony Benn, who throughout this conflict is a fair and measured commentator, would record his vote for the cuts. But Benn also described Healey's opening speech as 'the most formidable case in favour of the F111, calmly and quietly and with considerable power of argument'.[38] He logged Healey's central argument at this stage: that Britain's contribution to NATO by way of air force and ground troops was well below those of France and West Germany, that our best input would be the strike reconnaissance ability of the F111s, the only planes which could penetrate Eastern Europe.

George Brown, in another Cabinet Table note,[39] stated his own melancholy view of what was happening: 'No real foreign policy. No real close alliances. No effective and credible defence structure. – What we are being driven to is Crossman's favourite Little England posture. But God knows what's come over Jenkins.'[39] The voting ended in a tie and Wilson was forced into a declaration – for cancelling. A request for time and a reconsideration would have been hard to resist, so debate would be resumed on the 15th.

If 'very rough' is something of a motif at this point, a private note dated 5 December, from the Permanent Under-Secretary, suggests that roughness wasn't helping Healey's case. Ned Dunnett refers to 'a v. private message from Burke Trend. He said that you were having a difficult time but that you had a lot of solid support. He felt however that some of his support might weaken if you gave the impression that you were trying to bully-rag Roy Jenkins.'[40]

Trend was the Cabinet Secretary and a sensible moderate official. But a man in a corner fighting a duplicitous leader in a financial crisis is very likely to grow intimidating. It is a measure of what 'very rough'[41] meant in the Wilson Cabinet that Healey describes that afternoon's five-hour process by which the civilian cuts, including the school-leaving age and prescription charges were accepted, as 'went more easily'. Though alluding to the excellent and put-upon Health Minister, he adds with fellow feeling, 'but murder for Kenneth Robinson'.[42] A sense of the murder in the whole debate comes from another note pushed across the Cabinet table by Brown as Crossman pronounced in a cynical, non-committal way on the school-leaving age about which Brown cared fervently. 'I am fed up with this Jesuitical bastard. By Christ, if I have to go, I'll roast him unashamedly.'[43]

The idea of cancelling Concorde, not the Chancellor's proposal, was rejected, but Crossman's comment catches the cavalier despair of the situation. 'If we virtually abolish military aircraft, we still have to believe in civil aircraft, particularly if we're concerned about jobs in the aircraft industry.'[44]

Understandably Healey, who had been registering 'Very tired' a lot at this time, saw his children to a party on the Friday, then after doing a long interview with the *Sunday Times*, went off with Edna to the cottage they had recently bought in Withyham, Sussex, and watched Bob Hope's *Road to Hong Kong* on television.

His conversations in the pause before battle at the start of the next week involved the French Defence Minister, Pierre Messmer, the Ambassador, De Courcel, and the head of the Foreign Office, Sir Paul Gore-Booth; and, in a cryptic diary entry, he 'saw Jim Callaghan about the general interests – obviously wants to be PM.'[45] He also had a meeting with Roy Jenkins specifically to sustain 'friendly personal relations'.[46]

There would be a round of lobbying next day. Healey gained one supporter, Frank Longford, during this lull. But on Wednesday 10 January he would make a whole new approach to Tony Benn. On the Tuesday Dunnett, with or without his minister's authorisation, had carried his concern about 'bully-ragging' to the extent of apologising to a not-at-all shocked Benn for Healey's earlier F-speckled assault, while Healey's own approach to the Minister of Technology was 'totally different from the last meeting'.[47] He was now trying for less, a reduction in numbers of Fɪɪɪs rather than complete cancellation, which he perhaps ought to have looked for in the first place, and he had the figures for a different mix of cuts. He also saw Ray Gunter, 'very sound' – Gunter quite loathed Wilson – 'thinks TUC would want me as PM'[48] and again, 'Callaghan, as always, a little slippery.'[49] And next day, the 11th, he would work his way with varying responses through Michael Stewart, Fred Peart and Richard Marsh – 'OK but cynical and pessimistic.'[50]

On Friday 12 January the whole episode came to climax. Healey had arranged for the Chiefs of Staff to see the Prime Minister. George Brown arrived late – with good reason. He had been caught in an argument – 'a bloody unpleasant talk'[51] – by the US Secretary of State, to whom he had reported the Cabinet's then position: the decision to scrap the Fɪɪɪ and leave Singapore by 1970–71. In spite of the present debating respite, he had described them as unalterable decisions, presumably, given Brown's own furious convictions in the other direction, in the hope of extracting maximum reportable American outrage. Which he had got: 'Be British, George, be British – how can you betray us?'[52] he quoted Dean Rusk as imploring him. But the key point Brown stressed was not the Far East but the Persian Gulf, about which the Americans were 'desperately concerned'.[53]

His fear was that we had come to the end of an era in our relations with America and that the government was about to do irreparable damage. 'George,' he quoted an American official, 'as I understand it, you won't be in Asia; you won't be in the Middle East; and you won't be in Europe. What I want to know is where will you be? And what equipment will you have, to do what you say you have to do?'[54] Wilson's response was classic worst Wilson, a cocktail of spite and fantasy, saying that 'there were a lot of counter measures we could take against the Americans and that if they were difficult with us we would be able to withdraw our portfolio of investments.'[55]

Healey supported Brown's argument that we couldn't help the Americans in the Gulf at tolerable expense without being in Singapore and without the FI11; he therefore asked for an extra year and a reversal of the decision on the FI11. Jenkins, though he would later concede that withdrawal should take place nine months later, the end of 1971, which Healey had originally thought of as a compromise, successfully withstood the plea, arguing, sincerely enough, that there had to be a major shift in British foreign policy from the one obtaining since 1964 – actually since deep into the time of Macmillan and Sandys. It wasn't, for Jenkins, an argument about savings so much as about major strategic commitments. He and Brown recognised the same question and gave opposite answers.

When the debate shifted from East of Suez to the FI11, Healey spoke at great length – forty minutes, says Benn. Crossman's account is as reliable as that of any devoted enemy and consisted of ardent admiration for Jenkins and delight at Healey's failure. 'He plays the role of the young McNamara ... The supercilious sneering expert is always in danger in a British Cabinet.'[56] But importantly, Crossman has Jenkins saying, 'Yes I'm prepared to agree that Polaris at £20 million a year maintenance is worth keeping as long as we scrap the FI11.'[57]

This evidently drew from Longford clumsy and naïve thanks for Elworthy's briefing and a declaration of support for the FI11, but also the voting reversals of Cledwyn Hughes and Patrick Gordon Walker. Crossman is in raptures, but with every respect to Roy Jenkins, threatening the end of the fully installed British deterrent, independent or otherwise, in order to unthreaten it in return for scrapping a not yet delivered plane, sounds like a sensible but rather obvious strategy. In fact, for all Healey's and the Georges' exertions backstage and in Cabinet, the game was up. Crossman cackles of 'a vote of no confidence in the four pygmies on the other side of the table – Michael Stewart, George Brown, James Callaghan and Denis Healey – who had been running our foreign policy for four years'.[58]

Healey simply wrote that he was 'very depressed indeed'.[59] But Tony Benn, who had been watching his response to defeat, had nothing but admiration. 'Denis behaved with enormous courage and dignity in the face of a shattering blow quite as great for him as Devaluation was for Jim

Callaghan.'[60] Benn would evaluate other performances that day: 'George Brown was emotional, sensational, but immensely powerful in personality, Crosland rather niggling; Jim Callaghan trying to be weighty but without substance; Harold never quite equal to the occasion.'[61]

It is difficult, following Benn's account, to avoid the conclusion that the politician in Healey, not for the first time, showed itself badly underdeveloped. He understood the issues, his strategic thinking was large-minded, he made an impressive case, but lost through a want of the low arts of charm and alliance-forming. At the very start, over South African arms, he had fought a personally bitter campaign, however understandably, against Wilson at his most paranoid and vengeful. He conducted the main debate on an all-or-nothing basis when a smaller group of F111s for Europe would have been still serviceable and hard to resist. He threw weight about when he should have been stroking hair.

In his own memoir, Healey speaks of the CDS, Sam Elworthy, accusing him of giving way over the F111 in order to become Foreign Secretary,[62] just the sort of thing that a minister recently defeated on a central issue, and 'tired and very depressed', can do with. Behind the suspicion probably lies the meddling of Richard Crossman who would telephone Jenkins on the 14th, a Sunday, 'and talked to him again'* about the idea of Denis going to the Foreign Office. '"We have got to keep him in the government," I said to Roy. "We can't have both Denis and George retiring in a mass." Taking something of a risk, I went on, "Roy, you and I must give the impression to Denis that if he stays in the government we can get him into the Foreign Office when George goes."' There is more in the same self-regarding vein and he ends by congratulating himself that if both Wilson and Jenkins were willing 'even to consider having Denis at the Foreign Office, then their enthusiasm for trying to get into Europe must have cooled off'. And 'If so, that's good news indeed.'[63]

The notion of Healey becoming Foreign Secretary at that moment was on a par with Jenkins cooling on Europe. Healey himself was more concerned with calming down Air Marshal Elworthy: 'Very difficult.'[64] The CDS agreed next day not to go, 'though privately thinks I should'.[65] His own view of resignation was summed up in a private interview, all aides banished, requested by Peter Hill-Norton, Vice-Chief of Naval Staff. 'You've got to go. You haven't got a leg to stand on. You've been beaten. I saw it happen – If you were a man of honour, you'd resign,' said the admiral in his encouraging way. 'No I haven't got to,' replied the minister. 'I can do this job better than any other member of my party. Who would take my place if I resigned?'[66]

Hill-Norton, with his usual spiky generosity, quotes his words together with the view that Healey was absolutely right. Healey recalled a conversation

---

* Neither Crossman nor Jenkins tells us about the first time!

he had had with Antony Head, the Brigadier Head who had been Minister of Defence under Eden. Rather than push through Harold Macmillan's precipitate reorganisation plans and end conscription, Head had resigned. 'To his horror he saw that the Prime Minister's next visitor was Duncan Sandys; he realised that he had made a horrible mistake . . . You should never resign without knowing the name of your successor. I feared my successor might be Dick Crossman. So I stayed put.'[67] In fairness, Healey had less choice than he might have wished. He was a man more useful in government than dangerous out: he was a political celebrity. His resignation would have worried cognoscenti. But he had no faction, as Jenkins had, with which to menace a government. Again, his standing lay in an area without charm for the sort of MPs who rebel. Staying on and being useful made most sense.

Even to make way for a giant, Healey would not resign, nor would he ever let himself be shuffled around a succession of jobs in the futile solitaire player's way which Wilson visited upon so many of his colleagues. One minister who did go a year and more after having been thus messed about and punitively shifted from the Ministry of Labour to the ironically named Ministry of Power, was Ray Gunter. Tony Crosland would confide to Roy Jenkins, 'Ray did what we all wanted to do. He told me that he just couldn't stand that little man any longer.'[68] For Healey, business was a matter of trying, largely without much effect, to mitigate the new policy at a tidy-up Cabinet on the Monday, raising the idea of thirty-five instead of fifty F111s and getting nowhere but actually securing the nine months delay on withdrawal from Singapore, helped by a message from Sir Leslie O'Brien, the Governor of the Bank of England, later disputed, that sterling might actually be damaged by the implied panic of a too precipitate withdrawal. He records that the Chiefs were relieved that he had not gone and he had taken the view that he had better things to do than resign.

January 15 involved an all-day Cabinet, which had to take two telegrams from President Johnson speaking in Wagnerian terms about his personal dismay and 'a catastrophic decision'. They also heard of the fury of Lee Kuan Yew who had descended upon Chequers over the weekend threatening to withdraw Singapore's sterling balances.

There would also be parliament. Enoch Powell would make a shrill and embarrassing attack upon Healey, towards whom he had an animus only exceeded by his view of Ted Heath. Healey's own speech to the Commons on 20 March was a combination of rather grave historical reckoning up and vigorous defence by way of attack. The withdrawals to be made, he said, 'have brought fully home to the House that this is the end of two centuries of British history, an era which covers some of the brightest pages and some of the darkest, in the story of our people. It is the end of East of Suez in the sense in which the phrase has been used in public debate over the last few years.'[69]

And looking back at some of the wars which had been fought – Kenya, the

Gulf, Malaya, Borneo, East Africa and Southern Arabia – much of that had been 'an inevitable part of the process of disengaging from our old imperial role and in too much of it we were fighting against local nationalism'.[70] But where that had not been the case, those encounters had 'made a contribution to peace and stability of which we should always be proud. I am thinking now of the Gulf in 1961, of East Africa in 1964 and of the Far East during the three years of the confrontation, from 1963 to 1966 . . . This was the sense in which I and the Cabinet as a whole were East of Suez men. We believed that . . . Britain could make a military contribution of unique value towards peace and stability in the third world. I believe that still, as a general proposition.'[71]

The conflicts quoted had of course been bi-partisan efforts, the sort of thing the left wing had bayed against. But Conservative opinion was not mindful of the continuous seam. Hugh Fraser rumbled about . . . 'He is quite capable of telling even further untruths to add to those which he has told over the past few years.'[72] Even the serenely laid-back Reggie Maudling managed to make the foreign policy landscape look as if it had been sketched by William Blake. 'Then what will happen to Malaysia, Singapore and Hong Kong? Then what will happen even to India if the barrier against Communist expansionist forces – at present the American shield – is withdrawn?'[73]

This was a stronger statement than Healey would make privately of what might be feared, going well beyond his fine-tuning arguments for a rather longer stay and its necessary equipment. It is a small irony after such griev-ings that Iain Macleod, a pre-eminent figure in the Conservative Party when interviewed in 1969, would describe withdrawal from East of Suez as 'of no account'.[74]

When Healey, in his speech of 25 January, mocked the institutionalised uncertainty in Tory defence policy, something poised between muddle and cynicism, he was doing more than make a spirited defence. He was arguing, despite appearances, that he had achieved a greater degree of cohesion. 'I am the longest serving Defence Minister since 1950, and it has not been an alto-gether pleasant task.'[75] When the Tories in Macmillan's time had reneged on a policy – stopped this missile, instated that one, before cancelling *that*, all they had needed to do was to change the Minister of Defence – nine in thir-teen years. Peter Thorneycroft, a notable victim of the system, had said as much in a highly sympathetic speech in the Lords. Healey argued that 'the cancellation of Skybolt was not Thorneycroft's fault any more than the col-lapse of the AFVG [Anglo-French variable geometry plane] was mine.'[76]*

In his three years, said Healey, he had had 'to plan five separate reductions in defence expenditure, imposed partly by errors of economic judgement for which, I fully agree, I bear my due share of responsibility.'[77] But he would

---

* See account p. 470 et seq.

make two claims. 'I have made certain that as capability is cut, commitments are reduced accordingly.'[78] The Conservatives at that time were making promises to keep forces in Singapore without the planes or carriers to support them. Secondly, in his long term he had brought through a clutch of planes like the Harrier, which would actually happen. He had done the job continuously, taking blame and credit alike – he 'had never been one for abstaining'.[79] So, amid Opposition cries of 'Resign', he declined to do so.

In strategic terms something very important had happened: Britain had shipped anchor from long commitments with old obligations lying behind them. A good *political* case could be made for halting commitment, that we had done what could be done in a part of the world now unbossable for good or ill. The West would come to think back on Vietnam as a folly garlanded with the dead.

What was happening was a matter of timing. A great deal was being done in a flapping rush and in contradiction of undertakings clearly given. We did not look to be in charge of our geopolitical dispositions because we were *not* in charge of them. Withdrawal might fit Britain's strapped and writhing finances. But in the light of Singapore's fragility, the state of the Chinese government under Mao at his most paroxysmal and with the United States very powerful and very isolated, leaving so abruptly was the taking of a risk in the name of narrow and heavily stressed self-interest. The slower timetable and medium-term military commitment favoured by Healey and his Cabinet allies was a responsible and considered policy. As it was, things would work out all right on the night, but the gamble was a very large one reasonably resisted.

OTHER DEFENCE FRUSTRATIONS

Reforming the Ministry of Defence, assuaging the Chiefs and keeping them under knuckle, reducing expenditure, trying to stop expenditure being reduced too far, procuring the right ships and planes, finding the ships and planes places to move from and back to . . . the work of Healey across his six years in the job involved fighting on endless separate fronts.

One of these was unification, the idea going back to Macmillan and the Jacob/Ismay report. The idea was that the armed forces, as capable either of obstructing or making backs for each other, needed to be brought to heel, a single heel. Healey had responded at first with a Healeyism. He was engaged in the official policy of the government, trying to get defence spending down from 7 per cent of GDP to 5 per cent. 'You do not,' he said famously, 'conduct an appendix operation on a man while he is moving a grand piano on the stairs.' In fact he would always be cool about full-blown schemes of imperious centralisation. His bossy ways did not imply insensitivity to the grain of the services. Anyway the achieved objective, best seen in Canada, of a single air, land and sea force in a common dingy uniform, had little charm for him, and in dealing with the Chiefs, his ways would be Fabian.

The reforms of the mere Ministry had already been started and could be advanced. The rolling demotion of single-service ministries would be continued. What had once been Cabinet posts would go down and down. Non-single-service responsibilities – international policy, R and D, logistics, procurement, could be scattered among the ministers of state, while the single-service duties would be shifted to parliamentary under-secretaries, the scullions of office. Certain of those responsibilities would later become the main designations of new Ministries of State. His Minister of State for the Army, Fred Mulley, also functioned as Deputy Secretary with a general overview.

Healey, an admirer of the Pentagon group of critical analysts, the 'whiz kids in the Pentagon – Charlie Hitch, Alain Enthoven, Harry Rowen and co'[1] – was interested in common intellectual resources and consultation groups. The first White Paper created DOAE* (the Defence Operational Analysis Establishment) at West Byfleet, which, combining scientists and officers, was to keep the Ministry fully briefed technically. Healey therefore created a whole series of short-term committees to give him the information. 'The outcome,' says Sir Ewen Broadbent who served high in the Department, 'was a series of decisions on the three fronts of commitments, capabilities and individual items of equipment.'[2] These committees would concern the most important criteria of policy: avoidance of major operations outside Europe without allies, the addition of a nuclear strike aircraft to forces in Germany, withdrawal from Aden in 1968, and both the rejection of a new aircraft carrier and purchase of the American F111s.

Though service interests might clash within them, they served a common political military purpose. And when a conclusion was reached inimical to a particular service, a committee had either to make the best of things or to resign on principle. Healey also succeeded in establishing an all-service provision for security and intelligence. Public relations, the coming voodoo of the age, was also to function across the services.

So deep, however, were the rivalries of the Forces and perhaps even more so of the proud, fretful men who were the Chiefs of Staff – sometimes bright, always peculiar, these stars – that larger measures of unification were left to the conclusions of a report. The Healey diaries bristle with cryptic, busy references to 'Geraghty'. This was William Geraghty, a deputy under-secretary whose committee would examine 'the structure at all levels, both in the Ministry and Commands'.[3] Geraghty reported within a year, asking for 'a continuous defence review; to analyse systems and options; to exercise effective control over research, development and production; and to have maximum effectiveness in production.'[4] Geraghty recommended integration of forces over supply. In place of soldiers, sailors and airmen, Geraghty inclined towards having only 'personnel'.

The Department of Science too was still divided by three and wastefully done. Different costings by different parts of the Ministry obstructed progress. Even within the civil service organisation the committee saw too many overlaps and anomalies, contradicting the purpose of another new creation, the Defence Secretariat, which was supposed to be thinking on an all-defence basis.

Geraghty's literal-minded vigour could not be taken at a draught. The first

---

* That is, created it as a real force. Lord Cameron speaks of it in his memoir as 'souped up'.

concern was not to talk about it. A single clause in the 1967 White Paper took care of the parts adapted. Geraghty came at too hectic and crisis-riven a time for proper recognition. And, reporting in mid-1966, it accompanied the first griefs of economic crisis, which ran intermittently through to the great ministerial defeat of January 1968. Also it had too little to offer in the way of financial savings to justify the large element of civilian enhancement, which annoyed the Chiefs.

Ministers and civil service advisers did not need to clutch Geraghty as a manual. They had been living with the same debate and would make their own selective choices from a report whose strength lay in the sharp and prescient bits rather than the vision splendid.

But in the quiet way necessary, the report was profoundly influential. In 1967 came the establishment of two Ministers of State, one for administration, the other for equipment/procurement. Mayhew had probably made his contribution to this development. To put it in good Machiavellian terms, nobody looking after the navy would hereafter be in a job worth resigning from. And, in a cautious way, like amendment was made to the Staff, while the civil service pyramid began to flex a little with a general bringing together of civilian staff doing similar work for all the three service interests. Late in Healey's day, a committee under the Permanent Under-Secretary himself, the happy machinator, Sir James Dunnett, created more power of initiative for the CDS without his service colleagues and a strengthening of his Chief Adviser, Personnel and Logistics.

Healey had effectively decided what form integration should take. The Conservatives who had started the process would, under the astute Lord Carrington, do little or nothing to reverse it, despite backbench harrumphing. But centralising reform would always be an effort, an undertaking betwixt Hercules and Sisyphus. The coolest comment came from Fred Mulley when Defence Secretary: 'What Centre?'[5]

The effort involved is nowhere better illustrated than over PEG, the Performance Evaluation Group. Sir Michael Howard, in his excellent pamphlet,[6] praised Healey for the ability to go beyond the Chiefs, reach in and get the services of an officer at the rank of Major-General or Naval Captain to act for him. No one readily argues with Sir Michael, but that was perhaps more what Healey *wanted* to do, and it was made very hard for him and the officers concerned. PEG was tied in with American management techniques, a way of making the services look at their own virility symbols – the tank, the carrier and most immediately, the long-range strike aircraft.[7]

It was to have been the sharpest of all the question-asking, conclusion-reaching tools of intelligent government. PEG was central knowledge and thus central power. It was also set to work at the time of cuts and defeats when, as Jackson and Bramall put it, 'Each Chief had had his own cavalry.'[8] Grandy, the CAS, would lose the F111, Baker, the Army Chief, was losing six infantry battalions and half the Gurkhas, while Admiral Le Fanu inhabited a naval world prospectively without carriers and shrunk to the North Atlantic. Bubbling resentment was assured.

Of the upper-middle-rank officers chosen by Healey, one, Brigadier Younger, would be characterised by an observer as 'an awfully nice chap, but not all that terribly bright'. The naval man, Commodore, later Rear Admiral Colin Dunlop was a naval man first, honourable, impressed by Healey, but thoroughly loyal to his service with which he maintained full liaison. The exception was Neil Cameron, lean, earnest, Christian, Scottish, risen from the ranks by sheer ability and as naturally drawn to Healey as Healey to him. And Cameron narrowly escaped the hands of colleagues determined to shunt him into oblivion as HM Services' equivalent of a scab.

Constitutionally, the officers working in PEG had to report to the Chiefs, and the Chiefs stood ready to rubbish anything they said. But since its whole point lay in briefing the Secretary of State, the Chiefs, jealously negative, cut off PEG's access to information. Any report made without the full evidence would be weak and vulnerable, what the Chiefs intended. The whole business recalled the internal police inquiry known as 'Countryman'. Both were met with dragging feet, canteen curses and minimal co-operation.

However, in dealing with the RAF something could be done. Cameron was a whole-hearted believer in the mission and the ablest of the triumvirate. *His* Chief, Elworthy, was the best of the brass, and on good terms with Cameron. So 'on the whole I persuaded them that it would be to the benefit of the Service if I was fully briefed.'[9]

As Cameron tells it, such co-operation led to the one truly important piece of work – on the F111! PEG did not fault the aircraft dear to the Air Staff and accepted generally by the Chiefs. It looked rather at strategic needs. The retreat from major commitments East of Suez was already under way – Aden and South Arabia to be left in 1968, Singapore and Malaysia at this time scheduled for leaving in the early 1970s. Even before the great economic upheaval which culminated in January 1968, Healey's own halfway house of limited commitment implied fewer requirements than when the F111 had first delighted Elworthy's team. 'We concluded, however, having in mind the considerable equipment programme already in hand for the RAF, that there was no requirement.'[10] Deadly words!

For Cameron to lay such bullet-biting conclusions before the Chiefs, with his own man, Elworthy, sick in love with the aircraft, was an act of suicidal heroism. The Chiefs were massively affronted, their function usurped, their trophies recommended for confiscation. So angry were they that Healey did not keep up the provocation. Interestingly, though, while he would fight savagely to keep F111 against Jenkins's assault in 1968 through two long, bitter Cabinets, and would let PEG go, he prized and protected its main activist. He would appoint Cameron as Assistant Chief of the Defence Staff

(Policy) to head the Defence Policy Staff which he created as a less contentious thinking committee. And when, in the seventies, Cameron's career was being discreetly smothered with sideways appointments, Healey reached in and saw him back on to the path which would end with his ironic appointment as first CAS, then Chief of the Defence Staff.

PEG was, in short, something very contemporary: consultancy, but consultancy from within, the delivery of a dispassionate judgement *de bas en haute*. It was the sort of thing the chaps won't stand for and they didn't.

When Healey forsook carriers, the essential substitute lay in air bases. He would get no joy from the Australians, keen to be defended, not at all keen to provide territory from which the British would defend something else for the Americans. The Australians had sent forces to Vietnam and regretted it. The solution had to be islands. Gan, the British already had, but they coveted Aldabra. It lay off Mozambique, then controlled by undemocratic but helpful Portugal and accessibly near to similarly constituted South Africa. It stood at the western end of the Indian Ocean; build an airstrip on Aldabra and you had a great deal of air mobility.

Healey, the Chiefs and the Americans reckoned without Tam Dalyell (pronounced Dee'ell), 11th baronet and 31st Laird, descendant of a seventeenth-century Royalist, Black Tam Dalyell of The Binns, a man immoderately picturesque who spent much of the 1650s in Russia in the service of Tsar Alexei Mihailovich. It was of Black Tam that the Covenanters, whom he had knocked about, circulated memorable lines.

> The De'il and Dalyell begin with ane letter
> The Dei'l's nae guid, and Dalyell's nae better.

Healey felt the same way. The present Tam would later make endless difficulties with the West Lothian Question, and the *General Belgrano*, an elderly Argentinian battleship 'shot while trying to escape'. And over Aldabra, Tam was only just starting.

His *modus operandi* was – is – variations on an original theme, the inquiry, sometimes written, more often oral, nagging a minister to death with perfectly phrased, ever and again asked, theme and variations on an unanswerable question, all put with antique courtesy and limitless inveteracy. He had conservationist sympathies and caught the eye of Ashley Miles, former fellow of King's Cambridge, then holding the Chair of Pathology at London University, who provided him with detailed expertise on the fauna of Aldabra.

Early questions about threatened wildlife had been met by Healey and his juniors with the blank face of the departmental bat. They had a military contingency to look after and the welfare of recondite subspecies was not high on their priority list. Miles had confirmed that the MP was on the right track, that the ecology of the Indian Ocean *was* threatened. The pink-footed booby may be a humble species, but it made a wonderful headline. Liable to extinction, together with the flightless rail, and above all, the giant tortoise, it excited sympathy and left hanging above the Department an intolerable combination of reproach and derision. The notion of brutish aircraft, and their parasonic screams, harassing these sweet creatures to extinction in the service of the RAF and American Air Force was dreadful PR for the Ministry.

Dalyell lobbied at home, winning the sympathy of the Minister of Works, Bob Mellish: 'This geezer has a point.'* And he pressed on in the Commons where soon, of course, everyone else wanted to join in. To take a single day in July, Sir Tufton Beamish, the scholarly Conservative MP for Lewes, asked Healey 'what representations he has received regarding the ecological importance of Aldabra island';[11] Jeremy Thorpe asked him 'What use he will make of the island of Aldabra?'[12] and the difficult Tory, Nicholas Ridley, inquired, 'What is the estimated cost of building defence facilities on the island of Aldabra and for what will it be used?'[13] When Healey acknowledged having been lobbied by the President of the Royal Society leading a delegation 'representing a number of learned bodies, stressing the importance they attach to the full preservation of the existing ecology of the island'.[14] Sir Tufton murmured his ignorance as to why the government 'wished to develop a chain of island bases in the Indian Ocean'.[15] As such military purpose was not avowed, Healey took refuge in the magic marquee of diplomatic jargon. These would not be bases, but they might 'increase the flexibility of the deployment of our air forces by creating staging facilities in various parts of that ocean'.[16] At which, the Labour Member for Oxford, Evan Luard, asked for debating time.

The whole operation brilliantly illustrated what members of the legislature can do to disoblige the Executive. 'Denis,' says Dalyell, 'was fucking furious!' But he lobbied as vigorously in the United States, gaining the crucial ear of Bill Carey, head of the Science and Space Program in the Bureau of the Budget which, in US terms, is most of the power that matters to politicians, the spending of public money. Carey could wave him through for an attentive hearing to everyone short of the President: the Vice-President, for example, Hubert Humphrey, Don Hornig, the President's scientific adviser, Glen Seaborg of the Atomic Energy Commission, Ed Wonk, Secretary of the Marine Sciences Council, Congressman Wilbur Mills, chairman of Ways and Means, the ancient and godlike Senator Maclellan of Arkansas, chairman of the Appropriations Committee.

---

* All quotations from Tam Dalyell here come from a conversation with the author.

They all sent copies of the Parliamentary Questions to the Secretary of Defense, Robert McNamara. 'Tell us more,' said McNamara, he claims. Before he was through, Dalyell reckons that he had official America talking to Harold Wilson and asking anxiously, 'What *is* all this?' It was of course particularly maddening to Denis Healey. He was the man wired up in Washington and on terms of personal friendship with Bob McNamara. He was trying to do something, as asked, in the interests of Anglo-American military co-operation and here was a young backbencher blowing all his wires. 'Fucking furious' just about says it.

In a sense, this was a game whose point would disappear anyway, at least at the British end. Without the F111, which Jenkins would kill in January 1968, the giant tortoises of Aldabra would still have been threatened by US Air Force long-distance transport aircraft. But by late 1967 Aldabra, as the headlines put it, was saved and the Secretary of State for Defence had to draw on his limited resources of stoicism. 'It was sad really,' says Dalyell. 'My wife, Kathleen, and Edna Healey had been great friends and that rather cooled for a long time. Perhaps *I* should have been Denis's PPS. It might have helped both of us!'

Another grief for Healey was in the Anglo-French variable geometry aircraft. This was one of Hill-Norton's 'five planes which the Royal Air Force did not get'. Getting on decent terms with the French in the early days of the Labour government was important in itself. Healey personally had been distrusted a little because of his sympathy with post-war Germany. He was doubted more extensively because of his obvious closeness to the United States. De Gaulle, who would rule in France until 1969, detested the American link and would, after all, take France out of NATO in 1966. Healey accordingly was an Anglo-Saxon bearing gifts. Healey's biographers quote sources saying that, '"Healey had displaced McNamara as the villain of the piece in Charles de Gaulle's demonology" because of his determined bid to keep France in NATO "virtually on American terms."'[17]

And Healey had once told a tea meeting of *Socialist Commentary* that *Mongénéral* was 'a bad ally in NATO, and a bad partner in the Common Market'[18], the sort of true statement for which one has to publicly apologise. He had nevertheless pushed hard for co-operation in France and in particular technical co-operation. He had plenty of friends among the French military, among whom Healey's technocratic qualities were appreciated. He was a natural for the Écoles Normales which do for France what Oxbridge does for Britain without the social overtones. 'Had he been French, he would still have ended up as Minister of Defence – he's born to it,' said a French minister.[19] So, in 1965, he had explored collaboration. There were ideas already undertaken: the Jaguar fighter/trainer, the Martel airborne missile. Healey's particular project was the swing-wing or variable geometry aircraft, then the acme of new and 'exciting' technology. The project was everywhere proclaimed, budgeted for, and was part of the argument for the discontinuing of the TSR2. But this was to reckon without the French protectionist instinct and simple costs. It was widely known, before it would be admitted, that France was pulling out of the deal.

Again Dalyell was informed – known troublemakers receive information – and MPs' questions were parried by Healey and Wilson while last-minute attempts were made through the French Defence Minister, Pierre Messmer, to save the undertaking. Maurice Edelman was, as a Coventry MP, very much agitated about 'the very serious reports from France that the AFVG project may be cancelled and the catastrophic effect that would have on the employment situation in the aircraft industry'.[20] Wilson had in the customary form 'nothing to add' to what had been said in previous Defence Reviews. But he dropped a hint. 'This is of course a joint venture between ourselves and France and it requires two parties to continue with it.'[21]

Finally, on 5 July 1967, Healey made a statement. 'The French government have informed Her Majesty's Government that they have decided that for budgetary reasons, they must withdraw from the Anglo-French variable geometry aircraft project.'[22] There would be Tory haymaking. Patrick Wall asked if 'the whole of our Defence Review has been shown to be completely "phoney"?'[23] John Farr asked if there could be 'a 100 per cent British alternative flying by the late '70s to try to revive the position?'[24] and Frederic Bennett shouted out, 'The TSR2?'[25]

There existed a quasi-Arthurian myth among the dimmer military Tories. Sir Stephen Hastings had written a book called *The Murder of the TSR2*. Freddie Bennett in the Commons thought it would rise again. 'With respect,' said Healey, 'if we had gone along with the TSR2 programme as the former Conservative Government had conceived it, not only would we have been bankrupt on defence, but we should have had no money in the kitty whatever to support any research and development project in the next six years for our own industry.'[26]

Healey fought the Tories, not the French by whom he had indeed been warned nine months before. And during that time 'I worked very hard . . . to see whether we could see a way round that difficulty.' He had been reassured by the French in January that the problem had been overcome; now they had had second thoughts. And he took the opportunity of a sideswipe at the enemies of defence ministers everywhere, usually in Ministries of Finance, by exonerating Messmer. 'I could not wish to collaborate with a more valuable partner on a project of this nature.'[27]

In terms of hard policy, worse things could have happened. Healey would find alternative partners in Italy and Germany. Helmut Schmidt as Minister of Defence proved a key ally, with whom he launched the Multi-Role Combat Aircraft project, the fruit of which was the Tornado. As Healey claimed, it would be 'the backbone of the West European air forces for many years'.[28] And better French business turned up. The excellent Jaguar carried on as a project and was successfully produced, as were a group of helicopters, the Puma, taken by the RAF, and the Gazelle by the British Army; all good, working, efficient craft, though as Field-Marshal Carver remarks, not so joint in purchase. The Lynx helicopter, developed under that project from a British design, was not taken by the French when produced.[29]

And variable geometry itself was a sixties fashion in aircraft design which did not permanently take. It would be replaced by the delta-wing concept which has had a much longer life. Healey's refusal to share the tragic conclusions of the Tories or their Jacobite memorialising of the TSR2, would triumph over the VG débâcle. But the sheer ability to be knocked down and get up again was mainline Healey, to be seen again at the Treasury.

STUMBLING OUT OF THE SIXTIES

The period which followed devaluation, then the first Jenkins Budget and its cuts, was bleak for Labour far beyond the Ministry of Defence where the F111 was mourned. There was a grave economic situation underlying everything, the party had lost public support, and by-elections rubbed the fact in, while Cabinet members varied in their hatreds of other Cabinet members. The sort of anger which Brown, Thomson and Healey had focused, counterproductively, on the Prime Minister was replicated by other ministers and MPs on other issues. Late in July 1969, after sixteen months of murky water had washed under government bridges, Tony Benn could write of Wilson that he 'just felt contempt for him'.[1]

There was a more general depression after the events of November 1967. Edward Short, wholly loyal to Wilson personally, says, 'We felt our legs kicked from under us, everything we believed in had been destroyed.'[2] The postponement of the planned raising of the school-leaving age was poison in many more Labour mouths. And as the 1967 devaluation was not quick and conclusive in the financial markets, everyone from the Chancellor down, lived in fear of new blows and new humiliations.

Healey, long and steadily contemptuous of Wilson, did not discourage opposition to the Prime Minister, and Benn anxiously quotes Geoffrey Goodman of the *Mirror*, that 'Denis Healey was pouring stuff into the *Daily Mirror* including the voting figures on critical issues in the Cabinet to persuade Cecil King that Harold Wilson was weak.'[3] The febrile King was indeed up to no good and the air had been thick with conspiracy talk for some time. The chairman of IPC, and thus of the *Daily Mirror*, Labour's one friend in the tabloid press, contemplated the many failings of Wilson and his government and pushed businessmen's exasperation especially after devaluation, to the crazy point which required a discontented army Argentinian-style for conclusion. But before reaching this absurd climax, he simply talked coalitions, replacement of Wilson, governments of all the talents, the boardroom commonplaces. He sought Healey's company at lunch and is entered in the diary matter-of-factly, without excitement, though he had made it clear to others that he fancied the Defence Secretary for head of a coalition. But Healey confides no hopes about, or faith in, King to his private record.

More significantly, despite the bitterness of the struggle over F111, Healey was able to keep up decent social relations with Jenkins. On 10 February, a month after the great conflict, he was the guest in East Hendred of Roy and Jennifer 'at lovely ex-vicarage',* followed by a walk on the Berkshire downs and 'Chat with Roy about Budget problems'.[4] Such equanimity would be rewarded in his constituency at the end of the month in a party meeting: 'Fifty there, personally enthusiastic to me.'[5] He had travelled the day before to Swadlincote as guest of honour at George Brown's constituency annual dinner. 'George drunk and effusive alternately.'[6] It was almost the last anyone would see of George Brown the Cabinet minister.

Healey was aware of the constant low-level friction of the Cabinet and noted on a facing page of the diary: 'Great weakness of the Cabinet under Wilson is that interdepartmental consultations always produce an equilibrium of contradictions which cannot be brokered unless ministers will weigh them differently according either to financial or ideological quantifications. Failing that, we need a strong sense of direction and long-term objectives. Given Wilson's tendencies, we flounder.'[7]

On 15 March, the splendours and miseries of Cabinet life were on private view. Jenkins, hit by a wave of sterling sales and with gold reserves horribly low, was advised to close the London gold market and thus, deftly, the more important foreign exchange market. Emergency financial surgery in Britain demands the gold-frogged futilities of Privy Council and Royal Assent. Brown, who had been out of reach, finally informed Wilson's Private Secretary, Michael Halls,† that he took a mighty objection to the procedure. At a midnight Privy Council, the Queen proved chatty. Peter Shore who, not having been told, didn't know why he was there, was brought into the presence ahead of the Chancellor seeking the suspension. '"Mr Shore goes in first because he is a Secretary of State" said an equerry!'[8]

In fact, Brown had a case. The job had to be done, and quickly, but it was being done by small committee, and furtively. Both Crosland and Michael Stewart were unhappy about it. But Brown came to the same after-the-event,

---

* Described by Crossman as 'ramshackle old vicarage'.
† Like Jenkins's Private Secretary, David Dowler, he would die very young with over-stress attributed as a cause.

late-night Cabinet meeting, stormed at Wilson and eventually stormed out
for ever. Healey's account of events contradicts general assumptions of
Wilson's reasonable conduct. Flown back himself from a remote military station, he had been consulted by Jenkins, then, attending the late Cabinet, he
observed, 'George Brown found out – Wilson lied about trying to locate
him. Crosland and Marsh brought Brown to PM to explain about lack of
consultation. Wilson tried and failed to get Brown drunk. 3 am. Jenkins
took charge thereafter.' He describes Brown, back at the Commons, up late
and getting difficult, talking 'openly about resigning and what had happened
in front of Labour and Tory MPs'.[9]

It was the end of an able man as often enchanting as intolerable. A contemporary commentator spoke of 'the cold fish and the hot potato', but
Wilson too was a man of irrational impulses and sudden quick-burn rages.
Brown did indeed drink – self-destructively – not that Wilson was an
abstainer. But the evidence, of Jenkins as well as Healey, is clear that he was
not drunk on the night of 15–16 March. Brown merely responded more
explosively in an atmosphere gas-filled for explosion. The Foreign
Secretaryship now had to be distributed, and it went not to Healey but back
to Stewart. Roy Jenkins, arguing with Wilson on the phone against Stewart
and for Healey, found the deal done and ready for television. The preference
simply made Edward Short's point cited earlier that Wilson did not want a
major talent in a post where he wanted to play himself.

Healey had three-quarters of an hour with Wilson next day and received
a deluge of explanation and an irrational flurry of absurd job offers. 'After
beating about the bush – butter wouldn't melt in his mouth – stated I must be
angry not to be FS – No – disappointed. Choice of me, Roy, Tony, for
Chancellor, me, Tony, Michael for FS – needed a quiet type after George. I
said – No – poor administrator, could not take a grip on an issue . . . Did I
want a new job – Technology, Education, Housing or First Secretary . . .?'[10]

Healey found the episode, as anyone might have, a weird experience. He
did not formally reject the First Secretaryship, whose terms remained cloudy,
but over the next few days and after some consulting with colleagues, he successfully pushed it away. Wilson had tried to bait the trap with an
inducement. Having just denied Healey the job he wanted and was best
qualified for in the government, Wilson pointed to long-term celestialities.
'He tried to suggest [that] if I had a home job, I might succeed him! – might
leave when done as long as Asquith.' After this strange exhibition of low (and
obvious) cunning, Wilson evidently concluded in Uriah Heep mode, 'He finished with loathsome hypocrisy on George.'

In such a climate, no one felt confidence. Three of Healey's own juniors,
Merlyn Rees, James Boyden and Maurice Foley, confided to him that they
were 'upset at lack of leadership in the PLP'.[11] Cecil King at this time was
canvassing many Labour politicians at lunches in his *Daily Mirror* suite.

Many of them talked a great deal. King later published such indiscretions in his diaries. Healey and Jenkins were probably his favourite people. Though flecked with megalomania, King had reasonable taste. Both men would live to congratulate themselves on having said nothing worth quoting. In the Chancellor's case, his query of something said by his shadow, Iain Macleod, had brought forth the transcript of Macleod's most recent lunch and confined Jenkins thereafter to thoughtful silences. Healey seems to have been saved from damning himself in print, not by discretion so much as his own correctness, best summed up by King himself early in the acquaintance. 'I don't think Denis has any high opinion of Harold Wilson, but he is scrupulous in not making any criticism himself. At the same time, some of my more critical remarks passed unchallenged.'[12]

Beyond the busy King, Healey was hearing good quality gossip and seeing journalists. Callaghan told him he thought that Stewart would like to go to the Home Office. He feared that Wilson would bring the sycophantic and absurd George Thomas into the Cabinet. He also thought Healey should stay where he was. A day or two later, Douglas Houghton, Callaghan ally and Chairman of the PLP, also opposed the First Secretaryship option unless it went with a large hunk of proper responsibility like Health and/or Social Security. Other friends, like George Thomson and Michael Stewart, huddled round, Stewart hoping that Denis would replace him,[13] though Houghton, generally a friend, would tell King that 'Denis Healey does not like the House of Commons and the House does not like him.'[14]

The comments of others to King vary interestingly. Iain Macleod, himself the most vivid and vital figure on the Tory front bench, thought Healey 'the ablest of the Labour Ministers',[15] but Ted Heath described him to Cecil King as 'intolerably arrogant', adding that he 'had been this when they were both (with Roy Jenkins) at Balliol'.[16] And rather later, in March 1969, Reggie Maudling* though liking Healey, found him 'unbelievably arrogant in the House'.[17]

Journalists also had him in career focus. First Auberon Waugh,† then a *Times* tandem of William Rees-Mogg and Charles Douglas-Home took him to lunch. For Healey, press lunches had so far been occasional or departmental, but he was at this stage lapsing into fairly vigorous back-alley politics, if Wilton's can be called a back alley. The attention, though flattering, signified only that the press, having heard about the fight, wanted to watch it. But some reports were wildly wrong. Ian Aitken claimed in print on

---

* Healey's own (later) comments on these two rate Maudling as 'a brilliant pragmatist whose idleness was not wholly affected', and Heath as 'the Widmerpool of politics – a man for whom luck and application made up for a lack of natural distinction'. (*The Time of My Life, op. cit.*, p. 149)

† Waugh recalled his keenness on Wilton's restaurant and an enthusiasm for oysters combined with intense dislike of Harold Wilson. (Conversation with the author.)

1 April that Jenkins and Healey were 'at daggers drawn'.[18] In fact, Jenkins was regularly in touch, calling him on the strength of another of Wilson's obsessive late chats, to say that he thought Defence would be safe, but that he 'still talks of me needing a home job'.[19]

Wilson, whose chief therapy was reshuffles, kept this one simmering. He saw Healey on 3 April, was 'very friendly and talked about further tinkering – fewer Cabinet meetings, a steering committee and 3 new committees', but not the job. Finally, on 4 April, he saw Wilson – 'new volte face – clear [he] wants me to stay at Defence.'[20] At the end of the day he also heard from his drawn-dagger colleague, Jenkins, that Barbara Castle would replace Ray Gunter at Labour. There were complications to all this. Jenkins had not wanted Peter Shore at the DEA since Shore's ineptitude would hold up his prices and incomes legislation. Wilson suggested Castle, too strong and thus difficult for Jenkins. The entire DEA thing plus the floating title, First Secretary, now relinquished by Stewart and then offered to Healey, was a relic of the years 1963–4 when soothing George Brown with a spare coronet and a department neither the Treasury nor the Foreign Office but big enough to double Cabinet friction, had been the preoccupation. Healey had nearly been saddled with a title, into which might have been put DEA responsibilities – subordinate to Jenkins, no good to either of them – or something, almost anything, else.

The final outcome had Jenkins keeping a line of authority at the Treasury cluttered only by the Prime Minister, Healey staying where he was, and Barbara Castle being given the First Secretaryship – meaninglessly – to go with a Ministry of Labour now become the *Department* of Employment and Productivity. What would happen when, in 1969, she tried actively to do something about productivity by confining the unions' interests would weigh beyond a dozen titles.

Wilson had also confirmed another enemy. Raymond Gunter, a serious trade union figure, former President of the Transport Salaried Staffs Association, had been watching Wilson's way of doing business with mounting scorn for some time. He was now shuffled into the Ministry of Power, a post notoriously ill-named and generally seen as the back vestibule. Meanwhile his old Ministry, which he had called 'the bed of nails', was decked in bunting for Castle's triumphal entry. As already noted, Gunter, having brooded, walked away in June, making his anger generally apparent.

Unhappiness was widespread. Maurice Foley, a talented Healey colleague, talked anxiously to Denis about getting back to his old job outside politics and would soon be gone. All of Wilson's shuffling and hovering over chess pieces was counter-productive. Healey, in a rewarding job and with a military man's instinct to swear deeply and obey orders, took it very well. But he had an excellent claim on the FO, with colleagues chorusing support. Wilson had run round in a circle.

At the first meeting of the new Cabinet, Healey remarks with his usual dispassion, 'Cabinet – complete waste of time – bad start to new regime.'[21] The reshuffle unsatisfactorily accomplished, Healey himself sensibly took a holiday in Belgium and northern France, looking at Van Goghs and eating mussels and chips as he had on his first cycling trip to the Continent thirty-two years before.

Otherwise he concentrated on business, making a tacit agreement with Jenkins 'not to be seen with smoking pistols in their hands', pistols for Wilson presumably. With another Defence Review to get through, the Buccaneer, ultimate replacement for the F111, had to be fought for, successfully. In early July he is shepherding his White Paper through a tricky Cabinet: 'Opposition from Jenkins, Crossman, Castle, Callaghan, Gardiner [the Lord Chancellor], but support from Peart, Mason [who had replaced Gunter at Power], Shackleton and Benn, PM more neutral . . .'[22] But he got it through!

That wasn't all. The Tunku and Harry Lee made descents upon Healey to worry aloud about Communist infiltration and each other. There would be another visit to the Far East – meetings, talks with officers, a conference of ministers, 'awful waffle from Holyoake',[23] Prime Minister of New Zealand. And there were rounds and rounds of meetings with businessmen in the defence line. Of one Saturday meeting Denis speaks of 'Very tiring day for me as chairman: Wheeler a bit too obliging, Sebastian de Ferranti wild . . . Jim Clark of Plessey off the point, Jim Pearson sensible . . . Ned Dunnett (the Permanent Under-Secretary!) a bit tiddly. Finished at 9.30. Drove through Dorking to cottage arrived 11pm dog tired.'[24] The entry next day says: 'Too tired to think. Walked with [unclear] and Cressida in morning. Slept in afternoon. Home in evening and worked on my speech for Woodworkers.'[25]

Even though the major reforming days at Defence were tailing off, so that a move to another good department would have been welcome, the pressure of work and the not universally useful meeting and talking of government life had not eased at all. Years later Cressida would remember, 'Mum had once again made a lovely lunch and Dad came down with his papers and carried on working at the table, oblivious to it all. Mum asked him to at least stop working for lunch and Dad just saying it was a choice between him being at the table working or having lunch in his study as he worked.'[26]

However, one important thing now changed politically. On 30 May, Cecil King, having buzzed around the chairman of the Coal Board, the Deputy Governor of the Bank of England, and Lord Mountbatten, produced a particularly strident leader page article in the Mirror, made overt talk of sedition and was finally hoist with his own frantic petard and removed from his position. Two days later, Tony Benn was writing in his diary, 'I am sure the reconstruction of the party is the most important task. I believe it can be done on the basis of stronger trade unions and a PLP with a larger part to play. The student power movement, the Black Power movement and the discontent among trade unionists are very powerful and important new forces in society, and I believe that the Labour Party has got to enter into a creative relationship with them.'[27] One scourge had been wonderfully removed; another (wholly well intended) awaited its hour.

Meanwhile Callaghan remained the leading old-style malcontent. He and Healey worked most of the time in comfortable conjunction. Northern Ireland, soon to begin its dreary travails, brought Home and Defence Secretaries necessarily together, but relations were good anyway. They would be described rather later as 'the junta'. But a small episode in September indicates how easily one may jump three fences to the wrong conclusion. A note pushed across the Cabinet table from Callaghan to Healey read:

Denis,
I'm feeling hungry. I want a steak at the Steak House. What about it? Are you free?

Jim[28]

It should, in that throbbing atmosphere, have been deeply sinister. But after an account of his farm-buying enterprise with Gordon Denniss, Callaghan, as privately recorded by Healey, talks coolly round issues and personalities. He 'thinks [Harry] Nicholas will be popular at Transport House, Jenkins lobbying hard on being able to speak at Conference, told Jim to oppose would be "unfriendly act" – George Brown is opposing and will stay on as deputy leader. No point in opposing Harold – what will reshuffle do? Worried about sterling falling further through Hong Kong and Kuwait.'[29] On the Guy Fawkes Night scale of conspiracy this is dud-sparkler stuff, though it was clearly more interesting than Healey's entry of a few days later: 'Lunch with young dumb Sultan of Brunei – father the real power.'[30]

Other scribbled Cabinet table comments of Callaghan's are pleasantly disrespectful. During the contribution of Roy Jenkins, his predecessor has written:

Thoughts of Mao Callaghan
Every chancellor at some time discovers the truths that in his predecessor were thought to be prejudices.[31]

Callaghan could afford to be content about Harry Nicholas. The elderly, fussy and second-rate Deputy General Secretary of the T&G represented George Brown's revenge with Callaghan joining in. Wilson had wanted the party General Secretaryship to go to Anthony Greenwood, upon whose loyalty he could completely rely. At the NEC on 24 July, Brown, still on the National Executive, moved in and nominated Nicholas. He was supported by Callaghan, all this taking place in Wilson's outraged presence. A vote of the committee produced a majority of 14:13 for the T&G man. It was a process of deepening the Cabinet's misery, humiliating its head and intensifying ministerial enmities already jumping with venom. Healey talked politics with Callaghan but kept himself at a wise and grown-up distance from any such goings-on.

At Blackpool in October, he awarded marks, finding Michael Stewart's speech in the foreign affairs debate, an annual event getting ever more painful at this time, 'lucid and sound, but unconvincing'; he thought Walter Padley 'awful', and 'heard Harold speak quite well but failed to get standing ovation'.[32] Wilson's rating is not mentioned until the Cabinet season properly resumes and then only as 'Think Harold safe for time being.'[33] From an extra-Cabinet chat at the same meeting, he minutes Crosland's view of Jenkins '(Tony thinks Roy conceited and tricky).'[34]

This was still not a happy government. Ted Short, not a grandstander, made it grimly clear to Wilson and the rest of the Cabinet that he was deadly serious about resignation over education cuts. He would be hauled back only after an intense struggle which Healey compressed: 'Long Parliamentary committee on Ted Short's demand for more money, Roy lost temper with Jim.'[35]

Healey had anyway quite substantial enough business of his own. The Harrier aircraft, originally the jump-jet, was another potential victim of the rush to cut, and Healey recorded with some pleasure a Defence and Overseas Policy meeting at which four ministers, Jenkins, Crosland, Jack Diamond and Reg Prentice, had been set against him and that he had won his immediate argument for it. He had also had to defend the Chieftain tank, against the surprising opposition of Michael Stewart. The references to extreme tiredness recur heavily at this time.

He was dealing by now with a completely different hand of Chiefs, George Baker having become CGS, Michael Le Fanu CNS and John Grandy CAS. Baker was an admirable soldier, but very conservative, Le Fanu, an amusing and clever man, while Grandy was given to worrying. But Healey's joy among his military colleagues was the Vice-CGS, Michael Carver. 'Carver in, brilliant and on the ball as usual'[36] is a representative entry.

But other departmental business shrank to inconsequence in the light of the economic crisis, something which spilled into the personality game. Shirley Williams told Tony Benn that 'Harold and Roy were going to resign today, according to City rumours and this had led to a tremendous flight from sterling.'[37] On the BBC's *World at One* Crossman denounced the story as the work of the Gnomes of Zurich.[38] But it was a flight just the same. On Friday 5 December, the gilt-edged market went abruptly down and over $100 million was lost on adverse trading in sterling. On the Tuesday of the next week, £100 million was lost in forty minutes, a figure which became £200 million by the time Jenkins got back from the emergency meeting about the first £100 million. As it happened, excellent trade figures were known to the Treasury but were not scheduled for immediate announcement. With help from Wilson, who managed to hint at good news whose formal announcement ahead of schedule might have started more panic, the very worst would be over by the end of the week.

There is a curious parallel across eight years between the two chancellors and their respective worst times. Healey would write about a day in 1976 when for a full 24 hours 'I was entirely demoralised,'[39] after which recovery became thinkable and duly happened. Jenkins describes a Winter's Journey as bleak as Schubert's – taken on party business to Newcastle, Sunderland, Middlesbrough, Bishop Auckland and finally, driven by Jim Tinn, a local MP, one made in the dark through a defile in the Pennines, to Carlisle. 'It was almost pitch dark at 9.00 as I read the panicky headlines of the newspapers and never seemed to achieve more than reluctant half-light all day . . . I was much pursued by the press at every point . . . The Sunday newspapers at Euston were even worse than the Saturday one had been at Bishop Auckland.'[40]

It would come right in the end and none of the economic anxieties of 1969 would prove as deeply grievous as those just gone through. Jenkins could fairly say that his journey across the Pennines 'was a classic example of the darkest hour being the one before the dawn'.[41] But the government had been very near the end of its resources.

The prevailing mood in the Cabinet could be measured at its extreme point in Crossman. A fortnight before, on November 22 at a time when that fragile pound and shuffling movements in the rates of franc and mark were the preoccupation, he could be heard outside the Cabinet room booming 'at the top of his voice: "Of course this is going to be inadequate, of course it's going to be inadequate and everybody knows we ourselves shall have to devalue again soon."'[42] This, said Benn with startling bitterness 'is Dick the great leaker, an incredibly inadequate man like Hugh Dalton. He just can't keep his mouth shut.'[43]

If this was business of the most deadly serious kind, 10 December was 'Warning the Plotters' day. Healey's news pellet was 'PM threatened to reshuffle cabinet if Jim didn't stop attacking him.' According to Benn, Wilson told his Cabinet 'that four senior ministers had told him that one member of the Cabinet had been going round stirring things up, indicating conspiracy against Harold's own leadership, and that if this went on, without further ado, he would simply reconstruct his Government'.[44]

An unhappy government brooded upon the friction between Prime Minister and Chancellor and the peculiar bitterness of an economic crisis refusing to go away and feeding unhappiness with yet further prospective cuts. So the bad feeling of 10 December is in the conspiracy column, while what happened in the main Cabinet meeting the day before, comes under 'economic argument'. Jenkins presented a paper suggesting five areas in which, 'to give him room to manoeuvre', major cuts might be made. One of them was defence. Healey would take no more. And in his diary he can say devastating things in the space of a stretched haiku: 'SEP on expenditure

1970/71 – I threatened resignation if another major defence cut, strongly supported by the PM [took place].'[45] In fact, as things turned out and as newspaper and financial panic were dissipated, a refusal to slash again the things he had responsibility for, worked.

Healey, after this *démarche*, talked with Wilson about a prospective visit to Nigeria and observed him 'Soapily friendly'. In the absence of more wholesome goodwill and with the Conservatives in December increasing their lead in the poll to 20 per cent, soapy friendliness would have to do in this melancholy committee. For once, Crossman's defeatist instincts expressed something serious. He commented on the low attendance at a meeting of an important backbench group – on communications. 'The old Left turns up religiously at party meetings, the forty or fifty bloody obstreperous people who are always voting against us are to be found in the tea room, but the new Centre, the people who are for parliamentary reform, who believe in communication, the wonderful new faces from the techs, are no longer active members of the House ... Their first reaction was to demand reform, but now they have lost interest.'[46]

In fact, the substantive economic developments of 1969, though not dazzling, were firmly on an upward course. Politics might lag behind them, there would be bad polls and worse by-elections to come. There would also be economic wobbles, but the economy was becoming decently underpinned and the raw panic of December 1968 was past.

As with the Major government, the economy was recovering handsomely, but politics was something else. The party had lost its cohesion and was thinking in purely factional terms. Wilson had lost caste, Jenkins was Son of Gaitskell, surrounded by people more Jenkinsite than Jenkins: Taverne, Marquand, Rodgers, if not quite his future nemesis, David Owen. Owen, his boss thought, was 'able but lazy'.[47] His boss was Denis Healey. As to the group, Healey was not so little of a politician as to be without a friendly ear at the Anti-pope's court. Alan Lee Williams would periodically call on the Defence Secretary to be debriefed on their meetings and intentions.

Healey at this time experienced, quite pleasantly, another of Wilson's lurches into man-management At a lunch involving Marcia Williams, the press secretary, Gerald Kaufman and Roy Jenkins's indispensable John Harris, it was suggested, 'I should mastermind election campaign and oversee Transport House – not a clue or for what, as good as promised me FO if Michael went.' Healey was rarely moved by Wilson in a giving – or talking about giving – mood. This coolness extended to poor Mary Wilson who, at this lunch, he thought a 'mixture of Mrs Feather and Mrs Miniver'.*[48]

---

* 'Mrs Miniver' played in the film by Greer Garson, was a British upper-middle-class housewife, quietly staunch during the Second World War. 'Mrs Feather' was the dithering staccato character created by Jeanne de Cassalis.

Callaghan was Callaghan, a former holder of great office who now held another, lesser but commensurate. A first-rate professional politician, he too had been demoralised, but he had the resilience of his hard beginning and unprivileged ascent in life. As Wilson thrashed about, emptily threatened and manoeuvred under lights, Callaghan recovered a full sense of being better at the job, Wilson's job. A saying in the late sixties ran: Q: 'Who will succeed Harold if he's run over by a number 11 bus?'* A: 'Jim will be driving it.'

And Callaghan would not make the mistake made twenty-five years later by Norman Lamont. He kept his enmity for the Prime Minister to a small circle of acquaintance and loose alliance, Healey one of them, through which, in a talkative trade, it was extended to the Parliamentary Party and friendly lunching journalists. He made no declarations of war, no public self-justifications. Nobody was told, everyone knew. Across 1968 James Callaghan was not so much disloyal as available for disloyalty. He was Home Secretary yet, normally a dangerous job given police indiscipline, prison warders' violence and latterly, black and brown faces. But over Ireland, which would loom horridly in 1969, and race, in respect of which he would talk softly and act without illusions, Callaghan would play his hand extraordinarily well. Harold Macmillan had attributed everything to 'Events, dear boy, events.' Jim Callaghan worked steadily in his Queen Anne Street office and waited for them.

For the moment, early in the year, events suddenly became simply absurd. A local coup two years earlier in the not very important Caribbean island of Anguilla had severed it and the 6000 population from federation with the not very much more important grouping of St Kitts and Nevis, a federation imposed Sandys-style. The Americans were exercised. There was febrile talk about the Anguillan independence leader, Ronald Webster, having plans to establish a casino paradise in the style of Batista's Cuba, not normally the sort of thing to trouble a United States government. This was all speculative, with the one clear fact being a general disinclination on Anguilla to return to the unpopular Mr Bradshaw, Prime Minister of the Federation. Comparisons were made with Rhodesia. The British Cabinet met.

The situation was Harold Wilson-sized. Anxious meetings were held, a hapless Whip, William Whitlock, was sent out barely long enough for Healey to report 'Whitlock chased off island.'[49] On Saturday 13 March he records getting, at his cottage in Withyham, 'FO paper on force to return – clean up Mafia. Received in late evening. No political objection whatever.' Healey's own instinct was sceptical. He records a meeting with the trusted Elworthy (CDS until 1971) and they 'decided to oppose unless politics clear'.[50]

---

* It was always a number 11. They go down Whitehall, cross the T-junction with Downing Street and might hypothetically account for an absent-minded Prime Minister.

At a DOPC meeting held after the Cabinet, Healey had argued, 'Better something than nothing; better nothing than something silly.' He also asked, 'Wait a bit. Where's our intelligence on the strength of the island? We might need a battalion of troops and once we'd got there, how would we get off again? . . .'[51] By contrast, Callaghan was keen: 'very strongly for in first, organise afterwards . . . Roy mute. Harold, Michael worried at Rhodesia analogy.' Eventually Healey, though complaining bitterly about lack of solid intelligence, agreed to prepare something: 'In end agreed to work out plan over weekend.' But 'I said make clear not under Bradshaw.'[52] On the 17th 'the A[ttorney] G[eneral] says legal but would be contested. Leaks begin and build up all day. PM hysterical.'[53]

At one earlier stage of this melancholy farce, the Prime Minister had announced to colleagues, 'You will wish to know that another wave went in last night.' 'Another wave' turned out to be six metropolitan policemen.[54] Healey's plan at any rate involved doing the wrong thing properly and sending three hundred paratroopers from Antigua to occupy the island, from which they would withdraw six months later.

The episode was important if only as an illustration of the personalities concerned. Stewart, always too intense, had become convinced of a major calamity. Wilson, wanting to cut a figure, had been farcically decisive. Jenkins was wisely silent but did not resist. Healey was instinctively sceptical but performed his good soldier routine. Crossman had said immortally, 'Don't let's delay for the sake of another week's intelligence . . .'[55] And, by an irony now endemic in this Cabinet, Callaghan had been the strongest advocate of unplanned action, but Wilson would get the blame.*

He could hardly complain. Prime ministers are supposed to be able to recognise a howling nonsense before they turn it into D-Day. Wilson had managed to parody himself, but no one had stopped him. Anguilla was the sort of small, unnecessary excitement which, as it ends in derision, weakens the constitution of a government, a shattering blow with a pig's bladder.

What Wilson attempted next was *not* unnecessary, but the blow it provoked was very nearly fatal. The Industrial Relations Bill was one of those things entirely right and utterly wrong, upon which the unlucky, a category now including Wilson, sometimes alight. Trade union power in Britain had increased, was increasing, and ought to have been diminished. The advocate of limiting it in 1969 was Barbara Castle, old leftist but with eyes to see and courage to fight. (Her devoted press officer at this time was a former *Guardian* journalist and strong Labour supporter called Bernard Ingham.)

---

* Not just Wilson. An obituary by Tom Dalyell in 2001 in the *Independent* spoke with great bitterness of the scapegoating and political ruin of his friend, William Whitlock.

The power of the unions had been nagging government for a long time. An inflationary climate fed everything that was worst in the British system. Moderate men no longer looked big as they had in Will Lawthar's and Arthur Deakin's day. A loudmouth like Lawrence Daly and an ingenious but malignant chatterbox like Clive Jenkins became representative figures.

The Oxford economic training and Lancashire Catholic's predilection for conciliation of George Woodcock had been replaced at the TUC by Victor Grayson Keir Hardie Feather. Charming, good on television, but greatly vain anyway, Feather was vainer yet of the power of the General Secretary of the TUC, power derived from the aggressive acts of individual unions. When the Trade Disputes Act of 1906 began to be grossly abused, Vic Feather was not the man to fight it. A good and generous decision in its day, the immunity from tort it bestowed in all disputes had become a lethal weapon in the strikers' market emerging since the mid-fifties.

Late in this course of change, Lord Donovan, a Lord of Appeal and former Labour MP, had been asked to report. And to boil down a great many words, he had proposed voluntary restraints plus plant bargaining, something which was developing anyway to no great economic advantage. Since 'voluntary' meant optional, Donovan offered an evasion of the question he had been asked. Only a minority report by Andrew Shonfield of the *Observer* faced up to the need for legal sanctions – penal clauses – against acts illegal in any other context. To their great moral credit, Mrs Castle, now Minister of Labour, and Wilson himself, backed naturally by the anxious Chancellor, resolved upon a braver option. The only historic criticism to make of Barbara Castle's White Paper, *In Place of Strife*, was that the business of making it law was approached in a leisurely way when it needed speed and surprise. They were cutting with the grain of public feeling and against that of the movement to which they belonged. And that movement commanded a majority in the House of Commons. It was to be a case, very rare in Britain, of the executive being overruled by the legislature.

The proposal presented James Callaghan with an issue over which he would oppose Wilson in ways perfectly warranting his dismissal from the Cabinet. His opposition went public again as early as 26 March, during what Professor Morgan calls 'one of the most remarkable meetings of Labour's National Executive ever held'.[56] When the NUM man, Joe Gormley, moved that 'the NEC should reject legislation designed to give effect to the proposals in the white paper', Callaghan, the Home Secretary, bound by collective responsibility over government business, voted for it, and the motion passed by 15 to 6 with four other members of the government, Jennie Lee, Alice Bacon, Fred Mulley and Eirene White, withholding support.

Healey (and Jenkins) publicly deplored what Callaghan did – he called the action 'shabby',[57] but he shows no private sign of excitement on the question. The diaries contain no comment after this episode nor after the Cabinet of 2

April, which he does not actually mention. On 24 April he has, pushed across the table to him, another note from Callaghan

Denis,
    What a way to run a railway

Jim[58]

This was not about the Industrial Relations Bill, but Wilson's prevaricating behaviour over Ulster. It had, though, the broadest application.

The quarrel had deepened across the spring, involving not only conflict about the bill itself but speculative chat about a Cabinet which should be rejigged, with Callaghan specifically in mind. It was to be the tent from which the Home Secretary, looking out or looking in, would be active. Crosland on 7 April told Healey his thoughts – Fred Peart to go, an Inner Cabinet to be created and Callaghan put into it. On the following day, Healey had an hour with Wilson, 'dog-tired and rambling', who also favoured an Inner Cabinet, of which Fred Peart would of course be a member, together with 'me, Roy, Barbara and perhaps Stewart' – no Callaghan. With his taste for anticlimactic calm, Denis went down next day to the family's recently acquired cottage in Withyham and 'cut hedges and fitted carpets'.[59]

This was probably the only grown-up reaction. For the inner Cabinet was Wilson's fearfully contemplated device for cutting Callaghan down to size. Eventually he did exclude him, something which served only to establish that the Home Secretary had to be affronted because he was too important to sack. As part of the same twitchy Prime Ministerial reaction, the Chief Whip, John Silkin, originally appointed to take a soft line, was sacked at the beginning of May – for taking a soft line. This was done without Wilson informing Barbara Castle, his key ally, and she, according to Healey, 'told Hattersley to tell Harold what she thought of him'.[60] Silkin was replaced by Robert Mellish, a distinctly rough diamond, who yet later would give Wilson the stark news that the bill could not pass.

The mood which could make colleagues desert government legislation, could make them desert the Prime Minister. Healey was being informed by his source, Shirley Williams, of an explosive state of affairs: '50–75 of 150 non-left and non-payroll ready to write to Houghton* against Harold. Ivor Richard sourly confident of victory, Roy frightened will [get] out of control, worried effect on Sterling if Harold was to be dragged out kicking and screaming.'[61] Healey was hearing similar numbers from the journalist, Alan Watkins.

---

* Douglas Houghton, Callaghan's old Inland Revenue associate and close ally, elder Labour statesman and Chairman of the Parliamentary Party.

In fact, events would come to the full boil in the next couple of days when this same Houghton had made a speech damning any step which separated Labour from the trade union movement. For a number of years, Houghton had done a weekly problem-solving broadcast for the BBC. It was called *Can I help you?*

Events kept many Tory newspapers very happy and carried over into the Cabinet of 8 May. As Healey tells it, Callaghan began by saying he thought they would not win the election. Wilson 'spouted nonsense on Houghton's PLP speech while he, Healey, had said that it wasn't unconstitutional, with Mellish supporting him. Meanwhile Crossman told Callaghan to get out. Wilson said, "I won't get out and leave a choice of successor open. No one else could form a government." Stewart said this was true.' It was much more complex than that, but expressed in Healey's handwritten, minimal note in cable-ese, one still gets the dreadful drift. Advised by his Permanent Secretary, Philip Allen[62], Callaghan stayed on – as Home Secretary and bone in throat.

The bill was not going to pass. Resentment had grown huge and reflected different strands: the trade union interest in and out of parliament outraged at correction and right-wingers now conscious of Wilson's personal vulnerability, Callaghan, who was putting the unions' case, and almost everyone seems to have had a sense of the perfect impotence of government and leader. It would be later that Healey would coin the phrase, 'If you're in a hole, stop digging.' But it never had more perfect application.

He was, though, putting in a contribution. The calamitous 'Why don't you get out?' Cabinet was followed the next day by a joint meeting of Cabinet and NEC which of course included a number of leading unionists, notably Gormley, author of the earlier motion, who now said sorrowfully that the government had given the impression 'that it didn't trust the trade union movement'.[63] Healey reckoned that 'my speech went well',[64] which is as vainglorious as he gets. Tony Benn spoke of 'a tremendous Leader-of-the-Party sort of speech by Denis. He said that he was an old Transport House man and all we needed was a switch of 1 per cent of resources and defence had given that, and that there was a risk that we would get into opposition and destroy ourselves.'[65]

Even so, Healey's mind seems to have been genuinely preoccupied with departmental questions and foreign business. He goes to Germany, he goes to Washington, takes note of Jenkins's Budget, hears distressing news from his deputy, Gerry Reynolds, in great pain and very soon to die. He is active on Ulster, just starting to bubble, looks after the visiting Italian President and Prime Minister.* But until the moment of explosion, he fails to register any excitement about what would become a Cabinet war, except in the report of

---

* Ironically, the very Giuseppe Saragat and Pietro Nenni between whom the young Healey had tried to mediate back in 1948.

his intelligencer, Williams, on the Jenkinsite 1963 group: 'some believing Harold finished already'.[66] And he notes the attitude of the party General Secretary at a meeting on Ulster: '[Harry] Nicholas playing to Callaghan a bit.'

In fact, Healey, like Jenkins, was too busy, if not under quite such remorseless pressure, for the cloak-and-dagger stuff. His opinion of Wilson was no higher, but he strongly supported trade union reform. He would go on being what he always was, a very busy departmental minister and a dependable member of the Cabinet. Barbara Castle might note his physical manner in Cabinet: 'Denis Healey . . . spends a lot of time muttering under his breath and stabbing viciously at his blotter. I suspect his resentment against Harold is profound.'[67] Edward Short might observe that when it came to doodling, Wilson produced neat, rectilinear lines in the way of an architectural sketch, Healey would do brutal, thick-lined, scowling portraits.[68]

But when it mattered, Healey was loyal. He would note without comment flattering suggestions, as from Owen, that he might be a major beneficiary of any coming earthquake. He was perhaps contemptuously loyal, but he was not playing a hand against the Prime Minister. And Wilson knew it. The offer made on 12 March that Healey should become general overlord of the election signalled the fact. But the job itself had astounded him and he felt no affinity for the work. He discussed the offer with Jenkins, whose Jeeves, John Harris, had actually been at the lunch where it was made.

It would have involved playing a major adjudicating part over policy, occupying the full focus of public attention next only to the Prime Minister during the campaign. The function was close to that which the Conservative Party sensibly gives to its Party Chairman. It meant being talked about and speculated over by the Alan Watkinses and Auberon Waughs. As Healey realised, it was also kindly meant. 'By now I had become the Prime Minister's favourite.'[69] But though Wilson was 'mortified' at the rejection, he would not touch it.

A shift might have been welcome. But the role of 'election supremo' would have been a purely political post and Healey, despite his readiness for a fight, generally kept himself at a decent arm's length from pure politics. He would have been doubtfully good at it, having more vigour than nuance. The least silken of men, he would have been direct, healthy, without slyness, perhaps attracting the sort of public warmth he would find in the eighties Opposition. But the style which later brought forth 'She glories in slaughter' might well have managed further and better quotations for the Conservative press. He was anyway well out of things. Defeat was as generally expected during most of 1969 as it was felt to be unthinkable in the run-up to the election. Ordinary prudence advised against becoming the election supremo who lost the election.

In midsummer Denis and Edna gave lunch at Admiralty House to Cecil King and his wife, Ruth. They were on genuinely friendly *a quatro* terms, and

King's fall (and his incendiary foolishness) made no difference. Healey thought Callaghan was looking to defeat at the election, assuming

> that Wilson would now be anathema to the trades union movement, who would welcome Jim as the Leader of the Parliamentary Party after the defeat. Denis, or at any rate his wife, harbours a hope that Wilson may pull it off and win the next election. Denis feels he himself is gaining support in the PLP and that events are moving his way. I don't think he really wants the premiership: I think he feels he is doing a good job at Defence and is content to remain there. He is not far-sighted, takes the financial outlook fairly complacently. He is nice; he is tough; he would be a far better P.M. than Wilson.[70]

King might have had a crazy streak, but that is no bad assessment.

Now that the economy was soundly set up again, a state of affairs which Labour, by its antics, had helped the country to overlook, Jenkins contemplated their futures. 'Saw Roy Jenkins on defence budget then general chat. Obviously gloomy – wants to leave Treasury for FO! Me for chancellor especially if shift of policy is inevitable.'[71] That offer would have been accepted delightedly, but it wasn't made. However, relations with the Prime Minister continued happily enough. He speaks of a much more relaxing lunch with Harold Wilson at the end of May.

But the inevitable collapse of the Industrial Relations Bill was taking place, stone by crumbling stone. Since Callaghan on that celebrated occasion, the 8 May Cabinet, had said that the bill could not pass, things had not improved. Indeed another remark of Callaghan's at that time, that they should not talk of 'sink or swim' on the bill, but 'sink or sink', was proving prophetic. Exclusion from the 'Inner Cabinet' had indeed not worked.

On 5 June, the TUC held a special conference when the card vote supported its correct line by a majority of 9:1. A general retreat of Cabinet ministers, including customary sound loyalists, followed, clear intimation that the Parliamentary Party was now too deeply aroused to opposition for slapping down. Short, Mason, Mrs Hart and Cledwyn Hughes all pulled back. Roy Jenkins would join them, though he speaks almost penitently of doing so. He 'had not wanted a government smash', but Wilson and Castle 'badly though they had mishandled tactics, were now showing signs of desperate courage, and it was humiliating to desert them'.[72]

Three days after Healey's lunch with Wilson, the Prime Minister had arranged a dinner at Chequers in semi-secret with the main union leaders, Jones, Scanlon, Feather among them. But they offered no concessions worth having. As Roy Jenkins later wrote, 'They decided they had the interior lines of communication, dug in and waited for the investing forces to disintegrate.'[73] Healey, up in Leeds, had an uncharacteristically rough meeting with the city party which was trying to instruct MPs. He was kept in touch with the state of the bill by Jenkins and returned for a Sunday meeting of the Inner Cabinet only to record, 'Nothing very clear happening.' Wilson, two days later, was 'very vague on IR bill'.[74] Healey had his own practical task of getting a Forces pay increase accepted and very quickly succeeded. Eddie Shackleton had been 'flabbergasted to find Treasury had accepted my line on pay'.[75]

Healey reliably and steadily supported the bill. His interventions in Cabinet were almost all helpful, Mrs Castle only wincing once when, at the 8 May Cabinet (held on a Sunday!), he acknowledged Feather's smartness: 'Denis, usually adamant, said Vic had manoeuvred brilliantly.'[76] But he would differ from Jenkins at this same meeting when he wanted to measure support in Cabinet, underlining a figure now obviously low. 'Harold said it was too early to do that and Denis, who had now rallied, backed him up. Roy persisted: we ought to discuss this evening what we should do if the TUC refused to continue negotiating the "most favourable outcome". Denis and I were all against this; it was entirely the wrong mood in which to go into negotiations.'[77]

He was not part of the next day's special meeting with the TUC, but he did attend the Cabinet which followed that highly negative experience. Ministers were trying to hold the position to which they had retreated. The penal clauses in the original bill were now offered in cold storage to be activated only in extreme circumstances, which circumstances Wilson, by nod and wink, was assuring the unions would never arise. The option was to put things off by a year. In Healey's view, Wilson at this Cabinet 'threw it all away at the end by saying difference between cold storage and postponement very small'.[78]

Healey himself favoured postponement. As he told Barbara Castle at a Coop rally in Nottingham, he had seen Wilson ahead of a visit to the Far East, to say that 'there was little to be gained by going for "cold storage" as against postponing the Bill until next year with a view to seeing what the TUC could do.'[79] Castle's objection that this would 'tell everyone that the TUC has won'[80] has a melancholy all its own. The TUC had won. But when she said she should perhaps evacuate the rocking boat by resigning, Healey was emphatic. 'To lose the one minister whom the public believe has shown determination and guts would be a terrible blow to the government's credibility.'

On 18 June, it was the Cabinet itself which, in Benn's account, was 'postponed and postponed'. It finally assembled to hear Wilson announce 'a victory for everyone'. The unions would sign a solemn and binding agreement to follow a voluntary code on industrial action. 'He then went on to describe what a triumph he's had.'[81] Different people saw different things. Roy Jenkins described the final Cabinet with some warmth.

'Wilson behaved with a touch of King Lear-like nobility. He sounded fairly unhinged at times and there was a wild outpouring of words, but he did not hedge and he did not whine . . . It was a sad story from which he and Barbara Castle emerged with more credit than the rest of us.'[82] But the defeat was comprehensive and the final flimsy, word-spinning attempt to deny defeat, annihilated most of what remained of Wilson's reputation. The Sunday papers 'were full of briefings by Harold on how certain ministers had let him down'.[83]

Healey, who had been, quite as fortuitously, in the Far East during the 1966 financial crisis, had just arrived in Sydney from Bombay. Once again he was not missing very much. On the moon, American astronauts were landing. In the United States, calamity at least came big, Senator Kennedy driving off a narrow bridge on Chappaquiddick Island and Miss Kopechne drowning. In Britain, Harold Wilson was telling Tony Benn that Judith Hart was 'a prattling woman', that Dick Marsh and Tony Crosland were 'always leaking', before asking that Benn 'should keep an eye out for plots'. Wilson consoled himself with the strange rhetoric, 'Isn't there always magic in my reshuffle just as there's magic in my honours list . . .'[84]

It was at this point that Tony Benn wrote, 'I went out shaken by this, having concluded that the man had gone mad, ought to be removed, that the great case for the parliamentary system was that it did remove people. I just felt contempt for him. I just feel Harold is finished.'[85]

ELECTION 1970 AND AFTERMATH

This had been the low point of the two Labour governments of 1964–70. Things were never again quite so bad, but recovery would lift ministers rather into hubris than serenity.

In such times there was no substitute for being busy. Northern Ireland, which Callaghan was handling with some toughness and a full understanding of its vast importance, was also Healey's business. It had become a military commitment. On 19 August, at an Ulster summit at Downing Street, Wilson, Callaghan and Healey met James Chichester-Clark, now Prime Minister of Northern Ireland, Faulkner, his ambitious deputy, and the Home Minister, Porter.

Healey indicated no awe at the Unionist leadership. He thumbnailed Chichester-Clark as 'county colonel, farmer, not quick', Brian Faulkner as 'dapper little bridge player – too ingratiating' and Porter as 'nervous, defeated little man'. However, the Ulstermen had come to offer a highly conciliatory stance, willing to put all authority under the General Officer Commanding. Though this should not be the present commander, General Sir Ian Freeland who, ministers obscurely thought, 'did not suit us'.[1]

The Home Secretary was rather thrown at being deprived of a fight. 'Jim very miffed, surly and hostile – his fox shot, but in fact [we] got all we wanted from it.'[2] This undertaking known as 'The Downing Street Declaration', which also planned the closing of the brutally sectarian B Special police and the establishment of an Ulster Defence Regiment under effectual discipline, was the greatest step towards dismantling the old 1922 Northern Ireland state before Heath imposed direct rule. Healey noted that their only difficulty with the Ulstermen came over an inquiry into the RUC, one postponed but not avoided.

Healey would have liked to help secure the border by cratering it at key points, but did not get his way. Returning in September from his French holiday, he noted without irony, 'Pleasant day reading up Ulster.'[3] He would in fact be exercised by the problems on the ground in Northern Ireland for the ten remaining months Labour held office. He would tell Cecil King that Ulster might be a bigger threat to the government than any other. His diary comment on that momentous meeting, notably understated, expressed something rare for Northern Irish affairs: 'No one very silly.'[4]

When the management committee (Inner Cabinet) met at the start of 1970 to talk election dates, counsels were divided. Healey noted that 'Roy on whole for autumn. Harold obviously wants spring.'[5] The difficulty lay in the organisation. A few days later he reported on 'Boring campaign committee – appalling mediocrity of Transport House.'[6] His next regular visit to Leeds yielded some constituency opinion: 'Ted Naylor on prices and profits, Gabb, good leftwinger* – "more people feel themselves involved."'[7] But returning next day to another management committee meeting, he found Wilson 'rattled' at the Conservative Party's Selsdon Park programme. This was Heath's famous adoption, signalled by a weekend conference in a Surrey hotel, of a species of paper Thatcherism before the real thing.

The ineffective preparation was not for nothing. Wilson seems always to have been attached to the idea of an early election. At a 'dull management committee' on 20 April it was a case of 'Harold obviously thinking of a Spring election.' And such was the urgency that it was succeeded by another 'dull management committee' on 21 April.[8] For Labour's position seemed to be improving across 1970. It was being quite sensible over the economy. Jenkins writes of the Treasury being 'obsessed with 1964 guilt'[9] a reference to their complicity in the overspending of Reginald Maudling as chancellor. The chancellor quietly informed Douglas Allen, his Under-Secretary, that he 'was going to be a little, but not much more, generous than he wanted'.[10] There would be no election-buying in the budget of 1970.

Though a budget characterised by Jenkins himself as moving out of neutrality only by a hundred million or so disappointed backbenchers with seats to lose, nothing in the polls suggested he was wrong. The first figures published after its presentation in April, showed Labour back in the lead (by two points) for the first time in three years. And with a surplus of £39 million on visible account alone, this appeared to be the sort of April Browning had had in mind.

So at the end of the month, the 29th, the management committee met. Healey noted Wilson 'worried about blame if he chooses wrong', and stressing the importance of the pending World Cup from which, England disappearing early, no benefits would flow. Healey himself did not want to

---

* Douglas Gabb, later his constituency agent.

rule out July and warned on possible trouble in the Caribbean and recession in the US economy. Jenkins, who had taken a week's holiday in Ireland, was on his own admission, non-committal and 'must have sounded like Crosland',[11] notoriously given to reserving judgements. Fred Peart, who preferred October but thought 'June was OK if you can win',[12] was close to the wobbling norm. Crosland, out-Croslanding himself, said that 'it depended on the polls.'[13] Wilson who, according to Jenkins, murmured about a date which would make him Prime Minister for a day longer than Asquith, was perhaps the most resolute person present. Healey simply grew more and more exasperated: 'Campaign committee dull as usual' and 'Cabinet waste of time.'[14]

The rewards of this time were hypothetical. For when the Prime Minister came to contemplate a Cabinet formed after a Labour victory, Healey was both marked down for the highest promotion and paid a signal compliment. On 13 May, Wilson told Jenkins his choice of election date. It should be Thursday 18 June (something revealed to the management committee on 14 May). This accomplished, the Chancellor would move to the Foreign Office, while Healey would go to the Treasury. That was the promotion; the compliment was that he would be replaced by Fred Peart at Defence, 'which department, Wilson said, had experienced a strong minister for sufficiently long that it could do with a weak one who would please the generals'.

The difficulty of not actually winning the 1970 election would stale the charm of a gesture frozen in intent like the lovers and celebrants of Keats's Grecian urn. But it did confirm the passing of a Wilson 'full of the wickedness of Denis Healey'. It would also send Healey's driver, Jim McCaul, informed like all ministerial drivers ahead of the Cabinet, into a pre-emptive shift to chauffeuring the Chancellor, one which landed him with four years of driving Anthony Barber![15]

Wilson told Healey that although there was a risk of the US economy hitting trouble and passing on problems, his central message was 'Labour confident, the Tories demoralised.' In fact, the British economy would shortly strike problems all its own: notably the first bad trade figures for some time, distorted in part by the purchase of the first jumbo jets. At a time when trade figures still worried voters and politicians, this was unpleasant news, upon which Jenkins had glumly sat, knowing what he could not disclose but having learned it too late to pull Wilson back. Even so the very decent local government results for Labour in May seemed to make Wilson's point.

Healey would be busier at this election as a national figure than ever before. He would share press conference duties at Transport House with Wilson whom he noted on day one as 'very friendly'. He did the foreign press briefing before making off for East Anglia, speaking at Whittlesey and Peterborough, then next day to substantial audiences at Rushden and Wellingborough.

He was coming back to London most days and substituted for Wilson at Transport House on 4 June, handling a row which had broken out over a

Tony Benn speech blazing at Powell. It alleged that 'the flag that was being raised in Wolverhampton was getting to look more and more like the flag that fluttered over Belsen.'[16] Such talk was hardly wisdom, and since it was said in reproach to Heath who had fired Powell after the 'grinning Piccaninnies' speech in 1968, hardly fair.

Healey, having noted blithely that 'all polls now give us 5% lead',[17] next day shared the press conference and heard Wilson privately 'furious with Tony Benn'.[18] He then went back north to Leeds and his first fighting ground, Otley, where, perhaps ominously, he spoke to '30 people including Conservatives'.[19] He spent the day after in Leeds working a shopping centre with parliamentary and local party colleagues like Stan Cohen and Douglas Gabb. And since Labour politics have been anxiously ethnic since long before the *Empire Windrush* docked, he attended what Labour always called a social, at the Irish Club, guest of the Moynihans, his chief links with Irish Leeds. The evening was 'More Irish than believable, with Irish songs, dancing and music. Went well.'[20]

Leaving Harold Wilson to handle the press conference on Monday, the Defence Secretary flew to Venice for a NATO meeting to talk with Melvin Laird, Nixon's Defense Secretary, whom he liked and respected. And since such gatherings not uncommonly take place in Palladian villas filled with pictures, he luxuriated amid Bellinis and Tintorettos. Wednesday took him back to running the press conference with Wilson and Jenkins before a meeting on Ulster and departure by RAF Andover to Brussels for a planning meeting with Defence ministers, including an increasingly close ally, Helmut Schmidt.

At this stage – Wednesday 11 June, mid-campaign – just as Healey was developing an eye infection, Wilson chose to confirm his place in the reshuffle which would never be – 'Treasury for me'.[21] He went next to campaign in west London for his PPS, Ivor Richard, joined by 'nice young Tony Banks, candidate for East Grinstead'.[22] He still had ministerial business, notably finding a replacement for the CNS, Michael Le Fanu. Admiralty matters were followed on the Friday with a visit to Preston, scene of such anxiety in the mid-sixties over TSR2. Saturday saw him back at the press conference and doing a meeting for Alan Williams. Sunday meant writing an article for the *Daily Telegraph*, then going to London for a TV discussion: 'Muggeridge perverse, Shirley Williams excellent . . . I spoke too much.'[23]

On that Sunday, the papers came out with an array of polls so diverse as to put all pollsters to shame, if they knew the meaning of the word. But though running from 2–12 per cent, they all at any rate ran the same way – Labour – and so piled delusion upon false hopes. From Monday Healey was given over almost completely to Leeds, noting many meetings poorly attended. The great days of four meetings every night, each a hundred and more strong, were gone. Chiefly he encountered very bad organisation – 'wasted an hour and a half . . . to go around a council estate in Pudsey'[24] – before coming back to his own constituency for 'tremendous reception' at Seacroft, another meeting at Beachwood and a descent upon Harehills Labour Club.

But while these forms of worship and ceremony were taking place, the horrid trade statistics which Jenkins had kept under his coat in the style of the Spartan youth and the fox, were released – surely with consequences. Any kind of poster-paint bad news, however little understood, comes three days before an election with special force.

Since the world went on despite elections, Healey spent part of the next morning, Tuesday, talking to his office 'about Ulster reinforcements'[25] before doing two factory meetings, one at Montague Burton's, a vital constituency employer. It rained and attendance was thin. On the last day, 17 June, Healey visited two parts of the constituency for advertised open meetings. One had a good crowd, the other, Foxgrove, nobody. Polling day, Thursday, yielded a reality to jar on Labour ears with the first result, David Howell's victory at Guildford with a swing of 5.7 per cent. In Healey's own seat, the swing was slightly below the national figure and he was safely returned. But the whole campaign ended succinctly with, 'Bed at dawn after wake at Yorkshire Television.'

It had been one of those elections – 1992 was another – where a consensus forms (part poll figures, part general view), which consensus is cut down by events; with perhaps a sudden shaft of perception – a poll number or a particular speech – suggesting towards the end of the campaign the reversal that is coming. There was no equivalent in 1970 of Neil Kinnock's Sheffield speech, 'Stone cold drunk on words alone', as Donald Dewar put it. It is hard to think that that rather righteous speech by Benn was significant enough to shift the ground. The rotten and rather misleading trade figures may well have been. Or perhaps an election simply reminded people that they disliked the government. The early polls had cheered Labour, as they would in 1992. But while Heath was campaigning in Greenford in Middlesex, he was brought news of the first poll putting the Tories ahead. It seemed to put energy and conviction into the Tory leader. The phrase 'Labour confident, Tories demoralised' had suffered the common chemical shift from triumphalism into irony. The charmless photo-poster which had fixed a frozen glare on voters for three weeks, 'Edward Heath, Man of Principle', suddenly leapt Ruddigore-like from the walls. With a plurality of just under a million votes and a majority overall of 30, one 1930s Balliol man made it to Downing Street.

The chores and forms of defeat had to be accomplished, farewells at the Ministry, a drink with Roy Jenkins, a last meeting of the management committee at Number 10, 'Harold ridiculously undaunted', assorted goodbyes – notably warm ones with the dying Admiral Le Fanu – a Savoy lunch with the Chiefs and, with a final bump, hiring a lorry to shift belongings from Admiralty House to the Healeys' house in Highgate.

Observers of that other surprise Conservative victory in 1992 recognised that the Tory right wing bitterly regretted an inhibition in their ability to quarrel with the leadership – not that they stayed inhibited for long. Defeat in 1970 freed the Labour Party for the contest of blaming and counter-blaming at which it excelled. Policy disputes, over Europe and the measure of socialism to be adopted, and rival cults of personality, Jenkins and Benn, were all now free to blossom like Mao's hundred flowers. The full orchidaceous growth would come only after the *next* defeat, in 1979. But the early part of the Heath government was a good time for practice.

Defeat changed responsibilities. Healey did *not* get the Treasury even in ghostly form. It seemed sensible for Jenkins to stay put as he was placed to catch out an incoming chancellor with his accumulated expertise, something he swiftly did at the expense of Heath himself. Meanwhile Denis was solaced with the shadow form of the long desired Foreign Office. It had the value of involving yet more of the travel to which life, and career, had accustomed him.

He had the sense not to stand for the deputy leadership vacated by George Brown's defeat at Belper. Douglas Houghton's remarks about Healey and the House of Commons not getting on was, to a mild degree, also true of the PLP. He had done little or no politicking, his debating style was instructive and abrasive in equal parts, demonstrating the qualities of a brusque, clever don admired for his grasp of an unpopular subject. His chief claims were negative – those of a non-factionalist – a right-wing non-factionalist. But as, on this occasion, voting would be wholly factional, he did well to avoid the fate of Fred Peart, squeezed to 42 votes by Michael Foot and the winner on 140, Roy Jenkins. Though as Jenkins himself says, the advantage of being deputy leader was felt only by Attlee and Foot, and Foot could have done without it. Getting no joy out of the deputy leadership was, for Denis, a pleasure still to come. However, despite Houghton, Healey was popular enough with the Parliamentary Party to be voted into second place on the ballot for the Shadow Cabinet – behind James Callaghan.

In opposition, the capacity of the Labour Party to give itself a bad time was to be fully tested. A great part of the ordeal would flow from the shift in Tony Benn's thinking, from eclectic idealist devoted to expensive technology to late embracer of the sixties' spirit, whose excesses he would communicate to the seventies. Left-wingery would now take on at least two distinctive forms: hostility to Europe and the rise of a new kind of trade unionism at a time when trade union authority still flourished in the party. Frank Cousins, muddled but half-amenable, had been replaced by the more formidable Jack Jones, a Liverpudlian given the names 'James Larkin' for the Irish firebrand. The affable old Catholic mafioso, Bill Carron, had given way at the Engineers to Hugh Scanlon, Marxist and golfer, a Mancunian of greater good humour, but quite hard enough left to be getting on with. The rise in the early seventies, of the young Arthur Scargill, a shrill Messianist attached to his own dingy star, left these two (and his own bleak Communist outrider, Michael McGahey) looking comfortable.

Europe, which would come to the boil in July 1971, would complicate things even further. There had been argument enough when Wilson and Brown had made Britain's application back in 1967 only to be frustrated by the calcified phobias of General de Gaulle. The grumbling then was sufficiently low-level to make trouble only within the Cabinet. In opposition and with the Conservative Party, as ironically, near uniformity in support, the making of common cause with Heath was impossible. From the point of view of Jenkins, the situation was clear. Going in was the right thing to do. Wilson was essentially in favour; a strong line taken now would carry party and country and make Wilson look and be a statesman in the history books.

Jenkins spoke to him along such lines in May 1971, adding, unwisely, a parallel with Gaitskell over CND (not Gaitskell over Europe). Wilson's career had been devoted to remembering what Gaitskell had done, and not doing it. His predecessor had made an almighty stand of principle over unilateral nuclear disarmament, endured consequent bitter hatreds and won himself an honoured tomb. He had also, over Europe, made a speech of atavistic nationalism recalling the fighting at Vimy Ridge in 1917 and our consequent obligation to New Zealand sheep farmers. Jenkins cherished Gaitskell's memory, and over Europe, entirely disagreed with him. Wilson detested Gaitskell's impassioned making of stands – and over Europe entirely disagreed with him! His compromise was to refuse the stand of principle and accommodate the prejudices. The appliers for membership in 1967 would, on grounds only theologically distinguishable, oppose membership in 1971.

Healey had fewer problems. He never was and never would become 'a good European': application had been a policy submitted to, not embraced, in 1967. He could now see good practical reasons for belonging, but had not become an enthusiast. For Callaghan, this was pure opportunity. He, like Healey, had never been exactly keen, and exposure on his Sussex farm to the low fixes of the CAP had not improved his view (despite the high product prices which they entailed), but in May 1971, he would edge the tiller in a patriotic direction. He spoke of 'a complete rupture of our identity', muttering sepulchrally of 'a French continental-European approach'[26] and invoking 'the language of Chaucer, Shakespeare and Milton' as threatened. 'French,' he said, 'is the dominant language of the community.'[27] This was a strange taking of Gaullist day-dreams at their face value and an attempt to make our cultural flesh creep. This was Jim, the populist, stirring up trouble and putting himself, without further down-payment, into the good books of Jack Jones and Hugh Scanlon. Otherwise the non-leftist anti-EEC stance rested upon a mixture of Atlanticism and English particularism, as well as better arguments like the labyrinth of transfer payments sustaining the Common Agricultural Policy, a thing devised by the French – for the French.

For left-wing opponents, Europe was a capitalist ramp where it wasn't a German plot. It stood barring the way to further and better acts of national-isation. The Americans approved of it. It ran in parallel with NATO. There was a whiff of the priestly cassock about something instigated by the noto-riously Catholic politicians, Monnet and Schuman. The only point of real affinity between Labour rejectionists was a shared exaltation of the Commonwealth, that gilded husk, dear to so many.

Healey was a relatively minor player in all this, oddly echoing the uncer-tainty of his leader, allegedly writing a pro-European article for the *Mirror* one week and speaking against Europe soon after. Healey himself insists that the *Mirror* piece, 'Why I changed my mind', was a balancing of the pro and con cases, described by the *Guardian* as 'by no means euphoric', and that his own position was one of 'If our economy is strong when we go in we should reap a splendid harvest. If it is weak, the shock could be fatal.'[28]

Essentially he identified with Wilson, seeing him now as a reasonable man rightly refusing to disown Europe, as heavy Conference pressure wanted, and confining opposition to this entry *on the terms*, the too willing terms, negotiated by Heath.

It was part of a general reconciliation with Wilson, now a much easier leader to work with. There might be a specific reason for this. Edward Short has his own thoughts on the possible slow inception of Wilson's illness, describing one of the late Cabinets dealing with pre-election policy as being chaotic in the way the most difficult meetings had never been. Wilson, he says was 'a great taker of leaks', fleeing to the bathroom, usually meeting the Cabinet Secretary instead and coming back some time later with a formula for an exhausted Cabinet to embrace. On this occasion he came back with nothing and the Cabinet stayed incoherent. Perhaps, he feels, the mellowing of Wilson and the decline of suspicion were part of some self-knowledge, a perception of the terrible Alzheimer's to come.*

Healey himself mockingly calls his own autobiographical chapter on 1970–74, 'Entr'acte', and at its head, quotes Coleridge's poem 'Limbo', which speaks of

> . . . Time and weary Space . . .
> . . . unmeaning they
> As moonlight on the dial of the day!

But he was still in politics. His standing with the Parliamentary Party yo-yoed. Having come second in the Shadow Cabinet ballot in 1970, he fell to last place in 1971, straightforwardly a withdrawal of pro-EEC votes. He

---

* Conversation with the author.

was however also elected – for the first time – to the NEC. Both advances reflected a degree of respect from colleagues and the complex sub-democratic electorate of the national party. Healey had held the wrong job. He still held a number of wrong opinions. He had made no serious forays into charming his voters. But he was as nearly there on merit as the system permitted.

Some time was spent early on in conversation with John Diebold, a major figure in the pioneering days of computers, who sought Healey as deputy chairman of his company. But the diary is full of unease that any businessman might be in some way dubious and lead him unawares into discredit. This was entirely unfair to Diebold, but there would always be something of the Labour Party puritan about Denis. He was coming round to a more tolerant view, but business never charmed or fascinated him. This would lead him to reject a far grander and more splendidly remunerated place as chairman of Arnold Weinstock's GEC in 1979. Having bought from that company as minister, he thought it wrong to sell for it as ex-minister. Healey's sense of right was so strong that he never needed to talk about ethics. Employment would come instead from journalism, initially from the *Sunday Times*, not then the Murdoch mega-brute, which retained him for a quota of major articles.

Meanwhile, having been made Shadow Foreign Secretary, he meant to enjoy the post, doing what he most enjoyed – going to places, asking questions and finding things out. In September 1970 he went to South Africa, where his main guide would be a South-west African of German, indeed Nazi background, Horst Kleinschmidt, who had become a passionate opponent of apartheid. He met almost at once, and greatly took to, a student leader called Steve Biko who, with a political science lecturer, Rick Turner, undertook a 550-mile trek into Zululand. Biko would be heard of by most people outside South Africa when, in 1979, he was first beaten insensible by prison warders, then thrown in the back of a truck for a hundred-mile trip over rough track to hospital, in consequence of all which he died.

Another encounter would be with Nelson Mandela, then only eight years into his life sentence at the Rivonia trial, the death penalty having been a possibility, and not yet the burnished emblematic figure in Western eyes which he would become. Healey found him fit and surprisingly up to date on outside information. And after passing through a 'Chicago-type white suburb' near to the former gold diggings in central Johannesburg, he visited Soweto, '600,000 to a million in little bungalows scattered on the hills'. He saw '15–22 people in 2–3 room flats' and noted a school population of 93,000 with '7/8 secondary schools'.[29]

But South Africa and China, which Healey also visited and assiduously inspected, were foreign theatres, producers of well-stocked minds in shadow foreign ministers. By contrast, Europe for Labour in 1971, was a sump of hatreds and divisions. The Heath government, weakened by the death a month after its election of Iain Macleod, replaced as Chancellor with the limp Anthony Barber, was committed with very few dissenters to joining the EEC. Heath had talked about 'the full-hearted consent of the British people'. Rhetoric perhaps, but anyone electing Heath as Prime Minister in 1970 knew what they were getting. In fairness, they must also have thought they would be electing a potential reapplier in Wilson. But the word 'referendum' would now come up, inspired not by Sir James Goldsmith but by Tony Benn. Labour would in due course swing against Europe with a peculiar virulence, drawing an unhappy Harold Wilson at its chariot wheels and finally brushing Roy Jenkins into resignation from the deputy leadership.

To lose Macleod, whom one Tory called 'our trumpeter', was to drastically lighten the palette, diminish both ferocity and charm, and leave the Tory Party literal-minded, painstaking and bureaucratic. Jenkins compares him with Joseph Chamberlain, Canning and F. E. Smith, insolent, entertaining, full of adversarial theatre. To lose Jenkins himself was to deprive Labour of his own large talents, wit, literacy *and* numeracy while, ironically, alienating the Gaitskellites on the one issue where Gaitskell would have been against them. The losses left a decelerating Wilson sunk in fuddled agnosticism, with a diminished appetite for politics, fending off the ambition of Callaghan and the strange new sincerities of Tony Benn, in opposition to an Edward Heath as imperious some of the time as he was irresolute for the rest of it.

The French had pressed for, and Heath accepted, mischievous and unfair terms, the most iniquitous of which was the impudent invention of a Common Fishing Policy ultimately ruinous to British inshore fishermen. The bland words of his negotiator, the huffily uncommunicative Geoffrey Rippon, about settling details 'over coffee and cognac', measured the insensibility of the government in its haste to achieve the main aim, the proclaimed vision. This would be balanced by the attitude of much of Labour, and certainly of Healey, that Europe was not a centrally important thing, not worth a row in the party, and that 'vision' was for sissies. The conflict between the two parties' official attitudes would come to resemble a war between astigmatism and myopia.

Healey at this time had swung into utilitarian support of application. Benn, on the same day, describes him as a supporter in principle, though one who thinks entry will generate unpopularity.

> Denis said he didn't think Heath could promote the EEC unless the Tories carry it through the House without Labour support, but if we were going in, the sooner the better because the Government that took us in would lose a general election. Denis said he had changed his view; having been strongly opposed to it before, he was now in favour of entry because if we stayed out we would lose money. We had the problem of coping with Japan and if we were outside any bloc, we really would suffer. Politically, he didn't think it would be significant.

Without drawing breath, he has Healey interestingly concluding that 'There was little prospect of monetary union.'[30]

The explosion on Europe was not foreseen. Wilson had spoken soothingly to a Jenkins who asked him for a free vote in the Commons, saying that he had high hopes of getting the party to support entry and that a free vote was something to fall back on 'at the worst, the very worst'.[31] But the Callaghan speech, French linguistic imperialism and all, frightened Wilson. The leader had been humiliated in office by Callaghan whom he feared in the best Richard II and Bolingbroke sense. The thought of Jim flourishing the national identity like a severed head paralysed him.

The leaders of Labour opinion were strung out along their own complications. Wilson had been convinced since 1967 that entry was sensible. Callaghan was honestly prejudiced against Europe and as honestly ambitious to run the party. Benn was still sympathetic, but was moving left and at odds with the Jenkins group – 'They are genuinely pro-Europe (I give them credit for that), but they also see a last opportunity to do to the Labour Party what they failed to do over disarmament and Clause 4, namely to purge it of its trade union group and of its Left.'[32] Healey had no emotional attachment to Europe and viewed it purely as a market. On a balance of arguments, he favoured entry, but did not think it worth the blazing candle of another great party row.

On top of all this, Benn was fervent for a referendum, desiring it as a good in itself, something with which Healey could hardly have disagreed more. But as the argument continued, one thing became clear to Benn about his leader. After a meeting with Wilson a month after Callaghan's intervention, the younger man was convinced that 'He is totally obsessed with the leadership question now.'[33]

As Heath completed his negotiations, the Labour Party entered a long and embittering wrangle. Party Conference at Brighton 1971 came down massively against Europe. A subsequent meeting of the Parliamentary Party registered 87 supporters of entry into Europe with 157 against. The Shadow Cabinet's official motion to that meeting for rejecting present terms was carried by very similar figures (159:89). And on what really mattered, the taking of a free vote, that liberty was rejected by 140 to 111. The last and most eloquent word came from Charlie Pannell, Healey's colleague from Leeds: 'I can't turn overnight; Europe is an act of faith which has grown and never more strongly than now. It is not for those who have ratted on three-line whips to try and impose one now.'[34] At the Shadow Cabinet meeting preceding it, which Healey described as 'Very bad tempered'[35], Callaghan would be attacked by his oldest and closest friend, someone going back before parliamentary days, Douglas Houghton, a committed European.

Interestingly, Healey's position in this argument would be defined by something else said by Houghton: that Labour's Commons motion should 'assert in principle, but reject terms'. This temporised, but far less disgrace-fully than the final formula, and would have salved many consciences. However, as Healey added bleakly, 'Only *I* agreed!' The issue was now too sulphuric for compromise.

For Wilson, having given Jenkins assurances and been unable to deliver, would turn on the Jenkins group to say that 'he had been wading in shit for 3 months to allow others to indulge their consciences.' Healey in his memoirs approves of this as a judgement of events. But it was a snarled surrender, rough boy language employed from a position of abjection. Healey himself, in a debate back in July, had been guilty of similar truculent weakness, saying that 'we were entering the Market on the basis of information as false as that which had led the Americans into the Vietnam War.'[36]

As he acknowledged to himself, 'Speech went badly – fell between stools.'[37] Tony Benn, not a malicious commentator, described it as 'the most awful speech'. Healey's trouble over Europe was not a return of his hostility to the whole idea of five years earlier, nor that he was being uncomplicatedly opportunistic. He was being weak. He had made his support for entry on candid business grounds. He had also spoken very realistically of supporting businessmen and recognising the need for profits, not natural Labourspeak in 1970. But faced with a terrible fight, he would argue for party unity on the opponents' terms. He despised Harold Wilson, but in the conduct of this struggle, it was harder than it should have been to distinguish him from Harold Wilson.

To state the obvious, Europe fragmented the Labour right. The element identified with strong defence, the American connection and cool about further nationalisation, which had combined with social liberals and constitutional reformers, would falter because a sufficiently large piece of its membership, mostly, but not exclusively, working class and union-connected, followed Callaghan into opposition over entry. The bottomless stupidity of partisanship also meant that entry achieved by a Conservative government seemed tainted to people ready to swallow entry by Labour. And the requirements of regi-mental discipline, putting the party first, completed the operation.

The gainers from the fight were the left, almost uniform in their abhor-rence of foreign capitalist conspiracies. 'Frank Allaun talked of the untold misery if the Government went in.'[38] Such people enjoyed new union back-ing under new union leaders. Victory over the Castle bill had demonstrated that strength, and frightening vituperation over the coming Conservative industrial relations legislation would demonstrate it again. They had acquired winning-side psychology at the very moment when their opponents in the party had split.

But the Commons vote on entry was a rebelling issue. Forced beneath a three-line whip when Heath had declared a (rather bogus) free vote for the Tories, 69 pro-Europeans voted in favour and 20 abstained. Following the party's intestinal line, they would have defeated the legislation by a margin of 46. It was an issue of party against principle. Lips were curled on all sides. Party colleagues of the day before were now 'rats' and 'traitors', epithets exchangeable with 'hacks' and 'lobby fodder'.

For the moment, the fabric of the right held up. Benn, in whom ambition appears like temptation in a morality play, had stood for the deputy leadership against Jenkins in October 1971, winning only 46 votes. But a Shadow Cabinet in March (Healey absent abroad) proposed a Commons motion calling for a referendum. It would later carry only narrowly in the PLP, but in the Easter recess Jenkins resigned. He was most influenced by Wilson's having supported the motion and generally shown himself willing to join whatever he couldn't beat. This would be the main distinction (on many issues) between men of moderate outlook. And, beyond the issue of Europe, it would occur throughout the rest of opposition and after 1979 when the protection of office was lifted again. Benn was surfing on the new left-wing wave; others, Wilson and Healey among them, looked out at the tide, deploring it, hoping for a turn and getting splashed.

The effect of all this in low political terms was to occasion a reshuffle, magical or otherwise. With Jenkins withdrawing, his Treasury brief would be taken by Healey, while the Foreign Office job would pass to Callaghan. In even lower terms, Callaghan, without specifically trying, had brought about the elimination of Jenkins from the Labour Party game. The deputy leadership he vacated would be one quarrel avoided. The surprise but sensible winner, Edward Short, has his own judgement. Healey and Callaghan were the obvious contenders.

> They knew this, but they also knew that Tony C and Michael F were only a short way behind. Whoever won the Deputy Leadership would have a head start when the Leadership became vacant. It was therefore in both their interests to ensure that there was a candidate who could beat Foot and Crosland but who would not be a candidate when Harold went. I believe that they colluded (but I have no proof!) to persuade me to stand. This I did – with hindsight rather foolhardily – and won.*

The departure of Roy Jenkins was compounded by the more drastic departure of his close friend (and once Healey's PPS), Dick Taverne. Taverne, outspoken, unfootsoldierly, was also a devoted European; and, literally, a Dutchman, he was a damned foreigner anyway. He was to have been the first notable prospective victim of a new initiative by the left – to get rid of right-wing and/or pro-European MPs. In Healey's Transport

---

* Letter to the author.

House days there had existed, ironically for deployment against local parties too sympathetic to Stalin, a form of central command politics. Healey had instigated its use against the Nenni telegram-senders. One of Wilson's measures, not so much libertarian as currying left-wing favour, had been to discontinue this approach as he ended the Prescribed List for candidates.

In principle, this should have oxygenated politics. In practice, it laid local parties open to alliances of local union hard left and new junior zealots with a gift for the interminable. Meetings prolonged past midnight helped shed an already ageing and tiring normal membership, and the now radicalised parties turned their attention to a clean-out of 'right-wing MPs'. Taverne made a stand against this and because of his decisive action, the project never quite took off. For when his local party in Lincoln deselected him, Taverne, with no back-stop support from a depressed and disempowered headquarters, coolly resigned from parliament, precipitating a by-election in which he would stand.

The flaw in the constituency parties' claim that they represented democratic autonomy was that they were commonly more hermetically sealed-off from the working and voting world even than Transport House. They were democratic in terms only of very small arithmetic. Taverne pitched at the voters of Lincoln over the heads of the party and, in passing, shrugged off the polite restraints which party membership had imposed. He described Harold Wilson with painful precision as 'the past master of the pre-emptive cringe'. Lincoln led to much dutiful hoop-jumping by MPs on behalf of the official candidate, an unimpressive character called John Dilks. The Chief Whip, Robert Mellish, himself crudely right-wing, tried to make the entire Parliamentary Party put in an attendance. Some refused, more came sheepishly. At the top, Healey, the good party man, made a robust appearance for the official nominee. Tony Benn, outraged to have the by-election sprung during Party Conference, responded with words encouraging newspaper liftmen to exercise censorship against editorialists supporting such treason. It was not a wise intervention.

Roy Jenkins, as he puts it, 'had to go to ground like a skulking fox',[39] but to Lincoln he did not go. And Taverne won a smashing victory in March 1973, turning his 4000 official majority of 1970 into one of 13,000.* The rift within Labour ran blood and, specifically, the weakness with which Wilson had straddled and appeased was put under a bright light. The quarrels of eight years on were being vividly rehearsed.

Meanwhile Labour would accept Benn's referendum on Europe as policy,

---

* This victory would fail to stick over the next two years only because Taverne would be faced, freakishly, with two general elections, always worse for rebels, across eight months. He was finally defeated in his third contest by a Miss Margaret Jackson who, as Mrs Margaret Beckett, became a strong supporter of Europe and a member of Mr Blair's Cabinet.

if elected, and would furiously oppose Conservative legislation on industrial relations. It could hardly have been otherwise. The defeat suffered in 1969 over *In Place of Strife* had determined all thinking on the subject. But the union-organised opposition was brutal, public and ugly. Labour MPs trailed behind, dancing or slinking according to their wisdom. At the marches and street demonstrations, echoing the chant 'Kill the Bill, Kill the Bill', its leaders looked like captives at a Roman triumph.

43

THE DESCENT TO FEBRUARY 1974

If Edward Heath had been a skilled politician, he might well have pushed Labour into opposition for three parliaments. They were, in their favourite word, 'demoralised'; he was doing something inherently popular. His industrial relations legislation was directed at modest restraints on a union power very widely resented, not least by working-class women. It might have been more skilfully drafted, avoiding penal clauses whose enforcement would make martyrs, but the real failure was one of nerve. Iain Macleod was never more missed.

Good ministers like Robert Carr and Lord Carrington, Healey's successor at Defence, could be quietly persuasive. But Heath himself would start with the frozen bumptiousness of a functionary expecting compliance and, when denied, would look around for ways out. Compromise can be a civil service virtue. In the strip cartoon of adversarial politics, it is read as the first step to climb-down. Tough but rational policies, like the closing of the bankrupt Govan shipyard, were fled from as if no one was watching, as if no one perceived the weakness displayed.

For a period from the late sixties to the early eighties, government, all government, would grant political precedence to trade union power because that power was exercised with the confidence which wins. Healey had watched Wilson losing one fight; he now, as Shadow Chancellor, saw Heath losing another. He would inherit the Treasury at a time when the primacy within the British state of craft and labour organisers was received wisdom. As Heath by juddering degrees wasted a golden opportunity, nobody grew re-enamoured of the Labour Party. A by-election was won at the expense of the sitting Tories at Bromsgrove in 1971. But Labour would not actually gain another seat in an election until Fulham in 1986.

Rarely have an opposition and a government failed in parallel so comprehensively, the quarrels of the one offsetting the blunders of the other. But the Conservatives made their mistakes in government, which is usually the more important place. Heath's abrupt flight from the Selsdon Park principles had been nothing if not wholehearted. The Chancellor, Anthony Barber, a man of private quality and fair mind, was not a strong personality. Shifted by Macleod's death from entry negotiations in Brussels to the Chancellorship, he would essentially be a non-arguing-back minister under whom the Treasury retreated from its customary role of command or at any rate denial.

And the Heath government, after that Selsdon phase, tended ever more in the direction of solving problems through expansion, concluding with its own version of Reginald Maudling's 'dash for growth' policies of 1962–4. Heath would seek 'to prove what Maudling and [Sir William] Armstrong had been unable, or not given time, to prove, that a massive reflation could bring the era of Stop–Go to an end'.[1]

The entire post-war culture assumed very high to full employment with the same lazy habituation that the pre-war culture had accepted a very high (and little compensated) disemployment during the troughs of the remorseless cycle. With unemployment reaching 900,000 in October 1971, Barber adopted a Bank of England document, *Competition and Credit Control*, in November. It involved principally a major increase in the money supply. Despite the statistics, the National Union of Mineworkers broke with post-war precedent and struck, essentially, for primacy among public sector workers. After six weeks, and humiliatingly, it won, and a jeering and enraged young official called Arthur Scargill made his name. A succession of spuriously judicial settlements, usually headed by the benign non-economist, the Lord of Appeal, Lord Wilberforce, began its desolating course. The government surrendered, next, to a creation of the Labour government, a bankrupt Tony Benn fix, an unreal agglomerate called Upper Clyde Shipbuilders. Ministers surrendered, spending large quantities of money, at least in part because the Chief Constable of Glasgow thought that necessary to maintain public order.

The Heath government, despite bursts of unreal optimism, lived in acute fear, widely shared, of national breakdown. There was hysteria in the air. The economy had dragged its slow length for years, the puerile violence of the student revolts faced supercession by the adult violence of men in heavy boots. The notion of telling the public that it was mightily over-employed and must expect a major fall in job numbers was so fearful a thing that all impulse, if not all sense, was for evading it, for the economic equivalent of hiding under the bedclothes.

Heath was not alone in his belief that 'massive' (his favourite word) expansion, involving as massive an increase in public expenditure, was the answer. The major newspapers agreed with him and indeed worried at his caution. The Labour Opposition agreed with him. Labour had made great play in 1964–6 about the deficit which Maudling had left them, but they had never had bad feelings about 'the dash for growth'. In a wistful sort of way, it was their sort of thing, but wisely, they had never dared try it. And with rare exceptions like Sir Donald MacDougall, few economists were signalling to Heath to stop. Growth was to do all – by way of a floating currency, by way of deliberate spending plans like the grotesque local government reorganisation of Peter Walker, by tax cuts, by regional grants and (more sensibly) written-off depreciation of plant.

Barber's recurring proclamation that breakneck expansion would produce 5 per cent growth for eighteen months represented a body-swerve round gravity for which all – miners, investors, manufacturers and government ministers – should have prizes. When Heath/Barber got it hopelessly wrong, they got it hopelessly wrong in the best and widest of company. In fact, the balance of payments began to deteriorate badly and the borrowing requirement, the PSBR, swelled up by the time of Barber's 1973 Budget to £4423 million.

There would be a body of criticism beyond Enoch Powell, magnificently right about the economics but distorted with personal hatred for Heath, Europe, America and piccaninnies. But the judgements of people like Samuel Britten and Peter Jay would come a little later, and the Chancellor hearing them would be Denis Healey. The chief critic of Heath's economics would be Macmillan's old friend, events. The dollar was devalued and more American protection applied, commodity prices went up with a single grim consequence. Inflation took off anyway, but was mightily reinforced by that consequence: the decision of the oil producers to respond to a vast growth in demand by putting up the price fourfold. This meant that 'in 1974 Britain would be paying £2.5 billion more for 5 per cent less oil than had been imported in 1973.'[2] By November 1973, the deficit on the balance of payments projected by the National Institute for Economic Affairs for the year ahead had worsened from £350 million, its August forecast, to £2100 million![3] Healey had written an article for the Sunday Times in June 1973 prophesying a major rise in oil prices and had been sacked from his retainer and the piece spiked for its absurdity.

But despite this felicitous perception, Healey himself was struggling. He was, like Chancellor and Prime Minister, without economic training. He had the assumptions of the economically enlightened, Gaitskell, Wilson, Crosland and Jenkins, but not the full doctrine. This would help him later as Chancellor to ditch a Keynes in whom he had not been brought up in faith at the seminary. But for the moment, he was treading water uneasily. His speech to the Commons on 19 December 1973 was very far from the masterful swings round the houses regularly given on Defence. He did not come to terms with the inflation nor the horrendous slippage in the balance of payments. He concentrated on Barber's cuts, the true point about which was that they came after monstrous unreasoning spending and that after such expansion, abrupt economies carried no more conviction than a forlorn incomes policy.

Instead Healey stuck with the pain and suffering, criticising Barber for making them at all, and made a great issue of a highly disputed claim that there might have been a shortfall of 1.5 billion in the government's expenditure. And he turned readily to the solutions of the 1940s. We needed to reduce our consumption of Arab oil, so why wasn't the Chancellor rationing it? He posited 'manpower shortages in vital industries as justification for exceptional increases in wages'.[4] This was what the TUC were effectively saying, but only thinkable as a short-term way off the incomes policy hook. There was no question of criticising the hook. And Healey echoed his call in the 1940s for stern measures against expenditure on corrupt imported Camembert. He announced, 'The Chancellor could have increased taxes on luxuries such as fur coats, wines and brandy to subsidise the basic foods.'[5]

This and a list of anti-middle-class tax measures was pretty desperate stuff, missing both the main economic point and the depth of the crisis for a haze of broad-brush schmaltz. He ended with a charge that Barber wished 'to fight the next war against the working people of this country'. This was nonsense, as the standard Labour and trade union abuse of Heath always had been. Heath both felt sympathy for, and was afraid of, the British working class. He had failed all right, but failed by carrying Labour measures beyond the point where sensible Labour people were willing to carry them. He had employed precisely the Keynesian principles which Labour politicians had made their own.

He was, though, applying them as Keynes would never have done, near the top of the cycle. If he was blaming the NUM for behaving like organised labour at the end of an unsuccessful incomes policy, Heath did so after sustained over-spending undertaken as an alternative to an assault on gross over-manning. As an argument, Healey's was unworthy and not sufficiently above the characterisation of the Prime Minister by the drunken Scottish miners' leader, Lawrence Daly, as 'Benito Heath'.

It was not long before Peter Jay in *The Times* would quote Matthew Arnold's 'Dover Beach', a great and beautiful poem on the long lapsing of Christian faith, marking its 'melancholy, long, withdrawing roar'. That was happening now to Keynsianism which Heath, as sorcerer's apprentice, was misapplying to destruction. Healey, for all his bounce, is truthful about himself. His comment is harder than anything said here: 'my response to Barber's package of spending cuts in December 1973 was so stumbling and inadequate that many of the colleagues wondered whether I was up to the job.'[6] He was showing both the self-knowledge to recognise failure and the aptitude for quick, fierce study, and on 6 February, the day the election was formally called, he would speak again with quite different grasp and effect.

The steps to crisis and election were plain enough. All incomes policies enjoy early success in the rigid phase, all are vulnerable to invalidation with renewed flexibility. A freeze works against one cause of inflation, wages, but not, at once, on the symptom, prices. And as prices continue rising, it ceases to work against wages. Wage earners come out of freezes hungry and difficult. Heath and Barber achieved explosion.

The NUM, its councils dominated by Scargill, now President in Yorkshire, celebrated a year of incomes policy by demanding an increase of 35 per cent. Fighting it meant another unprepared war which the miners would win, precipitating equivalent increases all round in the public sector. The TUC tried to rescue Heath. The NUM claim, if granted, would, against all union practice, not be used by other major unions as a precedent for their own claims. Switching from soft to hard as an assertion of pride, also of reasonable doubt that the TUC could deliver, Barber and Heath rejected this and, to conserve the fuel they had not stockpiled, put the country on a three-day week. A miners' strike was voted by pithead ballot to commence on 31 January 1974. Anthony Barber, addressing the Commons, spoke of preserving government of our affairs 'by the rule of reason, by the rule of Parliament and by the rule of democracy', seeing as the alternative, 'chaos, anarchy and a totalitarian or Communist regime'.[7]

The government's only remaining card was an appeal to the country in this spirit. In fact, that government must in all circumstances, including a renewed mandate, have let a big increase through, breaking the terms of its parliamentarily anointed incomes policy. But with that mandate, it might have managed a longer-term picking up of the scattered pieces – in politicians' rhetoric, clearing up the mess they themselves had left behind. The election was first proposed for 7 February, and if Heath had stuck to it he must have won. He had to make his chosen issue credible and immediate. No one asking 'Who governs Britain?' could afford to create the time in which to half-answer the question with further concessions and the words 'Well, not me.'

Heath would be accused by Labour and Enoch Powell alike with invoking a bogus question to win an election in a niche of opportunity. That overstates Heath's guile and his intellectual grasp. Enoch Powell would charge fraud, but it wasn't fraud, it was fumble. Heath had uncomprehendingly summoned up an inflation which could turn into hyperinflation. This had both provoked and armed the unions. He had genuinely sought conciliation with workers by way of the very inflation in which Scargill swam. He was engaged in a struggle to the death with the consequences of his own actions. But it would take a brighter and more resolute man than Heath, cynically and with open eyes, to play that conflict through for a victory to be betrayed at leisure. He did the commonplace wrong thing; he compromised, was seen to compromise and came slowly to a political stop.

The election itself was tragi-comedy. The poll postponed in weakness to 28 February, the campaign began on 6 February with a fall in the stock market to *below* 300! Sterling fell at the same time, but the first polls of the campaign taken by the *Daily Telegraph* on 7 February gave the Tories a three point lead: 42.5 per cent to Labour's 39.5. Into which numbers leapt the taut, intense, flashing-eyed person of Enoch Powell.

'Mr Powell will not stand in "an essentially fraudulent election",' read the headline. The object, said the speech, 'of those who have called it is to secure the electorate's approval for a position which the government itself knows is untenable in order to make it easier to abandon that position subsequently'.[8] Like so much of what Powell said, it was a brilliant part-truth with the essential part missing. His renunciation of his seat came on the same day as an NOP poll showing the Tories nine points ahead. The Labour leader entered the campaign proper in Wales: 'Riotous welcome for Mr Wilson in Cardiff'.[9] It can hardly have been for his message. Wilson was quoted as calling for a fresh start. As inconsequentially, Norman St John Stevas, shadow Arts Minister, said in Dover that the 'Tories have become the party of the beautiful people. For the stronghold of the philistines – look to the ranks of our opponents.'[10] Meanwhile a voter in Lincoln expressed relief at the Tory candidate against Dick Taverne this time *not* being Jonathan Guinness who had stood, calamitously, at the by-election.[11] He was 'dreadful. Made you feel he would hang the serfs from the castle walls if he could.'

Two statements on the economy complemented one another. Enoch Powell said that in 1972 'we set out upon a course of causing inflation because we decided wrongly that it was politically more advantageous to maintain and increase the going rate of inflation.' James Paget, a 58-year-old miner, told Tony Benn campaigning in Burnley, that people like himself had 'more than kept up with the standard of living'. They were better off than under Labour.

Healey, with the Treasury in anxious view, intervened with prophecies of incendiary inflation. 'The news you have just been learning about from last month's price increases means that your cost of living will go up 25 per cent this year if you send the Conservatives back.'[12] In an election of strong assertions which string together like a necklace of non-sequiturs, Heath spoke next about strength. 'Mr Heath insists that strong government is main issue,'[13] said *The Times* headline, reporting a photo-opportunity with beer glasses that weekend in the bar of the Plough Inn, Cadsden, near Chequers. In Portugal, which had had strong government since 1932, the Prime Minister, Dr Marcello Caetano, cited the words of his mentor, Dr Antonio Salazar: 'There is no strong state where the government is not strong.'[14] Dr Salazar had been dictator of Portugal for forty years and any comparison with Mr Heath, blamelessly constitutional and fizzling out after three years and seven months, would be profoundly unfair, but his own shoulder-padded rhetoric invited unfairness.

On the Monday next, Denis Healey squeezed the rich until the pips squeaked. That is the form in which his speech has been passed around political company. In fact he started by talking about the profits made in food retailing. Harold Wilson, ambling half-heartedly round a supermarket, had claimed to have broken a finger-nail on the triple layer of price stickers on a tin of beans. It was a flash of the dazzling old Wilson of 1963–4, the superlative Leader of the Opposition. Healey joined in, saying that he would act over the profits made 'by food manufacturers and retailers', before undertaking to 'squeeze the *property speculators* until the pips squeak'.[15] He took aim at Lord Carrington who 'had made £10 million profit selling land at 30–60 times its price as agricultural land'. Healey also promised 'to wring the neck of the Housing Finance act'.[16] It was all high-class Healey Beelzebub, but not a prelude to the guillotine in Trafalgar Square.

As the election campaign developed, Powell's vivid presence allowed the EEC to be raised on the right when he agreed to speak for an organisation demanding withdrawal. But Powell used this platform to urge voters to vote Labour. Powell would hardly have acted as he did – in the teeth of his own interests – if he had not thought that the Labour leader would stick with anti-Europeanism. To do so, even in his decline, was to underestimate Harold Wilson. He also thought the Conservatives would win the election. Even though Joe Coral thought so too – odds 22 February, Conservatives 3:1; Labour 7:1[17] – he was plain wrong. Much more to the point were the figures released three days before Election Day, a trade deficit of £383 million which *The Times* remarked as 'the largest monthly trade deficit that Britain has known'.[18] Callaghan, in a mood of sincere and characteristic pessimism, caught the dark mood very well. 'Britain is punch drunk,' he told a meeting.

Healey's own part in the election involved the heaviest national commitments he had yet taken on and correspondingly less time in Leeds. He started in Wales: Bridgend, 'very useful meeting 150',[19] then Ogmore, did the *Today* programme with Geoffrey Howe on the Monday, following it with an hour's programme encountering Robin Day before, on the Wednesday, 'very long day indeed', when he did the formal TV reply to the Chancellor's speech, went to his own adoption meeting in Leeds, saw *The Times* correspondent and came back (sleeping badly) overnight. Next day he shared a press conference with Wilson, did interviews with a Canadian commentator and Belgian TV. Sunday involved *Weekend World* and a debate with Barber, then Shropshire to speak in Labour's only local seat, the Wrekin, and win a standing ovation, draw breath and be interviewed by Austin Mitchell, before concluding with a 'good meeting'[20] at Wolverhampton.

Monday took him to a poorly attended meeting at Wellingborough, more TV, then on to Lincoln. 'Looked at Cathedral,' he notes tourist-wise, 'had tea at White Hart',[21] finally rounding up speaking for Ted Bishop at Newark. Either Healey or Transport House failed to insist from the start on three-day runs on a given circuit with local accommodation booked. Perhaps under the stress, Denis's comments grow less and less *simpatico*. One not-to-be-named candidate, a woman, is described as 'revolting',[22] another as 'typical local Irish bullshitter'. But at his next venture, Ipswich, visited immediately, the candidate may be identified. He was 'nice Ken Weekes!'

After this, Healey went on to Braintree for the well-known journalist, Keith Kyle, neither damned nor blessed as candidate, and another five rounds with Robin Day, then on to Castle Bromwich and Yardley, and be interviewed by Irish TV, 'dull'! He moved easily on to Manchester, and a pitch at the seat held in the vacant name of Winston Churchill by his grandson and an interview – with James Bellini – before going to speak for the two Stockport MPs. He also managed a reconnaissance at the Midland Hotel with Joel Barnett, soon to be his chief lieutenant at the Treasury, and a phone conversation with Harold Wilson. The 23rd being a Saturday, this had to be North Wales, Bangor and Connah's Quay, then Flint for Barry Jones, later his PPS.

The week of the poll took him to Dover, Rochester and Gravesend: 'V. good meeting'.[23] The next day, though spent in Leeds accompanied by Edna and Cressida, was dominated by the dreadful trade figures, worst ever seen, upon which the Shadow Chancellor fell and devoured. Healey came together with Jenkins as a Treasury double for the party's press conference, as well as doing yet another TV debate with Geoffrey Howe and Nancy Sear, the Liberal Party's Lady Violet substitute. Polling Day itself was the usual round of the polling stations, a ritual serving politicians in the office of a cargo cult.

Healey's last contribution to the contest had been bitter beyond his normal punishing style. Heath's phrase 'Who governs Britain?', while it begged the question of who had made it so much harder to govern, meant extensive focus on the union leaders, some of whom, like Arthur Scargill, were genuine extremists. Healey blazed at Heath for waging a campaign of 'the worst, most corrosive emotion, based upon fear and hatred of the miners'. It reminded him of Churchill's wild speech of 1945, the one comparing Labour with the Gestapo. The problem, he ended, was economic, not military. Despite Joe Coral and Dr Caetano, it chimed in with the public view. Healey himself would have a majority of 10,500 in the poll which, on 28 February, reduced the Conservative vote by more than 1.2 million while docking that for Labour by only 500,000.

With 301 seats to the Conservatives' 297, Labour had won a contest by reason of its unpopularity growing more slowly.

44

THE TREASURY –
GETTING IT WRONG 1974–5

In a drawer in the long attic of the Healeys' Sussex home is an impressive state document, dated 5 March 1974. In it, Elizabeth the Second withdraws the licence of her 'trusty and well beloved Counsellor Anthony Perrinott Lysberg Barber'. Instead, 'Our especial Grace trusting in the wisdom and fidelity of Our right trusty and well beloved Counsellor Denis Winston Healey' . . . she 'by these Presents constitute and appoint him to be Our CHANCELLOR AND UNDER TREASURER OF THE EXCHEQUER'.

Parchment, the royal seal and words of glittering mystical anachronism proclaim Harold Wilson's choice of Finance Minister after the electorate had made its own narrow and hesitant selection of Harold Wilson as Prime Minister. Another document tells us the central assumption of the political class about its age. Dated October 1973, six months earlier, in Heath and Barber's time, it is the guest list for the *Financial Times*'s dinner in honour of Victor Feather. The chairmen of a dozen major companies, Cabinet ministers, Permanent Under-Secretaries, the Chiefs of the Defence Staff, the better sort of editor and the Director-General of the CBI are gathered in respect.

Now it would clearly be wrong in a society now less stuffily class-conscious and more respectful of workers and their leaders, actually to object to the honouring of the genial-sardonic and widely popular Yorkshireman who was General Secretary of the Trades Union Congress. But this gathering marked, not civility but the balance of economic and political power. Tony Benn remarks Mr Feather's view of ex-ministers: 'Vic has absolutely no time for politicians, especially former members of a Labour Cabinet, and it is hard not to be insulted by him . . . as far as Vic is concerned, a Minister and certainly a Labour Minister is no more than an MP who has got somewhere.'[1]

Such confidence was perfectly warranted. The long ascent of the trade unions through the fifties and sixties when 'industrial action', as it was respectfully called, had been steadily successful in getting what was wanted, was not in dispute. By 1973 a newspaper's Labour or union correspondent was called the 'Industrial Correspondent'. They drank deeply with general secretaries and could assure colleagues, with some complacency, of any move in business towards greater efficiency or better production, that 'Jack (or Hughie) won't stand for it.' Tony Benn took note after talking with Feather, that as a Cabinet minister he would not now be able to visit strikes. That dinner, attracting the cream and essence of civil service, private industry and a Tory Cabinet, said the same thing.

Ted Heath had tried to impose statutory pay policy on the unions, had also tried a non-interventionist free market approach and had been humiliated beyond the wont of the unluckiest governments. His laws, mandated by the electorate to whom they had been set out before the polls, had been rejected, ignored, marched against and, in all but form, destroyed. The general view of Labour politicians was that Ted had simply failed to be political. To be political translated as being realistic, cynical, avoiding the fights one was certain to lose, being, if you like, weak, but at least being weak pre-emptively. In this sense, Wilson was going to be very political indeed.

As for Healey, according to Roy Jenkins, he became Chancellor only after a weekend hiatus in which Jenkins had been told, via Marcia Williams and Terence Lancaster of the *People*, that his appointment was the Prime Minister's 'own unforced desire'. However Bernard Donoughue, the political academic who would head a 'political unit' serving Wilson, rang to relay Wilson's message 'that he had been unable to break the Healey/Callaghan matrix' so would Roy like to be Home Secretary again?

Jenkins, reasonably enough, sees himself as readier to take hard and necessary lines. That is not to be doubted, but together with the defensive trench dug between him and his friends and the rest of the Labour Party, such readiness was a reason why he would not be appointed. Wilson was dithery, unwell, already informing intimates of his intention to stay for only two years, and probably in early mental decline. But he was not going, by way of strident assertion, to make the mistakes of 'Edward Heath, Man of Principle'. Healey, though not primarily a politician, was shrewd enough to go in the same direction. Ironically, where Heath had declined from a firm stand almost to the liquidation of all purpose, Healey, serving Wilson then Callaghan, would move from soft to hard. And before they were through, Victor Feather's most powerful colleagues would be showing those nonentities, Labour Cabinet ministers, a degree of accommodation not dreamt of in 1974.

The team which Healey gathered around him at the Treasury, where ironically he worked out of the Air Force Board Room, was made up of clever men. Edmund Dell, who had served in the earlier Wilson government both at Trade and, under Benn, at Technology, would be the first and most consistent voice in favour of what turned out to be the right answer. This was to be as little political as possible and as much economic, prejudiced as it were in favour of solvency. He was thus noted as the most right-wing member of the government, unwearyingly lucid Magog against Tony Benn's visionary Gog. That conflict, unnerving as it must have been within the Cabinet Room, is part of the excitement and energy which marked these years: government under huge external pressures certainly, but government also by argument. Dell also had a residual touch of old Communist's taste for hard categories, saved or damned, not entirely unlike Healey.

Also in the Cabinet and, if not in the Treasury, certainly dancing all around it, was Harold Lever, Chancellor of the Duchy. Few politicians have been as much liked, even loved, by colleagues including civil servants, as Lever. He was rich but had the good humour rather than the pride of wealth. He was easily and comfortably clever, entirely kind and charitable, gifted to gain friendship, something which extended to the left who theoretically disapproved of his business background but couldn't get angry with him. He had also become exceptionally close to Harold Wilson.

The difficulty with Lever is that 'the opinions he held and the influence he exerted, were inappropriate in the circumstances of 1974.'[2] Lever was a fixer. His fixes made him a friend to new public expenditure, which he could so often see ways of paying for. He was called right-wing because he disliked inflation and understood business objectives, but his fixes were all forms of sophisticated borrowing. The crisis, which Labour had inherited and now proposed to nourish, required a sustained course of not spending and not borrowing. Lever favoured painless methods and, outside a delusively cheerful interim, there were none. He would finish on the reforming side, but for some time he would facilitate further travelling down (and down it was) the wrong track.

Joel Barnett, the Chief Secretary, was another agreeable, able man with lines to business. With the new Minister of State, Robert Sheldon, he had made up a triumvirate with Dell in their days in Manchester running a political Coffee House, and he shared the general optimism, if not the full sunshine economics, of Lever. He had the agreeable contradictions of a soft-hearted accountant

At the Treasury, key civil servants included Derek Mitchell who would develop into the most market-minded of civil servants. Douglas Wass was a natural Keynesian and would be sympathetic, in the face of crisis, to a strong devaluation. Leo Pliatzky, yet another Mancunian, would much later make the simple and devastating discovery that the Treasury had been over-counting its debts. This was something which, amid shoals of heroic departmental errors, floating now into spurious deficit and a credit quite as bogus, had required Chancellor, Cabinet, the City and creditors to get things wrong in all sorts of amusing and terrifying ways.

Argument would be conducted at a high and expert level, with Dell the first and clearest voice for a hard and early striking line. For much of the time that debate was one between him and Lever with, as Dell says about one occasion, 'Joel Barnett cheering on Harold and Bank officials cheering me on. Denis Healey maintained an impartial chairmanship.'[3]

The Labour Party would not face a Treasury united for arguing back. The Treasury, after all, had not mounted any very strong resistance to the Heath/Barber policy of open-road inflation. The post-devaluation period, 1968–72, showed spending power up by 17 per cent. Output per man on the slightly longer period from 1967 to 1972 was up 15 per cent, and following the 1967 devaluation, output overall up by 13 per cent, with the working population for the same five-year period down by 1 per cent and employment by 2 per cent.[4] The increase in output per man was appreciably superior to that for 1961–6. If not brilliant, none of this was worrying. But as the last years also showed, the rate of strikes, increasing steeply from the mid-sixties until they hit a record figure in 1971, constituted even greater reasons for caution – reasons, too, for fearful avoidance of unpopular courage. Psychologically, things had to get worse before they could begin to get better. They did.

One might have expected the Treasury and Healey to be much more fearful of any sort of expansion than they were. In fact, the Treasury would offer up in early June 1974 two policy options. The optimistic Case 1 favoured growth at the expense of the balance of payments. Case 2 meant taking action earlier and rather more drastically. Healey went for Case 1 to serve the preoccupying purpose of growth. He met with no direct opposition from the company. Only Dell argued back, and when the most junior figure present, Christopher France, told him later that he shared his unease, Mitchell remarked that when the minister's mind was made up, it would have done no good to have intervened.[5]

A fear would soon be expressed by another civil servant, Sir Douglas Henley and by Mitchell that borrowing, made apparently easy by the coming availability of North Sea oil, would encourage 'the Government to take the most cowardly position on this and allow things to drift'.[6] Dell favoured a Case 3, doing yet more to speed adverse payments back towards balance. The left were full of horror stories about how the Treasury embraced and seduced new chancellors, yet here they were weakly offering a softer option to a policy already under-strength. 'I wished,' said Dell, 'the Treasury reputation corresponded with Treasury performance.'[7]

Labour was trying to reconcile many things. It had inherited a wage explosion, that 31½ per cent demand by miners and all the contingent public sector wage awards, the quadrupling of the price of oil by OPEC, which had made grief for the Heath government and, softly waiting, a general condition of deficit to which markets, currently quiescent, would eventually react. At the same time, the leadership, losing control of its domestic policy-making machinery, had set itself perfectly absurd objectives.

Before the election, on 13 May 1973 at one of its most calamitous NEC meetings ever, no small compliment, Labour had opted for the creation of a National Enterprise Board which should superintend the nationalisation of twenty-five leading British companies. The outcome of the debate had seemed clear. Lever, Crosland and Shirley Williams had argued at the joint affair that the whole thing was suicidal. But two eccentric switches caused a crazy motion to be carried. Unfortunately one member, John Chalmers, switched from opposition to abstention. And worse, among the accredited safe right-wingers was John Cartwright MP from the Co-op. In scorning the proposal generally, Healey had asked – and the quip is often quoted without awareness of its horrendous context – if comrades wanted Marks & Spencer to be run like the Co-op? (This was before Sir Richard Greenbury.)

It was the sort of rumbustious tactlessness familiar enough in Healey, but the reaction of Cartwright, a future defector to the SDP, to vote for an off-trolley left-wing motion out of bruised self-esteem was puerility. Harold Wilson, who had talked about using a veto against the idea later, had flinched from actually voting himself. He would however succeed, at the grim 1973 Party Conference, in having the specific motion mysteriously lost by procedural manoeuvre. But Labour remained, against its leaders' judgement, in favour of extensive but unspecified nationalisation.

It was also the prisoner of something called the 'Social Contract'. The phrase of Jean-Jacques Rousseau became as official policy a triumph of rhetoric over arithmetic. Labour knew about wage inflation. This was the inflation that dare not speak its name. But Labour claimed in relation to the unions what British governments of all colours do in respect of the United States: a special relationship.

An agreement between Labour Party and TUC offered a 'strategy covering a wide area of the social and economic life of the nation: food subsidies, price controls, housing and rents, transport and a redistribution of income and wealth combined with a policy for increasing investment in industry'.[8] All this was supposed, in the document's own boiled prose, to 'engender the strong feeling of mutual confidence which is necessary to control inflation and achieve sustained growth in the standard of living'. Elsewhere Denis Healey would quote ruefully the opinion of Joseph Schumpeter: 'the real problem is labour . . . Unless socialisation is to spell economic breakdown, a socialising government cannot possibly tolerate present trade union practice . . . As things actually are, labour is of all things the most difficult to socialise.' Healey added succinctly, 'I spent my five years as Chancellor discovering how right he was.'[9]

The idea behind the Social Contract was that if money's worth were made over to union members by the state, there would be a general pulling back from excess demands of a kind to be lit up soon after as inflation statistics. In reality, as prices rose, union members and leaders concurred in bettering them.

The shift to the left, though the unions had voted for it, was something different and very much the crow on Healey's other shoulder. Labour's election and decision-making process was nominally democratic, if labyrinthine. Actually in the constituencies, it was miserably small scale, very tired and readily tilted, and in the often locally indistinguishable unions, almost hermetic and shiftable by the election of a key official on a 10 per cent vote. The colour of the commitments reflected a system which weighed Labour activists above Labour voters.

The Wilson government ought to have economised sooner and cut deeper, reserving to itself Scandinavian-type social democratic plans for a time when the economy had ceased to be vulnerable. That, after all, was what the Scandinavians did. But in activist politics, tentative and delayed economies were seen as an affront. The watchword among activists was dismay shading into 'betrayal'.

The only left-wing success had been won by the unions against Ted Heath, a 'success' crying out for inverted commas. Arthur Scargill had been aided by Heath – public service wage thrusts all round, things looked for to spend money on, new big council buildings, new big councils, new big prices. In response to which the miners were now up for their 31½ per cent on-year increase. This was the defeat of state and capitalism; now was the time for the party to be radical and effective, the time for 'an irreversible shift of power to working people'.

So Labour would trudge into office bearing an 'industrial strategy'. It involved a power to intervene and save/take over companies – shipbuilding and aircraft manufacture were in focus – also the separate creation of 'planning agreements'. Nobody quite knew what a planning agreement was. But industrialists feared 'unreasonable commitments against the interests of their shareholders and employees'.[10] Crosland, during the previous year's rancorous debate, had argued that the consequence of the price controls they involved 'would be a disastrous squeeze in profits'.[11] Healey had seen enough to make an understated prophecy: 'We must warn everyone against expecting too much. We might have to cut public expenditure.'[12]

With threats of extensive nationalisation tempered by Wilson only from the murderously specific to the menacingly general, the potential effect upon business and market confidence was clear. As for the government, they held 301 seats. Their election programme contained things in which they did not believe but had to make gestures towards. One apparently unavoidable gesture had been the waking up at midnight on 4 March of the Permanent Secretary at the Department of Trade and Industry, Sir Antony Part, to tell him that it was being broken into three, with the appointment to its large core, now a Department of Industry, of Tony Benn.[13]

Sir Antony and Mr Benn would be polite to one another at the highest chivalric level, only returning to diary and memoir to hesitate dislike.

Metaphorically I would watch his finger tightening on the trigger and when I judged he was about to fire I moved my head to one side. With any luck I heard the bullet smack harmlessly into the woodwork behind me.[14]

'Well I'm sorry but as far as I'm concerned, my work as a manager or a Minister is nothing like as important as my work as an educator and a spokesman – speaking for people.' Of course Antony Part doesn't understand that . . . He just comes along and warns me that I've crossed the Rubicon, that I've done this and that. At a suitable moment, after the election, I may ask for him to be replaced because of a breakdown of confidence between us.[15]

The person to ask would be the Prime Minister whose feelings towards Benn left Sir Antony looking positively indulgent. Bernard Donoughue, advising Wilson, was in a position to know: 'Mr Wilson decided in the summer of 1974 that he would try to provoke Benn to resign . . .'[16] But, as with all Wilson's blasted-heath mouthings, the prospect was slight.

Beyond the tribulations of an unwanted industrial policy, at once disruptive, expensive and calculated to scare the markets, there was the subsidiary matter of a general election. Labour were a minority government with a plurality of four seats and the untrustworthy tolerance of the minor parties. Healey's first Budget had thus to be at least two things: a response to the actual state of the economy – whatever that was, and there was some argument about it – and a handling of the finances so as to make no enemies with votes.

Calls made with hindsight for greater slashing vigour and the clenching of teeth, are anachronistic. Healey's talk about being political was realism. As Chancellor of a minority government, its leadership split from its activists and facing an unwelcome policy burden while at the same time trying to improve the party's parliamentary foothold, 'political' was the least he could be. Being political in his first Budget meant that small increase in income tax (with a less small tilt against unearned and higher earned incomes), provision for more public housing, an increase, bitterly regretted, in corporation tax, talk but not yet action about taxing gifts *inter vivos* and wealth tax, rent controls for privately rented properties and a significant increase in pensions and the food subsidies promised under the Social Contract. It is best viewed as an election budget, though on the (wildly wrong) figures available, it tried not to be inflationary. Effects differed from intentions.

The criticism of Healey himself by the Policy Unit[17] was that in the early months and beyond the election, he was very slow to act (and very reluctant to communicate with them or the rest of the Cabinet through position papers). Healey was unsure of himself. As his great capacity for work and understanding gave him full comprehension, uncertainty would be replaced by fascination and intellectual debate within the Treasury. His old Private

Secretary at Defence, Frank Cooper, tells of meeting Edna Healey shortly after the shift to the Treasury, asking 'How is he getting on?' and being told by that shrewdest of Cabinet wives, 'Oh Frank, you know Denis – it takes him a full six months in a department before he knows more about it than the people who've been running it.'[18] That catches the familiar breezy assurance, but it covered great uncertainty.

But even in this seven-month parliament, preoccupied as government was, there were warnings. Andrew Graham of the Policy Unit produced a paper on which Wilson was briefed in May, suggesting 'that we were on course for hyper-inflation, inevitable devaluation and a likely Treasury response that would demand public expenditure cuts and statutory wage controls'.[19] Only the last bit was wrong.

But Healey was very conscious of the volcanic potential underfoot. He told a meeting of the barely formed Cabinet in March of a balance of payments badly in deficit, inflation a menacing 15 per cent, increases required by nationalised industries, the need to hold public expenditure severely down. Apart from the wretched subsidies under the Social Contract, plus a cost-of-living increase in pensions, he wanted to bar new spending. His own professional concern, defence, should suffer cuts. As for Mr Benn's beautiful and extravagant beloved, Concorde, that kept aircraft, it should go.[20] Early talk of economy met early frustration.

A central, almost unavoidable mistake lay in not cancelling threshold payments. Established by Heath in October 1973, they provided for automatic increases in inflation above a set trigger point. This would lie 7 per cent above the inflation rate at that date. If reached, every 1 per cent increase thereafter in the Retail Price Index would automatically release a 40p weekly increase in pay. It was crazy folly. But the quadrupling of oil prices made the folly dance. Healey inherited thresholds at the same time as he inherited inflation. Even without the oil crisis, we would have been badly hit, but Heath had written in automatic increases in unit labour costs.[21] In the view of a Policy Unit economist, Gavyn Davies, failure to kill off thresholds added between 5 and 10 per cent to inflation.[22]

There would, before October 1974, be eleven triggerings, amounting to £4.40 per head across the board. In a purely economic world, the legislation should have been instantly repealed by Healey and the thresholds repudiated. But it wasn't a purely economic world. This Labour government could not contemplate cutting Heath's losses without direct conflict with the unions. Sense in these circumstances was not a runner.

Healey was thinking of taking £500 million out of the economy. But taking money out of the economy in the deflationary way any chancellor succeeding Barber would naturally favour, meant putting up taxes and this was an election year. As it was, he settled for taking out £200 million and a penny increase in direct taxation.

With such burdens subscribed to the making of it, a budget would be murderously difficult. Healey himself, listening intently to a roomful of economic advice, played, as he thought, safe. He would issue in April 1974 a budget which he believed to be 'broadly neutral'.[23] The Policy Unit grumbled that it was only 'mildly progressive', one in which 'food subsidies and indirect taxes largely cancel out . . . very little in it for the wage earner'.[24] Even on the figures available to him, he should, if consistent, have been harsher, not lying low against political outrage at deflation in any form. As, however, the Treasury had presented him with figures estimating the forecast PSBR at £3400 million, and his reductions looked next year to a figure of £2700 million, it was a nightmarish experience to announce in April 1975 debt at £7600 million. Healey had been given nonsensical numbers. Thinking that he was talking neutral and acting deflationary, he was doing his substantial bit for inflation. A chancellor liable to be censured for spending too much needs to know how much he is spending.

Edmund Dell argues that there was a sort of perverse luck in this. It was more important, he says cynically, to announce a cut in the PSBR than to make it.[25] The markets in the short term saw a move made at any rate in the right direction. Had the figures been judged anything like right by the Treasury, the fight which climaxed nearly three years later, in December 1976, would have taken place there and then. The rallying of senior ministers behind Healey and, most important of all, the emergence of a fundamentally stronger character as Prime Minister were horribly delayed.

The contest would have been staged ahead of an election, before Christmas, with Tony Benn at the zenith of his party power in a Cabinet led by the endlessly pretending, inflating and flinching Harold Wilson. But if the gap between the real figures and those received had not existed, a crazy sum equivalent to slashing 5.4 per cent of GDP, would have had to be done.

The Treasury still looked forward with more pessimism than ministers. A note from the Policy Unit's chief economist, Andrew Graham* speaks of 'The Treasury expecting statutory controls later in the year, the chancellor just beginning to worry about inflation, other ministers not fully facing the inflation likely this year and next.' With earnings likely to be 'up 20–25% this year', it was, he added optimistically, 'a dangerous situation, very like 1964–67.'[26]

Ministers by contrast, contemplated both a crisis and a general election, some minds alerted, others disposed to spend money, all of them concerned to win the election. Donoughue in a note to Wilson summed up coming divisions. 'Healey will increasingly want control of inflation but not want further subsidies, lower unemployment or the financing of [i.e. borrowing for] the balance of payments deficit. Foot will oppose further pressure on the

---

* Now Master of Balliol.

TUC, but will favour faster redistribution and lower unemployment – a freeze in the autumn would be his resignation issue.'[27]

Healey was being told, by way of the OECD figures, that the deficit would be high, but was sceptical of the very worst numbers. He was, however, very mindful of that threat of inflation around 20 per cent, the South American foothills, by the end of the year. But he was hearing good news about commodity prices. So, inflationary rising wages became a preoccupation. Healey was attracted by the paradoxical notion of compartmentalising an anti-inflationary package of tax moves *and* reflationary measures – not nonsensical, but difficult and risky. Dell, whose whole function at the Treasury was to second-guess and argue back, opposed the whole concept.

Not doing anything at all at this juncture struck him as more sensible, and a fight ensued between them, with the Paymaster ready to resign. 'The whole incident might be described as a flaming row.'[28] Essentially Dell, furthest from pure politics of all ministers, saw the package as cynical, otherwise political. And he argued across subsequent, friendlier meetings that ever larger Budget deficits were being run up to sustain employment. So they were. Healey, not at all cynically, but very much following the assumptions of the time, replied that unemployment at 550,000 could not be explained by technicalities. It had to be tackled.

We risk being out of tune with the mind-set of politics across the fifty years from the 1930s to the late 1970s, with its general horror of unemployment. By the autumn of 1974, unemployment had risen to 640,000. Joel Barnett summed it up: 'There was a sort of collective guilt complex round the Cabinet table which led to expenditure on "employment measures" that were far from being cost effective.' The Chief Secretary, in charge of expenditure, noted: 'The trouble for me, in trying to restrict expenditure on the more dubious schemes, was that this "guilt complex" clouded rational discussion.'[29]

But the undertaking to fight unemployment would only ever be expensive mitigation. Barnett recorded the throwing of money and its largely bouncing off.

We said then 'The underlying trend appears to be upwards . . .' We little knew just how much upwards. It rose at one point to 1.5 million, and was kept to around that level only by spending huge sums of money on so-called special employment measures – a euphemism for subsidies to firms so that they should keep on staff . . . We were also undoubtedly financing overmanning to the tune of hundreds of millions of pounds more in many parts of the public sector.[30]

Reckoning that perhaps 400,000 of further unemployment had been prevented in the private sector, he had no illusion that this was economically justifiable.

It was Healey's misfortune, or perhaps his great creative challenge, to come to his responsibilities at the changing point in economic thinking. He would straddle old assumptions and new departures just as he would be under pressure from an exasperated market and the old incomprehensions of departmental colleagues. His adjustments, as he shifted from old certainties to rasping new evidence, were the response of the quickest brain in the political leadership to desperate developments. But nothing happened overnight. The learning curve sloped gently at first. Talking to Wilson and his adviser in Downing Street in late May, he was described as 'characteristically buoyant . . . exports and the balance of payments were looking better and the Treasury was forecasting annual growth for the Gross Domestic Product of 4 per cent per annum through to 1979 . . . he also pointed out that the Treasury wished to see an effective sterling depreciation of around 3 per cent per annum in order to maintain Britain's export competitiveness, given the expected high domestic inflation.'[31]

The same observer, Bernard Donoughue, conveys the full spirit of the times in his next words. 'The Prime Minister enquired about unemployment prospects, but his mind was more on immediate electoral prospects and this distraction was even more apparent at the beginning of August.'[32]

In fact, the July Measures shrank from the projected £1500 million to £900 million. Healey cut VAT by 2 per cent, authorised more money for food subsidies, and introduced measures of rate relief where increases went above 20 per cent. He would tell the Commons that this would add only £200 million to demand by the end of 1974 and put £340 million on to the PSBR.[33] Joel Barnett, mildest of men, excoriates the VAT cut, 'a move in absolutely the wrong direction. We should have been increasing indirect taxes, not reducing them . . . What was transparently disproportionate was the percentage we took in direct taxes (income tax) as against indirect taxes (VAT, drink, tobacco, and so on).'[34] This of course is now the fixed orthodoxy of government, with ministers taking pennies off income tax in the manner of laying incense at a shrine, while pushing VAT to 17½ per cent. But 'Having once moved the basic VAT rate in the wrong direction . . . Denis never felt able to move it back up again.'[35] It was Labour culture; income tax was progressive and hit the rich, VAT fell like rain on the rich and unrich alike. They were against it. So the Policy Unit which, like the Treasury it distrusted so much, was focused upon incomes policy as the solution, deplored the economies. 'I see we are returning to Selwyn Lloyd [notable for a string of (necessary) cuts in 1961] . . . The Prime Minister has his head in the sand. Incomes policy is the only alternative to massive unemployment.' And even for the Unit's economists, electoral considerations weighed. Despite Heath's general folly, 'his incomes policy nearly won him the election.'[36]

The impending election brought out the worst in everyone. Healey indulged, in July, in one piece of low and brazen politics inexplicable in someone of his general honesty and calibre. Taking the three latest recorded months' figures for inflation, low because it was summer and because of the short-term measures just taken, he annualised them and spoke of inflation at 8.4 per cent. It was dreadful statistical practice, terrible long-term politics – a handle thrust into enemy hands for years of twisting – and as tricky-looking as it was tricky. From a man who in his November Budget statement would dismiss economic forecasting as 'extrapolation from a partially known past, through an unknown present, to an unknowable future according to theories about the causal relationships between certain economic variables which are hotly disputed by academic economists',[37] it was desperate cynicism.

The general election had been intended as a liberation, the government to be free to clench teeth and do necessary things, not least to move Tony Benn out of his expensive job. One of that minister's victories, achieved without informing colleagues in the spirit of true democracy, calls for which are to be found throughout his diary, was to ensure the continuation of Concorde. Beautiful and ruinous, a triumph over sense and arithmetic, the aeroplane would continue to be built, providing, as the evilly disposed softly remarked, extensive employment in Benn's Bristol constituency. The only consolation was that numbers were kept down to sixteen. Jacques Chirac, the French Minister with whom he colluded, talked about hundreds! Even so, moving Benn out, down or sideways was a prospective act with many friends.

Certainly the election was a card in the government's game with the markets. Abnormal circumstances were recognised, a working majority seen as a space for a government to rule without clogs and inhibitions. But the election itself was anti-climactic. Heath made no attempt to fight Labour. He was physically burdened by a thyroid complaint which, temporarily but drastically, diminished his energy and alertness. The food subsidies of the Social Contract would be retained, said the Conservatives, pensions increased every six months, mortgages pegged at 9 per cent, the Industrial Relations Act would, 'in the National interest', not be reintroduced – and Britain would be put first.[38]

Tony Benn became the object of much malevolent press scuttle, but also of more credible stories that he would be shifted. Healey's main contribution to the campaign had been to claim that the balance of payments deficit had been halved and with it, interestingly, the growth of the money supply, a statistic only just beginning to be bandied about. Healey at this point would be no monetarist, but he was practising a sort of inadvertent monetarism by pushing up interest rates to attract overseas funds which had no other pressing call to come here.

Wilson's political actions over the seven months of this parliament were described as 'a careful exercise: mellowing the manifesto'.[39] Benn's Green Paper on a National Enterprise Board (NEB) and nationalisation had been superseded by a White Paper whose planning agreements should be voluntary and thus harmless. The NEB became a handy facility for dubious investments, not at all for irreversibly transferring anything very much except public money. Wilson functioned like an owlishly wise head of the civil service, consigning visionary notions to high-sounding oubliettes. The White Paper was entitled 'The Regeneration of Britain'!*

Where Benn had used the bristling Nelsonian language treating private business as a species of French Navy: 'Securing the compliance' of companies, the final draft was Dr Wilson's syrup, talking about 'partners' and a 'closer, clearer and more positive relationship'[40] – froth, but benign froth. Benn had been allowed to produce a draft of the new White Paper. In Cabinet in June, Wilson, with colleagues behind him, turned savagely on paper and minister alike, 'a sloppy and half-baked document, polemical, indeed menacing in tone'. When Wilson produced his own soft-spoken draft, Benn described it as 'absolutely crazy'. But a major shift of policy had been made and a major defeat inflicted upon him. Except that, for Benn, defeats never quite mattered. As Joel Barnett would observe in another context: 'Imagine a brand new squash ball: put a grand piano on top of it and when you release it, the ball springs back to life.'[41]

The election, for which so much mellowing had been done, produced a result at once quizzical and malign. Labour's share of the poll actually went down by 180,000 votes – the Conservatives on 10,464,817 were 1.4 million votes down and had never before polled so poorly. But in terms of seats, the rewards for Labour were meagre and denying. They gained only 17 – 319 to everybody else's 316 – in a House where 49 seats were held by assorted Nationalists and Liberals. The Nationalists were on a roll generally with 11 seats in Scotland, and 3 in Wales, but the Liberal vote had gone briskly down. This would be reflected, before the new parliament was out, in devolutionary legislation and a Commons pact with the Liberals.

However, with a lead of 42 over the Tories, then as now unlikely to find coalition partners, Labour were stronger than disappointment suggested. Beyond this, everyone could look forward to the referendum on Europe which Tony Benn had all but obtained and consequent deepening splits within Cabinet and party.

Whatever exuberances Healey might indulge on his short excursions into partisan politics, he could claim fairly enough in October 1974 to be a man entirely preoccupied. Just occasionally he escaped. On 19 August, it was his good fortune when the stock market took one of its nasty turns to be on holiday in Corsica, 'enjoying lovely bathe at the Gorge bridge',[42] and unreachable despite having left several phone numbers. Edmund Dell, deputising, had anxious conversations with Wilson in the Scillies, Harold

---

* The phrase had been thought of before as a title for Barber's reflation programme, but Tory ministers had rejected it.

Lever in Deauville, and Shirley Williams in Tunis. Dell tried to use the situation to weaken the White Paper on the NEB further. But the stock market having gone down, went up again, and though Healey recorded being disturbed that night – 'disturbances by revolver shots after sinister trio called at hotel'[43] – Dell's three interlocutors seem not to have been involved.

The election had taken place on 10 October with sufficient goodwill to let Labour govern, but the skies had begun to darken before then. The fall and recovery in the stock market, which had agitated Dell, was more warning than blip. As a percentage of domestic income, profits had fallen in a year from 11 to 8 per cent, among other things, pushing up debt. The stock market took its cue and steadily fell across the latter part of the year, ending 1974 at just under 150. Healey had had sharp words in early August with his advisers. Why had they until recently been telling him that the CBI was badly overselling the case on company liquidity?[44] He had increased corporation tax from 50 to 52 per cent in his Budget and had spoken of profits 'doing rather well'. Chancellors, even political chancellors, do not make such assertions without thinking about it and Healey had heard the anxious protests of Sir Michael Clapham of the CBI.

Tony Benn had been at the meeting. 'Michael Clapham said there was deep disquiet about the Budget; there was no incentive to invest, nor to export; nothing to curb inflation . . . Large companies were only just maintaining their investment programme. There would be a down-turn next year and liquidity would be made worse. The pay crunch would come because the Budget was inflationary.' The CBI sounded absolutely licked. 'Like all these businessmen, they are trying to run a system that doesn't work any more. They want confidence which is essential for investment – then they refuse to invest.'[45]

Learning that he had been wrong and doing something about it was Healey's great strength. (His own record of the 6 August meeting says no more than 'Useful meeting with Wass and others on fears of industry.'[46]) But as Sir Donald MacDougall, now at the CBI, would comment, the bit about profits doing well 'was true on a *historic* cost basis . . . but no one seems to have told him that they were doing disastrously badly on a *replacement* cost basis after allowing for inflation. Nor do his advisers appear to have recognised that the outlook for company *liquidity* was very poor indeed.'[47]

What appears to have happened is that company liquidity, seemingly very high in the third quarter of 1973, had nose-dived in the last quarter and fallen further partly because of Heath's three-day week. What happened next was that stock appreciation between 1971 and mid-1974 had sharply increased in proportion to gross trading profits. Companies were paying taxes on inflated stock values when the stocks needed to be replaced. The first Budget had been inflationary by reason of those wrong figures, the July Budget had nearly been intentionally reflationary. It was the state of business which influenced the shape of Healey's third Budget in November.

Budgets at this time were serial affairs, strings of adjustments across the seasons of the year. The next would be on 12 November and preliminary discussions were on foot as the July Measures went into the House.[48] But the sense of oncoming crisis grew as the date approached, and the corporate problem was fully acknowledged. The Policy Unit was making its own flesh creep in response to Treasury ideas being floated. Accepting notions discussed on public expenditure would mean: 'Increase in school meal charges, no hospital starts for two years, raising family allowances by only half the increase in the RPI, no Christmas bonus.'[49]

Devaluation was an option. At a Treasury meeting on 20 September the advocates and opponents clashed. Kenneth Berrill and Hans Leisner had a paper in, 'arguing that we should still keep exchange rate policy well to the fore'. Derek Mitchell argued that there might be 'a loss of confidence if we were seen to be deliberately forcing the exchange rate down'. Dell, noting all this, thought that while Douglas Wass wanted to act in this way, 'Denis Healey's prejudice is clearly against taking action on the exchange rate.'[50]

Another meeting at the Treasury on 25 October considered the coming crisis as they faced the hideous PSBR figures. Healey would be announcing a PSBR not of £2.7 but £6.3 billion. The estimate for 1975/6 would be, incredibly, £8.5 billion. The wrong numbers had come home and would shortly be perching on the roof. Nicholas Kaldor, still a licensed Treasury auxiliary, was highly critical of what had been done in July and desperately anxious about the balance of payments but, unlike his old bubbling self, no longer sure what to do about them.[51] The Treasury group minded very much that 'these people', industrialists, were failing to invest through lack of profits. There were arguments only about how to help – one option involved relaxing the Price Code and its absurd productivity deduction which barred companies from passing on more than 50 per cent of wage increases to prices. This piece of nonsense had been intended to restrain wage increases, but simply ensured that employers, caught between demands and punishments, should suffer losses in profits, prospects and ability to employ.

The government's self-wrought fetters came on show. Healey's own diary entries are the customary primped compressions. In Cabinet, 'Roy Jenkins isolated v Foot [Jenkins was hawkish at this time] . . . Michael Foot lobbying me on TUC . . . Shirley Williams on price code.'[52] But fleshed out by Dell, they contain the substance of how uncomprehending interest groups and shibboleths bound a Labour chancellor across 1974. Michael Foot felt that the TUC would be very angry at abolition of the productivity deduction. Measures helping the profitability of industry were beneficial to the workers the TUC represented; would make, or at any rate save, real jobs for them. They would however, by offending the TUC, weaken the pointless Social Contract. But for believers, support for the Social Contract had become the cry: 'Great is Diana of the Ephesians.'

Then again, Shirley Williams, apart from being Minister for Prices, an illusion wrapped in a public office, thought that the price codes did deter some employers from putting up prices.[53] The fact that an increase in the RPI caused by lower barriers against passed on wage increases was only the *symptom* of inflation did not feature. This was a time when the growth in earnings had risen to 20 per cent. What Healey finally did, surrounded by so much advice, was to reduce the corporation tax he had incrementally raised in his first Budget, while judiciously relaxing Price Code regulations enough to give £800 million of relief to companies and another £800 million through allowances on stock appreciation.

It was, if not the best of both worlds, two moves in broadly the right direction, and over the years, corporation tax would dwindle into a marginal and largely voluntary donation. There would also be some relief in a recovery of the stock market from absurdly low to very low. But most things were actually getting worse – unemployment for one and the PSBR for another. The level of debt was discrediting the main alternative to drastic, expenditure-cutting action, the Lever/Crosland policy of borrowing. Showing through it with a touch of hysteria was the disastrous end-game of all-over reliance on borrowing, default!

Thomas Balogh, perpetual left-wing economist, member in the sixties of Wilson's malign kitchen Cabinet, set out proposals for a swap debt with Saudi Arabian lenders: 15 million barrels of oil annually lent to Britain over five to six years, to be repaid out of British oil royalties after the North Sea fields were opened up. The idea of borrowing oil rather than money was perfectly reasonable, providing the rate of interest was kept down. But Balogh showed his hand by saying that 'he had come to the conclusion that it would, if necessary, be easier to default on oil debts.'[54]

Balogh would argue more fully later that because we were running up a frightening burden of debt, the time would come when Britain defaulted. She would do it nicely, not with refusal to pay but with a request, South American-style, for rescheduling. It was a proposal situated between scoundrelism and despair. Healey was initially interested in the honest half of the deal, which failed to develop because the interest involved looked too high and because there was political embarrassment in staking what the SNP called 'Scotland's oil' as a swap commodity.

Dell has the last word. 'During Healey's visit to Saudi Arabia, the subject of oil borrowing was not raised. The UK Government did not borrow Saudi oil. Nor did it default.'[55] Healey might have been learning his advanced economics still, but no proposal could have been further from his constant streak of financial puritanism.

But the contemplation of such notions was eloquent of the direction in which Lever's and Crosland's thinking had carried them. Their path of dalliance now followed a course steeper and more twisted. Likewise devaluation; Harold Lever, of all people, was by October 1974 deploring currency depreciation as the soft option. The trouble was that it was ceasing to be an option. The full effects of the oil price-hike were now being felt. A prospective improvement in the export/import balance was crushed by oil price effects.

In his Budget statement in April 1975, Healey would, in neutral language, make a bleak admission: 'Foreign currency borrowing helped substantially to finance the current account deficit in 1975 and borrowing by public sector bodies under the Exchange Cover Scheme has already made an important contribution this year.' In the flat, ephemeral language of ministerial reassurance Healey was saying that it began to be thinkable that we might not be able to finance the deficit on the balance of payments.

A sense of things had come from Healey's words earlier at the Economic Strategy Committee (the principal forum for the Treasury to answer and explain). 'The key question is, can we go on borrowing? We are living 5 to 6 per cent above our earnings. It will be very much harder to borrow 3 billion this year; maybe we will have to go to the IMF or the OECD and suffer supervision.'[56]

The Treasury and the Policy Unit had long been agreed on one thing, a form of incomes policy. Robert Armstrong, the Prime Minister's Private Secretary, Douglas Wass, head of the Treasury, and Gordon Richardson, Governor of the Bank, were agreed in January, so the head of the Policy Unit was told, 'that a wage freeze was unavoidable'.[57] The TUC Conference had voted for £30 a week minimum. It had been thought of by government, the General Secretary, and indeed by Lionel Murray as a target at the end of two years. It was becoming clear that 'everyone regards this as something to be achieved this year and there have already been settlements at the £30 minimum'.[58]

The Policy Unit had put up their own proposals: public spending cuts plus import controls or tariffs (Tony Benn's sort of thing) directed at the balance of payments, and some response to wage inflation. For the moment though, officials were speaking for themselves. Healey at this stage was still averse to heavy deflation and his thoughts early in 1975 turned to heavier taxation.

He was also saddled with a series of forecasts – on inflation, the balance of payments and unemployment. Should they be made public? Healey's puritanism was strictly financial. No Stafford Cripps, he saw no reason to arm political opponents with information – too rich a diet would not be good for them. 'Will it not make it all the more difficult to carry through my policy if people know the assumptions on which it is based? . . . Why should I put weapons in my opponents' hands?'[59] By opponents, he was thinking of everyone in the Labour Party whose reaction to very bad projections on unemployment would be of the high-spending, protectionist order which it was his business to stop.

Ironically, some people in the Treasury itself, by no means as hard-faced as a good Treasury should be, were now floating import controls, surcharges on imports and subsidies on exports. This was happening precisely as the Benn alternative, or 'B Strategy', was being pushed hardest. It was proclamation of a B-Strategy manifesto by Benn on 25 February which provoked Healey's hard words about borrowing. And he went on to say that Benn's list – selective import controls, rationing and allocation of some imported materials, work sharing, 'Tax increases on the basis of greater egalitarianism' and a further slipping down of sterling – 'would produce a run on sterling, a cut of 6 per cent in our living standards – and he is trying to freeze the pattern of production.'[60]

On 6 March 1975, Healey briefed Treasury ministers on his close consultations with Wass, Mitchell and others. Their preoccupation had been the expectation of a PSBR which would be too high – talk was now of £10 billion – and ought to be got down. He agreed – one option was a modified protectionism, an import surcharge/export subsidy. There might be deflation, which Dell wanted, or devaluation, favoured by Barnett, Sheldon and John Gilbert.[61]

Healey might still flinch from heavy deflation, but he was not going to undertake any measure of protection and, though inclined to some borrowing, grew ever more wary of the tendencies of Harold Lever, the Chancellor of the Duchy recently visiting the United States seeking new wells to tap. Healey was moving by degrees to a harder line, to which borrowing was obstacle, option and irrelevance all at once. The Budget of March 1975, which Donoughue affably describes as 'a rag bag', was so only in that it contained both tax increases and the first cuts in expenditure. There was just one word for what he now tentatively contemplated – deflation. What would begin to emerge from the argument on all hands would be rejection of palliatives – Lever's borrowings and the Benn/soft Treasury impulse towards protection – in favour of recognising the true enemy in the swollen PSBR.

The issue was not 'if' but 'how?' Ideas were permutated like a football coupon. Nicholas Kaldor wanted a heavy deflationary package, detested further depreciation of the currency, favouring import surcharges and export subsidies. Barnett, Sheldon and Gilbert, as noted, favoured some depreciation. Dell disliked protectionist measures as a temporary fix, but would live with some as the price to get a deflationary package. He was joined by Richardson at the Bank in wanting £2 billion out. Kaldor and Dell agreed to defer the protectionist element while concentrating on the deflation.

But Donald MacDougall's successor as Chief Economic Adviser to the Treasury, Bryan Hopkin, was an inactivist, against not only subsidy/surcharge but any attempt at serious deflation. A dedicated Keynesian, he favoured a neutral budget with perhaps another attempt at anti-inflationary legislation, proved useless since Heath's time. The blind fears of the politicians of February 1974 also lingered in some civil service hearts. In Dell's view, the Treasury panicking a month or two earlier had by early March lost either the appetite for action or its nerve. Healey remarked sardonically at one point that the very word 'package' would put terror into his Cabinet colleagues.

As the March Budget was prepared, there was a swirl of consultation, Treasury, party and trade unions contributing. Healey's stamina and verve across an obstacle course of idea-crunching was noted. He nearly killed protection stone dead early on, keeping it only so as to retain studies on the scheme. He watched Gordon Richardson and his deputy at the Bank, Kit McMahon, embrace Kaldor in concerted opposition to the devaluations of either 20 or 10 per cent favoured by Barnett and Robert Sheldon. Though, sadly, Sheldon's call for a return to 10 per cent VAT failed to carry, Denis still preferring direct tax – 2 per cent more – up to 35 per cent. And a species of super VAT at 25 per cent for luxuries went through – yet another echo of punishing Camembert in 1946. In the same punitive spirit he would put up the price of a bottle of spirits by 64 pence. With beer going up by a mere 2p, there was a political message here.

Essentially the drift was now in the right direction, but it was more drift than thrust. The Treasury, having begun with anxiety and zeal, had been in part calmed by a couple of months of decent trade figures and some suggestions of world trade improvement. The Chancellor, traversing a snowstorm of ideas, had rejected the worst of them and embraced a measure of deflation. He was reducing the PSBR by £1.25 billion, but the original Treasury call, now reneged on by the Treasury, had been for £2 billion.

Cabinet and Treasury inhabited separate worlds. However short the measures might fall, they shocked the colleagues. Joel Barnett observed those for whom 'it was the worst crisis since 1931'.[62] He heard Shirley Williams, princess of moderates, worry about 'Traditional Treasury deflation'.[63] Tony Crosland, the great putter-off, asked for 'prolonged debate to consider an alternative Budget strategy',[64] this on 25 March before a budget scheduled for 15 April! To which Barnett mildly returns his own Treasury man's epitaph: 'we had already had our extended debate, and had come to our reluctant conclusion.'

The Cabinet response followed the Cabinet's essential state of mind – weakly unhappy. 'Denis spelt out his economic analysis and measures competently if a trifle wearily. Everyone shook their heads, but no one protested seriously. We all know that, whatever the reasons that got us into the mess we are in, we have little alternative.'[65] Harold Lever, 'for once said he backed the Chancellor 100 per cent.'[66] Mrs Castle's final words on the subject have a distinct poignancy. 'Once again, I felt caught up in that sense of inevitability when social democratic dreams come up against the realities of the mixed economy.'[67]

Healey had been a better friend to Barbara Castle, her department and its social democratic purposes than to immediate economic priorities. In a government less anxious about the activists, the unions, the PLP and its manifesto, she should, however sweetly, have been brought up against a lot more reality very much sooner. And any melancholy felt now was the merest trailer for the grief to come. She had had a private encounter the day before. 'Denis was at his most affable and relaxed . . . The borrowing requirement was terrifying. He just had to cut back public expenditure. The Social Contract wasn't working. Inflation was getting out of control . . . He was getting away with it in the current year by tax increases, but he was reaching the limit of them . . . He sounded so reasonable and anxious to take everyone's views into account.'

He worked on other colleagues. 'Talked to Michael Foot about budget – he took it very well.'[68] Not everyone was so accommodating. He would be hoist with his very own petard and 'got through unscathed except for Defence – Mason fought hard.' Roy Mason had inherited the old Denis Healey job. Also there were civil service pitches, 'Douglas Wass tried to get me to drop mixed rate VAT at last minute – failed.'[69] And there was the Queen 'friendly but not very interested'.[70] The Commons delivery, at two hours length, was 'received dully in the Commons',[71] but at a meeting of the parliamentary party, he won support by a margin of 2:1. Not doing enough, but doing far too much, he could hardly have hoped for more.

Relaxing next evening, as he had every right to, with a visit to the ballet (*Sleeping Beauty*) and attending a supper given by the property king, Sir Max Rayne, he noted the worrying approval of the amiable arch reflationist, Reginald Maudling: 'v. complimentary on budget.'[72] Healey had got it wrong in a sense which was almost inevitable in a party elected, to its own surprise, on a manifesto at perfect odds with the economic situation. A natural optimist as well as a trainee-Chancellor (like most chancellors), he had made the mistakes which were wanted of him. He had been given desperately wrong figures, he had found himself among civil servants notably political in the conflict-evading sense and with colleagues to whom all retrenchment came as an unpleasant and resented surprise. However he had shrugged off the false armour of large borrowings, had come to accept, if not quite proclaim, a measure of deflation. Crucially, with unemployment rising, he had set out to reduce demand.

This was a break with what had been called Keynesianism – not that one can see Keynes objecting. It was a clear break and a historic one. Healey had done too little, too anxiously, in his latest Budget, but he would never be a Reggie Maudling, clever but light-heartedly reckless. The Budget, for all its tentativeness, indicated the beginning of the end of being a political chancellor – and of getting it wrong.

THE TREASURY – REALITIES, 1975

Politics came first in the Wilson government. Deference had been shown to Benn and his industrial policy because of the disposition of power. That authority was ebbing, partly in response to events, very frightening events, in the economy at home and abroad, partly because Benn had invested furiously in the referendum – it was very much *his* referendum – on ratifying membership of what was then called the Common Market. After a two to one victory for entry on 5 June, Benn's position had slipped.

When, on 9 June, Wilson announced the reshuffle, Barbara Castle went to see the Secretary for Industry. 'Tony Benn was sitting at his desk, a figure of tragedy surrounded by a cortege of political advisers ... the curtains were drawn against the brilliant sun. "Have you heard anything?" I asked. "Yes," he replied, "I am to be moved to Energy."'[1] Wilson, it may be recalled, had talked in the sixties about 'my reshuffles' with all the pride of an old-style actor about 'my public'. But there was something terrible and emblematic about it. Wilson had been told by Eric Varley, who would take on Industry, that the move could only be done by a straight swap. If Benn resigned, he, Varley, would follow. *Per contra*, he had been told by Jenkins that any balancing move against Reg Prentice, the right-winger at Education, would be unacceptable. He offered Prentice a slanting-down move to Overseas Development (inside the Cabinet). In the process, he was delighted to demote Judith Hart, a meagre pillar of the left, to a job *outside* the Cabinet.

This would produce, through the best part of forty-eight hours, the sort of kicking and screaming which Wilson's ministers did best, including a descent upon the Prime Minister, on behalf of Hart, by Castle, Foot and Benn. 'After nearly an hour of this,' wrote Barbara, 'I suddenly took pity on Harold, having to show infinite patience after a long and exacting day.'[2] It was the

relative good fortune of Denis Healey to spend the eleven years of his ministerial career, however 'dog tired' or 'completely exhausted', across two great
stretches in two incontestably proper jobs.

Benn's shift, desperately wanted by Wilson who had behaved with steady
offensiveness to a rebel minister he essentially hated, had only been made
possible by the referendum.

The measure of how difficult the taking of necessary severe measures had
been for Wilson was underlined. Harold Lever, rather earlier, had been
poignant and unanswerable. 'You know, I love Harold,' Lever had said, 'but
I have to acknowledge that he is a complete coward.' He recalled that
Wilson, forgetting Benn's authorised absence from a Cabinet, had been 'like
a cat on hot bricks' thinking he had resigned. Lever also described an earlier
and desperate Wilson ploy. 'Apparently the content of this deal was that
Harold Wilson would sell out to Jack Jones and Michael Foot on the
Common Market if they supported him against Benn.'[3]

Politics accomplished, it would be possible at a special Cabinet at
Chequers on 20 June to take the economy seriously. 'Denis came next,' wrote
Barbara Castle,

> more sombre than I have seen him for a long time . . . The problem, he
> said, was more urgent than any of us realized. On the balance of pay-
> ments deficit we had done better than anticipated, but output would
> still be falling at the end of the year and inflation was 'terrifying' . . .
> Borrowing could stop 'overnight'. Anything could trigger off a disas-
> trous run on the pound and force us into 1 billion's worth of public
> expenditure cuts *this year*. There was not a minute to waste. 'We must
> have a credible policy by the end of July.' And if we were to get inflation
> down to single figures, we couldn't go beyond 10 per cent for wages or
> £5 a week.[4]

Tony Benn walked down those handsome stairs with John Silkin . . . 'I just
pointed my finger at Ramsay MacDonald.'[5]

But a great deal had had to happen first. The reason why the Chequers
meeting was taking place, why policy was now changing out of sight was
that the Social Contract had not merely failed in the ordinary way of failure,
it had made bad unimaginably worse. The defensive money had been spent
and the problem of a multiplied petrol price was now compounded by an
inflation very much of our own fashioning. Other countries had passed on
the oil hike, deflated, taken the pain at once and, by the spring of 1975, had
got through their worst inflation – the US now well below a high of 11 per
cent, Japan at 12–13 per cent after touching 25 per cent, Germany a steady
6–7 per cent.[6]

In Britain the rate went implacably up, with retail prices at 20 per cent.

The settlements made in the wake of the 1973 pit strike now looked like a base camp for who knew what ascent. Talk grew wilder until wage claims of 40–50 per cent were seriously expected. Retail prices had been rising by more than 20 per cent, the fastest peacetime increase for three hundred years, though the stock market after touching below 150 had come back to 300. By April 1975, unemployment was close to 900,000, the point at which Heath had panicked in 1971, and it was rising by 30,000 a month.[7] Though, as the economic analyst Nick Gardner points out, this was the product less of disappearing jobs than of population growth.

Healey had talked in May of planning 'for the individual programmes of a £3 billion cut in public expenditure by 1978–79 and studying the consequences for our overall political policy'.[8] As Barbara Castle candidly says, such advance viewing of developments was the approach of her own civil servants. In their different ways, Crosland, Castle, Benn and Wilson himself had come down against the latest paper. 'Wedgie,' said Barbara, 'was at his most apocalyptic . . . Denis's proposals would put our microeconomic strategy in a straitjacket. It would mean that we couldn't have a strategy for saving jobs. The movement will not accept this. It is a parallel with 1931, when the government of the day refused to accept protection and gave us a depression instead.'[9]

Healey argued that public spending had gone heavily up (he used the measure about to be revised down by Leo Pliatzky, but the actual increase wasn't in doubt), and that income tax had more than trebled as a percentage of family income. He spoke of the need for 'draconian cuts', but in May he faced a body of settled immobility. Though one substantial voice on his side at this time was Callaghan's. 'Jim said gloomily that the Cabinet itself should be looking at the other alternatives, such as restraint of wages.'[10]

As well he might. Healey himself, speaking of the Railwaymen's pay claim, recorded at the same meeting, 'Crosland wants to concede 30 per cent without a fight'[11] – which they did. The Cabinet, with Crosland providing a slick of intellectualisation, stood ready to make inflationary wage settlements, content at the rise in both public expenditure and direct taxation, much of it undertaken to persuade the unions not to seek inflationary wage settlements. The Cabinet of 22 May perfectly illustrates the impossibility of Healey's position. To rebuke him from hindsight for not moving earlier is to miss the point that when he was finally ready for drastic action, he would face a road block manned by Cabinet colleagues. Of all ministers, Dell apart, Healey was the one most alerted for action but when not met by incomprehension, he encountered a deep faith in procrastination.

Such contempt for economic gravity could not continue indefinitely. Even ministers could not entirely ignore evidence coming under the Cabinet Room door. Scaring figures on inflation produced anxiety, scaring figures on unemployment helped concentrate minds. The Social Contract had been conjured up first in a pamphlet of Tony Benn's.* Picked up and used rhetorically by a rather different Callaghan at Party Conference in 1972, it flourished in the climate of fear created by union victories over governments. The 'social wage' of the Social Contract had been estimated at £1000 per head of the population[12]. It had remained easy, in the face of such losing-side psychology, for public sector workers to cheerfully break through any guidelines. There had been a spat between Reg Prentice, when at Education, who accused the unions of 'welshing', and Michael Foot, something less than a trained economist, who accused him of 'economic illiteracy'. Foot reflected a Labour government selling in a buyer's market – and trading on unsecured credit. Events had done their work. The new, rising and again rising unemployment figures, whatever the sophisticated caveats, would change the terms of political trade.

Beyond that, the awfulness of the other figures, particularly for inflation, told the unions that Healey, even had he wanted to, could not redescribe Heath's U-turn. And Healey no longer did want to. The recent running seminar of Treasury life had, along with the rather vivid facts, unmade his attachments to Keynes. Not being an economist, he had fewer sentimental attachments. It wasn't a faith. As Healey and his Treasury team moved towards harder money and limiting debt, their chief Cabinet antagonist would be Anthony Crosland who had drunk deepest at that spring.

Healey would soon be placed to talk to the union leadership – and they to listen – soon, but not quite at once. The TUC disapproved of the April 1975 Budget. David Basnett of the G and M, an outstandingly dim figure, said that 'we had got to get away from all this one-sided exhortation about wages. The Social Contract did not mean exhortation: it meant creating an atmosphere, and we had got to realize that the budget hadn't helped.'[13] Jack Jones, soon a genuine and reliable ally, would hear Healey's warnings as being 'like an old time reactionary crying "Bring back the Cat"'.[14] But behind the resentful tone stood realities. Michael Foot, the unions' best friend, Cabinet spokesman and softest touch, had been shocked by the package of expenditure cuts in the April 1975 Budget: 'it would make our relations with the TUC impossible.'[15] For Joel Barnett, 'the next two pay rounds were the best we were able to obtain from the TUC.'[16] It was after the hardening of lines and the strengthening of pressures that ministers, coming out of submission mode, would find the unions ultimately responsive. The obvious irritation which Healey engendered in Jack Jones would be a sort of compliment.

Jones was a man of some quality, dour, hard-bred in real poverty, a puritan, rarely a bad thing, a veteran of the Spanish Civil War and invincibly true to his socialism. It was natural for him to be adversarial, with working

---

* *The New Politics*, Fabian pamphlet, 1970.

people and the unions as *his* side requiring to be fought for. Perhaps most importantly, he was both an autocrat and a man of his word. The sort of idle-mindedness by which the union side of an agreement was simply not delivered, natural to the slatternly Basnett, was not for Jack.

Winning him to an agreement in the first place would be a laborious busi-ness. Union leaders were very reluctant to believe that wages could be the cause of inflation. Having played a major and very brave part in confining wage increases, with the hoped-for consequences, Jones says in his autobi-ography, 'I do not accept that wage increases are the root cause of inflation; they are a reaction to rising prices and therefore, feed inflationary trends.'[17]

But half the trouble with the union leadership had been that all attempts at co-operation with ministers had foundered on their inability to deliver. Edward Heath had closed on an agreement with the Miners' President, Joe Gormley, which Arthur Scargill, and a sense of open-ended strength in enough miners, then brutally destroyed. From anarchic Fleet Street, home of the ghost shift and treble time, Bill Deedes, editor of the *Daily Telegraph*, observing the pleasant print union headquarters ringing the home counties, from which non-binding assurances freely came, spoke of 'The Emperors in their Summer Palaces'. But Jones had recognised the crisis, and in Aberdeen, in April, had talked to the Scottish TUC Conference, begging unions to respect and keep the Social Contract. 'How else but with unity between the trade unions and the Labour government are we going to fight rising unem-ployment and the redundancies that are taking place?'[18] And he meant to deliver.

Getting strong terms for the agreement would be a laborious business, but Jones had followed the Aberdeen speech with another in Bournemouth, which spoke of flat rates, a single cash sum rather than a percentage. Now his own union, the Transport and General, was a cumbersome assembly, a Portuguese empire of scattered parts. But like most general unions, it served large numbers of the unskilled and lowly paid. To speak in Bournemouth of a single figure which should 'apply to all people at work – MPs, judges, civil servants and other workers'[19] – was in no way ingenuous. 'Other workers', often members of the T&G, would get good percentages, people up the earnings ladder would get bad percentages. The term, 'differentials', would fill columns on its own before the government fell in 1979. But when we have seen Anthony Crosland wanting 'to concede 30% without a fight', when Lionel Murray of the TUC, with inflation at 20 per cent, had said 'that the going rate for wage increases was already 30 per cent',[20] Jack Jones was indi-cating an inkling of sense and salvation.

As Healey groped towards some kind of trade union shift from pre-emp-tive demand, Treasury thinking had moved towards an incomes policy. Statutory or voluntary was the issue. That there should be restraints was no longer doubted, and on the day the Cabinet had brushed him aside, the CBI, earlier hostile to the idea, came firmly down in favour. There was convergence, as there very well should have been. Inflation in June stood at 26 per cent, while hourly wage rates were up on the year by 32 per cent.[21] The TUC unhelpfully suggested a flat rate of £10. Healey records on 13 May the laconic note: 'Len Murray in – a bit aggressive at first, then v. friendly. Not much hope of help from TUC.'[22] That had been true for a long time. Jones would complain that the research staff at Congress House much preferred the wage-vetting machinery of the mid-sixties.

Events threw enormous onus upon Healey's personal courage and will-power. The soft options to any sort of incomes policy were still in the air. Michael Foot wanted another £2.5 billion in food subsidies to soften the impact of rising prices, Shirley Williams wanted an inflation tax. There was a strong tendency to confuse the Retail Price Index with inflation. Healey's private comments on his colleagues grew rougher. 'Roy and Mulley weak,' he wrote on 11 June, 'Foot quite terrible.'[23] Where union matters were concerned, such politicians were ruled by the dreadful word 'unacceptable'. Nothing which the unions found 'unacceptable', however necessary, could be done. Like 'requirement' in 'Public Spending Borrowing Requirement', it had an imperious ring. Resistance to that railway pay claim was unacceptable. The original ministerial offer breached guidelines on pay which the government itself had just set out. 'Michael Foot and Eric Varley greeted with total disbelief the idea that we were going to keep to the guidelines in this case.' When, said Varley, 'Ministers actually face the facts of this situation, they will say it is absurd to imagine we are going to get a guideline settlement.'[24] Another word, 'demoralisation' had been done to death by resentful backbenchers in the sixties. From an intelligent minister this *was* demoralisation.

How exactly the major policy shift came to be made is a question with several answers. In June, the May inflation figures came out.* They stood at 25 per cent, a nice, round, Argentinian sort of number. The Treasury knew what it wanted, so did the Policy Unit; the difference between them, making it voluntary or statutory, was a good deal less important than it looked. Then of course there was that referendum result. Suddenly there was a purely political shift, summed up by the words of Judith Hart at her 7 June dinner party for Foots, Benns, Baloghs, Shores and Harts. 'Peter [Shore] wanted us to go and see Harold, and Judith agreed: "Yes, we should tell Harold he mustn't now humiliate the Left."'[26] He didn't, but he got rid of Judith Hart! As for Benn, after having 'to run the gauntlet of Bernard Donoughue and Joe Haines' before 'Harold had looked at me with his little piggy eyes', he had

---

* Tony Benn dining with left-wing colleagues at the splendid Gay Hussar, thought the combined cost to himself and his wife worthy of note – £10![25]

been moved, down or across according to taste, but where Industry and all its griefs were concerned, plainly out. In Wilson's accustomed way, the action was limp enough, but it signified.

And with pressures easing one way and increasing the other, Wilson would come trembling up to the red and yellow signal for the economy. He had told Healey that he would support anything except a statutory wages policy, but by the turn of June/July, he was ready to amend that some distance. On 12 June, to Healey, he 'waffled'. But a week later Wilson told Bernard Donoughue 'that "something must be done" about the way wages were rising and asked me for suggestions'.[27] June 20 1975 was the occasion which had turned Tony Benn's eye to the portrait of Ramsay MacDonald, the day-long meeting of the Cabinet on inflation and incomes. Healey's contribution was categorical and downright.

'Anything could trigger off a run on sterling, which had already cost us $500 million to support. The rail strike could, or indeed a rail settlement.'[28] He was arguing for a target of 10 per cent annual inflation and, as he noted, only Foot opposed this.[29] The money equivalent of 10 per cent was £5. Unless inflation was got down to OECD levels by September of 1976, they would be facing unemployment at two million. Jenkins supported Healey and made a specific call for the policy to be statutory, with sanctions, and was asked by Foot, 'Are you suggesting putting people into prison?'[30]

Healey heard the arguments out, conceding nothing, and would end quite as emphatically.

> We should announce a credible policy soon because the Arabs and the shop stewards are both threatening us.* We must have the acquiescence of the unions. The Government must tell the TUC that 10 per cent is the maximum for pay increases, and formula agreements must not be more than 12.5 per cent in total. There must be a monitoring body. The voluntary versus statutory choice is false because we want specific sanctions, a wages fund for the public sector that would cut off *jobs* if the increases were too high, but not *investment*, because that would be burning our own seed corn.[31]

The last point, according to Tony Benn, was the only one on which Wilson disagreed with him.

The assumption between Foot and Jones had been that any policy on wages should be wholly voluntary. And as to the tariff, first thoughts had been for a flat rate increase of 15 per cent. It was a very long way from

---

* The relevant Arabs here were the Kuwaitis, ready, with the Nigerians, to pull funds out of tremulous sterling.

adequate, but it was half that climactic increase for the Railwaymen. The Policy Unit came up shortly after with £5, in Donoughue's recollection the suggestion of Joe Haines, the Prime Minister's dapperly viperish press secretary. Actually the number was not new in press conjecture. They were also talking in terms of 'a battery of sanctions' against over-paying employers.

Meanwhile the CBI was thinking on parallel lines – with one of its officials, Ron Owen, engaged in extensive discussion with Jack Jones. The union man had also wanted a cut-off to exclude the undeserving rich, who should get nothing, and a year-on-year adjustment. The CBI preferred a percentage, but saw Jones's point about the saleable simplicity of a cash sum.[32] This was something which Len Murray would echo at the June meeting of the TUC General Council. The General Council would be asked to endorse specific terms, followed by painfully extracted confirmation at Conference in September.

Things were happening. On 26 June, the special committee of senior ministers known as MISC met. Healey says no more than: 'Jim fairly firm. PM confident.' On 30 June, Wilson went to the Royal Agricultural Show at Stoneleigh and made a Harold Wilsonish speech, blithe, flinching and comfortable, discounting the incomes policy he had virtually agreed at Chequers on 20 June. While this was happening, Gordon Richardson, Governor of the Bank, arrived at Healey's office with news. 'Richardson in with Wass and Mitchell – "Sterling collapsing". Tell him to see PM.'[33] Wilson had heard the news back in Warwickshire, with his own complacencies hardly transcribed onto the wires. Healey, after his own scheduled working lunch with the CBI command, Campbell Adamson and Ralph Bateman plus Donald MacDougall, spoke to Wilson who 'agreed to go for statutory wage controls v. employers'.[34]

At which point, reports diverge. According to Bernard Donoughue: 'The famous Treasury "bounce" technique had been launched, with the Bank of England as a powerful ally.'[35] For Dell it was not the Treasury which was bouncing government, but the markets. And do chickens newly come home, bounce? After Richardson was gone, Wilson and Healey met in the MISC committee. According to Donoughue, he and Haines had looked over a midnight Treasury paper bristling with criminal sanctions which they with difficulty persuaded Wilson to reject, and the Prime Minister went through characteristic circuits of hard and soft before coming down against it.

Healey reports a late conversation with Wilson after his return from Stoneleigh and being told that he 'would after all support a statutory pay policy, providing the legal sanctions were directed only against employers who conceded too much, and not against workers who demanded too much. Then I persuaded the relevant ministerial committee to put such a statutory policy to the full Cabinet.'[36]

This echoes very closely the diary record: 'Saw PM and he agreed to go for statutory wage controls v. employers.'[37] Healey's handwriting has physician's tendencies, but the word is 'employers'! He also records a visit from Murray. 'Len Murray in – took it quite well.'[38] Clearly, Murray was not being briefed about and taking quite well, proposals for criminal sanctions against workers. The only person who reacted adversely at the MISC meeting was Michael Foot, who threatened to resign.[39]

Too much should not be made of the question and nobody's honour is at issue. We are talking interpretations. Donoughue's quarrel is essentially with the Treasury. But who was the Treasury? The paper was clearly seen by him and he notes it as borrowing language from early seventies Heath government proposals. But Wilson himself, at the time of its issue, has Healey not at the Treasury but at Number 10;[40] again, a ministerially approved paper would normally go to the Cabinet, as this did not. What this all sounds like is an unapproved Treasury draft for Healey and Wilson to look over. The root of this may be a preoccupation among people as disparate as Benn and Donoughue about the limitless and sinister resource of the Treasury.

This was of course the first instinct of most of the Cabinet next day, 1 July. Healey outlined the facts: sterling's horrid fall, those threatened Kuwaiti and Nigerian withdrawals from sterling – liable to be made, they had said, if it fell below $2.17 – the fact of depreciation now being marked specifically against the dollar. In the light of all this, said Healey, he did not want further expenditure cuts doing nothing here and now for inflation and only increasing unemployment. What he *did* want was the wage policy now being forged with the TUC so as to target inflation in September 1976. Jack Jones was by now arguing for £8. The government, said Healey, should not go beyond £6 a week, otherwise 10 per cent (actually it is slightly more). He had to get out a statement to the Commons that afternoon.

The immediate response seems to have been wooziness, notably from Harold Lever who hadn't taken it well. He was very depressed and worried about getting TUC approval. Michael Foot, chief mourner for the old ways, was convinced that a 10 per cent legal limit constituted a return to a statutory policy. And what about the miners? 'What if the miners went on strike against the 10 per cent limit? We would have to let current arbitrations through, but what about the indexation agreements? He didn't believe the TUC would accept a 10 per cent figure. He believed that we could get 12 per cent by negotiation and this would be worth more than anything else.'[41] Foot, a man given to transferred loyalties, was either thinking Jones's thoughts for him or treating the union man's negotiating positions as immovable rocks.

There was also surprisingly little solidarity from Callaghan. 'We shouldn't go into details on wages and prices today: merely make a firm statement of our intention and determination to get inflation down and take all the measures necessary to achieve it. We ought to state our target for wages publicly, which we never yet have done.'[42] Healey exploded at this, saying with some bitterness that he had done so three times and getting an immediate withdrawal from Callaghan. Wilson made great play of his anxiety – he had lain awake till 3 a.m. His proposal was for general powers, in the style of what had been done in 1966, which would become law only by subsequent regulation. Healey himself noted support from 'Roy, Tony Crosland, Shore, Peart, Reg [Prentice], Short, PM' and opposition from 'Foot, Benn, Castle, Varley, Jim', while putting 'Elwyn Jones, Mellish on fence with Shirley'. He then drafted a statement for the House and flung himself into explaining the same things to a different set of people.

His statement to the Commons that afternoon speaks of 'discussions with the TUC and CBI about measures to secure a drastic reduction in the rate of inflation . . .' For citizens, this was 'the overriding priority. It is a pre-condition for reducing unemployment and increasing investment.' They were, he said, 'determined to bring the rate of domestic inflation down to 10 per cent by the end of the next pay round and to single figures by the end of 1976.' (They didn't, but it was both decent intention and useful assertion.) To make the policy stick 'we propose to fix cash limits for wage bills in the public sector so that all concerned may understand that the Government is not prepared to foot the bill for excessive settlements through subsidies or borrowing or by loading excess costs on the public through increases in prices and charges.' While ministers 'much preferred to proceed on the basis of a voluntary policy agreed with the CBI and TUC', that agreement had to meet its targets. Otherwise 'the Government will be obliged to legislate to impose a legal requirement on both public and private sector employers to comply with the 10 per cent limit.'[43]

Eric Heffer, who had resigned as a Minister of State, saw movement towards 'a statutory incomes policy which is contrary to our election pledges'. And he reminded Healey of the pleasures of Bennism, 'an alternative economic strategy . . . advocated by some of his hon. Friends'.[44] Healey simply referred him to recent statements by union leaders 'that it is not possible to bring down the rate of inflation, as we undertook to do, without achieving a substantially lower level of payment settlements in the next pay round than in the last'.[45] Geoffrey Howe, for the Conservatives, grumbled fairly enough that the attempt 'to grapple with the nation's problems' was being made 'at last'.[46] But any member of the Heath government speaking as he did, of 'profligacy, dissension and incompetence', was at a disadvantage. Healey did, though, respond sympathetically to Howe's concern at the Price Code bearing heavily on private business. Patronised by John Pardoe, a leading and arrogant Liberal whom he would later deathlessly record as 'Denis Healey with no redeeming features',[47] the Chancellor said coolly, 'I suppose I must welcome the offer of support by the hon. Gentleman.'[48]

But the real political flavour of the day came with the intervention of

Norman Atkinson. Much more than the sweet-natured Heffer, Atkinson, a Manchester MP with matching mind and voice, resentful, slow and aggrieved, embodied the ostentatiously proletarian left. His hostility, essential to all credibility in a sensible chancellor, was forthcoming: 'totally unaccept-able to both the TUC and the annual conference of the Labour Party . . . defiance of the manifesto upon which we contested the last General Election'.[49] Healey, jeered at by some Conservatives, was polite, but grave in his reply. The government were 'paralysed . . . [Hon. Members: 'Oh'] – and prevented from taking action to bring unemployment down as long as [Interruptions] . . . inflation is running at current rates'.[50]

Privately, he referred to himself as 'very exhausted', but still had to face an hour-and-a-half visitation by Len Murray and his deputy, David Lea. 'Len v. sharp, controlled friendly-boxing.' Healey then, a human being as well as a chancellor in a crisis, went back to his family, including his newly returned younger daughter. 'Flopped home, Cressida arrived, very well and happy.'[51] Healey was now heavily occupied, his life a febrile shuttle between unions, employers, backbenchers and, most trouble of all, a dithering cabinet. Jones telephoned him next day. 'I told him the form. He told TGWU conference I ruled out a statutory pay policy! Sterling fell 10 points . . .' In the middle of all this General Sir John Hackett materialised in a state of blithe self-preoc-cupation. 'Shan Hackett in – wants a peerage.'[52] Next day he spent three hours at Congress House, where he was able to talk to Hugh Scanlon, the ostensibly hostile left-wing leader of the Engineers. Healey, on the strength of this, could now reckon him 'personally sympathetic'.[53]

On 4 July he had another meeting with Murray and his deputy, David Lea, at the Treasury, both 'v. helpful', as well as dealing with trouble at Burmah Oil, and another with the Deputy Governor of the Bank, Kit McMahon. After which he went off to Leeds for constituency work – 'sorting things out with Bannerjee, long surgery at S. Nicholas' – before another surgery in the afternoon. The visit at least got him to a concert of the Black Dyke Mills Band: 'V. good.'[54]

Monday 7 July had him at a lunch with the CBI accompanied by helpful Michael Foot and Shirley Williams. 'Michael making difficulties about my legislation.' He was unimpressed by the clumsy General Secretary of the CBI, Campbell Adamson – 'Adamson made a muck of it.' He then, in the corporate way essential at the time, went on to the TUC's Economic Committee, a gathering marked by 'a lot of tension. Scanlon/Fisher* wanted sanctions [on employers] . . . Bed at midnight, *very* tired.'[55]

The next day the Committee accepted all that Healey had asked of them. 'Jack Jones very helpful,' he adds, underlining the words. Fisher was still

---

* Alan Fisher, General Secretary of NUPE.

worrying that they might be being too good to the private sector. The only obstacle in the way was 'the difference between a cut-off at £7000 and £10,000'. But he records being 'warned off taking of reserve powers'. Suitably admonished, he 'rushed to PLP', a 'Very good meeting', only to encounter the Prime Minister in a characteristic state, 'Very friendly. Worried about Michael.' A meeting of MISC, which continued until 10.30, went well on most of the proposed developments, notably local government spending and a penal Price Code. But argument about reserve powers continued, with Wilson and Healey supporting the idea, Crosland and Williams veering towards support, Eric Varley uncertain and 'Michael strongly against'. There was also a meeting at the Treasury provoking some asperity, but nothing new in his creative relationship with Dell – who looked forward to expenditure cuts.[56] Dell noted 'usual clashes between Healey and myself'.[57]

After a day of the same sort of thing on the 9th, another MISC meeting, another encounter with David Lea* of the TUC, yet another with the CBI, 'Fairly easy',[58] and attendance at the NEC which was nothing of the kind: Ian Mikardo churning trouble, the Chancellor angry and exasperated. Mikardo ended a tirade against policy and the lack of contact with 'The Party' 'in a crescendo of viciousness'.[59] Healey wondered where some of his colleagues lived. Miners in his constituency had said to him, 'It's about bloody time.' The protective comment of Shirley Williams as Healey grew more angry, 'Denis has been under terrible strain all week,' was a formidable understatement.[60]

The Cabinet of 10 July was a morning-and-afternoon affair awash with emotion, so much so that it went lunchless, merely breaking for quarter of an hour for tea at 12.30. Foot in particular talked about the government being destroyed by the Cabinet if reserve powers on wages were taken. Healey, 'looking rather irritated',[61] repeated what he had noted in his diary, that only the level of cut-off – £7000 or £10,000 – remained in dispute with the unions. Benn asked, 'Is this an alternative to expenditure cuts or is it, as I believe, the first step?' and Roy Jenkins said flatly, 'We've got to do both.' Healey's central concern was to have the Cabinet understand 'credibility with the country's creditors'. The term 'global economy' had not yet been coined, but the essential division lay between those who understood that Britain was in a market and known there to be badly overdrawn and those who worried about party and union feelings.

Healey now had a TUC vote in his favour. But the Social Contract had been carried overwhelmingly and the unions' obligations under it not met. The present policy was backed only 19:13. Fearful and encouraged by

---

* Healey formed, and kept, a very high opinion of Lea as a sensible, non-ideological, hard-working official who responded to evidence.

Wilson in his choice of speakers, the Cabinet ducked reserve powers. There was a 10:9 majority against doing anything so upsetting to the unions. The Cabinet had been 'given a timid steer by PM' and Healey wondered to his diary if he had fought hard enough: 'Felt very uncertain whether I should have forced it.'[62] A note from Sir John Hunt, the Cabinet Secretary, suggested that Healey should stress that 'The one surest thing to start an immediate run on the pound is if stories get around that the Chancellor lost on this.'[63] Perhaps with such thinking in mind, Wilson, nerveless on Thursday, would on Friday in the Commons speak of 'powers in reserve'.[64]

But what had finally emerged was *not* a voluntary policy. Although Healey agreed not to expressly state reserve powers, in ghostly and threatening fashion they were there. 'I *would* be prepared to announce that legislation has been drawn up to deal with non-compliance which would not constitute reserve powers, only a threat to take reserve powers if necessary.' Faces, in particular Michael Foot's, were being saved. 'How would the TUC react?' Castle asked Foot. 'They'll be very relieved,' he replied, grinning with relief himself. 'He would have been in an impossible position if we had lost.'[65]

Much more significant long term was the response to Benn's question: Was not Len Murray, the General Secretary of the TUC, 'inflexibly opposed to reserve powers?' Healey's reply corresponded with the realities. 'Len has been told by the government that it has the right to make decisions for itself after taking account of TUC views.'[66] He understood this even if Wilson was still afraid of it. Down the sixteen-month defile of the government, this was a momentous remark, something which Healey could not have said before and which only two or three other ministers would have *wanted* to have said. When Benn opposed the key central paragraphs of Healey's White Paper, *The Attack on Inflation*, which 'pushed for higher profits in the hope that this will lead to investment through the market mechanism . . . pre-Keynesian and a recipe for a major slump',[67] he found himself alone. He noted in that strange, quarrelling, but family-like atmosphere, that when tea came, Wilson put out his, Benn's, special blue mug which seemed reserved for the days with the really bad news!

On the other hand in the absence of statutory powers Healey would not get the full reduction in inflation he had set himself. The retail price index had risen by 25 per cent across 1975. Over 1976 it fell but to 15 per cent, not the 10 per cent which he had wanted. £6 amounted to somewhere between 11 and 12 per cent not the 10 per cent he had sought and which the CBI would have liked to specify. An exchange of fire between Dell and Donoughue is eloquent. Treasury civil servants had been speaking with open contempt of Ministers. 'A pity,' replied Dell, 'that they had reason for such contempt!'[68] Another note from Hunt says of a particular paragraph in the paper, that it 'is cosmetic for the gnomes. It says public expenditure must be contained (which it must): & says massive cuts would only come if this policy failed. It implies nothing for the decisions which Cabinet will have to take . . .'[69]

Meanwhile, the struggle over detail continued and in Jack Jones's rather grumpy narrative, the demonology of the Treasury is maintained. They had wanted percentages and 'only grudgingly gave way to a flat-rate approach. Healey who was putting the Treasury arguments, then stuck at £5 while I had been pressing for £7 or 8. It became a hard negotiating session, but I came down to £6, reluctantly, but in order to get an agreement. We then pressed for the increase to apply only to wages and salaries under £7000 a year. Healey insisted the figure ought to be £10,000 and we finally settled on £8500 which indicates the haggling which went on.'[70]

Jones, though grumbling about satisfying forces outside Britain, decided, as he says, 'to see it through' and would fight hard, which in his case was very hard indeed, to get the policy over Council and Conference fences which were anything but formalities. Jones went further than this. He gave a serious telling-off to the left – 'obviously,' wrote Barbara Castle, 'a reaction to the Arthur Scargills of this world who are up to no good at all. Jack has thrown his hat over the windmill in an overt and unequivocal determination to save the Labour Government.'[71]

One reason for such intervention was the belief that Foot and Benn 'were ready to resign at the drop of a hat'.[72] Michael Foot might easily have done so. On Tony Benn, Bernard Donoughue is less trusting, remarking in a different context, 'It seemed transparently clear to a detached observer that there was no humiliation which Tony Benn would not swallow to stay in the Cabinet.'

Benn's own response to the breakthrough of Healey's incomes policy on 1 July had been conveyed to his press spokesman, Bernard Ingham, two days later. He saw four options: enduring it from the inside, opposing it from the inside, coming out and opposing constructively or coming out against it destructively. 'I thought opposing it from the inside was perhaps the best thing to do.'[73] In this spirit he arranged to brief Ian Aitken of the *Guardian*. Questioned on 10 July by Ingham, anxious for a press statement, Benn said that 'the movement wanted us to stay in'.[74] Jack Jones had less to worry about than he thought.

Another and essential weapon in the struggle against inflation lay in cash limits. Directed at public spending, their implications for pay levels followed naturally. Defeatism over public service wage settlements and the unions' notions of what was 'acceptable' would increasingly face disobliging arithmetic. The immediate arrangements were rough-and-ready, waiting upon the next financial year. But as the civil servant most involved, Leo Pliatzky (from late 1975, Second Secretary at the Treasury), observed, 'What was needed was a first stage discipline to prevent ministers from increasing the volume of programmes beyond the figures which had just been agreed with such difficulty.' They couldn't stop the Minister of Transport lengthening a road, but they could prevent him building a new one.[75] Interestingly, Pliatzky also noted that Healey was 'more sensitive to the monetary dimension of policy than some of his advisers'.[76]

Politically, the essential thing was that ten days after Healey had set out cash limits in his statement, they were specifically endorsed by Wilson. In most prime ministers, automatic support for a policy accepted from his Finance Minister would be natural practice. Given Wilson's flaccid response to hard choices – witness the Stoneleigh speech – on-the-record support was something to cherish. And on 11 July, Wilson gave open support to Healey's undertaking 'to employ the system of cash limits more generally as a means of controlling public expenditure in the short term'.[77]

Cash limits most immediately meant that programmes agreed at constant prices were then shifted into prices of the day, and a ceiling imposed as to how much money could be put up. Instead of waiting for the inflation figure and providing cash to cover it, an advance figure was to be given, stating the limits. Healey's White Paper *The Attack on Inflation* specifically said that 'the Government's purchases of goods and services will have to be cut back if prices rise too high.'[78] By April 1976, cash limits would have been sophisticated and fully set out in a White Paper of their own. The process by which money had been spent, debt incurred and public sector pay knocked cheerfully on, would now begin to be taken in hand and subjected to that sinister and useful thing, Treasury control.

Cash limits are a bridge between direct attempts to restrain wage inflation and the reduction of public expenditure. Once Healey was through the portals of the 1 July Cabinet meeting which changed (or acknowledged the change) of so much, he was into the business of specific cuts. There would be an important Treasury meeting on 8 July and a Cabinet at Chequers on 10 July. One area requiring immediate attention was local government. Current expenditure there had grown in ways to make the term 'exponential' look tame. Across four financial years and two governments, with the Conservatives as at least equal culprits, it had risen by almost 40 per cent.

Another was health. Barbara Castle had come away from the 10 July Cabinet, which had excluded formal taking of reserve powers, with Healey's parting shot in her ears: 'Cabinet will appreciate that as the package is weaker than I would like, that will make it all the more necessary for us to be tough over public expenditure.'[79] She was told by her anxious advisers, one of them Jack Straw, that a paper from the Chancellor and a Treasury document, *The Medium-Term Assessment*, required immediate response on £2 billion overall cuts for 1978–9.

In the remaining months of 1975, Healey would be locked in debate about the extent and nature of cuts. Harold Wilson had let himself say in his statement after the July deal with the unions, 'We reject panic cuts in expenditure.'[80] Joel Barnett remarked in the very next sentence of his never malicious memoirs, 'By the autumn, we were making further large cuts, indeed very much larger than those announced in the Budget.'[81]

Discussion of the White Paper on public expenditure began on 4 August at Chequers, inconclusive, discursive, a species of awayday for the Cabinet, with Benn in full, but little regarded flow. It was of course confused by the statistic estimating public spending at 60 per cent of GDP, something which Roy Jenkins remarked 'threatened a plural society'. This would duly be put right early in 1976 after Leo Pliatzky, visiting Canada, had noticed that the Canadian government was worried about much the same overspend as Britain but had public spending down as a mere 42 per cent of GDP. Yet the Canadians seemed to be counting different things. The British, unlike any other similar industrialised country, had been listing all capital investment in the nationalised industries, including trading surpluses and depreciation funds, as public expenditure. By Western industrialised practices, this was clearly the wrong column.

The cash volume of spending by the United Kingdom government would fall automatically by £7.7 billion after the changes went through parliament in 1976, changes which were neither fix nor whitewash, but better, more accurate accounting. However, having the real numbers in the low-to-middle forties rather than at the ruinous-sounding sixty mark did not diminish the actual problem. What mattered was the *direction* taken by the share of public spending from GDP. The ratio moved from 39 per cent in 1973 to 44.2 per cent in 1974 to 46.2 per cent in 1975, an increase of close on a fifth.

The serious opponents of the Chancellor throughout would be Anthony Crosland and Harold Lever. For Crosland, fear of spending having an incendiary effect on inflation was a fallacy. Spending was supposed to squeeze resources and thus crowd out private investment. But given heavy and rising unemployment and world recession, there was no pressure on resources. Healey's argument was that he was projecting forward, not asking for immediate cuts. These should be addressed to the years 1977/9 when, by any reasonable expectation, the world should be humming again. His concern was the amassing of a burden of debt, already fearful in a country which was borrowing a fifth of what it spent and more. He had been advised that the take would increase from a current 20 per cent for 1975/6, not as planned to 21½ per cent, but to 24 per cent. His fear was that the whole benefit of North Sea oil and gas, recently set in flow, might be lost.

Joel Barnett remarked, 'For now I had the impression Cabinet was either not listening or did not want to hear the unpalatable facts.'[82] He also felt that although Healey was on top of the facts, he did not quite stamp his authority on colleagues. August in Buckinghamshire – a meeting which everyone present recalls as pleasant, Barbara Castle bringing her dogs, Harold Wilson making a kindly fuss of them, right and left, Foot and Castle, Healey and

Barnett, bantering together – 'We chi-iked each other over a glass of wine'[83] – was not the occasion for grim resolution or threats of resignation. They would come.

Events in their customary way intervened. The Treasury could show in its National Income Forecast that the PSBR was going unpleasantly up, rising in 1975/6 by 5 per cent of GDP. A number of options were contemplated: import controls, a further devaluation – by 7 per cent – or an application to the IMF for a loan. The implication for Healey, who had come a long way from his optimism in 1974, was that cuts should be found, cuts on a large scale.

Across the autumn of 1975, a problem intervened, perhaps only a medium-sized horror but involving about 6 per cent of the money to be wrested from colleagues. Denis Healey *was* a strong Chancellor and he had ahead of him a major course of resolute and unpopular action. But he was not always conducting the orchestra and when it played low-grade schmaltz, he would find himself following. For, as Healey and his team bent ministers' minds to the saving of money, Wilson was still ready, as the occasion arose, to spend it. In the case of Chrysler, which ran from October to December 1975, a time of maximum struggle for expenditure cuts, he was abetted by Harold Lever.

This American motor company was established unprofitably in the form of Chrysler (UK) at Linwood in Scotland. It rejoiced in a ruthless, unsuccessful management and an atrocious workforce devoted to low production, absenteeism, and instant 'industrial action'. Chrysler Linwood was one of the worst plants in a spavined motor industry where, as Wilson remarked in Cabinet, 138,000 working days had been lost in disputes that year.[84] Benn had talked in his evangelical way about saving a lame duck. 'Lame duck' was a tough-sounding phrase when first used by Edward Heath, whom it had subsequently humiliated. Wilson, butch and epigrammatic, as always in the early stages, replied that Chrysler was a *dead* duck. He would end by funding its resurrection.

Chrysler's Chairman, John Ricardo, and his associates (which seems the right word) 'looked and talked', said Bernard Donoughue, 'like a Hollywood version of Chicago hoods from the 1930s'.[85] Ricardo came to Chequers for dinner with Wilson, washed his hands of further company spending and, with a certain Sicilian aplomb, invited the British government to find the survival money. Otherwise full unemployment and redundancy costs would be left with the government. He knew his man. Seats were being lost to the Scottish Nationalists. The government had a choice of arithmetics. Wilson thundered in the Commons about the blackmail of the management and the Luddism of the workers – and in due, inevitable course, caved in. But the manner of the caving was horribly instructive about the Cabinet.

Eric Varley, now at Industry and showing unexpected steel, was content in

Cabinet on 25 November that the company should go under. 'The NEB don't want it. Vauxhall are afraid we might help Chrysler. Ford don't want it.' Benn denounced Healey and spoke of 'a massive further step towards industrial suicide'.[86]

Healey's own judgement was against the succession of schemes flowing from Lever. A Cabinet Table note to Lever of 5 December says, 'I told you I would play straight on any assessment I made. Nowhere in the papers is it made clear that Scheme B is an offer to pay towards future losses but places on us half or more of past losses and *all* future losses. Even now Shirley [Williams] doesn't understand this when she says "as Chrysler are not paying 35m if they wind up, they can pay extra redundancy".'

And the same note moves across to another notion buzzing about at the same time – protection. 'As you well know, temporary import controls are useless to help but effective to cause us great damage. Help!' And he adds, 'If we were back at the beginning I would support you – and I did. But we are now in a difficult and more dangerous situation.'[87]

For some time the resistance looked to be succeeding, with Lever growing despondent. 'Cabinet on Chrysler,' wrote Healey. 'Lever now against help. Edmund brilliant. Most against redundancy payment. Michael Foot v. passionate. In end by majority for sensible line.'[88] But by 8 December, a Monday – weekends can be deadly for sensible lines – the tone had changed, and he wrote with no pleasure of a meeting of MISC. 'General if reluctant support for rescue on new terms. Varley furious with Lever's interference.'[89]

The Department of Industry had wanted to fight. 'This was *par excellence* a case,' Sir Antony Part commented later,[90] 'for skilled objective analysis by the Civil Service and a case for Ministers, in the light of that analysis, to decide how much weight to give to the strong political factors.' The skilled analysis could have been done on the back of an envelope. The chief political factor was Harold Wilson.

'Harold Lever and I knew,' wrote Bernard Donoughue, 'that the Prime Minister wished to settle at almost any price in order to avoid the unemployment and the threat of resignation from his Scottish ministers, who feared riots at Chrysler's Linwood Plant.' That useful Scottish word 'feardie' turns up again in a ministerial context. Lever took on an ambassadorial role negotiating with Chrysler, for Wilson, usurping the function of a justifiably outraged Varley evidently close to resignation.[91] There was a bitter exchange between Dell, unreservedly supporting Varley, and Lever, over the latter's cavalier treatment of his Cabinet brief when pursuing his real one – from Wilson – in a campaign of open-ended appeasement. Lever would later apologise for an attack on Dell in Cabinet. But he was met in kind. 'I've rarely seen Edmund so angry,'[92] wrote Joel Barnett, lamenting 'the bogus argument of de-industrialization, and the even more bogus argument that somehow you save real jobs by spending huge sums in a lost cause'.[93]

On 10 December, after much losing-side negotiation, Varley reiterated his view and Tony Benn wrote, 'The majority of the Cabinet undoubtedly supported Eric Varley, but Harold Wilson was worried about it and after a great deal of struggle, Harold Lever suggested that he could save some babies being thrown out with the bathwater.'[94] And on December 12 Wilson announced a rescue operation. The extent of the likely commitment was put by Varley at £184.5 million. Healey then presented to Cabinet an elaborate defence of a complete U-turn by the Government – by saying 'that Chrysler had done a complete U-turn.'[95] His argument concerned Iran, a major and cringed-to holder of sterling. The Shah's Finance Minister having told him that Britain would lose credibility in Iran if it failed to act, the absence of any concession on import controls from either the US or the EEC commission and the fact that redundancy payment involved establishing a precedent. The deal involved 8000 redundancies. A large lump sum was expended, plus an undertaking to pay 50 per cent of future losses. The company would later be sold by Chrysler to Peugeot.

There were excuses. It was a time of many bankruptcies and/or crises, Burmah Oil, Alfred Herbert, the tool makers, and the ineffable British Leyland, Labour's own golden albatross. Commercial contracts and ties in Iran added a complication. But Chrysler was the embodiment of politically-fuelled weakness, a general instinct to appease, postpone, walk away from confrontation. The narrow price was £155 million, the broad one, international identification as soft touch ever and again running scared. 'Harold was worried about it', 'The Prime Minister wanted to settle at almost any price . . .!'

As for Healey, his acceptance inspired Tony Benn with hopes that the whole shift in economic policy might be reversed. He saw Healey differentiating himself from 'the real Right which consists of Roy Jenkins, Shirley Williams, Reg Prentice, Fred Mulley, Roy Mason and Eric Varley'(!). Benn didn't rule out Healey giving up entirely on his wider strategy, 'but I wouldn't rule it out because he is entirely without principle.' As a general comment this is more than absurd. Healey was required to fight on a series of bitter fronts, and Wilson's fears meant one more wearying battlefield when prime ministerial support on broad policy was essential. (Mrs Thatcher incidentally followed with similar acts, over British Leyland, the Clegg award to teachers, and the first miners' strike.) But any minister trying to be realistic in Harold Wilson's Cabinet enjoyed a mighty handicap.

This painful diversion took place during an autumn given over by Treasury ministers to getting for real the cuts they had won in principle. On 20 August, Wilson had made a national appeal on television 'Tough and piggy-eyed and though the message sounded reasonable, it was the Ramsay MacDonald line all over again,'[96] wrote Benn.

Any hopes Benn might have entertained about a shift of policy induced by lack of principle had been discounted by yet more events. That rise in the PSBR had been crucial. The tone of the press was growing hysterical. It was possible for a talented, but sometimes silly journalist, Peregrine Worsthorne, to write in the *Sunday Telegraph* that such was the power of the trade unions that the old orders would have to turn to the army.[97]

The encircling gloom had also created agony in the Treasury. The advice coming to Healey was now violently contradictory. There was an End of the World School, one very senior civil servant talking of slashing cuts right down to the closing of hospitals. Hopkin, the Chief Economic adviser, wanted a war on credit cards, Leo Pliatzky, never extreme, suggested going steady, while Alan Lord, an expansionist in this crisis, wanted to cut taxes. The Mandarins resolved things at one meeting by saying to the Chancellor in terms that they could not give him a unified Treasury view.[98] The scheming monolith stood self-confessed as an unresolved colloquy. The autumn months marked no sharp, immediate purpose driven coolly through, rather they showed argumentative reduction of wide differences to a consensus full of options.

Healey's relations with his civil servants through these crises are described by those who attended the meetings as 'Socratic dialogues', Socratic that is, by their style of provocative assertion and response, not through any gentle exposition of clear and certain truth. Healey was frequently rough and rude, unsurprisingly facing such pressure. He also made, deliberately, many changes of debating front to tease out argument. He once, during one of these excursions, provoked Sir Bryan Hopkin to the return, 'Mr Chancellor you are a casuist.'[99] But enough would be taken from Treasury discussion to serve the ultimate conclusions at the MISC meeting in October – heavy cuts with an optional loan from the IMF as fallback.

It was at the October MISC meeting that Callaghan, political in a different sense, had supported Healey with the words 'Let us do the tough things now and get them out of the way.' As the next year would demonstrate, that didn't guarantee getting them out of the way. Healey carried that thinking and some very tough measures to the Cabinet meeting of 13 November, one which fully deserved the cliché rating, 'key'. He told the Cabinet that cuts must go as high as £3.75 billion. Debt was accelerating and threatening all the rewards of oil and gas in the North Sea. The borrowing requirement was £12 billion. (It wasn't, but Pliatzky had yet to speak.) Public expenditure was up 18 per cent, and public spending would be up in the next financial year by 4 per cent instead of the hoped for 1.5 per cent.

Oddly, here his most bitter opponent at the outset was Edward Short, perhaps as a former Minister of Education, also as Leader of the House looking at things in terms of revolts in the PLP. 'I find some of the Treasury's assumptions incredible,' he said. And other essentially friendly, right of centre people, like Roy Mason and Merlyn Rees, were unhappy. Mason talked about 'quite appalling political effects' while Rees objected to being hit with a round sum rather than shown a clear set of priorities. Crosland was against the full extent of demands, but acknowledged the gravity of the circumstances and was willing to accept £2 million of cuts. Nothing momentous could be achieved in so talkative and spirited a Cabinet in a single meeting. The cuts were, in Cabinet terms, the doing of three meetings, 13 November and 9 and 11 December.

Meanwhile in November, Healey informed the Commons of his application to the International Monetary Fund for a stand-by loan, the right to draw in the IMF's own complex banking units, the equivalent of just under a billion pounds. It was both re-insurance (not enough as it turned out) and a measure of the seriousness of things. Along with the bad news about the PSBR, it cut serious opposition to a democratic minimum. Spending ministers would grumble into their diaries, but the Chancellor got his numbers. However in the Labour Party's not-to-be-despised questioning and debating way, to get consent one argued the case all the time. Healey and Joel Barnett, a very tired Chief Secretary, got their breakdown among departments. Wilson could say on the ninth that thanks to earlier bilateral talks, £2600 million of the £3750 had been gathered in. At Health, Mrs Castle tried in vain to ignore inflation. 'I fought desperately,' she says at one point. Wanting to surrender no more than £200 million, she first retreated to £300 million. But 'Joel was adamant he wanted £508 million!' And defeated, she concludes 'I sat back limp.'[100]

A wry note to Healey from Sir John Hunt, observes 'we have done very well: and are now straining to get to a magic figure of £3750 [million]. We have just taken £50m off food subsidies on the assumption that inflation & unemployment will be cured. Could the Treasury take a lower figure for debt interest? Interest rates should fall with inflation and so with the PSBR.'[101]

Healey went into the whole process with a clear bargaining position. He stated a number to the Cabinet and kept one back for himself and the office. They must not, he told ministers on December 9, have cuts of less than £3.75 billion for 1977/8. Behind this lay a resolution, known to colleagues, that with cuts below £3 billion, he would actually resign. It was not a fight he was going to lose. 'Harold ran with very loose rein. No conclusion'[102] was how Healey described the meeting of 9 December.

Perhaps the Chancellor's most indignant and obdurate opponent that morning was the Minister of Defence, Roy Mason, also concerned like Healey that we were losing the confidence of the Shah of Iran. Mason was told not to worry, as he had been doing, vocally, about the effect on NATO. Healey had spoken to Helmut Schmidt. He had been worried but now understood what we were doing and objected no more. Even so, Mason resisted Healey's initial call for cuts of £350 million, displaying enough of what Barbara Castle admiringly called his 'ferocious fluency' to get away with cuts of only £275 million, later whittled down further. But Fred Mulley was rolled over on overseas students at Education, though Wilson quietly ring-fenced the Open University, one of the best things he personally, had ever done. The Environment were done for £225 million with Peter Shore left the perfect freedom of inserting the knife at points of his own choice.

Wilson performed mental arithmetic, and announced final bloc savings of £1033 million, short of the total by £172 million. At which Healey waived further twisting of arms. 'Denis looked noble at this,'[103] said Mrs Castle drily. All cuts by all governments in all crises are artificial, done for show, usually unfair and commonly in the wrong places. But things worth doing had been cut back because for nearly a year virtually the entire government had refused to recognise either the overspend or the inflation. The doing for show had taken place in response to grim figures for the PSBR and in the hope that the markets which had lain quiet, would be pre-empted before they noticed them too. A graceful Cabinet note from Roy Jenkins was warm and eloquent, beginning 'I know you must be appallingly exhausted' and concluding 'Yesterday was a frankly magnificent end to a very difficult process.'[104]

Healey had laboured painfully, a toiling, brave Chancellor brushing unpopularity away. By the time the cuts were approved, he had already suffered retribution. At Party Conference in October, he had recorded in his stoic way, 'Harold garrulous. I defeated for NEC.' He had fallen in that annual festival of bloc votes and prejudice, to a bad second place among the two runners-up.

But Conference was remarkable for something more surprising than that. Ian Mikardo, faux bonhomous and authentically malevolent, had indicated in a hand-out what he would say at a Tribune meeting, the eternal, booked-solid side-show to any decent Labour Conference in the pre-Nuremberg days. At the Spanish Hall of the Blackpool Winter Gardens he would blame Healey and Jones as twin sellers-out of the trade unions and the workers. Barbara Castle was there. 'Suddenly out of the crowd where he had been standing, leapt Jack Jones, up onto the platform, jabbing an accusing finger at Mik like an Old Testament prophet pronouncing his doom . . .' Jones had no microphone . . . 'but he stood there for a full minute, jab following jab with inarticulate shout after inarticulate shout. It was electrifying.'[105] Also therapeutic and the measure of Jack Jones's commitment to promises made.

Healey's Blackpool appearance was more conventional, but still startling. In the diary after noting his defeat, he also remarked, as calmly, 'standing ovation for speech, which was nice.'[106] He had quoted a general of Frederick the Great who, disregarding a foolish order, sent back the message 'Please tell his Majesty that after the battle my head is at his disposal. But during the battle I propose using it in his service.'[107]

It was the sort of remark, as pertinent as literate, which only the really interesting and worthwhile politicians could call up. It was a splendid speech,

pitched to intelligence, with intervals of fun – on the Tory proposals to bring
the exiled rich back by lower taxes: 'If the top rate of income tax were 50 per
cent, it would cost us £400 million. That would mean getting 8000 pop
stars earning £100,000 a year back to Britain. Even if we could do it, the
thought of 8000 Bay City Rollers . . .?' (Laughter and applause.)

It was long in hard realities if rough prose. 'The horrible truth is that in
recent years, for every unit of extra investment we have had in Britain, we
have only got half the return the Japanese have got and only 75 per cent of
the return the French and Italians have got.'[108] Also 'In 1955, a family on
average earnings paid only 16 per cent of its income in tax. Now it pays
nearly twice as much in tax, 29 per cent.' There was no way, he told delegates
that they could have 'substantial increases in public expenditure without
putting a substantial increase in tax burdens on the average working man
and woman'.[109]

Beyond that, Healey did what he was always game for. He took on enemies, lightly deriding a Clive Jenkins snarling his animus and demanding
open-ended borrowing and industrial protection. 'I will say one thing: I do
not want to be lectured by any member of our movement on the need for
import controls when they ask their own trade union to provide them with
a Volvo' (*Applause*).[110] By the end Healey had made an appeal outside the
NEC constituency of grudge and committee, and made it not for the party
office he had lost, but for endorsement of the harsh requirements he had met
in the economy. And the words in italics on the record read '(*standing ovation*)'. Historically, Labour Conferences are not fond of standing ovations.
Routine largesse for the Conservatives, they are grudged by Labour
Conference in a thoroughly monetarist spirit. Healey was a chancellor who
had held wages and was cutting spending, but his success that day was not a
triumph of humour and rhetoric over hard circumstances. He had given delegates, however deftly a hard lesson and indicated his own shift out of public
spenders' optimism into the hard market rules of the economy – into realities.

46

'BEAUTIFUL DAY, STERLING GOING DOWN',
1975–6

Those excited words of Perry Worsthorne about the Establishment turning to the army may simply underline the wisdom of modern Greeks in calling newspapers 'ephemera'. But his mood echoed a wider anxiety and social panic. Book titles alone, contemporary or retrospective – *Goodbye Great Britain*, *The Writing on the Wall*, *Britain in Agony* – convey the message.

It was a period of politics outside politics, heavily publicised though less heavily subscribed fractions and sub-parties – Socialist Workers' Party, International Marxist Group, Workers' Socialist League, Workers' Revolutionary Party, International Socialists – what the French call 'Grupuscules'. The Communist Party of Great Britain seemed placid and official by comparison, though an element in the CPGB, the industrial group around Peter Kerrigan, had done real harm to the economy. They had achieved this through unofficial and official strikes and exploitation of archaic working practices, things rooted ironically in the very conservative craft union tradition deriving from Alexander MacDonald in the 1850s.

The trade union establishment, once safely bossed by heavy-booted men of immoderate moderation, Bevin, Deakin, Lawther, Sam Watson, had fallen to left-wingers who differed from the parliamentary left in having practical power. In practice, classic left-wing new leaders, Jack Jones and Hugh Scanlon, had reached that sane and constructive agreement with Labour ministers over pay. But in the general blur of anxiety, they were tossed into the general nightmare by a press frightened and happy to be frightened. It was the conservative and apolitical tradition of low production through craft practices and job protection which had done most harm slowly over a long period, already a recognisable drag on any wheel that turned in Harold Macmillan's day.

The miners, often tragic victims – seen by themselves as heroic, often simply heroic – were a model of such thinking. Macmillan used to say that there were two forces he would never take on: the Roman Catholic Church and the National Union of Miners. He had nearly turned Catholic as a young man, he had led miners on the unspeakable Front, and not all Macmillan's tears were fake. But at the time of the Second Vatican Conference, he was out of date about the first. As for the miners, their strength lay in the perception of their strength, also in a decent respect for men who did their work and ran their risks. Ironically, perhaps the very best of all the moderate leaders of British unions had been Will Paynter, a Communist. But Paynter was a Pickwickian Communist, attached to the Party for auld lang syne's sake, and a man of perception who understood that pits would close. Paynter sought simply to get very good deals, the run-down of uneconomic pits on the union's timescale with proper redundancy money and, where possible, industrial replacement. He used the unuttered ferocious thought of a pit strike enhanced by memories of 1926, to get things peacefully for his members.

But grown-up unionism stopped in the pits with Paynter. Arthur Scargill, still a voice in the provinces, not yet even President of his own Yorkshire area, had turned miners' conservatism to his own purposes. And Scargill, an operatic personality, self-preoccupied on behalf of the workers, unimaginably like Thatcher in his conceit and shabby messianism, but lacking her controls, was explosive. The strike of 1971 owed something to Yorkshire and Scargill, the one of 1973 was driven by them. The blunderbuss which Paynter kept hanging on the wall Scargill itched to fire. He succeeded and Heath, advancing without preparation, retreating without resistance, turned Scargill into the most important man in British unionism. He had brought down a government, not a very good government, but something to be getting on with. He later gave an interview to the Magazine *Marxism Today*, talking of 'extra-parliamentary' roads to socialism which even not very excitable people took to mean violence. He was the exponent of 'flying pickets', intimidatory groups sent to impose loyalty.

The emblematic picture in the mind of every Cabinet Minister in February March 1974 was of Capper, Chief Constable of Birmingham, borrowing Arthur Scargill's loud hailer, his own having symbolically broken down, to tell his officers to close the gates of Saltley power station so that supplies could not be delivered and energy not be generated. It was at the very least, good Leninist theatre. More to the point, it was the police preventing resistance to a strike. It was the sort of thing to which over-reaction was very natural.

The politics of the Labour government, especially where Michael Foot was concerned, had been those of appeasement. His first piece of legislation was the Employment Protection Act, a name lasting through the long disemployment which followed, but better called the Trade Union Enhancement Act. He was chiefly anxious to accommodate, of all things, the closed shop: exclusion from employment of any non-member of the trade union commanding there. One consequence would be to take over most of the hiring and firing function of a business from the employer. Foot, oddly and cantankerously contemptuous of the small questions of the employee and his free choice, had stood ready with legislation to transfer the dock labour schemes, powers which had made London and Liverpool by-words for ruin, to non-scheme ports like Felixstowe, thriving unacceptably *without* a closed shop. The Foot scheme had been aimed, at the request of Jack Jones's Transport and General Workers' Union, at inland termini on canals and cold storage depots within fifteen miles of any waterway.

The very language recalled seventeenth-century legislation, the Five Mile Act, which tried to prevent non-Anglicans from congregation within five miles of any charter town. Brilliantly lobbied against, the Fifteen Mile Act did not eventually pass into law. But business not being in any way interested in the mere principle of freedom, there were plenty of boardrooms ready to do those deals with unions which guaranteed a smoother flow of production.

It is impossible to say how far the febrile quality of British politics – demonstrations, strikes, auxiliary disputes, the quite obvious lack of authority in the managements of companies – played in the failure of confidence expressed in 1976 in a succession of withdrawals from sterling. Healey as the Chancellor could pull many levers – interest rates, a wages policy, public expenditure. He could not make investors feel secure. Contrary to a common view, capitalism is not a conspiracy, it is a congeries of self-interested acts based on available data, some of it good, some of it useless. Its financial markets do good and ill largely by inadvertence. The trouble with capitalism is not self-interest, but the quality of the information and the inescapable requirement to follow other people doing the same thing. That 1967 story of Wilson's and Jenkins's resignation, resoundingly and demonstrably false, created a succession of shuddering 100 million dollar withdrawals. Healey, inheritor of adjustments made after the oil crisis, was the custodian of a floating pound. If anything fell now it would be sterling.

And, underlying everything irrational, uneconomic and potentially violent, was the press, that strange British thing, virulent, hysterical, apocalyptic, seeming to be sleep-walking through a disaster film. There was deep trouble, the press talked catastrophe. We are told that it is easy to make judgements with hindsight. That is why we make them and why they are so much better judgements. Looking back, it is clear that all the hysterias, left-wing, middle-class and press, *were* overdone. Equally clear is the fact that the dull steady men were right: the policemen who did not fire on demonstrators, the senior officers for whom the notion of involvement in politics was unthinkable and the trade union leaders like Hugh Scanlon saying 'We have seen the abyss' and turning away from it.

By early 1975, the government, pushed on by Healey, the Treasury, the

Bank and, in measure, the Policy Unit, were turning the economy towards orthodoxy. The supposed bogeys of unionism were part of the undertaking. Bennism, a potent scare stimulant, was visibly in retreat. Distress on the left did not register but the message of reshuffle and political attenuation was apparent. Sterling paying above the odds in interest rates, but still retaining the support of OPEC countries, stood fairly steady at $2.05, nothing to do us credit as a trading nation but not actually falling over. The PSBR, always the potential occasion for panics and plunges, was indeed looking grim at the end of the year, but had it not generated the sort of spending cuts which are supposed to calm markets?

The ultimate steady man had been Denis Healey. And very soon to everyone's surprise, he would be joined by that other, almost professionally steady man, James Callaghan, victim of other financial crises, a burnt child with a healthy fear of fire. On the face of things, convalescence with prospects of recovery was scheduled for Britain. The right steps were being taken, the right people were in charge. It was reminiscent of the reform ministers of Louis XVI, Turgot and Necker. Vast chronicles of error and neglect may pass in a dream, but it is frequently upon the head of the reformer, making progress but necessarily drawing attention to the reasons why progress ought to be made, that plaster and masonry actually falls.

The government had, in November 1975, obtained a stand-by loan from the IMF. This was equal-partner business without parental supervision and penalties. Contemplated at a Treasury ministers' meeting in August,[1] it was supposed to bridge our difficulties. Unfortunately, much of what had been going right for Britain reflected how bleak things were. The trade deficit was nicely down – by half from 1974 – but only because domestic demand had fallen. Also what the Americans call an inventory recession was taking place. We were too poor to import as much as we had. The rich, commodity-exporting countries knew as much and loved sterling ever less. Worrying about the Shah was natural. Worrying about Nigeria was endemic. At the back of this was the possibility of easing our predicament by devaluation. During the Treasury debate, it was very much the option to import-control, but with imports down through impoverishment, the appeal of that diminished. Nicholas Kaldor, an ardent devaluer in the sixties, was now furiously against it, as were Derek Mitchell and a surprisingly stern Harold Lever. Douglas Wass was its keenest advocate, with support from Hopkin and Michael Posner. Richardson, Governor of the Bank, could see the case for depreciation but, like Healey, feared losing control of such a move. Melancholy discussion quietly went on in the background of the uncomprehendingly resentful Cabinet arguments about cuts, a tinkling but terribly important obbligato.

Healey was even sharper about sterling depreciation than over import surcharges. He saw it provoking the large holders of sterling like Nigeria and starting a general run. And the message of the forecasts did nothing to lighten the mood. World recovery would sweep away, they said, any improvements registered in the balance of trade. As Miss Prism tells Cecily, 'The chapter on the fall of the rupee you may omit. I find that even these metallic matters have their sensational aspect.'

Britain went into 1976 having done a great deal by way of stern measures in an era of flammable politics. But if everybody knows there is an insurmountable problem and no one quite knows how to surmount it, circumstances have a way of taking over. There are several theories about the fall of sterling in March 1976. 'Backing into a quiet devaluation' was a phrase attributed to one unnamed Treasury official. People who believe in Treasury bounces will find a malicious intent, those who think things frequently go wrong without intention will put their trust in blunder.

What factually happened on 4 March 1976 was that with sterling having enjoyed a small upswell, the Bank of England sold pounds and, on the next day, lowered minimum lending rate. The pound was already, at $2.05, below the point, $2.20, at which Nigeria and Kuwait had threatened wholesale withdrawal. The surrounding circumstances were brittle, watchers with a direct interest were horribly alert and intent. One theory is that the Bank was not trying to nudge the pound down, but to make a little money. To 'cream off dollars' is the phrase, and it implied a belief that the pound was strong enough for such raids. Any conspiracy was also a blunder, any blunder was a big one. No one quantifies any supposed intention at Bank or Treasury above devaluation of 5 per cent. But the response of the oil producers was to sell all receipts made in sterling at once. In seven days, the Bank is thought to have spent $500 million to prop up the pound. Other estimates, in the *Banker* and *The Times* respectively, reckoned that '$750 million went in 11 days and one billion dollars over two weeks.'[2] As a creaming-off of dollars, it had not been a success. By July, sterling had fallen by 12 per cent, an aspect sensational enough to make ministers respond with Cecily's reply to Miss Prism, 'Horrid political economy!'

Evidence of clear Bank understanding of what specifically it should do is not available. The authorities there were the prisoners of their own uncertainty; a half shot failing was almost inevitable. But if there were ever a plan, it is overwhelmingly unlikely to have had government endorsement.

In the Treasury some sort of fall in the currency had many patrons. For the devaluers, the term current in Treasury circles had earlier been the 'Big Step'. This was seen as the alternative option to simply floating down. A recurring theme with this group at the Treasury was the advantage of permanent devaluation, as exemplified by France. It was a line France had followed before, during the thirties, meeting the slump with the franc already heavily marked down. This had produced, during that depression, to quote a later *New Statesman* piece, 'a gentle, bobbing inflation'.[3]

British inflation in the mid-seventies was not gentle, nor did it bob. However, just before March 1976, talk seems to have been about a move from $2.05 to perhaps $1.95. This was a little step, perhaps the product of the temporary optimism which allowed pounds to be sold. A big step, a candid devaluation of perhaps 12.5 per cent might, in markets subject to volatile psychology, have worked.* All we know is that floating, on what became a Zambesi in flood, did not.

The cutters of public expenditure attracted suspicion, especially Derek Mitchell because he had been part of a consulting group of international bankers with Karl-Otto Poehl, Jacques de la Rosière and Edwin Yeo. Labour opinion was ready to smell conspiracy in gatherings. Mitchell is firm that he was concerned, first, to put the case of Britain's reformed and fundamentally sound position to these colleagues; also that everything *they* said was at once reported fully to Healey who appreciated the information.

There is another reason to discount ministerial intent. Harold Wilson at this time was making ready to resign – he had made intimations in the ears of particular cronies like Haines much earlier. The man settling for a particular departure date because it would give him a few days longer in office than Asquith, would have countenanced nothing which even risked marking that leavetaking with a wheel falling off the economy. As for Healey, he had the sense not to get into a personal panic. His diary remarks on the dullness of that day's Cabinet and he went, as he had planned, to see Freni and Raimondi in *Simon Boccanegra*. Privately cool, he urged as much on colleagues. The visit of the Governor next morning produces the Attlee-esque comment, 'Gordon in about run on sterling – told him to keep calm,'[4] before settling down to a long meeting about his Budget. Life continued as it must, even for a Chancellor whose currency has been shot beneath him. 'Cut hedge, cleared gardens, made fire'[5] is a weekend entry a few days later. And as normal life continued, so did normal politics.

It was wisdom, however furious the efforts to buy off the slide, not to panic before colleagues. Sound currencies reflecting sound economies are not speculated against, dollars can be creamed off by their central bankers without calamity. Healey had to get the economy right before sterling would come right. And Healey's own uncertainty is reflected in his calm. He could see the arguments for a devaluation and those against. Britain would grow more competitive in the short run, something offset by higher raw material costs, but such costs could work against the already very promising deal with the unions on pay. And as he noted in the memoirs, 'once a trend changes, it's very difficult to check it where you want it . . .' His wry conclusion to the fall

---

* The (inadvertent) big step of September 1992, admittedly in circumstances of low demand, was hugely effective whatever the political cost.

in sterling was one of 'mixed feelings, like the chap who saw his mother-in-law go over Beachy Head in his new car'.[6]

But this is hindsight. Edmund Dell recalls that 'Healey intensely disliked policies which involved the depreciation of sterling. He was always fearful that sterling would fall out of control. His only decision had been to defer a decision.'[7] What he could also see was that if his actions – over a wage deal in June–July and over expenditure cuts in December – had proved too little for the market, Cabinet colleagues resisting so much and giving way so painfully demonstrated oblivion to events. This was most cruelly true of Crosland, the Social Democratic thinker who, behind a grand insouciance and the belief that he was far better qualified to be Chancellor, had responded to realities with theory.

In the contest which Wilson now precipitated, Healey would never have been chosen as party leader. There was room for one left-wing candidate, Foot, and one right-winger, Callaghan. He very nearly did not stand at all, asking Joel Barnett what he should do. The dilemma was simple: he was not strong enough to win, he was too strong not to run. But he probably scored lower than he might have done for a single chance reason. On 10 March the government suffered a defeat after being petulantly defied by the left wing. A natural majority was wiped out by 35 left-wing abstentions.* This is the sort of thing which happens to governments with small majorities. John Major was to be lacerated by it, through the disloyalty of his right-wing enemies. A vote of confidence the next night and the political fluff blows away.

But Healey, ahead of the anticipated vote, spoke contempt. '"He must have gone off his rocker" I muttered. "If he hasn't lost us this vote, he ought to have done." But of course he hadn't and the emptiness of the abstainers' gesture was shown when they meekly filed into the government lobby . . .'[8] Healey noted of the next day's confidence debate: 'Uproar when I spoke, Heffer furious – but all knuckled under.'[9] Cited as irrepressible wildness, a reason why he could never be leader, it might be better remembered as rough courage in a time of much flinching. But though perfect diplomacy would not have elected Healey in 1976, he might, if forewarned and suitably dull that night, have had a dozen or more extra votes and his marker placed further forward for the real chance of 1980. His reaction when the first ballot was announced on 25 March, giving him only 30 votes (seven less than Tony Benn, himself squeezed in the rush to Foot), was spartan: 'I, 30 (disappointing).'[10] For no very good reason, he stayed in the race and gained little by it – 38 votes on the second ballot to Foot's 133 and Callaghan's 141, the

---

* Later understood by Benn in terms of 'the EEC, Eric [Heffer]'s dismissal, unemployment, high prices, devaluation, divergence from the manifesto, Chrysler, the TUC, corporatism.'

Crosland and much larger Jenkins vote going fairly obviously to Callaghan. The final outcome gave Callaghan 176 to Foot's highly creditable 137.

Callaghan as Prime Minister would ultimately be a great improvement on Wilson. He balanced avuncularity with ruthlessness, not enough of the latter to despatch Tony Benn, enough with some vengeful recollections of 1969, to sack an outraged Barbara Castle and dismally replace that spirited woman (and silence her helpful diary) with the comprehensive nullity of David Ennals. The government also lost Short by resignation, the pre-emptive move of a man long at war with the new premier. Callaghan gratefully accepted and expressed to Short the importance of his deputy leadership now going to Michael Foot.[11] The unions' uncritical friend, first in the first ballot, was both irresistible and after his showing, suddenly a thinkable candidate for leader. He had the support of what would be called the hard and soft left. He also indicated the extent of the parliamentary party's propitiatory instincts. Constituency truculence muttering re-selection, occupied many minds and a vote for Foot confidingly acknowledged at the local Labour Club was excellent insurance.

The rest of the Cabinet moves were cautious. Crosland got one of the Great Offices, the wrong one for him and sadly too late, succeeded at the Environment by the voluble europhobic Shore, himself followed at Trade by Dell. With Jenkins very shortly afterwards withdrawing from British affairs to the presidency of the European Commission, Merlyn Rees, Callaghan's friend and election standard-bearer, would, in a very early reshuffle, go from the greater griefs of Northern Ireland in a terrible time to the customary ones of the Home Office. Roy Mason would then become the toughest and most unequivocally unionist Northern Ireland Secretary in the post's thirty-year history. One unrecorded impulse of Callaghan's, quickly suppressed, was noted by Healey. 'Jim nearly sacked Silkin [the left-wing Minister of Agriculture], wanted to give Kinnock a job, but not as reward for rebellion.' He also reports Foot trying to advance Tribunites including Norman Atkinson, most unintelligently obstreperous of backbenchers. Amazingly, 'Atkinson wanted cabinet rank.'[12]

The cast of British politics was more than reshuffled, it had a new shape altogether and now leaned, despite Foot's advance, perceptibly to the right. For Healey, Callaghan was a good choice. And though Dell would grumble that he 'took seven dangerous months to learn the job', even that astringent critic grants him to have been 'an excellent Prime Minister until he ducked the general election decision in the autumn of 1978'.

He had been Chancellor of the Exchequer. He knew how hard the work was and how much at odds with colleagues chancellors under financial pressure had to be. His relations with Healey were very good, the chat at the steakhouse, the sinister meeting which was not a sinister meeting, indicated the ease and affinity between the two men. Callaghan, wanting to talk about his farm plans after a feverish Cabinet meeting, turned to Healey for congenial company. The phrase 'Callaghan–Healey nexus' was not wholly fanciful. He would not have spoken to the parliamentary left in the way of Healey's March speech, but he shared the sentiments. He was not tied to the left by old association like Wilson. He was cautious where Wilson was nervous; and though only a little bolder, he lacked Wilson's flinching kindliness.

But Callaghan had chosen a hard time for his ascent. The Policy Unit's briefing, more attentively heard by the new Prime Minister, indicated on Callaghan's second day of office, 5 April, that sterling, at $1.88 nastily below any half-intended nudge to $1.95, was vulnerable to a further devaluation of perhaps 15 per cent. Callaghan the Chancellor had resigned days after devaluing sterling to $2.40![13] The immediate concern was to hold the dykes of the voluntary pay policy, the pride and joy of Prime Minister and Chancellor. And rightly so – it worked, it was getting inflation down. From a fearful high of almost 27 per cent in August 1975, the rate would be down to 12.9 per cent by July 1976. Healey had worked hard on his personal relations with the union leaders. Indeed, one witness at a meeting attended by Jack Jones when Wilson's resignation was announced, heard him rather like the idea of Healey as premier.[14]

One central idea for Callaghan was to use his excellent relations with the unions to build up the sort of permanent understanding which makes the Swedish trade union federation, LO (Lands Organisation), integral to government and fully alerted to its economic problems. The Conservatives would quickly call this 'corporatism', yet British unions had been so far from central command, so touchy on the shop floor, that the aspiration would come to conclusive grief in the grim winter of 1978–9. But in the shorter term, remarkable things would be achieved. The foundation was sensibly social. A monthly dinner to discuss anything current would be held. It would be attended by the six union leaders on the NEDC, affably known as 'the Neddy six' – at inception Jack Jones, Lionel Murray, David Basnett, Alf Allen, Hugh Scanlon and Geoffrey Drain – together with Prime Minister, Chancellor and Michael Foot with Kenneth Stowe* also present and taking an unofficial note. They were conservative as to cuisine, with a fixed menu of smoked mackerel, steak-and-kidney pie, followed by ice-cream with black cherries, the only exception to this being Hughie Scanlon's request for *goujons* of sole.[15] They are not to be mocked; a responsible and informed trade union leadership might not ultimately be enough, but it helped.

Dell regularly muttered at Healey for having pet projects mostly to do with industry, all directed at pleasing the unions. 'He always attempted to do

---

* Now Sir Kenneth, Private Secretary to Wilson, then Callaghan, as Prime Ministers, later Permanent Secretary at the DHSS.

something for them when he was contemplating other, less popular steps, like the £2 billion *extra* allowed to trade, industry and employment over the period 1975/9.'[16] But if less cost-effective than *goujons de sole*, the concessions represented the spending of money in return for something. As the Callaghan administration braced itself for market wrath following PSBR and balance of payments figures which frightened them, the need not to lose wage restraint, indeed to pin it back further, intensified. Healey's major move in his April Budget of 1976 was directed to union members. There would be tax relief, first without condition on the first £370 million of earnings, then, subject to a wage agreement being made at a lower rate – 3 per cent – further relief of £1 billion. It was all very dubious constitutionally. TUC leaders were functioning as a co-opted part of government and the result of the joint deliberations would be handed to the Commons for an assent hardly more doubtful than Her Majesty's. But like so many dubious things, it worked.

Circumstances contradicted Crosland's belief in the autonomy of an internationally indebted social democratic state. Benn's siege economy, socialism behind tariff walls, had few charms, but unlike Crosland's thinking, it was internally logical. As for the Cabinet, they had begun in March 1974 full of certainties. Two years on, they were to face a course of melancholy submissions, first by offering unsuccessful economies aimed at keeping out the Brokers' Men, then to those very persons, otherwise the IMF. The really objectionable side to government relations with the unions had come from Michael Foot with his union-pleasing assaults on the 'Lump',* and the legislation aimed at extending dock-scheme union command to cold storage depots and waterway outlets. However, the ultimate happy frustration of such schemes did not hinder Healey's business with the unions.

Unhappily, so much of the left-wing agenda, including the measures of nationalisation, was against the government's interests in those very markets. If the unions cut into the theoretical sovereignty of an elected ministry, so did sellers of sterling. Constitutional nicety was infringed on all sides, not least by the government itself. On 27 May, Callaghan, soldiering on with the Aircraft and Shipbuilding Nationalisation bill, saw it carry by a single vote in the Commons and that vote the illicit action of a member who had been paired.†[17] 'We cheated,' said Tony Benn righteously.[18] With sterling sliding to the $1.70 mark, nationalisation wasn't worth the candle, let alone the fix.

While such headless legislative chickens lived out their ordained destiny, Healey was reasoning successfully with Jones, Scanlon, Murray, Basnett and

---

* Self-insured or uninsured freelance labour.

† The system by which individuals in the major parties agree to cancel out each other's absent vote, keeping party scores level.

Alf Allen of the Shopworkers', with other union leaders secure behind. And in the spring of 1976, he pushed for a second year's more stringently anti-inflationary agreement. Not 10 per cent or its cash form, but 5 per cent or better was the first objective, nicely in parallel with fellow Social Democrats in Federal Germany where a cut in actual living standards had been accepted with deals narrowly between 5.2 and 5.4 per cent.[19] Healey was being very ambitious, for Germany had not engaged in anything like the same depth of over-spend and debt in the opening year of the OPEC price rise. Also German unions, like those of Sweden and not at all like Britain's, were self-disciplined, highly centralised and economically literate.

Very unusually, Healey's diary, normally entered however cryptically every day, is at this time full of jumps and days omitted altogether. It was a period of intense pressure and anxiety. He spent most of late April and early May in and out of meetings with the TUC, with the pound slipping away in the corner and with Wass at one point suggesting that minimum lending rate should be raised by 1½ per cent. On 25 April, on his way to Bonn for talks with the German Foreign Minister and Bundesbank chairman, he records, 'Sterling very nervous, Gordon Richardson saying will collapse in two days.'[20] The 27th is marked by 'Sterling a bit calmer but not much.'[21] On the 28th, the TUC are in, asking for more than he can allow – a formula for minimum earnings, percentage and maximum take which read £3 : 6 % : £5. His comment is 'Very stubborn. Got rougher.' Healey responded by warning 'No tax reliefs if 6%'[22] and he agreed to a further private talk with Len Murray. This takes place on the last day of the month and he is assured that the TUC will come down to £2.50 : 5% : £3.50, something to be achieved 'by forcing Alf [Allen]'. Meanwhile, 'Jack won't let Hughie fall through.'[23]

A day later Healey held a secret meeting at Number 11, at which the maxima and minima and the percentage equivalent are again wrangled over: 'They went down with great difficulty to £2.50, 6%, £4 after I said I couldn't offer tax reliefs. They promised to go further if possible. I suggest £2.25, 4%, £4. Talk again Tuesday.'[24]

A note from Len Murray expresses the psychology of such bargaining perfectly.

Denis,
    Oughtn't we to take a break?
    £3 floor – £5 limit expressed as 6% represents defeat. If it can be expressed to represent 3% on wage *rates*, victory.
    We ought to talk.

                                                                              Len

On the Tuesday, at 5.30 p.m., they gathered for a long night's number-swapping which, after he had returned from a 10 p.m. vote and heard their 'maximum offer', would be only half spent. The meeting finally ended at 3.30 a.m. That offer was £2.50 : 5% : £4. Healey's response was: 'Suggested they come down to 4½% and leave out £50 m of PE [Public Expenditure]. They wouldn't budge. Saw Jim. Jim met them, but didn't push further.' After further discussion, he says simply 'all exhausted when finished' and then, after talking for an hour to his officials about presentation including the next day's press conference, he adds, 'Hardly slept. Read papers at 7 a.m.'[25] But Murray's point was taken and accepted. The deal would be described fairly enough as 3 per cent on wage rates plus tax concessions. And it would, in fact, produce a figure of less than 5 per cent overall, something to be ratified by a special TUC conference in June.[26] The vote in favour when that conference met on 16 June was massive. This meant, of course, that the union leaders, owners of bloc votes, had dealt and delivered. Actual membership opinion was another thing and bubbling far left activist discontent yet another.

Callaghan, talking to Helmut Schmidt on 13 May, spoke in football man- agerese about 'Denis and all the rest of the lads' having pulled it off.[27] The deal, for Britain, as for Germany, would represent a real reduction in wage levels. Michael Foot, a witness with Shirley Williams of much of the pro- ceedings, wrote a note characteristically warm and kind, but by no means overstating things, describing the settlement as 'a Herculean feat on your part, a sustained piece of intellectual argument with people who are born arguers themselves . . . Only those who actually saw it can have the remotest idea of what it involved and what combined persistence and intelligence were required to secure it. Quite possibly it has changed the whole prospect for the country and the Government; at least it has given us the chance to survive. And the achievement was overwhelmingly yours.'[28] No one should argue with that.

The Labours of Hercules were nine. The Labours of Healey simply carried on where the last one left off. His next concern lay with another bout of public expenditure cuts. The unions didn't like them, but they knew they were coming and this increasingly sophisticated leadership, however gnarled in negotiation, was more or less reconciled to them. But he encountered a dif- ficult prime minister, observing on 13 May, 'Cabinet on Civil Service cuts – Jim a bit chippy.' On the next day it was 'Chat with Douglas Wass – a bit obsessed about 5%.'[29] Healey's gift for shrugging off crisis, and its attendant mad, stressed hours, to enjoy with Edna their cottage at Withyham, shows with the weekend entries in the diary: 'Perfect day again. Bought books at Halls' [a Tunbridge Wells bookshop he favoured] and 'Cleared plum trees . . . perfect day'.[30]

The irony was that whatever was difficult to get past colleagues, became easier as things got worse. The pound having started to fall, saw no reason to stop. Eventually the further round of cuts, yet further propitiation of the gods of the market, would become painfully do-able to a Cabinet which had thought that, in the previous December, it was through with such horrors. But first, the soft option rode again. Leo Pliatzky put it gently: 'One opinion which was urged upon the Chancellor with characteristic persuasiveness was that the most sensible and also the most painless course was to borrow our way through the situation; we should raise loans enabling us to put funds in the shop window on a scale large enough to demonstrate that there was plenty of backing for the pound and that speculators against it would burn their fingers.'[31] Harold Lever had the ear of Callaghan, and Pliatzky speaks of argument being 'heated, and opinion went in first one way then another. The scene of discussion shifted between the Treasury building and No. 11 frequently involving Harold Lever as well as the Chancellor and the Chief Secretary.'*[32]

It is not difficult to sense the panic of an office responsible for a currency now out of hand, an office full of people thinking in opposite directions. And even the soft option could be operational agony: '2 *June Wednesday*. Very heavy pressure – lost 4c, recovered 1c. Tories fussed, asked for statement.' Callaghan's concern at this time was to offer reassurance, messages being sent in the way of a panoramic Private Godfrey to 'BBC TV, Radio 4, ITN, NBC, LBC saying "Don't panic".'

The Treasury, and Healey with it, settled instead for worrying and neighbourly contradiction: '3 *June* Big meeting. Gordon wanted IMF, Douglas nothing (Both at Nottingham GS together).' He also made a note of Callaghan's wish to borrow in Europe.

Next day he made tentative approaches to the IMF: 'Enquired without commitment of Burns and Simon.† Before Gordon rang Burns, Zijlstra rang to offer $4-5 b. Simon rang to ask me to see Fed. Arthur told Gordon not satisfied with Simon's approach ... Decided we wanted £2 Bn US, $1 Bn Europe.' The first object seems to have been a direct US loan and on the Saturday (5 June) Healey spent three hours talking with Burns: 'told him everything. He wanted us to go straight to the IMF ... Leo returned. Rang Simon. Simon put pressure on Burns – needed currency $2 b. ... told Gordon to press on by phone with others (NB European Whit holiday).'

As Burns was dragging his feet about specific action, Sunday was spent in Sussex, now a base for triangular phone conversations through Richardson, successful in Europe, then a return to London, then hearing 'Arthur agreed to Monday'. Eventually the discussion hardened to a successful conclusion. The Bank of England had, by way of five days of frantic urgency, found lines

---

* Still Joel Barnett.

† These were, respectively, Arthur Burns, chairman of the Federal Reserve, and William Simon, Secretary of the US Treasury.

of credit worth $5.3 billion – money from the Bank of International
Settlements, the US, Switzerland and most of the G10 excepting France and
Italy, strapped for cash themselves.[33] But Healey noted doubt as to whether
pressure could be lifted without a change of policy.[34]

Getting the loan was rational and the lenders largely willing, since sterling
was by now almost certainly undervalued, the markets, after their long quiescence, having done a relentless dog-and-trousers act. The current account
deficit was under £1 billion, down from a high of £3.3 billion in 1975, and
inflation was falling in line with these improvements. But what had now been
so painfully extracted was a bundle of short-term loans, for which repayment
would start in six months' time. Large as the sum was, it was fairy gold and
never likely to soothe markets inclined by psychology and calculation to selling. The Lever approach had been tried and had worked for a very short
time. An orthodox market man like Dell argued that the reduction of debt by
yet more cuts was the precondition of recovery. The additional good news that
the miners had accepted the second year's pay agreement, if only by a vote of
53 to 47 per cent, ought to have mattered far more than it did. But the economy was into a new contest.

For sentiment was against us rather than arithmetic. It was odd that
Britain's virtue, secured largely by Healey, was being thrown back in her face.
Healey himself argues that the markets had a mania that the Treasury
planned a bear coup. It was their conviction, he writes, that 'we were determined to contrive a big fall in the pound, so of course they did not want to
hold sterling.'[35]

The inadvertent earlier folly of the Treasury talk – in circulated papers and
who knows in what less than perfectly private places – about the 'Big Step'
seems, quite calamitously, to have become market folklore. *Talk* about
options – in this case no more than limited moves for a reduction of ten or
twelve cents – had done more harm than any actual devaluation done quickly
early in the year, the full price for a Treasury unable to present the Chancellor
with a unified Treasury view.

There was one other irony, a huge one. In his conversations while raising
the loan in early June Healey had spoken to Witteveen of the IMF, finding
him 'Friendly but worried about PSBR'. It would of course be revealed some
time later that the figures which very reasonably worried the IMF chairmen
(and the markets) were £2 billion too high. The Treasury genius for coming
up with wrong figures came like a millstone to a drowning man. Not drowning was now to be Healey's chief concern.

The hope, never a promising one, was that the existence of the loan would
calm the markets and help the pound. He did not want either the economic
or political griefs of a new sheaf of cuts in public spending. But the markets
took note, not that we had an access of funds, but that we had needed them.
There was to be no remission. It was clear soon enough to Healey that he

must cut again. The markets might push sentiment to the point of irrationality, but they commanded all authority. As Housman wrote in a quite other context:

> Keep we must if keep we can
> These foreign laws of God and man.

Leo Pliatzky would, six weeks later, explain to Tony Benn the pressures which the Chancellor was under. 'The factors which had influenced the Treasury to go for public expenditure cuts were first, that the Governor of the Bank of England had been in two or three times in June and demanded £3 billion's worth of cuts immediately, and second, that the Treasury was deeply wounded by the general charge that public expenditure was out of control. It was probably true when Tony Barber was there, but certainly not now, because the cash limits are a noose round everybody's neck.'[36] Derek Mitchell's judgement was that the cuts had to be undertaken because of sentiment. If the markets wanted a specific form of reassurance, then that reassurance had to be given.[37]

Actually getting the cuts was a Cabinet grief which Healey found 'appallingly difficult'.[38] The objective that blazing summer of drought was a billion pounds, but since he found micro-measures to help industry worth while, he confided to Pliatzky the intention of raising a little over that billion to pay for them.

Healey might suffer but he had at least the consolations of relevance. Tony Benn reports at this time, 9 May 1976, a conversation with Anthony Crosland in which the new Foreign Secretary says that 'Jim was jealous of him for having got on well with Kissinger' and furthermore that by calling President Ford's office through his wife, who had been at Vassar with Anne Armstrong, the US Ambassador, he had had it agreed 'that at the dinner at the White House, though it would be white tie, the Foreign Secretary could come in a black tie'.[39]

Benn was taken aside by Callaghan on 21 June and told: 'I have a real problem on public expenditure. I am sure, indeed I know, that Denis is going to have to ask for huge public expenditure cuts next month, £1 billion, £2 billion, I don't know. How are we going to handle this in a way that doesn't damage the party?' He was concerned to have consultations, but knew that anything said to the NEC would leak. They settled on a paper from Benn, with a copy to go personally to Callaghan. 'I said "I know that view won't get through because the Chancellor always wins in the cabinet."'[40] Callaghan's mind at this time was fluid. Beyond the cuts, if they failed, lay the conditional loan which he hated to contemplate. So this exchange is best treated not as cynical man-management, but as a door kept open to other options.

Talk of depreciation continued. A Policy Unit note of 27 June had observed that 'A further decline in the exchange rate would be needed to maintain current competitiveness through 1976,' also that even if all went well with the wage settlements, there was still 'a very serious risk that sterling holders will try to remove some or all of their funds'. It suggested that 'The Treasury should be asked about sterling guarantees.'[41] This would represent assurance to sterling holders that they would not be losers. Across the crisis, Callaghan would develop an increasing yearning to be rid of sterling's status as a reserve currency. It gave one position and prevented one from keeping it up.

Healey had broad Prime Ministerial support but always had to work for it. Six days later, he heard from the Chief Secretary: 'Meeting with Mandarins, Joel on PE – it looks likely to get more than £1 b and successful if that will do the trick. Tax increase we all leave to incomes policy and industrial revival.'[42] Benn also records Healey at an economic strategy meeting. 'He gave a general review about confidence and how the pound could drop, all the usual arguments that are used to persuade you to give up what you want.'[43] But the pound *was* dropping.

Formal Cabinet discussion began on 6 July with Michael Foot pre-soothed by the Prime Minister. But Peter Shore, difficult over his Environment fief in his bilaterals with the Chief Secretary, went on being difficult in Cabinet. As Healey puts it, 'Peter v. emotional.'[44] The Policy Unit were also unhappy. It was, said a memorandum of 11 July, 'the wrong time'. The TUC and PLP might feel 'legitimate anger at having to swallow this after virtually accepting a legal cut in wages'. It had been, said the note, an assumption that restraints were 'an alternative to spending cuts'.[45]

The Cabinet of 15 July was a bitter affair if one listens to Tony Benn: 'I think that the British Establishment is now infected with the same spirit which afflicted France in 1940, the Vichy spirit of complete capitulation and defeatism . . . Denis sat there scarlet. He always blushes when he is in difficulty and the argument is gaining force.'[46] But in Healey's account, business was done satisfactorily: 'Jim handled cabinet well. Decided £1 b cuts in first ¾ hour. Roy Mason forced to £100m, Fred Peart £25. Shirley £75 re extra on food subsidies.'[47]

Cabinets were now as frequent as budgets and on 29 July, a Monday, an unusual date and a bad sign, cuts worth £994 million were painfully agreed, something which would have satisfied Callaghan. But Healey, listening now to Mitchell's market-minded advice, refused to take any shortfall which might make the markets punish us yet further. Mitchell had in fact told him that even a simple billion might not be enough for this market. By a mild fiddle, the consequent cut in debt interest was counted in to make up the round billion. And Healey added to this the politically less painful imposition of a surcharge on employers' National Insurance contributions, allowing him to go to the Commons and speak of £2 billion saved.

Naturally enough in a man talking to more immediately important groups than the House of Commons,* he was upbeat. In his April Budget speech, he had 'expected our gross domestic product, which fell during 1975, to grow by about 4 per cent and manufacturing output to grow by about 8 per cent in the year to mid-1977.' But it was better than that. 'In fact the recovery has proceeded faster than I expected, led by a vigorous growth in exports. On present policies I would now expect GDP to increase over the next 18 months from the first half of 1976 at an annual rate of 5 per cent and exports of goods and services by 11 per cent . . . I would expect unemployment to start falling before the end of the year . . . Money supply [M3] has grown well within the guidelines I set at the time of the Budget.'[48]

However, inside the bouquet was the sharpened knitting needle. 'Next year the recovery of the economy is likely by itself to reduce the PSBR only by something like £1 billion to about £10½ billion. This alone will not be enough . . . I must therefore look to public expenditure for a major contribution and I am announcing now, in advance of the usual White Paper, public expenditure reductions of £1 billion . . .'[49] In announcing the 2 per cent increase in employers' contribution to National Insurance, Healey also made a statement about debt policy. Further action 'in the tax field', he said, 'is needed to reduce the PSBR to £9 billion'.[50] It was the gentler alternative to Income Tax or VAT increases, but the whole package had Norman Atkinson telling the Chancellor that 'he may have won the confidence of international creditors but he has certainly lost the confidence of the Labour movement.'[51] For the moment, international creditors bulked rather large. The trouble was that, although the displeasure of Mr Atkinson ought to have helped, he hadn't won their confidence either. Mitchell, for one, envisaged the arrival of the IMF. 'Over these months there was an increasing sense of inevitability that Britain would have to apply.'[52]

The Labour Party and the Cabinet busied themselves with other things, like devolution – 'No enthusiasm on question in Cabinet'[53] – the sun shone and Denis Howell, a sensible junior minister from Birmingham, was put in charge of the water we didn't have.† But only one thing really mattered. And as Healey acknowledges, it was a good thing that he followed the July Measures with a decent holiday – Wales and the Western Highlands of Scotland, topped out with a quick draught of the Edinburgh Festival: Berganza in *Figaro* and *Carmen*, Alan Rickman in *The Devil is an Ass*, a

---

* He also spoke to the country, adding casually in his diary 'TV – Robin'.
† Actually Howell had an inspirational scheme for laying piping down a requisitioned M4 fast lane to save the parched West of England, before, quite thoughtlessly, it started to rain continuously.[54]

respite that he and Edna delighted in – for 'the next four months were to be the worst of my life.'[55]

There was an episode of the markets on 24–5 August, such as when he was in Corsica the year before, and passing almost as quickly: calls to Healey in Ullapool to authorise part of the loan (he set a limit of $150 million) being spent to quieten the markets, which it did. But this was no blip, more of a preliminary salvo.

Sterling during that incident fell to $1.73. It did nothing very terrible for most of September until two prospective unofficial strikes, at British Leyland and among seamen, provided less reason than pretext for more selling, which followed on 7 September. The Movement did its thick-headed bit to punish the Labour government further when, on 8 September, the NEC voted in favour of proposals to nationalise insurance companies and the leading banks. Not even the announcement next day of the death of Mao Tse Tung cheered the capitalists up.* On 8 September, the National Union of Seamen made the strike official. On 9 September, the Bank gave up on support for the pound after expending $400 million over those eight days to keep it at $1.77. It now fell by more than three cents.

To his other misfortunes Healey could add the burglary of his cottage in Withyham. But he could have well done with his larger concerns ending so happily. 'Nothing taken but bottle of gin(?)' he surmised on the day when he was compelled to raise minimum lending rate by 1½ per cent, adding a poignant note: '£ up to $1.75 83 – at one time.'[57]

One reason for giving up support for the pound was the prospect of not having the resources to do the supporting. The date of the midsummer loan was looming and, in the way of short-term loans, it had to be repaid in the short term. Another three months' renewal could be had, but that would be all. The experience of July, August and September told Callaghan and Healey what October, November and December would probably be like. As Dell put it, 'How long could he hang on against the market's disbelief when the stand-by was repayable not later than 9 December?'[58] For behind the standard sterling crisis lay the coming about of what had been predicted earlier – that we might not be able to finance the debt. The problem was to sell that debt, which is to say sell gilt-edged securities. Gilt-edged are more or less advantageous to buyers as interest rates go up or down. This fuels a rewarding pessimism. Because the market expected to make more money from a government forced to raise interest rates, it declined to buy at current rates, obliging governments to pay up, a gentlemanly form of blackmail fulfilling its own profitable expectations. It was enough to give one a frisson of sympathy for Tony Benn.

---

* Tony Benn observed that 'he certainly towers above any other twentieth century figure I can think of in his philosophical contribution and his military genius'.[56]

On the side of hope, Douglas Wass thought that the increase in MLR had improved things, and though not enough to prevent recourse to the IMF, should make its conditions less heavy. But at the start of September, sterling had stood at $1.77; MLR went up on 10 September – and on 27 September Sterling fell below $1.70. On the same day, Edwin Yeo, Under-Secretary at the US Treasury and prominent Brokers' Man, already in London, saw Healey and Richardson. Healey's reading matter over the weekend of 25–6 September, whose beautiful weather he noted, had been *The Friends of Eddie Coyle*,* which concerns a man trying to escape murder at the hands of confederates – unsuccessfully.

'Beautiful day, Sterling going down,' Healey wrote on 27 September, adding 'Saw officials about intervention, and Lever who agreed to soothe bankers and blackmail allies into giving support.'[59] The intervention was for $500 million and it was not enough. September 28 was the date for departure to, of all ironies, the conference of the IMF in Manila. 'Packed in morning. £ still falling heavily. Gordon in just before I left Downing St. £ fell the whole morning. Out to airport. Decided to stay. Back to London. Series of meetings, 3% loss.'[60] This was the midwinter of the economy and of Healey's fortunes as Chancellor. A wage restraint policy now in its second year, a rolling succession of spending cuts, agonies with the Cabinet, real improvements in inflation, the balance of payments and production all achieved, and still the blows fell.

Healey was now caught in a hiatus. Rather than be trapped for seventeen hours out of telephone communication, he had made the immediate judgement to stay in Britain. He was trying to avoid worsening the panic but the panic worsened anyway. His opening diary entry for 29 September reads like an item on the catalogue of doom: 'Strike at Ford's.' He had not, at first, ruled out later attendance at Manila. But three hours were given over, back at the Treasury, to the next course of action and that, they agreed, was application to the IMF. Edwin Yeo called: 'Ed Yeo rang sympathetically suggesting squeezing bears via money supply . . . Advised Yeo to come over and argue it out.' He decided against Manila altogether and instead did what he could for general reassurance, the main reason for staying, by giving a television interview to the BBC's chief economic commentator, Dominick Harrod. Assurance took the menacing form of warning what sort of breakdown might occur if we resisted an IMF deal.

But there was another consideration. The loan was now reckoned essential, but it would be conditional, and the conditions would be hateful. The Cabinet would resent them, the Parliamentary Party would be furious, the activists of Conference would be out of their minds. And in Blackpool the

---

* By George V. Higgins.

Labour Party's annual Conference was assembled. What was said to them mattered beyond the exhalations of delegates, it would go round the world. Callaghan used that day to make a remarkable speech written by his son-in-law, Peter Jay, one with which Healey was far from being in full agreement but which resonantly indicated retreat from Keynes and reflationary public spending as central economic philosophy. Famously he said, 'We used to think that you could just spend your way out of a recession . . . I tell you in all candour that that option no longer exists, and that in so far as it ever did exist, it only worked . . . by injecting a bigger dose of inflation into the economy, followed by a higher level of unemployment . . . That is the history of the last twenty years.'[61]

At first, Callaghan had not wanted his Chancellor to come to Blackpool. 'Jim doesn't want me in Blackpool – weaken repair of calm. Could not speak from platform.' So having done so much heavy labour, but with the application to the IMF in and the pound feverishly up on the 29th and 'fragile but stable' on the 30th, Healey had very little to do and went to see the curator of the National Gallery, Michael Levey, to look over Flemish paintings for the office, a soothing act in a lull for someone with every need of both.

Suddenly Callaghan changed his mind: '11.30 Jim wants me in Blackpool.' Held up at the airport by rain, he finally made it to the Lancashire resort by 3.00 p.m. And at 4.30, confined by the Labour Party's implacable devotion to procedural absurdity, a Chancellor of the Exchequer facing the second great financial crisis of the century and seeking to explain to party and country the circumstances in which harsh steps should be taken to save a vertically falling currency, was permitted to speak for five minutes from the floor.

By a delicate irony, he spoke to a motion deriving from that earlier NEC resolution and proclaiming:

> This conference believes that there can be no advance to and maintenance of full employment except by means of a planned economy and public control of all sources of money supply for commercial and industrial investment . . . Only by the creation of a state monopoly of credit and finance, with a state bank and a state credit corporation under the control and management of the democratic organisations of the working class, could integrated socialist planning be instituted . . .

Among six steps enjoined by the resolution, the most immediately resonant was the one which should 'put an end to capitalist speculation and profiteering on the money market, the hub of the entire economy'.

Never have the snows of yesteryear glittered so poignantly. However, such demands indicated the atmosphere in which Healey would speak. The Conference would hear Norman Atkinson, now Party Treasurer, say, to applause: 'If we are to restore confidence in this country behind a socialist banner and a socialist programme, then unfortunately we have to sacrifice the confidence of those who are now telling us what the terms are for us borrowing their money.' In the reported text Healey's short speech was spattered with the italics of response – *Shouts from the floor* (three times), *Interruption*, *Cries of dissent*, and *Shout of 'Resign'* but also *Applause* (four times) and *Laughter and applause*.

Distance lends a light irony to past conflicts, but over a period of about fifteen years from the late sixties onward, Labour conferences would be vulnerable, sometimes to spasms, sometimes to prolonged agonies of rage and intolerance. They, as much as any point of policy, gave impetus to the ultimate founding of the SDP, and one of the MPs who would join that exodus specifically identifies this occasion as his own turn-off point. 'In my case it goes back to the 1976 conference. There were a lot of very unpleasant people there, who just didn't give a damn about trying to save this country's currency. Healey was on his way to an IMF meeting and was brought back to the conference from the airport. And he was booed all the way to the rostrum. I was horrified. I hated it; that bloody mob, those clenched fists, those pointing fingers.'[62] Anyone familiar with Labour conferences in those years knows what he is describing, and over the turn of the decade, it would actually get worse. But that never named witness underlines the strength and virtue of Healey at his best. If he was horrified by the brutalism of the arena, he was not alienated. He was going neither to cringe nor turn away. As Barbara Castle liked to say, 'His Irish dander was up.' He had come, as he said, 'from the battlefront' and across his five officially authorised minutes, he was going to fight.

The speech itself was the sort of plain, forceful, urgent thing which Healey did better than anyone. Callaghan had used handsome marmoreal words to say that things would never again be what they had been. Conference goers had caught the liturgical quality and felt themselves in church. Healey, by contrast, took on the left on a specific panacea, the selective import controls which had been rattling around Whitehall – from Francis Cripps's desk in Tony Benn's Ministry, but with more caution in the Policy Unit, indeed in the Treasury itself. Healey himself had prodded them inquiringly in office discussion. They were taken on at Blackpool as simple fallacy. But he began from the heart.

'There are some people who would like to stop the world and get off, and I do not blame them, it has not been an easy world in recent months. They say "Let's go to a siege economy," but a siege economy of a rather odd type, a siege in which we stop the imports coming in, but we demand total freedom for the exports to go out ...' Shouted at from the floor, he turned on the shouters: 'Oh yes, you want the exports to go out, you want the jobs in the engineering factories to increase as the exports increase, but you want to stop other people having the advantage of selling their goods to us.' Having raised the image of a general tariff war, he said, 'I ask you to consider seriously, do you not believe there are trade unionists in Germany, in France, in the United States who are considering exactly that type of siege economy themselves?' He was giving the delegates, and Tony Benn and his parliamentary friends, an open engagement over an argument long bubbling just below ground. Open engagements involve annoying people, always Healey's greatest weakness as a politician and his greatest charm to admirers.

The new protectionism was a theory out of the Cambridge school, so Healey had a go at Cambridge: 'It is possible, theoreticians can argue, as the gurus of this particular proposal in Cambridge do argue, that in the long run it will work, providing you cut public expenditure four or five times more heavily than this government has had to cut it, but that is in the long run and how long do you think this government would run in the circumstances I have described?' If Conference did not want the Tory alternative,

> then we have got to stick to the policy we have got. I am going to nego-
> tiate with the IMF on the basis of our existing policies, not changes in
> policy, and I need your support to do it. But when I say 'existing poli-
> cies' I mean things we do not like as well as things we do like. It means
> sticking to the very painful cuts in public expenditure (*Shouts from the
> floor*) on which the Government has already decided. It means sticking
> to a pay policy which enables us . . . to continue the attack on inflation
> (*Shout of 'Resign'*).[63]

Tony Benn acknowledged 'a bold and vigorous speech' and the fact that 'parts of the Conference cheered him' but he concluded, 'I couldn't even clap him, his speech was so vulgar and abusive.'[64] Healey's own relaxed comment thirteen years later was, 'When I sat down, the cheers were much louder. So were the boos.'[65]

Healey had spoken as a classic free trader and while it could be argued that the United States practised protection to her own great advantage, the US was, by reason of her resources and physical self-sufficiency, an exception to all rules. Healey was combating, in the persons of Norman Atkinson and a sneeringly jocose Ian Mikardo, the more plausible arguments, seventy years before, of the Tory right wing in the person of Joseph Chamberlain who at least had an overseas empire to rely on.

Healey's unwillingness to follow Wass into a substantial deliberate cur-
rency depreciation was always evident, though what we had suffered was more substantial inadvertent devaluation. He had looked at the possibility of selective import controls and they conflicted with his understanding that we were part of a larger trading world whose terms had to be complied with. He might rightly feel that the real economy was moving in all the desirable directions and that we were the victims of a market looking for a better price

for its gilt-edged holdings. But he also knew that we had been vulnerable to the whole chapter of atrocity because of the sins of the previous thirty years – low productivity, industrial turmoil, the localised protectionism of the closed shop and heavy job demarcation, such an economy as no Harold Lever could mend. The effect of import controls would be to perpetuate everything wrong that had got us into this hole. It meant doing things uncompetitively and thus badly, the keeping of a basket case comfortable in its basket. While lacking Dell's sturdy masochism, Healey could see the point in some form of crunch. In the terms of his own later epigram, he was going to stop digging.

THE TREASURY – THE BROKERS' MEN

Once away from the slightly mad politics of the Blackpool Conference – the motion demanding 'public control of all sources of money supply for commercial and industrial investment' had been passed – the government returned to its own source of money supply, the IMF. Healey's formal application to the Fund had been for $3.9 billion, less than the earlier, mixed-source, loan, but less time-confined. It was in fact 'the largest sum then ever asked of them'.[1]

The decision could not be kept close after Johannes Witteveen, its managing director, had been informed. Unfortunately for the remaining British team in Manila, Wass, Mitchell and William Ryrie, executive director of the IMF, here wearing his hat back to front, had met the full force of Arthur Burns's personality. Between facing the activist left at Party Conference and asking Burns for money, there was not much to choose. The other people in the American corner were standard hard money-men who took a severe line. But reference to the 'crustiness' of the chairman of the Federal Reserve was limp. Arthur Burns was not Badger from *The Wind in the Willows*. He was the sort of rough customer around whom obituarists commonly edge their way with words like 'robust' and 'forthright'. Christopher McMahon, Deputy Governor of the Bank of England, recalls the meeting simply as 'appalling'.

But at this stage, Callaghan began to play a hand of his own. If these were the Brokers' Men, then he was Baron Hardup concerned to pay as little as possible. Callaghan had been Chancellor, but what he understood was politics, a rather Lyndon Johnson sort of politics – pressing flesh, calling in favours, relying on long-standing contacts, principally with other politicians, his sort of people. What this meant immediately was talking to Gerald Ford in America and Helmut Schmidt in West Germany and using intermediaries, ours and theirs. Accordingly Harold Lever would resume his pilgrimage while Callaghan himself, very Lyndon Johnsonishly, would pick up the phone to call a head of government.

There are different views of these exertions which filled much of the next two months. To Bernard Donoughue, they are a great achievement, what happened 'When Jim took over'. To Derek Mitchell, who quotes the cruel observation of Burns about Lever, 'Who *is* this guy?', the entire exercise had 'so far as I can see, no effect whatever'.[2] Burk and Cairncross, chroniclers of the whole course of events, see perhaps a limited mitigation won by Callaghan's efforts.

But Healey had other and immediately important work to do. He was not a monetarist in Ted Heath's derisive sense of a one-club golfer, still less in the literalist, percentage for percentage, school of Milton Friedman. But he had increasingly come to think that the volume of money in circulation seriously mattered. And he was concerned, above all things, to sell gilts. The money supply had gone up in the early part of 1976. Gilts were the means to absorb and control it. He would write a decade later that he had been persuaded by the Governor of the Bank 'that we needed to raise interest rates to 15% which was unheard of in those days . . . But I was also persuaded by him that we could get them down again within the year to 12 or 10 per cent which was roughly the level of inflation.'[3] They would do better than that.

All Callaghan's instincts were against doing anything of the sort. It was one more tribulation for a battered Cabinet returned from the trenches of the Fylde coast. The proposal would be damned in Cabinet, he knew, by just about everybody, and the prospect of the Crosland people and the Benn people making common cause was restrained now only by tribalism.* On 6 October, Healey met his Treasury colleagues, Alan Lord and Douglas Wass, the latter, as he noted, 'dog-tired, off plane from Manila'.[5] With Wass he went for a tough, but friendly, argument with an unresponsive Prime Minister, at this time intent only on seeing the German Chancellor about a safety net for sterling. Alan Lord chiefly recalls the unresponsiveness, noting that Callaghan, puffy and slumped, 'looked as if he had been beaten up with rubber hammers'.[6] Healey says, 'I insisted that we go for 2% on MLR.'[7] It was what Richardson in particular had been asking for and it was a big step in its own right, 15 per cent, outbreak of war numbers.

Callaghan, who had received a paper from Donoughue 'v. alarmed at MLR rise', gave no immediate answer. After dictating some letters in his

---

* David Hill, adviser/adjutant to Crosland then Hattersley, spoke to Frances Morrell, Benn's equivalent, only to be told that 'the Bennites were not willing to play that game with the Crosland group. Hill was left with the distinct impression that Morrell was speaking for Foot, Shore, Silkin, Orme and Booth as well as for Benn.'[4]

office, Healey, taking Wass with him, came back. 'He refused 2% MLR, will invite Schmidt to meet him Saturday on safety net. Would let me argue for MLR 2% in Cabinet. Said I would.'[8] Now came the single occasion when Healey was wholly ready to resign. He went back to his office and called the one colleague he could count on for support, Edmund Dell. But their conversation was not concluded when Kenneth Stowe, as Private Secretary, put his head round the door and, as Healey tells it, said 'Excuse me, Chancellor, the Prime Minister has asked me to tell you that he was only testing the strength of your conviction. Of course he will support you.'[9] 'Great Relief,' says Healey's note. But as he also recorded, '(this after asking Hunt if I really intended to force the issue in Cabinet).'[10]

That was a euphemistic way of putting things. The scenario to which Callaghan had opened himself, and for which Healey had tendered, was of the Chancellor making his case with the Prime Minister standing at ease, having his proposal crushed by the Cabinet and, on a rejected proposal to take stern measures, resigning. Relations had not been at their best. Callaghan, perhaps influenced by the Policy Unit, had toyed with the idea of splitting the Treasury – for Healey's own good, of course – and had been told that the move would not be accepted. The Chancellor, for all his cheerful bombast, did not as a rule do tests of will. But on this occasion, quite straightforwardly, he did one and won.

And economically he was proved entirely right. The earlier hike to 13 per cent had helped sell some gilts; the next rise was recognised on the markets as a condition precedent. The jump might be drastic and sensational, provoking every sort of newspaper noise, but it did exactly the job it was intended to do. (Healey also threw into his operation a requirement for special deposits to the value of £700 million.) What followed was a demonstration of monetary growth. The target for the next year's money supply growth stood at a range of 9–13 per cent. The growth actually achieved would be 7 per cent! The complaints of Peter Shore and Tony Benn made at the following morning's Cabinet and their calls for import controls were quietly being made redundant.* Healey handled colleagues with dramatic directness, telling them that morning that unless the rate went up 'the pound would go down the drain'.[11]

In the long term, this was the most important act taken by anybody in the flurry of action and pretend-action which would follow. At a cost to jobs and housing, a market running on masochistic sentiment and the expectations of prospective takers holding out for a better price was accommodated. No one noticed, but once gilts were being steadily bought and the debt funded, the

---

* Cabinet, of course, before a committee was established to resolve such matters, had no say except comment on movements of interest rates.

real reason for the siege would be over. However, before the long term, comes the short term. And in the short term, a foolish article on 24 October by the rather crass city editor of the *Sunday Times*, Malcolm Crawford, stating, incorrectly, that Britain had agreed a level for the pound at $1.50, caused a three-day nightmare with reverberations lasting longer. The consequent fall of 7 per cent brought it close to that number. The words used were 'The Fund thinks that sterling should be let down to about "$1.50 against today's $1.64."' In reality, although individuals on the IMF team like the Australian, David Finch, favoured a reduction and had said so, the term 'The Fund', implying a finished, agreed corporate intention, was flatly wrong.

There was also at this time a flurry of 'Healey Must Go' pieces. This was nothing new. Thoughtful colleagues had been talking to promising journalists at least since the application to the IMF. Notably there had been a piece of characteristic magisterialism from Peter Jenkins in the *Guardian*, written a week after he had quizzed Crosland in some detail during Conference at Blackpool on his own economic strategy. The column called for Healey to be replaced, stated that 'the Prime Minister had always intended at some point to swop Mr Crosland and Mr Healey in their jobs',[12] but added that it was doubtful if Crosland would become Chancellor because he had irritated Callaghan 'by his intellectual squeamishness and inverted snobbism'.[13] On top of such speculation, Barry Jones, Healey's dedicated PPS, was reporting hostility in the Parliamentary Party.[14]

Apocalypse was in the air. Peter Jay had written of 'Rampant inflation, falling employment, industrial decay, administrative breakdown, social and political chaos'.[15] Susan Crosland's observation, 'By the beginning of November, the pound was near ruin,'[16] cannot have seemed unreasonable at the time. Crawford's unsustainable story had exploded in thin mountain air and moved more than rocks. On 28 October, sterling had fallen to £1.535. But in David Hume's words, 'There's a deal o' ruin in a nation' – and in a currency. Big as all this looked, it was ephemeral fire, a burning-off of gas. Gilts sold like mince pies at Christmas; the talk of literal bankruptcy, of not being able to fund the debt, passed out of the argument.

As for sterling, after the horrors of October it would steadily recover until the year end when it would stand close to $1.70. The IMF negotiations would follow, they would be vastly disagreeable, but would not be accompanied by a still falling pound. Dell's judgement is pertinent: 'As things were, the credit justly accrued to Healey. Healey may at times have been mistaken in his policies, he may have been too much of a "political" chancellor, but now that his back was to the wall, he fought like a lion. If he and the Government were to survive, the next few months would require all his considerable courage and moral and intellectual strength ...' But then, 'In surviving and winning through the next few months, nothing less than the courage of a lion would have sufficed.'[17]

Meanwhile, a line in hopeful despair came from the Conservatives. Peter Tapsell, a front-bench spokesman, speaking with the authority of a gilts market specialist, suggested in the House of Commons that the IMF desired to see the PSBR reduced not to £9 billion but six. While Margaret Thatcher, who complained that public sector cuts had not hurt, also offered the view that cuts of between £5½ and £6 billion could be made.[18]

Healey's own statements to the Commons stress monetary arguments. In July he had 'indicated that the increase in the money supply as broadly defined – M3 – during the current financial year, should be in the region of 12 per cent. Any significantly higher figure would risk repeating the experience of 1973.' His monetary guideline in July

> was fully consistent with the provision of sufficient finance to support the increase in exports and investment on which the Government's economic strategy rests – and with the figure of £9 billion for Domestic Credit Expansion* . . . However, it became apparent in recent weeks that we were not achieving sales of Government stock on the scale sufficient to ensure that monetary expansion would keep to the guideline I set . . . It is probable that the foreign concern about our ability to control the money supply was a major factor in pressure on the exchange rate in the last few weeks.[19]

So indeed it had been. And a refusal to buy gilt-edged, otherwise government stock, had been the calamity feared all round. But already, less than two weeks on from his key move, Healey could announce, 'In banking October, however, we have already achieved over £1 billion net of gilt sales with the effects of this and future months of the new stocks still to come.' But nothing Healey said in making a defence of broad economic policy as he justified the immediate act of raising MLR, was quite as effective a summing-up of recent history and real causes as the words he quoted from the *Investors' Chronicle*. Writing on 1 October, that journal of finance capitalism had said,

> To see it in perspective we need to go back to 1973. In that year, money supply on the broader definition increased by not far short of 30 per cent. Inflation over the year was 12 per cent . . . The way was being prepared for the wage explosion of 1974. In other words, not only was Britain pointing in the wrong direction in almost every aspect of its economic management, but the country seemed determined to move even faster down the wrong road . . . [But today, by contrast] Most of the figures – wage increases, inflation rates and above all, government

---

* An alternative to PSBR in measuring current indebtedness.

borrowing requirement – are still frightening. But three years ago all of them were moving in the wrong direction. Most of them are now moving in the right direction.

But the point to focus on is the largely unsung change which has already taken place in Britain. So far it has taken place without revolution or even without the social collapse which was being widely predicted two or three years ago. The danger remains. But it was three years ago that the rest of the world should have been going short on Britain – not now when we are making progress – if slow – in dealing with the consequences of that period of collective insanity.[20]

Meanwhile Callaghan, who looked on the IMF mission as a species of negative Magi, set about a series of embassies and excursions directed at specifically political figures. Such lobbying of heads of government was intended to confine the injury and offence done by the visitants. The German Chancellor came to spend a weekend at Chequers on 9 and 10 October. It was a far less rewarding exercise than the Prime Minister had hoped for. Schmidt had the freedom of a man who has just won an election; he was an anglophile and Social Democrat, though at least as orthodox in his economic thinking as Dell. And what Callaghan wanted from him was direct help in finding a 'safety net' for the sterling balances with which, since the Policy Unit had raised the question, he had become animated. In some Treasury opinion, a better word might have been 'obsessed'. His Private Secretary more sympathetically sees it as an extension of Callaghan's exceptionally happy time at the Foreign Office where his talent for 'being political', with foreign heads of governments and ministers, had been enjoyable and fairly successful.[21]

His evangelism on the reserve currency went to the extent of getting his wife, Audrey, to forsake public dinner small talk for commercial breaks on the balances. Derek Mitchell, finding himself placed one evening next to Mrs Callaghan, was interested to have her turn to him and say, where one might have asked for the bread rolls, 'What we need is a good safety net for the sterling balances.'[22]

However, German reserves were held in dollars and while Schmidt fiercely resented Germany's consequent role in financing the US deficit, any underwriting of British balances with a part of these funds *and* US government help, would need full US support if it was to work. This support, unsurprisingly, was not forthcoming. The German government's authority, a fact which neither Callaghan nor Lever seemed fully to weigh, was sharply confined. The Bundesrepublik was a pioneer in Europe in the separation of central banking from the political executive. Schmidt had no powers to instruct the Bundesbank, a state of affairs which its chairman, Otmar Emminger, guarded with quiet purpose.

The German option would prove largely chimerical, and anyway, sterling balances were less important than Callaghan thought. As Sir Samuel Goldman, a former Second Secretary at the Treasury, said in a letter to *The Times* of 17 November, we should not 'use the reserve role of sterling and the sterling balances as an alibi or an excuse for weaknesses which lie much deeper, and exaggerate the help which a partial funding of the balances alone would bring us'.[23] The problem of the sterling balances was that depositors, seeing a failure of the British economy – inflation, balance of payments problems, falling currency – tended to get out of them. The answer, said tiresome people, was not to practise economic failure in the first place. Goldman's word, used quite gently, 'alibi', was a painful truth.

Schmidt made it clear that dealing with the IMF must come before anything could be done about the balances. As for hopes that Germany would use its influence at the IMF to soften the blow, genuine sympathy did not cause Germany to make any move in this direction. The Americans in IMF, anxious that this might have happened, would send Yeo to see Schmidt who told him plainly that Germany was doing no such thing. A Cabinet Table note of 27 October to Healey from Shirley Williams could have told the Prime Minister as much. She had had 'a long talk with Klaus von Dohnanyi'.*

'He shares a house with Dr Poehl, the German Pu-S.† He believes we could get a massive loan, but only in return for clear rational goals on PSBR, inflation, exports, etc – but made by HMG since he says Germans would not want to be seen to be interfering . . .'[24] This passed on the realities. Germany was indeed truly sympathetic, but her financial authorities would throw good money only after good economics. It was a long way from the slightly fantasising tone of some of Callaghan's remarks.

Callaghan, at this time, nursed hopes and felt resentments. Compare and contrast the report of Dohnanyi's insider views with 'Helmut Schmidt has got $32 billion dollars in reserves. They could fund the entire sterling balances. He's from Hamburg and they all like the English.'[25] He had added that 'Helmut Schmidt and I are going to have a long, comprehensive financial talk with nobody present from the Foreign Office, nobody from the Treasury, they'll wreck it.'[26] The Treasury had produced some crucially wrong numbers, but the assumption of a destructive purpose on their part was unjust

---

* Formerly German Minister of Education and later Deputy Minister of Finance, he was the man who would obtain favourable terms with German money for Lord Carrington and Ian Gilmour (and an ungracious Margaret Thatcher) over agricultural rebates after the Fontainebleau summit in 1980. (See Lord Gilmour's splendid *Dancing with Dogma*, Simon & Schuster, 1992.)

† It is no reproach to Shirley Williams for not knowing that, amazingly in a German high official, Karl-Otto Poehl had somehow neglected to obtain the Ph.D without which such persons are thought improperly dressed.

and hyper-suspicious. It did nothing to help his Chancellor that Callaghan was at this time listening with excessive sympathy to Crosland. Dell recounts a fleeting encounter in early November in a Commons corridor when he was talking to Healey. 'Callaghan came up to us and said: "Tony Crosland tells me that it is all a bankers' ramp like 1931. I think I agree with him." Before Healey could make any response, Callaghan walked off into the Chamber. Healey turned to me in near despair; "What can I do now?"'[27]

Another Callaghan departure was to use television to threaten the Americans. Appearing on *Panorama* on 25 October, a week ahead of the IMF delegation's arrival, he dropped heavy hints of non-co-operation in NATO. Perhaps, he said, we might not be able to maintain the troops currently stationed in Germany. From the man who would let Britain in for the grotesque open-ended costs of the Chevaline missile delivery system, it was an odd, improbable thing to threaten, a shaking of the fist from a position of not quite fully comprehended weakness. By making heavy weather of sterling balances on that programme, he also put water between himself and the Treasury (and by implication Healey) – 'I would love to get rid of the reserve currency. I am not sure that everybody in the Treasury would, or maybe in the Bank. But from Britain's point of view I see no particular advantage in being a reserve currency at all.'[28]

Crosland meanwhile, despite urgent requests from Callaghan for Cabinet secrecy, was busily talking to his press contacts and, across the long crisis, the *Guardian* would print tracts of Cabinet dispute, tracts in their official form now absurdly confined under the thirty years' rule. That newspaper would also, on 25 November, carry a story from Peter Jenkins that Callaghan had withdrawn his support from Healey. Benn attributed this to Lever since he was a friend of Peter Jenkins.[29] It seems unlikely as a deliberate act, given the affection between Lever and the Chancellor.*

These are the by-blows of stress, and with the IMF pending, there was quite enough of that. In due course, Callaghan would work his cautious way round till he stood back to back with Healey when it mattered. He was also, as Benn's honest account makes clear, open to the various options which colleagues might like to throw at him, listening to Benn himself with more than courteous interest.

The essential difference between Callaghan and his Chancellor was that Healey, after a long period of adjudicatory agnosticism, had come firmly to the conclusion that an IMF-approved solution was the only one which would work. Callaghan resented the idea of further expenditure cuts, the generally

---

* A charming Cabinet Table note from Lever says to Healey, 'You will posthumously rehabilitate me as you recall how delicately, considerately and *privately* I pushed my views.'[30]

recognised price of getting the PSBR, *as wrongly computed*, down to $9 billion. That was very human since the whole point of the July cuts had been to get down to $9 billion and the political price implied would be high. He was also hearing from the Chairman of the Parliamentary Party, Cledwyn Hughes. Hughes, doing his job as liaison man, warned him on 4 November that because of the prospective stickiness of the PLP, 'a balanced package should be sought, including import controls'.[31] But like Healey, Callaghan had to deal with the numbers he had, the official numbers. Not to do so was to invite all the things unconfident markets can do – had just done. The stoic in Healey was simply getting on and doing the job.

Politically, it was a very hard time for Healey. He had all the griefs of actually negotiating with the IMF; he would, he knew, be advocating yet more cuts of the kind Labour people hated; and after two and a half years at the Treasury, he would take the blame. He had had custody while things, already bad, came to be seen as bad. The hard line held to since the turn of 1974 had a great deal to its credit, but the achievement did not show and the pain of the cure kept increasing. Healey's standing in the party was not high, and Callaghan's grand excursion was hardly a gesture of confidence in his Chancellor. Although fully capable of meeting rough with rough, he would record the unpleasantness with the usual Spartan calm. A joint Cabinet/NEC meeting of 19 October in which he was personally attacked appears as 'Shirley v. good. I. Mikardo confected a row.'[32]

Instructively and encouragingly, Healey's visit to Leeds on 5–6 November yielded nothing worse than 'a slightly grumpy party meeting' and he was told by his chairman, Ashoke Bannerjee that '[social] benefits ought to be lower compared with earnings',[33] a facing-up-to-realities among the low-paid not available to most of the Cabinet. As detailed cuts came to be discussed, Healey would horrify Tony Benn by arguing for not giving that year's upgrading to benefits.

A sense of the oppression and political isolation under which the whole Cabinet lived speaks from a short Cabinet note from Shirley Williams:

> Denis,
>
> I was truly appalled to learn (confidentially) that the Sunday Times has decided to run a campaign about economic successes and offered their material to the BBC in case they wanted to do programmes on it; and that the BBC told them they were only interested in material on failure.
>
> Shirley[34]

Meanwhile Callaghan's excursion remained a mystery tour. Schmidt would tell the British Prime Minister on the telephone on 5 November of 'an unexpected offer that was to be of tremendous reassurance during the difficult weeks that followed'.[35] The offer remains an enigma wrapped in a mystery.

Probably, think Burk and Cairncross, this was something to do with funding sterling balances.

There was a direct contradiction between Schmidt's tone, 'tremendous reassurance during the difficult weeks', and the hard detail of German financial help. This was almost certainly due to no duplicity on the part of Schmidt, a man of unnerving bluntness, nor to wishful thinking on his part, another non-characteristic. More likely he underestimated how precisely his banking authorities would guard the sharp division between their authority and his – 'Abgrenzung' is the word which says it in German. The best he could do was to bid Pieske, Germany's man on the IMF, to press for restraint. And Callaghan would say bitter things about both Germany and the United States before he was done.

The IMF mission arrived in London on 1 November, a party of six, headed by an Englishman, Alan Whittome, late of the Bank of England.* And a cold coming they had of it. Placed in Brown's Hotel, off Piccadilly, under assumed names, in the mystifying manner with which a Sherlock Holmes story, 'The Six Central Bankers' perhaps, might open. They were then kept kicking their heels less like creditors than up-market asylum seekers suspected by the authorities of being bogus. The delay had most to do with Callaghan's pride and intransigence, but it owed something to sheer uncertainty in the Treasury about the facts. Healey spoke on 3 November to the Cabinet's Economic Strategy Committee. They faced a choice of forecasts: 'One assumed wages at 10 per cent, another at 20 per cent.' What mattered was a single objective: 'We must get the actual IMF loan and if possible, also fund the sterling balances if we can . . . We must show the IMF the forecasts and head them off from wanting to disrupt the industrial strategy or the social contract . . .' On top of all this, 'the PSBR had risen to £11 billion from £9 billion, where it had been in July, because of unemployment and the MLR.' He hoped to avoid making a direct offer to the IMF, but he wanted 'to avoid a demand by them for fiscal measures'.[36] The IMF were going to demand cuts, that much was certain. One faction in the Treasury, notably Mitchell and Lord, agreed with them, another headed by Wass did not.

As for Healey, a memorandum from Gavyn Davies at the Policy Unit of 9 November says: 'Treasury officials are pushing Healey to go for £2 billion of cuts, but Healey's personal feelings are not clear. He has no arguments for the Treasury position except the IMF pressure. I do not know if the IMF would accept less than £2 billion, but do know that Treasury officials *think* they want at least £2 billion.' Healey might have replied that no argument mattered as much as IMF pressure.

---

* Who died in 2001.

The Policy Unit was also informing Callaghan of the NIESR [National Institute for Economic and Social Research] figures on the projected PSBR, which were enormously heartening at a mere £8.5 billion.[37] Against this, it was the Keynesian NIESR which had signalled a persistent statistical green light to Edward Heath during his advance towards hyperinflation. The Unit also demonstrated that by the test of monetary control, though West Germany far outstripped the US, Britain and a ragingly profligate Italy, the British performance was actually better than that of the United States.

These, of course, were things which Healey knew very well. They were part of the *Investors' Chronicle* argument. As for the true figure for the PSBR, like everyone else with responsibility, he knew that he didn't know. Sir Derek Mitchell says today that what was at issue in the markets was not the reality, but the sentiment, a sentiment which would only respond to a decisive act, useful or otherwise, be it a major act of deprecation earlier or the promise of major public expenditure cuts now. Indeed, he adds, the promise was more important than the actual cutting.[38] In that climate of market sentiment Maurice Peston, then advising Roy Hattersley and opposed initially to the cuts, put it succinctly. 'I think Denis was right. If the IMF had said that the entire cabinet had to jump off Westminster Bridge, you would have had to jump off Westminster Bridge.'[39]

Uncertainty ruled. If the Treasury, having been at the match, didn't know the half-time score, the IMF and especially the dominant American voices, were as impervious as the BBC to the good news. They had lately been in Italy, a cheerful and surviving basket case whose statistics were sufficiently fluid to diminish confidence in those of any other country on the Fund's itinerary. The mission also had a healthy fear simply of failing. They expected sovereign governments to dislike them and seek influence from other governments and generally diminish their writ. This was a very American affair. The actual US member of the mission, Bill Dale, was little noticed. But Edwin Yeo called every sort of shot, and officially, Yeo's status within the IMF was barely ceremonial, but he was Under-Secretary at the US Treasury, speaking at will with the Chairman of the Federal Reserve and the Treasury Secretary, Bill Simon.

Such an organisation so wired could also act imperiously beyond the edge of propriety. In Portugal a year later, dealing with the left-of-centre government of Mario Soares, American liability to come over unconstitutional in other countries would show at the IMF. A briefing, seen in Downing Street, showed the IMF staff explicitly asking the Western governments of the United States, Germany, Japan and Britain to 'withhold financial and economic aid in order to create a foreign exchange crisis which would bring the Soares Government to its knees and force it to accept the harsh IMF prescriptions',[40] something which James Callaghan, splendidly, refused to touch. The Americans had vacillated between hysterical despair, ready to write

Portugal off to Communism, and vicarious financial coercion. Callaghan had been a steady good friend to that country and its democrats, of whom Mario Soares was the leader.*

But on this darkling plain, action, as Derek Mitchell argues, had to impinge upon perception. The numbers might be whatever they secretly and arithmetically were. The market which could tear sterling away from the slow recovery she had been making since 28 October and drive the successful interest rate hike (soon to start its descent) to South American levels, knew only what it perceived – the wrong debt figures. 'The hedgehog knows one thing,' said Isaiah Berlin's memorable Greek quotation, 'but it is a big thing.' This was not a clever hedgehog and the thing it knew was wrong, but for people trying to hold the British economy together against hysterical collapse, it was enough.

Amazingly, ignorance even extended to the British press. The right-wing newspapers would later damn Healey as 'the rubber chancellor' when he had pushed his colleagues to the furthest point of the possible. *Per contra*, parts of the BBC were convinced that Derek Mitchell was a species of enemy agent. He recalls an edition of *Panorama* in which the ever offensive John Pardoe spoke of 'treason' committed by an unnamed man engaged in selling the country short, his words accompanied by a film shot of Derek Mitchell walking in the street.

Edwin Yeo, not a man for official denials, would have none of it. 'Callaghan got madder than Hell at us,' he said. 'I know he thought there was a conspiracy between the British and the American Treasuries, but there was not. Derek Mitchell fought all the way. He never once said "This is what they think, but I think this."'[41] The categorical statement is important here because Healey and Mitchell were undoubtedly now arguing essentially the same line and it was not Callaghan's line. Healey's own comment was terse: 'Pardoe traduced Treasury.'[42]

What would emerge by early–mid November would be an arithmetical gap. Although the IMF, correctly, thought the Treasury estimate of the PSBR too high at £11.2 billion† and edged it down for working purposes to £10.5 billion (still too high), their cure was outstandingly drastic. Healey, reflecting Callaghan, had declined to give them a British estimate of what was needed, so they made their own. As a condition of the loan, they sought cuts in public expenditure of £4 billion. Just to make life more difficult for a Chancellor caught between colleagues unwilling to bite the bullet and Fund

---

* Kenneth Morgan hints in his *Callaghan* at a fascinating story to be told in 2005–6, when embargoed papers come free.

† A figure which in a time heavy with untraced leaks, Healey up in his constituency, first heard on Radio Leeds![43]

officials lining it with steel, he noted on 5 November, 'Lost Workington and Walsall, but Jim robust.'[44] The fact of by-elections having, since the early 1960s, become routinely hellish for governments does not make the fall to a position of minority status when engaged in a historic financial crisis, less hellish.

Callaghan's response to the Fund's ugly numbers was to make further excursions over the top of banking bureaucrats to heads of government. This time it would be to President Ford. Gerald Ford, appointed to the Vice-Presidency on the disgrace of Spiro Agnew before being elevated to the Presidency on the disgrace of Richard Nixon, was less well placed than any head of a US government ever to pull rank. The approach was made well before the US presidential election which Ford lost, diminishing an already modest body of authority. He was/is a decent, likeable man, politically sane and no sort of fool. But any response from Ford was always going to come filtered through Treasury and State Department guidance. Harold Lever would be passed through the hands of Simon, Kissinger and Burns.

Callaghan sought a US funding of sterling balances to take the place of the IMF negotiations. What Healey wanted was, through those negotiations, to reach the least painful conclusions possible. He expected, directly or through his closest officials, to speak with Whittome and Witteveen; the balances were an additional anxiety, but not for him the *res* of the argument. This also meant having specifically British figures on cuts, and he and Douglas Wass agreed that they should be armed to do this below the figure of £9 billion.

Though he and Callaghan consulted on everything that mattered, it was often the differences which showed, as on 11 November when he 'tried v. hard to get Jim to give Wass flexibility for meeting dinner with Whittome, but he wouldn't budge an inch – grumpy and moody to Stowe.'[45] He was also catching the backlash of IMF delegates' anxiety about Callaghan's hostility to their presence. Whittome had told Wass that he believed Callaghan would withdraw the invitation to the IMF. 'Asked Jim to confirm this was *not* his view.'[46]

Finally that day Healey himself had a first meeting with Whittome, 'v. bright, skilful, diplomatic'. They agreed that Lever in Washington should not meet Witteveen. And he was talking to the official traveller himself. 'Long, tiring meeting with Lever – passionately against any deflation at all – misgivings about his meeting with Yeo, Simon.'[47] This was on the Thursday. Next day he went with Callaghan to Rambouillet to speak with Giscard and Raymond Barre, French President and Premier, about support for the sterling balances campaign. Having asked another civil servant, Peter Thornton, to help look for savings in the civil service, Healey then worked on his way down to Withyham, before drawing breath and 'slept till 11 am!'[48] before working on his rhododendrons and roses.

Healey went to the TUC/NEDC dinner gathering: 'useful but not much progress'. There was a meeting with civil servants looking forward to likely cuts, followed by the droning pronouncements of the Lord Mayor's Banquet: 'Boring beyond belief. Jim good but platitudinous, Coggan* awful.'[49]

While Lever met people in Washington, Healey and his officials had to prepare for the cuts required, whatever the precise demands of the IMF, which no intercession with President Ford would stop. On 16 November, Douglas Wass related Whittome's belief that the cut in the PSBR should be a big one. There is also a curious cryptic reference to his having said that Schmidt was 'v. anti-British'.[50] This suggests a very narrow definition of anti-Britishness and reflects Yeo's reassuring visit to Hamburg where he found the federal Chancellor solidly behind IMF policy.

Something of the tension which made this crisis so enthralling, if fearful, was that things ran parallel with one another. Lever was in Washington on behalf of Callaghan, running talks with the US Treasury, State Department and eventually Ford himself, all aimed at substituting an underwriting of sterling balances for the whole operation. But for all that, Callaghan would meet the Cabinet on 17 November to talk about reducing the PSBR through public expenditure cuts. By the end of the month, lines of conflict would be drawn again, with Callaghan and Healey on one side while the Cabinet either assented or joined with those alternative alternatives, Benn and Crosland. Roy Hattersley, a devoted admirer of Healey before and after, had several arguments with him and at one point upset him by drawing a comparison between the Chancellor bending grimly to his task and the prisoner/officer commanding British prisoners of war building the bridge on the River Kwai who, over-focused, became enamoured of the task itself.[51]

Despite the edge between Healey and Callaghan, it is not profitable historically to deepen the conflict between them any more than they themselves sought to protract it. They had been split over interest rates. Healey had got his essential way, but the trumpetings of Malcolm Crawford had violently disguised the actual success of that move, and even after 28 October, the long-term strong effect would make its point only incrementally. On sterling balances, Healey had no objection, but he never thought that any such deal could replace agreement on the least hard terms that could painfully be got from the IMF.

As for Lever's mission, any incidental softening, which Healey did not expect, would be welcome. But he and the Treasury feared a collapse in their own negotiations, generated by IMF resentment at moves going over their heads. Yeo's journey to Hamburg was a demonstration of a touchy alertness to such moves. While Callaghan, though he had been more than flirting with other voices, knew at bottom that the hated IMF was death and taxes – not to be escaped.

---

* The Rt Rev. Donald Coggan, Archbishop of York then Canterbury, not an exhilarating speaker.

Harold Lever's crusade to Washington would be reported in different ways by different people. To Lever himself, it was a triumph. To Edwin Yeo, he would leave Washington 'as empty as a bone-dry bucket'.[52] To the Policy Unit, the Prime Minister was taking over and lifting the whole act. The reality seems to have been that Lever, after briskness from the US Treasury people and warm words from Henry Kissinger, enjoyed a brief high point with a sympathetic Gerald Ford, quickly snatched back by the departments who clarified his conversational warmth and responsiveness to no commitment.

Mitchell, there on separate business, heard Burns's expressions of incomprehension as to what Lever was about. He was asked by the chairman whom Lever was seeing and told him that the chief target was Kissinger. 'At which,' says Mitchell, 'he gave the nearest a banker can get to an unearthly laugh.'[53] The point being, he says, that Kissinger knew nothing about economics and did not pretend to. Time spent talking to him about economics was time wasted. In the conclusive words of Bill Ryrie, British member of the IMF team, Lever's presentation in Washington 'just didn't seem to be taking the problems seriously and this just confirmed the US view that we had to go through with this. This was the last throw to get some American influence to moderate the IMF line, and I think it convinced Callaghan that it wasn't going to succeed and he had to bite the bullet.'[54] Healey never gloated about any of this, but he had been biting bullets for some time and had been damned for it pretty widely.

Lever did indeed emerge with a promise, which would be kept, for a deal on the sterling balances, but he had quickly had to take a major step down, assuring the Americans that Britain was not 'seeking the sterling balances deal as an escape from the IMF'.[55] To say this was to surrender the whole point. We could have a deal on the sterling balances, but only on the understanding that we first met IMF conditions! The sterling balances deal of 1977, *after* the crisis, was worth having, but it was a lesser, subordinate and posthumous deal. As Callaghan's biographer briskly puts it, 'There was no specific US help in the short term at all, and the talks with the IMF went on as though Lever's visit to Washington had never taken place.'[56]

But the shouting was not all over. The Cabinet might contemplate the cuts to be made, but this was still the future conditional tense. Healey was seeking a contingent agreement on the PSBR, also authority to talk direct to the IMF instead of through Wass and only to Whittome. Callaghan was telling his Cabinet that, whatever might be minuted, only with *their* consent would an agreement with the IMF be made. Formal negotiations with the delegation, as distinct from Wass's dinners with Whittome and Healey's almost furtive drinks with him, only began on 19 November.* The Treasury wanted

---

* Perhaps symbolically, the Cabinet had gathered for a group photograph, more or less smiling, on the 18th!

a PSBR of £10 billion for the year 1977/8 and were already thinking about selling BP shares, but there was a minority Treasury view that the pre-crisis reforms had done the substantial trick and that nothing needed to be added.

The mission wanted cuts of £3 billion in '77/8 and 4 billion in '78/9. That was 6 per cent rising to 8 per cent off public expenditure. As Leo Pliatzky, the Second Secretary, remarked, 'It was never on the cards that Treasury ministers would put such proposals to Cabinet, let alone succeed in getting approval for them.[57] To put things in perspective, the impossibilist line of the IMF was issued at a time when *The Times*, whose editor, William Rees-Mogg, had a fixation with the convertibility of gold, was calling for cuts of £5 billion.'[58]

This excess of zeal was met in turn by much journalistic talk, not all of it from journalists, about the collapse of society, totalitarian options, men on white horses and the matter being taken to the streets. Callaghan talked like this to Schmidt and Ford, the catastrophe chat of persuasion. This was the time of Arthur Scargill, flying pickets and 'extra-parliamentary politics'. A dispute over the non-trade union Grunwick photo-developing company led to a species of near-siege on behalf of the closed shop. Meanwhile Tony Benn was much taken with 1931 when a Labour government had resigned rather than submit to bankers' demands for cuts.

Callaghan would promote with Schmidt and Ford what he called the three-legged stool: a smaller cut, one billion, in the PSBR, a safety net for sterling and import deposits. Healey and the Treasury negotiated – with the mission, and then with the Cabinet. On 19 November, he 'saw Douglas [Wass] v. depressed. Whittome threatens to go home if we don't budge.' On the same day, however, he 'saw PM with Douglas – v. relaxed, helpful but oscillating between doing nothing and doing everything.'[59] Intriguingly, on that very day, Whittome set out his stall and price, and Healey brought off a quarter-per-cent fall in MLR, noting sterling's improvement to $1.59 and the sale of £400 million government securities on long tap, precisely the small, vital signs of things getting better now most needed. As he listed Whittome's prices in terms of the PSBR required – £9 billion debt for 1977/8, £6.5 billion for 1978/9 – Healey after the figure '£9 b.', adds in brackets '(hopefully ten)'. Whether this larger allowance is a personal aside only, or something nodded to by Whittome, isn't clear.

He would now be shuttling between Whittome and the Cabinet, often conveying the impossibility of the one to the other. On the 22nd, there would be a special meeting with Callaghan, Crosland, Lever and officials. The safety net and its dependence on an IMF deal is spelt out. Healey comments, 'Roughish time' and adds, 'PM tries to get convergence, but others would not.'[60] Healey put up with a great deal at this time. John Cole, then the *Guardian*'s political correspondent, who speaks of 'The Chancellor's appalling load of work and anxiety' as he fights 'great waves of tiredness to maintain at least the appearance of his normal ebullient nature', also notes that Healey 'resented his lack of support in Cabinet [and] contrasted ministers' disloyalty with the behaviour of union leaders, Jack Jones and Hugh Scanlon . . . [who] went on television to defend government policy, even though this put them in trouble with their own members. Their support sometimes brought Healey, the cold logician, close to tears.'[61]

The argument continued next day. 'Cabinet all morning – no support now except from Reg [Prentice] and Edmund.' The others, he noted, offered either nothing or supported the Crosland compromise: '£500 in BP £500 pe [public expenditure]'. Healey saw Whittome, warned him of the situation and advised him to seek a meeting with the Prime Minister. Callaghan 'cabled Schmidt and Ford for support'.[62]

Cabinet opposition was mobilising. At its heart was Tony Crosland who had a coherent optional view, that the IMF's demands were irrational and unnecessary, and that if we made limited proposals ourselves and then supported them à l'outrance, their bluff would be called. On 22 November, in Crosland's room, there met Harold Lever, Shirley Williams, David Ennals, and Roy Hattersley with Bill Rodgers arriving halfway through.[63] Lever was quoted by the Financial Times: 'confident that we could borrow what we needed without having to cut public expenditure.' A tiny sidelight on the lack of killer purpose here was that Crosland, moving spirit and intellect of the internal opposition, could not be present because he was at a Palace dinner for the President of Venezuela. Machiavelli or Metternich, confronted by the futilities of Foreign Office hostessing, would have sent a Minister of State. In fairness, John Cole also noted that Crosland was 'sensitive to the Chancellor's feeling of hurt and did not want to make compromise more difficult'. Conversations with the Guardian's man were therefore marked with 'a lack of our normal combative candour'.[64]

The Left opposition met the same day, Nicholas Kaldor telling Benn and Peter Shore that 'it was essential for the life and safety of the Labour Party that any cuts should be rejected and that Callaghan's bluff should be called.'[65] Kaldor was also promoting the import deposit schemes and direct import controls which he had promoted to no greater effect when he was at the Treasury. For a time it looked, to excitable journalists, that the Chancellor and the Treasury might be defeated.

But next day (23 November) in Cabinet, again cut short for ridiculous dancing of attendance on the President of Venezuela, Crosland would set out his case: nominal cuts of a billion, half of it coming from the Burmah Oil sale, after which, 'if you demand any more of us we shall put up the shutters, wind down our defence commitments, introduce a siege economy.' This, thought Crosland, 'would be sufficient to persuade the Fund to lend the money without unacceptable conditions. Politically, the IMF could not refuse the loan. If the Government keeps its nerve, it could insist on its own terms – could limit the cuts to "window dressing" – to appease the irritating and ignorant currency dealers . . . We have,' he added, 'to stop paying Danegeld.'[66]

The mood at this time was threatening to Healey, with Tony Benn noting the opinion of Michael Foot 'that Jim was going to come down against Denis, and Denis might resign'.[67] Benn himself acknowledged that nothing would be more ruinous to the pound than such a departure, adding with more humour than usual, 'In order to keep Denis you have to have more deflation, but the trick is to keep Denis and have less deflation.'[68]

Despite Callaghan's calls to Schmidt, Healey noted that 'it was now a matter for the IMF negotiations and the British Cabinet.' And at a significant meeting on 24 November, between Chancellor and Prime Minister, they 'decided not to have substantial division on IMF at Cabinet'.[69] Healey also records seeing Karl-Otto Poehl, Schmidt's State Secretary. He would see him again on the 26th and was, we know, short and unwelcoming towards him,[70] the perhaps inevitable consequence of the whole German game having been played by Callaghan over the head of Healey. Whittome, whom the German sought out, was quite as angry, feeling thoroughly got at by Callaghan. They met, not in Whittome's suite, but 'in the darkest corner of the hotel' because, said Whittome, 'I'm sure they bug my phone here.'[71] Perhaps paranoia, perhaps standard British practice!

Poehl and Whittome, doing their jobs, neither of them offence-giving triumphalists, caught the exasperation spun off by four-handed, two-purpose diplomacy. Healey's account of the second Poehl meeting is neutral: 'Poehl in – wanting final settlement after UK puts bid in. Neg[ative] on Fund, US, Germany.' He also describes a meeting with Callaghan and Wass: 'V. relaxed and helpful', and the state of press comment: 'Press indicating Callaghan-Healey split etc.'[72] Thursday's Cabinet (25 November) had been preliminary, '1½ hours on IMF, general chat', but not relaxing. 'I spoke strongly at the end and shook many of them.' He had also been trying, without much success, to have his office work out the consequences of first-year cuts at PSBRs of, respectively, £9½, £9, and £8½ billion, an enterprise which had produced an 'appalling, confused paper'.[73] But he was trying to negotiate around those numbers.

After the meeting with Poehl on Friday 26 November, he had another with Whittome, a 'warning debrief' before going down to the cottage in Sussex 'appallingly tired'. But he was back on the Saturday to meet Larry Kline, an emissary of Jimmy Carter, the President-Elect, learning only what he must have guessed, that the Democrat would not attempt to influence events ahead of his inauguration.[74] On the Sunday, after noting a *News of the World* story, 'Knives out for Healey', he did something more useful and talked to the US Secretary of the Treasury.

Simon, on an official visit to Moscow, had broken his visit in London hoping to nudge progress along. Meanwhile Poehl, bidden by Schmidt to convey a note to Ford and generally do his best in Washington for the British, had met Burns and distanced himself, rather unprofessionally, from the letter Schmidt had sent to Ford, one which had enraged the readily enraged chairman of the Fed. 'Arthur, I am a civil servant,' Poehl had said. 'I have to obey orders, and I have instructions to tell you that we are supporting Callaghan and the British for political reasons and because of the partnership in Europe and all this kind of thing.'[75]

The pound being down, Simon cannily bought English clothing at a crisis-induced discount. Yeo, already in London, was invited over to Wells of Mayfair, Simon's tailor. Thereafter a sort of levée was staged. The participants recall meeting various Treasury people, presumably emissaries of Healey, at the Mayfair outfitters. But they also met Healey, saying for his record only that they were 'with us on front loading* and rate policy', while Yeo 'practically confessed to positioning Whittome'.[77] That the Deputy Secretary to the US Treasury should do this to the director of an international agency was the sort of power-political reality which Callaghan so resented.

But Karl-Otto Poehl was now telling Schmidt that the IMF were not to be moved. Callaghan (and Crosland) would learn this at a European Council meeting on 29–30 November. Breakfasting together in Brussels on the 30th, Callaghan had heard from Schmidt a general verdict which he would pass on next day to Healey. Schmidt, combining flattery and bathos, had told Callaghan that he 'should be a Churchill for Britain in Europe'. Callaghan had declared his inability to decide between Healey's line of broadly accepting the IMF's deflationary remedy and Crosland's desire to respond to a modest offer with defiance – ('J said v. uncertain between me and Crosland')[78] – Schmidt had said that he too was facing deflation in Germany. Unemployment there, he thought, would rise to 1.3 million, there was a 'profound lack of confidence' in that country.

Then, with words which would have confirmed all Tony Benn's suspicions, Schmidt had suggested that 'Jim and Heath† (!) should coalesce', adding that his own coalition partner, Hans-Dietrich Genscher, 'thinks UK must not be favoured'. He also urged the British Prime Minister to see Witteveen. 'Others think we are bluffing.'[79] Despite the blarney and the eccentric reading of English politics, this would be crucial for Callaghan. The horse he had backed had warned him about the going. So enlightened, he spoke discouragingly on the plane to his Foreign Secretary.

Tony Crosland had embodied the intelligent opposition to Healey. Since

---

* This is intriguing and not quite clear. 'Front loading' was the putting of the greatest burden on cuts in the first year of the three likely to be involved. Healey had been keen to spread the pain more heavily into a later year when, as he rightly suspected, the economy would be flourishing. It has generally been thought[76] that the IMF and Americans were very much against it.

† No longer, of course, Conservative leader.

the interest rates affair, Callaghan had inclined sharply to his way of thinking, treating his Chancellor as a questionable option. He now told Crosland that when it came to the essential Cabinet meeting, he would be on the other side. 'Jim very confident and relaxed, said that he would support Denis.'[80] Quite why Callaghan should be 'very confident and relaxed' is not clear. Crosland, who would show a great deal of dignity at this moment, simply said that 'he was sad about his conversation with Jim on the flight back'.[81]

After the superfluities of a Commons debate, 'Howe poor, Reggie attacked monetarism'[82] and Healey himself doing effective knockabout against Mrs Thatcher, the Cabinet would get down to the resolution of its griefs. Callaghan's shift would help frustrate the camarilla forming against the Chancellor. On the same day, 30 November, Crosland and his friends had held a meeting which Susan Crosland calls 'disappointing'. Support was slipping. 'Bill Rodgers had gone over to the Prentice–Dell hard line. Shirley and David Ennals were undecided what was best to do since they now seemed likely to save some of their departmental budgets ... Tony and Harold Lever and Roy Hattersley alone were unchanged in their opposition to the IMF's terms.'[83]

What happened next would be crucial: a meeting between Witteveen and Callaghan. The shadow-boxing had gone on too long, but Witteveen came at the express request of President Ford. The meeting, probably starting at 8.45 a.m., says Sir Kenneth Stowe, Callaghan's Principal Private Secretary, involved just Witteveen and Callaghan with only Stowe else present. But Healey's diary, however terse, gives the account of a participant. It is short and calm but dramatic in the way of the un-self-conscious: 'Witteveen in to see PM. Says must be shift to export investment, reasonable M3, cut in PSBR not by tax increases. Strongly for cuts in income tax and [illegible], cut by £1½–2bn in pe next year. I told him out of question ...'[84]

Callaghan's biographer suggests something altogether more angry, describing the exchanges as 'blunt and acrimonious', and describes how Callaghan 'turned savagely on Witteveen, accusing him of being oblivious to the impact of mass unemployment on the British economy and imperilling British democracy itself'.[85] Callaghan's own memoirs omit the event altogether. But the best of all available sources is Sir Kenneth Stowe. The meeting, he says, had been kept the tightest of all tight secrets, being organised by Stowe himself – VIP suite at Heathrow, Witteveen taken by government car not to Downing Street but the Cabinet Office (by the back door), then afterwards whisked away just as discreetly. The meeting itself involved no row, no shouting match.* It lasted about forty-five minutes and its crux was Witteveen

---

* There is a conflict of evidence here. Professor Morgan's account is of Sir Kenneth describing to him an acrimonious meeting. We are in the impossible field of recollection and glossing across more than twenty years and must settle for the fact that a meeting took place.

asking for cuts of £2 billion and Callaghan saying that £1 billion was the limit for the British Cabinet. This difference of view was acknowledged and no conclusion reached there and then.

Callaghan, according to some accounts, had expected a longer exposure of the Dutchman to the arguments of British political realities. This, as Burk and Cairncross report it, led to the near snub of Witteveen, saying that he had a cocktail party to host in Washington that night. But the single eye-witness has no impression of snub or rejection and concludes that the short meeting, handily held halfway through the interminable Cabinet discussions, finally helped impress Witteveen with the limits up against which he had come.

But Callaghan would tell the Cabinet the next day, 2 December, that Witteveen wanted £2 billion of real cuts; these, with no time span quoted, were presumably a variant of the £1½–2 billion for 1977 which Healey had already told him were out of the question. Healey had had his staff prepare that 'appalling' paper on a series of PSBRs between £9.5 and £8.5 billion.

Witteveen was not an easy person to deal with. It is not in dispute that any hard line maintained by Whittome, with whom Healey had very good relations, derived from Witteveen's Washington instructions and that he wanted expenditure cut by '£2 billion in 1977–78 and by up to £3 billion in 1978–79'.[86]

Callaghan himself, in his autobiography, gives the next move to Healey, delivering 'a brisk homily to the IMF' indicating that they could go no further than they believed to be necessary to get the economy into balance. If the IMF then refused a loan, the government would ask the Queen to dissolve Parliament and we would call a general election on the issue of the IMF versus the people. With this message ringing in their ears, the IMF negotiators had made a hurried departure for Washington. 'I had not given the Chancellor any authority to threaten a general election, but I was quite happy that he should have done so.'[87]

This, as Callaghan tells it, is rather compressed and slightly confusing. Getting the sequence right turns on what we mean by 'the IMF'. Healey did not beard or denounce Witteveen. Putting together various reports, including Healey's own in *The Time of My Life* and his diary, 'the IMF' here meant first Witteveen, encountered twice, before and after Cabinet deliberations, but then, crucially, Whittome and Witteveen together, with whom he lunched on 1 December. 'Told them problem. Took them to PM again. PM promised to support me on £1 Bn cuts next year. Saw Lever who is softening – encouraged Jim.'[88] It was, incidentally, at *this* point, after making the concession of support over the £1 billion, that Callaghan related to Healey his dismaying conversation with Schmidt on 30 November.

The business of speaking plainly to the IMF proceeded to its next stage only after the vast, grinding Cabinet of 2 December which Healey disposes of in two lines: '2nd Dec Thursday, Long cabinet – I said £1½–£2 bn. Jim supported. Crosland and Hattersley opposed in a [illegible] way.'

More of that Cabinet in a moment. Healey, seeking to extract more flexibility from Callaghan, found him still doggedly communicating with other
heads of government. 'Saw Jim again. Telegrams to Ford and Schmidt, I
pointed out Jim had *not* refused £2 bn 1978–9, he refused to budge. Told
Whittome the result – he thought Witteveen would want more.'[89]

It was only on the next day after so much ferrying of information, putting
of cases and alerting interlocutors to each other's positions, that Healey
would issue his warning, invoke the Queen and a united Labour Party and
generally lay down the law. His entry for 3 December begins: 'Dog-tired. Saw
Wass also v. tired. Whittome rang to say Witteveen wanted 1½, 2½, 3!' [pro-
jected cuts for the next three financial years].[90] After some small parley with
the CBI, the narrative continues, relating a subsequent conversation with the
delegate. 'Then Whittome; warned him we would prefer electoral defeat in
loyal LP [Labour Party] than 1931. He promised to seek compromise. Finally
offered formula for contingent increase in 1978/79.' If the details of
Whittome's offer are denied us, clearly this was momentous, a key response,
a trembling prospect of breakthrough. But no heroics are struck. Healey
rolls on with normal life: 'Off to Leeds. Annual Dinner . . . Jim seemed to
welcome Whittome formula.'[91]

After a weekend of hearing about his daughter's old passion having
become too complicated and talk of a possible new boyfriend, going to a
local bazaar and doing neighbourhood chores, plus, on the Sunday, a lunch
with Gavin Astor* and the Dean of Canterbury, Healey got together with
Wass on the Sunday evening to agree a paper for Callaghan on three things,
'IMF – safety net – formula.'[92]

Callaghan had been sensibly strengthened by separate conversations with
Jack Jones and Len Murray who 'gave me every encouragement to maintain
a Labour Government even if it meant taking some decisions the TUC would
not like and would oppose'.[93] All serious division between Healey and
Callaghan was now behind them and they had a meeting next day 'about
handling Cabinet on cuts'.[94] The Cabinets of early December would resolve,
first, if the IMF deal should go through at all, something which had to be
done while argument about the exact terms was taking place. They would
then settle what forms the necessary cuts would take. The opposition to an
IMF agreement so menacing in mid-November – 'Knives into Healey',
columns by Peter Jenkins calling for the Chancellor to be replaced – was
crumbling, but in the way of much crumbling, it made enough noise.

The gathering of 1 December was inundated with position papers, fourteen of them. Healey got in early, answering a query of Benn's. He had talked

---

* This was no jaunt. The government was trying to help the *Observer*, an Astor interest, with problems of its own.

to Simon and knew that 'trying to bully the Fund won't help us. The US are being very difficult, there is no bilateral borrowing available to us, even if the Fund helps us, but if a safety net is required, the US would be prepared to look at it. Henry Reuss, Chairman of the House Banking Committee, is being very helpful. If the Fund helps us, he'd try to clear it through Congress.'[95] He added that import deposits would meet with no favour.

Benn called for protection, attracting a wide range of fire – Callaghan, Williams, Rodgers, Peart and Lever – before Healey asked him, 'Where would you get the foreign currency to fund us if we had exchange controls?' Peter Shore came next, more credible and temperate and asking for control of imports only by way of our entitlements under GATT and certain EEC provisions, but vulnerable, as Healey noted, to the fact that he took no account of the PSBR.

Crosland did not help his case with the grand statement, 'I think the proposals I wish to put forward will command more support than Tony's or Peter's.' Languid grandeur did him no favours. His tone was quite extreme, scornful of the bankers rather than, like Benn, darkly fearful. His plan, requiring importers to put down cash in advance, had the advantage that it might cut the PSBR, and he quoted a similar paper from the Policy Unit. But as Edmund Dell commented later, he was 'moving from an attack on the deflationary effect of an agreement with the IMF, to restrictions on trade'.

In the process, he lost Shirley Williams, concerned about the plan accentuating poor-country poverty, also the devoutly free-trading Harold Lever. Crosland had alienated other friends by his patent readiness to run down Britain's contribution to Western defence. He might have had a good case in being sceptical about the full utility of this, but James Callaghan was the last man who would accept it. But Crosland's actual extremism lay in airy talk of blackmailing the IMF and everybody else with non-compliance, a sort of politicised sulk. The word 'cavalier' was often used about Crosland by his admirers. With the implied good humour and hedonism of an *enjoyable* socialism, no sensible person would quarrel, and this was probably Crosland's great political contribution. But that word has other meanings, casual indifference to consequences among them.

Crosland was now going through the motions of an opposition which had been both principled and a serious runner. After the Cabinet, he would seek out Roy Hattersley, now his only real supporter, and tell him that the game was up. 'In Cabinet tomorrow,' his widow reports him saying to the Prime Minister, 'I shall say I think you're wrong, but I also think that Cabinet must support you.'[96] It was a graceful and honest conclusion, but perhaps inevitable, after the combined impact of Callaghan's breakfast with Schmidt and the successive Whittome/Witteveen encounters.

On 2 December, Healey spelt out hard numbers. The first stand-by loan of \$1.6 billion would have to be repaid almost immediately. If it were paid without a fresh access from the IMF, we should then have exactly £2 billion of reserves to hand. He needed to cut the present PSBR of £10.2 billion (wrong number, but the one everybody was counting), otherwise he would get no loan from the IMF and would not be able to borrow from anyone else. But, once agree to that reduction, we could borrow again and would have a safety net for the sterling balances. He waved Helmut Schmidt, now something of a bogey figure, at the colleagues. He might be to the right of Milton Friedman,* but the world agreed with him. Callaghan now supported Healey, and the Cabinet assented to £1 billion of public expenditure cuts, half-a-billion dollars of Burmah shares to be sold, with Callaghan still making gesture talk about import deposits which would come to nothing.[97]

Broad-term Cabinet assent was one thing, it was still necessary to crunch the final numbers. Healey could now face Whittome, and through him Witteveen, with terms which he thought fair himself, finally agreed with colleagues. Talk of resignation and an election if the IMF stuck to its rigidities, should not be seen as bravado. Healey could not go back to the Cabinet for worse, wouldn't get it, didn't want it. For once it was Witteveen who was in the weaker position. The pure cuts would be a billion only. It was at this point that the Healey–Whittome–Witteveen–Whittome–Healey trialogue produced an invitation from the Chancellor of the Exchequer that the managing director of the International Monetary Fund 'should take a running jump', a suggestion coupled with that promise to go to the country.

The IMF response was restrained. Callaghan was called at Chequers on 4 December and told that the Fund wanted to talk again. Essentially the IMF, through Whittome, would now reduce their demands for the second year with the proviso that if growth were as high as 4 per cent, the British would make further cuts. No such large growth was anticipated, any further cuts were hypothetical, a get-out handy for the IMF's stern reputation. They had backed down. As the historians of the crisis put it rather primly, 'Too much had been invested in negotiations for them to fail. Presumably this had been Healey's appraisal, and his brutal negotiating manner at least made it clear that a line was being drawn in the dirt.'[98] It was indeed. The ultimate figures were to be for expenditure cuts of £1 billion for 1977/8 and of £1½ billion for 1978/9, much lighter than feared and Healey, wanting the heavier payments to come later, had avoided front-loading. The British were also authorised, secretly, to forgo later IMF tranches if the balance of payments should go into surplus early.

At this stage, one has the impression that Healey and Callaghan had played hard and soft policemen, soft line/hard line, cup of coffee/rubber

---

* Literalist school American monetarist, then much invoked to frighten socialist children.

truncheon. Whether they had fully intended to, is very doubtful. But they had worked together, conveyed the same message, finally closed a door which the Fund did not push against further. Callaghan does deserve great credit. The embassies and excursions had *not* persuaded Ford or Schmidt to redirect the Fund officers. And the sterling balances were not so central as the Prime Minister thought. But Callaghan understood mood music, knew when to stage a show. By getting into Cabinet business, he both indicated real action on cuts and could demonstrate the impossibility of getting more blood from this stone.

Edmund Dell objects to the politics dragged into an economic situation. But the politics worked and Dell, so often admirable, does sometimes approach the pains and penalties of this affair in the style of the flogging headmaster saying, 'Boys, I do this to save you from the gallows.'

As for the Cabinet, the first and truly political step had been agreed before the final agreement with the IMF. The left met and talked over resignation, with only Stanley Orme having to be persuaded to stay. Benn's friends outside the Cabinet urged him to walk out, but he saw no use in the move. Healey could now get the cuts. They might be less onerous but they still hurt, and getting them would be a two-day labour. However, no one could play a Cabinet like Jim Callaghan. He had allowed a great deal of indignation (and earnest thinking) to spend itself. He did the avuncular bit but could also put on a show of calculated temper, swapping threat for caress, if that might work.

Joel Barnett, as Chief Secretary, writes of 6/7 December's cut-making Cabinets as a connoisseur. He had effectively gone round the congregation with the collection plate. 'We then got down to the detail, and I managed to ensure that decisions covered the two years 1977/78 and 1978/79. We began with defence and I got £100 million and £200 million respectively.'[99] A total of £50 million was knocked off Overseas Aid for each year; food subsidies, that desperate piece of social contracting from the early seventies, were ended. Then Peter Shore, who had a complex and needy empire at the Environment, fought hard over water. The Welsh Secretary, John Morris, was supporting him, observing that following that year's North African weather, savings could create problems if there were drought, when with a flash of lightning and an immediate downpour, the gods declared themselves for the Treasury.[100]

Shore ceded something here, but his other chief concern, housing, was quietly left till later. More money came from an agreed increase in the price of gas, then state-owned, and in telephone charges, but notions of cutting pensions in the civil service and nationalised industries were prudently dropped. Eventually, by lunchtime on Tuesday the 7th, the Cabinet had put together cuts worth £954 million.

But if that looks to the arithmetical eye as good going, there had been a high price in attrition and general unhappiness. The Cabinet seems to have been out on its feet. Most ministers had gagged at one economy which

Healey wanted for its own sake. To stall for a year the automatic uprating of benefits was something a Labour Cabinet feared to contemplate. But Healey, who argued that most cuts didn't attack waste, was strongly reinforced by the judgement of his chairman in Leeds, Ashoke Bannerjee, who understood that lower-paid workers were resentful of levels of unemployment pay lapping close to their wage levels. 'We would be swept out of office by the anger of the low paid if we didn't deal with the level of benefits,' the Chancellor said.[101]

He and Callaghan also knew that the immediate alternative, housing cuts, would disemploy serious numbers of productive workers in the building trade. Against this stood fear, reinforced by the Whips, that the Parliamentary Party might revolt on the question. As Healey himself put it, 'Got close, but no one was prepared to legislate now on benefits. Jim lost his temper.'[102] Healey and Callaghan both understood that in a situation where so much floated upon sentiment, falling short even by a small amount of an agreed notional number, had a look of dangerous incompetence about it and there were ancillary costs looming. So, genuinely or by design, 'Jim lost his temper.'* The Prime Minister threatened that he and Healey would present their own final package to the PLP and parliament. When the Cabinet resumed at eight in the evening, off-edge and realistic, it would take until 10.30 p.m. to meet slightly enlarged commitments – £200 million for each year.

These, the extra costs, had nothing to do with the IMF, but were add-backs for industrial and more congenial employment ends, found through excise taxes and some delayed starts in road and water developments. Housing also suffered reductions. But the stalling of social security up-rating was gratefully escaped. Tony Benn sighed his relief at this. However, in the light of what would happen in 1979, failure to maintain the differentials between hospital porters or gravediggers and recipients of the Giro cheque looks distinctly misguided.

The government had done what it had to do. There would be further events before the year was out, a bitter and confusing argument about the formal document, the Letter of Intent. This was a statement of proposed conduct of economic policy during the term of obligation to the Fund. Donoughue, for the Political Unit, sent a dramatic late message telling the Prime Minister to insist on all numbers being spelt out, specifically on Domestic Credit Expansion, that alternative measure to the PSBR of indebtedness. In fact, it involved a falling rate of spending with DCE to fall from £9 billion in 1976/8 to £6 billion in 1978/9 and the prospect of a further cut of

---

* Healey later reassured Joel Barnett that the anger was unfeigned and the outcome one 'of real tiredness'. Barnett murmured, 'I am not sure.'[103]

£500 billion at current prices if circumstances required it. There were also M3 targets set.

This, according to Donoughue, led to a bitter verbal assault by Callaghan on Healey, deemed either to have connived at tougher terms or to have let the Treasury and IMF slip them past him. Healey himself makes no reference to any row. Doubtless something happened. As certainly, Healey did not let such things worry him. The whole argument was a ghostly one. He had been sharply aware of monetary targets for a long time now. He was perfectly aware that he had been dealing over the PSBR with supposititious figures liable to be revised down, something the Policy Unit's economists had pointed out! He took a highly philosophical view of promises made longer term to the IMF. Hence his concern to avoid front-loading and postpone heavier reduction until it might not be needed. The PSBR for 1976/7, the source of all this grief, would turn out to have been not £10.6 but £8.5 billion. Any promises came ready met. The numbers were indeed about to be very good indeed.

What remained were separate statements to the Commons on 15 and 21 December. Joel Barnett reported of the first: 'His credibility was at a very low level, and the House was unsympathetic; he was received with jeers by the Tories and stony silence from our side ... Denis looked very weary at the end.'[104] Dell sees it differently: 'He met less hostility from his back-benchers than expected. Perhaps they were learning a lesson. If you do not like your bank manager, do not let him become your lender of last resort.' Healey who, having brought the real economy away from inflationary spiral, had for months carried the prospect of technical national bankruptcy before wrestling with the calamitous requirements of creditors, with only two declared allies in the Cabinet, had reason to *be* very weary. But he was unfazed and commented on the debate characteristically. 'Not so bad,' he wrote.

In the second speech to the Commons, he acknowledged what he had seen in the economy from early on. 'I have described on earlier occasions the malignant interaction last autumn between the fall in the exchange rate, the increase in the money supply, and the level of domestic interest rates. No one who had the responsibility for watching the interaction, sometimes from minute to minute, in the Treasury, could doubt the need for measures to break this vicious circle.'[105] He then stressed the importance of resisting front-loading: 'I decided, with full agreement from the IMF, to spread the necessary adjustment over two years rather than one and to put the main burden of the consequent reduction in demand on the second year since in the first year our economy is already likely to be running well below its full capacity.'[106]

A Conservative, Ian Gow,* asked Healey: if interest rates should not fall, would 'he undertake that he will reduce further substantially in April the

---

* Later murdered by the IRA.

public sector requirement in order to achieve that fall in interest rates that he recognises to be essential?'[107] Healey would give no such assurance. He would not need to. The question was wistful masochism. Over the year October–October 1976–7 interest rates fell from 15 to 5 per cent, while during 1977, official reserves rose from $4.1 billion to $20.6 billion. And by the end of 1977, the pound stood at $1.90, higher than Healey wanted it, all DCE targets had been met and inflation stood at 10 per cent, with Britain able to invite the IMF to reallocate part of its drawing entitlement to some harder, more needy case.[108]

During a miserable year climaxing in perfect nightmare, Callaghan was entitled to credit. He had impressed his willingness to be difficult upon delegates and shown exceptional skill in handling the Cabinet. But for Healey, who had taken the anxiety and rage of his own party and the scorn of a shrill press, left and right, and undertaken the day-to-day watching of the fever, the word 'triumph' would not be too much. It *was* heroic and nobody else could have done it. 'Under Socialism who will do the really dirty jobs?' 'Denis Healey.'

A QUIET TIME AND AFTER

Now I ask you Comrades seriously, do you think we can possibly solve the problems of Capitalism with the programme Denis Healey has outlined? . . . unemployment is the product of capitalism. (*Applause*) Until you solve the problem of Capitalism you will not eliminate unemployment, and do not sit there in your seats, Comrades, and kid yourselves there is any other way to solve the basic problem . . . I would ask Comrades that you seriously consider Composite 26 because it is only Composite 26 which lays down a series of ways that we can tackle the problems of Capitalism because quite honestly I am sick to death of Socialism being presented to us as some pretty little package of social reforms once we have got the economy back on its feet. There is only one way to get the economy back on its feet and that is with Socialist and not Capitalist measures . . .[1]

Punctuation seems out of place in the speech of Julie McLean, Liverpool councillor and representative voice of the Militant Tendency. One can see a single hand chopping in the classic Tendency style as the sentences work themselves into fully completed circles. But it is only funny now. In volume (and volume came), it was frightening, and people were growing afraid of it. Callaghan, Healey, the whole Labour Party, would be facing that semi-autistic rant and the pure hatred which went with it, across a dozen conferences and across who knows how many local branches, from the early seventies onward. It would rise to screaming point in 1980–81, culmination of what Stephen Bird, curator of the Museum of Labour History in Manchester, calls 'the period of the Party's insanity'.[2]

Yet the government led by James Callaghan was entitled to a great deal of credit. After agonies, the economy was coming right, the Brokers' Men receded Cheshire-cat-wise – not that they had ever smiled much – and the whole IMF imposition would soon be gone. Callaghan was crisp, capable, and undeluded. Even the problem of a small majority, destroyed at by-elections, would be got over with some insouciance in the Lib-Lab Pact.

What was wrong was the archaic structure of the Labour Party, not democratic when serving a moderate leadership and no more democratic when the left moved into key places. Labour was the creation of people like Ernest Bevin, strong users of office and small committees. But the general line, sustained for most of Labour's active career by Bevin, Will Lawther, Arthur Deakin, Sam Watson and other union leaders, could claim to be on a fair wavelength with Labour voting opinion in the country, never mind the marginal opinion Labour needed to win. The party's vulnerability, once that strong-wristed control weakened, was already apparent in the programme proclaimed and partially enacted during 1974–5. The first Social Contract was directed both at responding to inflation in an inflationary way (to the advantage, short term, of unionised workers), and appeasing left-wing strength on the NEC and at Conference.

Michael Foot, quixotically devoted to a working class of his own Bohemian imagination, had given unions partial power of dismissal and exclusion. Tony Benn had run his own industrial policy, propping failed companies, itself an expensive and futile hobby, more importantly, talking about and looking to wholesale nationalisation. Wilson might detest Benn and treat him extremely badly in Cabinet, but neither he nor Callaghan would remove him. And despite an extremely bad climate for business generally, the government had shown early readiness to decree price levels, imposing upon businessmen both loss and interference. In a country of inherently moderate instincts, this bob to the left had invited the Thatcherian reply and bitter consequences when high unemployment grew higher and boots were on other feet.

Labour were in a false position, striking attitudes they didn't believe in, making enemies they didn't need. But Tony Benn's own position was coherent, if only within tight and hermetic limits. He was offering socialism. This was supposed to be a socialist party, wasn't it? What was wrong with that? Benn's problem was that it was also supposed to be a democratic party and the Benn gospel, syndico-Messianism, large public ownership, direct workers' control, co-ordinators of shop stewards edging out managers and discouraging investment, had no majority appeal whatever. Intuitive knowledge of this had always kept Labour from being socialist in Tony Benn's sense of socialism. Dick Taverne's local referendum in Lincoln had demonstrated that. The huge, if squandered, burgeoning of support for the SDP would show it again. Bennism rested upon a democratic fallacy, majority support within a small (and permanent) minority.

James Callaghan embodied at his best a reformist, pro-worker but this-worldly Labour Party that could be voted for by enough people for the normal purposes of politics. But Callaghan had both inherited the follies of 1973–5 and suffered the things which go wrong for governments anyway. He would also have to deal with the rise of Scottish nationalism, a sour-mouthed Kraken stirring in remote waters, and he governed on a thread of a majority, one to be bound up by fixes and deals – at doing which no man was more adept.

But the real tribulation of Callaghan's leadership was that he could make things work, actually make them work well, and govern with much sense only as long as he *was* governing. With Labour in office, Jack Jones and Hugh Scanlon could be persuaded to the second and useful Social Contract. Denis Healey could save the currency and the prospects of a stable, growing economy because the folly of party could be subordinated to the require-ments of government. Callaghan and Healey could go over the heads of muttering activists to the nation because nation and government had some-thing to say to one another. But out of office, the leaders of a party are naked and vulnerable to the party's mood and manias.

And as participatory politics shrank, the party shrank with it to small, clenched, virulent groups flying upon extravagant rhetoric, resentment, fan-tasy and an inveterate malice which had to be seen to be fled from. The unions would call the shots then, and union conduct, especially after the departure of Jack Jones who would retire with a Companionship of Honour earned many times over, in 1978, would be determined too often either by nonentities like Jones's visionless successor, Mostyn 'Moss' Evans, or camar-illas of far leftists, CP, Trotskyite or extragalactic. These, understanding local concentrated power, would cast their votes by the hundreds of thousands in the teeth of the known, even the polled views of union members. Tony Benn, an honourable, high-intentioned man who saw himself as a democrat and spoke the word 'democracy' in earnest, would assault and fetter the party by means democratic in a fashion to stretch the word 'Pickwickian'.

Out of office, the fate faced by Labour was that, having acquitted itself better than creditably in power, it had become, of all ironies, unfit *not* to govern. Callaghan knew this better than anyone. His concern to win the next election ran beyond the ordinary politician's inclinations. He needed to win short in order not to lose long. As far as the economy went, the prospects would be excellent. In Healey's phrase, 'An agreement with the IMF is like the Seal of Good Housekeeping.'[3] (He also spoke in classicist's exaltation of 'The Golden Apples of the Hesperides lodged with the IMF.'*) Only half of the loan was ever used, creditworthiness was restored and indeed Britain sat back to enjoy the tribulations of the United States under Jimmy Carter,

---

* One of the Labours of Hercules.

whose high moral tone, high spending, perfect manners and ability to annoy without trying – a Carter aide had monitored the price of the wine served to the visiting Vice-President – rather recalled Tony Benn.

So far had the climate changed that Healey would become active within the IMF itself, being appointed chairman of the Fund's Interim Committee, a job for which, he could remark luxuriously, he now had time. Such was his standing at the end of his time in the dock that he was invited onto the bench. Indeed Witteveen's job as managing director of the Fund, Healey was told more than once in 1978, was his for the asking. He declined, partly, as he says, because he didn't want to be an international bureaucrat, and partly, as he doesn't say, because he was now much more of a leading politician than he had been and was rather enjoying it. Healey, the clever toiler, saving money and phasing out aircraft carriers, was evolving into an instantly recognised face and with a national standing only below the Prime Minister's. Never an obsessive aspirant to the highest place, he could hardly have avoided thinking about it now. And in its grim way this was fun.

He could also attend Labour Conference in 1977 and take a little enjoyable credit: 'Last year when I spoke to Conference I had come, straight, as I said, from the battlefield. This year the battle is won,' adding teasingly, 'and I am bringing back a certificate from Washington to prove it.'[4] The rise in the pound had 'knocked between 2 and 3 per cent off the rate of inflation. To do that by way of subsidies, as some of you have asked, or through tax cuts would have cost £3000 million by cutting other forms of social expenditure . . . Every household has gained from it and every young couple buying a house is paying £200 a year less on a new mortgage.'[5]

He spelt out the consequences of a package, put through in July of that year. He had made tax reductions specifically to offset prospective wage demands. His Finance Act, claimed Healey, 'puts enough money through tax cuts into the pocket of an average married man with two kids on two thirds of average earnings, about 55 quid a week, enough to cover the whole increase in prices over the 12 months to next July even without a wage increase . . .' It would all be, he added, 'a hell of a sight more sensible a way to face the problem than a mad scramble for the biggest wage increase anybody can get, in which, you know from bitter experience, the weakest go to the wall. (*Applause*)'

Outside the Colosseum, the life of the government moved perilously, but on a mild upward curve. It suffered the intimations of tribulation ahead when, in December 1976, Reg Prentice, a minister stalwart through the crisis, was threatened in his constituency with reselection. Prentice cut his losses and resigned, though he did not quite give up politics. The Ministry lost a major talent when, early in 1977, Anthony Crosland suddenly collapsed with a stroke, dying a few days later on 19 February. Quirks and disappointments notwithstanding, Crosland had been a first-rater, an original thinker, true to his own reasoned-out principles, not the sort of man who would enter today's incurious display politics. His replacement, the swiftly rising David Owen, boosted by Callaghan's son-in-law, Peter Jay, was brave, brusque and difficult, and would be a major player in a game four years away.

Only a month before, Roy Jenkins, already retired from the Cabinet, formally left parliament to take up the presidency of the EEC Commission. Two of the great names of post-war Labour politics were gone, though in the case of Jenkins, incarnation-jumping would bring him interestingly back. On top of which, Edmund Dell, not famous nor established as a comparable name, but a superb intelligence for all his transferred masochism, would in 1978 be offered a City chairmanship (Guinness-Peat), would undertake to serve out the rest of the parliament first, and be grumpily told to go by Callaghan. Talent and strong characters, all in the party's sane tradition, were slipping away.

There was another matter raised by Crosland's death. There had been much talk of, at some stage, switching Healey and Crosland. In February 1977 the real task of the Treasury was done. Healey might have been shifted to a territory where he was an accredited expert, if one thinks that the foreign policy of a country set in its modest place and uncritical Atlanticist groove, provides a substantial post. Callaghan's clear reasons for taking no chances were good enough. Conviction of escape from the wood was a very sophisticated opinion not shared by voters or ministers. The best possible hand was needed at the Treasury; the FO was a suitable place for experiment.

The immediate problem for the government was their majority. Crosland's Grimsby seat, where there had been outstanding mutual affection, was narrowly held by the television journalist Austin Mitchell. But Labour had lost their nominal majority anyway and unofficial reliance upon the Nationalists and Liberals was too brittle. The SNP, a group rich in febrile personalities, was going through a triumphalist phase, obtaining devolution proposals from an unhappy Cabinet.

Doing a proper deal with the Liberals, a party limping after the bizarre personal activities of its departed leader Jeremy Thorpe, made sense and was accomplished, an alliance of people who didn't want an election, the sort of thing which happens in politics. Teeth had to be clenched, not least Healey's, in dealings with the affront-giving Liberal Treasury spokesman, John Pardoe. Joel Barnett describes a meeting late in 1977 when Pardoe called for much larger income tax cuts than Healey, the Treasury or common prudence would tolerate. Healey spoke his mind on the inflationary potential of the Liberal scheme and Pardoe walked out. 'The official record noted: "The meeting ended abruptly."'[6] Pardoe then talked widely about his achievement. 'His considerable ego was much boosted by his letting it be known that he had walked out on a tough Chancellor,'[7] and at Barnett's suggestion, the Chief Secretary and David Steel attended future meetings, 'if only to hold their coats'.[8]

David Steel, the Liberal leader, was no sort of fool, but inexperienced and conciliatory, and he was played by Callaghan too successfully for too little by way of concession. Closer and longer-lasting ties would have been valuable, but this was a time of narrow party patrialism. The Lib–Lab pact of 1977 had to suffice.

And in basic political terms, Labour began imperceptibly to prosper. The Conservative lead in the polls had leapt almost vertically in the last four months of 1976 and stood above 20 per cent by December as Healey slogged through his fifteenth round with the IMF. It now fell and went on falling, less quickly but reliably, across 1977, finally after an undulating 1978, turning into a small Labour lead in October when a by-election in Northumberland registered a swing to Labour.[9] The pact would hold. In Scotland the SNP's cocksureness would be rebuffed by two by-elections already written off for Labour by knowing journalists. Two figures with major careers before them, Donald Dewar and George Robertson, would retain respectively Glasgow Garscadden and Hamilton in April and May 1978, natural Labour seats which had been despaired of. A slow return to President Harding's 'normalcy' was being made.

Pursuing that objective back at Great George Street, Healey had continued, because of the terms of the Letter of Intent, to observe the dietary laws of monetarism, while denying it as God's law. He did this by targeting, among the wide selection of measures, the growth of M3. He quotes with cool approval a Treasury civil servant, Jasper Hollom, that in doing so he 'was redesigning his cross'.[10] The serious problem for the government, pleasing and worrying at the same time, involved a sterling recovery beyond the ideal point for competition. Half-hearted attempts were made to get the pound down. But this was not March 1976 – sold short, the pound stayed where it was.

Another concern was the EMS, parent body of the ERM, which Healey quickly came to reject despite its friends at Foreign Office and Bank (and Callaghan's sympathetic interest fuelled by his persistent hostility to the Treasury). The pound was going up further than was wanted for exports, but the price of keeping it down by EMS-approved means would have been a 30 per cent expansion of monetary growth, the last thing Healey intended. The EMS was the creation of Helmut Schmidt whom he respected enormously, and Giscard, the French President, fellow aesthete who would discuss Harold Pinter with him, but a man clever chiefly in the sense of ingenious contrivance. Healey saw it as impractical systematisation only able to compel weak economies and made lopsided in the process. Supported by Edmund Dell and opposed by Harold Lever, the customary formation, he kept out.

The same Dell would mildly criticise Healey in the latter part of his stewardship, again for 'politics'. Having been careful, with the money measures and most other things throughout 1977, Healey unconscionably recognised the advent of a general election and gave a stimulus to the economy of £2.5 billion in all, £2 billion of it for 1978/9. It is the sort of thing governments generally do and was not in the league of Reggie Maudling dashing for growth or Edward Heath spending money with his eyes shut. But the PSBR moved up again, ironically to the £8.5 billion mark where it had really been in the crisis year, a figure representing 5.25 per cent of GDP.[11] It would mean some renewed external market pressure and a higher MLR.

It is one thing to deplore politics in a chancellor whom strict economics may require to be a model of world-forgetting frugality. But the Labour government, having inherited the consequences of drunken-sailor economics and only begun its reform course a year later, in 1975, was in no position, with a general election eighteen months away, to press on to yet further heroics against inflation. If inflation were to be tackled at root, it needed, as Dell says, a new mandate and four years of elbow room. There is a cultural difference also. We have again become accustomed to very low inflation, screams being heard if it creeps above 3 per cent. But historically, rising inflation had been the tolerated norm ever since R. A. Butler left the Treasury. By 1962 a chancellor's uncalled-for resistance to champagne reflation had cost Selwyn Lloyd the thrust of the first of the long knives.

Healey and Callaghan were not going back to that. Their lapse, in the style of the housemaid's baby, would be a very little one. Healey's autumn Budget of 1977 was cautious beside the call of the Policy Unit for £3 billion of immediate reflation, spreading a rather smaller sum over two years, and it was shrewdly directed through tax allowances at take-home pay. It was a political act which worked politically, producing the first good opinion polls for three years, including a brief Labour lead of 0.5 per cent in December 1977.[12] Healey had one great battle to fight and win.

North Sea oil and its revenue were now flowing. That was capable of adding £3–4 billion in 1980 and by 1985 perhaps £5 billion. All Healey's earnest pamphleteering in the forties about not using foreign currency looked to its reward here, a burden of foreign exchange splendidly reduced. His own intentions towards the revenue were entirely prudential. He 'urged that the oil revenues be used for long-term investment and paying off liabilities'.[13]

Tony Benn, by contrast, had his own visions of manufactures renewed through major investments and a festival of nationalisation – more Meridens, more Leylands. Time and energy were expanded while position papers on sense and nonsense were presented to the Cabinet's liaison committee with the PLP. Healey's insistence on debt repayment and general revenue purposes would indeed be upheld, not least after the sardonic exertions of Lever and Barnett.[14] Perhaps the ultimate rejection of the Benn option was planned as demonstration of the government's good sense. Slapping it down at once would have sent a stronger message and saved Healey one more chore in the service of the obvious.

But the feelings and numbers were good. Unions were until quite late talking the language of consultative, planned-ahead restraint. The TUC annual conference in September 1977 had endorsed an earlier General Council vote to support renewal of a twelve-month deal on wages. All statistics are imperfect, but those for real personal disposable income after ten quarters of almost continuously falling or standing still (123: third quarter of 1975, 115: third quarter of 1977), show it moving firmly upwards reaching 128 in the last quarter of 1978.[15] Political and economic problems seemed, with only a slight lag, to run parallel. Doing the right things from early 1975 until the end of 1976, the government saw its popularity fall and fall. Getting credit for having done them by way of material wellbeing seemed to follow naturally in polls and by-elections.

Healey would put things squarely to yet another Party Conference, taking up where Julie McLean had left off.

When I spoke to conference twelve months ago, I predicted that the coming year would see a steady fall in unemployment and an increase in living standards, and the delegate who followed me said 'Tell us the old, old story.' What in fact happened in those twelve months? First of all I have put £3 billion of stimulus into the economy. The economy is growing at 3 per cent a year faster than average since the war. Inflation has been cut by over half. Living standards have been rising faster than in any other years since the war . . . Why do you think our position in the opinion polls has swung right round in the last twelve months? . . . above all, unemployment has been falling. There are 90,000 fewer people out of work now than there were twelve months ago.[16]

Healey pointed out that 'the *Financial Times* survey and the CBI survey show growing confidence throughout the economy,' and claimed that 'whoever wins the next election is going to inherit the best balanced economy, the best economic prospects of any government since the war.'

The consensus of midsummer would be that Callaghan and Healey had kept their nerve, turned the ship round and might now think of winning an election, something contemplated, even a year earlier, in perfect despair. Such an election would be natural in the early autumn of 1978. Labour had renewed its earlier tiny mandate four years before, but given the two-election year 1974, would have been in power for four years and eight months. With the numbers good, the public mood vastly recovered, Callaghan himself high in public esteem, and Margaret Thatcher as Leader of the Opposition, a distinctly flickering light, the old injunction *Carpe diem* looked pretty sensible.

There was something else: inflation in June 1978 stood at 7.4 per cent. A government re-elected on such figures would have a chance with its new mandate of still holding rising prices. Concessions had been made to stimulation which three exceptionally hard years made inevitable, but they were not gambler's concessions. Government spending as a proportion of GDP, which had stood 45.6 per cent at high-water mark in 1975/6 before coming down drastically to 39.8 per cent in 1977/8, had been allowed up for 1978/9 but only by an unsensational measure of 1.2 per cent to 41.4 from 40.4 per cent on revised Pliatzky figures for 1973/4.[17]

The Prime Minister failing to call the October election generally expected through the summer probably destroyed Healey's chance of the succession. But he seems to have played little part in making that decision. Kenneth Morgan has given a very full account of the process. The early consultations with Rees, Healey, Owen and Foot, the soundings round the Cabinet, the long retreat to Upper Clayhill Farm in Sussex in August 1978, the final dinner for trade union leaders, are all recounted.

The contributory reasons seem to have been Callaghan's own caution, the pessimism of senior whips, fearful talk conveyed by Michael Foot from nervous backbenchers and one private MORI poll indicating the uncertainty of such advantage as Labour now had. There was also a counter-precedent. Harold Wilson in 1970, perfectly certain of his wisdom in going early, had lost. Callaghan did not kill off the certainty of a solid Labour majority. But he almost certainly missed a result to keep Labour in the political game, and probably in power if only by the sort of working plurality which, with the Liberals, he had conjured into parliamentary authority. With no evidently intended irony, Healey would refer at Conference a month later to 1951 when Labour, in its exhaustion, went too soon into a general election, leaving the fruits of its exertion for Conservative delectation.

Healey, unlike the other three ministers consulted initially, Merlyn Rees, David Owen and Michael Foot, all clear postponers, seems to have been in two minds, thinking the economy might yet show more improvement, but worried about the effect on living standards not continuing during the winter. He would not be spoken to again on the subject until 18 August when Callaghan made a teatime call on a new neighbour. (Edna and Denis had moved only that year to Pingle's Place, between Seaford and Alfriston, the pleasing design of a pupil of Lutyens, whose garden is a last and beautiful roll of the downs.) The Prime Minister had decided against an autumn election and had come to tell his Chancellor.

Healey's comments in the memoirs are very much the stoic, non-self-justifying Healey. 'I warned him that the growth of output and living standards would be slower during the winter; but Jim thought that by the spring the longer experience of improving living standards would count for more with the voters. Neither of us foresaw the industrial troubles which lay ahead, or our defeat on devolution, which was in part their consequence.'[18]

The decision would be given to the public only on 7 September, when it came as an all-round shock in the Cabinet and the press and angered many colleagues. William Rodgers soon after said presciently that Labour had just lost the election. Roy Hattersley, who had heard an advance rumour from Dick Leonard of the *Economist*, was present. 'It was extraordinary. Jim said "I'd like to read you a letter I've sent to the Queen," and after pages of economic argument, it said "I am therefore not proposing to ask you to dissolve parliament at this time." There was a little ripple round the table. He said, "You're laughing now with relief. But you won't be laughing if we have a hard winter with the unions and we get forced out in the Spring." Then, absolutely typical of Jim, he said, "You can discuss it if you like, but I don't think you'll persuade me to write another letter to the Queen."'[19]

If nothing else, the decision had been a successful secret. A general assumption about the autumn had been made and the Prime Minister, enjoying the pleasures of surprise, had done nothing to correct it. The experience of the present writer, then a *Daily Express* leader-writer, was vivid and unforgettable. We had very early first edition deadlines in those days of old technology – 6.30 p.m., and I had written by late afternoon the standard comments of a Conservative middle-market paper on the next month's certain general election. At six we went idly into the office of the editor, Roy Wright, to gather round his television (another mark of the old times), for perfunctory assurance that what was everywhere assumed had definitely happened. Three or four sentences in, I jumped up and fled to the typewriter to turn out 550 quite different words at remarkable speed.

The annoyance of colleagues was intensified by Callaghan's tantalising hint-throwing at the TUC Conference on 5 September which, with its playful quotation of the Vesta Victoria music-hall song 'There was I, waiting at the Church', brilliant political theatre though it was, conveyed the general belief that while Mrs Thatcher might dally, the date was still on. The mystification added to the harm done. Callaghan seemed to have made fools of colleagues, union leaders, editors and the public. A hint of the later date would have avoided the shock, might even have allowed more argument in a Cabinet where a majority had been right against the Prime Minister. 'There was a startled silence,' wrote Joel Barnett, 'as mixed feelings sorted themselves out.' Relief at not immediately fighting an election was offset by the fact that 'most of us knew in our bones that hanging on was a mistake.' But all argument would be pointless. For he had said, 'I told the Queen of my decision last night.'[20]

But one point fascinates. At the union leaders' dinner held too aptly in a beautiful sunset,[21] only Hugh Scanlon favoured postponement of the election. Callaghan seems to have spent the evening arguing against the cream of the NEDC, all wanting an election in October. The best of them wanted it precisely to head off an explosion of wage claims. For rank-and-file activists were taking no talk of restraint from their leaders. Cynical leaders like Clive Jenkins and dumb ones like Moss Evans looked forward to a surge of major successful wage claims, returning us gaily and witlessly back to 1974–5. The responsible leaders knew that the Social Contract bottle had contained all the flammable pressure it could. The implication for *them* was that a newly mandated government might yet compel where the union leaders could no longer persuade. Instead Callaghan had subjected his own government to another annual round of wage claims, another bout at the threshold of year four, of trying to make incomes policy go on working. His motive, made clear to Kenneth Stowe, present on the spot, was conviction that the unions *generally* meant to follow up an election with a ruthless grab for inflationary wages.

Another of the many objections to postponement was that it obliged the government to stage a party conference. This for Labour was generally a bad idea, and in 1978, a conference meant exposure to a specific vote on incomes levels. With Jones both defeated at his own conference and retired, there could be no good news on the subject. A debate on *that* was something much better postponed than the general election.

What the country needed for a Labour solution to work was institution-alised understanding between government and trade unions, thought out long term with the numbers and the consequences of numbers faced up to, on the Swedish and German model. Real achievement had been managed short term through personal contributions, with Jones, Murray and Scanlon under-standing and leading. (Healey would mourn the government's failure – and that of the unions – to embrace the Bullock Commission with its good German thinking about *Mitbestimmung*, a union voice in management and union understanding of risks and losses.)

But for all the Conservative talk about the menace of corporatism, even the present structure was frail. The practical thing to do was to take a step back, patch up the least injurious bundle of settlements, get through an elec-tion intact, then with time in hand, seek to establish a new structure. Healey should have fought Callaghan, but seeing great difficulties ahead rather than the catastrophe which emerged, he proved on this occasion too ready a sub-ordinate.

If inflation was actually to be kept down, wage policy had to stay very tight. That meant, ideally, a norm well below 5 per cent. But it is in the way of all incomes policy to achieve a great deal in the first year in an atmosphere of mutual congratulation, something followed by difficulty, hard words and some success in the second, before falling apart in the third. The second Social Contract had been a remarkable affair, patient slogging by the princi-pals in pursuit of a sane and saving policy. Hugh Scanlon's remark about having looked into the abyss expressed it exactly. The abyss was South American, an Andean chasm, and we had been rescued from Chilean-Argentinian-style inflation by an act of all-round good sense.

But not only were the held-down wages coming into a testing year, there were fewer statesmen. Jack Jones had seen his union conference humiliatingly repudiate the whole approach. His own retirement would lead to the succession of Moss Evans, lacking courage, mind and energy to work even for mitigation of the mood.* The white-collar leader, Clive Jenkins, now bulked larger and Jenkins, part spiv, part leftist, wholly malevolent, would become a personal enemy of Healey. If Evans was an acceptance man, poor Terry Duffy who was elected in place of the retiring Scanlon was poor Terry Duffy. The candidate of the right and the Roman Catholic interest, succeeding the former Communist, he was brave, had great sweetness, but lacked the grasp to run a major union. Scanlon listened, understood and delivered. Duffy wanted to help, didn't understand, couldn't deliver.

The government, needing to hold inflation, had lost the trade union half of the act which had got it down in the first place. Any notion of falling inflation was out of the question. In the argot of the day, the unions wouldn't stand for it. Already in October 1978, within the upbeat language of Healey *gloriosus*, was buried a great anxiety. The catch-phrase of the hour, an old one refurbished, was 'free collective bargaining'. The unions had that written in their rubric, but in competent social democratic states it had been replaced by close governmental and union consultation, closet postponement of satisfaction and considerable macroeconomic sophistication.

Healey quoted a delegate on 'the blind play of market forces. But what else,' he asked, 'is unfettered free collective bargaining?' Why had they brought inflation down and increased employment? '. . . the reason is – you will not like this, some of you – it is the miracle ingredient, pay policy. If we had not had the support of the working people of this country in the past three years for moderate wage increases, we could not have brought down inflation and unemployment at the same time.'[23] Healey had begged in the same speech for support against inflation and loyalty to Callaghan. Neither would be much in evidence as the year fell. As for the miracle ingredient, it was being withdrawn.

A very high measure of responsibility has to lie with Callaghan. Not only had he put off the election and loosed the dogs of a conference predictable as crazy, he had gone out of his way to start a fight. Healey speaks with quiet regret of 'Our hubris in fixing a pay norm of five per cent without any support from the TUC met its nemesis, as inevitably as in a Greek tragedy.'[24] The 'our' there is fair up to a point. Healey had produced proposals for a White Paper in mid-July 1978, calling for continuation of pay policy and which mooted 5 per cent. Michael Foot gravely doubted the numbers. Stanley Orme, with excellent trade union contacts and sensibilities, defined the move

---

* Healey characterised him thus: 'he had no leadership qualities and little loyalty to the Labour Party.'[22]

as, not pay policy but pay restraint, and believed that it would fail. 'It's not an easy horse to ride and there's no easy ride. All we can do is try to persuade the TUC to go for moderation.'[25] The 'norm' of 5 per cent was fixed by the Cabinet on 20 July, an unhappy date for great enterprises. But everyone saw it as a rubber norm, liable to turn into an aspiration. 'Persuading the TUC to go for moderation' was to be the second theme of the music.

However the government, owing much to Callaghan's ability to stamp his authority on it, also 'ran into difficulties because of Callaghan's highly personal style . . . Callaghan took the decision to enforce the 5 per cent norm very much on his own, even in some isolation from the Chancellor of the Exchequer, and imposed his view on a somewhat cowed Cabinet in the course of 1978.'[26] Healey had been told back in Leeds by the local T&G regional officer, Ernest Hayward, someone he trusted implicitly, 'that it would be simply impossible to operate a national incomes policy for another year'.[27] But just as Callaghan had been 'obsessed' about sterling balances in 1976 (the only word, says Derek Mitchell,[28] which describes his attitude) so he would be obsessed with inflation in 1978. Late in the autumn, talking in the Cabinet Room to Alf Allen of the Shopworkers', one of the most moderate of union leaders, he would say, 'We've got to go for broke on inflation.'[29] Broke it was.

Although Healey fairly blames himself – 'We were blind to these warnings – I as much as any member of the Cabinet'[30] – he describes, without rancour, Callaghan's private preference for zero norm, his proposal at a meeting of a figure of a directive at 3 per cent, and his contradiction of his assault upon *In Place of Strife*. On the notion of an even lower figure than 5 per cent, Roy Hattersley recalls an approach to him from his Permanent Secretary, Kenneth Clucas, a civil servant of whom Callaghan approved, suggesting that perhaps 3 per cent might be a good idea. The implication was, says Hattersley, who did not think it a good idea, that he might like to advance it.[31] 'He [Callaghan] was,' said Healey, 'so disenchanted with the behaviour of the unions that he was contemplating legislation to control them.'[32] The serious criticism of Healey in all this is of his lack of insubordination. Callaghan was getting things wrong. The Cabinet, after its self-destructive exertions in 1976, was not making trouble. Healey, alone of ministers, had the authority to break in on the serene fallacy of the Prime Minister's private contemplations and say 'no'. The military instinct by which the brigadier follows the general served him poorly.

The most rational explanation for this arbitrary, provocative, more-than-the-market-would-bear and not otherwise very rational approach, is the example of West Germany.[33] Helmut Schmidt's government had managed to keep wages and inflation at the 5 per cent level. But that was in another country. The Germans had not reached a high degree of effective wage compliance through conference speeches. The psychology of a country which, having endured milliard mark loaves, had elected Hitler, lost a world war, then seen a brief unemployment level of 2 million, would combine with close and fully informed employer-worker institutions to make mature decision-taking the natural thing.

Another part of the problem lay in a personality trait of Callaghan. Where Wilson fantasised and talked like Micawber, Callaghan on occasion dipped into despair. He saw any concession in terms of the stone of economic recovery rolling all the way back down the hill. Healey and Foot were ironically united in wanting to make the best of a bad thing, talk, cajole, warn and get the least bad figures available in a bad year. Living to fight another day made better sense than laying on a conference for the benefit of the big-demand unions and the Conservative Party and then doing heroics.

The Prime Minister's stand gave him great press credit, he would be personally admired. But it had a touch of Samurai pride. Or rather Callaghan, the naval man, recalled the sort of admiral ready to go to the bottom taking his fleet with him rather than find a prudent haven. In doing so, he 'fatally antagonised the unions or at least his closest supporters like David Basnett, Alf Allen and Lionel Murray'.[34] Murray, 'letting his hair down', would tell John Cole that Callaghan 'had reverted to a bad habit from his Treasury days: he was too impressed by the Treasury's econometric models, and too little prepared to rely on his own very sensitive political instincts.'[35] In the light of Callaghan's foot-dragging obstruction and sour resentment when the Treasury was pointing out realities during the IMF crisis, this was darkly ironical.

Murray was profoundly unimpressed. 'We warned Callaghan that he would have industrial troubles if he tried to impose a 5 per cent wages policy. He was over-impressed by the quality of the Treasury printout and started thinking with his head rather than his stomach.'[36] Murray is quoted in the most recent study of the TUC as believing that the TUC might have been able to hold down pay deals in the 1978/9 wage round to 8 or 9 per cent, adding, 'Ministers thought they knew better than the General Council what trades unionists wanted.'[37] As for Denis Healey, who reckoned that the formula 'single figures' would have seen them through,[38] he was someone whose difficult job was being made impossible.

But although Callaghan made the central mistake, with Healey loyally sustaining it, many hands were involved in formulating it, including those of leading trade unionists. Roy Hattersley reports on one of the private ministerial/union leaders' dinner meetings taking place after the T & G's rejection of the wage formula. 'Denis argued very strongly for the 5 per cent. Denis suggested to Moss Evans that the T and G should have a recall conference. Moss said "You saw what they did to Jack Jones. What do you think they'll do to me?" And somebody – I think it was Alf Allen, certainly supported by Len Murray – said "Look, none of us can carry this in our unions. But if you blind it through, you'll get away with it." Denis is entitled to argue – I don't know why he never does – that the error was compounded by the TUC nod and wink. That was certainly what we thought we were doing. We thought we could blind it through and get away with it.'[39]

Healey was approached by the junior Prices minister, Robert Maclennan, deeply worried by the Ford deal and by the prospect of demand generally getting out of hand. Maclennan favoured the drastic course of a statutory incomes policy. They spoke calmly and rationally for three-quarters of an hour, Healey being entirely pleasant but very clear that he couldn't contemplate such an action. He was now close to the unions and he acknowledged, candidly, that his own future was wrapped up in them. Anything rational that could be done with them he was doing, but a frontal assault, as a statutory policy was perceived to be, was not a runner for him. Almost certainly it would also have been a policy impossible to sell to a Cabinet already battered and alienated by the rounds of price cuts. Maclennan's thinking falls into the category of 'Right thing to do, generally reckoned impossible.'[40]

At Conference, prophetically and ineffectually, Healey had singled out public service workers as those at the heart of the issue, arguing rationally with Alan Fisher, the handsome, eloquent, slightly unhinged spokesman for the public service union, NUPE. There had been free collective bargaining in the local authorities since 1919, Healey said, 'and the local authority workers have always been at the bottom of the pile'. Not unreasonably, he claimed credit for actual improvement through the £6 package of 1975. But then Fisher opposed a flat cash deal as much as a percentage. He wanted 50 per cent!

Healey in November, painfully and after weeks of work, attempted in close concert with Foot and Murray to minimise hurt through an agreed joint document. 'A statement which restored the position of helpful neutrality [the TUC Economic Committee] had been taken the previous year . . . not perfect, but the best ministers could hope for.'[41] In the judgement of John Cole, it would fall to the floor like dropped Meissen. The proposal, 'Collective Bargaining, Costs and Prices', involved the unions promising a 10 per cent norm in return for renewed price controls. It was lost at the TUC General Council entirely through incompetent absenteeism, one leader busy being interviewed in a studio, another voting against, as he thought safely, so as not to be committed, and Moss Evans who had talked about trying to keep wage demands under 10 per cent, having gone on holiday.[42] Murray felt no grief, regarding it as too much of a direction in a bad time for directions.

The Cabinet Pay Committee, chaired at first by Healey, later more often by Hattersley, seemed, said Joel Barnett, a constant attender, 'to meet almost round the clock'.[43] But the true crisis of autumn, Christmas and after, would start slowly and get worse. A long crisis in the hospitals would by common consent be grossly mishandled by the Health Minister, David Ennals, Barbara Castle's replacement, now her revenge. After maximum injurious exposure, it ended late and weakly with Ennals talking about the nurses being 'unique' and 'loved by everybody'. Other claimants, loved and unique or not, made their demands with the NHS figures in mind. There would be a miserable run-in with local government. Harold Lever had passed Healey a note saying that he could not treat the councils too badly. 'The louder the screams, the more popular we shall be.'[44] The screams now mingled with those of so many groups, and the government was *not* popular.

But it was not just low-paid public service workers who would make trouble. Ford Motors had had a good year, with profits of £246 million. Ford workers were doing less well than men at British Leyland, a company unwisely rescued by Benn. They both made large demands. Moss Evans's idea of conciliation was to call for a 30 per cent single-year increase at *both* plants.[45] After a five-week strike, they settled at 17 per cent, an object lesson in the economic consequences of Mr Benn. Leyland, a Lazarus among motor companies, had been told, following historic precedent, to take up its bed and walk, subsidised by the Department of Industry.

Ford gave the competition of a subsidised company as a reason for doing a deal, which Callaghan saw as perfect calamity. The calamity would be multiplied when the government attempted to use sanctions against Ford for breaking the guidelines. For this they needed legislation. All the non-governmental parties opposed it, and on 13 December, nine pillars of the lumpen left, which here included John Prescott, abstained, defeating the government. Ministers would leave for the Christmas recess with their majority at the next night's vote of confidence standing at 10 and the Lib–Lab Pact a memory. But not only was this aborted attempt at punitive incomes policy a bad mistake, Callaghan was being alarmist and thinking in headline numbers about Ford paying over the odds, where a quite genuine productivity deal made costs tolerable and the inflationary input so much less.

The sense of ice breaking under stumbling feet would be enhanced by something which Callaghan did not say, the famous 'Crisis, what crisis?' The words are those of a senior subeditor at the *Sun* who composed them for its headline. The actual words were 'I don't think other people in the world will share the view that there is mounting chaos.' But, together with the reproach that concerns were 'parochial',[46] they were quite bad enough since he was returning from a visit to Guadaloupe in early January. A meeting of world leaders to the Prime Minister, to everyone else it was a free luxury trip to the sunshine when hospitals and graveyards were working to rule and a lorry drivers' strike looked likely to stop food supplies. Before the black month was out, colleagues would hear Callaghan exclaim after a cautious response from Murray, 'The trouble is, the TUC simply don't believe there is a crisis.'[47]

Before making this unwise flight to the world stage, Callaghan had held a private meeting with Healey to express concern at settlements being made outside the norm in the private sector, also at the strike by local authority manual workers. They were demanding 40 per cent. Continuing to counterpoint the statesman role with plaintiveness, he also talked with Bernard Donoughue, telling the head of his Policy Unit, 'Bernard, it is all falling apart. I do not trust the Whitehall machine. I think ministers and their departments are quietly selling out. We are going to wake up soon and find that everybody in the public sector is settling for 20 per cent and the pay policy has been sunk.' Blaming the Treasury was a tedious bad habit of Callaghan's and it produced a corresponding savage scorn for him among some senior officials there. He was arguing that his strong line was being undermined, but if it had been less of a strong line and less masterfully presented, if the unions had been early consulted and listened to, the train of small explosions might not have been detonated.

The lorry drivers' strike owed nothing to the wickedness of the Treasury. It was another product of Moss Evans's idleness. He had delegated power to local union leaders as an easier way to popularity than helping the government get the chestnuts out of the fire before they turned to carbon dust. It had started in Scotland on 4 January as Callaghan left for the French West Indies, involved a claim for 20 per cent which, by 11 January, would be made official and defended to a helpless Callaghan by an uncomprehending Evans.[48] By then, it had got out of hand and Evans, thoroughly scared, would find reasserting the authority of Bevin, Deakin, Cousins and Jones impossible.

A series of stoppages by ASLEF, the engine drivers' union, was the merest cherry upon what would cleverly be called 'the Winter of Discontent', words by William Shakespeare – *Richard III*. As for the famous refusal to bury the dead, it started on 21 January naturally enough in Liverpool. To complain that the Conservatives and their newspapers overstated their case was pointless, that is what oppositions are for. Foot and Healey, Jones, Scanlon and Murray had put together an immediate cure for the hyperinflation of 1975. Keeping the deal, any deal, together would always be intolerably difficult by the end of 1978.

Healey could be blamed for stubbornly adhering to a norm of 5 per cent, which made sense in terms of inflation and the currency but was wholly unsaleable. He was, though, more willing than Callaghan to fit some flexibility into the official rubric, trying in November to draft a document which pulled the unions into at least a common acknowledged purpose. Callaghan, the Policy Unit complained, had stopped listening to them, and he had been afflicted by a monarchical style and black defeatism. His words to Joel Barnett, banteringly offering to swap his accountancy job of Chief Secretary with the Prime Minister, 'I think you'd get the better of the deal,'[49] were meant as a joke, but it was a sour and instructive one.

As for union leadership, allowing for obvious exceptions, too much of it was low grade, inspiration-free, cowardly, afraid of its local incendiarists, rationalising like Evans that 18–19 per cent wasn't that much really and running before a mob which its failure to lead had set loose. The Cabinet would reach the stage where the central issue was whether or not to declare a national emergency. That observation which Healey likes to quote, made fifty years before by Joseph Schumpeter, about the greatest danger faced by a socialist government coming from organised labour, had settled on the roof.

When the norm was effectively surrendered on 18 January 1979 with so-called 'underpinnings' aimed at the lower paid, raising it to something nearer 9 per cent, it was Healey who set himself to pull the unions into an agreement. He started talks at once with the TUC, looking forward to a new understanding with the unions. David Lea, Murray's endlessly reliable deputy, would be much involved, and the link to the Prime Minister was Kenneth Stowe, Callaghan's Private Secretary.[50] They were looking frantically before an election, as they might have looked with leisured reflection after one, for a Social Contract Mark III.

The government had another nine months before it must face an election, but by mid-January it was close to using troops and Healey appears to have been one of the group of ministers, with Rodgers, Barnett and Shore, who looked to military provision of street cleaning, grave-digging and lorry driving as some relief for the afflicted civilian population. If that was the stick in Healey's mind, his discussions with Lea and others were a sort of talking carrot.

But when, on 22 January, four major unions led by the T & G called out one and a half million workers for a French-style one-day strike, Callaghan and his government were utterly lost. Joel Barnett, involved with the Contingency Committee meeting under the Home Secretary, Merlyn Rees, recalls the plans for coping with the effects of successive strikes, named military-style by civil servants – '"Brisket" for the road haulage dispute, "Bittern" for the growing ambulance drivers' dispute and "Nimrod" for the water workers' action'[51] – all full of detail but with very little idea of what could actually be done. And one group of civil servants would soon be on strike themselves.

No stick was going to work, and the civil service, short of respect for a prime minister sullenly hostile to them, solidly resisted proposals for militarising the solutions. In particular, Sir Clive Rose, head of the Continuity Unit, and Sir Patrick Nairne who had run it previously, came down emphatically against any military intervention except in the matter of burying the dead who, in Liverpool, were now stacked in a warehouse! But late in the day, the carrot would come in handy. Murray, who had originally wanted the flexibility to let the leadership bring off increases at the 8–9 per cent level, now had a government officially and by convolutions authorising a norm which worked out at 8.8 per cent,[52] when the numbers hammering at the door recalled the Argentinian figures of 1975.

Murray understood the arguments Healey had put forward back in November. UK unemployment at 5.4 per cent was relatively low by comparison with like countries, economic growth the fastest in Europe, current account in balance and inflation 'cut more dramatically than in any other part of the world',[53] making moderate settlements, ideally under 5 per cent, best for everyone. He hadn't thought such numbers workable. The minutes of the TUC's meeting at the Treasury on 19 December had read: 'The TUC recognised the government's concern to avoid a sudden lurch from a restrictive to a free pay situation.' It had added in the same sentence, 'but the government should recognise the need at least to move steadily and by agreement in the direction of giving more scope for meaningful negotiations on particular problems in the public and the private sector.'[54]

But events, strike upon strike, actual or feared crisis on road and rail, settlements which made nonsense both of Callaghan's stand and the authority of a union leadership, had destroyed over three months a mutual trust working almost brilliantly for the previous three years.

Callaghan's stolidly imperious line had angered the most temperate union figures. The sight of the government's hard-won recovery being thrown away on the picket line and out of the loudest mouths of people whom the Neddy Six couldn't control, had created unprecedented bitterness among ministers. A dinner was called to attempt the re-creation of goodwill. It was heavily stage-managed so that Callaghan, currently *non grata*, would turn up for coffee. But there was nothing to report and before the entrance could happen, Michael Foot of all people, best friend of the unions in the Cabinet over four years, exploded at Moss Evans, beside whom he had been seated, 'You've fought against everything you've ever stood for.' Healey, speaking his mind on union conduct, provoked an outraged Jack Jones who made to walk out, only for Foot, reverting to his normal peacemaking instincts, to go round the table, put his arm round him and keep him in the company.

But Murray, understanding that a political act was needed, was unwilling to give up. One day in January, David Lea paid an unreported visit to Downing Street, visiting not the Prime Minister, but Kenneth Stowe; and they sat, unknown to history and unminuted, alone in the Cabinet Room, Assistant-General Secretary and Principal Private Secretary. Lea said, 'It would be something if we could get six words on to a sheet of paper.'[55] From that meeting stemmed a working party, with Stowe in the chair and involving Lea, for the Treasury, Geoffrey Littler, working direct to Healey, also Peter Le Chaminant. It would meet in the small dining room of Downing Street with Callaghan occasionally putting his head through the door to express appreciation and give encouragement. It prepared the way for a big meeting on 5 February 1979, involving Callaghan, Healey, Foot and Eric Varley with, as Stowe puts it, 'the Barons'. The meeting involved some mutual admission of fault, the government's economic anxieties, and the unions' problems with hard-and-fast norms. A document was authorised to be prepared at high speed to proclaim the areas of accommodation.

The agreement was put together during heavy negotiations in the next week or so and confirmed at a meeting with the Prime Minister on 14 February, St Valentine's day. Identification with the date was inevitable, though the term, 'Concordat', with its echoes of Mussolini and the Pope in 1929, was odd. But concordats are supposed to be accommodations between the secular and the divine which, at the end of the 1970s, may have seemed about right.

The St Valentine's Day Concordat was described by Joel Barnett as 'a reasonably useful TUC document', its 'voluntary code designed to prevent the worst forms of secondary picketing'.[56] Roy Hattersley, more ardent, spoke of it containing 'some nuggets of gold'. *The Economy, the Government and Trade Union Responsibilities* may sound like a Peter Greenaway film, but it was a grown-up attempt to lay down principles for the future.

Paragraph 23, while aspiring to European living standards, agrees that 'If we are to achieve this, we must match the average European performance on inflation as well as growth.'[57] Paragraph 12 is a disavowal of the acts of the previous two months. 'The TUC emphasises the vital necessity of maintaining supplies and services essential to health and safety of the community; of maintaining plant and equipment, and sustaining livestock during industrial disputes.'[58] Paragraph 26 acknowledges that 'major factors – productivity, investment, industrial structure and industrial relations – are within our control'.[59]

Any joint statement, especially one issued as a patching mission in a crisis, risks vapid generality. But at paragraph 27, it moves on to follow this up. 'Therefore, given the facts of our international position, we must set ourselves the task of aligning our inflation rate to that of our main overseas competitors, and that means getting our annual inflation rate, within three years from now, down to 5 per cent and holding it there.'[60] No one has recall, twenty years and more on, of who said what. But it is surely not altogether fanciful to hear the voice of Healey insisting upon the last twenty or so words, not one of them vapid or generalised. The TUC had made a remarkable commitment to see 5 per cent as a desirable objective – only within three years indeed, but even so, it was a creditable foundation.

Perhaps much of what was said was obvious or should have been obvious. It had not been so to the crazed Fisher or to a host of local activists. The St Valentine's Day Concordat, an attempt at picking up the pieces of the Social Contract, points forward to a renewed approach to a model of close-monitored, number-watching co-operation of labour and government. And gradually, things did set about improving. Large concessions had been made to the most dangerous strikers, 20 per cent to lorry drivers, 14 per cent to water workers, but despite the intrusion of the new strike among civil servants in the middle rank and professional CPSA (Civil and Public Services

Association), the water was receding from the sea wall, strikers were beginning to go back.

But any chance of the Concordat working economically required it to work politically, to buy time and soothe public recollection. It was not a *good* chance – the Conservative lead had hit 19 per cent at one point. But it was not necessarily hopeless. Healey would write, 'I believe that if we had struggled on a little longer we might have cut Mrs Thatcher's majority by a few seats for each week we moved further away from the Winter of Discontent.'[61] That sounds optimistic. A similar recovery had indeed been managed in the polls across 1977, but the bad news of 1975 and 1976 had been statistical. Not burying the dead had an immediacy not easily dispelled.

But Labour did have time if it had the nerve – and if Callaghan's old guileful arts had been revived to charm the Liberals or anyone else with a spare vote in the Commons. Thatcher's lead in the polls during the campaign would move about between a high of 13 and a low of 2 per cent. And Callaghan himself understood the situation perfectly clearly. 'I want two or three more months,' he would tell his Private Secretary.[62] However, to quote Healey again, 'By March Jim was exhausted and dispirited.'[63]

Brutally, Callaghan had by now lost his touch. In solitary retreat, he had passed up the election which could have been won. In a remote and imperious way, he had provoked his best allies in the TUC with a line as rigid as it would prove brittle. He had failed to make the connection between his own pleasant and flattering role among the top people in the Caribbean and cold wet voters enduring siege at home. And on his return, as his own adviser, Tom McNally would remark,[64] he had ignored every rule of public relations by the sort of chat with journalists which laid veins open to knives. Now he was exhausted and recurringly depressed. Looking back on the period of inertia at the turn of the year, he would say, 'For three weeks I let the country down.' Kenneth Stowe, to whom he said it, remarks that Callaghan was a patriot and it hurt him that he had not done enough.[65]

Generally debilitated, he was in no position to cope with more things going wrong and when, late in March, over a motion of confidence following the frustration of Scottish devolution, they did go wrong, it was the end. Callaghan, whose mood had swerved between elation and despair, was not ready to head off a Commons vote threatening defeat by the sort of all-out manoeuvres and accommodations which had worked in the past. The prospect of devolution had kept the SNP and the milder Plaid Cymru loyal to Labour in the Commons. The effective wrecking of devolution by the 40 per cent *of votes cast* requirement of the Cunningham Amendment took away the incentive for a highly calculating loyalty. Faced with a collision over an SNP vote of confidence, Callaghan wanted to meet it full on, to live or die by it.

Michael Foot tried very hard to avoid the buffers – new talks, a new bill, a positive response to the Scot Nats. From the angle of all rational Labour self-interest, he was right. An SNP, given a new shot at its goal, would surely prop Labour while daffodils grew over the winter.

When Foot reported on his efforts, unwisely making calls after 11.30 at night unwelcome to Callaghan, he had an unwilling audience. Healey had talked to Callaghan on 14 March about the coming Budget and found him 'fed up about intriguing to stay in office. I tried to bolster him.' On 22 March he noted, 'Cabinet on devolution, Jim absolutely refused give a date. Hattersley – Michael Foot pressed him, question a muddle as usual.'[66] Foot had had a pre-meeting ahead of the Cabinet and reported, 'His patience had suddenly snapped. He wanted to invite the election and the decision that would lead to it.'[67]

The saving of the government to fight an election in more hopeful conditions would have involved small deals with the Welshmen, a pipeline in Northern Ireland, fixer's politics. And James Callaghan, supreme fixer, ultimate doer of deals, felt disgust at it all. Roy Hattersley who had been working hard on Ulster Unionist votes, remarked without admiration that 'Jim was going to go down like a noble Roman.' And down they all went on 28 March, defeated 311:310 with Enoch Powell, eternal spoiler, deciding late at night to oppose the government and a group of back-benchers, echoing 1945, fall with triumph, singing 'The Red Flag'. Among them was Neil Kinnock.

Exhaustion probably played a greater part in Callaghan's embrace of that vote than role-playing. Labour politicians of that generation had been obsessed with not making Clement Attlee's mistake of 1951, of letting exhaustion and a small majority force them to the polls. Out of exhaustion and a small majority, they did exactly that. Meanwhile, Callaghan, having missed the opportunity of an early election which carried a good chance, would give up on a late general election with at least some chance. It was the worst of all middle ways and it had failed.

The Prime Minister resolved, another solitary act, to see the Queen, only for Tom McNally to find him sitting in a chair, head in his hands. Government transport, like so much else, had miscarried and a desolate Callaghan told his press officer, 'I can't even get a car to take me to the Palace.' There was nothing left to lose except the election.

49

TWO DEFEATS AND A VICTORY

At the Labour Conference of October 1979 at Brighton Tom Litterick, a left-winger whose behaviour sometimes suggested disturbance, went to the tribune carrying a bundle of papers, to extol the efforts of NEC members preparing the party's manifesto for the general election. 'Then,' said Litterick, throwing a couple of hundred sheets up in the air to cascade on to the conference floor, 'up gets Jim!'[1] However, the election of 1979 had begun with a more substantial explosion than that. The House of Commons, still sitting on 30 March, heard a dull detonation: the sound of the Conservative spokesman on Northern Ireland, Airey Neave, being murdered by either the IRA or its rival, INLA, who had attached a bomb beneath his car.

Tom Litterick would die not long after. But he had both caught the coming mood of a vengeful left and told a truth. Callaghan, having been imperious with the Neddy Six, the Cabinet and finally with Michael Foot, had in a series of early April meetings, turned his imperiousness rather more reasonably on to the NEC and the joint Cabinet–NEC committee handling the manifesto. The first gathering on 2 April started at six-thirty in the evening and ended, insanely, at three-thirty next morning. A grim sort of affair, no civil servants about Downing Street as they were on strike, provision only for sandwiches and drinks at 8 p.m. and midnight (no tea for Tony Benn, the dedicated abstainer had to drink ginger ale), it was cheered up by the celebration of Benn's fifty-fourth birthday. 'At one stage Denis leaned over and said "You're being very helpful. Why are you so cheerful?" I said it was my birthday in half an hour, so when midnight struck, Denis announced, "It's Tony's birthday," and Jim started singing, and then everybody joined in . . . The whole evening was a funny mixture of table-banging, shouting at each other and slightly nostalgic sentimentality,' wrote Benn, adding, 'There was a lot of conning and overawing going on.'[2] A measure of the level of argu-ment was the remark of Moss Evans that rather than acknowledge the Winter of Discontent, Labour should stress their success in avoiding a national emergency!

The Frank Allauns, Joan Maynards, Eric Heffers and Norman Atkinsons attended, but almost nothing they favoured was let through by a Callaghan still Prime Minister and party leader. Plans from Benn for intervention in industry were flatly turned down, so that *The Labour Way is the Better Way*, a notably uncrisp title, headed a document determined to give mini-mum offence. Nuclear weapons were to be retained which, as Callaghan had already bought the Chevaline delivery system in secret, is hardly surprising. A notable casualty was a proposal to abolish the House of Lords. 'Jim very tough on House of Lords,' wrote Healey.[3] The exchange between Callaghan and Eric Heffer was prophetic of things to come. On their lordships, Callaghan, according to Benn, said, 'I won't have it. I won't have it.'

Eric said, 'What do you mean, you won't have it? Who are you to dictate? Who do you think you are? You are just a member of the party.'

'Well,' said Jim, 'I won't have it.'

I said, 'You can't do that.'

'I can.'

'No you can't . . . [People] will say "We joined the party. We've got this through, we've elected an MP and we want him to implement our policy."'

Jim said, 'You'll have to change the leader.'

I said, 'That's making it a personality issue, not a political issue at all.'

'Well I won't do it. I am the leader of the party and I have to decide what is right. I have responsibilities that I have to take and I won't do it.'

It was an instructive exchange and would take mighty and distorted shape soon after the general election.

Along with fox hunting, their Lordships' House was protected as much by Callaghan's innate conservatism as by the ordinary electoral prudence which blocked minimum pay for agricultural workers – 'couldn't really be done without our appearing to adopt a policy of statutory pay control'[4] or a com-mittee to examine the nationalisation of banking.

The seven-hour meeting of 6 April, thought Healey, whose diary gave precedence to the pound, still rising after a cut in MLR, 'went OK except for ritual protest from Heffer, Skinner, Maynard. Rushed to train.' A permanent distinction between Healey and Benn is the canyon-like gap in the seriousness with which their diaries treat political discussions. On this meeting, Benn has three pages of octavo, Healey has been quoted in full.[5]

Healey would have a prominent part in the campaign, as would Shirley Williams. Both featured at the wish of Callaghan anxious to stress the Labour Party's financial authority and its representation, in Margaret Thatcher's first election as leader, by a nicer sort of woman. A flavour of the arson in the dressing-rooms behind this soothing stage management came with the resignation of a left-wing candidate, James Dickens,* because his local party, not finding him left-wing enough, had endorsed his election address by a margin of only 18–14!⁶

Healey's election was taken at the run, starting in Yorkshire supporting Derek Enright who would become a well-liked MP, dying sadly early. He was required widely for TV and radio: '*Points of View* Robin Day – only moderate', and debating with Christopher Tugendhat, a liberal Tory and European of a kind now almost extinct, an encounter with Peter Walker and the *Today* programme whose invited audience contained, he thought, '300 extremists'.⁷

Then it was back to Robin Day, whose phone-in 'went well', also a television interview 'with Ian Ross on pay policy' followed by talking to an American columnist, Robert Vogl. After which, cryptically, he 'Did Manifesto' before going 'Off to King's Lynn. Nice Agent met me. 300 at good meeting.' From King's Lynn, it was 'off across Dutch landscape via Wisbech to Peterborough, evening meeting with 350 for Mike Ward.' Peterborough was the notorious shuttle seat which had passed back and forth since the mid-sixties between Sir Harmar Nicholls, Conservative, and Michael Ward, Labour, on majorities of as little as seven and three. This marginal, regularly employing the legal maximum of seven recounts without a wrong word, was a permanent reproach to Florida.⁸

Healey would, when in London, attend the campaign committee at Transport House and take on press conferences, as on 11 April 'with Jim and Shirley' before he 'rushed to BBC – [Vincent] Duggleby for *Money Box* with Geoffrey Howe – quite fun', then afterwards work at the office in consultation over posters with Edward Booth-Clibborn,† chairman of the publicity and advertising company who were taking over from Transport House. Almost immediately, it was off to Birmingham: 'Good quiet meeting Stechford', old Roy Jenkins territory, then to Stechford Town hall for 350 people: 'v. good meeting' – he liked the candidate as well – before coming back via Stratford and Oxford, getting home at '2 a.m. Dog-tired.'⁹

On 12 April a Thursday, Healey was back at the BBC debating with the amiable Geoffrey Howe again, and he later enjoyed a meeting with the American scholar, Sam Beer. But he had the sense not to drive himself impossibly, returning to Sussex to do some work at home, happy to have Cressida in the house. Contradicting Tony Benn Stakhanovism (and Denis

---

* He had replaced Reg Prentice who had progressed from right-wing Cabinet minister to resignation, to a safe Conservative seat at Daventry.

† Callaghan, fed up with so many things, was fed up with party headquarters, certainly as a source of publicity.

Healey Stakhanovism), he did some pottering, cleaned out the garden pool, shopped in Seaford and listened to a broadcast of *Cosi fan tutti*. Sunday was also, he said, 'a perfect day', so he cut the grass and avoided addressing the nation. The entry 'Worked on election and garden' says it nicely.

Stakhanov was up and running again by the 17th, electioneering in south London for Chris Price, Sam Silkin and Alf Dubs, pursued by TV cameras through Sydenham and some noise from a drunken element. Wednesday the 18th took him to Reading, then Aylesbury, Buckingham and Oxford. Life for a leading politician in demand at election meetings can resemble something between a royal progression and a picaresque novel. And from Oxford, where he had spoken for Evan Luard, Healey advanced next day to Newark for Ted Bishop, and Lincoln where, with the then leftish Margaret Jackson (now the rightish Margaret Beckett), he had 'good meeting', staying at the White Hart, 'v. comfortable'.

Next morning he 'looked at cathedral – lovely' before snaking northwards by way of Bedfordshire to reach Yorkshire for a walkabout in Normanton and a big meeting back in Leeds – 'Merlyn [Rees], Stan [Cohen], Joe [Dean]' – and a fighting encounter on Yorkshire Television with a local Conservative political editor, Bernard Dineen, 'very aggressive'. After which, same day, it was 'Off to Heckmondwike', then Halifax, for meetings.[10] Saturday 21 April, he was in Lancashire, Middleton – 'v. good walkabout', Manchester and Bolton (for Ann Taylor and David Young) – another walkabout, drinks at the Labour Club, then Nelson for Doug Hoyle – 'nice wife Pauline', and Clitheroe – 'Very good meeting', then a tour of the party clubs, 'v. well received', before finally returning to Preston for the night, not surprisingly 'dog tired'.[11]

Sunday was spent in Cumbernauld New Town and its vicinity, meeting its management and being shown the town. Among the company were 'impressive women' – Rosemary McKenna, the chairman, and Ann McGuire, treasurer,[12] both later to become MPs. There was no getting away from women. The next day in Scotland brought Helen Liddell, 'Bustling and pregnant'. The itinerary that day was Glasgow, Ayr, Crummock, Blackwater.[13]

Normally Healey is 'tired', 'dog tired' or 'appallingly tired' by night. Setting off for Manchester he felt 'Very tired' at the *start* of the day. He had, throughout, been keeping up on essential Treasury work, though he makes no description of contacts with the Labour leadership. It was a round of strenuous peripatetic activity, interspersing simple slogs through great parts of the country with media debates and interviews, friendly or inquisitorial, the 'very aggressive', the dandified celebrity Robin Day, with print journalists like Peter Riddell, then of the *Financial Times*, who 'wrote v. friendly piece'[14] or, accompanying him to Carlisle on the 25th, 'Peter Jenkins – friendly'.

Healey never complains. He announces dog-tiredness most nights, but is up and pleased to see Carlisle, Manchester again, Stockport, Buxton,

Eastwood, Long Eaton ('good meetings' both), before hurrying between Saturday and Sunday from the East Midlands to Eastbourne and a 2000-strong meeting organised by Alf Allen's shopworkers, pausing only to admire the luxuriant daffodils.

Monday, the Monday of election week, involves his return to London to take the press conference and indulge the first judgement of a privately close-mouthed election. He would be accompanied for this stretch by Derek Gladwin, sensible *apparatchik*, a General and Municipal official seconded to be campaign manager. 'He thinks (like me) more '59 than '45.' In 1945 Labour had a three-figure majority, in 1959 they were defeated by 100 seats. Behind the cheeriness, Healey saw nothing but defeat. Oddly, if polls are true at point of gathering, he and Gladwin were excessively bleak at that snapshot of time. The big Conservative lead of the early days lay between a low of 10 per cent and a high of 21 per cent. Those from 21 April to three days before Election Day, varied from 8 per cent to 3 per cent!

The actual result would be a Conservative lead of 7.2 per cent. Labour had started at the wrong point, steady double-figure advantage to the Conservatives against the 1–2 per cent Tory lead which Robert Worcester had shown Callaghan in the late summer of 1978, but they had subsequently moved in the right direction.[15] They had done something occasionally wryly claimed by the losing side: lost power and won the election. Ground had been made up. From the horrors of mid-January, when Alan Fisher and T & G branches were engaged full-time on Conservative wish-fulfilment, ministerial efforts and a well-conducted election had given Mrs Thatcher power but no landslide. It was the sort of defeat which a party, losing, reasonably hopes to reverse. Across the next few years that hope would be taken care of.

Final defeat on 3/4 May gave Healey much the same personal sequence of events that had attended victory in 1964: 'Bed at 5 a.m. – up at 8 off with Derek to London, very tired.' But afterwards comes a long list of the political dead, some in seats he had worked. They were over – the election, the government, Healey's life as a minister and Labour's control of itself.

The malediction upon Labour was that, so deep was the division between left and right, between radical activists and people running a political party, that war was acknowledged to be something waiting to happen once the civilities of office were shaken off. When the arena of Conference replaced the arena of parliament, current leaders became prophets unarmed. Tony Benn, sweetness and light compared to his followers, would talk about betrayal of the party.

And Benn would have his own view of Callaghan's bypassing of the apparatus and 'the party'. On 2 May, the day after mutually contradictory polls – Conservatives leading by 17 per cent and Labour ahead by 0.3 per cent – he would venture, not without schadenfreude, a melancholy estimate: 'Without any doubt the Tories are going to win. I'm not sure about their majority but my guess is that our own campaign ran out of steam because Jim didn't make use of the party at all. He ran a one-man band because the polls put him ahead of Mrs Thatcher and therefore he felt free to ignore the party, never mentioned the manifesto at all.'[16]

The concentration upon Callaghan had been at the insistence of professional advisers like Booth-Clibborn. Polls showed him running far ahead of Thatcher, making it the commonsense thing to do without either vanity or professional advice. As for the polls, the latest ones were remarkably close. The average error on five polls: MORI/*Express*, Marplan/*Sun*, Gallup/*Telegraph*, NOP/*Mail* and MORI/*Evening Standard* was an understatement of the Conservative lead by 1.7 per cent.[17]

But these are refinements. When Litterick did his rant at Brighton in October, delegates roared. As they did for an extraordinary, snarling-mouse address by the normally meek old Salford unilateralist, Frank Allaun, and when Ray Apps, a Brighton delegate and something of a fixture, said 'we have to recognise that . . . the starting point for reforms must be the nationalisation of the major monopolies and the financial institutions.'[18] The composite, no. 30, to which Apps spoke, called for 'a massive extension of public ownership of the profitable sectors of the economy . . . under democratic workers' control and management linked to a national plan of production [which] would enable us to produce to meet the needs of society and would end the chaos of production for profit'. It failed to pass but that was all the joy the leadership could take from a very unpleasant Conference. Composite 31, calling for an overhaul of the party in the name of accountability, 'the political education of the electorate in the party's beliefs', reaffirmation of Clause IV (the 'public ownership of the means of production distribution and exchange'), did carry. Its fulfilment, through a one-day constitutional conference and a new domestic election system, would plunge Labour into conflicts which provoked a split and underwrote defeat at the next two elections.

In a similar spirit, Conference carried a motion in favour of mandatory reselection. The sporadic practice which had already been putting MPs under menacing notice was now to be institutionalised. When Healey spoke, he defended Callaghan and Members of Parliament. Anyone who attended Labour conferences over this period will recall MPs herded on to a ramp, which reminded more sympathetic observers of the French First Estate at the Versailles General Assembly in 1789.[19] John Morris, Attorney-General in the Labour Government, said, 'I feel like a defendant in a People's Court.'[20]

Regardless of the ambience, Healey met full-on the almost unchallenged left-wing slogans about mass membership and mobilising 'the tremendous power and strength of this Labour movement'.[21] He had nothing to fear personally in Leeds. But Labour MPs, even in defeat, represented 11.5 million voters. 'You have now made it possible for them to say without any doubt that they now represent, not 11.5 million voters but under 300,000 constituency party members.' It was a characteristic Denis Healey speech in direct descent from the 1960 inquiry: 'Do you want your children to call you fools?'

He hoped that when comrades had 'got over the bad blood of electoral defeat', they would turn their efforts to policies which would regain the votes lost not to the Communists or Militants 'but to the Tories and Liberals'. They should accept that 'Conference resolutions do not change the laws of arithmetic, that if we try to run the country the way the National Executive runs the party finances, it will not be possible for the trade unions to bail us out (*Applause*).'

But as Benn told his diary on reselection, 'It has been the most amazing campaign and after five years of hard work we've carried it through. The MPs will just have to accept it. It means there are 635 vacancies for candidates in the next Parliament.'[22] Benn now looked forward to not being bullied any more by the union leaders. 'They got it wrong and they have to accept that the Party is entrusted to the NEC.'[23] His last diary thrust was to expect an attempt to remove Callaghan 'because they'll say he wasn't strong enough to beat the left'. This was quite wrong. Callaghan would suffer no assault except from a group of left-wingers in his constituency.[24] But his subsidiary remark was true enough. His opponents, the right-wing Labour MPs, 'only have a year to get Denis Healey elected by the PLP before any rule changes occur'.[25]

It was, if looked at calmly, all absurd, Leninism *après la lettre*, long, long *après* and at stark odds with all measurable public opinion. The change giving Tony Benn such joy had the essential qualities of a bowls club putsch. The party had shrivelled, had been shrivelling for a long time. Healey's figure of 300,000 active members implies around 500 members per constituency, a very flattering figure in many of them. One serious academic source states that 'Labour's individual membership by 1979 was down to about 250,000, of whom at most 1 per cent regularly attended party meetings.'[26] The public which had just given Margaret Thatcher, with all her dubieties, 43 per cent of the vote, had not done so out of disgust at Labour's inadequate socialist quotient. They would not kill James Callaghan to make Tony Benn king.

The substance of everything Benn had done in perfect sincerity over the five years he had spoken of, was a shift of power, irreversible or otherwise, from one clique to another. Most of what he said about the Labour leadership being unaccountable was true, and Callaghan latterly had given a depressing demonstration of power not so much corrupting as coarsening. He had made mistakes because he didn't listen, but not because he didn't listen to Ray Apps or Tom Litterick. Callaghan was popular nationally, much more so than Margaret Thatcher. A hostile verdict had been returned for a multiplicity of reasons, but failure to nationalise the financial institutions and the 220 largest companies was not high among them.

The Labour Party was about to throw itself into a struggle at once tragic, furious and tedious, in pursuit of a vote structure which should better represent groups of ennui-proof bores dedicated to ideas unlikely in the best of conditions to win so much as 5 per cent of the popular vote. Tony Benn, in so many ways a nice man, honourable and idealistic in ways both nonconformist and public school, but not without vanity or priggishness, was often right. His distrust of establishments, secret intelligence and the self-service of the high-up had/have much to be said for it. But he believed in an abstract good, a dream. His view of the workers and their state resembles Thomas Traherne contemplating corn which never should be reaped nor was ever sown. And as the children of the sixties grew, but before they grew up, he had allies – or disciples – ardent to harvest it. Healey would compare him to Gregers Werle, protagonist of Ibsen's *The Wild Duck*, 'who ruins a happy family in his pursuit of the ideal'.[27]*

The issue now was the succession. Callaghan told John Cole that he meant to stay just long enough 'to smooth the path for Denis Healey to succeed him'.[29] He told Healey that he would stay 'just long enough to take the shine off the ball'. In the event, Healey would face spin-bowling. Healey himself favoured an early move. As with the general election, difficult could get more difficult. He ought to have been well placed. In the autumn of 1979 he was elected top of the list for the Shadow Cabinet. But Clive Jenkins, an especial Healey enemy, victim of derisive comment at an earlier Conference, and David Basnett, vain, pliable, very much under Jenkins's influence, tried to persuade Callaghan to stay on until the new regime should obtain.

That, at least, Callaghan was proof against, but by then he would have lingered in office for a full year and a half after his election defeat, not announcing his departure until 15 October 1980. He had also told John Cole that he had expected an unpopularity to match defeat, but 'had been encouraged by the reception he was getting: when he emerged from a West End cinema, the crowds had applauded him.' There was no reason why they should not and, genuinely, he did want Healey's succession, but possibly the enjoyment of an Indian summer of uncontroversial public life helped him linger. The instructive contrast is with Malcolm Fraser, defeated that same year, 1980, as Prime Minister of Australia: 'There isn't room for two leaders in one party. You won't be seeing any more of me.' Healey speaks of having to put some pressure on him to move and of Callaghan being 'miffed'. Another view is that Callaghan's entourage, people like Jack Cunningham and the late Gregor MacKenzie, were thought to have been unsure of Healey as a force for holding the party together. Moss Evans was also urging this

---

* He also kept learning things about working-class life, turning at one point like a judge of the old sort confronting raw life, to ask what a mangle was.[28]

course. As late as September, Healey is recording a message that one of his former Treasury colleagues has been trying to persuade Callaghan to stay put. He checks it and records: 'v. doubtful'.[30] Certainly the former premier supported Healey in all the wrong ways. Similarly, Healey's PPS at this time, Barry Jones, speaks of having never heard a whisper of criticism of the leader.

Callaghan had made a calamitous mistake. In the time which he allowed for smoothing the way, everything grew rougher. Bill Rodgers, former Transport Secretary, made a speech at Abertillery saying, 'Our party has a year, not much longer, in which to save itself.'[31] What Labour would do on 31 May 1980 made no contribution to salvation. Callaghan, wanting to launch a policy statement, called a special conference, involving unaffordable expense, at Wembley. The description of the atmosphere as 'fractionally less poisonous than it had been at Brighton'[32] is the kindest thing that could be said about it. The new brutishness was very much on show. Healey, speaking in the afternoon, was accompanied all the way to the Tribune by cries of 'Out', 'Out', 'Out'. He varied the conventional opening by beginning, 'Comrade Chairman, friends and those who shouted "out".' Then, having done over Mrs Thatcher for 'returning to the thirties, not the 1930s, but the 1830s', he turned on the dominant presence of the day, the far left. Labour would not stop her if it took the advice of one speaker to 'sit on our hands and let the Tories take over and stay in power unless every dot and comma of our own particular ideology is accepted by the National Executive and the Party in its next election manifesto'.[33]

Then, with the Healey flair for a phrase, which weaker-hearted observers see as a fatal quality and others delight in, he added that no election would be won if 'we go on ideological ego trips or accept the clapped-out dogmas which are now being trailed by the toytown Trotskyists of the Militant group'.[34]

The conference was quite poisonous enough. One delegate delivered himself of: 'To the weak hearted, the traitors and the cowards I say: "Get out of our Movement. There is no place in it for you. Cross the House of Commons [sic], join Prentice and do the work he is doing at the present moment,"'[35] also, disturbingly, of Margaret Thatcher, 'My kids sit and watch the television set. If they could get their hands on her, they would rip the throat out of her.'[36] The speaker, Terry Fields of the Militant Tendency, would subsequently be selected for a seat in Liverpool, endorsed by the NEC, elected to parliament and, much later, on the insistence of Neil Kinnock, expelled. That career parabola rather profiles the coming short progress of Labour Party history.

Another delegate invited Callaghan to 'retire to his farm and make way for someone who will do a better job'. A Mike Davies of Hackney denounced 'the mealy-mouthed, shallow policies that our last Prime Minister and current Leader was putting forward today'.[37]

One victim of the conference was David Owen, who would later speak of standing at the back of the hall 'with his gorge rising'.[38] He was close to being shouted down and had to be protected by the chair, Lena Jeger, when he spoke for the defence policy of the previous government. Thus did one significant player begin to think of Bill Rodgers's 'year to save the party' as a hopeless option. Healey seemed unable to take the special conference too seriously. 'Party conference at Wembley. Dull and wet. Big militant group were rough on Jim, booed me a little, cheered Tony . . . David Owen booed loudly for arrogance.'[39] Owen's gorge was rising, Healey was shrugging off hostile noise. It was going to be an important difference.

For into the hiatus which Callaghan had created came talk of the return of Roy Jenkins, near the end of his presidency of the EEC Commission. Jenkins would not seek, and could not gain, the leadership of the Labour Party of which he was just about a member, in a parliament of which he was not. But as the legislative year, October to October 1979/80, passed and the scurrying left groups worked to perfect constitutional forms serving their own advancement, and as Benn's expectation of '635 vacancies for candidates in the next parliament' loomed in the imaginings of current MPs, two things would happen.

The weak and temporising would look to accommodation with the deselectors; appeasement would have its charms in the dim middle among those fillers of space, whom one Labour MP, Peter Snape, savagely characterises as 'the dossers'. Denis would have more to fear from mice than rats. Meanwhile the harder cases, those disposed to a fight, would look with ever more sympathy upon breaking away from a party quietly becoming intolerable. Well before the public lecture at which Roy Jenkins would delicately indicate such possibilities, the notion was in the air. Callaghan was, Healey sought to become, something called 'the Leader of the Labour Party'. Many people were drifting, across that dismal year, towards a belief that the Labour Party would cease to exist.

Beyond Wembley lay Bishop's Stortford. If Wembley was serious money for atrocious public relations, Bishop's Stortford, more precisely Whitehall College, once a distiller's mansion, now a trade union stately home, was a grim duty. A commission established for the purpose had to decide on a form for the new electoral college decreed by the 1979 Conference. The commission would have six delegates from the NEC. With a splendid disregard for even-handedness, the Executive sent six negotiators, Norman Atkinson, Frank Allaun, Tony Benn, Jo Richardson and, conceding something to the friendly end of the left, Joan Lestor and Eric Heffer. It would also handle mandatory reselection. Callaghan tried to have that postponed and was let down on the vote, not for the first time, by Moss Evans and left the meeting angrily. On the electoral college, the question was what share of the equity should go respectively to MPs, unions, constituency parties and the socialist societies. The recommendation emerging, 50 per cent for MPs, 25 per cent for unions, 20 per cent for constituencies and 5 per cent for the societies, was less than the Benn group hoped for. Despite 'wanting not to be bossed by the Unions any longer', he agreed with the left group, Campaign for Labour Party Democracy, in seeking 50 per cent for the unions.

But as Kenneth Morgan says, any left-wing disappointment was offset by the fact that the party leader had to accept the loss of half the MPs' authority.[40] Nothing could have been worse for Healey in the short term, for the Labour Party in the long. The PLP would choose the next leader but it would do so under a cloud of retributive menace. Mandatory deselection and the close prospect of collegiate elections were blades of the same scissors in dangerous hands. To vote, in the next few months, for a leader detested by the left groups running so many constituencies was to fight the new dispensation, to defy the masterful trend. The people who had shouted 'Out', 'Out', 'Out' at Wembley now had powers of retribution in a great number of constituencies. If Healey should defiantly be put *in*, the hell to be paid locally and severally, could not be calculated.

On the longer, general question of healthy parliamentary politics, MPs choosing the person who would, after all, lead *them,* did know, often in detail, the candidates concerned. A leader partially imposed from outside would have the job of leading a partially franchised Parliamentary Party which, alone, might never have chosen him. The actual vote cast by a Member of Parliament would quickly be made the business of a constituency party now equipped with the parallel power of deselecting him for voting the wrong way or refusing disclosure.* If the whole operation was Leninist, it also recalled the good old days before the Ballot Act when tenants-at-will declaimed their vote at the hustings before the squire's agent.

The degradation of Labour's people in parliament spoke the same hatred and distrust which had put them at Conference on a ramp resembling a mass dock. It was calculated to repel all talent and independence of mind. Comparison with the plastic counters of an East European People's Chamber was overstated but not fanciful. Laurie Pavitt, a mild, respected working member devoted to health questions, would say to a friend that life was now a total misery and that he positively crept back to his constituency party.[41]

Bishop's Stortford would create a bitter confrontation in Shadow Cabinet between Callaghan and Rodgers. He, Williams and Owen had publicly disavowed Bishop's Stortford, Owen in his very own rhyming scorn: 'fudging

---

* As was remarked in 1790s France, 'Those who blow on the flame are often consumed by it.' Norman Atkinson, dedicated, heavy-duty leftist, would be cited by a delegate from his own constituency as the sort of properly socialist MP with nothing to fear from deselection. But deselected he would be – by comrades in his Tottenham constituency party! – to make a speech dripping abjection worthy of Moscow 1937.

and mudging, mush and slush'; and they were savagely attacked for doing so by the leader who could be very unpleasant when he tried. 'It was all,' said one of them, 'very, very nasty.'[42] But with power shifting to the left on the NEC, apparently in the unions and more ferociously than ever at Conference, while the Parliamentary Party stood under threat, Callaghan's one redoubt, the Shadow Cabinet, was no longer a unified force loyal to the party leader. The prospective separatists put out a statement in the friendly *Guardian* and *Daily Mirror*. It spoke of 'growing anxiety about the Labour Party's commitment to parliamentary democracy, reinforced by the willingness of some leading NEC members to flirt with extremists who openly regard democracy as a sham . . .', adding that 'the argument may grow for a new democratic socialist party to establish itself . . .'[43]

The Gang of Three, as they were now called, and a significant part of the right-wing parliamentary grouping, the Manifesto Group, were now looking outside to an undertaking of their own. From Healey's point of view it was a setback. The rationale of his camp was that Denis should be supported as the alternative to the forces which had sprung up fully armed at Brighton in 1979. He was to be at once continuity from Callaghan, but stronger and more resolute. You knew his record, you knew where he stood, there had been enough criticism of him for bluntness in the past, he surely didn't need to talk splits or civil war. But such a quiet approach angered others.

Bill Rodgers, a putative rebel, reports middling men like Derek Foster, later Chief Whip, and Ken Weetch, the notably courageous MP for Ipswich, fed up with Callaghan's inertia, saying to him that 'the young pretenders (meaning Roy Hattersley, David Owen and myself) must rally round Denis Healey as the next leader.'[44] But he also describes Healey as unwilling to give this message to Callaghan. He had, said Healey, 'told Callaghan to toughen up. I replied that toughening up was what I hoped to see in *him* and I would help to rally his troops if he showed more fighting spirit.'[45] The phrase would recur.

There is about this dialogue something of the prefect speaking to the Second Master about concern over his slackness. Though Healey was not so idle as not to be able to inform Rodgers that another candidate for the leadership was materialising, Michael Foot. Rodgers acknowledges that, after five murderous years at the Treasury, Healey was tired, but deplores his absences on conferences in places like Japan. The Gang of Three wanted decisive action and were scornful of Healey for not hurrying to provide it. Pre-emptive scorn for patience would in the end bring about a very small party led by David Owen who embodied decisive action.

The preconditions of Labour Party recovery would be brought about over the next two years by untrumpeted union men like John Golding and David Warburton who would work – much as Rodgers had worked twenty years before – through the unions, to shift the NEC back to reason. But people who despised Callaghan for retreat, saw Healey as the continuation of such weakness by more cerebral means. In the language ironically of Tony Benn, there was now an alternative policy.

With reselection and a final form of electoral college looming, all Callaghan's good reasons for staying on had been frustrated. But having defeated him, the left was rather keen that the leader should stay. Clive Jenkins, whose union contained more Conservative voters than most, and had only 150,000 votes to cast at Conference, had gained formidable influence over David Basnett whose General and Municipal Union had 650,000. Basnett did not want a triumph for Bennism, but he did want both to play a grand part in events and to avoid unnecessary conflict, not a happy political cocktail. The two men made clear to Callaghan their strong wish that he should stay. They were joined by Moss Evans. During the Winter of Discontent, Basnett had been afraid to speak out against Alan Fisher whose rival union was denying those burials. Evans had given supine official status to the road transport strike. Both felt happy to express their confidence in the party leader. If not the last straw, it was a burdensome one.

Others wanted Callaghan to remain for more benign reasons. Adam Raphael of the *Observer* thought he should stay because he was the man best able to talk to the unions. With the NEC blatantly overreaching itself, perhaps Callaghan could rally the likes of Basnett to an ultimate reversal of the vote on reselection and the preparation of the manifesto. But Raphael also observed, 'His political stock is at its lowest point. Labour's election defeat was a personal one, a reflection on his judgement, both as to the timing and the ill-fated 5% pay norm. In the aftermath of that political disaster, personal despair understandably set in while Mr Benn and his allies wasted no time in laying in their stunning victories at conference. By the time Mr Callaghan roused himself to the danger it was too late.'[46] Such advisers and such admiration were not calculated to sustain morale.

At Conference meeting in Blackpool, 'By 5 million to 2 million, we voted to withdraw from the Common Market. That is sensational, a fantastic victory,'[47] wrote Tony Benn radiantly. Also in a nice disposition of millions, mandatory reselection was carried; 'the Conference nearly went berserk' wrote Tony. Finally, after a speech by Eric Heffer, Conference voted to support the principle of an electoral college for electing the leader and deputy leader. The details would be settled at a special conference in January. 'It was,' wrote Tony Benn, 'a most thrilling day.'[48] Healey recorded the same facts in neutral tones, nothing about being thrilled, and described the day's NEC as 'rowdy meeting'. It was the one at which a new variant of the college had been put through which offered 40 per cent to the members and 30 per cent each to MPs and unions. Callaghan had lost his temper, had threatened to drop all talk of party unity and openly advised MPs to go ahead and make their own choice of successor.

Healey's own speech was on the economy, accusing Mrs Thatcher of dragging a red-hot rake through the Midlands.[49] Preceding Benn's speech, apart from a throwaway half-line on prices and incomes, it picked no fights, not something often levelled against Healey. Benn himself urged the accomplishment, within days, of withdrawal of all authority afforded to the EEC and the taking of power, together with other acts of nationalisation, to control capital movements combined with abolition of the House of Lords, if necessary by creating a thousand peers. 'Comrades,' he added, as Conference contemplated a fortress socialism combining the best thinking of Fidel Castro and Eamon de Valera, 'this is the very least we must do.' Healey would later remark that even a single day would be too short a time in which to stop the flight of capital likely to follow such an announcement.[50]

Callaghan would not actually announce his resignation until 15 October, but resignation was the assumption on which the contending forces had been calculating since Bishop's Stortford. Power was dissolving in Callaghan's hands, the last days marked with newspaper headlines: 'Jim's Time is Up' in the *Observer* and 'Nevertheless Mr Callaghan should go' in the *Guardian*.

As the resignation was awaited with the date telegraphed, Healey returned on 8 October from a trip to Vienna, whose social democracy was to his own taste and consulted Barry Jones and Giles Radice who would run his leadership campaign. 'Barry indicating some movement to me from floaters. Hattersley offered help – not running.'[51] On the same day the BBC expressed the belief that Callaghan would leave and another rumour went round 'Silkin won't run. Everyone flabbergasted.'[52] On 13 October, Callaghan rang to assure him that his intentions were unchanged and he was told by Peter Jenkins that 'Shore would not make way for Foot.' Giles Radice, who had worked for the General and Municipal, worried about the attitude of Basnett.[53]

When resignation was formally announced and the first poll fixed, Tony Benn responded, on the advice of his wife, with thanks and the words, 'As to the future, nothing must be done that divides the Parliamentary Party from the Party in the country.' Adding, 'I said that several times.' His view of the illegitimacy of a merely parliamentary election would be endorsed in a poll of 250 constituency chairmen by Thames TV. Of these, just under 40 per cent thought it in order 'and 61.6 per cent said it was wrong'. As for the leadership, the same sample, 38.4 per cent, wanted Benn himself, 28 per cent Healey, 15 per cent Shore, 11 per cent Foot and 4.8 per cent Silkin. On those numbers, Benn reckoned that in a constituency election he would emerge, after eliminations, with about three-quarters of the vote. There would soon follow an earnest discussion at the Benns' Holland Park home, on the evening of 19 October, where Victor Schonfield, Chris Mullin, Reg Race, Frances Morrell, Audrey Wise, Norman Atkinson, Martin Flannery, Geoff

Bish and Ken Coates met to consider the question: '"Should Tony stand for the PLP election?" It was agreed that I should not.'[54]

The question of whether Michael Foot would stand was altogether more urgent. On the same day the title of an edition of the ITV politics programme, *Weekend World*, 'a party political broadcast of the right wing of the Labour Party',[55] was 'Can Healey be stopped?' The subtext was 'Will Michael Foot stand?' Geoffrey Smith of *The Times* thought that MPs would look at him and say 'Here is a man of 67, he's not in the best of health, it will probably be three years before there's a general election and the leader of the party must be prepared to serve some time beyond that general election.' For Foot 'this would mean serving for let us say about five years and that is not a realistic probability.' Brian Walden, a former Labour MP, agreed. 'Doubts like these seem to destroy Mr Foot's chance of stopping Healey. If Mr Foot does stand, he will win many votes from the left and some from the centre. But at the same time he will drive enough centrists over to Mr Healey to give Healey victory.'[56] It was a misreading touched by optimism. Foot might be elderly, objectively not up to five years of bombardment. But he was the last candidate to drive centrists across to Healey. He lacked personal enemies, Healey had quite a few. He was the natural continuation of Callaghan's ineffective post-election leadership. And, worst of all bad reasons, Foot was the soft option. The thought would wickedly be put about by Conservative papers that Foot, elected on the old, discredited parliamentary system, could be replaced a year later by a Benn heroically popular with the new electorate. Over the white head of Mr Foot the words 'interim' and 'cat's-paw' hovered disagreeably. But his candidacy evaded so many questions it was irresistible. The people who had wanted the leader to stay, when that was denied, wanted Foot to succeed. To the hard-headed left he was opportunity, to the soft, comfort.

It was agreed that Healey was the front runner. It was as clear that Tony Benn could not run. He regarded the parliamentary franchise as illegitimate, something he sought to sweep away, and it was the merest coincidence that he had no chance whatever of being elected by it. Eric Heffer, with whom he stood in a prickly relationship, played with the idea of running, wrote articles, gave interviews and debated with Shirley Williams to that end. But Heffer, a clumsily likeable figure – getting on, noisy, unthreatening, remote from the new conspiratorial style – was never quite serious politics.

John Silkin almost was. A rich solicitor married to the former film actress, Rosamond John, he had made two reputations, first as a soft-handed Chief Whip at the latter end of the first Wilson government, then as Callaghan's Minister of Agriculture, a notable table-banger in Brussels. His Permanent Secretary, Sir Frederick Kearns, held him in open contempt, but Silkin's exertions had been pro-consumer and unhelpful to British producers, not the standard approach in that Ministry. The reputation was moreover a foundation for playing the anti-EEC card. Silkin was more obviously self-seeking and opportunistic than the run of politicians. A scrutineer at a Shadow Cabinet election noticed a ballot paper with a single cross for Silkin and was assured by a colleague that this was his habitual practice.[57] Yet he was kind and warm, very hard to dislike.

For as long as Foot kept back, Peter Shore was taken seriously. The former head of Research at Transport House a decade after Healey's International job, he had been close to Wilson who would grow bitterly disillusioned with him over *In Place of Strife* which, not knowing a placeman's place, he readily opposed. Angular and thin to the point of emaciation, once compared to Smike, Shore had passed for a left-winger of sorts. There had been much Tory talk in the seventies about 'Benn and Shore'. But though his politics were idiosyncratic and mixed, he was a conservative figure, attractive fleetingly to the left because of a hostility to what was then called 'the Common Market' of an unremitting, not to say obsessive, sort.*

In those days before Jacques Delors charmed the TUC and Mrs Thatcher made Europhobia her own, opposition to Europe was largely a thing of the far left. Hatred of 'the Common Market' and calls to get out of it had figured heavily at Wembley, with Callaghan saying wistfully that we ought not to approach our problems with such an insular view. Shore, who declaimed 'England hath made shameful surrender of herself,' would be seen until quite late as the candidate of compromise acceptable to the left and to some people who would in no circumstances support Benn.

Michael Foot had natural appeal, but through the griefs of his leadership he also had considerable talent. He was a stump speaker with great rousing appeal. Donald Anderson recalls a conference of the Welsh TUC in 1979, addressed by Foot and John Morris. 'John had a formal typed speech and was fine. But Michael stood up and was brilliant off a single piece of paper. I looked at it later. He had five words written down.'[58] At their worst, those words dissolved into a warm haze of rhetoric, at their best they were very good. He could speak with the passion and moral conviction of the West of England Nonconformist pulpits to which the Foot family were accustomed. And he could be very funny even to a sophisticated audience. His assault on Keith Joseph, now emerging as the chief advocate of monetarism, compared him with a conjuror borrowing a spectator's watch, wrapping it in a silk scarf and hitting it with a hammer before saying 'Oh, I've forgotten how the next bit goes.'

He had a high culture, more English and more specifically literary than Healey's. Not many party leaders can write a life of Byron or be acknowledged experts on Hazlitt. He had been editor and rather uncomfortable

---

* It did not abate. He was to be heard long after in the Lords bringing into a debate about juries his fervent support for a man selling sweets in ounces.

friend to George Orwell, had edited both *Tribune* and the *Evening Standard* (one of many radical journalists, captivated by the mephitic dazzle of Max Beaverbrook). More important, though Foot could rant and denounce, he was essentially without malice. He did though, this paladin of unilateralism, grow not a little self-righteous in his reminiscent denunciations of appeasement, and he would in 1982 show a strange avidity for war in the Falklands, something repeated in the Balkans.

As for his ministerial record, it involved great patience and long constructive work in getting the unions onside for the second Social Contract. He had worried all the way through the hard decisions of the Callaghan government, so many of them Healey's, but had not resigned, had in fact loyally gone against his own instincts over cuts. He was violently attacked from the Conference floor for his defence of the former government. To those talking about 'traitors', Foot was part of the treason. To the new feral left he was an object of contempt.

But from the viewpoint of good government, Foot in office had in a negative sense been quite left-wing enough. If anyone had given the derisive term 'union barons' serious feudal meaning, it was Michael Foot. His time as a minister contained acts stupidly coercive of business. As observed, he promoted dock regulation when the collapse of Liverpool and London and the rise of Felixstowe were demonstrating the ruin of work by enforced employment. And he had only just been frustrated from imposing a closed shop at cold storage depots and inland waterway termini.

Against his virtues, there is a deadly little cameo of him in Edmund Dell's unpublished diaries. Foot attended a Treasury meeting for CBI people. 'Michael Foot seemed to be incapable of carrying on an ordinary, normal conversation. He had barely once looked at them. He was all the time thumbing his brief. He was exactly as he is in the House of Commons: totally absorbed, full of debating points and precious little substance.' As the meeting was ending, 'instead of letting them go Michael launched into this great speech . . . [he] went on for about ten minutes with this great exposition and then, probably to avoid anything else starting, the CBI withdrew.'[59]

He was an old romantic with not much head for administration. Born in 1913, he seemed much older, and his style, marked with odd traits of diction, stressing words not meant to be stressed and full of little bronchial pauses, came too close to the eccentric. Substantially, Foot was far less of an eccentric than Shore, but he was taken for one, which meant that he was not taken seriously. In a famous and widely resented passage, Orwell described fat, bald-headed men in pistachio-coloured shorts travelling upstairs on a bus, and someone saying under his breath 'Socialists!' Foot was broom-handle slim, had lots of hair, worn at virtuoso length, and was innocent of shorts. But he dressed socialist, and looked socialist – corduroys, cardigans, dark shirts and woven ties which made even people who reliably voted Labour sense difference. He was not at the time of his election much mocked, but he was horribly vulnerable to *being* mocked. Michael Foot was profoundly liked, often loved, within the Labour Party, even by the right. Indeed the reputation was parliamentary, the nicer Tories having a soft spot for the old radical.

But parliament is less conformist than mass opinion, and among the generality, Foot at his best probably rated as an oddity, a queer fish. In the hands of a few accomplished brewers-up of contempt and hatred, he would be turned into a village idiot. Defeat for the leadership would be a misfortune for Healey, but victory was to be plain tragedy for Foot.

As a candidate, Healey started strong, with a general expectation of winning. Obviously the rising far left abominated him and the MP given misery *à la* Laurie Pavitt, by his constituency party, would fear to register what he might be asked to reveal. But beyond that, Healey, though admired for accomplishment, had none of the Callaghan qualities, the handy clichés attaching to the sound man – safe pair of hands, avuncular manner, gravitas, bottom. He was a busy *Macher*, a departmental minister doing well, even brilliantly, but too busy, lacking in an old shoe relationship with the ranks.

He was direct and combative on the conference rostrum, something admired but thought risky. He could be downright rude and had, with specific brusqueries, made enemies among natural allies: Tam Dalyell, wanting for serious purposes – he has no other – to be included on a trip to Indonesia being treated as a freeloader;[60] Leo Abse, clever creator of excellent private member's legislation, seeing his bright son unintentionally patronised over the books he had been reading.[61] Robert Sheldon, a junior Treasury minister under Healey, had also been rubbed the wrong way.[62] They should, though, be set against people like Peter Hardy, South Yorkshire MP, who saw Healey, during Conference, take his retired miner father for a long comfortable talk on a seafront bench giving the old man perfect delight.[63] All the acts, both affront and kindness, will have been done without calculation.

Then again, the Parliamentary Party had seen relatively little of Healey sending up the Tories, as he would soon brilliantly do, still less of the endearingly funny Healey. Overworked departmental ministers commonly speak factually and in defence and are rarely much fun. There would be a different Healey during the bleak times ahead, witty, with a lighter touch and mocking the Tories rotten. That came with release from so many burdens, but it came too late.

He was by far the ablest candidate in practical and intellectual terms. He had courage and stamina. However cautious he might have to be over the interim, there was no serious doubt that he would work to make the Labour Party electable and sane. If that battle was worth fighting, Healey was in every Irish sense your only man. Unfortunately there were MPs for whom battles were dangerous and appeasement comfortable. Equally, there were others so ready for a fight that they wanted to have one with the whole Labour Party now.

The idea of a candid break and the creation of a new separate party was in the air. Its protagonists had learned from the far left a certain narrow concern with their own project. A phrase in Crewe and King's study of the SDP is that Healey 'showed no inclination to fight any corner but his own'.[64] The question that remark invites is 'What other corner should the candidate for that party's leadership be fighting?' He was placed in a tactical bind, needing the votes of people who, like him, wanted to restore the party intact to something like normality and the votes of people so angry with the leftward drift that they were ready to leave it.

To some of the first group he looked too combative, to the second he wasn't the fighter they were. One of the split-ists would speak contemptuously of Healey as a blusterer soft inside. 'Like Ferdinand the Bull, he would respond to the left by smelling the flowers and putting another of his classical records on the gramophone.'[65] The remark, shimmering with resentment, shows very little regard for what a candidate must do to hold a coalition together or indeed of Healey's steady, historic willingness to fight, both in debate and departmentally.

The compliment was returned. These people yearned to break away. The Healey of the forties, involved as observer and consultant counsellor during the Italian Party's split, was by experience and professional instinct, violently opposed to all breakaways. Within a party of the left, they did harm to the old party, achieved nothing after the first bubbles, for the new one, and chiefly helped to keep the party of the right in power. His prejudices would be proved immaculately correct. But in the autumn of 1980, being right didn't help. There was not a vote to spare.

In an atmosphere of distrust with the future schismatics, Healey did little to ease things. This was emphasised by a falling-out with Rodgers. With the leadership contest looming, a group was formed to look after Healey's interests. Having been away abroad, he returned, found not enough done and spoke as he could do, sharply, about some people not trying hard enough. Most people, especially Treasury civil servants, had learned either not to mind or to shout back.* Rodgers, intelligent and brave, but on his own admission during this period, badly stressed, took mighty affront.

Again, John Horam, chairman of the moderate Manifesto Group, remembers taking a small delegation to meet him and getting decidedly short shrift. Healey was trying hardest to get the votes of the centre, of people scared

---

* Alan Lord tells a story of Healey saying, 'This is the first piece of entire nonsense you have submitted,' and his replying, 'That, Chancellor, is probably because you have no answer to it,' and never looking back from Healey's laughter.

of their constituency parties, above all of party loyalists unhappy at the new snarling developments, but prejudiced against splitters. He thought and said to their faces that they had nowhere else to go. The Newcastle MP, Mike Thomas, a future SDP defector, was told just that: 'You have nowhere else to go.' He had been tempted when the SDP was founded, said Thomas, to send Healey a telegram, 'Have found somewhere else to go.'[66] But then as events from late 1982–3, including the general election result, would demonstrate, he hadn't!

A measure of all-round suspicion is that Barry Jones was asked by David Owen and Bill Rodgers to inspect their ballot papers.[67] The support is less significant than the need to prove it. And where Owen and Rodgers showed responsibility, others did not. For those most fraught and angry, the Samson option was available. It is generally accepted that at least three MPs who later left Labour, first voted against Healey. Tom Ellis, Neville Sandelson and Jeffrey Thomas seem clearly to have made that decision. Others are speculated about.* This was a two-stage election. Chances in the run-off rested upon calculation of sufficient strength on the first ballot. Allegedly, Harold Wilson, having voted for Healey in the first round, switched to Foot in the second! To have added as many as five to Healey's first-round total might have given him the impetus to win.

It was an election among 278 people. Accordingly, in a way which looks odd to posterity, souls were counted lovingly like large coin. Assurance came that 'David Clarke was OK' but that 'Terry Davies may vote for Silkin.'[68] Upon such things great calculations are made, and next day, Barry Jones rang Denis with an estimate. The assured votes seemed to be between 132 and 135.[69] Calls also went out to alert his allies, Eric Varley and Ernest Armstrong, to start the campaign. But at this time Healey, who had felt ill a few days earlier during a visit to the Midlands, fell quite seriously sick, registering a temperature of 102 and was treated by his doctor with antibiotics. Throughout the Friday and Saturday, 17 and 18 October, he 'felt terrible'.[70]

Still feeling ill and with Edna down as well, he dragged himself back on Monday the 20th, doing a string of interviews, questioned by Margaret Jay, Peter Sissons and John Tusa and also receiving a self-exculpatory phone call from David Basnett. There would be a moment of rest, a bubble of civility in mid-revolution, a little chat with Tony Benn who asked after his just published book. This was *Healey's Eye* and the product of his passionate hobby, photography. It would go on to be an outstanding success in terms of sales *and* esteem. Healey could tell Benn that 'they had sold 10,000 copies in a week which, I must say, is amazing.'[71]

---

* In his obituary of Sandelson in January 2002 in the *Independent*, Tom Dalyell quotes him as claiming seven cross voters. But enquiries have not yet yielded their names.

And on the same day, Michael Foot declared his candidacy. His wife had told him, it transpired, that if he didn't stand, Foot would be 'letting down your friends'.[72] The wife in question, Jill Craigie, sometime actress and film maker, was the object of much affection but no great esteem for her political sense. George Page, London Regional Chairman, would observe unanswerably, 'That bloody woman! Why didn't Michael marry Edna Healey?' Foot also insisted that he 'would have no truck with the notion of being a caretaker manager, an idea espoused by the far left of the party'.[73] As Fred Emery, *The Times* correspondent, wrote: 'The immediate consequence of the four-way race seems to have been the spiking of Mr Denis Healey's hopes of a first ballot victory.'[74]

The left were demanding that MPs should surrender their vote and follow their local management committees' instructions. It was a piece of characteristic ugliness and, sincerely enough, Foot expressed himself against it. The people putting pressure on *him*, he acknowledged, were union leaders. Those making personal appeals, he said, 'far exceeded anything he had expected'.[75] Numbers were of no account. Healey had a sheaf of general secretaries himself, Terry Duffy, Gavin Laird, Brian Stanley, Tom Jackson, Sidney Weighell and Joe Gormley. What had mattered was Clive Jenkins propelling the vacant prestige of David Basnett. Unions had as yet no votes to cast in this election, only backstairs influence. The time would come, a year on, when they would – to Healey's advantage.

Healey would not feel properly well until the Friday (24 October). An attempt would be made at this time to suspend the standing orders of the Parliamentary Party, and thus the election, until a college had been created. Healey noted the contribution of the ultra leftist, Ernie Ross, 'appalling'.[76] The move was defeated by 119 votes to 66 with 72 abstaining, a bad sign for Healey's campaign and highly symbolic. PLP votes are open and more people were too scared to defend their own authority than would actually vote for its immediate ending.

The next day, Tony Benn would find himself in the middle of a small tea-room fight.

> I sat down next to Jim Wellbeloved who was talking to Joan Lestor, and I heard him say, 'There'll be a split.'
> I said, 'I don't think there will be a split.'
> All of a sudden the atmosphere turned nasty . . .

After 'people had started to gather round' and he had been attacked, not least by the moderate left-winger, Joan Lestor, pointing out that she had resigned on principle and he had not, Benn records, 'The point was, they were having a collective nervous breakdown. They are in a state of panic, and the hatred was so strong that I became absolutely persuaded that this was not a Party I would ever be invited to lead, and nor could I lead it.'[77]

On Election Day, 30 October, Benn wrote, 'I voted last night for Michael Foot as Leader of the Party.'[78] He had written earlier in the month of 'the old lion . . . His usual line is to warn that we face the greatest crisis since Hannibal's march on Rome and that we must do nothing whatever that might interfere with total mental inactivity and 100 per cent loyalty to the leader whoever he may be . . .'[79] On the same day, Healey would be told by Austin Mitchell of his support and note the helpfulness of a young woman MP, Ann Taylor (much later Leader of the House and Chief Whip). What could be done had been done. At the weekend, as during economic crises, he cut the grass in Sussex.

Probably Healey missed a trick when he declined the *Guardian*'s invitation to contribute a case parallel with those of the other contestants. While distrust of the paper's ultra-left features editor, Richard Gott, may have played a part, the main motive seems to have been the one which keeps incumbents out of television debates in Britain: less arrogance than the anxiety of front runners not to say anything for fear of losing the lead they have. And as Roy Hattersley recalls, at least one MP, Phillip Whitehead, who complained that he was withholding open debate, rather priggishly refused to vote for him. Healey argued to allies like Hattersley that he didn't want to thrust his multilateralism and a view of Europe, friendlier than the backbench norm, in the faces of his electorate.[80]

On 4 November, Healey would have a final chat with Barry Jones who now expected a vote of 120 which, on arithmetical expectations, would have given him the sort of lead better not challenged on second ballots. The actual result was grimly short of what was necessary: Healey had only 112 votes. Seven fewer people had voted for him as, at the PLP meeting, had dared defy suspension of parliamentary leadership elections. Silkin had 38 votes and Shore 32; Michael Foot had 83. With 70 votes cast for candidates calling themselves left-wing, Foot was only 29 behind. Healey noted without comment that 'Michael voted for Peter,' adding 'Great depression.'[81] Benn was convinced that Foot would now win. Victory for 'the old lion', keen 'that we should do nothing whatever that might interfere with total mental inactivity', delighted him; 'that will be a tremendous event.'[82] Shore and Silkin followed one another into declarations, withdrawal and support for Foot. It was an election which would be determined on the first ballot. It was essential to have a lead pointing to victory. In Hattersley's view, another five votes at the first go would have put Healey in a position to win. Eric Varley, he says, was as campaign manager tearing his hair out because Denis wouldn't do the little extra things, the private meetings with doubters which would have tipped the result.[83]

What followed was arithmetical necessity. Healey held a meeting with his team, a last flurry of canvassing was done over the interim. But Barry Jones describes what happened on the afternoon of 10 November. Healey and he, with others, waited in the grand committee room of the Commons, Foot and the wife who had helped bring this about were in a small room off it. A woman clerk came anxiously in at 5.55 p.m. and held out a small tray to Healey. It contained a folded sheet of paper. As soon as he took it, she hurried nervously off. He read the result and nodded, saying nothing and showing no emotion of any kind. His vote had gone up to 129, Foot's to 139. This briefly anticipated the formal announcement at the PLP meeting. Foot in his habitual way quoted Aneurin Bevan to no very clear point. 'Never underestimate the passion for unity in the Labour Party.' Writing that night, Healey was matter of fact. 'Went grinning to PLP, short speech, said I'd run for deputy leader – tremendous cheering and relief, but anger on faces of hard left!'[84] Tony Benn thought what Healey said next 'odious' – 'that the party had to recover its electoral strength, because it has lost votes consistently over the last thirty years and those votes had not gone to extreme left-wing parties',[85] a plain truth soon to be illustrated in lights.

Frank Giles, editor of the *Sunday Times*, a neighbour and friend who saw them soon after, remarked that though Edna was distressed and thoroughly unhappy, 'Denis was completely stoical.' Barry Jones also saw 'Edna upset and Denis gently put his hand on her forehead.' And, confronted with the fears of his secretary, Harriet Shackman, he put his arm round her and said, 'Well, look at it this way Harriet, that's a whole lot of extra work you won't have to do.' Two last words are in order. Ian Aitken, political editor of the *Guardian*, splendid journalist, old-time Bevanite, but political realist, met Bill Rodgers that evening. 'He was over the moon. "It's marvellous," said Aitken, "I'm delighted" then added, "though it will be a disaster for the party."'[86] However, the killer comment probably rests with an unidentified left-winger who, a year or more later, was reported as saying, 'God, what fools we were not to choose Denis.'

A MAD WORLD MY MASTERS

Ja Poppa!
    Vot you dun to dat Mr Benn vid der leedle pointy needle; maybe you bin creep creep vun darg night? Nixt thign we kno his ligs fall off compledely. Larf? I koffed borcht all ober de newstpaper.

Yr frind
Tim[1]

The words, in the style of Hyman Kaplan, were written in the late spring of 1981 by the Healeys' son, Tim, another Balliol Exhibitioner, by then in New York. They commemorated the suffering by Tony Benn at the hands of Guillain-Barré's Syndrome, a form of polyneuritis which, in May, would put the New Pretender out of circulation for three months. Since, on 2 April, he had announced his candidacy for the deputy-leadership of the party, that ungrateful office which Healey had reluctantly taken up unopposed after defeat in November, sympathy in the Healey family could hardly have been managed. The feelings of High churchmen when York Minster was hit by lightning during the enthronement of the Broad Church Dr Jenkins were nearer the mark. Not that Healey wanted the position. 'The best job I ever had,' Healey once said, 'was International Officer of the Labour Party. The worst was deputy-leader of the party.'[2]

A defeated politician who has to 'go grinning' to the next party meeting is often expected to take the nominal second place as an act of grace, proof of 'a passion for unity', a way of grinning officially. Occasionally the post is worth having. Foot, ironically, had been deputy leader, while Attlee, raised to that place in a party of 51 after the calamity of 1931, had been seen as acceptable; enough a buggins to take the leadership four years later, after

George Lansbury's defeat at Conference. But broadly, the position is reserved for safe men not likely to seek the leadership, Jim Griffiths or Ted Short, or else it falls to the doomed and yearning, disappointed major figures like Herbert Morrison or George Brown. Healey early compared the job with the United States Vice-Presidency, described by Roosevelt's deputy, the laconic Texan, John Nance Garner* as 'a pitcherfull of warm spit'. It is a measure of the passion for unity in the party that this was immediately misunderstood as a description of left-wing backbenchers!

The deputy leadership is an aspidistra among offices, prominent but not useful. Conveniently but not pleasurably, it put Healey back *ex-officio* on the NEC – now a paradise of droners-on. One future colleague there, Betty Boothroyd, recalls with awe his responding to tedious wrangles with noisy preparation of his press archive by slashing noisily through a pile of newspapers with a dangerous clasp razor (known in the Healey family circle as 'the snickersnee'). Only the most intricately minded conspiracy enthusiast had expected this irksome honorific to provoke a dawn raid in the markets. But expectations could not comprehend the evangelical instincts of Tony Benn. The year 1981 would be largely concerned with a furious struggle between the two men for this dubious niche. And for once, bad prose would be in order. Sub-editors' vermilion about a life-or-death contest for the soul of the party would be fair comment. Michael Foot was too weak to lead the party, too cherished to be thrust aside. But a vote under the new rules, identical for both posts, which demonstrated hard left ascendancy in menacing parallel, would say all that needed to be said. Victory for Benn would have been the prelude to a beleaguered Foot throwing in a towel he should never have picked up.

But we anticipate. Healey, defeated on 10 November, found himself chairing a meeting on the form the next leadership election would take on 11 November. That was the state of telescoped intolerability into which the party (or, as Benn insists on casing it, 'the Party'), had got itself. (Another irony was that on the day after defeat, Healey was slated to speak to a women's organisation about 'The art of the possible'.) At the committee meeting he had found Foot, Orme, Silkin and Albert Booth favouring a mix of MPs, unions, constituencies and societies (*how* mixed being the real question), while David Owen and Bill Rodgers were calling for 'One man one vote'.

This was a clever shift by the right, intended both to invoke a wider franchise and enrol voters better disposed towards them. The plotting right, happy enough with the Venetian limits of a parliamentary franchise, had learned to adapt. The plotting left's position, after so much exalted talk about democracy, was to get just as much of that commodity as would do the trick and freeze it there. Labour politics was now running two scenarios. One

---

* Vice-President 1933–41.

was the achievement of a form of electoral system leading to the people ordering MPs to submit their ballot intentions to them,* electing a party leader in their own corrugated image.

The other involved departure from the Labour Party of a group of MPs forming a new party, running against Labour, splitting the vote and generally pulling down the pillars of the temple. Crewe and King's study, *SDP*, has a chapter on this period. It is called 'Anguish'! And as they remark, for most of the potential defectors, Foot himself, never mind Foot as Kerensky, Foot as cat's-paw, was quite objectionable enough. He was a unilateralist, a nation-aliser, a protectionist, a planner, but not of wages, a withdrawer from Europe and calamity in a general election.

Into such a crisis regularly comes a helpful man with a compromise. At the 11 November Shadow Cabinet Roy Hattersley offered a variant of the college, acceptance of the principle but with MPs enjoying 55 per cent of the total vote. It carried by 7 to 6 according to Healey's diary, by 8 to 7 say Crewe and King; and it infuriated people least inclined to temporise like Owen and Williams. In the eyes of Owen at least, Hattersley was a fudger and mudger with Healey not far behind.

The right's own runner, 'One Man One Vote' (OMOV), had a lot to be said for it. But the Parliamentary Party repeated its performance when choosing Foot. OMOV, which would have protected them by vaulting over the local management committees, was rejected at a PLP meeting by 74–60.[3] Healey himself functioned as an *apparatchik* supporting the Hattersley line (55 per cent for MPs had been agreed in Shadow Cabinet). It duly passed the PLP by the same unimpressive margin, 74–60, but with a great bloc of OMOV supporters against.[4]† The low turnout was perhaps the most important figure, apprehensive demoralised MPs unsure of what to do and doing nothing.

Although he would put on a cheerful face and sustain the general rumbustiousness, Healey was oppressed and unhappy. Richard Heller, who saw more of him privately at this time than anyone except Edna, says:

He suffered a lot of black dog, anger and frustration. Part of it was not the craziness, but the sheer boredom. In the deputy leadership year, 1980–81, the NEC was exactly balanced which meant that you had to attend every NEC meeting and the hard left kept them going as long as possible. But even worse than having to wade through all the party business at meetings you absolutely had to attend was the dependence on Michael Foot. We had 15, the baddies had eleven and Footie had

---

* This had received wide publicity when it was tried on the Manchester MP, Ken Marks, who admirably declined to submit.

† '68–59' say Ivor Crewe and Anthony King in *SDP*, OUP, 1995, p. 78.

four. You needed him for everything. And Michael was always very secretive about a vote and how he voted depended upon who he had been talking to.[5]

Even so, one thing had been perfectly certain from the start. Healey would have no part in any exodus from the Labour Party. Edna Healey was almost certainly more angry than Denis with the people who had rewarded his struggles at the edge of exhaustion by choosing an inferior candidate out of pusillanimous weakness. Had he felt tempted, one suspects that he would have met with no opposition from his wife. Edna, incidentally, was now a public figure in her own right with the brilliant reception of her first biography – of the banking heiress, philanthropist and Dorothea Brooke figure, Angela Burdett-Coutts. It was also inconceivable that Healey could share such an operation with Roy Jenkins. There was mutual respect, but 'All our lives we have rubbed one another the wrong way'[6] says Jenkins. Instead he joined Foot in trying to talk the defection down.

Not that he showed him much deference. Eric Heffer complained to Benn that the Shadow Cabinet of 19 November had been 'bloody awful. There was Denis Healey banging the table and shouting at Michael Foot. It was Denis trying to bully Michael . . .' Benn had to be told about Shadow Cabinet meetings. Having approached Foot for the Home Office portfolio, he had then collected only 88 votes and failed to be elected. Owen ominously had declined to stand. Rodgers had been elected, only for Foot, in the first of a series of inept moves, to offer him minor portfolios, thus helping cement the party of defection. Healey himself would take up the Foreign Affairs slot and he busied himself across the next six months with renewed overseas contacts, meetings, lunches and whatever, for the Chinese, the Romanians, the New Zealanders and East Germans, attending influential much-muttered-against gatherings, a Bilderburg conference and a Georgetown/Oxford seminar. He had an ally in the Defence spokesman, Brynmor John, and highly acceptable deputies in Ted Rowlands and Robert Maclennan. He also saw rather more of general Commons politics, learning from a Conservative Cabinet minister something later to be feasted upon by the whole nation. 'Saw Mark Carlisle – nice lawyer – Heseltine v. fed up with Thatcher.'

And amidst all this travail, it has to be remembered that the government, watching unemployment spiral to frightening heights, had become immensely unpopular. An opposition which, by way of compromise, got no further out of control and toned down its act, had apparently a great deal to play for. Healey himself and his close associates, George Robertson and Giles Radice,* would argue against defection with the leading defectors-in-waiting, Radice

---

* Both former officers of the useful G&M.

enduring finger-jabbing denunciation as 'rich and privileged' by an overwrought Bill Rodgers.[7] Healey was particularly concerned to save the soul of Shirley Williams whom he liked, but Robert Maclennan's mind was made up and Healey recognised as much.

Labour Party life continued in customary vein. A 'dreadful shadow cabinet' and a 'dreadful NEC' are recorded in December. At a slightly later NEC meeting, Healey would respond to a long Norman Atkinson chunter about 'Thinking through a fundamental transformation of the economy' (without troubling the Treasury), saying, 'I agree with Norman Atkinson when he said that we must think it through, and we shall watch with interest while he attempts that task himself.' The dialogue then took off.

ATKINSON: (*very angrily*) We shall watch your demise too.
ROY HATTERSLEY: What the hell does that mean?
ATKINSON: Well, what the hell did Denis mean when he said he would watch me thinking?[8]

Given so much, the diversions of village life in Sussex had something to be said for them. The headmaster of the Pilgrims' School, Seaford, thanks Denis for 'responding so promptly to our request that you honour us by starting the Pram Race from the Berwick Inn to The Cricketers'.[9]

Unfortunately the world and Seaford were mere background for the real stage of the party crisis. The first brick through the window came at the second special conference at Wembley on Saturday 24 January 1981. It was, Healey noted, 'orderly'. It was also disastrous. The Hattersley compromise had been cut back at the left-dominated NEC. Following a simple muddle by the AUEW which having committed itself to nothing under 50 per cent for MPs, refused to vote for the compromise offering them 40 per cent, and a further muddle by Syd Tierney, president of USDAW, a motion would be carried leaving MPs with only 30 per cent of the vote, equal with the constituencies, and giving 40 per cent to the unions.

'It will never be reversed,' said Tony Benn, adding sepulchrally, 'and nothing will be the same again.'[10] He was asked by the *Financial Times* if he might stand for the party's deputy leadership, replying 'If I am nominated I might. I shall certainly consider it.' Everything conspired to make it happen. Benn was cordially detested by the Parliamentary Party. Fearful as they were of constituency dictation, they had found only 88 votes for him in the Shadow Cabinet elections. Under the new rules, with 40 per cent voting strength for the unions, muscles were being invited to flex themselves. Ironically the response of Bill Rodgers to the new rules had been to resign from the Shadow Cabinet, leaving a space for the runner-up – Tony Benn!

Michael Foot, who had done his own loyal thing in government, was bitter about Benn's excursions. The latest of these was to propose binding

MPs, in response to the pending exodus, with a loyalty oath. This proposal was to be considered by the NEC. When Foot's new colleague came to see him, the conversation swiftly deteriorated: 'You're very soft on the right, buttering up Bill Rodgers all the time' and Foot's 'You try to fix votes in advance don't you?' until, on Benn's denial of that, Foot exploded, 'You're a bloody liar.'[11]

But the new rules had done their work. They were that last worse event which the most adventurous defectors had thought necessary for things to get better. The Council for Social Democracy was created on 2 February, a step intimating departure. Healey and Foot responded by holding a three-hour meeting with the 'Gang of Three', attempting to head them off. Healey's judgement was succinct: 'David Owen – Rodgers already decided to leave. Shirley unsure but still agonising.'[12] Over the interim before the formal departure, there was opportunity, grasped by all hands, for recrimination.

Healey would need all the solace he could get from university seminars and pram races. He has spoken of the four months of the IMF, September–December 1976, as the worst of his life. He had done the right but excruciating thing then, conjuring the hatred of the left and doing himself no good with enough other MPs to deny him the leadership. He now faced the second-worst time of his life. He had missed the chief job, seen the party stumble into an electoral system likely to deny him all hope of the succession, and precipitate a split perfectly capable of pushing Labour into third-party marginality. He now faced the possibility of a contest simply to keep things and himself standing where they were.

The notion of Benn seeking the deputy leadership under the new rules, began to crystallise in the spring, not least with the launch on 26 March of the Social Democratic Party, seen by Benn as 'a major media festival . . . unreal and potentially dangerous . . . reminds me of what Tawney said. The attack on the two party system, the attack on the democratic process, the attack on choice, the attack on debate, the attack on policy – all these have within them the ingredients of fascism.'[13] Healey had referred resignedly to a 'boring, bad-tempered NEC – Heffer row with me.'[14] There had been a number of these. For, if anything was a constant across those three months, it was the anger of Michael Foot at Tony Benn.

The greatest of Foot's concerns was that he should not contest the deputy leadership. Benn was a remorseless producer of papers and signer of resolutions. The latest condemned Healey for criticising the NEC. As he told a frayed Foot on 24 March, 'I believe there is a letter coming before the NEC tomorrow, which I have signed, just simply regretting the fact that the Deputy Leader of the Party, while giving fraternal greetings of the NEC, should have chosen to attack the NEC.' 'There you are,' Foot said. 'Every meeting will be like this and it will be like this all summer. It will ruin the Conference.'[15]

As parents sometimes say, 'It's not a bit of good talking to him.' On 29

March, a dozen of Benn's friends, Tony Banks and Chris Mullin among them, assembled at his Holland Park home for 'three hours' intense discussion' after which 'there was absolutely no doubt that I should stand as a candidate: it was unanimous.' It was, thought Benn, 'A very useful day and a historic decision taken collectively.'[16]

Understandably, Denis Healey remembered the date of declaring that candidacy as All Fools' Day 1981. Pedantically, it was actually released at 3.30 a.m. on 2 April, literally a dawn raid. Healey was in Germany at the time, attending the Anglo-German Koenigswinter conference, noting 'violent language' between German participants: arms for Saudi Arabia, a row between Helmut Schmidt and Karl-Otto Poehl over interest rates,[17] also noting Schmidt's detestation of the British Prime Minister: 'Violently anti-Thatcher – she has no friends or sympathy left in Europe.'[18] This was nine years before her semi-public outburst of hatred for Germany at another Koenigswinter gathering (Cambridge, 1990). Benn does not make the diary, and then only parenthetically, until the Sunday 4 April when Frank Field and Jack Straw, also at the conference, 'offer help v. Benn'.[19]

It was during this trip that Healey was asked officially if he would accept nomination as Secretary-General of NATO.[20] There had been an offer of that post in 1969. It was unlikely that he would have taken it whatever the circumstances. His refusal in 1969 derived from exasperation at the foot-dragging attitude to NATO of so many European governments, a function perhaps of European scepticism about a Soviet threat and the priority which Healey gave to modern thinking on defence.

But in terms of British politics the refusal was remarkable. He was fighting an ungrateful battle for a dogsbody's job which he might lose. His parliamentary colleagues had snubbed him over the post that mattered. He had an MP's salary augmented with occasional journalism. He would be sixty-four years old in August. Since 1964 he had put in eleven years of exhausting work as a minister. He was a foreign affairs and defence specialist, he loved the countries and people of Europe and knew their political leaders better than any British politician excepting possibly Edward Heath. He owed, as Edna strongly felt, no favours to a Labour Party lacking the courage to fight against its own destruction. His public message for the IMF, 'Sod off', would have been entirely in order. But there was no question of issuing it. NATO was politely declined.

The scornful view of those SDP people who had suggested, after Foot's victory, that Bill Rodgers should stand for the deputy-leadership 'without the slightest hope of winning, but on behalf of fifty or sixty colleagues who wished to cast a protest vote against Denis Healey's lack of fighting spirit',[21] was as wrong as wrong could very well get. The fighting spirit of Denis Healey would find expression in staying, seeing the whole tragicomedy through, as he describes it, by 'slogging on'. If Healey took the nice job and the money, he took the soft option, the good career move, then, with the SDP established and flourishing, the moderate, this-worldly, credible Labour Party would be without a leader.

He later wrote, 'I think that if Tony had won there would have been a great movement to get Michael to go early so that he could take over as leader. But I think that most of the country would have seen it as the definitive sign that we were turning into what they regard as a Marxist party . . . a lot of MPs would have joined the Social Democrats and the Party structure would have disintegrated.'[22] Certainly if he had turned away, Benn would have beaten any substitute. The split would have been more nearly equal and politics overall quite different. That might have been a good or a bad thing, but Healey's loyalty was to the Labour Party, an echo of Hugh Gaitskell at Scarborough, ready 'to fight, fight and fight again to save the party we love'. It was a fine irony that twelve months after being rejected as leader, Healey was offering his party leadership. It was now what he existed for.

None of which required an immediate overreaction to the challenge. Not getting excited became the right approach when Benn was at once hit by a flurry of reproaches and complaint from people generally classed as left wing, like Stan Newens, Oonagh McDonald and Stan Orme, while the member for Bedwelty, Neil Kinnock, was said to be organising staff at Transport House to sign a letter asking Benn to desist. Negative communication was extensive. 'Robin Cook urged me not to waste the next six months.' Even Clive Jenkins, sensing the end of the trouble which could usefully be made, presented him with a loving cup inscribed back and front 'Elections can be poisoned chalices, Tony' and 'Don't do it. Tony'.[23] 'There is,' admitted the dependable Stuart Holland, 'a lot of anti-Benn feeling in the Tribune Group.' When it met: 'John Prescott said, "Tony should back down or we should disown him."'[24] With large parts of the future Blair government indicating unhappiness, signs of the earth rearranging itself under feet are clear, at any rate to hindsight.

What would follow would be compared by the psephologist David Butler to an American primary election. The result would be announced at Conference in late September. A whole summer could now be given up to appealing to the three elements making up the new constituency. The parallel umbrella organisations under which Labour Party factions delight to walk, would spring into function if not always action, Benn served by the CLPD (Campaign for Labour Party Democracy), Healey by a group, 'Forward Labour', already working in parallel within the unions to shift the balance away from the left on the NEC. In the latter part of the campaign, American practice was also followed in the distribution of 2000 Healey badges, (loyally got up as Foot and Healey badges despite the leader's failure to go public for Healey) in red on a yellow and white background.

There would, however, only be time for Clive Jenkins's ASTMS

(Technicians) to come out narrowly on a poll of 28,000 for Benn and for SOGAT, the wonderfully dreadful printworkers, to do the same, and perhaps inevitably, for John Silkin to announce that he was standing too, the first rattle round the British equivalents of New Hampshire, before the 'leedle pointy needle' suddenly struck. Benn had been feeling ill for some time, unable to run or move quickly, his throat constricted and his hands tingling.[25] Accordingly he went to Dr Stein, his regular physician, who referred him to the consultant neurologist at Charing Cross Hospital, Clifford Rose, who put him into hospital at once for tests on 3 June. There he stayed until 20 June when Guillain-Barré was diagnosed and he was required to undertake 'a complete rest' of a couple of months.

Now Benn was a compulsive addresser of meetings, going gladly everywhere and speaking in any room booked to hear him. Peter Shore had asked him during the leadership campaign, 'I wonder if you have done more meetings than John Wesley?' Benn checked out and found that the great Methodist had made upwards of 40,000 sermons in his long life, whereas he had managed a mere two hundred a year over the previous ten years. (He thought Wesley 'must have counted every little stop'.)[26] Benn, also inclined to make the whole world his province, was now suddenly switched off and tucked up by doctors. No tenor with laryngitis can have felt more deprived. He had perhaps won a sympathy vote, while artillery trained on him, not least by an infuriated Foot daring him to challenge for the leadership, had to be stilled. The campaign was confined to newspaper articles and the scurrying of candidates' committees to implore unions. Othello's occupation was under interim suspension.

Meanwhile the SDP was enjoying what that party's chroniclers call its 'golden age', touching 50 per cent in the polls at one stage, while Michael Foot was stumbling badly, saying too much, issuing too much paper, and quoting Nye. Every characteristic endearing to Labour and Conservative politicians who knew him at Westminster, was horribly mockable under lights and cameras. The term 'Wurzel Gummidge', an ambulating scarecrow in a series of 1930s' children's stories, attached by *Private Eye*, began an exploitation by the tabloid right-wing press cruelly climaxing during the general election of 1983. As for the polls, Labour had stood at 46.5 per cent (Gallup) before the January Wembley conference. After that 'historic decision taken collectively', it fell by 11.5 per cent and would stay below the 33 per cent mark, almost, it seemed, for ever while Foot's own rating fluttered around 20 per cent, extraordinary in a new leader of an opposition to an unpopular government. Labour, facing ministers recording the worst economic numbers since before the war, found itself unable to function as an opposition, so preoccupied was it with the party itself. The quasi-Leninism of the new politics, 'the central role of the party', was showing that role as a farcical one.

Healey had major press support. Too much of this sustained Benn's not particularly extravagant view of gross right-wing bias. *The Times* of 3 September listed the known union backers, Bill Sirs, Terry Duffy and Tom Jackson, under the headline 'Top Union Men back Healey'. Its leader the same day declared him to be 'overwhelmingly more popular than the other two candidates and a symbol of the survival of the party. If Labour is to recover itself it becomes all the more important that Denis Healey wins.' Such comment from the gifted but idiosyncratic editor, William Rees-Mogg, was both well meant and true. But if there was an uncomfortable feeling about so much and so fervent upper Establishment support, there was even more so about the conduct of the lower Establishment, the simple viciousness with which *Sun* and *Express*, among others, attacked Benn personally.

In the *Sunday Express*, Michael Cummings, a superb draughtsman with the political perceptions of a shrill schoolboy, showed Benn in fascist rig with a hammer and sickle on his sleeve above the title 'Ein Volk, Ein Reich, Ein Führer', actionable if Benn could have been bothered. In the same spirit, the *Daily Express* reviewed Benn's pamphlet, *Arguments for Democracy*, comparing it with *Mein Kampf*. *The Times*, more gracefully, discussed Benn's inherited finances so as to make untrue imputations of tax evasion.

Given that Benn, for all his trance-like vanity and self-unacknowledged ambition, (what might be called his high opportunism), was/is an honourable and decent man, the rabidry of the tabloids and the slyness of their betters was hateful. It was also wildly irrelevant. What was actually to be feared, if Benn won and the likely contingencies followed – serial deselection, Vatican authority for a party Conference at odds with Labour voters and a manifesto proclaiming a siege economy under party guidance – was quite bad enough. But as a gun, it was pointing in only one direction, the Labour Party.

Some of the hysteria against Benn derived from the extreme unpopularity descending on the Thatcher government with unemployment on its way up to 3.5 million. The notion certainly lodged in many editorial/proprietorial minds that a Benn take-over of the Labour Party might coincide with the only moment in history when such a farrago might be electable. Benn himself said that a Labour landslide might be on the way. He was making flesh creep. Healey tried to crush extravagant speculations. The idea had also been put about that he might, if defeated, leave the Labour Party. It flew in the teeth of everything in his career and he was quick to knock the idea on the head.

Campaigning naturally intensified in September. Benn returned from his rest. Healey came back from a holiday in southern France ready to lay about him. He had the assistance of another Yorkshireman, the quietly indispensable David Warburton from the General and Municipal whom Benn thought 'a smooth young man', together with Giles Radice and Barry

Jones. Forward Labour dovetailed its plans to pull the NEC and party back to sense with those for the re-election of Healey. Warburton and his allies assembled 1200 contacts in the constituencies and set about spadework in the unions so that nothing would pass by default. They worked with another group, regular gatherers at the St Ermine's Hotel, Labour's favourite resort of conspiracy and so known as 'the St Ermine's Group'. Co-ordinated by Bryan Stanley of the Post Office Engineers, it drew in Terry Duffy of the Engineers and Roy Grantham of Apex (Professional, Executive, Clerical and Computer Staff), while John Golding, an MP on the NEC, acted as linkman outside the unions. The campaign, not just to re-elect Healey, but over a longer period to restore a moderate NEC and put the Labour Party back on the rails deserves a full study to itself. It came before red roses and mattered more.

While the two union groups worked primarily but not exclusively on unionists, Healey's allies in Westminster, Barry Jones, Giles Radice and his PA, Richard Heller, worked the Commons lobbies and corridors. 'Just about everybody,' said Heller, 'including the outright enemy. We wrote and talked to everybody even people like Michael Meacher.' He was particularly pleased to have turned Oonagh McDonald and Frank Field away from voting for Benn. The known Silkin supporters were a useful concentration of people seriously worth talking to. Heller recalls arguing that having made their point with a first preference, did they really want Tony Benn as leader of the Labour Party?[27]

Since the struggle was hot busy news, Healey had the television studios as his platform: *Newsnight* with John Tusa on 4 September – 'all went well', *Meet the Press* with Tony Howard on 6 September – 'went well', *Today* with Brian Redhead, and many more. He went to the TUC conference and showed himself on all social fronts. At the G&M party, he found 'Basnett cold and wet as usual', unlike Ken Dodd also met there – 'frenetic!',[28] and talked to SOGAT and NGA men (printers all) at their receptions. A TV public debate was noted in the style of Mr Jingle: '"Panorama" v. Benn, Silkin – good for me. Bad for party. Very noisy.'[29] Each candidate was to be interrogated by a trade union ally of his opponent. Benn, Silkin and Healey were backed by, respectively, Ray Buckton of ASLEF, the Beethoven-loving George Wright of the T&G, and Warburton. What should have been cross-examination and debate was interrupted by abuse from the auditorium beyond any definition of heckling. Happily, sound engineering rendered the transmitted programme altogether milder.[30]

A story splashed in the early autumn announced municipal defection: sixteen councillors in Islington, not then so potent a location, announced their mass departure for the SDP. But the main concern was the disposition of union votes. Unions were a law, or several quite different laws, unto themselves. Some consulted seriously by way of binding local ballots. Others concentrated power in the central Executive. One, as we shall see, would decide on the day between its members and its leadership. But the news was promising. The General and Municipal intended to hold full consultation and be bound by it: only Scotland, of its ten regions, was inclined to vote for Benn, the other nine being firmly for Healey.[31] The G&M was Basnett's union and Basnett had, a year earlier, done everything in his power to block Healey from the leadership.

Against which Benn recorded a nod-and-wink conversation with Sam Pemberton, chairman (a secondary post) of the Transport and General.

'He kept saying, "The best of fucking British luck to you, comrade. Just keep your head down this month and you'll be all right."' Benn noted, 'real hope that the T&G might vote for me on the first ballot of the deputy leadership contest'.[32] They didn't. Eight days later he was reporting a news story 'that the T&G is going heavily, by six regions to three, in favour of Healey'.[33] What was at issue was whether any of their members would actually be counted.

This was an age before consultant speech-making. If there were sound-bites extractable from Healey's roughneck literacy, listeners' teeth would crunch upon Greek and Latin syllables. He attacked the basis for the whole left surge of the previous eighteen months: 'a little, self–representing, self-appointed elite',[34] also the 'ideological narcissism' of Benn who was 'blackguarding the record of the governments he served in as betrayals of the British working class, and abusing Prime Ministers from whom he accepted office as mad monarchs who turned MPs into puppets'.[35] It came from the heart and it came urgently.

The deputy leadership had never been, for Benn or Healey, the *Ding an sich*. The question was the Labour Party – where the Bennite campaign had taken it, where it might take it yet. For all the froth, nothing was ever taken more seriously. Healey spoke to Foot 'about TGWU – Warned of disintegration if Benn wins'.[36] There was serious talk, especially among the Engineers, that if Healey lost, this would be the last time they would make an effort, talk also of disaffiliation with consequent loss of funds. This was a time before £2 million cheques from ennobled entrepreneurs.[37]

Central to Healey's argument was the long decline of the Labour Party and in whose favour it had declined. Peter Shore had spoken the day before, 9 September, of 'the massive erosion of Labour support over the previous two and a half years'.[38] The beneficiary, said Healey, had been Margaret Thatcher, not Michael McGahey.* They were losing votes, not to the Socialist Workers or the International Marxist Group, but to David Steel and Roy Jenkins.

---

* Immediate lieutenant in the National Union of Miners to Arthur Scargill, and as a member of the British Communist Party, the more reasonable man.

Violence hovered. At that televised debate Robin Corbett, one of Healey's parliamentary allies, was 'pushed about by Trots etc'.[39] It went beyond people in one audience. One of the ugly realities of Labour conferences across 1980–81 had been the replacement of the usual doorkeepers, cantankerous and unhelpful in the cherished Labour style, by fit young men commonly wearing leather and an aura of menace. 'Trots etc' is what one would have called them. Richard Heller recalls a general awfulness. 'It was deeply unpleasant standing up and saying you were going to support Denis. It was deeply unpleasant for me to say in Westminster South, my local party, what job I did.'[40]

The news, though, was promising. A breakdown of T&G intentions showed a 5:1 lead for Healey in the Northern branches, a 7:2 lead in Wales, and big advantages in Yorkshire and East and the Southern region. The left bloc of MPs had, fascinatingly, shown itself less than solid for Benn. Neil Kinnock, protégé of Foot, Education spokesman and rising talent, indicated that he would not be voting for him.[41] The notion of a 'soft left', people who saw nothing but trouble from exponential pursuit of the course followed since 1979, was materialising.

On 19 September, a ballot in NATSOPA (more printers) gave Healey 12,948 votes, twice the combined vote of Benn and Silkin. And on the same day, the Post Office Engineering Union under the notably sane leadership of Bryan Stanley, gave Healey 56,768 votes to fewer than 22,000 for the other two. Also on that busy 19th, Labour held another of its unnecessary meetings, 'a national rally' in Birmingham, a very Michael Footish undertaking which, in the party's masochistic way, also involved a four-mile march. People who go on four-mile marches to national rallies are not there for conversational stimulation. Healey, just returned from the civilities of the Soviet Union, later summed up the reactions: 'Hattersley bad time, Michael F. cheers, Orme dead silence, Heffer great cheers,' and of himself, 'Howled down by Bennites.'[42]

Healey would get a black mark for accusing Jonathan Lansman, Benn's 23-year-old and rather accomplished campaign aid, of running it from the floor. In fact he wasn't there. But the howling-down was real – and virulent. Healey's reaction at an NEC meeting a few days later was to suggest that 'since we financed these rallies, it just encouraged anti-Labour reaction and we should seriously consider whether it was worth having the rallies at all.'[43] Sensibly, though, he took Warburton's advice and made a full apology to Lansman.

Three voting elements were contributing to the outcome. The unions, with their 40 per cent holding in the business, claimed first attention. An MP was one vote and one 278th part of 30 per cent, a decent-sized union like NUPE was 600 votes. It was all remarkably like capitalism, capitalism as displayed during a contested take-over bid. Small investors would be courted, but first attention would focus on the building societies and pension funds, each with 3 and 4 per cent of the equity.

So NUPE was watched avidly. Today part of the public service union, UNISON, it represented cleaners, hospital porters, all sorts of unprivileged people. Benn, with his narrow majority among well-paid technicians and scientific staffs, looked to the bottom of the economic heap – with concern. As he would note on the day of the howling-down, 'The rumours that NUPE have gone bad on us are too strong to be disregarded.'[44] NUPE was still headed by Alan Fisher and Bernard Dix, gross offenders during the Winter of Discontent, men wilder and more extreme than Tony Benn at the high point of his enthusiasm. But NUPE had consulted its members by ballot. Whether the leadership would have accepted the result left wholly to itself cannot be guessed. But they were not left to themselves. A strong rumour developed, picked up first by Giles Radice, that Dix and Fisher planned to assert executive leadership over a ballot which could be called 'consultative'. 'We had lined up a legal application through a NUPE member to a judge in chambers to enforce the rules of NUPE. There was a press briefing to a major newspaper pointing to dirty work at the cross roads which nearly dropped Giles into a libel action. I said quite frankly that we feared a fiddle. It came out alright in the end, but we felt nervous enough to do that.'[45]

The outcome, when the union made the best of its virtue, was eloquent of the real state of play among the working class to which Tony Benn addressed his devotion. There was a disinclination at this stage to count chickens, but by D-Day, 28 September, Warburton's contacts inside NUPE had given him certain assurance and Healey felt able to write 'NUPE will vote for me.'[46]

But against this *The Times* would print on 22 September a headline: 'TGWU Puts Benn in Sight of Victory' – 'Short of a miracle, the union will cast its 1.25 million votes for Mr Benn.' Actually, under these rules and this arithmetic, it cast 1250. Their reporter described the delegation as being divided '21 for Benn, 12 against and 6 undecided'. It would add by way of editorial comment that 'It was incredible that the union should act against the wishes of its members. There was a real risk that Benn would be elected even though the PLP don't want him, the public don't want him and the rank-and-file membership of the Labour Party don't want him.'[47] What was in sight was the peremptory act of a union first consulting, then disregarding, its own membership. A consultation process did exist and had produced a view, but it had been the wrong view. As Alex Kitson explained: 'In the consultation, Denis Healey had attracted most support, but the Executive had balanced that verdict against Denis Healey's known opposition to the Union's position on withdrawal from the EEC and collective bargaining.'

The union executive, which in old, iron-handed, centralist style, made this resolve, had thirty-seven members, it was headed by Moss Evans and Alex Kitson and had four members also members of the Communist Party.

Although the British CP was dwindling apace and would, by the end of the decade, suffer its own fascinating split between 'Designers' and 'Tankies', it was not altogether bogey language to talk of CP influence. Boxing far above its weight in the unions, the Party was surprisingly influential at board level and, though bemused by the bubbling new Bennery, happy to throw a strategic handful of votes in its direction especially against so absolute an old enemy as Denis Healey.

Chris Mullin, briefly a Blair junior and an outstanding if under-used talent, then a Benn lieutenant, expressed fear that the Healey camp might exploit the situation. 'I imagine there will be an enormous cry of "foul play" in the hope of pressing a delay of the vote. Our view is that Mr Benn will win a majority even in the consultation process.'[48] Benn was opaque. 'The papers were full of attacks on the executive of the T&G for supporting me yesterday – "Votes hijacked" and all that. It's hard to know how to react. I refused to speak to the journalists and film crews waiting outside the front door.'[49]

A few days later, after arrival in Brighton for the Conference, he is musing about the conclusions of the computer of his youngest son, Joshua. 'Joshua was working on his computer and if the T&G and NUPE vote for me, then I'm home comfortably, even with forty abstentions and only 480 constituencies. If NUPE vote for Healey, but the T&G vote for me, I could just win if I could scrabble together a few more MPs and a few more constituencies . . .'[50] Back on the 22nd, he had taken the train to Leeds and a meeting in the great town hall. It was 'a fantastic meeting – with 2100 people inside and 2000 turned away'.[51] But it hardly compared with the vote of the Transport and General, now materialising, the biggest bloc in the hall – to be determined by thirty-nine delegates.

One blessing about Labour procedures was that they dealt with the unbearably big issues first – on the Sunday ahead of the debating – also before the election of the NEC. NUPE would be as good as their word. Their branches had backed Healey: the full 600,000 votes went to him. To his amusement, even the branch serving Benn's most sullen and resentful supporter, the MP, Reg Race,* had supported Denis, who later elaborately thanked him. '"Huh" he grunted, "lot of fucking IMG!"'[52]† The Transport and General followed its own rule, which was not to mandate but to leave the final decision to the delegation. Moss Evans, who had been seriously ill and had undergone an operation, was present but not active. The union, under continuous public attention and getting very bad publicity, acted defensively. The names of the four Communist Party members are not included on

---

* Lately fallen at Chesterfield as his successor.
† The International Marxist Group, a galactically challenged gathering to the left of everyone in sight and beyond prediction.

the delegation list, but close counsel was kept. It was everywhere understood that the union would be voting on the first ballot for John Silkin. It was Silkin's whole intention as a no-hope candidate to be a snapper-up of unconsidered trifles, if the T&G wedge can be so called. But smart calculations turned upon the second ballot. Healey himself succinctly records the message circulating in the brutalist block of the conference hall: 'False rumour TGWU would abstain.' David Warburton warned him against it. Never for a moment believing that this delegation would miss the chance to promote Benn, he wrote them off. Asked by Healey for an overall estimate, Warburton said that the second ballot would be almost literally 50:50.[53]

False the rumour was. The delegation, headed by Alex Kitson, cast their vote for Benn, the largest group of votes cast by anybody. The resolving of victory had now become indeed 'a scrabbling for a few spare votes'. And Warburton's judgement would be correspondingly true. The outcome of the first ballot, calculated in terms of percentages of votes which the chief teller, Danny Mangham, read out, was:

First ballot	Constituency parties	Trade unions	MPs	Totals
Tony Benn	23.483	6.410	6.734	36.627
Denis Healey	5.367	24.696	15.306	45.369
John Silkin	1.150	8.894	7.959	18.003

The numbers fed into Joshua Benn's computer had produced very similar conclusions, a credit to the staffwork of the camp, but for both Healey and Benn they were just fractionally above what had been announced.

While the Conference, running two and a half hours beyond normal adjournment time, debated South Africa – frequent Labour therapy – and Benn received two messages that he had won on the second ballot, though not from Joshua who now had Healey ahead on 51.3 to 48.7 per cent,[54] the real second ballot took place, and after a fraternal address was announced at 8.30 p.m. by Danny Mangham thus:

Second ballot	Constituency parties	Trade unions	MPs
Tony Benn	24.327	15.006	10.241
Denis Healey	5.673	24.994	19.759

This translated, after the arithmetic, into final totals of Benn 49.574, Healey 50.426.

The present writer heard the result relayed into the press room and chanced to be standing close to Edna Healey. A great buzz went up at the closeness of the score. She said, so that everyone immediately around could hear, 'Denis has won. Nothing else matters.' She was exactly right. So were the cameramen who pursued Tony Benn into a fish restaurant, only to be begged by Chris Mullin to leave him alone. Oddly considerate, they went instead and found the Healey party in the less proletarian premises of The Old Ship* drinking champagne![55] Seeking Benn first they recognised a prophetic order. This was the high-water mark of the left-wing tide. Two days later a number of leftists would stumble: Norman Atkinson defeated by Eric Varley for the Treasurership, Renée Short, Margaret Beckett, then in one of her left-wing phases, and Charlie Kelly all voted off the NEC. 'A disaster for us,' wrote Benn. There would be another disaster a year later as Forward Labour did its work in the unions.

The Benn people would understandably mutter about later defectors to the SDP who stayed to support Healey. But this was also a very bad result for the SDP. Notoriously, political pennies drop in agonised slow motion. The message that Labour had passed the crisis of the fever would not be apparent for a long time yet. There would be more by-elections to lose, more bad polls. But the dam-break, the detonation to send another seventy or eighty MPs across the floor and turn off the funds and affiliation of the Engineers followed by who knows who else, did not follow, would not now follow. The Labour Party would come limping through.

Healey had won by a sub-percentage, but he had won. And though Benn would stress his amazement and pleasure at having come so far, 'a staggering result',[56] his performance, stripped of its undemocratic element, was altogether less impressive. The T&G casting a vote as Ernie Bevin or Arthur Deakin would have cast it, but in direct defiance of the vote taken among its members, and of public wishes, had brought him thrillingly close. But without this crude contradiction of the membership, his performance amounted to a heavy majority in constituency parties notoriously contracted, plus a quarter of MPs and 15 per cent of union votes.

Two things were cumulatively crucial to Benn's defeat that day. The first was the mobilisation of a string of very small unions, minor craft unions in textiles and engineering, who usually didn't bother to vote and weren't bothered by candidates; blast-furnace-men, carpet weavers, loom overlookers, pattern-makers. Forward Labour circulated them and pulled in most to vote for Healey. Second and most ironical was the failure to support Benn on the second vote of thirty-seven members of the Tribune Group. Neil Kinnock

---

* A delightful hotel favoured historically by the Labour right, notably ETU, POEU and G&M men.

would be the most remarked, also Stanley Orme, Martin O'Neill, Jeff Rooker, Joe Ashton and Tom Pendry. Among the abstainers was Laurie Pavitt, who had spoken of the misery of creeping back to his militant constituency party. John Silkin had come in tremendously convenient. It was acceptable with a left-wing constituency party to vote for this ostensible leftist. It was, in the style of legal fictions, a political fiction. There was a double irony here. Back at Wembley, the left had wanted a maximum union vote and had got it by accident. Union opinion, where consulted, would be impressively hostile to Tony Benn. But the key finally turned against him would be parliamentary: the irrelevant, to-be-swept-away dross of MPs who had been penned in for the floor's contempt like the French nobility in 1789. Thus did the whirligig of time bring in his abstentions.

THE LONG DEFILE

Such had been the Labour Party's preoccupation with the Labour Party that it was not well equipped to emerge from Brighton 1982 and contemplate a Conservative government, by-elections, the SDP and, within six months, the Falklands conflict. While Labour had been engaged with the last writhing consequences of that 'useful day and historic decision taken collectively', the Liberals had held a public meeting at the fringe of their conference in Llandudno. At the Pier Pavilion the leadership of the SDP had come together with David Steel for the Liberals in a joint meeting presaging an alliance or Alliance. Labour was also faced with the incapacity of Michael Foot to lead a serious political party.

Nothing was resolved. The Left held power, but were losing it. In a year's time they would actually lose control of the NEC, but for the interim, they could make policy and commitments to a defence policy close to unilateralism when a poll showed Labour voters 59:33 per cent opposed to it, the sort of affront which too much regard for the wishes of activists is liable to yield. The Parliamentary Party was depressed, kicked about and resentful. Benn accused them, especially over membership of Europe, of being unable to come to terms with the fact 'that there has been a clear decision reached by Party Conference and the TUC on Europe.'

If that was characteristic Benn at this time, as typical would be the feeble good sense of Foot's reply: 'You know, you've got to be careful about the PLP. They've got a useful job to do.'[1] Within a day of that conversation, on 22 October, the by-election at Croydon North West showed a swing of 29.55 to the first and triumphant contesting Alliance candidate with Labour's vote down from 40 to 26 per cent.[2]

Like so much of what was happening, it lay beyond the reconfirmed deputy leader's power to do much about it. 'Down to Croydon in rain',[3] 'wrote NS article' and 'Saw Rumanian Foreign Secretary'[4] is the best of it, culminating in 'Stayed up late to watch our defeat at Croydon.'[5]

But Healey didn't pine. Richard Heller gave a contemporary account of his life in opposition so vivid and close to nature as to be worth quoting at some length. For Heller, Healey was 'The Man':

Some heavy steps in the corridor. The door crashes open. Some hummed vaudeville music on a rising beat: 'Yah Dah-de Dah-Dah – DAH.' Arms flung aloft to greet the applause for the *Star* . . . The Man moves to his desk. The huge EIIR briefcase thuds down beside the stack of mail.

'I was brilliant on TV last night.'

'You were rude and omniscient as usual.'

'I called Howe a Sado-monetarist' . . . He says in a faraway voice, 'That goes *there*, that goes *here*, that I'm going to keep in my file. At length he achieves harmony . . . He hands over a pile of newspaper cuttings. He has razored all the English morning national papers, ten journals, three foreign papers, two financial bulletins and yesterday's Hansard. There are already three full filing cabinets, Afghanistan to Zimbabwe in permanent suspense, one for domestic, one for the party. This contains two drawers labelled 'Goodies' and an equal number labelled 'Baddies' . . . 'What have I got today? . . . lunch for the King of G—PM's Questions. Then I want to dictate to Harriet Shackman. Then I've got this new Ambassador. The foreign affairs team. Then I've got to see Bugalugs.'

'Bugalugs?'

'Francis Pym [the Foreign Secretary].'

He peers intently at the next entry. 'It says Dracula.'

I look at my own diary. 'That's Dr Acola, chairman in exile of the N— Liberation Front.'

He makes a vampire face. The telephone rings. He answers as a Chinese laundry. 'Hah–lo–er. No. He not here. This steam plessing loom.' Then he puts the caller out of his misery. 'Yes. It is me. You could tell by the brows.' He listens and repeats for my benefit, 'Statement on land drainage in Wales. I can hardly wait.' He shuts his eyes.

'How many votes have we got tonight?'

'Several. They're trying to push through a lot of clauses.'

'I have to write a major speech for that bloody institute. I'll fit it in somehow when we're not voting.' He opens his eyes towards heaven. Palms upraised, he says passionately, 'What a life! What a life, eh?' Then, complacently, 'Rotten really.'

I indicate assent.

'Can you check a number of things? When did I last go to Cheshire and what did I do for Cheshire when we were in office? Remind me what were Carter's proposals for deep cuts in nuclear weapons. Can you get some stuff on the Health Service dispute? Oh and can you look into the sea?'

'The sea?'

'The Law of the Sea.' . . . [Later he dictates letters.] 'He's a twerp; she's forgotten what we did in office; they're a bunch of baddies.' When he gets to the constituency letters, his commentary becomes more detailed. At one letter he stops dead and gives the history of the family concerned for the last twenty-five years . . . [With another letter] beaming, he dictates, 'Dear Mr —, I was sorry to hear about your difficulties, but I am afraid I cannot help you since your MP is in fact Mr —, and I have sent your letter on to him. Heh-heh-heh.'

In due course, after a day doing many things like seeing the Foreign Secretary, and drawing animals on Richard's draft of a reply to a little girl who has sent him a letter with animals drawn on it, he greets the newly arrived Dr Acola.

The Man opens with his favourite conversation-killer: 'Now then, what did you want to tell me?'

Dr Acola wants to tell him quite a bit about the unity of democratic and progressive forces advancing on a broad front and of the iniquities of something called the Popular Movement for the Liberation of N—. The Man writes and writes on a pad. I fantasise what will happen to him at midnight? I look for a cross. At length he leaves . . . I glimpse The Man's notepad. It contains facts about N— and caricatures of vampires.

The Man stretches. 'Bloody Hell. I'm tired.' The phone rings. It is his wife. I can tell because he puts on the strangulated German voice. Then he sighs and says in a normal voice that he cannot come home, there is a series of votes, between which he will see people and write a major speech . . . I hear him say, 'I am now going to show my face in the tea room in a suggestive manner' and then 'I know . . . rotten life really.'[6]

But not all aspects of foreign affairs were as remote as the doings of Dr Acola. The really bad news – for Labour, for the Alliance – was the invasion of the Falkland Islands by the forces of General Leopoldo Galtieri. The reasons why the Argentinian military junta thought this was a possible undertaking make complex history. Conservative neglect of the defence they talked about, in pursuit of the cuts they were making, a garrison of eighty men, withdrawal of the frigate discouraging invasion, the long tease of a sale and lease-back proposal handled by an envoy, Nicholas Ridley, well known for his contempt for the islanders and the appearance in *The Times* of a piece, surely briefed, headed

'These Paltry Islands', all contributed. And on the morning of 2 April 1982, it looked as though they might cook the goose of Mrs Margaret Thatcher. What followed was a sort of justifiable Suez and, more to the point, a successful Suez. Over the prolonged period of journey out and short, quite bloody conflict, the air was full of patriotic enthusiasm tempered by dread of a single French-made missile killing a thousand troops.

The soldiers and sailors were very brave, but despite dreadful events like the sinking of HMS *Coventry*, the total of British deaths was kept below the point at which heroic bubbles burst. From this, with its thanksgiving service in St Paul's, Mrs Thatcher, who had struck an attitude which suited her, emerged resplendent, dug out of a hole of her own digging to enter the political rocket which was duly launched.

Michael Foot was, quaintly, a very suitable leader. The old radical, unlike most of his party, liked small wars. He would be gung-ho in the Gulf and more ardent yet to revenge the bombardment by the Serbs of Dubrovnik, where he had spent holidays. The man content with the bombing of Belgrade could have no problems over the Falkland Islands. Hazlitt would have been ashamed of him.

By a nice irony, Denis Healey and Tony Benn were in clear, if muted accord in disliking the idea of a shooting war, Benn from anti-militarist convictions, Healey from too shrewd a knowledge of what might happen if the risk were miscalculated. And since eleven of twenty-five bombs hitting British ships failed to explode, he had a point. Though one footnote to the war would be the important part played by aircraft carriers, or rather the through-deck cruisers which had replaced the larger ships Healey had cut out in the 1960s. The Falklands War was, however, one which no sailor, soldier or military technician would have foreseen and it had taken, not his economies, but those of Mrs Thatcher and her Defence Secretary John Nott, to make it possible.

But for a long period of preparation, belief that there would actually be that sort of war, with dead bodies in the water, was not strong. The expectations were for a bluffing match for which Britain's military quality was flawed by distance and lack of air cover. The odds were either that the US would lean on Argentina in our interests, or that the risk would show so steep that through one or other peace 'initiative', Britain would effect a climb-down which would be called something else. In the long meantime, the essential thing for Healey was to stop the left from pre-empting defeat, not least with calls for evacuation of the islands. Eric Heffer tried this on the NEC and Healey, who had hurried back from Greece, stopped him. 'Incredibly busy ... P[arty] C[ommittee] to box Heffer in on Falklands.'[7] Laudibly but calamitously, Heffer had wanted to 'ensure the safety and evacuation of the people of the Falklands ... and believes it is not in the best interests of the country to allow a jingoistic militaristic frame of mind to develop . . .' The one sure thing to emerge from April–June 1982 was that a jingoistic, militaristic frame of mind developed like wildfire, to the enormous career advantage of Mrs Margaret Thatcher.

Healey and Foot could see this and proposed a resolution saying that, when negotiations were entered into with a dictator, 'they must be based on a position of strength and that the British forces now sailing towards the Falkland Islands must be used to lead the Argentinian Government to an honourable settlement which has the support of the Falkland Islanders.'[8] Denis amused himself by quoting the book to which Michael Foot had contributed forty years before, *Guilty Men*, on the evils of appeasement. He also drew an essential distinction with the case of Suez. 'That had been undertaken in defence of property; this time it would be human rights.'[9] During the long wrangle, Joan Lestor, a nice woman from the soft left, asked Denis if he would use force and was told he would. A compromise resolution came down in favour of a position for strength and against jingoism, which on *that* NEC, was a good result.

But in the first week of a ten-week campaign, with ships still being assembled, politics seemed more real than war. Many weeks later Edward Heath would advise the Commons that the flotilla, having gone so far and proved its point, should now turn round. Thatcher, it was reckoned, would not survive climb-down. Her party, avid for action, had been at her throat during the first day's debate. Bonny fighter she was, there was nothing else she very well could be. And if military advice had finally been that an assault without air cover was suicidal, or if President Reagan's adviser, Jeanne Kirkpatrick, had carried the day, valuing the Argentinian regime – 'authoritarian not totalitarian' – above Her Majesty's Government, the Thatcher ministry would probably have fallen.

The difficulty was to stop the party's still leftish Executive from doing anything silly. So, as ships approached the South Atlantic islands, Healey records: 'NEC 10 to 3.30! ploughing through policy document. I blocked appalling Reagan letter'[10] or as Tony Benn put it, 'I moved an amendment to Michael's motion, but I was defeated by 14 to 9. Michael and Denis's motion – 100 per cent pro-Mrs Thatcher, even talking about 'our country' rather than 'the British government' – was carried by 15 to 9.'[11]

The attitude of Benn and the Left was not unreasonable. The crazy nationalism which had snatched the islands would end on 15 June with a thousand Argentinian and two hundred and fifty British soldiers and sailors dead, what is called an acceptable level. And ugly episodes like the sinking of the *Belgrano* never explained away, helped accomplish the security of 1800 islanders. Healey's private distaste for the consequent Union Jack triumphalism would surface a year later during the election campaign when he let slip the phrase about 'This woman who glories in slaughter'. But he and Foot had prevented the Labour Party from a stand which in the Mafeking mood of mid-1982 might have sunk it yet lower than it would soon go. It was an occasion for making the best of things and there would be plenty more of those.

Two forces would now make for major Labour defeat, the Falklands and the existence as a serious force of the Social Democrats. In developments after the Llandudno public accord, that party would stand, in modified harmony with the Liberals, under a name orotund and forgettable, the 'Social Democratic and Liberal Alliance'. The immediate concern of the Labour leadership was that this Alliance should not achieve a momentum which might lead to their taking Labour's place.

As things stood, Labour, shaken to its roots, the incremental recovery of moderate strength on the NEC badly undervalued, groups like the Militant Tendency virulently active, the loss of many highly educated people to the SDP and sustained hostile coverage in the press, ran great risks. There would be a period of genuine three-party politics. And though steadily ahead of the Tories for most of the explosive first two years of the Thatcher government, Labour could on Conservative recovery, have slipped into a spiral of rejection.

Public opinion polls show the Alliance across the last three quarters of 1981 rising from 27.7 per cent to 28.6 to 42.1, while Labour support, steady for the first two of these periods (37.8 then 38.7 per cent), falls after the great contest to 28.9 per cent against a frightening 42.1 for the Alliance. Labour would eventually regain a lead. But anxiety about the SDP would be a factor for two general elections. Meanwhile the Conservatives, solidly behind Labour across 1981, moved very close in the last quarter of that year, the time of the great Alliance surge. Then lifted by South Atlantic breezes, they took flight. Standing at 30.9 in the opinion polls January–March 1982, they moved in the next quarter to 44.4 per cent.[12] Confidence was perfectly voiced even before the final victory, by one Christopher Murphy MP, who stated that 'the Union Jack was flying again, not just as a symbol of sovereignty but as frontline banner for freedom, justice and democracy.'[13] Eric Heffer had been entirely right to fear jingoistic militarism.

From that time onwards, Labour no longer competed for victory in the next election. With things as bleak as such numbers showed them, with the left strategy having created a third party biting deep into Labour's side, desperate remedies grew attractive.

One was to make a clear stand against the militant group. They had been effective infiltrators in constituency parties, had helped select bizarre candidates in by-elections where Labour suffered perfect humiliation. They were a wholly autonomous, systematically disloyal group punching above their weight, punching, moreover, the party to which they nominally belonged. And there was now a report from the National Agent giving chapter and verse. Getting rid of them would be pleasure as well as duty, but there were good and bad ways of doing it. The means favoured on the NEC was a register of the supposed 7000 'supporters of the Tendency' – they acknowledged no membership.

Richard Heller saw this as an example of Foot's wayward leadership. The idea came from the Hughes–Hayward report of party officials. It was, he said, 'a damn silly idea, unconstitutional, unlawful, and it won Militant all sorts of friends and allies. But Michael collared the report at the start without consulting anyone, least of all Denis, and suddenly announced what a good idea it was. He never considered the arguments or asked what anyone else thought. But we, the good guys, had to go along with what he said.'[14] Denis was stuck with that, but he noted the shrewd judgement of Neil Kinnock who, as leader, would famously drive them out of the door. 'If we attack Militant we give them allies. We must get rid of some leaders of Militant rather than the 7000.'[15] In fact, with union backing, the register was established and wholly ineffective.

To Healey's great personal dismay, recovery of the NEC at Conference was offset by the carrying of a pure unilateralist motion from SOGAT. Calling also for the removal of all American bases, it passed in the absent-minded way of a Conference whose votes had just decimated the left on the NEC, passed moreover by a two-thirds majority, something to put it automatically into Labour's programme. Benn thought that Foot's fear of Healey resigning would nevertheless keep it out.

Metaphors about moving staircases and ancient Greeks trundling rocks up inclines have been used more than once, but the sheer genius of the institutional Labour Party in handing deadly weapons to its enemies before blaming a press it has fed with blood, beggared belief. But though Foot would, in fact, wave the unilateralist motion through when the manifesto was produced, Healey was not going to resign. He had slogged on before and he would slog on again.

The other option was a change of leadership. Michael Foot had, from the start, made only a negative impact. After a series of relaxed media and Commons performances, Healey was now much better known as a public person. He might not actually win the election, but on the evidence, he would leave them uncrushed and credible. In Australia, the local Labour Party's replacement of the unimpactive Bill Hayden with the loud-check personality of Bob Hawke would win it the first of several elections. The possibility of Foot's withdrawal in favour of Healey was mooted, taken seriously, Healey believes, by Foot himself. A dreadful by-election at Bermondsey involving Peter Tatchell, not then a gay campaigner (though evilly sniped at), more of an orthodox far-leftist, lost a chunk of working-class south London in a way beyond crediting: a majority of 12,000 in a smallish seat turned it into an Alliance one of 9000.

At that point, Foot started to receive messages from people in marginal seats dropping hints. He enjoyed, though, the anxious solicitude of the Conservatives. But Richard Heller does not trust either Foot's judgement or his goodwill.

Michael had a great belief in his own leadership and, rather like Attlee in respect of Herbert Morrison, he was determined to stay on so that Denis could not succeed. It was not animus against Denis, but he thought, 'It's my mission to represent this strand of the Labour Party and its beliefs and whatever it does to the party, I'm going to stay to embody them.' He ran to prevent Denis becoming leader. He stayed on to prevent Denis becoming leader. He was never, despite lots of initiatives, going to resign to make Denis leader.[16]

Margaret Thatcher had not, like Lord Salisbury, called a khaki election to cash in on military victory. It was a little too obvious, and unlike Salisbury, she had been furiously unpopular until very recently. Besides, the popularity of the Alliance, though dimmed by drums and trumpets, had been potent. Conservatives who had done their arithmetic, wanted a Labour recovery. The Alliance, though launched by Labour defections and taking Labour votes, looked more likely to take Conservative seats. And fighting an election against a doomed and written-off Opposition leader was not something to let slip.

Something was needed to steady Labour's shattered nerves and in the by-election at Darlington it was found. The death of Edward Fletcher, a stolid, leftish backbencher, threw open a swing seat usually electing a candidate from the winning side. Labour's choice of a delightful old fox of a former town councillor, Oswald O'Brien, who knew local politics backwards and the Alliance's smart, thoughtless picking of a regional TV presenter whose heroic ignorance would be exposed a week into the campaign, settled things. On 24 March, Labour won Darlington, the very worst thing they could have done. On a huge poll, 80 per cent, they took the seat by 2 percentage points over the Conservatives with the Alliance down to 10 per cent.[17] Healey had of course gone to the Durham railway and engineering town to speak for and 'chat with candidate, nice Ossie O'Brien'.[18] But in his PA's view, 'If we had lost Darlington Denis would have become leader and the election itself would have become a respectable contest.'[19]

An Alliance victory would have been the spur to a Labour coup, perhaps a coup by consent, with Foot recognising the impossibility of his position and Healey by emergency procedures, becoming leader. A poll taken at the start of the election would show 50 per cent of voters satisfied with Thatcher (not something which would last) and 19 per cent satisfied with Foot. One MORI poll which on 9 May would appear on *Panorama,* saw a switch from Foot to Healey converting a Conservative lead of 9 per cent to zero. Yet though Labour were only ever going to do badly in that election Pelion would be piled on Ossa in the form of a manifesto imposed by Foot very much in the take-it-or-leave-it spirit of Callaghan in 1979.

But whereas Jim Callaghan had tried to put Labour before the voters without embarrassing policies which they might not actually like, Foot with a maximum of incompetence and irrelevance, went the distance in a clumsily drafted call for huge increases in public spending, a price commission empowered for statutory controls, re-nationalisation of privatised industry, a 50 per cent rise in local authority housing expenditure, all that and a defence policy just reclaimed by Healey from total unilateralism. The phrase now quoted to death about 'the longest suicide note ever penned' was fair comment. Healey's only part in all this was to insist on promises to co-operate with NATO allies on defence spending and to put Polaris on the table for disarmament negotiation rather than remove it at once as a gesture of peace and love.* Overall, Foot's approach to the general election was a technicolour nightmare.

The Conservatives started ahead when the election campaign began in the second week of May, but they were ahead of Labour with the Alliance trailing. The Darlington effect had been felt, its leaders were on uneasy terms with each other; and Roy Jenkins, though this was not appreciated, was quite seriously ill with a debilitating hypothyroid complaint.† There was a squeeze to be effected if Labour were capable of it.

That was an assumption too far. Foot was horribly vulnerable to a press which Aneurin Bevan twenty-five years before, when it was much nicer, had called 'the most prostituted in the world'. But the man who says, quoting Shakespeare inaptly, 'Out of our way I say. You do assist the storm. That's what we say to the Tories. Out of our way'[21] is going to suffer.

Healey's position on defence was still acutely embarrassing. Apart from the cancellation of Trident, an excellent idea, he didn't actually agree with it. Putting Polaris, that sensible if elderly vehicle, up for negotiation did not for him mean scrapping it if negotiation failed. The manifesto – 'within the lifetime of the parliament' – did. He said, specifically invoking a trade union view of negotiations, 'We don't get rid of it unless the Russians cut their forces aimed at us.' Silkin directly contradicted him. Neither Foot, rushing the manifesto through Shadow Cabinet in an hour, nor Silkin, had any appreciation that whatever the technical arguments, people wanted to hear that we were doing something to defend ourselves and that charges of appeasement and weakness, however spurious, won votes.

The issue burned more fiercely as James Callaghan made a spoiling intervention. He stated at a meeting in Cardiff that 'The principal significance of nuclear weapons is political' and that unilateralism was deeply unpopular with voters. It was all true, but profoundly unhelpful; nuclear weapons were safe with Mrs Thatcher[22] who was not going to lose this election. The speech

---

* Healey was happy about one thing in the general lunge at defence – disengagement from Trident. This was the exponentially profligate development from the Chevaline which Callaghan had improperly smuggled through.[20]
† Hashimoto's thyroiditis.

was not the treachery which Eric Heffer and Alex Kitson naturally called it, but made in the middle of an election where Labour were trying to avoid humiliation and push back a third party, it was a blow struck against friends like Healey who were trying to hold the party together as a national force. It was not treachery, more like what passing Americans call friendly fire.

The advice which Healey gave at the upper echelon meeting (Shadow Cabinet plus NEC) went beyond his usual concerns, stressing the threats to civil liberties in the new Police Bill and the weakening of Citizens Advice Bureaux – 'amazing for Denis Healey', wrote Benn. Healey stressed the need for trade union restraint. 'The unions must accept responsibilities that go with the rights that the Labour manifesto would give them. For example, they have got to be concerned about the unemployed, the old, children, the sick. We will need a social wage – which will mean a smaller pay packet for some.'[23] Here, thought Tony Benn, was Healey already harking back to the old pay policy of earlier years which led to such a disaster. 'It's significant that the right-wing on the parliamentary side feel confident enough to say that.' So they did, but thanks to Foot's non-grasp of detail and precipitation of things, the unread manifesto could contain statutory powers for price control alone.

Healey tried hard to be fair and loyal. His first comment of the campaign, before he got on the road, would be: 'Watched Michael Foot do quite well on *Panorama*,' followed just as fairly by 'Campaign committee not v. useful'[24] and 'Short useless PLP.'[25] Then, leaving the committee pulling in different directions, he went with Edna down to Cardiff for the day, for a series of broadcasts and articles. The entry is always 'Wrote article for XYZ'. Though he had the services of Tom Burlison and Alan Donnelly as trail managers for much of the time, no office task force produced his speeches or what he would say in a party political broadcast. On the Monday he 'Scribbled PPB piece, at 6 recorded at studio'. That day, as on many others, he took the party's press conference at 9 a.m. and in the evening he would do *Newsnight*, complaining that in between, his visit to Leeds had been wasted with calls at empty factories.

As at earlier elections, the logistics were terrible: out of London, back to London, out again! Having done a day each in Cardiff and Leeds, he was off next to West Bromwich where appearing for Betty Boothroyd, he at least enjoyed himself, 'V. good meeting,' and did general walking about before being allowed to sleep in the Midland Hotel. He went with Hattersley to Bradford, then back to Leeds before sweeping back to London to write a piece for the *News of the World* on defence.[26] The 19th was Thursday so after recording for TV with Robert Kee, Healey was in Peterborough: interviews, listening to a reply by Norman Tebbit to his own earlier attack, going round a mail order firm, meeting Asians and, more surprisingly, meeting Roy Jenkins before being taken by Peter Jenkins 'to Cambridge in awful weather' for 'excellent meeting' then 'run to Stevenage' where he spoke for another candidate.[27]

His itinerary for the next few days alone – the idea that election campaigns last for three weeks is theoretical – took him to Leicester: three candidates, meeting Ugandan Asians, then Northampton and 'v. slow train to London' (20 May), a 'campaign committee rather badly run by Michael', a slow journey to Edmonton, Enfield, then Braintree and 'afternoon off working' before a meeting in Stepney Green for, of all people, Ian Mikardo, 'Not full because of Cup Final.'

He resumed next day with another press conference before flying to Edinburgh and another one, looked after there by Helen Liddell, now Secretary of State, then Stirling, 'good walkabout', an interview for the US with the legendary Walter Cronkite, then a flight to Newcastle for, among others, Nick Brown – the hungry generation, now in office, was getting Denis's best attentions.

After the meetings he was given a very decent dinner by the Geordies – 'Turbot and soufflé glace, cointreau, but far too late – dog tired. Stayed at County Hotel' (23 May); still in Newcastle – 'excellent walk around in shopping centre', then Wallsend for Ted Garrett, Sunderland – 'good walkabout' where he seems to have sung 'Torn a Sorrento' to some Italian workers – always a risk with Healey – Thornaby-on-Tees for an old people's home, a Radio One phone-in from Stockton town hall – 'V. nice Mayor' (Stockton was Bill Rodgers's constituency and would be taken by the Labour candidate, Frank Cook) (24 May). York for the difficult and rather tragic Alex Lyon who would also lose, occupied half a day before a train back to London where he learned of the Callaghan speech (25 May).[28]

He dealt with this as best anyone could, with a casual kick on the shins in an interview with Robin Day: 'Went very well.' Before setting off for Dover and Sealink staff and the NUM with its (then) two local pits, and an evening meeting at Rochester and back to London; Friday was 'Campaign Committee shambles', 'took good press conf. with Hattersley . . . heavy day in London . . . hard left in Kilburn . . . luxury buffet' at the ASTMS office in Hampstead, then Wood Green, 'with awful leftist – excellent meeting' before 'wasted time walking round Ilford' and a large meeting for Essex members (27 May).

After a Saturday in Dartford and the south-east London area and a Sunday worrying about his mother Win, indomitable but now very frail, he returned to find the campaign committee insistent that he and Roy Hattersley should take a higher profile. Next he took off to Lancashire – Nelson – 'good meeting but aged pessimists', after which another snap of the elastic band brought him back to London to record a party political (30 May). Thursday was LBC, a major radio station of the day, then North Wales, beautiful, interminable and quite irrelevant: 'Wrexham, race to Caernarfon, Betws-y-Coed 2½ hours, 1½ hours late, lovely country . . . excellent meeting for Bob Williams' (31 May).[29] This fell at the time of a burst of quite false press rumours that there had been a secret coup and that Denis had become *de facto* leader.

It was all very well and in its exhausting way, enjoyable. But Labour had begun the election with 36 per cent support in the polls and the Alliance with 20 per cent, not enough to do *well* against the Conservatives but enough to demonstrate that second place and renewed challenge were secure. Instead a horrible convergence was taking place. A private quarrel was taking place among the SDP, a party of highly strung people given to fretting, on account of Jenkins's debilitation. On top of which the Association of Liberal Councillors, a faction to themselves, in eccentric particularist hands resentful of the new links, put out a leaflet separating SDP and Liberal policies. It was all evidence of the Alliance schizophrenia which would lead to later self-immolation. And in the 1983 election it didn't matter a bit!

Denis's own contribution to Labour's trouble, with the remark about Mrs Thatcher glorying in slaughter, came at the start of June. But against this, he had spent his time modifying the manifesto message in the direction of continuing nuclear defence. It enraged the left, but the private polls told Labour that 'most people did not trust the party to defend the country'.[30] They also, as Heller recalls, told the party a week into the campaign that the replacement of Foot by Healey, still technically possible, would be worth 7 percentage points. And he recalls a campaign committee meeting at which 'no one had the bottle to say that the problem is the leader'.[31] He was a voice against the full unilateralist commitment which, with all voters polled opposing unilateralism by a margin of 77:16 and Labour voters nearly two to one against,[32] was just as well. The gaffe – he said later he had meant 'glories in conflict', true enough – was a silly thing to say, though it expressed a former soldier's dislike of the press/Thatcher 'Our Boys – Bash the Argies' celebration of war. She had, after all, quarrelled with the Archbishop of Canterbury for remembering the Argentinian dead at the public service. But it was not a major factor in an election going wrong on all fronts. The day after, Healey recorded 'awful press conference'[33] and soldiered on.

Foot was making the central mistake, to be followed by Neil Kinnock at Sheffield in 1992, of valuing speeches made to the faithful in however impressive numbers above making them to voters. The ardour of great loyal crowds in large halls created false confidence, loosened inhibition and put stress on the exultant language of leader and activists, priest and congregation. The Alliance panicked unnecessarily but did so in private, Foot's Labour Party maintained a serene public complacency in the teeth of crying evidence. The present writer heard Michael Foot, ironically at Darlington, in a great oration, storming on at alliterative but unenlightening length, about the evils of 'Thatcher–Tebbit Toryism'. The hall was packed, the response rapturous. But it was inward-directed politics aimed at the faithful. And the faithful were shrinking.

Healey would make his own judgement three months after the election in a report to the NEC. The election, he thought, had been lost 'in the three years which preceded it'. During that time, the party 'had acquired a highly unfavourable public image, based on disunity, extremism, crankiness and general unfitness to govern'.[34] Labour had regained a respectable second place well ahead of the Alliance in the months before the election. But the contest had been a sort of exhibition match, displaying an impression of oddity, extremism, even absurdity. Healey did a last *allegro energico:* Slough, Ealing, Manchester, Worsley, 'Balls-up at Horwich,' Bolton, Bury and his own Leeds East, followed by TV (with Robert Kee again), the campaign committee, the press conference, a flight to Barrow, then Carlisle – 'Excellent meeting with Ron Lewis – ovation' and flight back to London. On the Tuesday before Polling Day, it was press conference, Halifax, Huddersfield, Dewsbury, Batley and major TV (*First Tuesday* with Geoffrey Howe) and a final two days in the constituency.

When, on 9 June, the great axe fell, it killed. The Conservatives emerged with 397 seats, up from 339 in 1979. The Alliance had a mere 23 (17 Liberal, 6 SDP) against 11 Liberal previously. Labour had 209 against 269 at the last election. But the percentage figures were what mattered. Labour's 209 seats overstated its percentage support – 27.6 per cent – while the absurdly under-represented Alliance had 25.4 per cent of the vote. And in numbers, Labour were down from 11.5 to 8.5 million while the Alliance stood at 7.9 million. The government party of 1974–9 had narrowly escaped coming third. The experiment was over. The battles lost inside the party since 1979 had ensured a battle calamitously lost in the country in 1983.

Amid the ruins, there was no useful role for Foot. Though 'Quite characteristically, he broke a promise to inform Denis in advance when he intended to go. He announced it for Clive Jenkins at ASTMS without telling Denis in advance. There were a lot of occasions when perhaps through incompetence he didn't keep his promise.'[35] It was clear at once, short of a pending statement, that Foot would give up the leadership. It was perfectly possible now for Healey to have put his hand up. Though he knew about the bright talk of skipping a generation, had he asked, refusal would have been almost impossible. Labour, though it fights like cats, is full of sentiment. Healey had answered defeat with loyalty and good service. He had shone in parliament even more than in his drier ministerial years. He was, and would remain, very popular in the country.

He gave it thought and telephoned David Warburton to discuss things. The reply was that the union man would support him in every way, as he had during the deputyship contest. But he thought it only right to consider both his age and the state of the party. Healey would be seventy or just short at the next election and, frankly, Warburton didn't think there was any chance of Labour winning it. Healey thanked him for being honest, adding, 'That is the conclusion I am coming to.'[36] There was a similar message from Barry Jones: 'Better opt out quietly.'[37] And he briefed John Cole accordingly, observing on the same day 'All fairly safe for Kinnock and Hattersley'.[38] To that end he would advise Peter Shore also to stay out. By the sixteenth, his diary records him 'writing NoW article to help Hattersley.'[39] It is not indulgent to regard that laconic usefulness to someone else as typical.

He would have been doomed to re-enact Michael Foot's melancholy journey, leading a wounded party in his late sixties with, moreover, the younger men doing mental arithmetic and clucking tongues over any little slip. So he announced that he would not be standing, made graceful way for the skipping generation and applauded when 'the Dream Ticket' of Kinnock and Roy Hattersley appeared at the end of an unnervingly polite contest, to take the stand for photographers, each man wearing a buttonhole-rose and 'looking', said Michael White of the *Guardian*, 'for all the world like a gay wedding'.

Too often, the latter part of a great political career – Macmillan, Heath, Callaghan and supremely Thatcher – is marked with resentful disloyalties to successors who are second-guessed and smiled over, and in the Thatcher–Major relationship, crazily plotted against. Some politicians go dysfunctional and turn clean against the party which failed them, George Brown is a sad example. Healey continued what he had always been, a good Labour man, not tactful, not muffled, but reliably a friend to the current leadership. Continuing as Foreign Affairs spokesman for Neil Kinnock did, of course, keep him on the seminar and conference circuit, the foreign visits, academic gatherings and other pleasantnesses. Though only Healey, that complete academic manqué, as a civil servant had called him, would so much have wanted such things. But he was also being invaluable to Neil Kinnock. A nice man, sensible but desperately inexperienced and always liable to a touch of the junior Michael Foots, the new leader needed and got a public uncle, someone from the generation which had been skipped who would add weight to the experimental and uncertain Opposition.

No longer on the NEC, something which went *ex officio* with what was now Hattersley's deputy leadership, Healey was to be a willing campaigner and, by a delicate twist of fate, found as one of his earliest duties the rendering of assistance to Tony Benn. Benn's Bristol seat had been carved by the Boundary Commission, leaving him defending and losing a marginal. Eric Varley, offered the management of Coalite, had accepted and left, creating a by-election in Chesterfield where, in January 1984, Benn would be adopted. It was a safe seat, but every kind of malevolence could be expected from the tabloids. Healey's debt to Benn was one of devoted opposition, contradiction and trouble, culminating in the six months' grief of the deputy-leadership campaign. Benn made the invitation, a cheerful brass neck always having been part of his charm. Healey speaks of 'my moment of careless charity'.[40] As film footage demonstrates in the agonised wince of one member of the platform party, he modified it by stepping squarely on the foot of Eric Heffer as he went to the microphone.

This was perhaps a case of Healey's Bounty. The platform had been decorated with the embroidered banners which were the pride of Labour halls and trade union branches in pre-consultancy days. Benn had packed up his own NUM banner, Arthur Scargill's gift, from his Commons room before the election. The one on the platform at Chesterfield was on poles. And as Healey was speaking, – 'a great speech', said the candidate – comparing himself and Tony Benn to the ice dancers, Torvill and Dean, the poles quietly slipped out of vertical, bringing the great crimson banner in slow motion and with heavy symbolism, to the floor. The inability of anyone to stop laughing came as relief, certainly to a meeting which in principle had been an unnatural, if legal, act. It was, said Benn 'hilarious and impossible not to laugh uproariously'. They all went on to the nearest pub, the Hopflower, Healey played the piano and they sang together: 'Here we are again, happy as can be, all good pals and jolly good company.' He was, said Benn, 'extremely good and even the press were laughing'.[41] It is one of those moments, more important than much solemn stuff about innovative legislation, which ought to go into textbooks on the constitution. As pleasantly, Benn would be elected with an increase in his majority.

In Commons debate Healey would be a very damaging opponent of Mrs Thatcher. He once claimed, to Edna's annoyance, to hold the Prime Minister in affection, but it didn't show. The speech which contained that particular courtesy related to the abolition of trade union rights at the ciphering centre of British Intelligence, GCHQ at Cheltenham. Coming after forty years of peaceable, uncontested union establishment, this was a hysterical act which exasperated many Conservatives. Cheltenham's MP, Charles Irving, spoke of 'Some bright berk in the Foreign Office or more probably some bright berk in the US Embassy.' Ian Bancroft, the former head of the civil service, called it 'Breathtakingly inept; a further exploration of the bloody fool branch of management service.'[42] Healey's attack was, at thirty-five minutes, packed with fact and information – GCHQ was a Secretary of Defence's pigeon – and included an enlightening cameo of the Secret Service mind: 'When I assumed office as Secretary of State for Defence in 1964, I was told that the configuration of the Polaris submarine was the most closely guarded secret in my possession. On my next visit to New York I was able to buy a scale model of it, produced by the Metal Toy Company, for my children.'[43]

Near the end there was a flurry of punches. Geoffrey Howe, now Foreign Secretary, was 'hobbling around from one doorstep to another with a bleeding hole in his foot and a smoking gun in his hand'.[44] Having compared poor Sir Geoffrey to Marinus van der Lubbe of the Reichstag Fire, Healey delivered one of the great assaults of parliament* 'We are asking ourselves the question which was asked at the [Lubbe] trial: "who is the Mephistopheles

---

* The author was in the gallery and would hear nothing to compare with it for impact until the attack on Mrs Thatcher made in late 1990 by Sir Geoffrey Howe.

behind this shabby Faust?" The answer to that is clear. The handling of this decision by – I quote her own back benchers – the Great She-Elephant, she who must be obeyed, the Catherine the Great of Finchley, has drawn sympathetic trade unionists such as Len Murray into open revolt. Her pig-headed bigotry has prevented her colleagues and Sir Robert Armstrong from offering and accepting a compromise.'[45]

It was the sort of thing never done often, not now done at all, but always a possibility in parliament. Literate, allusive, mocking, silence-inducing, the verbal wit of politics, what Lloyd George, F. E. Smith, Disraeli and O'Connell could do and perfectly alien to the current *Zeitgeist*. The same wit had flashed in the previous parliament. Witness the tour of the Conservative front bench treated like a Safari Park with a friendly salutation to the Thatcher-detesting Lord Privy Seal, Sir Ian Gilmour, 'Then we come to the flamingo pool and see the Rt. Hon. Gentleman – elongated, pink and wet.'

Healey continued to enjoy life but he occasionally, on a moody day, picked little fights. John Biffen, another, more oblique, Commons wit, recalls being asked with Healey and their wives to a small dinner with journalists. He describes keeping his head down and avoiding giving offence or copy. 'But Denis was feeling stroppy. He picked on one chap – "That piece you wrote on Tuesday was absolute crap." And really we had a very good time until late in the evening when Edna looked at her watch and said, "Well Denis, I think we might go now. I don't *think* there's anyone you haven't insulted."'

He would early use his foreign affairs brief to put glosses on Labour's still voter-toxic unilateral commitments. Labour, in the early Kinnock days, was still ravelled in the knitting of the previous four years while Kinnock had prior convictions of his own which it helped to have someone else dilute. Geoffrey Howe had asked how Healey could square the circle of his concern for a Western nuclear alliance and Neil Kinnock's total renunciation of such weapons. 'For us in Western Europe,' said Denis, 'alliance with the United States is not more nor less important, nor just for defence, but to influence the United States in the exercise of their formidable nuclear power.'[46] As a commentator remarked, 'Circles can in shrewd hands be turned into irregular parallelograms.'[47]

He was in fact quite strikingly modifying his strategic views, producing a Fabian pamphlet and a long article in the American journal, *Foreign Affairs*, arguing for a NATO not armed with nuclear weapons itself while welcoming continued United States nuclear defence. This was what he had been opposed to in the 1950s when distrust of an American response seemed reasonable and when the Soviet Union's great conquests in Europe were recent. This, as he would point out in his memoirs, was only part of a wider amendment of strategic thinking adopted by the likes of Helmut Schmidt, Field Marshal Carver and Robert McNamara,[48] but he was violently abused for it by the dimmer Tories and called a twister trying to ingratiate himself with the left.

What he was actually doing, apart from the merits of a stand-off, was to let the American nuclear umbrella serve both European defence and a Labour Party which in pure political terms needed not to call itself unilateralist. And he was grimly amused to be told by increasingly unfrozen Russian inter-locutors that they couldn't understand Labour's insistence on a moral stand when it would obviously lose them the next election.

In fact, unfolding events in the Soviet Union echoed for Healey the hopes raised thirty years before when he was talking to Adam Rapacki and responding to his plan for zones of disengagement. He went to Russia with Neil Kinnock in 1984 and did what he always did, drank deep on acquaintance, conversation, discussion about defence, talk about the arts, anything to know the people and the country there as well as such contact could make possible. And the perceptible changes in the country he had first visited with Hugh Gaitskell in 1959 filled him with hopes. Healey's hard line was always part of a wider and much more responsive battery of responses. Life at this time was an education for Kinnock, a reappraisal for Healey; and at 67, he got exhilaration out of it. Cut off from the rest of the delegation outside the Kremlin, he got himself past a previously unyielding sentry by producing his old age pensioner's pass for the London buses.[49]

Domestically, the sense Healey had shown in trusting Labour to find its way again would be demonstrated in that Queen Mother of watering places, Bournemouth, when to cries of 'You rat, you bloody rat. You sold us yesterday. You sold us again today,'[50] Neil Kinnock finally turned full-frontally on Mr Derek Hatton functioning as surrogate for the Militant Tendency, surrogates for the wider far left. A Labour Party free of its manic incubus was being established. Though the SDP–Liberal Alliance would do well enough still to show Labour after the 1987 election only twenty seats stronger with ten million votes against the 8.5 million of 1983 and 30.8 per cent of the vote against 27.6 per cent. Only with the self-destruction of the Alliance, commenced during that election, would Labour get out of their mathematical hole of being one of three parties, scrambling for votes inside a two-party system.

Healey had stuck around and done everything possible to help Kinnock, even going with him on an ill-conceived pre-election visit to the White House when President Reagan addressed him as 'Mr Ambassador'. The result was immaterial to Healey. It had been one of those contests where the expected result happens as predicted. There was now no utility in staying on the front bench as a seventy-year-old Shadow minister for the job he had always wanted and would never get.

Envoi

WHAT FOOLS WE WERE NOT TO HAVE CHOSEN DENIS

Notoriously, Enoch Powell said that all political life ends in failure. But then, contemplating the failure of R. A. Butler in 1963 to use a group of willing resignations to force his own premiership upon his party, Powell also said, 'We gave him a gun and he wouldn't use it.' The distinction is not made between getting and doing, will and talent. Butler did not have stomach or energy for conspiracy and shoot-out, but he was an exceptionally good minister, from Education in the 1940s to his African mission in the early 1960s. The parallel with Healey is clear: good at doing, no talent for getting, a shortfall in ruthless will.

What exactly is failure anyway? Not surely, failure to win the highest office, irrespective of performance. Healey himself remarked somewhere that he was more concerned to do something than be somebody. And part of his appeal, a part that lasts, is that although of course ambitious, he had less of the obsessional drive for power than most men and women seriously in that race. It is impossible to imagine Healey, at Balliol, writing down on the back of a cigarette packet his schedule of ascent, with the premiership at the end with a date. He chased no card index of winnable seats. He had a go at Pudsey in 1945, did well, went happily off to his fascinating job at Transport House as International Officer and didn't show his head again through two general elections, until a seat in his own West Riding territory suddenly appeared.

He had a deep vein of the academic, and the shift into parliament left him doing much of what he had done before, writing analyses, preparing pamphlets, inveterately travelling, making acquaintances, name-dropping if you like, but hardly networking. Over defence and foreign policy issues, he arguably painted with too fine a brush in the 1950s, like the sort of lawyer more taken with a refined point of law than with getting us off.

He was the Labour Party's in-house intellectual, a sort of cerebral handy-man. This defined his relationship with Hugh Gaitskell, loyal, in agreement, but not of the blood, never in the way, never out of the way. It led to his being tagged 'a lone wolf', which cliché, like 'bruiser', would effortlessly replace thinking about him. A true lone wolf would have understood the full career value of the little distance between himself and the Gaitskellites, which became a larger distance from the Jenkinsites, and would have played a game of 'Vote for the Technocrat'. A lone wolf calculates and gives no offence. But from 'Can I get it into your heads, comrades, that Mr Khrushchev is not the George Lansbury type?' to 'You fucker, you fucker' addressed to Denis Canavan on the Commons floor, Healey *has* given offence, lots of it. Whether or not on the old definition that because he has usually intended to, it makes him a gentleman, it made him very little of a politician and nothing of a cal-culator. He has *wanted* to be a politician and tried to calculate, but the instinct wasn't in him. The in-house intellectual doesn't cabal or play ends against the middle. He reaches conclusions, tentative or dogmatic.

But because Healey went beyond being an intellectual, he also did things. One has to put side by side the examiner of theories and thinker-out and the decision-making, policy-trundling, executive minister. Healey belonged to a strange generation, born at the right time to read Kant and Aeschylus before getting troops and mesh-track off landing craft. His war had its brief requirements of heroism, but more important, it made him a taker of admin-istrative decisions. The accounts given here of Captain Healey getting some of his liberty ships diverted to Augusta from Bari because the harbour wasn't big enough, coping with rotten communications, then getting men and artillery by sea, road and rail up to Ancona, are part of the distinction between Denis Healey and Michael Foot.

So is the recollection of his junior minister at Defence, Roy Hattersley. He speaks of 'the bliss of working for somebody who had the subject absolutely at their fingertips, who knew what he wanted and pursued his own concept of defence policy with a degree of critical rigour which I have never seen from anyone else'. Sir Charles Elworthy, speaking of shifts in NATO's strategic think-ing, described these as 'a matter of Healey's intellect and McNamara's muscle'.[1]

He was a thinker but not a dreamer, something which helped define his political role. In the most creditable sense of the word, he was a pragmatist, someone who looked for the most intelligent way of doing the job. Like Butler, he was very happy with the very best civil servants. They too are com-monly intellectuals, if of a decently muted sort. They also are presented with problems which – we are describing the best of them – they do not want to fudge. To practicality, Healey added courage and its bottle-holder, physical stamina. His saga at the Treasury is one, first, of learning – from discussion, evidence and frightening experience – then of fighting the long, exhausting jungle war of persuading a Cabinet, almost all of whose members had learned none of these things, what must be done. Such intelligence, courage and willingness to hold through is likely to provoke charges of being a lone wolf. It is the compliment of incomprehension.

The other thing sustaining Healey was normality, extravagant, noisy, even irritating normality. The lone wolf liked company, liked buzz. His ministerial method involved much group discussion and argument. He might be provocative, as we have seen, once compelling Sir Bryan Hopkin who had been badly teased, to say 'Mr Chancellor, you are a casuist.'[2] But it was his comfortable, chosen way. He was an extrovert and a devourer of all experience – foreign countries, people, books, pictures, 'maximum extraction' in his son Tim's phrase. This is, as it were, unusual but normal. The pack-sensitive, but solitary, politician, mindful of his goal, is short of interests without use to him, unlikely to be really excited by a picture or a poem. He exists to succeed and gives his genius, if there is one, to succeeding. The question: what's in it for me? was not one Healey often asked. Instead he drank at every fountain which sprang.

At the same time this recognition of a wider life beyond politics, the Healey hinterland, subtly affected his political colouring. The two main factions of the Labour Party were bastions, peel towers, fortresses of retreat and security. A dozen reasons, starting in Czechoslovakia in 1947–8 and ending at the rate of inflation, put Healey on to one of those sides and, given his flair for offence, he wore its colours conspicuously. But he was a different kind of animal from the Gaitskell-to-Jenkins group. They were, exactly like the Tribune inner core, engaged in permanent self-identification with, and/or separation from, the other group who had become essentially enemy.

This was so strong a factor that, in ultimate crisis, the Gaitskell succession group were the Gaitskell succession group before they were members of the Labour Party. Given a sustained alienation, exile had long been their option. Healey had no complexities of soul, no anguish pulling him away. He was usually too busy for anguish, or hatred either, witness the comic bliss of Healey at Chesterfield supporting Tony Benn.

The party, he would have said, was being bloody silly. Fixing it would be a mixture of conciliation, ruse and patience. For a man who could flare up and who regularly said the wrong thing, he had a lot of patience. He looked at the Labour Party in its travails as the company he had travelled with for nearly forty years and wondered how it could be put right. Leaving to start again, like leaving for a highly paid, prestige-dripping job, wasn't worth ten minutes' thinking about.

The highest intelligence, practicality, courage, complete loyalty and a stupendous capacity for work are qualities which will last. They are also qualities which come to be appreciated. Healey did not attain the highest office though he surely succeeded in essentials in the two mighty jobs he undertook. But after the peaks, when he was no longer a runner, appreciation came, from party and public alike. The country liked Denis Healey, he was fun, he was cheeky, he was a human being, normal, if in an outsize way. He had no side or distance. And the true remark was made, by that left-winger quoted above – whom Barry Jones says could be multiplied many times – 'What fools we were not to have chosen Denis!' The country, alas, never got the chance, though polls showed him far ahead of the winners. They, the public, recognised substance and good humour. An old-fashioned public servant without the formality, a funny, talkative don, somebody from the North instantly liked in the South, he was on most wavelengths except those of faction-bound or panicking or calculating politicians. But because he was not obsessed with the highest office, that has been our loss not his grief.

He would stay in the Commons for another five years, completing forty years in Leeds (same constituency more or less, variously South-East or East) before making the customary British move down the hall to the House of Lords as Lord Healey of Riddlesden. He would there be an intervener and was widely sought by the media for opinion during crises, surprising no one who knew his open views over Suez and less public ones over the Falklands, by being a sharp critic of the Gulf War and a sharper one yet of the bombing of Belgrade and Afghanistan.

But the great activity of Healey's later days would be writing. His autobiography, *The Time of My Life*, was received with general delight, the *Economist* writing that 'No finer autobiography has been written by a politician this century.' Sales of 600 pages of contemporary history reflected reviews praising its sheer enjoyableness. It is a natural life, written easily, without self-importance.

Although he made exhaustive use of the diaries, which he can read, there is none of the clipped style of those volumes. But nor is it a ramble. Healey is an unpompous, friendly man whose life had been interesting and he set about talking us through everything from his Todmorden grandfather, the Irish tailor and economic migrant, to meetings with Mikhail Gorbachev. People loved it, they were quite right to do so. A second book, *My Secret Planet*, though often admired, sold much less well since it concerned poetry, music, art and such things. It was Healey who coined the phrase 'the hinterland' – actually he used it about Mrs Thatcher who hadn't got one – to describe every secret garden lying behind a public life. He tells us of *his* hinterland, anarchic and insulting soldiers' songs as much as Yeats and Virginia Woolf, his especial favourites. And it quotes and quotes at decent, enthusiastic length. Any youngster reading it would have an outline of the calamitous century and the omnivorous culture of a vivid but sensitive man living through it.

The family life continued happily enough, Tim and Jenny having both married and had families long since, Cressida finding a pleasant life in California. Edna's writing flourished, the current book a life of Emma Darwin. She used the rewards of very successful books – Angela Burdett-Coutts had been followed by a history of Buckingham Palace – to buy a couple of fields around Pingles to disappoint developers. Healey calls her 'the Landowner'. In 1997 came the eightieth birthday and a great party at which his secretary of twenty years, Harriet Shackman, a former Departmental Private Secretary, Sir Patrick Nairne, Neil Kinnock, Roy Jenkins and Edward Heath all said their affectionate things.

Perhaps the last, best word should rest with Neil Kinnock describing the four of them, husbands and wives, on what was then Leningrad station in the winter of 1984. 'As the small army of journalists and cameramen followed us on the long walk through the flickering snowfall, Denis and Glenys began to hum "Lara's Theme". As the march continued, Edna and I joined in, followed by the rest of the group. Denis and Glenys began to waltz, the people with us laughed helplessly.' It is no bad politician thus to be remembered for cheering everybody up. For the real Healey, the one with the hinterland, the one married to Edna, the one assailing waiters in Italian, can say with Michael Foot's hero Hazlitt, 'Well I've had a happy life.'

ENDNOTES

CHAPTER 1 BEGINNINGS: FAMILY AND SCHOOLING

1 Healey Papers (hereafter referred to as HP) – D4.
2 *The Time of My Life* (hereafter referred to as TTOML), Michael Joseph, 1989, p. 18.

CHAPTER 3 STUDYING AND CYCLING – OXFORD

1 Sir Edward Heath, *The Course of My Life*, Hodder & Stoughton, 1998, p. 47.
2 Roy Jenkins, *A Life at the Centre*, Macmillan, 1991, p. 29.
3 TTOML, p. 28.
4 Sidney and Beatrice Webb, *Soviet Communism* (Longmans, 1935), last pages of ch. 2.
5 'Journal of a Voyage to Greece', unpublished typescript, HP, passim.

CHAPTER 4 THE OXFORD BY-ELECTION

1 HP.
2 Ibid.
3 Ibid.
4 Christopher Mayhew, *Time to Explain*, Hutchinson, 1987, p. 29.
5 Mrs Szuszanna Schonfield. Conversation with the author.
6 TTOML, p. 37.
7 Bryan Magee relating conversation to the author.
8 HP – Q. M. Hogg election address, Oxford, 1938.
9 Patrick Gordon Walker, *Political Diaries 1932–71*, ed. Robert Pearce, The Historians' Press, 1991, pp. 86–7.
10 Ibid., p. 87.
11 Ibid.
12 Ibid.
13 Ibid., pp. 87–9.
14 Ibid., p. 253.
15 HP – Hogg election address, 1938, passim.
16 TTOML, p. 37.
17 Drusilla Scott, *A. D. Lindsay*, Blackwell, 1971, p. 254.
18 Ibid., pp. 248–9.

CHAPTER 5 SOLDIERING

1–15 HP – war diaries (D16 and 18).
16 TTOML, p. 50.
17–30 HP – war diaries (D18).
31 Dominick Graham and Shelford Bidwell, *Tug of War: The Battle of Italy 1943–45*, Hodder & Stoughton, 1986, p. 94.
32 TTOML, p. 55.
33 Graham and Bidwell, op. cit., p. 52.
34 HP – loose notes contained in war diaries (D18).
35–40 HP – book proposal, ch. III, paras 4, 9, 11 and 14.
41 TTOML, p. 60.
42 Graham and Bidwell, op. cit., p. 137.
43 TTOML, pp. 63–4.
44 Graham and Bidwell, op. cit., p. 98.
45 Chester Wilmot, *The Struggle for Europe*, Collins, 1952, p. 196.
46 Graham and Bidwell, op. cit., p. 392.
47–49 HP – book proposal, ch. IV, paras 4, 5 and 13.

CHAPTER 6 1945 AND BEYOND

1 Labour Party Conference Report (Blackpool), May 1945.
2 [Hansard] *Parliamentary Debates* (hereafter referred to as PD), 1945–6, vol. 427, col. 1715.
3 HP – archives.
4 Ibid., p. 68.
5 HP – press archives.
6 Ibid.
7 *Hugh Gaitskell 1906–63*, ed. William T. Rodgers, Thames & Hudson, 1964, p. 50.
8 HP – archives, electoral address.
9 HP – press archives.
10 Ibid.
11 Ibid.
12 Ibid.
13 Ibid.
14 Kenneth Younger, unpublished diaries.
15 TTOML, p. 79.
16 Isaac Kramnick and Barry Sheerman, *Harold Laski: A Life on the Left*, Hamish Hamilton, 1993, p. 555.
17 HP – D.
18 *The Political Diary of Hugh Dalton, 1918–40, 1945–60*, ed. Ben Pimlott, Jonathan Cape/LSE, 1986, p. 60.
19 HP – D.
20 Private interview, March 1999.
21 Ibid.
22 Quoted in Peter Hennessy, *Never Again, Britain 1945–51*, Jonathan Cape, 1992, p. 245.
23 Labour Party Conference Report, May 1945, op. cit., p. 115.
24 Alan Bullock, *Life and Times of Ernest Bevin*, vol. 1: *Trade Union Leader*, Heinemann, 1960, and vol. 3: *Foreign Secretary 1945–51*, OUP, 1985, p. 117.

25 Quoted in Anne Deighton, *The Impossible Peace: Britain, The Division of Germany and the Origins of the Cold War*, Clarendon Press, 1990, pp. 25–6.
26 Public Record Office FO 181/1023, 1 May 1946, quoted in Hennessy, op. cit., p. 259.
27 Bullock, op. cit., vol. 3, p. 135.
28 Ibid., p. 134.
29 Ibid.
30 *New Statesman*, 23 March 1946.

CHAPTER 7   BUREAUCRAT AND TRAVELLER

1 HP and National Museum of Labour History, Manchester – Spelthorne Memorandum.
2 Labour Party constituency circular.
3 Ernest Bevin, 'The Foreign Situation', FO 800/478/MIS/45/14, quoted in Bullock, vol. 3, op. cit., p. 193.
4 PD, 20 August 1945.
5 Ibid., vol. 450, cols. 1135–6, May 1948, quoted in Hugh Berrington, *Backbench Opinion in the House of Commons 1945–55*, Pergamon, 1973, p. 61.
6 TTOML, p. 83.
7 Ibid., p. 82.

CHAPTER 8   CARDS ON THE TABLE

1 HP – D, 14 April 1947.
2 Quoted from Hennessy, op. cit., p. 335.
3 Quoted from Bullock, vol. 3, op. cit., p. 396.
4 Kenneth Younger, unpublished diaries.
5 Bullock, vol. 3, op. cit., p. 398.
6 HP – press archives, also all subsequent press comment.
7 All from Anne Chisholm and Michael Davie *Beaverbrook*, Hutchinson, 1992, pp. 434–5.
8 HP – press archives.
9 HP – D, 24 May 1947.
10 HP – D. This and subsequent diary comment, 24–31 May 1947.
11 Ibid.

CHAPTER 9   CZECHOSLOVAKIA AND FRIENDS

1 HP – D, 12 June 1947.
2 HP – D. This and subsequent diary comment, June 1947–March 1948.
3 HP – press archives (1948).
4 Ibid.

CHAPTER 10   HUNGARY 1947–50

1 HP – D January 1947.
2 Unless otherwise stated, this and all subsequent diary comments, HP – D, 1947.
3 HP – D.
4 Ibid.
5 Ibid.

6 Ibid.
7 *The Curtain Falls*, ed. Denis Healey, Lincolns-Prager, 1951.

CHAPTER 11   FRANCE AND ITALY 1947–8

1 TTOML, p. 480.
2 HP – archives.

CHAPTER 12   *FEET ON THE GROUND* – A RESPONSE TO SCHUMAN.

1–6 *Feet on the Ground* (hereafter referred to as FOTG), Labour Party
Publication, 1948, pp. 3–8.
7 TTOML, p. 116.
8–16 FOTG, pp. 9–16.
17 TTOML, p. 115.
18–25 FOTG, pp. 20–23.

CHAPTER 13   'IL DOGMATISMO LABORISTO'

1 French communique translated in Cmnd. 7971/2, quoted in Edmund Dell,
The Schuman Plan and the British Abdication of Leadership in Europe,
OUP, 1995, p. 14.
2 Ibid., p. 15.
3 Dean Acheson, 'Present at the Creation Norton', 1969, quoted in Dell,
Schuman Plan, p. 111.
4 Kenneth Younger, unpublished diaries, my p. 11.
5 Pimlott (ed.), *Dalton*, p. 472.
6 Kenneth Younger unpublished diaries, my p. 10.
7 TTOML, p. 117.
8 Ibid., pp. 116–17.
9 Pimlott (ed.), *Dalton*, pp. 476–7 (all of extended quotation).
10 *European Unity*, Internal Labour Party Publication, 1950, p. 8.
11 Pimlott (ed.), *Dalton*, p. 475.
12 Quoted in Dell, *Schuman Plan*, p. 204.
13 *Daily Worker*, 13–14 June 1950.
14 *News Chronicle*, 13–14 June 1950, passim.
15 *Corriere della Sera*, 14 June 1950.
16 HP – D, 12–17 June 1950.

CHAPTER 14   SCHUMAN: THE COMMONS DEBATE

1 PD, vol. 476, 1950, col. 1919.
2 Ibid., col. 1921.
3 Ibid., col. 1953.
4 Ibid.
5 Ibid., col. 1976.
6 Pimlott (ed.), *Dalton*, p. 480.
7–9 *European Unity*, pp. 6, 7.
10 Quoted in Dell, *Schuman Plan*, p. 108.
11–14 *European Unity*, pp. 6–10.
15–18 Ibid., pp. 12–14.
19 *New Fabian Essays*, ed. R. H. S. Crossman, Turnstile Press, 1952, p. 169.
20 Ibid., pp. 174–5.

CHAPTER 15   THE CASE FOR REARMAMENT – 1951

1   *Rearmament – How Far?,* Fabian pamphlet, July 1951.
2   Michael Foot and Jennie Lee, *One Way Only,* Tribune Bevanite publication, 1951.
3   Quoted in Brian Brivati, *Hugh Gaitskell,* Richard Cohen Books, 1996, p. 124.
4   *Rearmament – How Far?,* op. cit.
5   Ibid.
6   Ibid.
7   Ibid.

CHAPTER 16   FROM LEEDS TO MORECAMBE – 1952

1   Benn, Unpublished Diaries, November 1956.
2   Edward Pearce, *The Lost Leaders,* Little, Brown, 1997, p. 157.
3   TTOML, p. 132.
4   Conversation with Douglas Gabb.
5   TTOML, p. 141.
6   Labour Party Conference Report, 1952.

CHAPTER 17   MAIDEN SPEECH

1   PD, vol. 500, 5th Series, 5–16 May, 1952, col. 1505.
2   Quoted in Frank Giles, *The Locust Years, The Story of the Fourth French Republic 1946–1958,* Secker & Warburg, 1991, p. 170.
3   Ibid., p. 164.
4   Alistair Horne, *Macmillan 1957–86,* vol. 2, Macmillan, 1988, p. 322.
5   Pimlott (ed.), *Dalton,* p. 504, mid-February, 1951.
6   Ibid., p. 596.
7   PD, vol. 500, 5th Series, col. 1498.
8   Ibid., cols 1498–9.
9   Ibid., col. 1499.
10 Ibid., col. 1502.
11 Ibid.
12 Ibid., col. 1504.
13 Ibid.
14 Ibid., col. 1505.

CHAPTER 18   EUROPEAN DEFENCE COMMUNITY

1   PD, vol. 495, Feb. 1951.
2   Saul Rose, 'Labour Party and German Rearmament', *Political Studies,* June 1966, p. 139.
3   Labour Party Conference Report (Margate), 1953.
4   Labour Party Conference Report (Scarborough), 1954.
5   PD, vol. 533.

CHAPTER 19   FIRE OVER SUEZ

1   Tony Benn, *Diaries,* 1: *Years of Hope 1940–62,* Hutchinson, 1994, p. 183.
2   Ibid.
3   TTOML, p. 169.
4   Hugh Thomas, *The Suez Affair,* Weidenfeld & Nicolson, 1967, p. 19.
5   Ibid., p. 23.

6   Ibid., p. 25.
7   Ibid.
8   Quoted in Alistair Horne, *Macmillan*, vol. 1: *1894–1956*, Macmillan, 1988, Chapter 15.
9   PD, vol. 557, 2 August 1956, cols 1618–19.
10   Ibid., col. 1619.
11   Ibid., col. 1620.
12   Ibid., col. 1606.
13   Ibid.
14   Ibid., col. 1604.
15   Ibid., col. 1608.
16   Ibid., col. 1616.
17   Ibid., cols 1616–17.
18   Ibid., col. 1617.
19   Ibid.
20   Ibid., col. 1612.
21   Ibid., col. 1613.
22   Ibid., col. 1624.
23   Ibid.
24   Ibid., cols 1624–5.
25   Ibid.
26   Ibid., cols 1625–6.
27   Ibid., cols 1629–30.
28   Ibid., col. 1630.
29   Ibid.
30   Quoted in Brivati, op. cit., p. 258.
31   Ibid., pp. 258–9.
32   Ibid., p. 259.
33   R. H. S. Crossman, *Backbench Diaries*, Hamilton/Hamish Jonathan Cape, 1979, p. 508.
34   Benn, *Diaries*, 1, p. 191.
35   HP – press archives.
36   Ibid.
37   Benn, unpublished diaries, 24 October 1956.
38   PD, vol. 558, 30 October, col. 1274.
39   Ibid., col. 1275.
40   Both ibid., col. 1290.
41   All ibid., cols 1290–91.
42   Benn, unpublished diaries, 31 October 1956.
43   Ibid., 31 October–6 November 1956.
44   Ibid.
45   Ibid.
46   Ibid., 7 November.
47   Ibid., December.
48   PD, vol. 558, 2 November, cols 1756–7.
49   Ibid., col. 1757.
50   Ibid.
51   Ibid., cols 1753–7.
52   Ibid., col. 1291.
53   Ibid., col. 1905.

54 Ibid., col. 1906.
55 Ibid., col. 1909.
56 Ibid., col. 1907–8.
57 TTOML, p. 170.
58 Crossman, *Backbench Diaries*, p. 540.
59 HP – press archives.

CHAPTER 20 RAPACKI, GAITSKELL AND HEALEY

1 TTOML, p. 179.
2 Ibid.
3 Ibid. and passim.
4 *A Neutral Belt in Europe*, Fabian Tract 311, 1958, passim.
5 TTOML, p. 180.
6 Ibid., p. 179.

CHAPTER 21 A NATO MAN AND THE MARCHERS

1 Jacquetta Hawkes quoted in Richard Taylor, *Against the Bomb: The British Peace Movement 1958–65*, Clarendon Press, 1988, p. 20.
2 Labour Party Conference Report (Brighton), 1957, p. 181.
3 'Dilemmas of the Cold War', reprinted in Healey, *When Shrimps Learn to Whistle*, Michael Joseph, 1990, p. 153.
4 US Congressional Report, Appendix, pp. 186–7 passim.

CHAPTER 22 BLUE STREAK AND LABOUR POLITICS

1 Taylor, op. cit.
2 Ibid., quoting David Boulton, unpublished MS.
3 Jacquetta Hawkes quoted in Taylor, op. cit., p. 20.
4 Taylor, op. cit., p. 287.
5 Labour Party Conference Report (Blackpool), 1959.
6 Ibid.
7 Ibid.
8 Ibid.
9 Healey, *The Race Against the H-Bomb*, Fabian pamphlet, March 1960.
10 Benn, *Diaries*, 1, p. 342.
11 Ibid., p. 343.
12 Crossman, *Backbench Diaries*, 11 May 1960, p. 845.
13 Brivati, op. cit., p. 354 and n., and Healey speaking to the author.
14 Brivati, op. cit., p. 354.
15 Gordon Walker, *Political Diaries*, p. 260.
16 Ibid., p. 259.
17 Ibid.
18 Ibid., p. 260.
19 Ibid., p. 259.
20 Healey, 'Interdependence', *Political Quarterly*, vol. 31, no. 1, January–March 1960, pp. 46–56 passim.

CHAPTER 23 THE DANGEROUS ROAD TO SCARBOROUGH

1 *New Statesman*, 30 April 1960.
2 Brivati, op. cit., p. 355.
3 *New Statesman*, 30 April 1960.

4   Gordon Walker, *Political Diaries*, p. 268.
5   Ibid., p. 268.
6   *The Race Against the H-Bomb*, op. cit.
7   Crossman, *Backbench Diaries*, p. 874.
8   Ibid., p. 874.
9   Ibid. and passim.
10 Benn, *Diaries*, 1, Labour Party Conference (Scarborough), 1960.
11 Labour Party Conference Report (Scarborough), 1960.
12 Ibid.
13 PD, vol. 640, March 1960.

CHAPTER 24   1960 AND AFTER

1   Brivati, op. cit., p. 385.
2   Bruce Reed and Geoffrey Williams, *Denis Healey and the Politics of Power*, Sidgwick & Jackson, 1971, p. 126.
3   TTOML, p. 222.
4   PD, vol. 668, 3 December 1962, cols 948 et seq.
5   Ibid., col. 948.
6   Ibid., col. 953.
7   Ibid., col. 980.
8   Ibid., col. 958.
9   Ibid., col. 958.

CHAPTER 25   WILSON SUCCEEDS

1   Brivati, op. cit., p. 415.
2   Ben Pimlott, *Harold Wilson*, HarperCollins, 1992, passim.
3   TTOML, p. 330.
4   Comment at the time to the author.
5   TTOML, pp. 302–3.
6   Ibid.
7   Crossman Diaries (1965).

CHAPTER 26   INTERVAL SCENE-SHIFTING

1   Quoted in Horne, *Macmillan*, vol. 2, p. 435.
2   Ibid., p. 441.

CHAPTER 27   PREPARING FOR THE MINISTRY OF DEFENCE

1   Horne, op. cit., vol. 2, p. 48.
2   Quoted ibid., p. 45.
3   Ibid., p. 47.
4   Quoted ibid., p. 49.
5   Quoted in Philip Ziegler, *Mountbatten*, Collins, 1985, p. 550.
6   Conversation with the author.
7   Ziegler, *Mountbatten*, p. 553.
8   Ibid., pp. 551–2.
9   Horne, op. cit., p. 502.
10 PD, vol. 684, 21 November 1963.
11 Crossman, *Backbench Diaries*, p. 1022.
12 PD, vol. 684, col. 1219.
13 Ibid., col. 1225.

14   TTOML, p. 274.
15   PD, vol. 684, op. cit., col. 1218.
16   PD, vol. 690, col. 455.
17   Ibid., col. 443.
18   Ibid., col. 457.
19   Ibid., col. 443.
20   Ibid., col. 459.
21   Ibid.
22   Ibid., col. 469.
23   Ibid., col. 465.
24   Ibid.
25   Ibid.
26   Ibid., col. 469.
27   Ibid., col. 475.
28   Ibid., col. 476.
29   Ibid., col. 475.
30   Ibid., col. 480.
31   Ibid.
32   PD, vol. 690, cols 483–4.
33   Lawrence Freedman, *Britain and Nuclear Weapons*, Macmillan/RIIA, 1980, p. 33.

CHAPTER 29   RUN-UP TO ELECTION 1964

1   Edmund Dell, *The Chancellors*, HarperCollins, 1990, pp. 252–3.
2   Ibid., p. 302.
3   Ibid., p. 299.

CHAPTER 30   ELECTION 1964 AND AFTER

1   *Yorkshire Evening Post*, October 1964.
2–3   Quoted at PD, vol. 725, col. 1770.
4   Ibid., col. 1769.
5–7   Crossman, *Backbench Diaries*, op. cit., p. 1038.
8   Lord Glenamara, interview with the author.
9   TTOML, p. 250.
10–14 HP – D30, pp. 2–7.
15   Conversation with the author, quoted in Pearce, *The Lost Leaders*, Little, Brown, 1997.
16   Conversation with the author.
17   Sir William Jackson and Lord Bramall, *The Chiefs*, Brassey's, 1992, p. 357.
18   TTOML, pp. 258–9.
19   Earl Mountbatten, *From Shore to Shore: Tour Diaries 1953–79*, Collins, 1989, p. 176.
20   HP – D, 25 January 1965.
21   Jackson and Bramall, op. cit., p. 328.
22–25 HP – D30, pp. 5–9.

CHAPTER 31   EARLY DAYS AS SECRETARY OF STATE

1   Kenneth O. Morgan *Callaghan: A Life*, OUP, 1997.
2   PD, vol. 702, col. 947.
3   Sir Henry Hardman in conversation, quoted in Reed and Williams, op. cit., p. 167.

4 Ibid., p. 169.
5 *The Crossman Diaries*, ed. Janet Morgan, Hamish Hamilton/Jonathan Cape, 1979, p. 89.
6 PD, vol. 702, cols 1028–30.
7 TTOML, p. 304.
8 HP – D.
9 PD, vol. 702, col. 1034.
10 Ibid., col. 1034.
11 Ibid., col. 1036.
12 *Crossman Diaries*, op. cit., p. 50.
13 Ibid., p. 50.

CHAPTER 32   TSR2

1 Field Marshal Lord (Michael) Carver, *Tightrope Walking: British Defence Policy since 1945*, Hutchinson, 1992, p. 72.
2 Ibid.
3 Private interview with Lord Hill-Norton.
4 Bramall and Jackson, op. cit., p. 365.
5–7 Report DPBG/P (65)1 DEFE 25/106, paras 7, 8 and 11.
8–9 HP – D, 6 and 12 January 1965.
10 Robert Pearce, in his introduction to Gordon Walker, *Political Diaries*, pp. 45–6.
11 HP – D, 7 January 1965.
12 HP – press archives.
13 All ibid., HP – D, January 1965.
14–15 CC (65) 5th Conclusions, CAB 128/39PH, 28 January 1965.
16–17 HP – D, 29 January and 1 February 1965.
18 TTOML, p. 273.
19 Private conversation with Lord Hill-Norton.
20 PD, vol. 706, 9 February 1965, col. 329.
21 PD, vol. 705, 1 February 1965, cols 724–30, and HP – D, 1 February 1965.
22 HP – D, 20–21 March 1965.
23 HP – D, 24 March 1965.
24 HP – D, 29 March 1965.
25 HP – D, 25 March 1965.
26–29 Ibid., 1 April 1965.
30–31 Crossman, *Cabinet Diaries* vol. 1, p. 191, 1 April 1965.
32 HP – D, 6 April 1965.
33 PD, vol. 710, 6 April 1965, cols 318–44.
34 Ibid., cols 325–6.
35 Ibid., col. 331.
36 Ibid., col. 341.
37 Ibid., 13 April 1965, col. 1265.
38 All ibid., cols 1171–89.
39 Reed and Williams, op. cit., p. 182.
40 PD, vol. 710, 13 April 1965, col. 1200.

CHAPTER 33   CARRIERS AND RHODESIA

1 All at HP – D, 22 November 1965.
2–3 Crossman, *The Diaries of a Cabinet Minister*, vol. 1: 1964–66, Hamish

Hamilton/Jonathan Cape, 1979 (hereafter referred to as *Cabinet Diaries* (8 October).

4 Ibid., p. 394 (29 November).
5 HP – D, 2 December 1965.
6 OPD (65, 52nd meeting) annexe.
7–8 Ibid., p. 4.
9–11 Ibid., p. 5.
12–13 Ibid., p. 6.
14 OPD (66, 11th meeting).
15–16 Ibid., p. 1.
17–18 Ibid., p. 2.
19 Ibid., p. 3.
20 Ibid., p. 4.
21 Ibid., p. 7.
22–24 Ibid., p. 8.
25 Cabinet Committee (66) Conclusions, p. 4.
26–27 All at HP – D, January 1966.
28 Barbara Castle, *Diaries*, vol. 1: *1964–70*, Weidenfeld & Nicolson, 1984, p. 492.
29 Conversation with Lord Hill-Norton.
30–31 HP – D, 25 January, 16 February.
32 PD, vol. 725, col. 265.
33 Conversation with Lord Hill-Norton.

CHAPTER 34   BETRAYING THE TERRIERS

1 HP – D, 29 July 1965.
2 Quoted in Carver, *Tightrope Walking*, p. 91.
3 Crossman, *Cabinet Diaries*, vol. 1, pp. 414–15.
4 PD, vol. 722, 1965, col. 1475.
5 Ibid., col. 1477.
6 Ibid., col. 1486.
7 Ibid., col. 1507.
8–9 Ibid., col. 1512.
10 Ibid., col. 1576.
11 Both ibid., col. 1584.
12–16 Michael Carver, *Out of Step: Memoirs of a Field Marshal*, Hutchinson, 1989, pp. 343–4 and p. 515.
17 PD, vol. 722, col. 1585.
18 Ibid., col. 1586.
19 Ibid., col. 1588.
20 Ibid., col. 1589.
21 Ibid., col. 1590.
21 Ibid., col. 1591.
23 Ibid., col. 1592.
24–26 Ibid., col. 1593.

CHAPTER 35   FIII

1–2 CC (66) 9th Conclusion, pp. 9–10.
3–5 Ibid., p. 5.
6–7 Ibid., pp. 7–8.

8   Private information.
9   Louis Heren, 'No Hail, no Farewell' (1970), quoted in John Baylis, *Anglo-American Defence Relations 1939–80*, Macmillan, 1981, p. 95.
10   H. G. Nicholas, quoted in ibid., p. 95.
11   CC (66) 9th Conclusion, op. cit., p. 8.
12   Ibid., pp. 8–9.
13–15 Crossman, *Cabinet Diaries*, vol. 1, pp. 455–6.
16–19 HP – D, 14–19 February 1966.

CHAPTER 36   DEFENCE DEBATE – MARCH 1966

1   PD, vol. 725, 22 February 1966, col. 242.
2   Ibid., col. 243.
3   Ibid., cols 244–5.
4   Ibid., 7 March 1966, col. 1748.
5   Quoted at ibid., col. 1749.
6–7 Ibid., cols 1754–5.
8   PD, vol. 585, cols 388–9, quoted at PD, vol. 725, col. 1760.
9   All at ibid., col. 1760.
10   Ibid., col. 1761.
11   Ibid., col. 1765.
12   Ibid., col. 1769.
13–14 Ibid., cols 1772–3.
15   PD, vol. 580, 23 January 1958, cols 1295–6, quoted at PD, vol. 725, col. 1775.
16–19 Ibid., col. 1782.
20–21 Ibid., col. 1791.
22–23 Ibid., col. 1792.
24   Ibid., col. 1809.
25–28 HP – D, 8 March 1966.
29   PD, vol. 725, col. 2042.
30   Ibid., col. 2044.
31   Ibid., col. 2045.

CHAPTER 37   AFTER SUEZ, EAST OF SUEZ

1   TTOML, p. 280.
2   Carver, *Tightrope Walking*, p. 53.
3   Quoted in Phillip Darby, *British Defence Policy East of Suez 1947–1968*, OUP/RIIA, 1973, p. 206.
4   Carver, *Tightrope Walking*, pp. 54–5.
5   Quoted in Tom Little, *South Arabia: Arena of Conflict*, Pall Mall Press, 1968, pp. 90–91.
6   Darby, op. cit.
7   Jackson and Bramall, op. cit., p. 347.
8   Little, op. cit., p. 115.
9   HP – D31, 17 June 1965.
10   HP – D31, 18 June 1965.
11–15 HP – D31, 16–19 June 1965.
16   TTOML, p. 282.
17–18 HP – D31, 20 June 1965.
19–20 Little, op. cit., pp. 146, 150.

21   Horne, *Macmillan*, vol. 2, p. 421.
22   TTOML, p. 284.
23   Carver, *Tightrope Walking*, p. 65.
24–25   PD, vol. 640, col. 1408, quoted in Chin Kin Wah, *The Defence of Malaysia and Singapore*, CUP, 1983, p. 60.
26   TTOML, p. 285.
27   Crossman, *Cabinet Diaries*, vol. 1, p. 95.
28   Chin Kin Wah, op. cit., pp. 67–8.
29   Quoted ibid., p. 69.
30   Reed and Williams, op. cit., pp. 205–6.
31–32   TTOML, p. 289.
33   Reed and Williams, op. cit., p. 206.
34–36   HP – D33, 7–9 July 1965.
37   Crossman, *Cabinet Diaries*, vol. 1, p. 540.
38   Quoted in Reed and Williams, op. cit., p. 215.
39   Carver, *Tightrope Walking*, p. 79.

CHAPTER 38   1966–7 – CRISES

1   Lord Glenamara, conversation with the author.
2   DEFE 10/511 610630, p. 1.
3   Quoted in Morgan, op. cit., p. 239.
4   Callaghan memo, 1 July 1966, Callaghan Papers, quoted in ibid., p. 242.
5–6   HP – D, 17, 19 July 1966.
7   Crossman, *Cabinet Diaries*, vol. 1, p. 574.
8   Tony Benn, *Diaries, 2: Out of the Wilderness 1963–67*, p. 458.
9   Crossman, *Cabinet Diaries*, vol. 1, p. 574.
10   HP – D, 21 July 1966.
11   Jackson and Bramall, op. cit., p. 371.
12–14   OPD (66) 122, 23 November 1966, pp. 1–2.
15–22   Ibid., pp. 10–12.
23   CC 34 (65) CAB 128/42/PH.
24–27   OPD (66), op. cit., p. 12.
28–32   CC 34 (67), 19th Conclusion, 11 April 1967, Section 4.
33   TTOML, p. 290.
34–37   CC 34 (67), op. cit., p. 3.
38   CC (67), 42nd Conclusion, CAB 128/42/Pt 2.
39–40   HP – D, 27 July.
41   HP – D, 26 July.
42   Cmnd 3357. Defence White Paper.
43   HP – D 34.
44   Dell, *Chancellors*, p. 340.
45   Quoted in Morgan, op. cit., p. 267.
46   Callaghan MS, quoted in Morgan, op. cit., p. 271.
47   Sir Alec Cairncross, unpublished diaries quoted in Morgan, op. cit., p. 272.
48–49   HP – D, 14 July 1967.
50–52   Castle, *Diaries*, vol. 1, pp. 325–8.
53   Crossman, *Cabinet Diaries: 1966–68*, vol. 2, p. 588.
54   HP – D, 29 November 1967.

CHAPTER 39 FIII AGAIN: 'APPALLING DAY AT NUMBER 10'

1   Conversation with the author, quoted in his *The Lost Leaders*, op. cit.
2   Dell, *Chancellors*, pp. 352–3.
3   Jenkins, op. cit., p. 222.
4   Private information.
5–6   Crossman, *Cabinet Diaries*, vol. 2, pp. 598, 603.
7–8   HP – D, 15 December 1967.
9   Crossman, *Cabinet Diaries*, vol. 2, p. 607.
10–11   HP – D, 20 December 1967.
12   Crossman, *Cabinet Diaries*, vol. 2, p. 607.
13   HP – D, 20 December 1967.
14   Jenkins, op. cit., p. 224.
15   HP – D, 20 December 1967.
16–17   Jenkins, op. cit., pp. 224, 225.
18   Quoted ibid., p. 223.
19–20   Ibid., pp. 224–5.
21   HP – D, 5 January 1968.
22   Jenkins, op. cit., p. 251.
23–24   HP – D, 20 December 1967.
25   Jenkins, op. cit., p. 226.
26–28   HP – D, 27–29 December 1967.
29–30   Ibid., 1–3 January 1968.
31   Tony Benn, *Diaries*, 3: *Office without Power 1968–72*, pp. 1–2.
32–36   HP – D, 4–5 January 1968.
37   Jenkins, op. cit., p. 648.
38   Benn, *Diaries*, 3, p. 3.
39–43   HP – D35, note cache attached.
44   Crossman, *Cabinet Diaries*, vol. 2, p. 638.
45–46   HP – D35, 9 January 1968.
47   Benn, *Diaries*, 3, p. 10.
48–50   HP – D35, 10–11 January 1968.
51   Benn, *Diaries*, 3, p. 12.
52   Crossman, *Cabinet Diaries*, vol. 2, p. 646.
53–55   Benn, *Diaries*, 3, pp. 12–13.
56–58   Crossman, *Cabinet Diaries*, vol. 2, pp. 647, 648, 635.
59   HP – D35, 12 January 1968.
60–61   Benn, *Diaries*, 3, pp. 15, 14.
62   TTOML, p. 273.
63   Crossman, *Cabinet Diaries*, vol. 2, p. 649.
64–65   HP – D35, 16 January 1968.
66   Interview with Peter Hill-Norton.
67   TTOML, p. 273.
68   Private information.
69   PD, vol. 757, col. 620.
70–71   Ibid., col. 621.
72   Ibid., col. 650.
73   Ibid., col. 644.
74   Private information.
75   PD, vol. 757, col. 633.
76–79   Ibid., col. 632–6.

CHAPTER 40   OTHER DEFENCE FRUSTRATIONS

1   Lord Cameron (Neil Cameron), *In the Midst of Things*, Hodder &
       Stoughton, 1988, p. 154.
2–4   Sir Ewen Broadbent, *The Military and Government from Macmillan to
       Heseltine*, Macmillan, 1988, pp. 31–3.
5   Quoted in Cameron, op. cit., p. 156.
6   Sir Michael Howard pamphlet: *The Central Organisation of Defence*.
7   Cameron, op. cit., p. 156.
8   Bramall and Jackson, op. cit., p. 374.
9–10   Cameron, op. cit., pp. 159, 162.
11–13 PD, vol. 749, 7 July, col. 1791.
14–16 Ibid., col. 1792.
17–19 Reed and Williams, op. cit., p. 185, 186.
20   PD, vol. 749, 29 June 1967.
21–26 Ibid., cols 1825–7.
27   Ibid., col. 1831.
28   TTOML, p. 274.
29   Carver, *Tightrope Walking*, p. 97.

CHAPTER 41   STUMBLING OUT OF THE SIXTIES

1   Tony Benn, *Diaries*, 3, 24 July 1969, p. 193.
2   Conversation with the author.
3   Benn, *Diaries*, 3, p. 37, 17 February 1968.
4–7   HP – D, 10 February, 25 February, 24 February and 6 March 1968.
8   Jenkins, op. cit., p. 237, 15 March 1968.
9–11   HP – D, 15 March 1968.
12   *The Cecil King Diary 1965–70*, Jonathan Cape, 1972, p. 70, 10 May 1966.
13   HP – D, 26–7 March 1968.
14–17 King, op. cit., pp. 203, 190, 204, 246.
18–19 HP – Press archives, 1 and 2 April 1968.
20–21 HP – D, 4 and 9 April 1968.
22–23 HP – D, both 4 July 1968.
24   HP – D, 25 May 1968.
25   HP – D, 26 May 1968.
26   'Edna and Denis', family tribute privately published, 1995.
27   Benn, *Diaries*, 3, p. 74, 2 June 1968.
28   HP – D36, papers cache, 10 September 1968.
29   HP – D, 10 September 1968.
30   Ibid., 23 September 1968.
31   Notes cache, op. cit., undated.
32   Ibid., 4 October 1968.
33–34 Ibid., both 31 October 1968.
35   Ibid., 28 November 1968.
36   Ibid., 19 November 1968.
37–38 Benn, *Diaries*, 3, pp. 132–3.
39   TTOML, p. 429.
40–41 Jenkins, op. cit., p. 271.
42–43 Benn, *Diaries*, 3, p. 127, 22 November 1968.
44   Ibid., p. 133, 10 December 1968.
45   HP – D, 9 December 1968.

46   Crossman, *Cabinet Diaries*, vol. 3: 1968–70, pp. 287–8.
47–49   HP – D, 10 and 12 March 1969.
50   Ibid., side note dated 14 March 1969.
51   Crossman, *Cabinet Diaries*, vol. 3, p. 416.
52   HP – D, side note dated 14 March 1969.
53   Ibid., 17 March 1969.
54   Richard Marsh quoted in Philip Ziegler, *Wilson: The Unauthorized Life*, Weidenfeld & Nicolson, 1993, p. 343.
55   Crossman, *Cabinet Diaries*, vol. 3, p. 416.
56–57   Morgan, op. cit., p. 334.
58   HP – D 36, notes cache dated 24 April 1969.
59   Ibid., 8–9 April 1969.
60–61   Ibid., both 6 May 1969.
62   Morgan, op. cit., p. 336.
63   Benn, *Diaries*, 3, p. 167.
64   HP – D, 9 May 1969.
65   Benn, *Diaries*, 3, p. 167.
66   HP – D, 30 April 1969.
67   Castle, *Diaries*, vol. 1, p. 426.
68   Conversation with the author.
69   TTOML, p. 340.
70   King, op. cit., pp. 261–2.
71   HP – D, 21 May 1969.
72–73   Jenkins, op. cit., pp. 290, 289.
74–75   HP – D, 12–13 June 1969.
76–77   Castle, *Diaries*, vol. 1, p. 665, 8 June 1969.
78   HP – D, 9 June 1969.
79–80   Castle, *Diaries*, vol. 1, p. 671.
81   All at Benn, *Diaries*, 3, p. 188, 23 June 1969.
82   Jenkins, op. cit., p. 290.
83   Benn, *Diaries*, 3, p. 188, 23 June 1969.
84   All ibid., 24 July, p. 193
85   Ibid., p. 193; see also first page of this chapter.

Chapter 42   Election 1970 and Aftermath

1–2   HP – D 37, 19 November 1969.
3–4   Ibid., 13 September and 19 August 1969.
5–8   Ibid., 14 and 20 January, 1 February and 21 April 1970.
9–11   Jenkins, op. cit., pp. 291, 292, 296.
12–14   HP – D, 23 May and 28–30 April 1970.
15   TTOML, p. 349.
16   Benn, *Diaries*, 3, p. 287.
17–20   HP – D, 4–5 June 1970.
21–22   Ibid., 11 June 1970.
23–25   Ibid., 14–16 June 1970.
26–27   Quoted in Morgan, op. cit., pp. 394–5.
28   TTOML, p. 359.
29   HP – D, 20 September 1970.
30   Benn, *Diaries*, 3, p. 325.
31   Jenkins, op. cit., p. 316.

32–34   Benn, *Diaries*, 3, pp. 347, 352, 380.
  35   HP – D, 19 October 1970.
  36   Quoted in Benn, *Diaries*, 3, p. 362.
  37   HP – D, 26 July 1970.
  38   Benn, *Diaries*, 3, p. 380.
  39   Jenkins, op. cit., p. 352.

CHAPTER 43   THE DESCENT TO FEBRUARY 1974

  1–3   Dell, *Chancellors*, pp. 386, 397.
  4–5   PD, vol. 866, 19 December 1973, cols 1358 and 1357.
    6   TTOML, p. 368.
    7   PD, 6 February 1974, col. 1242, quoted in Dell, *Chancellors*, p. 399.
    8   *Times*, 8 February 1974.
    9   Ibid., 14 February 1974.
   10   Ibid., 16 February 1974.
   11   Ibid., 15 February 1974.
   12   Ibid., 16 February 1974.
13–14   Ibid., 18 February 1974.
15–16   Ibid., 19 February 1974.
   17   Ibid., 22 February 1974.
   18   Ibid., quoted in Dell, *Chancellors*, p. 397.
   19   HP – D, 9 February 1974.
   20   Ibid., 17 February 1974.
   21   Ibid., 18 February 1974.
   22   Ibid., 20 February 1974.
   23   Ibid., 24 February 1974.

CHAPTER 44   THE TREASURY – GETTING IT WRONG, 1974–75

    1   Benn, *Diaries*, 3, p. 350, 17 June 1971.
    2   Edmund Dell, *A Hard Pounding: Politics and Economic Crisis 1974–1976*, OUP, 1991, p. 28.
    3   Ibid., p. 65.
    4   All figures quoted in Nick Gardner, *Decade of Discontent: The Changing British Economy since 1973*, Basil Blackwell, 1987, p. 33.
    5   Dell, unpublished diaries, Bodleian Library, Oxford, p. 117, 21 June 1974.
    6   Ibid., p. 60, 7 June 1974.
    7   Gardner, op. cit., p. 65.
    8   Harold Wilson, *Final Term: The Labour Government, 1974–1976*, Weidenfeld & Nicolson/Michael Joseph, 1979, p. 43, quoted ibid., p. 14.
    9   Joseph Schumpeter, *Capitalism, Socialism and Democracy*, Harvard rev. edn 1946, quoted TTOML, p. 378.
   10   Dell, *A Hard Pounding*, op. cit., p. 90.
   11   Quoted in Mark Wickham-Jones, *Economic Strategy and the Labour Party*, Macmillan, 1996, p. 91.
   12   Benn, *Diaries*, 3, 9 July 1971, quoted in Wickham-Jones op. cit., p. 88.
   13   Sir Antony Part, *The Making of a Mandarin*, André Deutsch, 1990, p. 167.
   14   Ibid., p. 172.
   15   Benn, *Diaries*, 3, p. 187.
   16   Bernard Donoughue, *Prime Minister: The Conduct of Policy under Harold Wilson and James Callaghan*, Jonathan Cape, 1987, p. 54.

17   Lord Donoughue, private conversation.
18   Private conversation with Sir Frank Cooper, quoted in the author's *The Lost Leaders*, op. cit., p. 179.
19   Donoughue, op. cit., p. 56.
20   Castle, *Diaries*, vol. 2, p. 142, quoted in Dell, *A Hard Pounding*, p. 30.
21   Gardner, op. cit., p. 45.
22   Quoted in Kathy Burk and Alec Cairncross, *Goodbye Great Britain: The 1976 IMF Crisis*, Yale UP, 1992, p. 14.
23   Quoted in Dell, *A Hard Pounding*, op. cit., p. 14.
24   Political Unit Collection (PUC), 11 April 1974.
25   Dell, *A Hard Pounding*, p. 14.
26   PUC, 17 May 1974.
27   Ibid.
28   Dell, *A Hard Pounding*, p. 78.
29   Joel Barnett, *Inside the Treasury*, André Deutsch, 1982, p. 50.
30   Ibid., p. 49.
31   Donoughue, op. cit., pp. 56–7.
32   Ibid., p. 57.
33   PD, July 1974, cols 1048–53, quoted in Dell, *A Hard Pounding*, p. 80.
34   Barnett, op. cit., pp. 32–3.
35   Ibid., p. 33.
36   PUC, Andrew Graham, 2 August 1974.
37   Quoted in TTOML, p. 381.
38   Castle, *Diaries*, vol. 1, p. 188.
39   Phillip Whitehead, *The Writing on the Wall*, Michael Joseph, 1985, p. 129.
40   Quoted in Wickham-Jones, op. cit., p. 138.
41   Barnett, op. cit.
42   HP – D, 19 August 1974.
43   Ibid.
44   Dell, *A Hard Pounding*, op. cit., p. 82.
45   Benn, *Diaries*, 4: *Against the Tide 1973–7*, Hutchinson, 1989, p. 130.
46   HP – D, 6 August 1974.
47   Donald MacDougall, *Don and Mandarin: Memoirs of an Economist*, John Murray, 1987, quoted in Dell, p. 38.
48   Barnett, op. cit., p. 33.
49   PUC, 19 September 1975.
50   Dell, unpublished diaries, op. cit., p. 270, 20 September 1974.
51   Dell, *A Hard Pounding*, op. cit., p. 112.
52   HP – D, 29 October 1974.
53   Dell, *A Hard Pounding*, p. 116 et seq.
54   Ibid., p. 116.
55   Ibid., p. 117.
56   Benn, *Diaries*, 4, p. 325.
57   Donoughue, op. cit., p. 6.
58   Dell, unpublished diaries, op. cit., p. 287, 17 October 1974.
59   Quoted in Dell, *A Hard Pounding*, op. cit., p. 122.
60   Benn, *Diaries*, 4, p. 325.
61   Dell, unpublished diaries, op. cit., pp. 369–40, 6 March 1975.
62–64   Barnett, op. cit., p. 64.
65–67   Castle, *Diaries*, vol. 2, p. 361 et seq., 14 April 1975.

68–69   HP – D, 9–10 April 1975.
70–72   Ibid., 14–16 April 1975.

CHAPTER 45   THE TREASURY – REALITIES, 1975

  1   Castle, *Diaries*, vol. 2, p. 410.
  2   Ibid., p. 414.
  3   Dell, unpublished diaries, op. cit., p. 104, early June.
  4   Castle, *Diaries*, vol. 2, p. 426, 20 June 1975.
  5   Benn, *Diaries*, 4, p. 405, 20 June 1975.
  6   Figures from Dell, *A Hard Pounding*, op. cit., p. 147.
  7   Gardner, op. cit., p. 55.
  8   Castle, *Diaries*, vol. 2, p. 398.
 9–10 Both ibid., p. 400, 22 May 1975.
  11 HP – D, 22 May 1975.
  12 Dell, *A Hard Pounding*, p. 150.
  13 Quoted ibid., p. 153.
  14 Jack Jones, *Union Man*, Collins, 1986, p. 296.
15–16 Both Barnett, op. cit., p. 64.
17–19 Jones, op. cit., pp. 296, 295, and quoted on p. 296.
20–21 TTOML, p. 394.
  22 HP – D, 23 May 1975.
  23 Ibid., 11 June 1975.
  24 Dell, *A Hard Pounding*, pp. 151–2.
  25 Benn, *Diaries*, 4, p. 403, 18 June 1975.
  26 Ibid., p. 387, 7 June 1975.
  27 Donoughue, op. cit., p. 63.
  28 Benn, *Diaries*, 4, p. 404.
  29 HP – D, 20 June 1975.
30–31 Benn, *Diaries*, 4, pp. 404–5.
  32 Dell, *A Hard Pounding*, p. 160.
33–34 HP – D, 30 June 1975.
  35 Donoughue, op. cit., p. 67.
  36 TTOML, pp. 394–5.
37–38 HP – D, 30 June 1975.
  39 TTOML, p. 395.
  40 Wilson, *Final Term*, quoted in Dell, *A Hard Pounding*, p. 165.
41–42 Castle, *Diaries*, vol. 2, pp. 440–2.
  43 PD, vol. 894, cols 1189–90.
44–46 Ibid., cols 1192–3.
  47 TTOML, p. 403.
  48 PD, vol. 894, col. 1193.
49–50 Both ibid., col. 1198.
  51 All at HP – D, 1 July 1975.
  52 Ibid., 2 July 1975.
  53 Ibid., 3 July 1975.
  54 Ibid., 5 July 1975.
  55 Ibid., 7 July 1975.
  56 All ibid., 8 July 1975.
  57 Dell, unpublished diaries, op. cit., p. 143, 8 July.
  58 HP – D, 9 July 1975.

59–61   Castle, *Diaries*, vol. 2, pp. 452–3.
62   HP – D, 10 July 1975.
63   HP – misc. end papers, 10 July 1975.
64   PD, vol. 895, col. 904.
65   Castle, *Diaries*, vol. 2, p. 456.
66–67   Benn, *Diaries*, 4, pp. 414–15.
68   Dell, *A Hard Pounding*, pp. 172–3.
69   HP – D, misc. end papers, 10 July 1975.
70   Jones, op. cit., p. 298.
71   Both Castle, *Diaries*, vol. 2, 456.
72   Jones, op. cit., p. 298.
73–74   Benn, *Diaries*, 4, pp. 413–14.
75–76   Leo Pliatzky, *Getting and Spending: Public Expenditure, Employment and Inflation*, Basil Blackwell, 1982, pp. 138–9.
77   PD, vol. 895, 11 July 1975, col. 1190.
78   *The Attack on Inflation*, Cmnd 6151, quoted ibid., p. 138.
79   Castle, *Diaries*, vol. 2, p. 456.
80–82   Quoted in Barnett, op. cit., pp. 68–9.
83   Castle, *Diaries*, vol. 2, p. 485.
84   Benn, *Diaries*, 4, p. 460.
85   Donoughue, op. cit., p. 53.
86   Benn, *Diaries*, 4, all at pp. 466–7.
87   HP – D, misc. end papers, 5 December 1975.
88   HP – D, 5 December 1975.
89   Ibid., 8 December 1975.
90   Part, op. cit., p. 177.
91   Donoughue, op. cit., p. 53.
92–93   Barnett, op. cit., p. 73.
94–95   Benn, *Diaries*, 4, pp. 477–8.
96   Quoted in Ziegler, *Wilson*, p. 448.
97   *Sunday Telegraph*, 16 November 1975, quoted in Benn, *Diaries*, vol. 4, p. 461.
98   Denzil Davies MP, private conversation.
99   Castle, *Diaries*, vol. 2, p. 595.
100   HP – D, misc. end papers, 11 December 1975.
101   Ibid., 9 December 1975.
102   Castle, *Diaries*, vol. 2, p. 602.
103   HP – D, misc. end papers, 12 December 1975.
104   Castle, *Diaries*, vol. 2, p. 512.
105   HP – D, 30 September 1975.
106–110 All Labour Party Conference Report (Blackpool), 1975, pp. 200–204.

CHAPTER 46   'BEAUTIFUL DAY, STERLING GOING DOWN', 1975–6

1   Dell, *A Hard Pounding*, p. 193.
2   Burk and Cairncross, op. cit., p. 31.
3   Untraced, author's own recollection.
4   HP – D, 4 March 1976.
5   HP – D, 14 March 1976.
6   Ibid.
7   Dell, *Chancellors*, p. 422.

8   Castle, *Diaries*, vol. 2, p. 687.
9   HP – D, 11 March 1976.
10 HP – D, 25 March 1976.
11 Conversation with Lord Glenamara.
12 HP – D, both 20 April 1976.
13 PUC, Graham, 6 April 1976, also quoted in Morgan, op. cit., p. 523.
14 Private conversation with Lord Lea.
15 TTOML, p. 396.
16 Dell, *Hard Pounding*, pp. 189–90.
17 Morgan, op. cit., p. 528.
18 Benn, *Diaries*, 4, p. 572, 27 May 1975.
19 Morgan, op. cit., p. 528.
20 HP – D, 25 April 1976.
21 Ibid., 27 April 1976.
22 Ibid., 28 April 1976.
23 Ibid., 30 April 1976.
24 Ibid., 2 May 1976.
25 All ibid., at 4–5 May 1976.
26–27 Morgan, op. cit., p. 529.
28 Quoted in TTOML, p. 397.
29–30 HP – D, 14–16 May 1976.
31–32 Pliatzky, op. cit., p. 148.
33 TTOML, p. 427.
34 All at HP – D, 2–5 June 1976.
35 TTOML, p. 427.
36 Benn, *Diaries*, 4, p. 593, 9 July 1976.
37 Conversation with Sir Derek Mitchell.
38 TTOML, p. 428.
39 Both Benn, *Diaries*, 4, p. 576.
40 Ibid., pp. 582–3, 21 June 1976.
41 PUC note, 27 June 1976.
42 HP – D, 25 June 1976.
43 Benn, *Diaries*, 4, p. 588, 2 July 1976.
44 Ibid., 6 July 1976.
45 PUC note to PM, 11 July 1976.
46 Benn, *Diaries*, 4, p. 595, 15 July 1976.
47 HP – D, 15 July 1976
48 PD, vol. 915, 22 July 1976, col. 2010.
49 Ibid., col. 2012.
50 Ibid., col. 2017.
51 Ibid., col. 2024.
52 Cited in Burk and Cairncross, op. cit., p. 51.
53 HP – D, 17 July 1976.
54 Private conversation.
55 TTOML, p. 428.
56 Benn, *Diaries*, 4, p. 609.
57 All at HP – D, 10 September 1976.
58 Dell, *A Hard Pounding*, p. 235.
59–60 HP – D, 28 September 1976.
61 Quoted in Dell, *A Hard Pounding*, p. 236.

62   Unidentified SDP, MP, quoted in Ivor Crewe and Anthony King, *SDP: The Birth, Life and Death of the Social Democratic Party*, OUP, 1995, p. 26.
63   Labour Party Conference Report (Blackpool), 1976, pp. 318–19.
64   Benn, *Diaries*, 4, p. 616.
65   TTOML, p. 429.

CHAPTER 47   THE TREASURY – THE BROKERS' MEN, 1976

1   Dell, *A Hard Pounding*, p. 326.
2   Private conversation.
3   Healey article in the *Institutional Investor*, June 1987, quoted in Dell, *A Hard Pounding*.
4   Susan Crosland, *Tony Crosland*, Jonathan Cape, 1982, p. 379.
5   HP – D, 6 October 1976.
6–7   Conversation with the author.
8   Both HP – D, 6 October 1976.
9   TTOML, p. 431.
10   HP – D, 6 October 1976.
11   Quoted in Stephen Fay and Hugo Young, *The Day the £ Nearly Died*, *Sunday Times* reprint, 1978, p. 20.
12–13   Quoted in Crosland, op. cit., p. 372.
14   HP – D, 25 October 1976.
15   Quoted in Morgan, op. cit., p. 553.
16   Ibid., p. 376.
17   Dell, *A Hard Pounding*, pp. 239–40.
18   PD, vol. 917, 11 October 1976, cols 47, 49.
19   Ibid., cols 43–4.
20   Quoted ibid., col. 52.
21   Private conversation.
22   Private conversation.
23   *The Times*, 17 November 1976, quoted in Dell, *A Hard Pounding*, pp. 256–7.
24   HP – misc. papers, 27 October 1976.
25   Benn, *Diaries*, 4, p. 624.
26   Ibid.
27   Dell, *A Hard Pounding*, p. 251.
28   Quoted in Fay and Young, op. cit., p. 25.
29   Benn, *Diaries*, 4, p. 657.
30   HP – misc. papers, undated, in D 46, October 1976.
31   Morgan, op. cit., p. 543.
32–33   HP – D, 19 October 1976.
34   HP – misc. papers, October 1976–June 1977, vol. 46, no precise date.
35   James Callaghan, *Time and Chance*, Collins, 1987, p. 432, quoted in Burk and Cairncross, op. cit., p. 65.
36   Benn, unpublished diary, quoted in Burk and Cairncross, op. cit., p. 71.
37   Memo from Bernard Donoughue to Prime Minister, 16 November 1976.
38   Private conversation, December 2000.
39   Private conversation.
40   Donoughue, op. cit., pp 95–6.
41   Fay and Young, op. cit., p. 25.
42–44   HP – D, 5 November 1976.

45–47 Ibid., 11 November 1976.
48 Ibid., 13 November 1976.
49 Ibid., 15 November 1976.
50 Ibid., 16 November 1976.
51 Conversation with Roy Hattersley.
52 Fay and Young, op. cit., p. 29.
53 Conversation with the author.
54 Burk and Cairncross, op. cit., p. 82.
55 Interview with Harold Lever, 1989, in Burk and Cairncross, op. cit., p. 82.
56 Morgan, op. cit., p. 545.
57 Pliatzky, op. cit., p. 153.
58 Dell, *A Hard Pounding*, p. 249.
59 Both at HP – D, 19 November 1976.
60 HP – D, 22 November 1976.
61 John Cole, *As It Seemed to Me*, Weidenfeld & Nicolson, 1995, p. 163.
62 HP – D, 23 November 1976.
63 Dell, *A Hard Pounding*, p. 258.
64 Cole, op. cit., p. 163.
65 Dell, *A Hard Pounding*, p. 259.
66 Crosland, op. cit., pp. 377–80.
67 Benn, *Diaries*, 4, p. 656.
68 Ibid., quoted in Dell, *A Hard Pounding*, p. 262.
69 HP – D, 24 November 1976.
70–71 Burk and Cairncross, op. cit., p. 90.
72–74 All HP – D, 26, 25, 27 November.
75 Interviews quoted in Burk and Cairncross, op. cit., p. 91.
76 Dell, *A Hard Pounding*, p. 274.
77 HP – D, 28 November 1976.
78–79 All HP – D, 1 December 1976.
80–81 Crosland, op. cit., pp. 380, 379.
82 HP – D, 30 November 1976.
83 Crosland, op. cit., p. 380.
84 HP – D, 1 December 1976.
85 Morgan, op. cit., p. 547.
86 Burk and Cairncross, op. cit., p. 103.
87 *The Man Who Did the Dirty Work* – A Film Portrait of Denis Healey, produced by Michael Cockerell for the BBC, 1989.
88 HP – D, 1 December 1976.
89 Both ibid., 2 December 1976.
90–91 Ibid., 3 December 1976.
92 Ibid., 5 December 1976.
93 Callaghan, op. cit., pp. 438–9.
94 HP – D, 6 December 1976.
95 Benn, *Diaries*, 4, p. 66, 1 December 1976.
96 Crosland, op. cit., p. 381.
97 Dell, *A Hard Pounding*, p. 270.
98 Burk and Cairncross, op. cit., p. 103.
99–100 Barnett, op. cit., pp. 105, 106.
101 Benn, *Diaries*, 4, p. 683.
102 HP – D, 7 December 1976.

103–104 Barnett, op. cit., pp. 106, 110.
105–107 PD, vol. 923, 21 December 1976, cols 483–5.
108 Dell, *A Hard Pounding*, p. 286.

CHAPTER 48   A QUIET TIME AND AFTER

1 Labour Party Conference Report (Brighton), 1977, p. 175.
2 Letter to the author.
3 TTOML, p. 435.
4–5 Labour Party Conference Report (Brighton), 1977, p. 174.
6–8 Barnett, op. cit., p. 142.
9 D. E. Butler and Denis Kavanagh, *The General Election of 1979*, Macmillan, 1980, diagram, p. 29.
10 TTOML, p. 434.
11 Dell, *Chancellors*, p. 447.
12–14 Morgan, op. cit., pp. 575–8.
15 Economic Survey quoted in Butler and Kavanagh, op. cit., p. 24.
16 Labour Party Conference Report (Blackpool), 1978, p. 220.
17 Quoted in Pliatzky, op. cit., p. 172.
18 TTOML, pp. 461–2.
19 Conversation with Roy Hattersley.
20 Barnett, op. cit., p. 154.
21 Morgan, op. cit., p. 641.
22 TTOML, p. 468.
23 Labour Party Conference Report (Blackpool), 1978, p. 221.
24 TTOML, p. 462.
25 Barnett, op. cit., p. 162.
26 Morgan, op. cit., p. 649.
27 TTOML, p. 398.
28 Conversation with the author.
29 Conversation with Sir Kenneth Stowe.
30 TTOML, p. 398.
31 Conversation with Roy Hattersley.
32 TTOML, p. 398.
33 Pliatzky, op. cit., pp. 172–3.
34 Morgan, op. cit., p. 649.
35 Cole, op. cit., p. 182.
36–37 Robert Taylor, *The TUC – From the General Strike to New Unionism*, Palgrave, 2000, pp. 238–9.
38 TTOML, p. 398.
39 Conversation with Roy Hattersley.
40 Conversation with Robert Maclennan.
41 Cole, op. cit., p. 182.
42 Morgan, op. cit., p. 657.
43 Barnett, op. cit., p. 160.
44 HP – D, end papers, 1978.
45–46 Morgan, op. cit., pp. 655, 661.
47 Barnett, op. cit., p. 174.
48 Morgan, op. cit., p. 663.
49 Barnett, op. cit., p. 173.
50 Morgan, op. cit., p. 666.

51–52   Barnett, op. cit., pp. 171, 174.
53–54   Taylor, op. cit., p. 241.
    55   Conversation with Sir Kenneth Stowe.
    56   Barnett, op. cit., p. 176.
57–60   *The Economy, the Government and Trade Union Responsibilities*, TUC
        publication, February 1979.
    61   TTOML, p. 463.
    62   Conversation with Sir Kenneth Stowe.
    63   TTOML, p. 463.
    64   Morgan, op. cit., pp. 661–2.
    65   Conversation with Sir Kenneth Stowe.
    66   HP – D, 22 March 1979.
    67   Quoted in Morgan, op. cit., p. 682.

CHAPTER 49   TWO DEFEATS AND A VICTORY

     1   Labour Party Conference Report (Brighton), 1979.
     2   All Tony Benn, *Diaries, 5: Conflicts of Interest 1977–80*, 1989, p. 484.
     3   HP – D, 2 April 1979.
     4   Benn, *Diaries*, 5, p. 486.
     5   HP – D, 6 April 1979.
     6   Butler and Kavanagh, op. cit., p. 180.
     7   HP – D, 9 April 1979.
     8   All at ibid., 10 April 1979.
     9   All at ibid., 11 April 1979.
 10–14   Ibid., 20–25 April 1979.
    15   Butler and Kavanagh, op. cit., p. 264.
    16   Benn, *Diaries*, 5, p. 492.
    17   Butler and Kavanagh, op. cit., p. 265.
 18–19   Labour Party Conference Report (Brighton), 1979, pp. 286, 289.
    20   Author's conversation.
    21   Labour Party Conference Report (Brighton), 1979, p. 287 (Ray Apps).
 22–23   Benn, *Diaries*, 5, pp. 545–6.
    24   Morgan, op. cit., p. 712.
    25   Benn, *Diaries*, 5, p. 546, 5 October.
    26   Crewe and King, op. cit., p. 33.
    27   TTOML, p. 470.
    28   Conversation with Donald Anderson.
    29   Cole, op. cit., p. 216.
    30   HP – D, 24 September 1980.
 31–32   Crewe and King, op. cit., pp. 36, 39.
 33–34   Labour Party Special Conference Report (Wembley), May 1980, p. 259.
 35–37   Ibid., pp. 251, 250, 247.
    38   Crewe and King, op. cit., p. 36.
    39   HP – D, 31 May 1980.
    40   Morgan, op. cit., p. 716.
    41   Conversation with Donald Anderson, MP.
 42–43   Crewe and King, op. cit., pp. 46–7.
 44–45   William Rodgers, *Fourth Among Equals*, Politicos, 2000, pp. 190–91.
    46   *Observer*, c. September 1980.

47–48 Benn, *Diaries, 6: The End of an Era, 1980*, Hutchinson, 1992, pp. 31–2, 1 October 1980.
  49 Labour Party Special Conference Report (Wembley), 1980, p. 27.
  50 Crewe and King, op. cit., p. 49.
51–52 HP – D, 8 October 1980.
  53 Ibid., 13 October 1980.
54–55 All Benn, *Diaries, 6*, p. 38, 19 October 1980.
  56 All at a transcript of *Weekend World*, 19 October 1980.
  57 Conversation with John Horam.
  58 Conversation with Donald Anderson.
  59 Dell, unpublished diaries, p. 90, no date ? September 1974.
  60 Conversation with Tam Dalyell, MP.
  61 Conversation with Leo Abse.
  62 Conversation with Robert Sheldon.
  63 Conversation with Peter Hardy, quoted in the author's *The Lost Leaders*, op. cit.
64–66 Crewe and King, op. cit., p. 44, 74.
  67 Conversation with Barry Jones.
68–70 HP – D, 13–18 October 1980.
  71 Benn, *Diaries, 6*, p. 39, 20 October 1980.
72–74 *Times*, 21 October 1980.
  75 HP – D, 28 October 1980.
76–77 Benn, *Diaries, 6*, p. 43.
  78 Ibid.
  79 HP – D, 4 November 1980.
  80 Conversation with Roy Hattersley.
81–82 Benn, *Diaries, 6*, p. 44, 4 November 1980.
  83 Conversation with Roy Hattersley.
  84 HP – D, 10 November 1980.
  85 Benn, *Diaries, 6*, p. 46, 10 November 1980.
  86 Rodgers, *Fourth Among Equals*, p. 203.

CHAPTER 50 A MAD WORLD MY MASTERS

   1 TTOML, p. 482.
   2 Conversation with Denis Healey.
   3 HP – D, 13 November 1980.
   4 Ibid.
   5 Conversation with Richard Heller.
   6 Private conversation and elsewhere.
   7 Crewe and King, op. cit., pp. 91–2.
   8 Benn, *Diaries, 6*, p. 87, also quoted in the author's *The Lost Leaders*, op. cit.
   9 HP – misc. papers, December 1980.
  10 Benn, *Diaries, 6*, p. 70, 24 January 1981.
  11 Ibid., pp. 75–6, 26 January 1981.
  12 HP – D, 2 February 1981.
  13 Benn, *Diaries, 6*, p. 113, 28 March 1981.
  14 HP – D, 25 March 1981.
  15 Benn, *Diaries, 6*, p. 111, 24 March 1981.
  16 Ibid., p. 113, 29 March 1981.
  17 HP – D, 2 April 1981.

18 Ibid., 3 April 1981.
19 Ibid., 4 April 1981.
20 TTOML, p. 481.
21 Rodgers, *Fourth Among Equals*, p. 203.
22 Quoted in Whitehead, op. cit., pp. 405–6.
23 Benn, *Diaries*, 6, p. 120.
24 ibid., p. 121.
25 Ibid., p. 132, 19 May 1981.
26 All ibid., p. 45, 7 November 1981.
27 Conversation with Richard Heller.
28 Both HP – D, 9 September 1981.
29 Ibid., 13 September 1981.
30 Conversation with David Warburton.
31 *Times*, 7 September 1981.
32 Benn, *Diaries*, 6, p. 146, 8 September 1981.
33 Ibid., p. 148, 17 September 1981.
34 *Times*, 11 September 1981.
35 Ibid.
36 HP – D, 15 September 1981.
37 Conversation with David Warburton.
38 *Times*, 10 September 1981.
39 HP – D, 22 September 1981.
40 Conversation with Richard Heller.
41 *Times*, 18 September 1981.
42 HP – D, 19 September 1981.
43 Benn, *Diaries*, 6, p. 152, 23 September 1981.
44 Ibid., p. 149, 19 September 1981.
45 Conversation with David Warburton.
46 HP – D, 28 September 1981.
47 *Times*, 22 September 1981.
48 Ibid.
49 Benn, *Diaries*, 6, p. 151, 22 September 1981.
50 Ibid., p. 153, 26 September 1981.
51 Ibid., p. 151, 22 September 1981.
52 TTOML, pp. 483–4.
53 Conversation with David Warburton.
54 Benn, *Diaries*, 6, p. 154, 28 September 1981.
55 Conversation with David Warburton.
56 Benn, *Diaries*, 6, p. 154.

CHAPTER 51 THE LONG DEFILE

1 All at Benn, op. cit. p. 161, 21 Oct 1981.
2 Butler and Kavanagh, *The British General Election of 1983*, Macmillan 1984, p. 330.
3 HP – D, 19 October 1981.
4 Ibid., 19–20 October.
5 Ibid., 22 October.
6 Richard Heller article, *The Observer*, May 1983.
7 Ibid., 5 April 1982.
8 Quoted in Benn, op. cit., p. 206, 5 April.

9   Conversation at that time with Denis Healey.
10 HP – D, 26 May.
11 Benn op. cit., 26 May.
12 All figures from Crewe and King, op. cit., p. 552.
13 *Daily Telegraph* Commons Sketch, 25 May 1982.
14 Conversation with Richard Heller.
15 HP – D.
16 Conversation with Richard Heller.
17 Butler and Kavanagh, op. cit., p. 332.
18 HP – D 16 March 1983.
19 Conversation with Richard Heller.
20 TTOML, pp. 455–6.
21 Butler and Kavanagh, op. cit., p. 90.
22 Morgan 'Callaghan', op. cit., p. 726.
23 All at Benn, op. cit., p. 283, 6 May.
24 HP – D, both 9 May.
25 Ibid., 10 May.
26 Ibid., 16–18 May.
27 Ibid., 19 May.
28 Ibid., all 21–25 May.
29 Ibid., all 27–31 May.
30 Butler and Kavanagh, op. cit., p. 279.
31 Conversation with Richard Heller.
32 Butler and Kavanagh, op. cit., p. 282.
33 HP – D, 2 June.
34 Quoted in Crewe and King, op. cit., p. 278.
35 Conversation with Richard Heller.
36 Conversation with David Warburton.
37 HP – D, 12 June.
38 Ibid., 12 June.
39 Ibid., 16 June.
40 TTOML p. 507.
41 All at Benn, op. cit., p. 337.
42 Quoted at PD, vol. 27, Feb 1984 col. 35.
43 Ibid. col. 38.
44 Ibid. col. 41.
45 Ibid. col. 41–42.
46 *Daily Telegraph* Commons Sketch, 23 March 1984.
47 Ibid.
48 TTOML p. 533.
49 TTOML p. 525.
50 *Daily Telegraph* Commons Sketch, 2 October 1985.

ENVOI

1   Conversation with Roy Hattersley.
2   Conversation with Denzil Davies.

BIBLIOGRAPHY

Annan, Noel, *Our Age: Portrait of a Generation*, Weidenfeld and Nicholson, 1990.

Barnett, Joel, *Inside the Treasury*, André Deutsch, 1872

Bartlett, C. J., *The Long Retreat: A Short History of British Defence Policy, 1945–70*, Macmillan, 1972

Baylis, John, *Anglo-American Defence Relations 1939–80*, Macmillan, 1981

— (ed.), *British Defence Policy in a Changing World*, Croom Helm, 1977

Beckett, Francis, *Enemy Within: The Rise and Fall of the British Communist Party*, John Murray, 1995

Beckett, Ian, and Gooch, John (eds), *Politicians and Defence: Studies in the Formation of Defence Policy 1845–1970*, Manchester University Press, 1981

Benn, Tony, *Years of Hope: Diaries, 1, 1940–62*, ed. R. Winstone, Hutchinson, 1994
Out of the Wilderness: Diaries, 2, 1963–67, Hutchinson, 1987

— *Office without Power: Diaries, 3, 1968–72*, Hutchinson, 1988

— *Against the Tide: Diaries, 4, 1973–76*, Hutchinson, 1989

— *Conflicts of Interest: Diaries, 5, 1977–80*, Hutchinson, 1989

— *The End of an Era: Diaries, 6, 1980–90*, Hutchinson, 1992

Berrington, Hugh, *Backbench Opinion in the House of Commons 1945–55*, Pergamon, 1973

Brivati, Brian, *Hugh Gaitskell*, Richard Cohen Books, 1996

Broadbent, Sir Ewen, *The Military and Government from Macmillan to Heseltine*, Macmillan, 1988

Bullock, Alan, *Life and Times of Ernest Bevin*, vol. 1: *Trade Union Leader*, Heinemann, 1960; vol. 3; *Foreign Secretary 1945–51*, Oxford University Press, 1985

Burk, Kathy, and Cairncross, Alec, *'Goodbye Great Britain': The 1976 IMF Crisis*, Yale University Press, 1992

Butler, D. E., and Kavanagh, Denis, *The General Election of 1979*, Macmillan, 1980

— *The British General Election of 1983*, Macmillan, 1984

Callaghan, James, *Time and Chance*, Collins, 1987

Cameron, Lord (Neil Cameron), *In the Midst of Things*, Hodder & Stoughton, 1986

Carlton, David, *Anthony Eden*, Allen Lane, 1981

Carver, Michael, *Out of Step: Memoirs of a Field Marshal*, Hutchinson, 1989
— *Tightrope Walking: British Defence Policy since 1945*, Hutchinson, 1992
Castle, Barbara, *The Castle Diaries*, I: 1964–70, Weidenfeld & Nicolson, 1984; II: 1974–76, Weidenfeld & Nicolson, 1980
Chin Kin Wah, *The Defence of Malaysia and Singapore*, Cambridge University Press, 1983
Chisholm, Anne, and Davie, Michael, *Beaverbrook*, Hutchinson, 1992
Clutterbuck, Richard, *Britain in Agony: The Growth of Political Violence*, Faber, 1978
Cole, John, *As It Seemed to Me*, Weidenfeld & Nicolson, 1995
Crewe, Ivor and King, Anthony, *SDP: The Birth, Life and Death of the Social Democratic Party*, Oxford University Press, 1995
Crosland, Susan, *Tony Crosland*, Jonathan Cape, 1982
Crossman, R. H. S., *The Crossman Diaries 1964–70*, ed. Janet Morgan, Hamish Hamilton/Jonathan Cape, 1979
— *The Backbench Diaries of Richard Crossman, 1951–64*, ed. Janet Morgan, Hamish Hamilton, 1979
— *The Diaries of a Cabinet Minister*, I: 1964–66; II: 1966–68; III: 1968–70, Hamish Hamilton/Jonathan Cape, 1975, 1976, 1979
— (ed.), *New Fabian Essays*, Turnstile Press, 1952
Darby, Phillip, *British Defence Policy East of Suez 1947–68*, Oxford University/RIIA, 1973
Deighton, Anne, *The Impossible Peace: Britain, the Division of Germany and the Origins of the Cold War*, Clarendon Press, 1990
Dell, Edmund, *A Hard Pounding: Politics and Economic Crisis 1974–1976*, Oxford University Press, 1991
— *The Chancellors: A History of Chancellors of the Exchequer 1945–90*, HarperCollins, 1996
— *The Schuman Plan and the British Abdication of Leadership in Europe*, Oxford University Press, 1995
Donoughue, Bernard, *Prime Minister: The Conduct of Policy under Harold Wilson and James Callaghan*, Jonathan Cape, 1987
Fay, Stephen and Young, Hugo, *The Day the £ Nearly Died*, Sunday Times, 1978
Freedman, Lawrence, *Britain and Nuclear Weapons*, Macmillan/RIIA, 1980
Gardner, Nick, *Decade of Discontent: The Changing British Economy since 1973*, Basil Blackwell, 1987
Giles, Frank, *The Locust Years: The Story of the Fourth French Republic 1946–58*, Secker & Warburg, 1991
Gordon Walker, Patrick, *Political Diaries 1932–71*, ed. Robert Pearce, The Historians' Press, 1991
Graham, Dominick and Bidwell, Shelford, *Tug of War: The Battle for Italy 1943–45*, Hodder & Stoughton, 1986
Grant, John, *Member of Parliament*, Michael Joseph, 1974
Grove, Eric J., *Vanguard to Trident: British Naval Policy since World War II*, Bodley Head, 1987
Hattersley, Roy, *Fifty Years On*, Little, Brown, 1997
Heath, Edward, *The Course of My Life*, Hodder & Stoughton, 1998
Hennessy, Peter, *Never Again, Britain 1945–51*, Jonathan Cape, 1992
Horne, Alistair, *Macmillan*, I: 1894–1956; II: 1957–86, Macmillan, 1991
Hunter, Leslie, *The Road to Brighton Pier*, Arthur Barker, 1959
Ignotus, Paul, *Hungary*, Ernest Benn, 1972

Jackson, Robert, *Rebels and Whips: An Analysis of Dissension, Discipline and Cohesion in British Political Parties*, Macmillan, 1968

Jackson, Sir William, and Bramall, Lord, *The Chiefs*, Brassey's, UK, 1992

Jefferys, Kevin, *Anthony Crosland*, Richard Cohen Books, 1999

Jenkins, Roy, *A Life at the Centre*, Macmillan, 1991

Johnson, Franklyn, A., *Defence by Ministry: The British Ministry of Defence 1944–74*, Duckworth, 1980

Johnston, Sir Charles, *The View from Steamer Point*, Collins, 1964

Jones, Jack, *Union Man*, Collins, 1986

Kaiser, Philipp, *Journeying Far and Wide*, Charles Scribner's Sons, 1992

Keohane, Dan, *Labour Defence Policy since 1945*, Leicester University Press, 1993

Kilfoyle, Peter, *Left Behind*, Politico's, 2000

King, Cecil, *The Cecil King Diary 1965–70*, Jonathan Cape, 1975

Kramnick, Isaac, and Sheerman, Barry, *Harold Laski: A Life on the Left*, Hamish Hamilton, 1993

Lewis, Roger, and Owen, Roger, *Suez*, Clarendon Press, 1989

Little, Tom, *South Arabia: Arena of Conflict*, Pall Mall Press, 1968

MacDougall, Donald, *Don and Mandarin: Memoirs of an Economist*, John Murray, 1987

Mayhew, Christopher, *Time to Explain*, Hutchinson, 1987

Minkin, Lewis, *The Labour Party Conference*, Allen Lane, 1978

Morgan, Kenneth O., *Callaghan: A Life*, Oxford University Press, 1997

Mountbatten, Earl, *From Shore to Shore: Tour Diaries 1953–79*, Collins, 1989

Part, Sir Antony, *The Making of a Mandarin*, André Deutsch, 1990

Pearce, Edward, *The Lost Leaders*, Little, Brown, 1997

Pimlott, Ben, *Harold Wilson*, HarperCollins, 1992

— (ed.), *The Political Diary of Hugh Dalton, 1918–40, 1945–60*, Jonathan Cape/LSE, 1986

Pliatzky, Leon, *Getting and Spending: Public Expenditure, Employment and Inflation*, Basil Blackwell, 1982

Radice, Giles, *Socialism with a Human Face*, Civic Press, 1981

Reed, Bruce and Williams, Geoffrey, *Denis Healey and the Politics of Power*, Sidgwick & Jackson, 1971

Rodgers, William T., *Fourth Among Equals*, Politico's, 2000

— (ed.) *Hugh Gaitskell 1906–63*, Thames & Hudson, 1964

Rolph, C. H., *Kingsley: The Life, Letters and Diaries of Kinsley Martin*, Victor Gollancz, 1973

Rothschild, Joseph, *Return to Diversity: A Political History of East Central Europe since World War II*, Oxford University Press, 1989

Schumpeter, Joseph, *Capitalism, Socialism and Democracy*, Harvard University Press, rev. edn, 1946

Scott, Drusilla, *A. D. Lindsay*, Basil Blackwell, 1971

Short, Edward, *Whip to Wilson*, Macdonald, 1989

Taylor, Richard, *Against the Bomb: The British Peace Movement 1958–65*, Clarendon Press, 1988

Taylor, Robert, *The TUC – From the General Strike to New Unionism*, Palgrave, 2000

Thomas, Hugh, *The Suez Affair*, Weidenfeld & Nicolson, 1967

Webb, Sidney and Beatrice, *Soviet Communism: A New Civilisation*, Longmans, 1935

Whitehead, Phillip, *The Writing on the Wall: Britain in the Seventies*, Michael Joseph, 1985

Wickham-Jones, Mark, *Economic Strategy and the Labour Party: Politics and Policy-Making 1970–83*, St Martin's Press, 1996
Wigg, Lord, *George Wigg*, Michael Joseph, 1972
Williams, Philip (ed.), *The Diary of Hugh Gaitskell 1945–56*, Jonathan Cape, 1983
Wilmot, Chester, *The Struggle for Europe*, Collins, 1952
Wilson, Harold, *Final Term: The Labour Government 1974–76*, Weidenfeld & Nicolson/Michael Joseph, 1979
Ziegler, *Mountbatten: The Official Biography*, Collins, 1985
— *Wilson: The Authorized Life*, Weidenfeld & Nicolson, 1993

Unpublished Papers

The Healey Papers (HP-1935–83)
Healey Diaries (HP–D) 1935–83
End papers and Cabinet Table notes 1964–70, 1974–79 (HP-Misc.)
Proposal by Denis Healey for Unpublished Transport Section of a projected history of the Italian campaign
Unpublished diary of Tony Benn 1956 (Benn Unpublished)
Unpublished Diary of Edmund Dell 1974 and 75 (Bedleian – permission of Mrs Suzanne Dell (DUC – Dell unpublished collection))
Cabinet papers 1964–68 (PRO)
Miscellaneous papers from Museum of Labour History Manchester
Policy Unit papers (Bernard Donoughue collection)
D. E. Butler Election Studies 1945– Interview archive material

Interviews

Leo Abse, Donald Anderson MP, Lord Barnett (Joel Barnett), Tony Benn, Harold Best MP, Stephen Bird, Lady Boothroyd (Betty Boothroyd), FM Lord Carver, Lady Castle (Barbara Castle), Susan Crosland, Tam Dalyell MP, Denzil Davies MP, the late Edmund Dell, Lord Donoughue, Adm. Colin Dunlop, Sir Christopher France, Douglas Gabb, Frank Giles, Lord Glenamara (Edward Short), Lord Hardy (Peter Hardy), Lord Hattersley (Roy Hattersley), Richard Heller, Adm. of the Fleet Lord Hill-Norton, John Horam MP, Lord Jenkins (Roy Jenkins), Barry Jones MP, Lord Judd (Frank Judd), Lord Lea (David Lea), Alan Lord, Robert Maclennan, Bryan Magee, Sir Derek Mitchell, Sir Nicholas Monck, Lord Moore (Phillip Moore), Lord Morgan, Sir Patrick Nairne, Giles Radice MP, Adam Raphael, Lord Richardson (Gordon Richardson), Szuszanna Schonfield, the late Roger Stott, Sir Kenneth Stowe, Lord Taverne (Dick Taverne), Lord Thomson (George Thomson), David Warburton

Newspapers and reports

Corriere della sera, *Daily Express*, *Daily Herald*, *Daily Mail*, *Daily Mirror*, *Daily Telegraph*, *Daily Worker*, *Economist*, *Guardian*, *New Statesman*, *News Chronicle*, *Spectator*, *Sun*, *Sunday Express*, *The Times*, *L'Unita*, *Yorkshire Evening News*, *Yorkshire Evening Post*
Labour Party Annual Conference Reports, 1945, 1952–4, 1957, 1959–60, 1975–80 (Museum of Labour History, Manchester)
Special Trades Union Congress March 1973 Report:
Economic Policy and Collective Bargaining in 1973.
Joint statement by the TUC and the Government Feb 1979:
The Economy, the Government and Trade Union Responsibilities.

Publications by Denis Healey

Books

(ed.) *The Curtain Falls: The Story of the Socialists in Eastern Europe*, Lincolns-Prager, 1951
Neutralism, Ampersand, 1958
Healey's Eye: A Photographic Memoir, Jonathan Cape, 1980
The Time of My Life, Michael Joseph, 1989
When Shrimps Learn to Whistle, Michael Joseph, 1990
My Secret Planet, Michael Joseph, 1992
Denis Healey's Yorkshire Dales: A Celebration of the Yorkshire Dales Landscape, Dalesman, 1995

Labour Party and Fabian Society Publications

Approach to Foreign Policy, 1947
Cards on the Table, 1947
Feet on the Ground, 1948
'European Unity', 1950
The Race Against the H-Bomb, 1960
A Neutral Belt in Europe?, 1958
Labour and a World Society, 1985
Beyond Nuclear Deterrence, 1986

Parliamentary Debates

1945–6 vol. 427
1948 vol. 450
1950 vol. 476
1951 vol. 495
1952 vol. 500, and vol 510
1953 vol. 518
1954 vol. 533
1956 vol. 553 to 558
1957 vol. 561, and 562
1958 vol. 580, and 585
1959 vol. 604
1960 vol. 640
1962 vol. 668
1963 vol. 684, and 690
1964 vol. 702, and 706
1965 vol. 710, and 722
1966 vol. 725
1967 vol. 749–50 and 757
1973 vol. 866
1974 vol. 871
1975 vol. 894–5, and 909
1976 vol. 915–17, and 919–23
1977 vol. 929–936

INDEX

Spinelli, Altiero, 103

Stalin, Joseph, 31, 59, 69, 78, 86, 110; Bevin's distrust of, 68; Cold War, 70; Beaverbrook on, 90; vetoes Marshall Plan, 117; May Day celebrations, 118; DH's case for rearmament, 148; death, 165, 166, 187; Khruschev denounces, 191

Steel, David, 506–7, 558, 565

Sterling, General William, 270

Stewart, Michael, 230, 257, 270, 272, 278, 282, 313, 337–8, 367, 368, 369, 373

Stockwood, Mervyn, 200

Stoddart-Scott, Colonel Malcolm, 57, 63

Stowe, Sir Kenneth, 459 and n., 476, 493, 512, 519, 520, 522

Strachey, John, 23

Strang, Sir William, 35, 130

Strauss, Franz Josef 213, 265

Straw, Jack, 442, 553

strikes, Winter of Discontent, 518–22

Suez Crisis (1956), 152, 168–82, 198, 222, 234, 290, 310, 568, 569

Suez Group, 170–1

Suharto, General, 332

Sukarno, General, 319–20, 321, 322, 323, 332, 336–7

Sun, 265–6, 517, 529, 556

Sunday Express, 556

Sunday Telegraph, 289, 447

Sunday Times, 208, 239, 338, 351, 393, 402, 477, 482, 546

Swinton, Lord, 240, 249

Szakasits, Arpad, 98, 104 and n., 105, 106, 107, 108

Tapsell, Peter, 478

Taverne, Dick, 375, 397–8 and n., 405, 503

Territorial Army (TA), 278, 280, 291–6

TFX/F111 see F111 aircraft

Thames TV, 537

Thatcher, Margaret, 21, 74, 162, 228, 344, 446, 452, 478, 509, 511, 532, 539, 553, 558, 578; and Rhodesia, 226; Winter of Discontent, 522; 1979 election, 522, 525, 528–9, 530; unpopularity, 556; Falklands War, 568, 569; 1983 election, 572, 573, 576; GCHQ debate, 579–80

Thomas, George, 369

Thomas, Ivor, 53

Thomas, Sir Leslie, 180

Thomas, Mike, 543

Thomson, George, 344–5, 346, 348, 349, 369

Thorez, Maurice, 78, 110

Thorneycroft, Peter, 232–3, 237–41, 243, 271, 307, 355

Thorneycroft (company), 298

Thorpe, Jeremy, 293, 362, 506

The Times, 89, 90–1, 92, 93, 108, 133, 176–7, 178, 252, 254, 257–8, 262, 291, 405, 406, 455, 480, 489, 538, 544, 556, 560, 567–8

Tito, Marshal, 53, 80, 108, 111, 114, 183n., 191

Todmorden, 4, 5

Togliatti, 78, 80, 110–11

Tomney, Frank, 175

trade unions: and nuclear weapons, 204; Industrial Relations Bill, 377–80, 382–3; power of, 390–1, 400, 408–9; Social Contract, 412, 415, 422, 430–1, 432; 1975 economic crisis, 431–2; Employment Protection Act, 452–3; Callaghan's relations with, 459; DH's relations with, 459–62; structural problems in Labour Party, 503; second Social Contract, 504, 512, 521, 540; and failure to call election in 1978, 511–12; incomes policy, 403, 434–40, 509, 512–21; Winter of Discontent, 518–22; and Labour deputy leadership contest, 557–8, 559–64; 1983 election, 574

Trades Union Council (TUC): nuclear weapons policy, 220; Ray Gunter and, 351; Vic Feather becomes General Secretary, 378; and Industrial Relations Bill, 382, 383; incomes policy, 403, 434–40, 509, 513–21; miners' strike, 404; Social Contract, 412, 422; minimum wage, 424; 1975 economic crisis, 431, 433; DH's relations with, 460, 461–2; St Valentine's Day Concordat, 521–2

Transport & General Workers' Union (T&G), 67, 68, 94, 372, 557; and unilateral disarmament, 199, 214–15, 217; and incomes policy, 432, 438, 514, 515; dock labour scheme, 453; Winter of Discontent, 519, 528; and deputy leadership contest, 558, 559, 560–2, 563

Treasury: postwar economic situation, 121; sterling crisis, 263; 1966–7 economic crisis, 338, 348–9; see also Healey, Denis: as Chancellor

Trend, Burke, 350

Tribune, 218, 540

Tribune Group, 449, 554, 563–4

Truman, Harry, 76, 86, 89, 142

Tsakos, Basil, 25–6, 56

TSR2 aircraft, 238–9, 240, 241, 257, 260, 261, 264, 267–77, 297, 364

Tunisia, 40–2

Turton, Robin, 225

Tynan, Kenneth, 30

Udall, Stewart, 201

Uganda, 223

Ulbricht, Walter, 56

Ulster see Northern Ireland

UNESCO, 86

Union for Democratic Action, 134–5

UNISON, 560

Unita, 109, 110

United Nations, 60, 85, 87, 88, 93, 172, 178, 179, 181

United States of America: Second World War, 48–9; in postwar period, 69; Spelthorne Letter, 73, 75; Labour foreign policy, 87, 88, 91–2; Marshall Aid, 109–10, 111–12, 115, 121; and Schuman Plan, 143; atom bomb, 147; DH's case for rearmament, 151, 152, 160; DH's affinity with, 156–7;